LINCOLN ~~CHRISTIAN~~ ~~COLLEGE~~ SEMINARY
1978

THE GULAG ARCHIPELAGO

Also by Aleksandr I. Solzhenitsyn

The Gulag Archipelago I-II

Letter to the Soviet Leaders

Candle in the Wind

The Nobel Lecture on Literature

August 1914

A Lenten Letter to Pimen, Patriarch of All Russia

Stories and Prose Poems

The Love Girl and the Innocent

The Cancer Ward

The First Circle

For the Good of the Cause

We Never Make Mistakes

One Day in the Life of Ivan Denisovich

Aleksandr I. Solzhenitsyn

THE GULAG ARCHIPELAGO

1918–1956

An Experiment in Literary Investigation

III-IV

Translated from the Russian by Thomas P. Whitney

HARPER & ROW, PUBLISHERS

New York, Evanston, San Francisco, London

1817

THE GULAG ARCHIPELAGO 1918–1956: AN EXPERIMENT IN LITERARY INVESTIGA-
TION III–IV. Copyright © 1974 by Aleksandr I. Solzhenitsyn. English language
translation copyright © 1975 by Harper & Row, Publishers, Inc. All rights
reserved. Printed in the United States of America. No part of this book may be
used or reproduced in any manner whatsoever without written permission
except in the case of brief quotations embodied in critical articles and reviews.
For information address Harper & Row, Publishers, Inc., 10 East 53rd Street,
New York, N.Y. 10022. Published simultaneously in Canada by Fitzhenry &
Whiteside Limited, Toronto.

FIRST EDITION

Designed by Sidney Feinberg

Library of Congress Cataloging in Publication Data

Solzhenitsyn, Aleksandr Isayevich, 1918–
  The Gulag archipelago, 1918–1956.
  Translated from the Russian.
  1. Political prisoners—Russia.   I. Title.
HV9713.S6413   365′.45′0947   73–22756
ISBN 0–06–013911–0
ISBN 0–06–080345–2 (pbk.)

83 84   4 3

Contents

PART III

The Destructive-Labor Camps*

■

"Only those can understand us who ate from the same bowl with us."

Quotation from a letter of a Hutzul* girl, a former zek

THE DESTRUCTIVE-LABOR CAMPS

NOVAYA ZEMLYA

Murmansk

Monchegorsk

KOLA

Amderma

Naryan-Mar

Kem

Solovetsky
Islands

Archangel

Ukhta

Knyazh-Pogost

Svir

GULF OF FINLAND

Kronstadt

Kargopol

Ust-Vym

Kotlas

Vychegda

LENINGRAD

Novgorod

Totma

Solikamsko

Staraya Russa

Kady

Berezniki

Rybinsk

Jaroslavl

Molotovsk

Permo

RIGA

Dvina

Volokolamsko

Ivanovo

(Nizhni Novgorod)

MOSCOW

GORKY

KAZAN

Katyno

Moscow

MINSK

Smolensk

Ryazan

Oka

KUIBYSHEV

Kaluga

Penza

Syzran

Tambov

Kuznetsk

Saratov

Voronezh

Volga

KIEV

Dnieper

KHARKOV

Kamyshino

Donets

Don

Dniester

STALINGRAD

Shakhty

Rostov

Don

Volga

Odessa

Krasnodar

Astrakhan

Sevastopol

Kuban

BLACK SEA

TBILISI

Yana

Indigirka

Lena

Lena

noyarsk
Taishet ● ●Bratsk

Lake
Baikal

BAIKAL-

Nerchinsk

Irkutsk

Dzhida ○ AMUR

REGION

Labor   Railroads
camps ●━┼┼┼┼┼● built by convicts   ┏┓┏┓┏┓ Canals

0   300   600   900 km

© by Scherz Verlag

Solzhenitsyn, July, 1946, as a prisoner in the Kaluga Gates Camp, Moscow

There is no limit to what should be included in this part. To attain and encompass its savage meaning one would have to drag out many lives in the camps—the very same in which one cannot survive for even one term without some special advantage because they were invented for *destruction*.

And from this it follows that all those who drank of this most deeply, who explored it most fully, are already in their graves and cannot tell us. No one now can ever tell us the *most important thing* about these camps.

And the whole scope of this story and of this truth is beyond the capabilities of one lonely pen. All I had was a peephole into the Archipelago, not the view from a tower. But, fortunately, several other books have emerged and more will emerge. In the *Kolyma Stories* of Shalamov the reader will perhaps feel more truly and surely the pitilessness of the spirit of the Archipelago and the limits of human despair.

To taste the sea all one needs is one gulp.

Chapter 1

■

The Fingers of Aurora

Rosy-fingered Eos, so often mentioned in Homer and called Aurora by the Romans, caressed, too, with those fingers the first early morning of the Archipelago.

When our compatriots heard via the BBC that M. Mihajlov claimed to have discovered that concentration camps had existed in our country as far back as 1921, many of us (and many in the West too) were astonished: That early really? Even in 1921?

Of course not! Of course Mihajlov was in error. In 1921, in fact, concentration camps were already in full flower (already even *coming to an end*). It would be far more accurate to say that the Archipelago was born with the shot of the cruiser *Aurora*.*

And how could it have been otherwise? Let us pause to ponder.

Didn't Marx and Engels teach that the old bourgeois machinery of compulsion had to be broken up, and *a new one created* immediately in its place? And included in the machinery of compulsion were: the army (we are not surprised that the Red Army was created at the beginning of 1918); the police (the militia* was inaugurated even sooner than the army); the courts (from November 22, 1917); and the prisons. How, in establishing the dictatorship of the proletariat, could they delay with a new type of prison?

That is to say that it was altogether impermissible to delay in the matter of prisons, whether old or new. In the first months after the October Revolution Lenin was already demanding "the most

9

decisive, draconic measures to tighten up discipline."[1] And are draconic measures possible—without prison?

What new could the proletarian state contribute here? Lenin was feeling out new paths. In December, 1917, he suggested for consideration the following assortment of punishments: "confiscation of all property . . . confinement in prison, dispatch to the front and forced labor for all who disobey the existing law."[2] Thus we can observe that the leading idea of the Archipelago—*forced labor*—had been advanced in the first month after the October Revolution.

And even while sitting peacefully among the fragrant hay mowings of Razliv* and listening to the buzzing bumblebees, Lenin could not help but ponder the future penal system. Even then he had worked things out and reassured us: "The suppression of the minority of exploiters by the majority of the hired slaves of yesterday is a matter so comparatively easy, simple and natural, that it is going to cost much less in blood . . . will be much cheaper for humanity" than the preceding suppression of the majority by the minority.[3]

According to the estimates of émigré Professor of Statistics Kurganov, this "comparatively easy" internal repression cost us, from the beginning of the October Revolution up to 1959, a total of . . . sixty-six million—66,000,000—lives. We, of course, cannot vouch for his figure, but we have none other that is official. And just as soon as the official figure is issued the specialists can make the necessary critical comparisons.

It is interesting to compare other figures. How large was the total staff of the *central* apparatus of the terrifying Tsarist Third Department, which runs like a strand through all the great Russian literature? At the time of its creation it had sixteen persons, and at its height it had forty-five. A ridiculously small number for even the remotest Cheka provincial headquarters in the country. Or, how many political prisoners did the February Revolution find in the Tsarist "Prison of the Peoples"? All these figures do exist somewhere. In all probability there were more than a hundred such prisoners in the Kresty Prison alone, and several hundred returned from Siberian exile and hard labor, and

---

1. Lenin, *Sobrannye Sochineniya* (*Collected Works*), fifth edition, Vol. 36, p. 217.
2. *Ibid.*, Vol. 35, p. 176.
3. *Ibid.*, Vol. 33, p. 90.

how many more were languishing in the prison of every provincial capital! But it is interesting to know—exactly how many. Here is a figure for Tambov, taken from the fiery local papers. The February Revolution, which opened wide the doors of the Tambov Prison, found there political prisoners in the number of . . . seven (7) persons. And there were more than forty provinces. (It is superfluous to recall that from February to July, 1917, there were no political arrests, and after July the number imprisoned could be counted on one's fingers.)

Here, however, was the trouble: The first Soviet government was a coalition government, and a portion of the people's commissariats had to be allotted, like it or not, to the Left SR's, including, unhappily, the People's Commissariat of Justice, which fell to them. Guided by rotten petty bourgeois concepts of freedom, this People's Commissariat of Justice brought the penal system to the verge of ruin. The sentences turned out to be too light, and they made hardly any use at all of the progressive principle of forced labor. In February, 1918, the Chairman of the Council of People's Commissars, Comrade Lenin, demanded that the number of places of imprisonment be increased and that repression of criminals be intensified,[4] and in May, already going over to concrete guidance, he gave instructions[5] that the sentence for bribery must be *not less than* ten years of prison and ten years of forced labor *in addition*, i.e., a total of twenty years. This scale might seem pessimistic at first: would forced labor really still be necessary after twenty years? But we know that forced labor turned out to be a very long-lived measure, and that even after fifty years it would still be extremely popular.

For many months after the October Revolution the prison personnel everywhere remained Tsarist, and the only new officials named were *Commissars* of prisons. The brazen jailers went so far as to create their own *trade union* ("The Union of Prison Employees") and established an *elective basis* for prison administration! (The only time in all Russian history!) The prisoners were not to be left behind either—they, too, had their own internal self-government. (Circular of the People's Commissariat of Justice, April 24, 1918: prisoners, wherever possible, were to be brought into self-verification and self-supervision.)

4. *Ibid.*, Vol. 54, p. 391.
5. *Ibid.*, Vol. 50, p. 70.

Naturally such a free commune of convicts ("anarchical licentiousness") did not correspond to the needs of the dictatorship of the progressive class and was of sorry help in purging harmful insects from the Russian land. (And what could one expect—if the prison chapels had not been closed, and our Soviet prisoners were willingly going there on Sundays, even if only to pass the time!)

Of course, even the Tsarist jailers were not entirely a loss to the proletariat, for after all theirs was a *profession* important to the most immediate purposes of the Revolution. And therefore it was necessary to "select those persons of the prison administration who have not become totally calloused and stupefied in the patterns of Tsarist prisons [And what does 'not totally' mean? And how would you find that out? Does it mean they had forgotten 'God save the Tsar'?] who can be used for work at the new tasks."[6] (Did they, for example, answer precisely, "Yes, sir!" and "No, sir," or turn the key in the lock quickly?) And, of course, the prison buildings themselves, their cells, their bars and locks, although in appearance they remained exactly as before, in actual fact had acquired a *new class content*, a lofty revolutionary meaning.

And nevertheless, the habit of the courts, right up to the middle of 1918, of keeping right on, out of inertia, sentencing "to prison, to prison," slowed the breakup of the old machinery of state in its prison area.

In the middle of 1918, to be exact on July 6, an event took place whose significance is not grasped by everyone, an event superficially known as the "suppression of the revolt of the Left SR's." But this was, in fact, a coup d'état, of hardly any less significance than October 25. On October 25 the power—the government—of the Soviets of Workers' and Peasants' Deputies was proclaimed, whence the name *Soviet power*. But in its first months this new government was very much beclouded by the presence in it of other parties besides the Bolsheviks. Although the coalition government consisted only of the Bolsheviks and the Left SR's, nonetheless, in the membership of the All-Russian Congresses (the Second, Third, and Fourth), and of the All-Russian Central Executive Committees (VTsIK's) which they elected, there were still included some representatives of other

6. *Sovetskaya Yustitsiya* (a collection of articles, *Soviet Justice*), Moscow, 1919, p. 20.

socialist parties—SR's, Social Democrats, Anarchists, Popular Socialists, etc. Because of this fact the VTsIK's possessed the unhealthy character of "socialist parliaments." But in the course of the first months of 1918, by a whole series of decisive measures (supported by the Left SR's), the representatives of the other socialist parties were either expelled from VTsIK (by its own decision, an original parliamentary procedure) or else were simply not allowed to be elected to it. The last non-Bolshevik party, which still constituted one-third of the parliament (the Fifth Congress of Soviets), was the Left SR's. And the time finally came to get rid of them too. On July 6, 1918, they were excluded in toto from VTsIK and from the Council of People's Commissars. Thereby the power of the Soviet of Deputies (by tradition called the "Soviet") ceased to stand in opposition to the will of the Bolshevik Party and took the form of the Democracy of a New Type.

Only on this historic day could the reconstruction of the old prison machinery and the creation of the Archipelago really begin.[7]

And the direction of this desired reconstruction had long since been understood. After all, Marx himself had pointed out in his "Critique of the Gotha Program" that productive labor was the only method of prisoner correction. It was clear, of course, as Vyshinsky explained much later on, that what was meant here was "not that kind of work which dries out the mind and the heart of a human being," but "the miracle worker [!] which transforms people from nonexistence and insignificance into heroes."[8] Why is it that our prisoner must not chew the rag or read nice little books in a cell, but must labor instead? Because in the Republic of the Soviets there can be no place for forced idleness, for that "forced parasitism"[9] which could exist in a parasitical society, for example in Schlüsselburg. Such idleness as this on the part of prisoners would have very simply been contrary to the bases of the work structure of the Soviet Republic as defined in the Con-

7. In the clumsily high-flying language of Vyshinsky: "The process, unique in the world, possessing genuine universal historical significance, of creating, on the ruins of the bourgeois system of prisons, those 'houses of the dead' which were built by the exploiters for the workers, of new institutions with new social content." A. Y. Vyshinsky (editor), *Ot Tyurem k Vospitatelnym Uchrezhdeniyam (From Prisons to Rehabilitative Institutions)*, Moscow, Sovetskoye Zakonodatelstvo Publishing House, 1934, preface.

8. *Ibid.*, p. 10.

9. *Ibid.*, p. 103.

stitution of July 10, 1918: "He who does not work does not eat." Consequently, if the prisoners were not set to work, they were, according to the Constitution, to be deprived of their bread ration.

The Central Penal Department of the People's Commissariat of Justice,[10] which had been created in May, 1918, had immediately begun to send off to work the then-existing zeks ("began to organize productive labor"). But this legislation had been proclaimed only after the July coup—to be precise, on July 23, 1918 —in "Temporary instructions on deprivation of freedom":[11] "*Those deprived of freedom who are capable of labor must be recruited for physical work on a compulsory basis.*"

One can say that the camps originated and the Archipelago was born from this particular instruction of July 23, 1918 (*nine months* after the October Revolution). (Someone may enter a reproach that this birth was premature?)

The necessity of forced labor by prisoners (which was anyway quite clear for everyone by then) was further clarified at the Seventh All-Union Congress of the Soviets: "Labor is the best means of paralyzing the disintegrating influence . . . of the endless conversations of prisoners among themselves in the course of which the more experienced instruct the newcomers."[12] (Aha, so that's why!)

Soon after that there began the Communist "subbotniki"*— "voluntary Saturdays." And that same People's Commissariat of Justice issued an appeal: "It is essential to teach [the prisoners] to become accustomed to Communist, collective labor."[13] In other words, the spirit of the Communist "subbotniki" was to be applied to the *forced-labor* camps.

And that is how that hasty epoch instantly heaped up a mountain of problems which it took decades to sort out.

The bases of *corrective-labor policy* were included in the Party program at the Eighth Congress of the Russian Communist Party (March, 1919). The complete organizational structuring of the camp network throughout Soviet Russia coincided rigidly

10. After the Brest-Litovsk Peace the Left SR's left the government, and the People's Commissariat of Justice was headed by Bolsheviks.
11. These instructions continued to exist during the whole course of the Civil War, right up until November, 1920.
12. *Otchyot N. K. Y. VII Vsesoyuznomu Syezdu Sovetov* (*Report by the People's Commissariat of Justice to the Seventh All-Union Congress of Soviets*), p. 9.
13. *Materialy N. K. Y.* (*Materials of the People's Commissariat of Justice*), Vol. VII, p. 137.

with the first Communist *subbotniki* (April 12–May 17, 1919): the decrees of VTsIK on camps for forced labor were issued on April 15, 1919, and May 17, 1919.[14] Under their provisions, camps for forced labor were obligatorily created (by the provincial Cheka) in *each provincial capital* (if convenient, within the city limits, or in a monastery or on a nearby country estate) and also *in several counties* as well (although for the time being not in all of them). The camps were required to accommodate *no fewer than three hundred persons* each (in order that the cost of the guard and the administration should be paid for by the prisoners' labor), and they were under the jurisdiction of the Provincial Penal Departments.

The early forced-labor camps seem to us nowadays to be something intangible. The people imprisoned in them seem not to have said anything to anyone—there is no testimony. Literature and memoirs, when they speak of War Communism, recall executions and prisons, but do not have a thing to say about camps. And nowhere, even between the lines, nowhere outside the text, are they implied. So it was natural for Mihajlo Mihajlov to make his mistake. Where were those camps? What were their names? What did they look like?

The Instruction of July 23, 1918, had the decisive fault (noted by all jurists) that nothing was mentioned there about class differentiation among the prisoners, in other words that some prisoners should be maintained in better conditions and some in worse. But it did outline the labor system—and that is the only reason we can get any picture of what they were like. The workday was set at eight hours. Because of the novelty of it all, the hasty decision was made to pay the prisoners for all their work, other than camp maintenance, at 100 percent of the rates of the corresponding trade unions. (Oh, what a monstrous thing! The pen can hardly bear to write it!) (They were being compelled to work by the Constitution, and they were also being paid according to the same Constitution—logical enough!) It is true that the cost of maintenance of the camp and the camp guard was deducted from their wages. For "conscientious" prisoners there was a special benefit: to be allowed to live in a private apartment and to come to the camp for work only. And release ahead of term

14. *Sobraniye Uzakonenii RSFSR za 1919* (*Collection of Legislative Acts of the R.S.F.S.R. for 1919*), No. 12, p. 124, and No. 20, p. 235.

was promised as a reward for "special labor enthusiasm." And in general there were no detailed instructions on the regimen, and every camp had its own. "In the period of building a new governmental system, taking into account the *great overcrowding of places of confinement* [!—my italics—A.S.] there was no time to think about the regimen in the camps. All the attention was being directed to *unburdening the prisons*."[15] Something like that reads like a hieroglyphic from Babylon. How many questions immediately suggest themselves: What was going on in those wretched prisons? And what were the social causes of such overcrowding? And is one to understand the matter of *unburdening* the prisons to mean executions or dispatching prisoners to camps? And what did it mean by saying it was impossible to give any thought to the regimen in the camps? Did this mean that the People's Commissariat of Justice did not have time to safeguard the prisoner against the arbitrary actions of the local camp chief? Is that the only way this can be read? There were no instructions about the regimen, and in the years of *the Revolutionary Sense of Justice* every petty tyrant could do just as he pleased with the prisoners?

From the meager statistics (all from that very same collection, *Soviet Justice*) we learn: in general the work in camps was menial. In 1919 only 2.5 percent of the prisoners worked in workshops, and in 1920 only 10 percent. It is also known that at the end of 1918 the Central Penal Department* (what a moniker—it makes the flesh creep!) sought the establishment of agricultural colonies. It is known that in Moscow several brigades made up of prisoners were established to carry out repairs on water pipes, heating systems, and plumbing in nationalized buildings. (And these apparently unescorted prisoners wandered about with monkey wrenches, soldering irons, and pipes through the corridors of government organizations and institutions, in the apartments of the bigwigs of those times, summoned by their wives by telephone to carry out repairs—and were never mentioned in any memoir, in any play, or in any film.)

But the forced-labor camps were nonetheless not the *first* camps in the R.S.F.S.R.

15. *Materialy N. K. Y., 1920*, Vol. VII.

The reader has already read the term concentration camp—"kontslager"—several times in the sentences of the tribunals (Part I, Chapter 8) and concluded, perhaps, that we were guilty of an error, of making careless use of terminology subsequently developed? No, this is not the case.

In August, 1918, several days before the attempt on his life by Fanya Kaplan, Vladimir Ilyich Lenin wrote in a telegram to Yevgeniya Bosh[16] and to the Penza Provincial Executive Committee (they were unable to cope with a peasant revolt): "Lock up all the doubtful ones [not "guilty," mind you, but *doubtful*— A.S.] in *a concentration camp* outside the city."[17] (And in addition "carry out merciless mass terror"—this was before the decree.)

Only on September 5, 1918, ten days after this telegram, was the Decree on the Red Terror published, which was signed by Petrovsky, Kursky, and Bonch-Bruyevich. In addition to the instructions on mass executions, it stated in particular: "Secure the Soviet Republic against its class enemies by isolating them in *concentration camps*."[18]

So that is *where* this term—*concentration camps*—was discovered and immediately seized upon and confirmed—one of the principal terms of the twentieth century, and it was to have a big international future! And this is *when* it was born—in August and September, 1918. The word itself had already been used during World War I, but in relation to POW's and undesirable foreigners. But here in 1918 it was for the first time applied to the citizens of one's own country. The switch in meaning is easily comprehended: concentration camps for POW's were not prisons but a necessary precautionary concentration of the POW's. And so, too, for doubtful compatriots extrajudicial precautionary concentration was now proposed. For an energetic mind which could visualize barbed wire surrounding prisoners who had not been tried, the necessary term was right at hand—concentration camps.

And while the forced-labor camps of the People's Commissariat of Justice belonged to the category of *general places of*

16. To this now forgotten woman was entrusted at this time—via the line of authority of the Central Committee of the Party and of the Cheka as well—the fate of all Penza Province.

17. Lenin, fifth edition, Vol. 50, pp. 143–144.

18. *Sobraniye Uzakonenii za 1918 (Collection of Legislative Acts for 1918)*, No. 65, p. 710.

confinement, the concentration camps were in no sense "general places," but were under the direct administration of the Cheka and were maintained for *particularly hostile* elements and for *hostages*. True, in the future, prisoners would be sent to concentration camps by tribunals as well; but people never tried kept pouring in automatically, sent there only *on the basis of hostility*.[19] For escape from a concentration camp the sentence was multiplied by *ten*—also without trial. (This was in tune with the times: "Ten for one!" "One hundred for one!") Consequently, if a prisoner had a five-year sentence and escaped and was caught, then his sentence was automatically extended to 1968. For a second escape from a concentration camp, execution was prescribed (and, of course, was punctiliously carried out).

In the Ukraine, concentration camps were created somewhat later—in 1920.

But the creative thinking of our young Soviet justice did not content itself with this. Very shortly, even the concentration camps, which would seem to have had a firm class foundation, came to be considered insufficiently severe, insufficiently purposeful. In 1921 the Northern Special Purpose Camps were founded (not for nothing was that label, *special*, attached to them). They had as their acronym SLON.* The first such camps arose in Pertominsk, Kholmogory, and just outside Archangel itself.[20] However, these places were evidently considered difficult to guard and unsuitable for large concentrations of prisoners. And the gaze of the higher-ups naturally fell on the nearby Solovetsky Islands ("Solovki"), with their already built-up establishments, and their stone buildings, located twelve to twenty-five miles from the mainland, sufficiently close for the jailers, and sufficiently distant to discourage escapees, with no communication with the mainland for half the year—a harder nut to crack than Sakhalin.

And once Solovki had been selected and established, recollections of the forced-labor camps, the concentration camps, and the

19. Vyshinsky, *op. cit.*
20. The magazine *Solovetskiye Ostrova* (*The Solovetsky Islands*), 1930, No. 2–3, p. 55. From the report of the Chief of Administration of SLON, Comrade Nogtev, in Kem. When nowadays tourists are shown the so-called "Camp of the Government of Chaikovsky," at the mouth of the Dvina River, one would have to be in the know to realize that this was one of the first Northern "Special Purpose Camps."

Special Purpose Camps vanished from the popular mind! Because Solovki was not kept secret in the twenties, and in actual fact ears buzzed with Solovki. They openly used "Solovki" to scare people with. They were publicly proud of Solovki. (They had the brass to be proud of it!) Solovki was even a symbol. There were as many jokes about it in vaudeville acts as you can imagine. After all, classes had already disappeared (whither?), and Solovki itself was soon to come to an end. Subscriptions to the internal camp magazine, _The Solovetsky Islands_, were boldly sold throughout the Soviet Union.

But the camp rootlets went deeper, deeper, and it is simply that we have lost count of their places and traces. There is no one now to tell us about most of those first concentration camps. And only from the last testimony of those few surviving first concentration camp inmates can we glean and preserve a little bit.

At that time the authorities used to love to set up their concentration camps in former monasteries: they were enclosed by strong walls, had good solid buildings, and they were empty. (After all, monks are not human beings and could be tossed out at will.) Thus in Moscow there were concentration camps in Andronnikov, Novospassky, and Ivanovsky monasteries. In the Petrograd _Krasnaya Gazeta_ of September 6, 1918, we can read that the first concentration camp "will be set up in Nizhni Novgorod in an empty nunnery. . . . And _initially_ it is planned to send five thousand persons to the concentration camp in Nizhni Novgorod." (My italics—A.S.)

In Ryazan the concentration camp was also set up in a former nunnery (Kazansky). And here is what they say about it. Imprisoned there were merchants, priests, and so-called "war prisoners" (as they called captured officers who had not served in the Red Army). But there was also another segment of the prisoner population which fitted into no simple category. (For example, the Tolstoyan I. Y——v, whose trial we have already read about, was kept here.) Attached to the camp were workshops— a weaving shop, a tailor shop, a shoemaker's shop—and there was also repair and construction work in the city—"general work"* (in 1921 they were already calling it that). To this the prisoners were taken by convoy, but those who worked as individual craftsmen, because of the kind of work they did, were allowed to go without convoy, and the citizens fed the latter in their homes. The population of Ryazan was very sympathetic toward the *deprivees*, as they were called. (Officially they were called not prisoners but "persons deprived of freedom.") A passing column of them would be given alms (rusks, boiled beets, potatoes), and the convoy guards did not try to prevent their accepting such gifts, and the deprivees divided everything equally among themselves. (At every step—customs *not ours*, ideology *not ours*.) Those deprivees who were especially fortunate got positions in their specialized fields in institutions (for example, Y——v, on the railroad). They then received passes which permitted them to walk around the city (but they spent the night in camp).

Here is how they fed them in a camp in 1921: half a pound of bread (plus another half-pound for those who fulfilled the norm), hot water for tea morning and evening, and, during the day, a ladle of gruel (with several dozen grains and some potato peelings in it).

Camp life was embellished on the one hand by the denunciations of provocateurs (and arrests on the basis of the denunciations), and on the other by a dramatics and glee club. They gave concerts for the people of Ryazan in the hall of the former noblemen's assembly, and the deprivees' brass band played in the city park. The deprivees got better and better acquainted with and more friendly with the inhabitants, and this became intolerable—and at that point they began to send the so-called "war prisoners" to the Northern Special Purpose Camps.

The lesson of the instability and laxity in these concentration camps lay in their being surrounded by civilian life. And that was why the special northern camps were required. (Concentration camps were abolished in 1922.)

This whole dawn of the camps deserves to have its spectrum examined much more closely. And glory to he who can—for all I have in my own hands is crumbs.

At the end of the Civil War the two labor armies created by Trotsky had to be dissolved because of the grumbling of the soldiers kept in them. And by this token, the role of camps in the structure of the R.S.F.S.R. not only did not diminish but intensified. By the end of 1920 in the R.S.F.S.R. there were eighty-four camps in forty-three provinces.[21] If one believes the official statistics (even though classified), 25,336 persons and in addition 24,400 "prisoners of war of the Civil War" were held in them at this time.[22] Both figures, particularly the second, seem to be understated. However, if one takes into consideration that by *unloading prisons*, sinking barges, and other types of mass annihilation the figure had often begun with zero and been reduced to zero over and over, then perhaps these figures are accurate.

According to the same source, by October, 1923, at the beginning of the cloudless years of NEP (and quite a long time before the *personality cult*), there were being held: in 355 camps —68,297 persons deprived of freedom; in 207 reformatories—48,163; in 105 homes for confinement and prisons—16,765; in 35 agricultural colonies—2,328, and another 1,041 minors and sick persons.[23]

And there is another expressive figure: on the overcrowding of camps (for the numbers of those imprisoned grew more swiftly than the organization of camps). For each one hundred accommodations for prisoners there were: in 1924—112 prisoners; in 1925—120; in 1926—132; and in 1927—177.[24] Whoever has *done time* there knows well what camp life was like (in terms of places on bunks, bowls in the mess hall, or padded jackets)—if there were 1.77 prisoners for each allotted place.

Year after year other forms of existence for prisoners were also tried, in a search for something better: for those who were not dangerous and not politically hostile there were labor colonies, corrective-labor homes (from 1922), reformatories (from 1923), homes for confinement, labor homes (from 1924), labor homes for juvenile offenders; and for politically hostile prisoners there were detention prisons (from 1922), and from 1923 on Special Purpose Isolators (the former "Centrals" and the future Special Purpose Prisons or TON's).

The creators of these forms saw in them a bold "struggle against making a fetish of prisons" common to all other countries

21. Tsentralnyi Gosudarstvenny Arkhiv Oktyabrskoi Revolyutsii (Central State Archives of the October Revolution) (henceforth TsGAOR), collection 393, shelf 13, file IB, sheet 111.

22. *Ibid.*, sheet 112.

23. *Ibid.*, shelf 39, file 48, sheets 13, 14.

24. A. A. Gertsenzon, *Borba s Prestupnosttyu v RSFSR* (*Struggle Against Crime in the R.S.F.S.R.*), Moscow, Juridical Publishing House, 1928, p. 103.

of the world, including the former Russia, where nobody could think up anything at all except prisons and more prisons. ("The Tsarist government, which had transformed the entire country into one enormous prison, had developed its prison system with some kind of particularly refined sadism.")[25]

On the threshold of the "reconstruction period" (meaning from 1927) "the role of camps *was growing* [Now just what was one to think? Now after all the victories?]—against the most dangerous, hostile elements, wreckers, the kulaks, counterrevolutionary propaganda."[26]

And so it was that the Archipelago was not about to disappear into the depths of the sea! The Archipelago would live!

Until 1924 there were very few ordinary labor colonies in the Archipelago. In those years *closed places* of confinement were predominant, and they would not grow less later on. (In his report of 1924 Krylenko demanded that the number of Special Purpose Isolators be *increased*—isolators for nonworkers and for *especially dangerous persons among the workers* (in which category, evidently, Krylenko himself would turn up later on). (This, his formulation, became a part of the Corrective Labor Code of 1924.)

Just as in the creation of every archipelago invisible shifts take place somewhere in important supporting strata before the picture of the world emerges before us—so here, too, very important shifts and changes in names took place which are now nearly incomprehensible to our minds.

At the very beginning there was primeval chaos, and places of imprisonment were under the jurisdiction of three different institutions: the Cheka (Comrade Dzerzhinsky), the NKVD (Comrade Petrovsky), and the People's Commissariat of Justice (Comrade Kursky). In the NKVD at first there was GUMZak (the Chief Administration for Places of Imprisonment, immediately after October, 1917), and then GUPR (the Chief Administration for Forced Labor), and then once again GUMZ.[27] In the People's Commissariat of Justice there was the Prison Administration (December, 1917), then the Central Penal Department

25. Vyshinsky, *op. cit.*, p. 431.
26. I. L. Averbakh, *Ot Prestupleniya k Trudu (From Crime to Labor)*, edited by Vyshinsky, Soviet Legislation Publishers, 1936.
27. Just as it is today, in the sixties.

(May, 1918) with a network of Provincial Penal Departments and even congresses of them (September, 1920), and this was then made to sound better as the Central Corrective Labor Department (1921). It goes without saying that such dispersal was to the disadvantage of the punitive-corrective business, and Dzerzhinsky sought the unification of administrations. And as it happened, at this point a little-noticed merging of the Cheka into the NKVD took place: after March 16, 1919, Dzerzhinsky became the Commissar of Internal Affairs as well. And by 1922, he had also succeeded in transferring all places of imprisonment from the People's Commissariat of Justice to himself in the NKVD (June 25, 1922).[28] And thus GUMZ of the NKVD kept ever expanding.

Parallel to this took place the reorganization of the camp guards. First these were the armies of the VOKhR (the Internal Guard Service of the Republic), and then VNUS (the Internal Service). And in 1919 they were merged into the Corps of the Cheka,[29] and Dzerzhinsky became the chairman of their Military Council as well. (Nonetheless, nonetheless, up until 1924 there were complaints about the numerous escapes, the low state of discipline among the personnel[30]—probably there were drunkenness and carelessness—their only interest lay in getting their wages.) And it was only in June, 1924, that, by decree of VTsIK and the Council of People's Commissars, military discipline was introduced into the corps of convoy* guards and recruitment of them through the People's Commissariat for the Army and Navy was inaugurated.[31]

And furthermore, parallel to this, a Central Bureau of Dactyloscopic Registration and a Central Breeding Establishment for Service and Tracking Dogs were created in 1922.

But at this same time GUMZak of the U.S.S.R. was renamed GUITU (Chief Administration of Corrective Labor Institutions) of the U.S.S.R., and then was renamed again—GUITL of the OGPU (the Chief Administration of Corrective Labor Camps), and its chief simultaneously became the Chief of Convoy Troops of the U.S.S.R.

28. The magazine *Vlast Sovetov* (*The Power of the Soviets*), 1923, No. 1–2, p. 57.
29. *Ibid.*, 1919, No. 11, pp. 6–7.
30. TsGAOR, collection 393, shelf 47, file 89, sheet 11.
31. *Ibid.*, collection 393, shelf 53, file 141, sheets 1, 3, 4.

And how much excitement there was! And how many of those stairs, offices, guards, passes, rubber stamps, seals, and signs there were!

And from GUITL, the son of GUMZak, derived our own Gulag.

Chapter 2

■

The Archipelago
Rises from the Sea

On the White Sea, where the nights are white for half a year at a time, Bolshoi Solovetsky Island lifts its white churches from the water within the ring of its bouldered kremlin* walls, rusty-red from the lichens which have struck root there—and the grayish-white Solovetsky seagulls hover continually over the kremlin and screech.

"In all this brightness it is as if there were no sin present. . . . It is as if nature here had not yet matured to the point of sin" is how the writer Prishvin perceived the Solovetsky Islands.[1]

Without us these isles rose from the sea; without us they acquired a couple of hundred lakes replete with fish; without our help they were settled by capercaillies,* hares, and deer, while foxes, wolves, and other beasts of prey never ever appeared there.

The glaciers came and went, the granite boulders littered the shores of the lakes; the lakes froze during the Solovetsky winter

1: And to Prishvin only the monks themselves seemed sinful in the context of Solovki. It was 1908, and in accordance with the liberal concepts of the times it was quite impossible to say an approving word about the clergy. And yet to us, who have survived the Archipelago, those monks–certainly seem angels. Though having every opportunity of eating their bellies full, they, in the Golgotha-Crucifixion Monastery, permitted themselves a fast dish, only on the great holidays. Despite the opportunity to sleep whenever they pleased, they kept vigil nights on end, and (in that same small monastery) day long, year long, and in perpetuity read the Psalter around the clock and prayed for all Orthodox Christians, living and dead.

1. The Solovetsky kremlin

2. The Herring Gates

nights, the sea howled under the wind and was covered with an icy sludge and in places froze; the northern lights blazed across half the sky; and it grew bright once again and warm once again, and the fir trees grew and thickened, and the birds cackled and called, and the young deer trumpeted—and the planet circled through all world history, and kingdoms fell and rose, and here there were still no beasts of prey and no human being.

Sometimes the men of Novgorod landed there and they counted the islands as belonging to their Obonezhskaya "pyatina."* Karelians lived there too. Half a hundred years after the Battle of Kulikovo Field and half a thousand years before the GPU, the monks Savvaty and German crossed the mother-of-pearl sea in a tiny boat and came to look on this island without a beast of prey as sacred. The Solovetsky Monastery began with them. After that the cathedrals of the Assumption and of the Transfiguration arose (Illustration No. 1: a general view of the Solovetsky kremlin from the direction of Svyatoye [Holy] Lake), the Church of the Beheading on Sekirnaya Hill (Illustration No. 3), and another score of churches, and another score of bell towers, and the smaller monasteries of Golgotha, the Trinity, Savvatyevsky, and Muksalmsky, and solitary retreats of hermits and ascetics in the remote locations. The labor of many went into the creation of all this—first of the monks themselves and subsequently of the peasants belonging to the monastery. The lakes were joined by dozens of canals. Lake water was delivered to the monastery by wooden pipes. And the most surprising thing of all was a dike at Muksalma (nineteenth century) made from "immovable" boulders somehow set in place on the sand spits. On Large and Small Muksalma fat herds began to pasture. The monks loved to tend animals, both tame and wild. The Solovetsky land turned out to be not only holy but rich too, capable of feeding many thousands.[2] In the vegetable gardens they raised plump, firm, sweet white cabbages (the stalks were called "Solovetsky apples"). All their vegetables were their own. And all of them were of the best quality. And they had their own greenhouses for

---

2. Specialists in the history of technology say that back in the sixteenth century Filipp-Kolychev (who had raised his voice against Ivan the Terrible) introduced a system of agricultural technology at Solovki that even three centuries later would have been respectable anywhere.

flowers, where they even raised roses. They developed fisheries—catch from the sea and from the "Metropolitan's fishponds" dammed off from the sea. In the course of centuries and decades they acquired their own mills to mill their own grain, their own sawmills, their own dishware made in their own pottery works, their own foundry, their own smithy, their own bindery, their own leather shop, their own carriage shop, and even their own electric power station. Even their elaborately shaped bricks and their seagoing boats for their own use—they made all themselves.

However, no development ever took place in the past, nor takes place in the present—and it isn't clear that it will ever take place in the future—without being accompanied by military thought and prison thought.

Military thought: It was impermissible for some sort of feckless monks just to live on just an island. The island was on the borders of the Great Empire, and, consequently, it was required to fight with the Swedes, the Danes, the English, and, consequently, it was required to build a fortress with walls eight yards thick and to raise up eight towers on the walls, and to make narrow embrasures in them, and to provide for a vigilant watch from the cathedral bell tower.[3]

Prison thought: How glorious—good stone walls standing on a separate island! What a good place to confine important criminals—and with someone already there to provide guard. We won't interfere with their saving their souls: just guard our prisoners![4]

Had Savvaty thought about that when he landed on the holy island?

They imprisoned church heretics here and political heretics as well. For example, Avraami Palitsyn was imprisoned here (he died here); and Pushkin's uncle, P. Gannibal—for his support of the Decembrists. And the last ataman of the Zaporozhe Cossacks, Kolnyshevsky (a distant predecessor of Petlyura?), when

---

3. And the monastery did have to defend itself against the English in 1808 and in 1854, and emerged unconquered; and in the conflict with the supporters of the Patriarch Nikon in 1667 the monk Feoktist opened a secret entrance and betrayed the Solovetsky kremlin to a boyar of the Tsar.

4. How much of humanity's faith was destroyed by this double duty of Christian monasteries as prisons!

he was already a very old man, was imprisoned here, and he was over a hundred years old when he was released after serving a long term.[5]

Incidentally, the ancient history of the Solovetsky monastery prison was the victim of a fashionable myth, disseminated only in Soviet times, during the period of the Soviet prison camp on Solovki, which deceived the writers of guidebooks and historical descriptions—and nowadays one can read in several books that the Solovetsky prison was a torture prison, that it had hooks for the rack, and lashes, and torture with fire. But all these were the appurtenances of interrogation prisons in the era before Empress Elizabeth, or of the Western Inquisition, and were not at all typical of Russian monastery dungeons in general, and were dreamed up here by an unscrupulous and also ignorant investigator.

The old Solovetsky Island people remember him very well. It was the *joker* Ivanov, who bore the camp nickname of the "antireligious germ." Formerly he had been a lay brother attached to the Novgorod Archbishopric, arrested for selling church valuables to the Swedes. He got to Solovki in 1925 and hustled about to escape general work and death. He had made antireligious propaganda among the prisoners his specialty, and of course became a collaborator of the ISCh (the Information and Investigation Section—which was named very candidly!). But in addition he excited the heads of the camp with his suggestions that many treasures had been buried here by the monks—and so they created a Commission for Excavations under his leadership. This commission kept on digging many months. But, alas, the monks had cheated the psychological calculations of the "antireligious germ": they had buried no treasures on Solovki. At this point, to get out of the situation with honor, Ivanov went around explaining the underground workshops, storehouse, and defense installations as prison and torture facilities. The torture instruments naturally could not be preserved so many centuries,

5. The state prison in Solovki existed from 1718 on. Visiting Solovki in the eighties of the nineteenth century, the Commander of the Armies of the St. Petersburg Military District, Grand Duke Vladimir Aleksandrovich, found the military garrison there superfluous and *he removed all the soldiers from Solovki.* In 1903 the Solovetsky prison ceased to exist. (A. S. Prugavin, *Monastyrskiye Tyurmy* [*Monastery Prisons*], Posrednik Publishers, pp. 78, 81.)

but the hooks of course (for hanging up carcasses) were evidence that there had been a rack here. It was more difficult to provide a basis for the finding that no trace of nineteenth-century torture had survived—so the conclusion was reached that "during the past century the regime in the Solovetsky prison had been significantly relaxed." The "discoveries" of the "antireligious germ" had come right at the most appropriate time, had in some degree reassured the disappointed administration, and were published in *The Solovetsky Islands* and subsequently as a monograph in the Solovetsky printing shop—and by this means successfully muddied the waters of historical truth. (This whole intrigue was judged all the more appropriate because the flourishing Solovetsky Monastery had been very famous and respected in all Russia up to the time of the Revolution.)

But when power passed into the hands of the workers, what was to be done with these malevolent parasitical monks? They sent Commissars, socially tried-and-true leaders, and they proclaimed the monastery a state farm, and ordered the monks to pray less and to work harder for the benefit of the workers and peasants. The monks worked, and their herring, which was astonishing in its flavor, and which they had been able to catch because of their special knowledge of where and when to cast nets, was shipped off to Moscow to be used for the Kremlin tables.

However, the abundance of valuables concentrated in the monastery, especially in the sacristy, troubled some of the leaders and overseers who had arrived there: instead of passing into the workers' hands (i.e., *their own*), these valuables lay there as a dead religious burden. And at that point, contradicting to a certain degree the Criminal Code but corresponding in a very genuine way with the general spirit of expropriation of the property of nonworkers, the monastery was set on fire (on May 25, 1923); the buildings were damaged, and many valuables disappeared from the sacristy; and, the principal thing, all the inventory records burned up, and it was quite impossible to determine how much and exactly what had disappeared.[6]

But without even conducting an investigation, what is our revolutionary sense of justice (sense of smell) going to hint to

---

6. And the *antireligious "germ"* also referred to this fire, explaining the difficulty in finding nowadays material proofs of the former prison cells and torture apparatus.

us? Who if not the black gang of monks themselves could have been to blame for the arson of the monastery wealth? So throw them out onto the mainland, and concentrate all the Northern Special Purpose Camps on the Solovetsky Islands! The eighty-year-old and even hundred-year-old monks begged on their knees to be allowed to die on the "holy soil," but they were all thrown out with proletarian ruthlessness except for the most necessary among them: the artels of fishermen;[7] the cattle specialists on Muksalma; Father Methodius, the cabbage salter; Father Samson, the foundry specialist; yes, and other such useful fathers as well. (They were allotted a corner of the kremlin separate from the camp, with their own exit—the Herring Gates [Illustration No. 2]. They were christened *a Workers' Commune*, but out of condescension for their total stupefaction they were left for their prayers the Onufriyev Church at the cemetery.)

And that is how one of the favorite sayings constantly repeated by the prisoners came true: A holy place is never empty. The chimes of bells fell silent, the icon lamps and the candle stands fell dark, the liturgies and the vespers resounded no longer; psalms were no longer chanted around the clock, the iconostases were wrecked (though they left the one in the Cathedral of the Transfiguration)—but on the other hand courageous Chekists, in overcoats with superlong flaps which reached all the way down to the heels, and particularly distinctive black Solovetsky cuffs and lapels and black-edged service caps without stars, arrived there in June, 1923, to set up a model camp, a model of severity, the pride of the workers' and peasants' Republic.

Whatever *Special Purpose* might mean had not yet been formulated and set forth in instructions. But they had of course explained this orally at the Lubyanka to the chief of the Solovetsky Camp, Eichmans. And he, on arriving at the islands himself, had explained it to his closest assistants.

∎

Nowadays you could not astonish former zeks or even just plain people of the sixties with the story of Solovki. But just let

---

7. They removed the fishermen from Solovki about 1930—and from that date on, the herring catches came to an end: no one could manage to find that particular herring in the sea any more, and it was as if it had completely disappeared.

the reader imagine to himself, if he will, a person of Chekhov's and post-Chekhov Russia, a person of the Silver Age of our culture, as they called the decade after 1910, brought up *then*, a bit shaken up by the Civil War no doubt, but nonetheless accustomed to the kind of food, clothing, and mutual verbal communication customary among human beings—and then and there he enters the gates of Solovki—Kemperpunkt, the Kem Transit Camp.[8] This transit camp in Kem was barren, without a tree or bush, Popov Island, joined to the mainland by a dike. And the first thing he would see in that naked, dirty pen would be a quarantine company (for they organized the prisoners there in "companies"—they had not yet discovered the "brigade") dressed *in sacks*. Just ordinary sacks: the legs stuck out down below as if from under a skirt, and there were holes for head and arms (impossible to imagine something like that, but what is there that our Russian ingenuity cannot overcome!). This sack the newcomer would avoid as long as he had his own clothes, but before he had even managed to examine those sacks well, he would see the legendary Captain Kurilko.

Kurilko (or Beloborodov, interchangeable with him) also came out to the prisoner transport column in a long Chekist overcoat with those frightening black cuffs which looked so utterly outlandish against the background of the old Russian khaki—like a herald of death. He jumped up on a barrel or some other suitable elevation, and he spoke to the new arrivals with unexpectedly strident rage: "Hey! Attention! Here the republic is not So-viets-ka-ya but Solovets-ka-ya! Get this straight —no prosecutor has ever set foot on Solovetsky soil! And none ever will! Learn one thing! You have *not* been sent here for correction! You can't straighten out a hunchback! The system here will be this: When I say, 'Stand up,' you stand up; when I say, 'Lie down,' you lie down! Your letters home are going to read like this: I'm alive, healthy, and satisfied with everything! Period!"

Struck dumb with astonishment, famous noblemen, intellectuals from the capital, priests, mullahs, and dark Central Asians listened to him and heard such things as had never before been heard or seen or read. And Kurilko, who had never

8. In Finnish this place is called Vegeraksha, i.e., "The Habitation of Witches."

made a splash during the Civil War, but who now, by this particular historical method, was writing his name in the chronicle of all Russia, got more and more worked up by each successful shout and turn of phrase, and kept formulating and spontaneously sharpening up still other, new ones.

And so, vainglorious and in full cry (and thinking maliciously inside himself: You prisoners, where were you hiding when we were fighting against the Bolsheviks? You thought you could sit the whole thing out in your nooks and crannies? And now they've dragged you here! So that's for your shitty neutrality! And I'm friends with the Bolsheviks, we are people of deeds!), Kurilko would begin his exercises:

"Hello, First Quarantine Company! . . . That's bad, it's not loud enough, once more! Hello, First Quarantine Company! . . . That's not loud enough! . . . You have got to shout 'Hello' so loud that they can hear you over there on Solovki, across the bay! When two hundred men shout, the walls have got to fall down! Once again! Hello, First Quarantine Company!"

Making sure that everyone was shouting at the top of his lungs and was ready to fall in his tracks, exhausted by shouting, Kurilko began his new exercise—the quarantine company was to run around a post:

"Legs higher! Legs higher!"

He was having hard going himself by now—like a tragedian before the final murder in the fifth act. And in the last hoarse croak of his half-hour of instruction, as a confession of the essence of Solovki, he promised those falling and those fallen, already prostrate on the ground: "I'll make you suck the snot from corpses!"

And that was just the first training session, intended to break the will of the newly arrived prisoners. And in the black, wooden, rotten, stinking barracks they would be ordered "to sleep on their sides"—which wasn't so bad either, because that was for those prisoners whom *the squad leaders* would squeeze onto the bunks —for a bribe. And all the rest would *stand* between the bunks all night (and anyone guilty of an offense would be set to stand, furthermore, between the latrine barrel and the wall).

And these were the blessed years of 1923 and 1925, before the great turning point, before the personality cult, before the distortions, before the violations. (And from 1927 on there was this in addition—that urki, thieves, would already be lying there on the bunks and snapping the lice off themselves into the midst of the standing intellectuals.)

While waiting for the steamship *Gleb Boky*,[9] they worked at the Kem Transit Camp, and some of them might be compelled to run around the post hollering incessantly: "I'm a sponger, I don't want to work, and I get in the way of others!" And an engineer who fell off the latrine barrel and spilled it on himself was not allowed in the barracks and was left outside to freeze in all his sewage. And sometimes the convoy would shout: "No laggards in the group! The convoy shoots without warning! Forward march!" And then, sliding the bolts of their rifles into position: "You trying to bug us?" And in the winter they would chase them out on the ice on foot, forcing them to drag the boats behind them and row across patches of water, and then in open water they would load them into the steamship's hold and shove so many in that before getting to Solovki several of them would certainly die—without ever seeing the snowy-white monastery inside the brown walls.

In his very first Solovetsky hours the newcomer might well experience the Solovetsky reception bath trick: He has already undressed, and the first bath attendant dips a swab into a cask of green soap and swabs the newcomer; the second one boots him somewhere down below, down an inclined board or a flight of stairs; down there a third bath attendant lets him, still confused, have a whole bucketful; and a fourth right off shoves him out into the dressing room, where his "rags" have already been tossed down from above however they happen to land. (In this joke one can foresee all Gulag! Both its tempo and the price of a human being.)

And that is how the newcomer swallowed the Solovetsky spirit! A spirit still unknown in the country as a whole, but which repre-

---

9. Named in honor of the Chairman of the Moscow Troika of the OGPU, a young man who never finished his studies:

"He was a student, he was a mining student,
   But passing marks* just never came."

(This was a "friendly epigram" which appeared in the magazine *Solovetskiye Ostrova*, No. 1, 1929. The censor was stupid, and he didn't understand what he had passed.)

sented the future spirit of the Archipelago created at Solovki.

And here, too, the newcomer would see people in sacks; and also in ordinary "free" clothing, new on some and tattered on others; and in the special Solovetsky short pea jackets made from coat material (this was a privilege; this was a sign of high position; that was how the camp administrative personnel dressed), with the so-called "Solovchanki," caps made from the same kind of cloth; and suddenly you would see a person walking about among the prisoners in formal tail coat, and no one was surprised, no one turned around to look at him and laugh. (After all, everyone came wearing what was his own. This poor chap had been arrested in the Metropole Restaurant* and so there he was, slogging out his sentence in his tail coat.)

The magazine *The Solovetsky Islands* (1930, No. 1) declared it was the "dream of many prisoners" to receive standard clothing.[10]

Only the children's colony was completely dressed. And the women, for example, were given neither underwear nor stockings nor even kerchiefs to cover their heads. They had grabbed the old biddy in a summer dress; she just had to go on wearing it the whole Arctic winter. Because of this many prisoners remained in their company quarters in nothing but their underwear, and no one chased them out to work.

Government-issue clothing was so precious that no one on Solovki found the following scene either astonishing or weird: In the middle of winter a prisoner undressed and took his shoes off near the kremlin, then carefully handed in his uniform and ran naked for two hundred yards to another group of people, where he was given clothes to put on. This meant that he was being transferred from the kremlin administration to the administration of the Filimonovo Branch Railroad[11]—but if he had been transferred wearing clothes, those taking him over might

---

10. All values turn upside down with the years, and what was considered a privilege in the Special Purpose Camp of the twenties—to wear government-issue clothing—would become an annoyance in the Special Camp of the forties; there the privilege would be *not* to wear government-issue clothing, but to wear at least something of one's own, even just a cap. The reason here was not economic only but was a cry of the whole epoch: one decade saw as its ideal how to join in the common lot, and the other how to get away from it.

11. They had dragged the railroad from Staraya Russa to Novgorod all the way over here.

not have returned the clothes or have cheated by switching them.

And here is another winter scene—the same customs, though the reason is different. The Medical Section infirmary is found to be infectious, and orders are issued to scald it down and wash it out with boiling water. But where are the sick prisoners to be put in the meanwhile? All the kremlin accommodations are overcrowded, the density of the population of the Solovetsky Archipelago is greater than that of Belgium—so what must it be like in the Solovetsky kremlin? And therefore all the sick prisoners are carried out on blankets and laid out on the snow for three hours. When they have washed out the infirmary, they haul the patients in again.

We have not forgotten, I hope, that our newcomer is a child of the Silver Age? He knows nothing of the Second World War or of Buchenwald! What he sees is this: *The squad leaders* in khaki pea jackets, stiffly erect, greet one another and the company leaders with salutes, and then they drive their workers out with long clubs—with *staves* (and there is even a special verb, which everyone understands, meaning "*to stave*"). He sees that sledges and carts are drawn not by horses but by men (several harnessed into one rig)—and there is also another word, *VRIDLO* (an acronym meaning a "Temporary Replacement for a Horse").

And from other Solovetsky inhabitants he learns things more awful than his eyes perceive. People pronounce the fatal word "*Sekirka*" to him. This means Sekirnaya Hill. Punishment cells were set up in the two-story cathedral there. And here is how they kept prisoners in the punishment cells: Poles the thickness of an arm were set from wall to wall and prisoners were ordered to sit on these poles all day. (At night they lay on the floor, one on top of another, because it was overcrowded.) The height of the poles was set so that one's feet could not reach the ground. And it was not so easy to keep balance. In fact, the prisoner spent the entire day just trying to maintain his perch. If he fell, the jailers jumped in and beat him. Or else they took him outside to a flight of stairs consisting of 365 steep steps (from the cathedral to the lake, just as the monks had built it) (Illustration No. 4: the view up Sekirnaya Hill as it is today). They tied the person lengthwise to a "balan" (a beam), for the added weight,

3. Church of the Beheading on Sekirnaya Hill

4. Steps up Sekirnaya Hill

and rolled him down (and there wasn't even one landing, and the steps were so steep that the log with the human being on it would go all the way down without stopping).

Well, after all, for *poles* you didn't have to go to Sekirka. They were right there in the kremlin punishment block, which was always overcrowded. Or they might put the prisoners on a sharp-edged boulder on which one could not stay long either. Or, in summer, "on the stump," which meant naked among the mosquitoes. But in that event one had to keep an eye on the culprit; whereas if he was bound naked to a tree, the mosquitoes would look after things themselves. And then they could put whole companies out in the snow for disobedience. Or they might drive a person into the marsh muck up to his neck and keep him there. And then there was another way: to hitch up a horse in empty shafts and fasten the culprit's legs to the shafts; then the guard mounted the horse and kept on driving the horse through a forest cut until the groans and the cries from behind simply came to an end.

Before even beginning his life on Solovki the novice was oppressed in his spirit simply by the fact of his endless three-year term. But the contemporary reader would be much too hasty if he concluded that this was an open and aboveboard system of destruction, of death camps! Oh, no, we are not so simple! In that first experimental camp, as in others afterward, and in the most comprehensive of them all, we never act openly. It is all mixed up, layer upon layer. And that is why it is so long-lasting and so successful.

All of a sudden through the kremlin gates rode some daredevil astride a goat. He bore himself with importance and no one laughed at him. Who was it and why was he on a goat? This was Degtyaryov. In the past he had been a cowboy.[12] He had asked for a horse, but there were few horses on Solovki, so they gave him a goat. What had he done to deserve the honor? Because he had been a cowboy? No, not at all, because he was the manager of the Dendrological Nursery. He grew exotic trees. Here on Solovki.

---

12. Not to be confused with the free Degtyaryov, the Chief of Troops of the Solovetsky Archipelago.

And so it was that from this horseman on a goat there arose a Solovetsky fantasy. Why should there be exotic trees on Solovki, where even the simple and reasonable vegetable economy of the monks had been destroyed, and where the vegetables were running out? Well, they were there because exotic trees at the Arctic Circle meant that Solovki, like the entire Soviet Republic, was remaking the world and building a new life. But where did the seeds and the funds come from? That's exactly the point: there was money for seeds for the Dendrological Nursery; there just wasn't any money for feeding the logging crews (where food was provided not according to norms but according to available funds).

And as for archaeological excavations? Yes, we have a Commission for Excavations. It is important for us to know our past.

In front of the camp administration building was a flowerbed. In it was outlined a friendly elephant—the acronym for "Solovetsky Special Purpose Camp" being SLON—"elephant." On the blanket on the elephant's back was the letter "U"—standing for "Administration." And that very same rebus was on the Solovetsky coupons which circulated as the currency of this northern state. What a pleasant, cozy little masquerade! So it would seem that everything was really very nice here, that that practical joker Kurilko had only been trying to throw a scare into us for nothing? And then, too, the camp had its own magazine—also called *Slon.* (The first numbers came out in 1924, typed, and from issue No. 9 on it was printed in the monastery printing shop.) From 1925 on *The Solovetsky Islands* had been published in two hundred copies, and had its own supplement— the newspaper *Novyye Solovki* (*New Solovki*). (We shall break with our accursed monastery past!) And from 1926 on subscriptions were accepted from the entire Soviet Union, and the run was a large one, and it was a big success.[13] Censorship of the magazine was evidently superficial; the prisoners (according to Glubokovsky) wrote joking verses about the GPU Troika—and they were passed! And then they were sung from the stage of the

---

13. And almost immediately it was broken off: the regime showed it was not in such a joking mood. In 1929, after the big events on Solovki and a general turn in all camps in the direction of re-education, the magazine was started up once again and appeared until 1932.

Solovetsky theater right in front of Troika Chairman Gleb Boky himself:

> They promised us gifts—a bag full—
> Boky, Feldman, Vasilyev and Vul!

And this bigwig liked it! (Well, after all it was flattering! You hadn't even finished school—and here you were, going down in history.) Then the chorus:

> All those who rewarded us with Solovki,
> We do invite: Come take your leisure!
> Sit here with us for three or five—
> You'll always remember them with pleasure!

They roared! They liked it! (Who was there to figure out that this was a prophecy?)

And impudent Shepchinsky, the son of a general who had been shot, then hung a slogan over the entrance gates:

"SOLOVKI—FOR THE WORKERS AND PEASANTS!"

(And this, too, was a prophecy after all! But it didn't go over well: they figured this one out, and they took it down.)

The actors of the dramatics troupe wore costumes made out of church vestments. They presented *The Rails Hum*. There were affected foxtrotting couples on the stage (the dying West)— and a victorious Red forge painted on the backdrop (Us).

It was a fantastic world! No, that scoundrel Kurilko had just been joking!

And then there was also the Solovetsky Society for Local Lore, which published reports and researches. For instance, about the unique sixteenth-century architecture or the Solovetsky fauna. And they wrote in such detail and with such scholarly devotion, with such a gentle love for their subject, that it really seemed as if these idle eccentric scholars had come to the island because of their passion for knowledge, not as prisoners who had already passed through the Lubyanka and who were trembling lest they end up on Sekirnaya Hill, or out under mosquitoes, or fastened to the empty shafts behind a horse. Yes, the very Solovetsky beasts and birds, in keeping with the spirit of the students of local lore, had not yet died out, had not been shot or expelled, were not even frightened. Even as late as 1928 a whole trusting brood of hares would come right up to the very edge of the road and watch with curiosity the prisoners being led off to Anzer.

5. The bell tower

6. Door under the bell tower arch

How had it happened that the hares had not been exterminated? They would explain it to the newcomer this way: The little beasts and birds are not afraid here because there is a GPU order in effect: *"Save ammunition!* Not a single shot is to be fired, *except at a prisoner!"*

So all the scares were just a joke! But a shout comes in broad daylight in the kremlin yard where prisoners are crowded as thick as on Nevsky Prospekt: "Make way! Make way!" And three foppish young men with the faces of junkies (the lead man drives back the crowd of prisoners not with a club but with a riding crop) drag along swiftly by the shoulders a prisoner with limp arms and legs dressed only in his underwear. His face is horrible—*flowing* like liquid! They drag him off *beneath the bell tower* (Illustrations Nos. 5 and 6: right there beneath the arch and through that low door—it is set into the bell tower foundations). They squeeze him through that little door and shoot him in the back of the head—steep stairs lead down inside, and he tumbles down them, and they can pile up as many as seven or eight men in there, and then send men to drag out the corpses and detail women (mothers and wives of men who have emigrated to Constantinople and religious believers who refuse to recant their faith and to allow their children to be torn from it) to wash down the steps.[14]

But why like this? Couldn't they have done it at night—quietly? But why do it quietly? In that case a bullet would be wasted. In the daytime crowd the bullet had an educational function. It, so to speak, struck down ten with one shot.

They shot them in a different way too—right at the Onufriyev cemetery, behind the women's barracks (the former guest house for women pilgrims). And in fact that road past the women's barracks was christened *execution* road. In winter one could see a man being led barefoot along it, in only his underwear, through the snow (no, it was not for torture! it was just so his footgear and clothes should not go to waste), his hands bound behind his back with wire,[15] and the condemned man would bear himself

14. And right now, there on the stones over which they dragged them, in that part of the courtyard secluded from the Solovetsky wind, cheerful tourists, who have come to see the notorious islands, *sock a volleyball* hours at a time. They do not know. Well, and if they did know? They would go on *socking* anyway.

15. A Solovetsky method which, strangely, was repeated with the corpses at Katyn Forest. Someone remembered—a matter perhaps of tradition? Or was it personal experience?

proudly and erectly, and with his lips alone, without the help of his hands, smoke the last cigarette of his life. (This was how you recognized an officer. After all, these were men who had gone through seven years on different fronts. There was an eighteen-year-old youth, the son of the historian V. A. Potto, who, when he was asked his profession by a work assigner,* replied with a shrug of the shoulders: "Machine gunner." Because of his youth, in the heat of the Civil War, he had never managed to acquire any other.)

A fantastic world! And that's the way it is sometimes. Much in history repeats itself, but there also exist completely unique combinations, brief in duration, and limited in place. One such example was our New Economic Policy—the NEP. And another was early Solovki.

There weren't many Chekists there at all (yes, and those who were may well have been in semipunishment status); no more than twenty to forty people held sway over thousands, many thousands. (At the very beginning they hadn't expected so many, but Moscow kept sending and sending and sending. In the first half-year, by December, 1923, there were already two thousand prisoners gathered there. And in 1928 in the 13th Company alone—the general-work company—the last in formation on count-off would announce: "The 376th! Ten in the unit!" And what that added up to was 3,760 men, and the 12th Company was just as large, and the 17th—which dug mass graves in the cemetery—was even bigger. And in addition to the kremlin companies there were already others in "kommandirovki"—temporary work parties: Savvatiyevo, Filimonovo, Muksalma, Trinity, and "Zaichiki"—the Zayatsky Islands.) By 1928 there were altogether about sixty thousand. And how many among them were "machine gunners," veteran soldiers with long service records? And in 1926 the inveterate habitual-criminal elements of all sorts began to flood in. And how were they all to be kept in check, kept from rebelling?

Only *by terror!* Only with Sekirnaya Hill! With poles! With mosquitoes! By being dragged through stumps! By daytime executions! Moscow kept pushing out prisoner transports without taking into consideration local forces—but neither did Moscow set limitations on its Chekists by hypocritical rules: everything done to maintain order was a fait accompli, and it was really true that no prosecutor would set foot on Solovetsky soil.

And the second method was a gauze veil with a fringe: the era of equality—and New Solovki! Self-guarding by the prisoners! Self-supervision! Self-verification! Company commanders, platoon commanders, squad leaders—all from among the prisoners themselves. And their own amateur stage shows and their own self-amusement!

And beneath this terror and this fringe what kind of people were there? Who? Genuine aristocrats. Career military men. Philosophers. Scholars. Painters. Actors. Lyceum graduates.[16] Because of their upbringing, their traditions, they were too proud to show depression or fear, to whine and complain about their fate even to friends. It was a sign of good manners to take everything with a smile, even while being marched out to be shot. Just as if all this Arctic prison in a roaring sea were simply a minor misunderstanding at a picnic. To joke. To make fun of the jailers.

So there was an elephant on the money and in the flowerbed. So there was a goat in place of a horse.

And if the 7th Company was made up of actors, then its company leader had to be Kunst. And if there was a person named Berry-Yagoda,* then he, of course, had to be the chief of the berry-drier. And that is how those jokes came about which got past the ignoramus censors of the magazine. And those songs. Georgi Mikhailovich Osorgin used to walk around and mock: "Comment vous portez-vous on this island?" "A lager comme a lager."

(And these jokes, this stressed and emphasized independence of the aristocratic spirit—these more than anything else irritated the half-beast Solovetsky jailers. One time Osorgin was scheduled

16. Here are a few of the Solovki veterans whose names have been preserved in the memoirs of those who survived: Shirinskaya-Shakhmatova, Sheremeteva, Shakhovskaya, Fittstum, I. S. Delvig, Bagratuni, Assotsiani-Erisov, Gosheron de la Foss, Sivers, G. M. Osorgin, Klodt, N. N. Bakhrushin, Aksakov, Komarovsky, P. M. Voyeikov, Vadbolsky, Vonlyarlyarsky, V. Levashov, O. V. Volkov, V. Lozino-Lozinsky, D. Gudovich, Taube, V. S. Muromtsev, former Cadet leader Nekrasov (was it he?), the financier Professor Ozerov, the jurist Professor A. B. Borodin, the psychologist Professor A. P. Sukhanov, the philosophers Professor A. A. Meiyer, Professor S. A. Askoldov, Y. N. Danzas, the theosophist Myobus. The historians N. P. Antsiferov, M. D. Priselkov, G. O. Gordon, A. I. Zaozersky, P. G. Vasiyenko. The literary scholars D. S. Likhachev, Tseitlin, the linguist I. Y. Anichkov, the Orientalist N. V. Pigulevskaya, the ornithologist G. Polyakov, the artists Braz and P. F. Smotritsky, the actors I. D. Kalugin (of the Aleksandrinka), B. Glubokovsky, V. Y. Korolenko (a nephew). In the thirties, near the end of Solovki, Father Pavel A. Florensky was also there.

to be shot. And that very day his young wife [and he himself was not yet forty] disembarked on the wharf there. And Osorgin begged the jailers not to spoil his wife's visit for her. He promised that he would not let her stay more than three days and that they could shoot him as soon as she left. And here is the kind of self-control this meant, the sort of thing we have forgotten because of the anathema we have heaped upon the aristocracy, we who whine at every petty misfortune and every petty pain: For three days he never left his wife's side, and he had to keep her from guessing the situation! He must not hint at it even in one single phrase! He must not allow his spirits to quaver. He must not allow his eyes to darken. Just once [his wife is alive and she remembers it now], when they were walking along the Holy Lake, she turned and saw that her husband had clutched his head in torment. "What's wrong?" "Nothing," he answered instantly. She could have stayed still longer, but he begged her to leave. As the steamer pulled away from the wharf, he was already undressing to be shot.)

But still someone did give them those three days. Those three Osorgin days, like other cases, show how far the Solovetsky regime was from having donned the armor of *a system*. The impression is left that the *air* of Solovki strangely mingled extreme cruelty with an almost benign incomprehension of where all this was leading, which Solovetsky characteristics were becoming the embryo of the great Archipelago and which were destined to dry up and wither in the bud. After all, the Solovetsky Islands people did not yet, generally speaking, firmly believe that the ovens of the Arctic Auschwitz had been lit right there and that its crematory furnaces had been thrown open to all who were ever brought there. (But, after all, that is exactly how it was!) People there were also misled by the fact that all their prison terms were exceedingly short: it was rare that anyone had a ten-year term, and even five was not found very often, and most of them were three, just three. And this whole cat-and-mouse trick of the law was still not understood: to pin down and let go, and pin down again and let go again. And that patriarchal failure to understand where everything was heading could not have failed entirely to influence the guards from among the prisoners also, and perhaps in a minor way the prison keepers themselves.

No matter how clear-cut the declarations of the class teaching, openly displayed and proclaimed everywhere, that the sole fate the enemy deserves is annihilation—still, it was impossible to picture to oneself the annihilation of each concrete two-legged individual possessing hair, eyes, a mouth, a neck and shoulders. One could actually believe that *classes* were being destroyed, but the *people* who constituted these classes should be left, shouldn't they? The eyes of Russians who had been brought up in other generous and vague concepts, like eyes seeing through badly prescribed eyeglasses, could in no wise read with exactitude the phrases of the cruel teaching. Not long before, apparently, there had been months and years of openly proclaimed terror—yet it was still impossible to believe!

Here, too, on the first islands of the Archipelago, was felt the instability of those checkered years of the middle twenties, when things were but poorly understood in the country as a whole. Was everything already prohibited? Or, on the contrary, were things only now beginning to be allowed? Age-old Russia still believed so strongly in rapturous phrases! And there were only a few prophets of gloom who had already figured things out and who knew when and how all this would be smashed into smithereens.

The cupola had been damaged by fire—but the masonry was eternal. . . . The land cultivated on the very edge of the earth . . . had now been laid waste. The color of the restless sea was changeable. The lakes still. The animals trusting. The people merciless. And the albatrosses flew to the Bay of Biscay to spend the winter with all the secrets of the first island of the Archipelago. But they would not tell their secrets on the carefree beaches . . . but they would tell no one in Europe.

A fantastic world. And one of the main short-lived fantasies was this: camp life was run by . . . White Guards! So Kurilko was . . . not a chance phenomenon.

Here is how it worked. In the whole kremlin the only free Chekist was the camp duty officer. Guarding the gates (there were no watchtowers) and patrolling the islands and catching escapees were up to the guard. Other than free people, they recruited into the guard ordinary murderers, counterfeiters, and other habitual criminals (but not the thieves). But who was there to take charge of the whole internal organization, who was to run the Administrative Section, and who were to be the company and squad commanders? Not, certainly, the priests, nor the sectarian prisoners, nor the NEPmen, nor the scholars, nor the students. (There were no few students there, too, but a student's cap on the head of a Solovetsky prisoner was considered a challenge, an impudence, a black mark, and an application to get shot.) It was former military men who could do this best. And what military people were there other than the White officers?

And thus, without any special deal and hardly as the result of any well-thought-out plan, the Solovetsky cooperation of the Chekists and the White Guards began!

Where were the principles of either? It is surprising? Astonishing? Only to someone used to social analysis on a class basis and unable to see differently. But to such an analyst everything in the whole world is bound to be astonishing, because the world and human beings never fit into his previously set grooves.

And the Solovetsky prison keepers would have taken the devil himself into their service, given that they had not been given "Red" personnel. It had been decreed: the prisoners should supervise themselves (in other words, oppress themselves). And who was there to whom this could better have been entrusted?

And as for the eternal officers, the "military breed," how could they forgo taking into their own hands at least the organization of camp life (camp oppression)? Just how could they stand aside submissively, watching someone else take charge incapably and mess everything up? We have already discussed earlier in this book the subject of what shoulder boards do to the human heart. (And just bide your time. The day will come when the Red commanding officers will be arrested too—and how they will fight for jobs in the camp guards, how they will long to get hold of a turnkey's rifle, just so as to be trusted again! I have already said that if Malyuta Skuratov had just summoned us . . .) Well, and the White Guards must have felt much the same: All right, we're lost anyway, and *everything* is lost, so what difference does it make, why not! Then too: "The worse, the better"—we'll help you make a hellhole out of Solovki, of a kind that never ever existed in *our* Russia, and your reputation will be all the worse. And then: All the rest of our boys agreed, so what am I supposed to do—sit in the warehouse as a bookkeeper like a priest?

Nonetheless, the most fantastic Solovetsky story was not just that alone but the fact that, having taken over the Administrative Section, the White Guards began to *put up a fight* against the Chekists! It's your camp on the outside, so to say, and ours on the inside. And it was the business of the Administrative Section to decide who worked where and who would be sent where. We don't meddle outside, so don't you meddle inside!

Not very likely, that! For after all, the Information and Investigation Section—the ISCh—had to have the whole inside of the camp speckled with its stoolies! This was the primary and the dreaded power in camp—the ISCh. (And the security officers were also recruited from among the prisoners—the crowning glory of prisoner self-supervision!) And that was what the White Guard Administrative Section—the ACh—took upon itself to do battle with! All the other *sections*—the Cultural and Educational Section and the Medical Section, which would have such great significance in future camps—were both frail and pitiful here. And the Economic Section, headed by N. Frenkel, was also merely vegetating. It engaged in "trade" with the outside world and ran the nonexistent "industry"; the paths of its future grandeur had not yet been plotted. So it was the two powers, the ISCh and the ACh, that fought it out. It began right at the Kem Transit Camp: The newly arrived poet A. Yaroslavsky approached the squad commander and whispered something in his ear. The squad commander bellowed out his words with military precision: "You were *secret*—so now you're *public!*"

The ISCh had its Sekirka, its punishment blocks, its denunciations, its personal case files on the prisoners, and had control of liberating prisoners ahead of time and executions. It also was in charge of censoring letters and parcels. And the ACh controlled work parties, reassignment from island to island, and prisoner transports.

The ACh exposed the ISCh stoolies in order to send them off on prisoner transports. The stoolies were pursued and fled and hid in ISCh headquarters—but they were pursued even there, and the ISCh rooms were broken into and the stoolies dragged out and hauled off to prisoner transports.[17]

(They were dispatched to Kondostrov, to logging camps. And there the fantastic story went right on. In Kondostrov the exposed

17. It is interesting that the dawn of the Archipelago thus began with the very same phenomenon to which the later Special Camps returned: with a blow struck at the stoolies.

and ruined stoolies published a wall newspaper entitled *Stukach* [*Stoolie*], and in it, with sad humor, they further "exposed" in each other such sins as "being overpampered" and the like.)

At this point the heads of ISCh brought *charges* against the eager beavers of the ACh, lengthened their terms, and sent them to Sekirka. But the ISCh defense was complicated by the fact that an exposed informer, in the interpretation of those years, was considered a criminal. (Article 121 of the Criminal Code: "disclosure . . . by an official personage of information not to be disclosed"—quite independently of whether disclosure took place intentionally or not and in what degree the individual was actually an *official* personage.) Consequently, exposed informers could not be defended and saved by the ISCh. Once caught they had only themselves to blame. Kondostrov was almost legitimized.

The height of the "hostilities" between the ISCh and the ACh came in 1927 when the White Guards broke into the ISCh, cracked the safe, seized and published the complete lists of stoolies —who thereby became hopeless criminals! After that, however, the ACh steadily declined: there were ever fewer former officers, and the percentage of criminals continually rose (for example, the "chubarovtsy"—as a result of the notorious Leningrad thugs trial). And gradually the Administrative Section was subdued.

Yes, and then in the thirties a new camp era began, when Solovki even ceased to be Solovki—and became a mere run-of-the-mill "Corrective Labor Camp." And the black star of the ideologist of that new era, Naftaly Frenkel, rose in the heavens while his formula became the supreme law of the Archipelago:

"We have to squeeze everything out of a prisoner in the first three months—after that we don't need him any more."

■

But where are Savvaty and German and Zosima? Who was it who thought of living below the Arctic Circle, where cattle can't be bred and fish can't be caught and breadgrains and vegetables don't grow?

Oh, you experts at ruining flourishing lands! So soon—in one year or two—to reduce the model agricultural enterprise of the monks to total and irreversible decline! How was it done? Did they plunder it and send away the plunder? Or did they destroy it all right there on the spot? And to be incapable of extracting

7. The Chapel of German

8. Preobrazhensky Cathedral: entrance

9. Preobrazhensky Cathedral (Church of the Transfiguration)

anything from the good earth while possessing thousands of unoccupied hands!

Only the free people there had milk, sour cream, and fresh meat, yes, and the excellent cabbage of Father Methodius. And for prisoners there was rotten cod, salted or dried; a thin gruel with pearl barley or millet grits and without potatoes. And there was never either cabbage soup or borscht. And as a result there was scurvy, and even "the office workers' companies" all had boils, and as for those on *general work*, their situation can be imagined. Prisoner transports returned "on all fours" from distant work parties—they actually crawled from the wharf on hands and knees.

The prisoners were allowed to use up nine rubles a month out of money orders from home—and there was a prison commissary in the Chapel of German (Illustration No. 7). And one parcel a month could be received, which was opened and inspected in the ISCh, and if you didn't bribe them, they would announce that much of what had been sent you was *prohibited*—grits, for example. In the Nikolskaya Church and in the Uspensky Cathedral the bunks rose—four tiers high. Nor was the 13th Company any less crowded in the block attached to the Preobrazhensky Cathedral (Illustration No. 9). Imagine the crowded mass of prisoners at that entrance (Illustration No. 8): 3,500 stampeding back to quarters on returning from work. It took an hour's wait in line to get hot water at the boilers. On Saturdays the evening roll calls dragged out till very, very late at night (like the former religious services). They were very particular about hygiene, of course: prisoners were forced to have heads clipped and beards shaved off (also all priests—one after another). In addition, they cut all the flaps off long clothing (particularly cassocks, of course), for they were a principal point of infection. (The Chekists had greatcoats which reached right down to the ground.) True, in the winter the ill and the aged sitting there in underwear and sacks could not make it to the baths from the company bunks. They were done in by the lice. (They hid the corpses under the bunks so as to get the extra rations—even though that was not very advantageous for the living: the lice crawled from the cold corpses onto the warm living survivors.) In the kremlin there was a bad Medical Section with a bad hospital, and in the remoter parts of Solovki there was no medicine at all.

(The sole exception was the Golgotha-Crucifixion Monastery on Anzer, a penalty work party, where they cured patients . . . by murdering them. There in the Golgotha Church prisoners lay dying from lack of food and from cruelty, enfeebled priests next to syphilitics, and aged invalids next to young thieves. At the request of the dying, and in order to ease his own problem, the Golgotha doctor gave terminal cases strychnine; and in the winter the bearded corpses in their underwear were kept in the church for a long time. Then they were put in the vestibule, stacked standing up since that way they took up less space. And when they carried them out, they gave them a shove and let them roll on down Golgotha Hill.[18])

At one time—in 1928—a typhus epidemic broke out in Kem. And 60 percent of those there died, but the typhus crossed to Bolshoi Solovetsky Island as well, and hundreds of typhus patients lay about in the unheated "theatrical" hall all at the same time. And hundreds likewise left there for the cemetery. (So as not to confuse the count, the work assigners wrote the last name of every prisoner on his wrist, and some of those who recovered switched terms with shorter-term cadavers by rewriting the corpses' names on their own hands.) And when many thousands of the Central Asian "Basmachi" rebels were herded here in 1929, they brought with them an epidemic characterized by black spots on the body, and all who fell ill with it died. It could not, of course, be the plague or smallpox, as Solovki people imagined it was, because those two diseases had already been totally wiped out in the Soviet Republic. And so they called the illness "Asiatic typhus." They didn't know how to cure it, and here is how they got rid of it: If one prisoner in a cell caught it, they just locked the cell and let no one out, and passed them food only through the door—till they all died.

What a scientific discovery it would be for us to establish that

18. This is an unusual name for a church and monastery, not encountered anywhere else. According to legend (a manuscript of the eighteenth century in the State Public Library, "Solovetsky Paterik" ["The Lives of the Solovetsky Fathers"]), on June 18, 1712, the monk-priest Job during an all-night prayer vigil at the foot of this hill saw a vision of the Mother of God "in all the glory of heaven"—and she said to him: "This hill from henceforth shall be called Golgotha, and on it shall be built a church and a monastery of the Crucifixion. And it will be whitened by the sufferings of countless multitudes." That is what they named it, and they built it there, but for more than two hundred years the prophecy was an empty one; and it did not seem likely that it would ever come true. But after the Solovetsky camp one could no longer say this.

in Solovki the Archipelago had not yet arrived at an understanding of itself, that the child had not yet guessed its own character! And then to observe how this character gradually manifested itself. Alas, it didn't work out that way! Even though there was no one to learn from, even though there was no one from whom to take an example, and even though it would seem that there was no hereditary element, nonetheless the Archipelago swiftly discovered and manifested its future character.

So much future experience had already been discovered at Solovki. The phrase "to extricate from general work" had already come into existence. All slept on board bunks, but there were nevertheless some who had individual cots. There were whole companies in the church, but some prisoners were crowded twenty to a room, and there were other rooms, with only four or five. There were already some who knew their rights: to inspect the women's prisoner transports and pick out a woman. (There were only 150 to 200 women for thousands of men, but later on there were more.) A struggle for the soft cushy spots through bootlicking and betrayal was already going on. They had already removed all the *Kontriki*—"Counter-Revolutionaries"—from office positions, to which they were then restored because the habitual criminals only messed everything up. The camp air was already thick with continual ominous rumors. The supreme law of conduct had already become: Trust no one! (And this squeezed and froze out the spiritual grace of the Silver Age.)

The free persons, too, had begun to enter into the sweetness of camp life and to taste its joys: Free families received the right to have the free services of cooks from the camp. They could always demand the services of woodcutters, laundresses, seamstresses, and barbers. Eichmans built himself an Arctic villa. Potemkin, too, a former sergeant major of the dragoons, subsequently a Communist, a Chekist, and then the chief of Kem Transit Camp, lived lavishly. He opened a restaurant in Kem. His orchestra was recruited from Conservatory musicians. His waitresses wore silk dresses. Gulag comrades who arrived from rationed Moscow could feast and frolic in luxury here at the beginning of the thirties. They were served at table by Princess Shakhovskaya and their check was only a formality, amounting to something like thirty kopecks, the rest being at the camp's expense.

Yes, and the Solovetsky kremlin—this was not the whole

Solovki. It was the most privileged place in camp. The real Solovki was not even in the monasteries (where, after the socialists were sent away, work parties were established). The real Solovki was in the logging operations, at the remote work sites. But it is precisely those distant backwoods that are most difficult to learn about nowadays, because *those* people did not survive. It is known that even at that time they did not allow the workers to dry themselves out in the autumn, that in winter they did not provide them with clothes or footgear in the deep snow, and that the length of the workday was determined by the *work norm*: the workday was completed when the work norm had been executed, and if it wasn't, there was no return to shelter until it was. And at that time, too, they "discovered" the device of new work parties which consisted of sending several hundred people to totally unprepared, uninhabited places.

But it would seem that in the first years of Solovki both slave-driving the workers and allotting back-breaking *work norms* took the form of periodic outbursts, transitory anger; they had not become a viselike *system*. The economy of the whole country was not based on them, and the Five-Year Plans had not been instituted. In the first years of SLON there was evidently no firm external economic plan. Yes, and for that matter there was no very careful calculation of how many man-days went into work for the camp as a whole. This was why they could suddenly switch with such frivolity from meaningful productive work to punishment: pouring water from one ice hole into another, dragging logs from one place to another and back. There was cruelty in this, yes, but there was also a patriarchical attitude. When slave-driving became a thought-out *system*, pouring water over a prisoner in subzero temperatures or putting the prisoner out on a stump to be devoured by mosquitoes had turned into a superfluity and a useless expenditure of the executioners' energy.

There is an official figure: up to 1929 in the R.S.F.S.R.—the Russian Republic of the Soviet Union—"only 34 to 41 percent of all prisoners were engaged in work."[19] (And how could it have been any different, in view of the fact that there was unemployment in the country at the time?) It is not clear whether work at servicing and maintaining the camp itself was included in this

19. Vyshinsky, *op. cit.*, p. 115.

or whether it was only "external" work. At any rate, work at servicing and maintaining the camp itself would not have been enough to occupy all the remaining 60 to 65 percent of the camp prisoners. This proportion found its expression at Solovki as well. Clearly throughout the twenties there were no few prisoners without permanent work (partly because of the lack of anything to wear outdoors) or else performing purely formal duties.

That first year of the First Five-Year Plan, which shook up the entire country, shook up Solovki as well. The new Chief of SLON, appointed in 1930, Nogtev (the same Chief of the Savvatyevsky Monastery who had shot down the socialists), reported, to the accompaniment of a "whisper of astonishment in an astounded hall," to *the free inhabitants* of the city of Kem, these figures: "Not counting its logging operations for its own use, which had grown at quite exceptional tempos," USLON had filled "external" orders alone for the Railroad Timber Trust and the Karelian Timber Trust: in 1926—63,000 rubles; in 1929—2,355,000 rubles (thirty-seven times greater!); and in 1930, the total had jumped another three times. Road construction for the Karelian-Murmansk region had been carried out in 1926 in the amount of 105,000 rubles, and, in 1930, six million—increased by fifty-seven times![20]

And that is how the once remote Solovki, where they didn't know how to make full use of the prisoners, came to an end. The *miracle-worker work* rushed in to assist.

Solovki was created via Kem Transit Camp. And via Kem Transit Camp Solovki, in its maturity, began, at the end of the twenties, to spread back to the mainland. And the worst thing that could now befall a prisoner was to be sent out on these work parties on the mainland. Previously the sole mainland points belonging to Solovki were Soroka and Sumsky Posad—coastal appurtenances of the monasteries. But now the advancing SLON forgot its monastery boundaries.

From Kem, through the swamps to the west, to Ukhta, the prisoners began to build a dirt road, "which had at one time been considered almost impossible to build."[21] In the summer they drowned and in the winter they froze. The Solovki prisoners

20. *Solovetskiye Ostrova*, 1930, No. 2–3, pp. 56–57.
21. *Ibid.*, p. 57.

feared this road to the point of panic, and for a long time the threat echoed and re-echoed over the kremlin courtyard: "What? You're asking for *Ukhta?*"

The second, similar road was from Medvezhyegorsk to Parandovsky. On its route the Chekist Gashidze ordered explosives set into a cliff and then sent KR's up on the cliff and through his binoculars watched them being blown up.

They say that in December, 1928, on Krasnaya Gorka in Karelia, the prisoners were left to spend the night in the woods as punishment for failure to fulfill the assigned norm of work—and 150 men froze to death there. This was a standard Solovetsky trick. Hard to doubt the story.

There is somewhat greater difficulty in believing another story: that in February, 1929, on the Kem-Ukhta road near the tiny settlement of Kut, a company consisting of approximately one hundred prisoners *was driven into the bonfire for failure to fulfill the work norm—and burned alive!*

I was told this story by one solitary person only, who had been close by: Professor D. P. Kallistov, an old Solovki veteran, who died recently. But I was never able to collect any corroborative testimony. (And maybe no one ever will collect any—and there is also much else about which no one is ever going to collect testimony, even one single solitary report.) But after all, why shouldn't people who freeze other people to death and who blow them up in an explosion burn them alive? Because the technology involved was no more complex.

Let those who prefer to put their faith in the printed word rather than in living people read about the road-building by this very same USLON, and by the very same zeks, in the very same year, except that the area was the Kola Peninsula:

"With great difficulty we built the dirt road along the valley of the Belaya River, along the shore of Lake Vudyarv to Kukisvumchorr (near the present Apatity) for a distance of seventeen miles, paving a swamp. . . ." (And what would you think it was *paved* with? The answer fairly leaps to the tip of the tongue, doesn't it? But it can't be set down on paper. . . .) ". . . with logs and sand embankments, leveling the capricious configuration of the crumbling slopes of the stony mountains." And then USLON built a railroad there in addition—"seven miles in a single winter month." (And why in one month? And why couldn't it have been postponed till summer?) "The task seemed insuperable—400,000 cubic yards of excavations. . . ." (North of the Arctic Circle! In the middle of winter! And they called it earth? It was harder than any granite!) ". . . performed solely by hand—with pick, crowbar and spade." (And did they at least have mittens?) "The work was delayed by the need for a multitude of bridges. Work went on for twenty-four hours a day in three shifts, and the Arctic night was sliced by the light of incandescent kerosene lanterns as clearings were cut through the pine woods and stumps were dug out, in the midst of snowstorms which covered the roadbed deeper than the height of a man."[22]

Now go back and read that over. Then close your eyes and picture the scene: You are a helpless city dweller, a person who sighs and pines like a character in Chekhov. And there you are in that icy hell! Or you are a Turkmenian in your embroidered skull-cap—your "tyubeteika"—out there in that night blizzard! Digging out stumps!

This was in those best and brightest twenties, before any "personality cult," when the white, yellow, black, and brown races of the Earth looked upon our country as the torchbearer of freedom.[23] This was during those selfsame years when they used to sing amusing ditties about Solovki from the nation's vaudeville stages.

And so, imperceptibly—via work parties—the former concept of the Special Purpose Camp, totally isolated on its islands, dissolved. And the Archipelago, born and come to maturity on Solovki, began its malignant advance through the nation.

A problem arose: The territory of this country had to be spread out in front of the Archipelago—but without allowing the Archipelago to conquer it, to distract it, to take it over or assimilate it to itself. Every little island and every little hillock of the Archipelago had to be encircled by a hostile, stormy Soviet seascape. It was permissible for the two worlds to interlock in separate strata —but not to intermingle!

And this Nogtev report which evoked a "whisper of astonish-

---

22. G. Fridman, "Skazochnaya Byl" ("A Fairy Tale"), *Solovetskiye Ostrova,* 1930, No. 4, pp. 43–44.

23. Oh, Bertrand Russell! Oh, Hewlett Johnson! Where, oh where, was your flaming conscience *at that time?*

ment" was, after all, articulated so as to initiate a resolution, a resolution by the workers of Kem, which would then appear in the newspapers and be posted in the villages:

> . . . the intensifying class struggle inside the U.S.S.R. . . . and the danger of war which is increasing as never before[24] . . . require of the organs of the OGPU and USLON even greater solidarity with the workers, vigilance. . . .
>
> . . . by organization of public opinion . . . a struggle is to be waged against free persons' rubbing elbows with prisoners . . . against concealment of escapees . . . against purchase of stolen and government property from prisoners . . . and against all kinds of malicious rumors which are being disseminated by class enemies about USLON.

And just what were those "malicious rumors"? That *people* were imprisoned *in camp*, and *without cause!*

And one more point: ". . . it is the duty of every person to inform. . . ."[25]

Disgusting free people! They were making friends with zeks. They were concealing escapees. This was a terrible danger. If an end was not put to it, there would be no Archipelago. And the country would be a goner, and the Revolution would be a goner.

And, therefore, to combat "malicious" rumors, honest progressive rumors were spread: that the camps were populated by murderers and rapists! That every escapee was a dangerous bandit! Lock your doors! Be frightened! Save your children! Catch them, turn them in, help the work of the OGPU! And if you knew of someone who did not help thus—*inform!*

Now, with the spread of the Archipelago, escapes multiplied. There was the hopelessness of the logging and road-building work parties—yet at the same time there was a whole continent beneath the feet of the escapees. So there was hope in spite of all. However, escape plans had excited the Solovki prisoners even at a time when SLON was still on a totally isolated island. The innocents believed in the end of their three-year term, but those who were foresighted had already grasped the truth that they would never see freedom in either three or twenty-three years. And that meant freedom lay only in escape.

But how could they escape from Solovki? For half a year the

---

24. In our country things are always increasing or intensifying *as never before*. They never ever get weaker.

25. *Solovetskiye Ostrova*, 1930, No. 2–3, p. 60.

sea was frozen over, but not solidly, and in places there was open water, and the snowstorms raged, and the frost bit hard, and things were enveloped in mists and darkness. And in the spring and for a large part of the summer there were the long white nights with clear visibility over long distances for the patrolling cutters. And it was only when the nights began to lengthen, in the late summer and the autumn, that the time was right. Not for prisoners in the kremlin, of course, but for those who were out in work parties, where a prisoner might have freedom of movement and time to build a boat or a raft near the shore—and to cast off at night (even just riding off on a log for that matter) and strike out at random, hoping above all to encounter a foreign ship. The bustle among the guards and the embarkation of the cutters would reveal to the islanders the fact of an escape—and there would be a tremor of rejoicing among the prisoners, as if they were themselves escaping. They would ask in a whisper: Had he been caught yet? Had he been found yet? Many must have drowned without ever getting anywhere. One or another of them reached the Karelian shore perhaps—and if he did was more silent than the grave.

And there was a famous escape from Kem to England. This particular daredevil (his name is unknown to us—that's the breadth of our horizon!) knew English and concealed it. He managed to get assigned to loading timber in Kem, and he told his story to the Englishmen. The convoy discovered he was missing and delayed the ship for nearly a whole week and searched it several times without finding the fugitive. (What happened was that whenever a search party started from the shore, they lowered him overboard on the opposite side on the anchor chain, where he clung under water with a breathing pipe held in his teeth.) An enormous fine had to be paid for delaying the ship, so they finally decided to take a chance and let the ship go, thinking that perhaps the prisoner had drowned.

Then a book came out in England, even it would seem, in more than one printing. Evidently *An Island Hell* by S. A. Malsagoff.[26]*

This book astounded Europe (and no doubt they accused its fugitive author of exaggerating, for, after all, the friends of the

26. And is this another book you have not read, Sir Bertrand Russell?

New Society could not permit themselves to believe this slanderous volume) because it contradicted what was already well known; the newspaper *Rote Fahne* had described Solovki as a paradise. (And we hope that the paper's correspondent spent time in the Archipelago later on.) And it also contradicted those albums about Solovki disseminated by Soviet diplomatic missions in Europe: fine-quality paper and true-to-life photographs of the cozy monks' cells. (Nadezhda Surovtseva, our Communist in Austria, received this album from the Soviet Mission in Vienna and indignantly denounced the slander about Solovki current in Europe. And at the very same time the sister of her future husband was, in fact, imprisoned at Solovki, and she herself was predestined to be walking single file in the Yaroslavl Isolator in two years' time.)

Slander or not, the breach had been a misfortune! And so a commission of VTsIK, under the chairmanship of the "conscience of the Party," Comrade Solts (Illustration No. 10), was sent off to find out what was going on there on those Solovetsky Islands (for, of course, they didn't have the least idea!). But in fact the commission merely rode along the Murmansk Railroad, and they didn't do much of anything even there. And they thought it right to send to the islands—no, to implore to go there!—none less than the great proletarian writer Maxim Gorky, who had recently returned to live in the proletarian Fatherland. His testimony would be the very best refutation of that repulsive foreign forgery.

The rumor reached Solovki before Gorky himself—and the prisoners' hearts beat faster and the guards hustled and bustled. One has to know prisoners in order to imagine their anticipation! The falcon, the stormy petrel, was about to swoop down upon the nest of injustice, violence, and secrecy. The leading Russian writer! He will give them hell! He will show them! He, the father, will defend! They awaited Gorky almost like a universal amnesty.

The chiefs were alarmed too: as best they could, they hid the monstrosities and polished things up for show. Transports of prisoners were sent from the kremlin to distant work parties so that fewer would remain there; many patients were discharged from the Medical Section and the whole thing was cleaned up. And they set up a "boulevard" of fir trees without roots, which were simply pushed down into the ground. (They only had to last a few days before withering.) It led to the Children's Colony, opened just three months previously and the pride of USLON, where everyone had clothes and where there were no socially hostile children, and where, of course, Gorky would be very interested in seeing how juveniles were being re-educated and saved for a future life under socialism.

Only in Kem was there an oversight. On Popov Island the ship *Gleb Boky* was being loaded by prisoners in underwear and sacks, when Gorky's retinue appeared out of nowhere to embark on that steamer! You inventors and thinkers! Here is a worthy problem for you, given that, as the saying goes, every wise man has enough of the fool in him: a barren island, not one bush, no possible cover—and right there, at a distance of three hundred yards, Gorky's retinue has shown up. Your solution? Where can this disgraceful spectacle—these men dressed in sacks—be hidden? The entire journey of the great Humanist will have been for naught if he sees them now. Well, of course, he will try hard not to notice them, but help him! Drown them in the sea? They will wallow and flounder. Bury them in the earth? There's no time. No, only a worthy son of the Archipelago could find a way out of this one. The work assigner ordered: "Stop work! Close ranks! Still closer! Sit down on the ground! Sit still!" And a tarpaulin was thrown over them. "Anyone who moves will be shot!" And the former stevedore Maxim Gorky ascended the ship's ladder and admired the landscape from the steamer for a full hour till sailing time—and *he didn't notice!*

That was June 20, 1929. The famous writer disembarked from the steamer in Prosperity Gulf. Next to him was his fiancée, all dressed in leather—a black leather service cap, a leather jacket, leather riding breeches, and high narrow boots—a living symbol of the OGPU shoulder to shoulder with Russian literature.

Surrounded by the commanding officer corps of the GPU, Gorky marched with long swift strides through the corridors of several barracks. The room doors were all wide open, but he entered hardly any. In the Medical Section doctors and nurses in clean robes formed up for him in two rows, but he didn't even look around and went on out. From there the Chekists of USLON fearlessly took him to Sekirka. And what was there to see there? It turned out that there was no overcrowding in the punishment cells, and—the main point—no *poles*. None at all. Thieves sat on benches (there was already a multitude of thieves in Solovki), and they were all . . . reading newspapers. None of them was so bold as to get up and complain, but they did think up one trick: they held the newspapers upside down! And Gorky went up to one of them and in silence turned the newspaper right side up! He had noticed it! He had understood! He would not abandon them. He would defend them![27]

They went to the Children's Colony. How decent everything was there. Each was on a separate cot, with a mattress. They all crowded around in a group and all of them were happy. And all of a sudden a fourteen-year-old boy said: "Listen here, Gorky! Everything you see here is false. Do you want to know the truth? Shall I tell you?" Yes, nodded the writer. Yes, he wanted to know the truth. (Oh, you bad boy, why do you want to spoil the just recently arranged prosperity of the literary patriarch? A palace in Moscow, an estate outside Moscow . . .) And so everyone was ordered to leave, including the children and the accompanying gaypayooshniki—and the boy spent an hour and a half telling the whole story to the lanky old man. Gorky left the barracks, streaming tears. He was given a carriage to go to dinner at the villa of the camp chief. And the boys rushed back into the barracks. "Did you tell him about the *mosquito treatment?*" "Yes." "Did you tell him about the *pole torture?*" "Yes." "Did you tell him about *the prisoners hitched up instead of horses?*" "Yes." "And how they roll them down the stairs? And about the sacks? And about being made to spend the night in the snow?" And it turned out that the truth-loving boy had told all . . . all . . . all!!!

But we don't even know his name.

On June 22, in other words after his chat with the boy, Gorky left the following inscription in the "Visitors' Book," which had been specially made for this visit:

"I am not in a state of mind to express my impressions in just

27. The gaypayooshnitsa—the GPU woman agent—who was Gorky's companion also exercised her pen, and here is what she wrote: "We are getting to know the life of the Solovetsky Camp. I went to the museum. . . . All of us went to 'Sekir-Hill.' From it there was a wonderful view of the lake. The water in the lake was coldly dark blue in color and around the lake was a forest. It seemed to be bewitched, and as the light shifted, the tops of the pines flared up, and the mirror-like lake became fiery. Silence and astonishing beauty. On the way back we passed the peat workings. In the evening we listened to a concert. We dined on local Solovetsky herring—small but surprisingly tender and tasty. They melted in the mouth." From *M. Gorky i Syn (M. Gorky and Son)*, Moscow, Nauka, 1971, p. 276.

a few words. I wouldn't want, yes, and I would likewise be ashamed [!], to permit myself banal praise of the remarkable energy of people who, while remaining vigilant and tireless sentinels of the Revolution, are able, at the same time, to be remarkably bold creators of culture."[28]

On June 23 Gorky left Solovki. Hardly had his steamer pulled away from the pier than they shot the boy. (Oh, great interpreter of the human heart! Great connoisseur of human beings! How could he have failed to take the boy along with him?!)

And that is how faith in justice was instilled in the new generation.

They try to tell us that up there on the summit the chief of literature made excuses, that he didn't want to publish praise of USLON. But how can that be, Aleksei Maximovich? With bourgeois Europe looking on?! But *right now, right at this very moment,* which is so dangerous and so complicated! And the camp regimen there? We'll change it, we'll change the camp regimen.

And he did publish his statement, and it was republished over and over in the big free press, both our own and that of the West, in the name of the Falcon and Stormy Petrel, claiming it was nonsense to frighten people with Solovki, and that prisoners lived remarkably well there and were being well reformed.

And descending into his coffin, he gave his blessing to the Archipelago.[29]

And as for the camp regimen, they kept their promise. The regimen *was reformed.* Now in the 11th Punishment Company *they were kept standing for a week packed against one another.* A commission came to Solovki, and it wasn't a Solts commission either, but an investigative-punitive commission. It delved into

---

28. *Solovetskiye Ostrova,* 1929, No. 1, p. 3. (This inscription is *not* included in Gorky's collected works.)

29. I used to ascribe Gorky's pitiful conduct after his return from Italy and right up to his death to his delusions and folly. But his recently published correspondence of the twenties provides a reason for explaining it on lesser grounds: material self-interest. In Sorrento Gorky was astonished to discover that no world fame had accrued to him, nor money either. (He had a whole palace full of servants.) It became clear that both for money and to revive his fame he had to return to the Soviet Union and accept all the attached conditions. He thereby became Yagoda's voluntary prisoner. And Stalin killed him to no purpose, out of excessive caution: Gorky would have sung hymns of praise to 1937 too.

things and, with the help of the local ISCh, came to understand that all the cruelties of the Solovetsky camp regime were the work of the White Guards of the ACh, and of the aristocrats in general, and partly of the students too (those very same students who since the past century had been setting St. Petersburg on fire). At this point the silly unsuccessful escape attempt of the insane Kozhevnikov (former minister of the Far Eastern Republic) together with Shepchinsky and Degtyaryov, the cowboy, was inflated into an enormous and fantastic plot by the White Guards, who were allegedly scheming to seize a steamship and sail away. And they began to make arrests; and even though no one confessed to such a plot, the case kept on growing, as did the arrests.

They had set themselves a figure of "three hundred." And they reached it. And on the night of October 15, 1929, having dispersed everyone and locked them up in quarters, the Holy Gates, ordinarily kept locked, were opened so as to shorten the route to the cemetery. They kept taking groups there the whole night long. (And each group was accompanied by the desperate howling of the dog Black, who had been tied up somewhere and who suspected that his master Bagratuni was being led off in each new group. The prisoners could count the number of groups being taken off by the number of periods of howling; but because of a strong wind the shots themselves were less audible. This howling had such an impact on the executioners that the next day they shot not only Black but also all the other dogs on account of Black.)

The executioners were the three fancy Dan junkies, plus the chief of the camp guard, Degtyaryov, and, no less, the Chief of the Cultural and Educational Section, Uspensky. (The combination was only superficially astonishing. This Uspensky's biography is what is called *typical*, in other words not the most common, but concentrating in itself the essence of the epoch. He was born the son of a priest, and that is what he was when the Revolution caught up with him. What did he have to look forward to? Security questionnaires, restrictions, exile, persecution. And there is no possible way to erase this from one's record, no possible way to change one's father. But no, Uspensky discovered there was a way: *he killed his own father* and declared to the authorities that he had done it *out of class hatred!* This was a healthy attitude, and almost not murder at all! He was given an easy sentence—

and he immediately rose in the camp in the Cultural and Educational line of work and was soon liberated, and here we come upon him as the free Chief of the Cultural and Educational Section, the KVCh, of *Solovki*. And as far as these executions are concerned, it is not known whether he volunteered or whether they suggested he reaffirm his class position. By night's end, at any rate, he was seen washing off the blood-soaked tops of his boots, one after the other, over a washbasin.) And in Illustration No. 19 it is perhaps he on the far right, though it may merely be someone else with the same name.

They were drunk and careless—and in the morning the enormous pit, only lightly covered over, was still stirring and moving.

Throughout October, and during November too, they brought additional groups from the mainland for execution.[30]

(Somewhat later the entire cemetery was leveled by the prisoners while a band played in the background.)

After those executions the chief of SLON was replaced: Zarin came to replace Eichmans, and it is considered that a new era of Solovetsky legality was thereby established.

However, here is what it was like. In the summer of 1930 they brought to Solovki several dozen religious sectarians who rejected anything that came from anti-Christ: they refused to accept any documents, including passports, and they refused to sign for anything or to handle any money. At their head was a gray-bearded old man of eighty, blind and bearing a long staff. Every enlightened person could clearly see that these sectarians could never ever enter into socialism, because that required having a great deal to do with papers—and that therefore the best thing for them to do was to die. And so they sent them off to Maly Zayatsky Island, the smallest in the entire Solovetsky archipelago—sandy, unforested desert, containing a summer hut of the former monk-fishermen. And they expressed willingness to give them two months' rations, the condition being that *each one* of the sectarians would have to sign for them on the invoice. Of course they refused. At this point the indefatigable Anna Skripnikova intervened; notwithstanding her own youth and the youth of the Soviet government, she had already been arrested for the fourth time. She dashed back and forth between the accounting office, the

---

30. In one of them Kurilko was shot.

work assigners, and the chief of the camp himself, who was engaged in putting into effect the humanitarian regimen. She first besought compassion for them, and after that she begged to be sent to the Zayatsky Islands with the sectarians as their clerk, undertaking the obligation of issuing food to them each day and conducting all the bookkeeping formalities for them. And it would appear that this didn't conflict in any respect with the camp system. And the chiefs refused. "But they feed insane people without asking for signatures on receipts!" Anna cried. Zarin only burst out laughing. And a woman work assigner replied: "Maybe those are Moscow's orders—we don't really know. . . ." (Of course, they were instructions from Moscow—for who else would have taken the responsibility?) And so they were *sent off without food*. Two months later (exactly two months because they were then to be asked to sign for their food for the next two months) they sailed over to Maly Zayatsky and found only corpses which had been picked by the birds. Everyone was there. No one had escaped.

So who now is going to seek out those guilty? In the sixties of our great century?

Anyway, Zarin, too, was soon removed from his post—for liberalism. (And it seems he got ten years himself.)

■

From the end of the twenties the face of the Solovetsky Camp changed. From a silent trap for the doomed *KR's* it was transformed increasingly into the then new, but to us old, species of generalized ITL or Corrective Labor Camp. The number of "especially dangerous criminals from among the workers" multiplied rapidly in the nation, and they herded the nonpolitical offenders and hoodlums to Solovki. Both veteran thieves and beginning thieves landed on Solovki. A big wave of women thieves and prostitutes poured in. (And when they encountered each other at the Kem Transit Camp, the women thieves yelled at the prostitutes: "We may steal, but we don't sell ourselves." And the prostitutes shouted back: "We sell what belongs to us, not stolen goods.") The fact of the matter was that a war against prostitution had been proclaimed throughout the country (not in the newspapers, of course), and so they rounded them all up in all the big cities and pasted a standard three years on all of them and drove many of them to Solovki. In theory it was quite clear that honest labor would swiftly reform them. However, for some reason they clung stubbornly to their socially humiliating profession, and while en route they asked to be allowed to wash floors in the convoy guards' barracks and seduced the Red Army men, subverting the statutes of the convoy service. And they made friends just as easily with the jailers—not for free, of course. They arranged things even better for themselves on Solovki, which was so starved for women. They were allotted the best rooms in the living quarters and every day new clothes and gifts were brought them, and the so-called "nuns" and the other KR women earned money by working for them, embroidering their underthings. And on completion of their terms, rich as never before, with suitcases full of silks, they returned home to begin an honest life.

And the thieves spent their time playing cards. And the women thieves found it useful to bear children on Solovki; there were no nurseries and by having a child they could get themselves released from work for their whole short term. (The KR women who preceded them had refused to take this way out.)

On March 12, 1929, the first group of juveniles arrived at Solovki, and from then on they kept sending and sending them (all of them under sixteen). At first they were quartered in the Children's Colony near the kremlin with those same showpiece cots and mattresses. They hid their government-issue clothing and shouted that they had nothing to go out to work in. And then they, too, were sent off to logging—from which they fled, switching all their names and their terms, and they had to be caught and thereupon sorted out all over again.

With the arrival of a socially healthy contingent of prisoners, the Cultural and Educational Section came to life. They campaigned for the liquidation of illiteracy. (But the thieves had not the slightest problem in telling the difference between clubs and hearts.) They posted a slogan: "A prisoner is an active participant in socialist construction!" And they even thought up a term for it too—*reforging*. (It was here that this term was invented.)

In September, 1930, came the appeal of the Central Committee to all workers for the development of socialist competition and the shock-worker movement. And how could the prisoners not be included? (If free people everywhere were being harnessed up, then wasn't it also necessary to put the prisoners between the shafts?)

From here on our information comes not from living people but from the book of the scholar-jurist Averbakh.[31]

And therefore we suggest that the reader may wish to divide this information by 16 or maybe by 256, and sometimes it even needs to be taken in a reverse sense.

In the autumn of 1930 there was created a Solovetsky staff for socialist competition and the shock-worker movement. Inveterate repeaters, murderers, and cutthroats suddenly emerged "in the role of economy-minded managers, skilled technical directors, and capable cultural workers." G. Andreyev recalls: they used to scream in one's face: "Come across with your norm, you KR." The thieves and bandits had no sooner read the appeal of the Central Committee than they threw away their knives and their playing cards and simply burned with thirst to create a *Commune*. They wrote into the statutes that the social origin of members must be either poor or middle-level peasant families or the working class. (And it need be said that all the thieves were registered in the Records and Classification Section as "former workers"—so that Shepchinsky's former slogan almost came true: "Solovki—for the Workers and Peasants!") And on no account would 58's be admitted. (And the commune members also proposed that all their prison terms be added together and divided by their number so as to arrive at an average term—and that on its expiration they should all be freed simultaneously! But notwithstanding the ·Communist character of this proposal, the Chekists considered it politically premature.) The slogan of the Solovetsky Commune was: "Let us pay our debt to the working class!" And even better was the one: *"From us—everything, to us—nothing!"*[32] And here is the ferocious penalty they thought up to punish members of the commune who were guilty of infractions: to *forbid* them to go out to work! (Now it would be quite hard to find a stiffer punishment for a thief than that!!)

Nonetheless the Solovetsky administration, which was not about to go as far as the cultural and educational officials, did not base its faith too heavily on the thieves' enthusiasm, but in-

---

31. I. L. Averbakh, *op. cit.*
32. This particular slogan, which was fully mature, was probably worthy of All-Union dissemination.

stead "applied the Leninist principle: 'Shock work—Shock maintenance.' " What this meant was that the commune members were moved into separate barracks where they got softer bedding, warmer clothing, and were fed separately and better (at the expense of all the rest of the prisoners, of course). The commune members liked this very much, and for the purpose of keeping all their fellow members in the commune, they established the rule that there would be no more expulsions from it.

This sort of commune was also very popular among *non*commune members. And they all applied for admission to the commune. However, it was decided not to take them into the commune but to create second, third, and fourth "labor collectives," which would not have all those privileges. And in any case, the 58's were not accepted in any of the collectives, even though in the newspaper the most impudent of the hoodlums instructed the 58's: It's time, really, it's time, to grasp that camp is a school for labor!

And the reports were flown by plane to Gulag headquarters: Miracles at Solovki! A turbulent turning point in the attitude of the thieves! All the passion of the criminal world had been redirected into shock work, socialist competition, fulfillment of the production and financial plan! And in Gulag they were suitably astonished, and they broadcast the results of the experiment.

And that is how Solovki began to live: part of the camp was in the "labor collectives," and their percentage of plan fulfillment had not simply risen but doubled! (And the Cultural and Educational Section explained this by the influence of the collective. But we know what it was—common garden-variety camp padding of work sheets—"tukhta.")[33]

The other part of the camp, the "unorganized" part (yes, and also underfed, and underdressed, and engaged in the heaviest work), failed, as one can well understand, to fulfill its work norms.

In February, 1931, a conference of Solovetsky shock brigades

33. I have been reproached with spelling this word incorrectly, and told that it should be written as it is correctly pronounced in thieves' jargon: *tuFta*. For *tuKHta* is the peasants' assimilation of it, just like "Khvyodor" for "Fyodor." But I like it: "tuKHta" is somehow akin to the Russian language, while "tuFta" is totally alien. The thieves brought it, but the whole Russian people learned it—so let it be "tu*KH*ta."

decreed "a broad wave of socialist competition to answer the new slander of the capitalists about forced labor in the U.S.S.R." In March there were already 136 shock brigades. Then suddenly in April their general liquidation was decreed—because "a hostile-class element had permeated the collectives for the purpose of causing them to disintegrate." (Now there's a riddle for you: the 58's were not allowed across the threshold, and so who was it who was causing them to disintegrate? What we have to understand is that the "tukhta" had been uncovered. They had eaten and drunk and made merry; they had counted things up, shed a few tears, and taken the whip to some so the rest would get moving.)

And the joyous hubbub gave way to the noiseless dispatch of the prisoner transports: the 58's were being sent from the Solovetsky mother tumor to far-off fatal places to open up new camps there.

Chapter 3

■

The Archipelago Metastasizes

Well, the Archipelago did not develop on its own but side by side with the whole country. As long as there was unemployment in the nation there was no feverish demand for prisoner manpower, and arrests took place not as a means of mobilizing labor but as a means of sweeping clean the road. But when the concept arose of stirring up the whole 180 million with an enormous mixing paddle, when the plan for superindustrialization was rejected in favor of the plan for supersupersuperindustrialization, when the liquidation of the kulaks was already foreseen along with the massive public works of the First Five-Year Plan—on the eve of the Year of the Great Fracture the view of the Archipelago and everything in the Archipelago changed too.

On March 26, 1928, the Council of People's Commissars (meaning it was still under the chairmanship of Rykov) conducted a review of the status of penal policy in the nation and of conditions in places of imprisonment. In regard to penal policy, it was admitted that it was inadequate. And it was decreed[1] that harsh measures of repression should be applied to class enemies and hostile-class elements, that the camp regimen should be made more severe (and that *socially unstable elements* should not be given terms at all). And in addition: forced labor should be set up in such a way that the prisoner should not earn anything from his work but that the state should derive economic profit from it. "And to consider it necessary from now on *to expand the capacity*

1. TsGAOR, collection 393, shelf 78, file 65, sheets 369–372.

of labor colonies." In other words, putting it simply, it was proposed that more camps be prepared in anticipation of the abundant arrests planned. (Trotsky also had foreseen this same economic necessity, except that he again proposed that a labor army be created by the compulsory drafting of people. The horseradish is no sweeter than the black radish. But whether out of a spirit of opposition to his eternal rival or whether in order to cut people off more decisively from the possibility of complaint and hope of return, Stalin decided to process the labor army men through the prison machinery.) Throughout the nation unemployment was abolished, and *the economic rationale* for expansion of the camps appeared.

Back in 1923 no more than three thousand persons had been imprisoned on Solovki. And by 1930 there were already about fifty thousand, yes, and another thirty thousand in Kem. In 1928 the Solovetsky cancer began to creep outward, first through Karelia, on road-building projects and in logging for export. Just as willingly SLON began to "sell" its engineers: they went off without convoy to work in any northern locality and their wages were credited to the camp. By 1929 SLON camp sites had already appeared at all points on the Murmansk Railroad from Lodeinoye Pole to Taibola. From there the movement continued along the Vologda Railroad—and so active was it that at Zvanka Station it proved necessary to open up a SLON transport control center. By 1930 Svirlag had already grown strong in Lodeinoye Pole and stood on its own legs, and in Kotlas Kotlag had already been formed. In 1931 BelBaltlag had been born, with its center in Medvezhyegorsk,[2] which was destined over the next two years to bring glory to the Archipelago for eternity and on five continents.

And the malignant cells kept on creeping and creeping. They were blocked on one side by the sea and on the other by the Finnish border, but there was nothing to hinder the founding of a camp near Krasnaya Vishera in 1929. And the main thing was that all the paths to the east through the Russian North lay open and unobstructed. Very soon the Soroka-Kotlas road was reaching out. ("We'll complete Soroka ahead of 'sroka'—ahead of

2. This was the official date, but in actual fact it had been there since 1930, though its organizational period had been kept secret to give the impression of rapid work, for bragging, and for history. Here, too, was "tukhta."

term!" The Solovetsky prisoners used to make fun of S. Alymov, who, nonetheless, stuck to his last and made his name as a *poet and song writer*.) Creeping on to the Northern Dvina River, the camp cells formed SevDvinlag. Crossing it, they fearlessly marched on the Urals. By 1931 the Northern Urals department of SLON was founded, which soon gave rise to the independent Solikamlag and SevUrallag. The Berezniki Camp began the construction of a big chemical combine which in its time was much publicized. In the summer of 1929 an expedition of un-convoyed prisoners was sent to the Chibyu River from Solovki, under the leadership of the geologist M. V. Rushchinsky, in order to prospect for petroleum, which had been discovered there as far back as the eighties of the nineteenth century. The expedition was successful—and a camp was set up on the Ukhta, Ukhtlag. But it, too, did not stand still on its own spot, but quickly metastasized to the northeast, annexed the Pechora, and was transformed into UkhtPechlag. Soon afterward it had its Ukhta, Inta, Pechora, and Vorkuta sections—all of them the bases of great independent future camps.[3]

The opening up of so expansive a roadless northern region as this required the building of a railroad: from Kotlas via Knyazh-Pogost and Ropcha to Vorkuta. This called forth the need for two more independent camps which were railroad-building camps: SevZhelDorlag—on the sector from Kotlas to the Pechora River—and Pechorlag (not to be confused with the industrial UkhtPechlag!)—on the sector from the Pechora River to Vorkuta. (True, this railroad was under construction for a long time. Its Vym sector, from Knyazh-Pogost to Ropcha, was ready for service in 1938, but the whole railroad was ready only at the end of 1942.)

And thus from the depths of the tundra and the taiga rose hundreds of new medium-sized and small islands. And on the march, in battle order, a new system of organization of the Archipelago was created: Camp Administrations, Camp Divisions, Camps (OLP's—Separate Camps; KOLP's—Commandant's Camps; GOLP's—Head Camps), Camp Sectors (and these were the same as "work parties" and "work subparties"). And in the

3. We are giving dates and places equal weight but beg the reader to bear in mind that all this was gotten through questioning people and comparing, so there may be omissions and errors.

Administrations there were Departments, and in the Divisions there were Sections: I. Production (P.); II. Records and Classification (URCh); III. Security Operations (again the *third!*).

(And in contemporary dissertations they wrote: "The contours of educational institutions for *individual* undisciplined members of the classless society are taking shape ahead of time."[4] In actual fact, when there are no more classes, there will be no more criminals. But somehow it takes your breath away just to think that tomorrow society will be classless—and does that mean that no one will be *imprisoned? Only individual* undisciplined members. Classless society is not without its lockups either.)

And so all the northern portion of the Archipelago sprang from Solovki. But not from there alone. In response to the great appeal, Corrective Labor Camps (ITL's) and Corrective Labor Colonies (ITK's) burst out in a rash throughout our whole great country. Every province acquired its own ITL's and ITK's. Millions of miles of barbed wire ran on and on, the strands crisscrossing one another and interweaving, their barbs twinkling gaily along railroads, highways, and around the outskirts of cities. And the peaked roofs of ugly camp watchtowers became the most dependable landmarks in our landscape, and it was only by a surprising concatenation of circumstances that they were not seen in either the canvases of our artists or in scenes in our films.

As had been happening from the Civil War on, monastery buildings were intensively *mobilized* for camp needs, were ideally adapted for isolation by their very locations. The Boris and Gleb Monastery in Torzhok was put to use as a transit camp (still there today), while the Valdai Monastery was put to use for a colony of juveniles (across the lake from the future country house of Zhdanov). Nilova Hermitage on Stolbny Island in Lake Seliger became a camp. Sarovskaya Hermitage was used for the nest of Potma camps, and there is no end to this enumeration. Camps arose in the Donbas, on the upper, middle, and lower Volga, in the central and southern Urals, in Transcaucasia, in central Kazakhstan, in Central Asia, in Siberia, and in the Far East. It is officially reported that in 1932 the area devoted to Agricultural Corrective Labor Colonies in the Russian Republic

4. Vyshinsky, *op. cit.*, p. 429.

alone—was 625,000 acres, and in the Ukranian Republic 138,-000.[5]

Estimating the average colony at 2,500 acres, we learn that at this time, without counting the other Soviet republics, there were already more than three hundred such *Selkhozy* alone, in other words the lowest grade and most privileged form of camp.

The distribution of prisoners between near and distant camps was easily determined by a decree of the Central Executive Committee and the Council of People's Commissars of November 6, 1929. (How they do manage to hit the anniversary dates of the Revolution!) The former "strict isolation"—detention—was abolished (because it hindered creative labor), and it was ordained that those sentenced to terms of less than three years would be assigned to the *general* (near) places of imprisonment, while those sentenced to from three to ten years would be sent to distant localities.[6] Since the 58's never got less than three years, that meant that they all flocked to the North and to Siberia —to open it up and to die.

And the rest of us during those years were marching to the beat of drums!

■

A stubborn legend persists in the Archipelago to the effect that *"The camps were thought up by Frenkel."*

It seems to me that this fanciful idea, both unpatriotic and even insulting to the authorities, is quite sufficiently refuted by the preceding chapters. Even with the meager means at our disposal we succeeded, I hope, in showing the birth of camps for repression and labor back in 1918. Without any Frenkel whatsoever they arrived at the conclusion that prisoners must not waste their time in moral contemplation ("The purpose of Soviet corrective labor policy is not at all individual correction in its traditional meaning")[7] but must labor, and at the same time must be given very severe, almost unbearable work norms to achieve. Long before Frenkel they already used to say: "correc-

5. *Ibid.*, pp. 136–137.
6. *Sobraniye Zakonov SSSR (Collection of Laws of the U.S.S.R.)*, 1929, No. 72.
7. Vyshinsky, *op. cit.*, p. 384.

tion through labor" (and as far back as Eichmans they already understood this to mean "destruction through labor").

Yes, and not even contemporary dialectical thought processes were needed to arrive at the idea of using prisoners sentenced to heavy labor for work in remote, little-settled areas. Back in 1890, in the Ministry of Railroads they decided to use hard-labor exiles in the Amur region for laying rails on the railroad. They simply forced the hard-labor prisoners to work, while exiles and deportees were *permitted* to work at laying rails, and in return got a reduction in their terms by one-third or one-half. (However, they preferred to get rid of their whole term all at once by escape.) And from 1896 to 1900, work on the Lake Baikal shoreline sector of the Trans-Siberian was carried out by fifteen hundred hard-labor prisoners and twenty-five hundred compulsorily resettled exiles.[8] Therefore the idea was by no means new, and not founded on progressive educational theories.

Nonetheless, Frenkel really did become the nerve of the Archipelago. He was one of those successful men of action whom History hungrily awaits and summons to itself. It would seem that there had been camps even before Frenkel, but they had not taken on that final and unified form which savors of perfection. Every genuine prophet arrives when he is most acutely needed. Frenkel arrived in the Archipelago just at the beginning of the metastases.

Naftaly Aronovich Frenkel, a Turkish Jew, was born in Constantinople. He graduated from the commercial institute there and took up the timber trade. He founded a firm in Mariupol and soon became a millionaire, "the timber king of the Black Sea." He had his own steamers, and he even published his own newspaper in Mariupol called *The Kopeck*, whose function was to slander and persecute his competitors. During World War I Frenkel conducted some speculative arms deals through Gallipoli.

8. However, generally speaking, the course of development in nineteenth-century Russian hard labor was in just the reverse direction: labor became ever less obligatory, withered away. By the nineties, even at Kari, hard-labor camps had been transformed into places of passive detention and work was no longer performed. By this time, too, the demands made on workers had been eased at Akatui (P. Yakubovich). So the use of hard-labor prisoners on the Lake Baikal shoreline sector of the railroad was most likely a temporary necessity. Do we not observe here once again the "two horn" principle, or that of a parabola, just as in the case of the long-term prisons (Part I, Chapter 9): one prong of increasing leniency and one of increasing ferocity?

In 1916, sensing the pending storm in Russia, he transferred his capital to Turkey even *before* the February Revolution, and in 1917 he himself went to Constantinople in pursuit of it.

And he could have gone on living the sweetly exciting life of a merchant, and he would have known no bitter grief and would not have turned into a legend. But some fateful force beckoned him to the Red power.[9]

The rumor is unverified that in those years in Constantinople he became the resident Soviet intelligence agent (perhaps for ideological reasons, for it is otherwise difficult to see why he needed it). But it is a fact that in the NEP years he came to the U.S.S.R., and here, on secret instructions from the GPU, created, as if in his own name, a black market for the purchase of valuables and gold in return for Soviet paper rubles (this was a predecessor of the "gold drive" of the GPU and Torgsin). Business operators and manipulators remembered him very well indeed from the old days; they trusted him—and the gold flowed into the coffers of the GPU. The purchasing operation came to an end, and, in gratitude, the GPU arrested him. Every wise man has enough of the simpleton in him.

However, inexhaustible and holding no grudges, Frenkel, while still in the Lubyanka or on the way to Solovki, sent some sort of declaration to the top. Finding himself in a trap, he evidently decided to make a business analysis of this life too. He was brought to Solovki in 1927, but was immediately separated from the prisoner transport, settled into a stone booth outside the bounds of the monastery itself, provided with an orderly to look after him, and permitted free movement about the island. We have already recalled that he became the Chief of the Economic Section (the privilege of a free man) and expressed his famous thesis about using up the prisoner in the first three months. In 1928 he was already in Kem. There he created a profitable auxiliary enterprise. He brought to Kem the leather which had been accumulated by the monks for decades and had been lying uselessly in the monastery warehouses. He recruited furriers and shoemakers from among the prisoners and supplied fashionable high-quality footwear and leather goods directly to a special shop on Kuznetsky Most in Moscow. (The GPU ran it and took the

---

9. I have a personal hypothesis about this, which I will mention elsewhere.

receipts, but the ladies who bought their shoes there didn't know that, and when they themselves were hauled off to the Archipelago not long after, they never even remembered the shop.)

One day in 1929 an airplane flew from Moscow to get Frenkel and brought him to an appointment with Stalin. The Best Friend of prisoners (and the Best Friend of the Chekists) talked interestedly with Frenkel for three hours. The stenographic report of this conversation will never become public. There simply was none. But it is clear that Frenkel unfolded before the Father of the Peoples dazzling prospects for constructing socialism through the use of prisoner labor. Much of the geography of the Archipelago being described in the aftermath by my obedient pen, he sketched in bold strokes on the map of the Soviet Union to the accompaniment of the puffing of his interlocutor's pipe. It was Frenkel in person, apparently on that precise occasion, who proposed the all-embracing system of classification of camp prisoners into Groups A, B, C, D, which left no leeway to the camp chiefs and even less to the prisoner: everyone not engaged in providing essential services for the camp (B), not verified as being ill (C), and not undergoing correction in a punishment cell (D) must drag his workload (A) every day of his sentence. The world history of hard labor has never known such universality! It was Frenkel in person, and in this very conversation, who proposed renouncing the reactionary system of equality in feeding prisoners and who outlined a unified system of redistribution of the meager food supplies for the whole Archipelago—*a scale for bread rations and a scale for hot-food rations* which was adapted by him from the Eskimos: a fish on a pole held out in front of the running dog team. In addition, he proposed *time off sentence* and release ahead of term as rewards for good work (but in this respect he was hardly original—for in 1890, in Sakhalin hard labor, Chekhov discovered both the one and the other). In all probability the first experimental field was set up here too—the great Belomorstroi, the White Sea–Baltic Canal Construction Project, to which the enterprising foreign-exchange and gold speculator would soon be appointed—not as chief of construction nor as chief of a camp either, but to the post especially dreamed up for him of "works chief"—the chief overseer of the labor battle.

And here he is himself (Illustration No. 11). It is evident

10. Aron Solts

11. Naftaly Frenkel

12. Yakov Rappoport

13. Matvei Berman

14. Lazar Kogan

15. Genrikh Yagoda

from his face how he brimmed with a· vicious human-hating animus. In the book on the Belomor Canal—the White Sea–Baltic Canal—wishing to laud Frenkel, one Soviet writer would soon describe him thus: " . . . the eyes of an interrogator and a prosecutor, the lips of a skeptic and a satirist . . . A man with enormous love of power and pride, for whom the main thing is unlimited power. If it is necessary for him to be feared, then let him be feared. He spoke harshly to the engineers, attempting to humiliate them."[10]

This last phrase seems to us a keystone—to both the character and biography of Frenkel.

By the start of Belomorstroi Frenkel had been freed. For construction of the Belomor Canal he received the Order of Lenin and was named Chief of Construction of BAMlag ("The Baikal-Amur Main Line Railroad"—which was a name out of the future, while in the thirties BAMlag was put to work adding a second track to the Trans-Siberian main line on those sectors where there was none). And this was by no means the last item in the career of Naftaly Frenkel, but it is more relevant to complete the account in the next chapter.

■

The whole long history of the Archipelago, about which it has fallen to me to write this home-grown, homemade book, has, in the course of half a century, found in the Soviet Union almost no expression whatever in the printed word. In this a role was played by that same unfortunate happenstance by which camp watchtowers never got into scenes in films nor into landscapes painted by our artists.

But this was not true of the White Sea–Baltic Canal nor of the Moscow-Volga Canal. There is a book about each at our disposal, and we can write this chapter at least on the basis of documentary and responsible source material.

In diligently researched studies, before making use of a particular source, it is considered proper to characterize it. We shall do so.

10. *Belomorsko-Baltiisky Kanal imeni Stalina, Istoriya Stroitelstva* (*The White Sea–Baltic Canal Named for Stalin; History of Its Construction*), Chapter 8.

Here before us lies the volume, in format almost equal to the Holy Gospels, with the portrait of the Demigod engraved in bas-relief on the cardboard covers. The book, entitled *The White Sea–Baltic Stalin Canal*, was issued by the State Publishing House in 1934 and dedicated by the authors to the Seventeenth Congress of the Soviet Communist Party, and it was evidently published for the Congress. It is an extension of the Gorky project of "Histories of Factories and Plants." Its editors were Maxim Gorky, I. L. Averbakh,* and S. G. Firin. This last name is little known in literary circles, and we shall explain why: Semyon Firin, notwithstanding his youth, was Deputy Chief of Gulag.[11]

The history of this book is as follows: On August 17, 1933, an *outing* of 120 writers took place aboard a steamer on the just completed canal. D. P. Vitkovsky, a prisoner who was a construction superintendent on the canal, witnessed the way these people in white suits crowded on the deck during the steamer's passage through the locks, summoned prisoners from the area of the locks (where by this time they were more operational workers than construction workers), and, in the presence of the canal chiefs, asked a prisoner whether he loved his canal and his work, and did he think that he had managed to reform here, and did the chiefs take enough interest in the welfare of the prisoners? There were many questions, all in this general vein, and all asked from shipboard to shore in the presence of the chiefs and only while the steamer was passing through the locks. And after this outing eighty-four of these writers somehow or other managed nonetheless to worm their way out of participating in Gorky's collective work (though perhaps they wrote their own admiring verses and essays), and the remaining thirty-six constituted an authors' collective. By virtue of intensive work in the fall and winter of 1933 they created this unique book.

This book was published to last for all eternity, so that future generations would read it and be astounded. But by a fateful coincidence, most of the leaders depicted in its photographs and glorified in its text were exposed as enemies of the people within two or three years. Naturally all copies of the book were thereupon removed from libraries and destroyed. Private owners also

---

11. Anguished by the vanity of authorship, he also wrote his own individual booklet about the Belomor Canal.

destroyed it in 1937, not wishing to earn themselves *a term* for owning it. And thàt is why very few copies have remained intact to the present; and there is no hope that it may be reissued—and therefore all the heavier is the obligation to my fellow countrymen I feel on my shoulders not to permit the principal ideas and facts described in this book to perish. It would be only just, too, to preserve the names of the authors for the history of literature. Well, these at least: M. Gorky, Viktor Shklovsky, Vsevolod Ivanov, Vera Inber, Valentin Katayev, Mikhail Zoshchenko, Lapin and Khatsrevin, L. Nikulin, Korneli Zelinsky, Bruno Yasensky (the chapter "Beat the Class Enemy to Death!"), Y. Gavrilovich, A. Tikhonov, Aleksei Tolstoi, K. Finn.

Gorky explained in the following way why this book was necessary to the prisoners who had built the canal: "The Canal Army Men[12] do not have the necessary vocabulary to express the complex feelings of reforging"—and writers do have this vocabulary, so they will help. He explained as follows why the book was necessary for the writers: "Many writers after becoming acquainted with the canal . . . got 'charged up' as a result, and this has had a very positive impact on their work. . . . *A mood is going to appear* in literature *which will push it ahead* and put it on the level of our great deeds" (My italics—A.S. And this is a level still palpable in Soviet literature today). And why the book was necessary to its millions of readers (many of them were soon to flow to the Archipelago themselves) requires no elaboration.

What was the point of view of the authors' collective on the subject? First of all: certainty as to the justice of all sentences and the guilt of all those driven to work on the canal. Even the word "certainty" is too weak: for the authors this question is out of bounds not only for discussion but even for mention. It is as clear to them as the fact that night is darker than day. Using their vocabulary and their imagery to instill in us all the misanthropic legend of the thirties, they interpret the word "wrecker" as the basis of the engineers' being. Agronomists who spoke out against early sowing (maybe in snow and mud?) and irrigation experts who provided Central Asia with water—all were indubitable wreckers to them. In every chapter of the book these

12. It was decided to call them this in order to raise morale (or perhaps in honor of the labor army which was never created).

writers speak only with condescension of engineers as a class, as of a foul, low breed. On page 125 the book accuses *a significant segment of the Russian prerevolutionary engineering profession of swindling.* And this is not an individual accusation, not at all. (Are we to understand that engineers were even engaged in wrecking Tsarism?) And this was written by people of whom not one was capable of extracting even the simplest square root (which even certain horses do in circuses).

The authors repeat to us all the nightmare rumors of those years as historical gospel truth: that workers were poisoned with arsenic in factory dining rooms; that it is not just a piece of stupid carelessness if milk from the cow on a state farm went sour, but an enemy's stratagem to compel the country to *swell up from starvation* (and that's exactly how they write). In indefinite and faceless terms they write about that sinister collective *kulak* who *went to work in a factory and threw a bolt into the lathe.* Well, after all, they are oracles of the human heart, and it is evidently easier for them to imagine this: a person has managed by some miracle to avoid exile to the tundra, has escaped to the city, and by some still greater miracle has managed to get work in a factory when he is already dying of hunger, and at this point, instead of feeding his family, he throws a bolt into the lathe!

Then, on the other side, the authors cannot and do not wish to restrain their admiration for the leaders of the canal works, those employers whom they stubbornly call Chekists, although it is already the thirties, thereby forcing us to use the name too. They admired not only their minds, their wills, their organization, but also them—in the highest human sense, as surprising beings. Indicative was the episode with Yakov Rappoport. (See Illustration No. 12: he does not look to be stupid.) This student at Dorpat University, who failed to complete the course there, was evacuated to Voronezh, where he became the Deputy Chairman of the Provincial Cheka in his new homeland, and then Deputy Chief of Construction at Belomorstroi. In the words of the authors, Rappoport, while on an inspection tour of the construction site, was dissatisfied with the way the workers were pushing their wheelbarrows along, and he posed an annihilating question to the engineer in charge: Do you remember what the cosine of 45 degrees is equal to? And the engineer was crushed and put to shame by Rappoport's erudition,[13] and immediately made corrections in his instructions aimed at wrecking, and the movement of the wheelbarrows immediately moved onto a high technological level. And with such anecdotes as these the authors not only enrich their exposition artistically but also lift us onto scientific heights!

And the higher the post occupied by the employer, the greater the worship with which he is described by the authors. Unrestrained praises are lavished on the Chief of Gulag, Matvei Berman* (Illustration No. 13).[14] Much enthusiastic praise is also lavished on Lazar Kogan (Illustration No. 14), a former Anarchist who in 1918 went over to the side of the victorious Bolsheviks, and who proved his loyalty in the post of Chief of the Special Branch of the Ninth Army, then as Deputy Chief of the Armies of the OGPU, and was one of the organizers of Gulag and then became Chief of Construction of the Belomor Canal. And it is even more the case that the authors can only endorse Comrade Kogan's words about *the iron commissar*: "Comrade Yagoda is our chief, our constant leader." That is what more than anything doomed this book! The glorification of Genrikh Yagoda was torn out, together with his portrait, from even that one copy of the book which survived for us, and we had to search a long time in order to find this portrait of him (Illustration No. 15).

This same tone permeated the camp leaflets even more strongly. Here, for example: "The honored guests, Comrades Kaganovich, Yagoda, and Berman, arrived at Lock No. 3. (Their portraits hung in every barracks.) People worked more quickly. *Up above* they smiled—and their smile was transmitted to hundreds of people down in the excavation."[15] And in officially inspired songs:

> Yagoda in person leads and teaches us,
> Keen is his eye, and his hand is strong.

13. And Rappoport got the meaning of the cosine all wrong. (*Belomorsko-Baltiisky Kanal, op. cit.,* p. 10.)

14. M. Berman—M. Bormann; once again there is only a one- or two-letter difference. Remember Eichmans and Eichmann.

15. Y. Kuzemko, *3-i Shlyuz* (*The Third Lock*), KVO Dmitlag Publishers, 1935. "Not to be distributed beyond the boundaries of the camp." Because of the rarity of this edition, we can recommend another combination: "Kaganovich, Yagoda and Khrushchev inspect camps on the Belomor Canal," in D. D. Runes, *Despotism,* New York, 1963, p. 262.

Their general enthusiasm for the camp way of life led the authors of the collective work to this panegyric: "No matter to what corner of the Soviet Union fate should take us, even if it be the most remote wilderness and backwoods, the imprint of order . . . of precision and of conscientiousness . . . marks each OGPU organization." And what OGPU organization exists in the Russian backwoods? Only the camps. *The camp as a torch of progress*—that is the level of this historical source of ours.

The editor in chief has something to say about this himself. Addressing the last rally of Belomorstroi officials on August 25, 1933, in the city of Dmitrov (they had already moved over to the Moscow-Volga Canal project), Gorky said: "Ever since 1928 I have watched how the GPU re-educates people." (And what this means is that even before his visit to Solovki, even before that boy was shot, ever since, in fact, he first returned to the Soviet Union, he had been watching them.) And by then hardly able to restrain his tears, he addressed the Chekists present: "You devils in woolen overcoats, you yourselves don't know what you have done." And the authors note: the Chekists there merely *smiled*. (They knew *what* they had done. . . .) And Gorky noted *the extraordinary modesty* of the Chekists in the book itself. (This dislike of theirs for publicity was truly a touching trait.)

The collective authors do not simply keep silent about the deaths on the Belomor Canal during construction. They do not follow the cowardly recipe of *half-truths*. Instead, they write directly (page 190) that *no one* died during construction. (Probably they calculated it this way: One hundred thousand started the canal and one hundred thousand finished. And that meant they were all alive. They simply forgot about the prisoner transports devoured by the construction in the course of two fierce winters. But this is already on the level of the cosine of the cheating engineering profession.)

The authors see nothing more inspiring than this camp labor. They find in forced labor one of the highest forms of blazing, conscientious creativity. Here is the theoretical basis of re-education: "Criminals are the result of the repulsive conditions of former times, and our country is beautiful, powerful and *generous*, and it needs to be *beautified*." In their opinion all those driven to work on the canal would never have found their paths in life if the employers had not assigned them to unite the White Sea with the Baltic. Because, after all, "*Human raw material* is immeasurably more difficult to work than wood." What language! What profundity! Who said that? Gorky said it in his book, disputing the "verbal trumpery of humanism." And Zoshchenko, with profound insight, wrote: "Reforging—this is not the desire to serve out one's term and be freed [So such suspicions did exist?—A.S.], but is in actual fact a restructuring of the consciousness and the pride of a builder." What a student of man! Did you ever push a canal wheelbarrow—and on a penalty ration too?

This worthy book, constituting the glory of Soviet literature, will be our guide in our judgments about the canal.

How did it happen that the Belomor Canal in particular was selected as the first great construction project of the Archipelago? Was Stalin forced to this by some kind of exacting economic or military necessity? Looking at the results of the construction, we can answer with assurance that there was none. Was he thus inspired by his spirit of noble rivalry with Peter the Great, who had dragged his fleet over portages along the same route, or with the Emperor Paul, in whose reign the first project for such a canal originated? It seems unlikely the Wise Man had ever even known of this. Stalin simply needed a great construction project *somewhere* which would devour many working hands and many lives (the surplus of people as a result of the liquidation of the kulaks), with the reliability of a gas execution van but more cheaply, and which would at the same time leave a great monument to his reign of the same general sort as the pyramids. In his favorite slaveowning Orient—from which Stalin derived almost everything in his life—they loved to build great "canals." And I can almost see him there, examining with love the map of the North of European Russia, where the largest part of the camps were already situated at that time. And down the center of this region the Sovereign drew a line from sea to sea with the end of his pipe stem.

In proclaiming this project it had to be proclaimed necessarily as *urgent*. Because in those years nothing which was *not* urgent got done in our country. If it had *not* been urgent, no one would have believed in its vital importance, and even the prisoners, dying beneath the upturned wheelbarrows, had to believe in that importance. Because if it had not been urgent, then they would not have been willing to die off and clear the way for the new society.

"The canal must be built in a short time and it must *be built cheaply!* These were Comrade Stalin's instructions." (And everyone who was alive then remembers what *the orders of Comrade Stalin* meant!) *Twenty months!* That was the time the Great Leader allotted his criminals both for the canal and for their own correction: from September, 1931, to April, 1933. He was in such a rush he would not even give them two full years. One hundred and forty miles. Rocky soil. An area abounding in boulders. Swamps. Seven locks in the Povenets "staircase," twelve locks on the descent to the White Sea. And "this was no Dneprostroi, which was allowed a long time for completion and allotted *foreign exchange.* Belomorstroi was entrusted to the OGPU and received *not one kopeck in foreign exchange!*"

So the plan looms more and more clearly: This canal was so badly needed by Stalin and the nation that it was not to get one kopeck of foreign exchange. Let *a hundred thousand* prisoners work for you simultaneously—what capital is more precious? And deliver the canal in twenty months! Not one day later.

That's when you rant and rage at the wrecker engineers. The engineers say: "We will make the structure of concrete." The Chekists reply: "There is not enough time." The engineers say: "We need large quantities of iron." The Chekists reply: "Replace it with wood!" The engineers say: "We need tractors, cranes, construction machinery!" The Chekists: "There will be none of that, not one kopeck of foreign exchange: do it all by hand."

The book calls this "the bold Chekist formulation of a technical assignment."[16] In other words, the Rappoport cosine.

We were in such a rush that we brought in people from Tashkent for this northern project, hydrotechnologists and irrigation experts (arrested, as it happened, at the most opportune time). With them a Special (once again *special*, a favorite word!) Design Bureau was set up on Furkasovsky Lane (behind the Big Lubyanka).[17] (Incidentally, the Chekist Ivanchenko asked the en-

---

16. *Belomorsko-Baltiisky Kanal, op. cit.,* p. 82.
17. This was thus one of the very earliest *sharashkas,* Islands of Paradise. At the same time people mention one other like it: the OKB—the Special Design Bureau—at the Izhora Factory which designed the first famous blooming mill for semifinished steel ingots.

gineer Zhurin: "Why should you make a plan when there already is a plan for the Volga-Don Canal project? Use it instead.")

We were in such a rush that they were put to work making a plan before surveys had been made on the ground. Of course we rushed survey crews into Karelia. But not one of the designers was allowed to leave even the bounds of the design office, let alone go to Karelia (this was vigilance). And therefore telegrams flew back and forth! What kind of an elevation do you have there? What kind of soil?

We were in such a rush that trainloads of zeks kept on arriving and arriving at the canal site before there were any barracks there, or supplies, or tools, or a precise plan. And what was to be done? (There were no barracks, but there was an early northern autumn. There were no tools, but the first month of the twenty was already passing.)[18]

We were in such a rush that the engineers who finally arrived at the canal site had no drafting papers, no rulers, no thumbtacks (!), and not even any light in their work barracks. They worked under kerosene wick lamps, and our authors rave that it was just like during the Civil War.

In the jolly tone of inveterate merrymakers they tell us: Women came in silk dresses and were handed a wheelbarrow on the spot! And "how many, many encounters there were with old acquaintances in Tunguda: former students, Esperantists, comrades in arms from White Guard detachments!" The comrades in arms from the White Guard detachments had long since encountered each other on Solovki, but we are grateful to the authors for the information that Esperantists and students also got their White Sea Canal wheelbarrows! Almost choking with laughter, they tell us: From the Krasnovodsk camps in Central Asia, from Stalinabad, from Samarkand, they brought Turkmenians and Tadzhiks in their Bukhara robes and turbans—here to the Karelian subzero winter cold! Now that was something the *Basmachi* rebels never expected! The norm here was *to break up two and a half cubic yards of granite and to move it a distance of a hundred yards in a wheelbarrow*. And the snow kept falling and covering everything up, and the wheelbarrows somersaulted off the gangways into the snow. Approximately like this (Illustration No. 16).

18. Plus several hidden—*tukhta*—months of the preliminary organizational period not reported anywhere.

But let the authors themselves speak: "The wheelbarrow tottered on the wet planks and turned upside down."[19] "A human being with such a wheelbarrow was like a horse in shafts."[20] "It took an hour to load a wheelbarrow like this"—and not even with granite, merely with frozen soil. Or a more generalized picture: "The ugly depression, powdered over with snow, was full of people and stones. People wandered about, tripping over the stones. They bent over, two or three of them together, and, taking hold of a boulder, tried to lift it. The boulder did not move. They called a fourth and a fifth." But at this point the technology of our glorious century came to their aid: "They dragged the boulders out of the excavation with a *net*"—the net being hauled by a cable, and the cable in turn by "a drum being turned by a horse"! Or here is another method they used: *wooden cranes* for lifting stones (Illustration No. 17). Or here, for example, are some of the first Belomorstroi machines (Illustration No. 18).

And are these your wreckers? No, these are engineering geniuses! They were hurled from the twentieth century into the age of the caveman—and, lo, they managed to cope with the situation!

The basic transportation at Belomorstroi consisted of *grabarki*, dray carts, with boxes mounted on them for carrying earth, as we learn from the book. And in addition there were also *Belomor Fords!* And here is what they were: heavy wooden platforms placed on four wooden logs (rollers), and two horses dragged this *Ford* along and carried stones away on it. And a wheelbarrow was handled by a team of two men—on slopes it was caught and pulled upward by a *hookman*—a worker using a hook. And how were trees to be felled if there were neither saws nor axes? Our inventiveness could find the answer to that one: ropes were tied around the trees, and they were rocked back and forth by brigades pulling in different directions—*they rocked the trees out*. Our inventiveness can solve any problem at all—and why? Because the *canal was being built on the initiative and instructions of Comrade Stalin!* This was written in the newspapers and repeated on the radio every day.

Just picture this battlefield, with the Chekists "in long ashy-

19. *Belomorsko-Baltiisky Kanal, op. cit.*, p. 112.
20. *Ibid.*, p. 113.

16. A work detail

17. The wooden cranes

18. The earliest machinery

gray greatcoats or leather jackets." There were only thirty-seven of them for a hundred thousand prisoners, but they were loved by all, and this love caused Karelian boulders to move. Here they have paused for a moment (Illustration No. 19), Comrade Frenkel points with his hand, and Comrade Firin chews on his lips, and Comrade Uspensky says nothing (and is this that patricide? that same Solovki butcher?). And thereby were decided the fates of thousands of people during that frosty night or the whole of that Arctic month.

The very grandeur of this construction project consisted in the fact that it was carried out without contemporary technology and equipment and without any supplies from the nation as a whole! "These are not the tempos of noxious European-American capitalism, these are socialist tempos!" the authors brag.[21] (In the 1960's we will learn that this is called . . . the "Great Leap Forward.") The whole book praises specifically the backwardness of the technology and the homemade workmanship. There were no *cranes?* So they will make their own—wooden "derricks." And the only metal parts the "derricks" had were in places where there was friction—and these parts they cast themselves. "Our own industry at the canal," our authors gloat. And they themselves cast *wheelbarrow wheels* in their own *homemade cupola furnace*.

The country required the canal so urgently and in such haste that it could not even find any wheelbarrow wheels for the project! It would have been too difficult an order for Leningrad factories.

No, it would be unjust, most unjust, unfair, to compare this most savage construction project of the twentieth century, this continental canal built "with wheelbarrow and pick," with the Egyptian pyramids; after all, the pyramids were built with the *contemporary* technology!! And we used the technology of forty centuries earlier!

That's what our gas execution van consisted of. We didn't have any gas for the gas chamber.

Just try and be an engineer in these circumstances! All the dikes were earthen; all the floodgates were made of wood. Earth leaks now and then. How can it be made watertight? They drive horses over the dikes with rollers! (Stalin and the country were pitiless to horses as well as to prisoners—because horses were a kulak animal and also destined to die.) It is also very difficult to

21. *Ibid.*, p. 356.

eliminate leakage at contact points between earth and wood. Wood had to be used in place of iron! And engineer Maslov invented rhomboid wooden lock gates. There was no concrete used in the walls of the locks. And how could they be strengthened? They remembered the ancient Russian device called "ryazhi"— cribs of logs fitted and joined, rising fifty feet high and filled with soil. Make use of the technology of the caveman, but bear responsibility according to the rules of the twentieth century: if it leaks anywhere, "Off with your head!"

The Iron Commissar Yagoda wrote to Chief Engineer Khrustalyev: "On the basis of available reports [i.e., from stoolies and from Kogan-Frenkel-Firin] you are not manifesting and you do not feel the necessary energy and interest in the work. I order you to answer immediately: do you intend immediately [what language!] . . . to set to work in earnest . . . and to compel that portion of the engineers [what portion? whom?] which is sabotaging and interfering with the work to work conscientiously? . . . " Now what could the chief engineer reply to that? He wanted to survive. "I admit my criminal softness . . . I repent of my own slackness. . . . "

And meanwhile it is incessantly dinned into our ears: *"The canal is being built on the initiative and orders of Comrade Stalin!"* "The radio in the barracks, on the canal site, by the stream, in a Karelian hut, on a truck, the radio which *sleeps* neither day *nor night* [just imagine it!], those innumerable black mouths, those black masks without eyes [imagery!] cry out incessantly: what do the Chekists of the whole country think about the canal project, what does the Party have to say about it?" And you, too, better think the same! You, too, better think the same! *"Nature we will teach—and freedom we will reach."* Hail socialist competition and the shock-worker movement. Competition between work brigades! Competition between phalanxes (from 250 to 300 persons)! Competition between labor collectives! Competition between locks! And then, finally, the *Vokhrovtsy*—the Militarized Camp Guards—entered into competition with the zeks.[22] (And the obligation of the Vokhrovtsy? To guard you better.)

But the main reliance was, of course, on the *socially friendly*

22. *Ibid.*, p. 153.

elements—in other words, the thieves! These concepts had already merged at the canal. Deeply touched, Gorky shouted to them from the rostrum: "After all, any capitalist steals more than all of you combined!" The thieves roared with approval, flattered. "And big tears glistened in the eyes of a former pickpocket."[23] They counted on being able to make use of *the lawbreakers' romanticism* in the construction. And why shouldn't the thieves have been flattered? A thief says from the presidium of the rally: "We didn't receive any bread for two days, but there was nothing awful in that for us. [After all, they could always plunder someone else.] What is precious to us is that people talk to us like human beings [which is something the engineers cannot boast of]. There are such crags in our path that the drills break. That's all right. We manage them." (What do they *manage them with?* And *who* manages them?)

This is class theory: friendly elements against alien elements as the basis of the camp. It has never been reported how brigadiers at Belomor ate; but at Berezniki an eyewitness (I.D.T.) says there was a separate *kitchen for the brigadiers* (all . . . thieves) and rations—better than in the army. So that their fists would get strong and they would know *for what* to put the squeeze on.

At the second camp there was thievery, grabbing dishes from the prisoners and also ration tickets for gruel, but the thieves were not expelled from the ranks of shock workers on that account; it did not cast a shadow on their social image, or their productive drive. They brought the food to the work sites cold. They stole clothes from the drivers—that was all right, *we'll manage.* Povenets was a *penalty site*—chaos and confusion. They baked no bread in Povenets but brought it all the way from Kem (look at the map!). On the Shizhnya sector the food norm was not provided, it was cold in the barracks, there was an infestation of lice, and people were ill—never mind, we'll *manage!* "The canal is being constructed on the initiative of . . ." KVB's—Cultural and Educational Battle Points!—were everywhere. (A hooligan no more than arrived in camp than he immediately became an instructor.) An atmosphere of constant battle alert was created. All of a sudden *a night of storm assault* was proclaimed—*a blow against bureaucracy!* And right at the end of the evening work the cultural instructors went around the administration rooms and

23. Y. Kuzemko, *op. cit.*

19. Frenkel, Firin, and Uspensky

20. Distribution of the food bonus

took by storm! All of a sudden there was a *breakthrough* (not of water, of percentages) on the Tunguda sector. *Storm attack!* It was decided: *to double the work norms!* Really![24] All of a sudden, without any warning, some brigade or other has fulfilled its day's plan by 852 percent! Just try to understand that! So a universal *day of records* is proclaimed! A blow against *tempo interrupters.* *Bonus pirozhki* are distributed to a brigade (Illustration No. 20). Why such haggard faces? The longed-for moment—but no gladness . . .

It seemed that everything was going well. In the summer of 1932 Yagoda, the provider, inspected the entire route and was satisfied. But in December he sent a telegram: The norms are not being fulfilled. The *idle loafing of thousands of people* must be ended. (This you believe! This you see!) The labor collectives are *dragging their way* to work with *faded* banners. It has been learned that, according to the communiqués, 100 percent of the total amount of earth to be moved to build the canal has already been excavated *several times* over—yet the canal has not been finished. Negligent sloggers have been filling the log cribs with ice instead of stone and earth! And this will melt in the spring— and the water will break through. There are new slogans for the instructors: *"Tufta[25] is the most dangerous weapon of counter-revolution."* (And it was the thieves most of all who engaged in "tufta"; filling the cribs with ice was, plainly, their trick.) And there was one more slogan: *"The cheater is a class enemy!"* And the *thieves* were entrusted with the task of going around *to expose "tufta" and verify the work done by KR brigades!* (The best way for them to claim as their own the work of the KR brigades.) "Tufta" is an attempt to destroy the entire corrective-labor policy of the OGPU—that's how awful this "tufta" is! "Tufta" is the theft of socialist property! That's how terrible that "tufta" is! In February, 1933, they rearrested engineers who had been released early—because of the "tufta" they'd discovered.

There was such élan, such enthusiasm, so whence had come this "tufta"? Why had the prisoners thought it up? Evidently they were betting on the restoration of capitalism. Things hadn't gone that way here without the White emigration's black hand being present.

At the beginning of 1933 there was a new order from Yagoda:

---

24. *Belomorsko-Baltiisky Kanal, op. cit.,* p. 302.
25. I accept "f" in "tufta" here instead of "kh" only because I am quoting.

All administrations were to be renamed *staffs of battle sectors!* Fifty percent of the administrative staffs were to be thrown into construction work (would there be enough spades?). They were to work in three shifts (the night was nearly polar)! They would be fed right on canal site (with cold food)! For "tufta" they would be put on trial.

In January came *the storm of the watershed!* All the phalanxes, with their kitchens and property, were to be thrown into one single sector! There were not enough tents for everyone. They slept out on the snow—never mind. *We'll manage!* The canal is being built on the initiative of . . .

From Moscow came Order No. 1: "To proclaim *a general storm attack* until the completion of construction." At the end of the working day they drove stenographers, office workers, laundresses onto the canal site.

In February there was a prohibition on all visits from relatives for the entire Belomor Camp system—either because of the danger of typhus or else because of pressure on the zeks.

In April there was an incessant forty-eight-hour storm assault —hurrah! *Thirty thousand people did not sleep!*

And by May 1, 1933, People's Commissar Yagoda reported to his beloved Teacher that the canal had been completed on time (Illustration No. 21: map of the canal).

In July, 1933, Stalin, Voroshilov, and Kirov undertook a pleasant excursion on a steamer to inspect the canal. There is a photograph that shows them sitting on deck in wicker armchairs, "joking, laughing, smoking." (Meanwhile Kirov was already doomed but did not know it.)

In August the 120 writers made their excursion through the canal.

There were no people in the area to service and operate the canal. And so they sent dispossessed kulaks ("special deportees"), and Berman himself picked the places for their settlements.

A large part of the "Canal Army Men" went on to build the next canal—the Moscow-Volga Canal.[26]

---

26. At the August rally of the Canal Army Men Lazar Kogan proclaimed: "Not far off is the rally which will be the last in the camp system. . . . Not far off is that year, month and day when by and large corrective-labor camps will not be needed." He himself was probably shot, and never did find out how sadly mistaken he was. And maybe when he said it, he did not believe it.

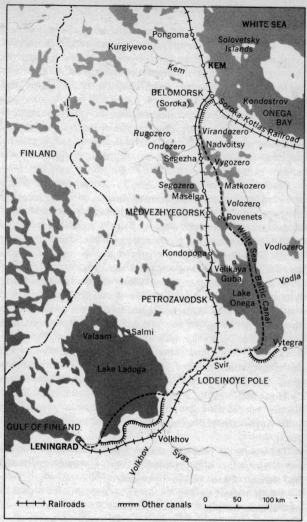

21. Map of the Belomor Canal

Let us turn away from the scoffing collective writers' volume.

No matter how gloomy the Solovetsky Islands seemed, the Solovetsky Islanders who were sent off on prisoner transports to end their terms (and often their lives) on the Belomor Canal only there really came to feel that joking had ended, only there discovered what a genuine camp was like, something which all of us gradually came to know later. Instead of the quiet of Solovki, there were incessant mother oaths and the savage din of quarreling mingled with indoctrinational propaganda. Even in the barracks of the Medvezhyegorsk Camp in the Administration of BelBaltlag people slept on "vagonki"—double-tiered wooden bunks anchored in pairs (already invented), not just by fours but by eights, two on each single bunk panel—head by feet. Instead of stone monastery buildings, there were drafty temporary barracks, even tents, and sometimes people out on the bare snow. And those transferred from Berezniki, where they had also worked a twelve-hour day, found it was worse here. Days of work records. Nights of storm assaults. "From us everything, to us nothing." Many were crippled and killed in the crowding and chaos in the course of dynamiting rocky crags. Gruel that had grown cold was eaten among the boulders. We have already read what the work was like. What kind of food—well, what kind could there have been in 1931–1933? (Anna Skripnikova reports that even in the Medvezhyegorsk mess hall for free voluntary employees they served only a murky dishwater with fish heads and individual millet grains.)[27] Their clothing was their own and was worn till it was worn out. And there was only one form of address, one form of urging them on, one refrain: "Come on! . . . Come on! . . . Come on! . . ."

They say that in the first winter, 1931–1932, 100,000 died off —a number equal to the number of those who made up the full working force on the canal. And why not believe it? More likely it is an understatement: in similar conditions in wartime camps a death rate of one percent per day was commonplace and common knowledge. So on Belomor 100,000 could have died off in

---

27. However, she recalls that refugees from the Ukraine came to Medvezhyegorsk in order to get work near the camp and by this means save themselves from starvation. The zeks called them over and *brought some of their own food from the camp compound for them to eat.* And all this is very likely. But not all were able to escape from the Ukraine.

just three months plus. And then there was another whole summer, and another winter.

D. P. Vitkovsky, a Solovetsky Islands veteran, who worked on the White Sea Canal as a work supervisor and saved the lives of many prisoners with that very same "tukhta," the falsification of work reports, draws a picture of the evenings:

> At the end of the workday there were corpses left on the work site. The snow powdered their faces. One of them was hunched over beneath an overturned wheelbarrow, he had hidden his hands in his sleeves and frozen to death in that position. Someone had frozen with his head bent down between his knees. Two were frozen back to back leaning against each other. They were peasant lads and the best workers one could possibly imagine. They were sent to the canal in tens of thousands at a time, and the authorities tried to work things out so no one got to the same subcamp as his father; they tried to break up families. And right off they gave them norms of shingle and boulders that you'd be unable to fulfill even in summer. No one was able to teach them anything, to warn them; and in their village simplicity they gave all their strength to their work and weakened very swiftly and then froze to death, embracing in pairs. At night the sledges went out and collected them. The drivers threw the corpses onto the sledges with a dull clonk.
>
> And in the summer bones remained from corpses which had not been removed in time, and together with the shingle they got into the concrete mixer. And in this way they got into the concrete of the last lock at the city of Belomorsk and will be preserved there forever.[28]

The Belomorstroi newspaper choked with enthusiasm in describing how many Canal Army Men, who had been "aesthetically carried away" by their great task, had in their own free time (and, obviously, without any payment in bread) decorated the canal banks with stones—simply for the sake of beauty.

Yes, and it was quite right for them to set forth on the banks of the canal the names of the six principal lieutenants of Stalin and Yagoda, the chief overseers of Belomor, six hired murderers each of whom accounted for thirty thousand lives: Firin—Berman—Frenkel—Kogan—Rappoport—Zhuk.

Yes, and they should have added there the Chief of VOKhR of BelBaltlag—Brodsky. Yes, and the Curator of the Canal representing VTsIK—Solts.

<hr />

28. D. Vitkovsky, *Polzhizni* (*Half a Lifetime*).

Yes, and all thirty-seven Chekists who were at the canal. And the thirty-six writers who glorified Belomor.[29] And the dramatist Pogodin *should not be forgotten either*.

So that tourists on steamers would read and think about them.

But that's the rub. There are no tourists!

How can that be?

Just like that. And there are no steamers either. There is nothing there that goes on a schedule.

In 1966, when I was completing this book, I wanted to travel through the great Belomor, to see it for myself. Just so as to compete with those 120 others. But it was impossible. . . . There was nothing to make the trip on. I would have had to ask for passage on a freighter. And on such vessels they check your papers. And I have a name which had been attacked. There would immediately be suspicion: Why was I going? And, therefore, so that the book remained safe, it was wiser not to go.

But, nonetheless, I did poke around there a bit. First at Medvezhyegorsk. Even at the present time many of the barracks have still survived. Also a majestic hotel with a five-story glass tower. For after all, this was the gateway to the canal! After all, things would buzz here with Soviet and foreign visitors. . . . But it stayed empty forever and ever, and finally they turned it over to a boarding school.

The road to Povenets. Stunted woods. Stones at every step. Boulders.

From Povenets I reached the canal straightaway and walked along it for a long stretch, keeping as close as possible to the locks so as to look them over. Forbidden zones. Sleepy guards. But in some places things were clearly visible. The walls of the locks were just what they had been before, made from those very same rock-filled cribs. I could recognize them from their pictures. But Maslov's rhomboid gates had been replaced by metal gates and were no longer opened by hand.

But why was everything so quiet? There were no people about.

---

29. Including Aleksei N. Tolstoi, who, after he had traveled over the canal (for he had to pay for his position), "recounted with excitement and inspiration what he had seen, drawing attractive, almost fantastic, and at the same time realistic pictures of the prospects of the future of the region, putting into his narrative all the heat of his creative passion and writer's imagination. He literally bubbled with enthusiasm in speaking of the labor of the canal builders, of the *advanced technology* [my italics—A.S.]."

There was no traffic on the canal nor in the locks. There was no hustle and bustle of service personnel. There were no steamer whistles. The lock gates stayed shut. It was a fine serene June day. So why was it?

And so it was that I passed five locks of the Povenets "staircase," and after passing the fifth I sat down on the bank. Portrayed on all our "Belomor" cigarette packages, and so desperately needed by our country, why are you silent, Great Canal?

Someone in civilian clothing approached me with watchful eyes. So I played the simpleton: Where could I get some fish? Yes, and how could I leave via the canal? He turned out to be the chief of the locks guard. Why, I asked him, wasn't there any passenger traffic? Well—he acted astonished—how could we? After all, the Americans would rush right over to see it. Until the war there had been passenger traffic, but not since the war. Well, what if they did come and see it? Well, now, how could we let them see it? But why is no one traveling on it? They do. But not very many. You see, it is very shallow, sixteen feet deep. They wanted to rebuild it, but in all probability they will build another next to it, one which will be all right from the beginning.

You don't say, boss! We've long since known all about that: In 1934, no sooner had they finished passing out all the medals than there was already a project for reconstructing it. And point No. 1 was: to deepen the canal. And the second was: to build a deep-water chain of locks for seagoing ships parallel to the existing locks. Haste makes waste. Because of that *time limit* imposed on its completion, because of those *norms*, they not only cheated on the depth but reduced the tonnage capacity: there had to be some faked cubic feet in order to feed the sloggers. (And very soon afterward they blamed this cheating on the engineers and gave them new "tenners.") And fifty miles of the Murmansk Railroad had had to be moved to make room for the canal route. It was at least a good thing that they hadn't wasted any wheelbarrow wheels on the project. And what were they to haul on it anyway —and where? They had cut down all the nearby timber—so where was it to be hauled from? Was Archangel timber to be hauled to Leningrad? But it was sold right in Archangel; foreigners had been buying it there since long ago. Yes, for half the year the canal is frozen anyhow, maybe more. So what was it needed for anyway? Oh, yes, there was a military necessity: in order to be able to shift the fleet.

"It's so shallow," complained the chief of the guard, "that not even submarines can pass through it under their own power; they have to be loaded on barges, and only then can they be hauled through."

And what about the cruisers? Oh, you hermit-tyrant! You nighttime lunatic! In what nightmare did you dream up all this?

And where, cursed one, were you hurrying to? What was it that burned and pricked you—to set a deadline of twenty months? For those quarter-million men could have remained alive. Well, so the Esperantists stuck in your throat, but think how much work those peasant lads could have done for you! How many times you could have roused them to attack—for the Motherland, for Stalin!

"It was very costly," I said to the guard.

"But it was built very quickly!" he answered me with self-assurance.

Your bones should be in it!

That day I spent eight hours by the canal. During this time there was one self-propelled barge which passed from Povenets to Soroka, and one, identical in type, which passed from Soroka to Povenets. Their numbers were different, and it was only by their numbers that I could tell them apart and be sure that it was not the same one as before on its way back. Because they were loaded altogether identically: with the very same pine logs which had been lying exposed for a long time and were useless for anything except firewood.

And canceling the one load against the other we get zero.

And a quarter of a million to be remembered.

■

And after the White Sea–Baltic Canal came the Moscow-Volga Canal. The sloggers all moved over to it immediately, as well as Chief of Camp Firin, and Chief of Construction Kogan. (Their Orders of Lenin for Belomor reached both of them there.)

But this canal was at least needed. And it gloriously continued and developed all the traditions of Belomor, and we can understand even better here how the Archipelago in the period of rapid metastasis differed from stagnant Solovki. Now was the time to remember and regret the silent cruelties of Solovki. For now they not only demanded work of the prisoners, they not only demanded that the prisoners break up the unyielding rocks with their failing picks. No, while taking away life, they even earlier crawled into the breast and searched the soul.

And this was the most difficult thing to bear on the canals: They demanded that in addition to everything else you *chirp*. You might be *on your last legs*, but you had to make a pretense of participation in public affairs. With a tongue growing numb from hunger you had to deliver speeches demanding over-fulfillment of plan: and exposure of wreckers! And punishment for hostile propaganda, for *kulak* rumors (and all camp rumors were *kulak* rumors). And to be on the lookout to make sure that the snakes of mistrust did not entwine a new prison term about you.

Picking up these shameless books where the life of the doomed is portrayed so glossily and with such admiration, it is almost impossible to believe that they were written in all seriousness and also read in all seriousness. (Yes, and circumspect Glavlit destroyed the printings, so that in this case too we got one of the last existing copies.)

And now our Virgil will be the assiduous pupil of Vyshinsky, I. L. Averbakh.[30]

Even driving in a single screw takes at first some special effort: The axis must be kept straight, and the screw has to be kept from leaning to one side. But when it has already begun to take hold, one can then free one hand, and just keep screwing it in and whistling.

We read Vyshinsky: "Thanks in particular to its educational task, our Corrective Labor Camp (ITL) is fundamentally counterposed to the bourgeois prison where raw violence reigns."[31] "In contrast to bourgeois states, the use of violence in the struggle against crime plays a role of secondary importance, and the center of gravity has passed over to organizational-material, cultural-educational, and political-indoctrinational measures."[32] (You really have to furrow your brains not to burst out: Instead of the club—the *ration* scale, plus propa-

30. Averbakh, *op. cit.*
31. Vyshinsky's preface to the collection *Ot Tyurem . . . , op. cit.*
32. Vyshinsky's preface to Averbakh's book.

ganda.) And here is some more: ". . . the successes of socialism also exercise their magical [! that's what's sculpted there: magical!] influence on . . . the struggle against crime."[33]

Following in his teacher's footsteps, Averbakh similarly elaborates: The task of Soviet corrective-labor policy is "the transformation of *the nastiest human material* [Do you remember *raw material?* Do you remember *insects?*—A.S.] into worthwhile, fully useful, active, and conscientious builders of socialism."

There is just the question of that little coefficient: a quarter-million of nasty material lay down and died, and 12,500 of the active and conscientious were liberated ahead of time (Belomor). . . .

Yes, and wasn't it back at the Eighth Party Congress in 1919, when the Civil War was still blazing, when they were still waiting for Denikin near Orel, when Kronstadt and the Tambov revolt were still in the future, that the Congress declared and determined: to replace the system of punishments (in other words, in general not to punish anyone at all?) with a system of *education*?

"Compulsory," Averbakh now adds. And rhetorically (already saving up for us the annihilating reply) he asks: But *how else?* How can one remake consciousness for the benefit of socialism if in freedom it has already become hostile to it, and camp compulsion is perceived as violence and can only intensify the hostility?

So we and the reader are caught in a blind alley—is it not true?

But that's not the end of it, and now he is going to dazzle us blind: productive, meaningful labor with *a high purpose!*—that's the means by which all hostile or unreliable consciousness will be remade. And for that, it seems, we need "to concentrate our work on gigantic projects which astound the imagination with their grandeur." (Ah, so that's it, that's why we needed Belomor, and we dunderheads didn't understand a thing!) By this means are attained "immediacy, effectiveness, and the pathos of construction." And at the same time "work from zero to completion" is obligatory, and "every camp inmate" (who is not yet dead as of today) "feels the political resonance of his personal labor, the interest of the entire country in his work."

Please notice how smoothly the screw is now going in.

33. *Ibid.*

Perhaps it is a bit crooked, but are we not losing the capacity to resist it? The Father marked a line on the map with his pipe, and is there some anxiety about justifying him? An Averbakh always turns up: "Andrei Yanuaryevich, here is an idea I've had. What do you think about it? Should I develop it in a book?"

But those are only frills. What was required was that the prisoner, while still confined in camp, "be indoctrinated in the highest socialist forms of labor."

And what was required for that? The screw had gotten stuck.

What muddle-headedness! Of course, *socialist competition* and *the shock-worker movement!* (Illustration No. 22.) What millennium is it, darlings, out of doors? "Not just work, but heroic work!" (OGPU Order No. 190.)

Competition for temporary possession of the red banner of the central staff! Of the district staff! Of the division staff! Competition between camps, construction sites, brigades! "Along with the transferable red banner a brass band was also awarded! For whole days at a time it played for the winners during work periods and during periods of tasty food!" (Illustration No. 26: There is no tasty food to be seen in the photograph, but you can see the searchlight. That was for night work. The Moscow-Volga Canal was constructed around the clock.)[34] In every brigade of prisoners there was a "troika" concerned with competition. Audit—and resolutions! Resolutions—and audit! The results of the storm assault on the watershed for the first five-day period! For the second! The intercamp newspaper was called *Perekovka—Reforging*. Its slogan was: "*Let us drown our past on the bottom of the canal.*" Its appeal: "Work without days off!" Universal enthusiasm, universal agreement! The leading shock worker said: "Of course! How can there be days off? *The Volga doesn't have . . . days off*, and it's just about to overflow its banks." And what about days off on the Mississippi? Grab him, he's a kulak agent! A point in the obligations undertaken: "Preservation of health by every member of the

---

34. A band was used in other camps as well: they put it on the shore and it played for several days in a row until prisoners working without relief or rest periods had unloaded timber from a barge. I.D.T. was in a band at Belomor and he recalls: The band aroused anger among those working (after all, the musicians were released from general work, had their own individual cots and their own military uniform). They used to shout at us: "Parasites, drones! Come here and get to work!" In the photograph neither this nor anything like it is shown.

collective." Oh, what humanitarianism! No, here's what it was for: "to reduce the amount of absenteeism." "Do not be ill, and do not take time off." Red bulletin boards. Black bulletin boards. Bulletin boards of charts: days remaining until completion; work done yesterday, work done today. The honor roll. In every barracks, honor certificates, "a bulletin board of reforging" (Illustration No. 23), graphs, diagrams. (And how many loafers were scurrying about and writing all this stuff!) Every prisoner had to be informed about the production plans! And every prisoner had to be informed about the entire political life of the country! Therefore at morning line-up (taken out of morning free time, of course) there was a "five-minute production session," and after returning to camp, when one's legs could hardly keep one upright, there was a "five-minute political session." During lunch hours prisoners were not to be allowed to crawl into nooks and crannies or to sleep—there were "political readings." If out in freedom the "Six Conditions of Comrade Stalin" were proclaimed, then every camp inmate had to learn them by heart.[35] If in freedom there was a decree of the Council of People's Commissars on dismissing workers for absenteeism, then here explanatory work had to be undertaken: Every person who today refuses to work or who simulates illness must, after his liberation, be *branded with the contempt of the masses* of the Soviet Union. The system here was this: In order to get the title of shock worker it was not enough merely to have production successes! It was necessary, in addition: (a) to read the newspapers; (b) *to love your canal;* (c) to be able to talk about its significance.

And miracle! Oh, miracle! Oh, transfiguration and ascension! The "shock worker ceases to feel discipline and labor as something which has been forced on him from outside." (Even horses understand this: Illustration No. 24.) "It becomes an *inner necessity!*" (Well, truly, of course, freedom, after all, is not freedom, but accepted bars!) New socialist forms of reward! The issuing of shock workers' buttons. And what

---

35. It is worth noting that intellectuals who had managed *to make their way up* to positions in management took advantage of these Six Conditions very adroitly. "To make use of specialists by every possible means" meant to yank engineers off *general work.* "Not to permit turnover in the work force" meant to prohibit prisoner transports!

22. Barracks posters:
"Complete the canal!"

23. "For a better life, for a happier life!"

24. "Even the horse
doesn't need the whip!"

25. Beneath the storm

26. A brass band at the canal

would you have thought, what would you have thought? "The shock worker's button is valued by the sloggers *more highly than rations!*" Yes, more highly than rations! And whole brigades "voluntarily go out to work *two hours before line-up.*" (What presumption! But what was the convoy to do?) "And they also stayed behind to work after the end of the workday."

Oh, flame! Oh, matches! They thought you would burn for decades.

Here it is: shock work! (Illustration No. 25.) A thunderstorm breaks, but we are going to work anyway! We are going to overfulfill the day's plan! Remark the technology. We spoke of it at the Belomor too: on the slopes a hookman hauls the wheelbarrow from the front—indeed, how else could it be made to roll upward? Ivan Nemtsev suddenly *decided* to do the work of *five men!* No sooner said than done: he moved seventy-two cubic yards of earth in one shift.[36] (Let us calculate: that is six and a half cubic yards per hour, one cubic yard every nine minutes. Just try it, even with the lightest type of soil!) This was the situation: there were no pumps, no wells had been readied— and water had to be fought off with one's hands![37] And what about the women? They used to lift, unaided, stones of up to a hundred and fifty pounds![38] Wheelbarrows overturned and stones struck head and feet. That's all right, we'll *manage!* Some- times "up to their waists in water," sometimes "sixty-two hours of unbroken work," sometimes "for three days five hundred persons hacked at the frozen earth," and it turned out to be to no avail. That's all right, we'll *manage.*

> With our battle spades
> We dug our happiness near Moscow!

This was that same "special, gay tension" they had brought with them from Belomor. "They went on the attack with boisterous gay songs."

> In any weather
> March out to line-up!

36. Kuzemko, *op. cit.*
37. *Ibid.*
38. The leaflet *Kanaloarmeika* (*The Canal Army Woman*), Dmitlag, 1935. (Not to be taken beyond the boundaries of the camp!)

27. Shock brigade

28. Meeting of a shock brigade

And here are the *shock workers* themselves (Illustration No. 27). They have come to the rally. On one side, by the train, is the chief of convoy, and on the left there is one more convoy guard. Look at their inspired and happy faces; these women do not think about children nor about home but only about the canal which they have come to love so. It is quite cold, and some are in felt boots, some in ordinary boots, homemade of course, and the second from the left in the first row is a woman thief in stolen shoes, and where better to go swaggering about in them than at the rally? And here is another rally (Illustration No. 28). It says on the poster, "We will build it ahead of time, cheaply and strong." And how do we reconcile all that? Well, let the engineers break their heads over it. It is easy to see in the photograph that there are shadows of smiles for the camera, but in general these women are terribly fatigued. They are not going to make speeches. And all they expect from the rally is a nourishing meal for once. All of them have simple peasant-like faces.[39] And the trusty guard got stuck in the aisle. The Judas, he so much wanted to get into that photograph. And here is a shock brigade, provided with the last word in equipment (Illustration No. 30). It is not true that we haul everything under our own steam! If we are to believe the camp artists whose works were exhibited in the KVCh—the Cultural and Educational Section—(Illustrations Nos. 29 and 31), then this is the equipment already in use at the canal: one excavator, one crane, and one tractor. Are they in working order? Perhaps they are broken down; isn't that more likely? Well, generally speaking, in winter it isn't very cozy out on the construction site, right?

There was one small additional problem: "At the time Belomor was completed too many triumphant articles appeared in various newspapers, and they nullified the terrorizing effect of the camps. . . . In the description of Belomor they overdid it to such a degree that those who arrived at the Moscow-Volga Canal expected rivers of milk and honey and presented *unheard-of* demands to the administration." (Presumably they asked for clean linen?) So that was it: Go ahead and lie as much as you

---

39. All these photographs are from Averbakh's book. He warned that there were no photographs of kulaks and wreckers in it (in other words, of the finest peasants and intellectuals). Evidently, so to speak, "their time has not yet come." Alas, it never will. You can't bring back the dead.

29. Winter on the canal (painting by camp artist)

30. Women's shock brigade

please, but don't get entangled in your lying. "Today, too, the banner of Belomor waves over us," writes the newspaper *Reforging*. That's a moderate statement. And it is quite enough.

In any event, both at Belomor and at the Moscow-Volga Canal they understood that "camp competition and the shock-worker movement must be tied in *with the entire system of rewards*" so that the special rewards would *stimulate* the shock-worker movement. "The principal basis of competition is *material incentive*." (!?!? It would seem we've been thrown about-face? We have turned from East to West? One hundred eighty degrees? Is this a provocation! Hold tight to the handrails! The car is going through!) And things worked out like this: On production indices depended . . . nutrition and housing and clothing and linen and the frequency of baths! (Yes, yes, whoever works badly can go about in tatters and lice!) And liberation ahead of time! And rest days! And visits! For example, issuing a shock worker's lapel button is a purely socialist form of encouragement. But let that button confer the right to a long visit out of turn! And by this means it becomes more precious than *bread rations*.

"If in freedom, in accordance with the Soviet Constitution, we apply the principle of *whoever does not work does not eat*, then why should we put the camp inmates in a *privileged* position?" (The most difficult thing in organizing a camp: they must not become privileged places!) The ration scale at Dmitlag was this: The penalty ration consisted of muddy water and ten and a half ounces of bread. One hundred percent fulfillment of norm earned the right to twenty-eight ounces of bread and the right to *buy* in addition three and a half ounces in the camp commissary. And then "submission to discipline begins out of egotistical motives (self-interest in getting a better bread ration) and *rises* to the second step of socialist self-interest in the red banner."[40]

But the main thing was time off sentence! Time off sentence! The socialist competition headquarters compiles a report on the prisoner. For time off sentence not only overfulfillment of plan is required, but also *social work*. And anyone who in the past has been a nonworking element gets reduced time off sentence, miserly small. "Such a person can only pretend, not reform! He must be kept in camp *longer* so as to be verified." (For example,

40. In his private life Averbakh probably began immediately with the second step.

31. Winter on the canal (painting)

32. "Volunteers"

he pushes a wheelbarrow uphill—and maybe he isn't working, but just pretending?)

And what do those who were freed ahead of time do? What do you mean, what? *They stay with the project.* They have come to love the canal too much to leave it! "They are so absorbed in it that when they are liberated they *voluntarily* stay at the canal, engaging in earth-moving operations right to the end of the project." (They voluntarily remain at work like that. As, for example, in Illustration No. 32. Can one believe the author? Of course. After all, they all have a stamp in their passport: "Was in OGPU camps." You aren't going to find work anywhere else.)[41]

But what is this? The machinery for producing nightingale trills has suddenly broken down—and in the intermission we hear the weary breath of truth: "Even the thieves were only 60 percent involved in competition. [It is pretty bad if even the thieves don't compete!] The camp inmates often interpret the special benefits and rewards as incorrectly applied"; "recommendations of prisoners are often composed tritely"; "very often trusties pass themselves off on recommendations [!] as shock-worker excavators and receive a shock worker's time off sentence while the real shock worker often gets none."[42] (And so it would seem, gentlemen instructors, that it was *you* who had not managed to rise to the second step?); "and there were many [!] who clung to feelings of hopelessness and injustice."[43]

But the trills have begun again, with a metallic ring. The main incentive had evidently been forgotten: "cruel and merciless application of disciplinary penalties!" OGPU Order of November

---

41. Averbakh, *op. cit.*, p. 164.

42. In our country everything is topsy-turvy, and even rewards sometimes turn out to be a misfortune. The blacksmith Paramonov received two years off his ten-year sentence in one of the Archangel camps for the excellence of his work. But because of this two-year reduction, he completed his term during wartime, and as a result, being a 58, he was not released, but was kept there "under special decree" (*special*, once again). Just as soon as the war was over Paramonov's codefendants, convicted with him in the same case, completed their ten-year sentences and were released. And he dragged out another whole year. The prosecutor studied his case and couldn't do a thing: "the special decree" remained in force throughout the entire Archipelago.

43. Well, and in 1931 the Fifth Conference of Justice Officials condemned this whole snakepit: "The widespread and totally unjustified application of parole and time off sentence for workdays . . . leads to *diminution of the impact of sentences*, to the undermining *of the repression* of crime, and to distortions *in the class line.*"

28, 1933. (This was at the beginning of winter, so they would stand still without rocking back and forth!) "All incorrigible loafers and malingerers are to be sent to distant northern camps with total deprivation of rights to any privileges. Malicious strikers and troublemakers are to be turned over to trial by camp collegia. For the slightest attempt to violate iron discipline prisoners are to be deprived of all special privileges and advantages already received." (For example, for attempting to get warm beside the fire.)

And, nonetheless, we have again omitted the main link—total confusion! We have said everything, but we didn't say the main thing! Listen! Listen! "*Collectivity* is both the principle and the method of Soviet corrective-labor policy." After all, there have to be "*driving belts* from the administration to the masses!" "Only by basing itself on collectives can the multitudinous camp administration rework the consciousness of the prisoners." "From the lowest forms of collective responsibility to the highest forms is a matter of honor, a matter of glory, a matter of valor and heroism!" (We often abuse our language, claiming that with the passage of the ages it has grown pale. But if one really thinks about this, it is not true! It becomes more noble. Earlier, in the manner of cabmen, we said "reins." And now "driving belts"! It used to be called "mutual back-scratching": You help me out of the ditch and I'll help you out of the swamp—but that smells of the stable too. And now it's collective responsibility!)

"The brigade is the basic form of re-education." (A Dmitlag order, 1933.) "This means *trust in the collective,* which is impossible under capitalism!" (But which is quite possible under feudalism: one man in the village is at fault, strip them all and whip them! Nonetheless it sounds noble: Trust in the collective!) "That means the *spontaneous initiative* of the camp inmates in the cause of re-education!" "This is *psychological enrichment* of the personality by the collective!" (No, what words, what words! After all, he's knocked us right down with this *psychological enrichment!* Now there's a real scholar for you!) "The collective *heightens* the feeling of human *dignity* [yes, yes!] of every prisoner and by this means *hinders* the introduction of a system of moral *repression.*"

And, indeed, please tell me: thirty years after Averbakh, it was my fate to say a word or so about the brigade—all I did was describe how things work there; but people managed to understand me in quite the opposite sense, in a distorted way: "The brigade is the basic contribution of Communism to the science of punishment. [And that is quite right, that is precisely what Averbakh is saying.] . . . It is a collective organism, living, working, eating, sleeping, and suffering together in pitiless and forced symbiosis."[44]

Oh, without the brigade one could still somehow manage to survive the camp! Without the brigade you are an individual, you yourself choose your own line of conduct. Without the brigade you can at least die proudly, but in the brigade the only way they allow you even to die is in humiliation, on your belly. From the chief, from the camp foreman, from the jailer, from the convoy guard, from all of them you can hide and catch a moment of rest; you can ease up a bit here on hauling, shirk a bit there on lifting. But from *the driving belts*, from your comrades in the brigade, there is neither a hiding place, nor salvation, nor mercy. You cannot *not want* to work. You cannot, conscious of being a political, prefer death from hunger to work. No! Once you have been marched outside the compound, once you have been registered as going out to work, everything the brigade does today will be divided not by twenty-five but by twenty-six, and because of you the entire brigade's percentage of norm will fall from 123 to 119, which makes the difference between the ration allotted record breakers and ordinary rations, and everyone will lose a millet cake and three and a half ounces of bread. And that is why your comrades keep watch on you better than any jailers! And the brigade leader's fist will punish you far more effectively than the whole People's Commissariat of Internal Affairs.

Now that is what *spontaneous initiative in re-education* means! That is *psychological enrichment of the personality by the collective!*

So now it is all as transparent as a windowpane, yet on the Moscow-Volga Canal even the organizers themselves still did not dare believe what a strong dog collar they had found. And there the *brigade* was kept in the background, and the *labor collective* was elevated to the position of highest honor and incentive. Even in May, 1934, half the zeks in Dmitlag were still

44. Ernst Pawel, "The Triumph of Survival," *The Nation,* February 2, 1963.

"unorganized"; *they were not accepted in* the *labor collectives*! They did take them into *labor cooperatives,* but not all of them: they did not take in priests, sectarians, or other religious believers (unless they renounced their religion—the game was worth the candle—in which case they were accepted with one month's probation). They began to take 58's into the labor collectives unwillingly, but only those whose terms were less than five years. The collective had a chairman, a council, and the democracy there was quite unbridled: the meetings of the collective took place only with the permission of the KVCh—the Cultural and Educational Section—and only in the presence of the company (yes, indeed, they had companies too!) instructor. It goes without saying that the collectives were given higher rations than the mob: the best collectives had vegetable gardens allotted to them in the compound (not to individual people, but, as on a collective farm, to supplement the common pot). The collective split into sections, and every free hour was filled with either checking the daily living routine or inquests into thefts and the squandering of government property, of publication of a wall newspaper, or delving into disciplinary violations. At the meetings of the collectives they spent hours in pretentious discussion of such questions as: How to *reforge* lazybones Vovka? Or Grishka, the malingerer? The collective itself had the right to expel its own members and *ask that they be deprived of time off sentence,* but, as a more drastic measure, the administration could dissolve entire collectives which were "continuing criminal traditions." (Which were not, in other words, immersed in collective life?) However, the most entertaining were the periodic *purges* of the collectives—of loafers, of the unworthy, of *whisperers* (who depicted the labor collectives as organizations for spying on one another), and of agents of the class enemy who had crept into their midst. For example, it was discovered that someone, already in camp, was concealing his kulak descent (for which he had, in fact, been sent to camp in the first place), and so now he was branded and purged—purged not from the camp but from the labor collective. (Realist artists! Please paint that picture: "The purge in the labor collective!" Those shaven heads, those watchful expressions, those fatigued faces, those rags on the body—and those enraged orators! Right here is a prototype [Illustration No. 33]. And for those who find it hard to imagine, well, this sort of thing took place in freedom too. And in China.)

33. Labor collective

And listen to this: "As a preliminary, *the task and the purposes of the purge were communicated* to every camp inmate. And at that point every member of the collective gave public accounting."[45]

And then, too, there was *exposure of fake shock workers*! And elections of the cultural council! And official rebukes to those who had done poorly at liquidating their illiteracy! And there were the classes in liquidation of illiteracy too: "We-are-not-slaves! Slaves-we-are-not!" And the songs too?

> This kingdom of swamps and lowlands
> Will become our happy native land.

Or, in the masterful words of Nikolai Aseyev, the poet himself:

> We Canal Army Men are a tough people,
> But not in that lies our chief trait;
> We were caught up by a great epoch
> To be put on the path that leads straight.

---

45. All the citations not otherwise credited are from Averbakh's book. But sometimes I have combined phrases from different places, sometimes passed over his intolerable prolixity. After all, he had to stretch it out into a dissertation. But we don't have the space. However, I have nowhere distorted the meaning.

Or, at the amateur theatricals, bursting from the breast:

> And even the most beautiful song
> Cannot tell, no, cannot do justice
> To this country than which there is nothing more wondrous,
> The country in which you and I live.[46]

Now that is what *to chirp* means in camp slang.

Oh, they will drive you to the point where you will weep just to be back with company commander Kurilko, walking along the short and simple execution road, through open-and-above-board Solovki slavery.

My Lord! What canal is there deep enough for us to drown *that* past in?

---

46. Song books of Dmitlag, 1935. And the music was called *Canal Army Music*, and there were free composers on the competition committee: Shosta kovich, Kabalevsky, Shekhter. . . .

Chapter 4

■

The Archipelago Hardens

And the clock of history was striking.

In 1934, at the January Plenum of the Central Committee and Central Control Commission of the Soviet Communist Party, the Great Leader (having already in mind, no doubt, how many he would soon *have to do away with*) declared that the *withering away* of the state (which had been awaited virtually from 1920 on) would arrive via, believe it or not, the maximum *intensification* of state power!

This was so unexpectedly brilliant that it was not given to every little mind to grasp it, but Vyshinsky, ever the loyal apprentice, immediately picked it up: "And this means the maximum *strengthening* of corrective-labor institutions."[1]

Entry into socialism via the maximum strengthening of prison! And this was not some satirical magazine cracking a joke either, but was said by the Prosecutor General of the Soviet Union! And thus it was that the iron grip of the Yezhov terror was prepared even without Yezhov.

After all, the Second Five-Year Plan—and who remembers this? (for no one in our country ever remembers anything, for memory is the Russians' weak spot, especially memory of the bad)—the Second Five-Year Plan included among its glistening (and to this very day unfulfilled) goals the following: "the uprooting of the vestiges of capitalism from people's consciousness." This meant that this process of uprooting had to be finished by

1. Vyshinsky, *op. cit.*, Preface.

1938. Judge for yourself: by what means were these vestiges to be so swiftly uprooted?

"Soviet places of confinement on the threshold of the Second Five-Year Plan not only are not losing but are even gaining in significance." (Not one year had passed since Kogan's prediction that camps would soon cease to exist at all. But Kogan did not know about the January Plenum!) "In the epoch of entrance into socialism the role of corrective-labor institutions as weapons of the dictatorship of the proletariat, as organs of repression, as means of compulsion and education [compulsion is already in the first place!] must *grow still further* and be strengthened."[2] (For otherwise what was to happen to the command corps of the NKVD? Was it just supposed to disappear?)

So who is going to reproach our Progressive Doctrine with having fallen behind practice? All this was printed in black on white, but we still didn't know how to read. The year 1937 was publicly predicted and provided with a foundation.

And the hairy hand tossed out all the frills and gewgaws too. Labor collectives? Prohibited! What nonsense was that—self-government in camp! You couldn't think up anything better than the brigade anyway. What's all this about political indoctrination periods? Forget it! The prisoners are sent there to work and they don't have to understand anything. At Ukhta they had proclaimed the "liquidation of the last multiple bunk"? This was a political mistake—were the prisoners to be put to bed on cots with springs? Cram them on the bunks twice as thickly! *Time off sentences?* Abolish that before anything! What do you want—that the court's work should go for nothing? And what about those who already have credits toward time off sentence? Consider them canceled! (1937.) They are still permitting visits in some camps? Forbid them everywhere. Some prison or other permitted a priest's body to be turned over for burial outside prison? You must be insane! You are providing an opportunity for anti-Soviet demonstrations. There must be an exemplary punishment for this! And make it clear: the corpses of deceased prisoners belong to Gulag, and the location of graves is top-secret. Professional and technical courses for prisoners? Dissolve them! They should have done their studying in freedom. And what about VTsIK—what VTsIK

2. *Ibid.*, p. 449. One of the authors, Apeter, was the new Chief of Gulag.

anyway? Over Kalinin's signature? And we don't have a GPU, we have an NKVD. When they return to freedom, let them study on their own. Graphs, diagrams? Tear them off the wall and whitewash the walls. And you don't even have to whitewash them. And what kind of payroll is this? Wages for prisoners? A GUM-Zak circular dated November 25, 1926: 25 percent of the wages of a worker of equivalent skill in state industry? Shut up, and tear it up! We are robbing ourselves of wages! A prisoner should be paid? Let him say thank you he wasn't shot. The Corrective Labor Code of 1933? Forget it once and for all; take it out of all camp safes. "Every violation of nationwide codes on labor . . . only on the basis of agreement with the Central Council of Trade Unions—the VTsSPS"? Do you really think *we* are going to go to the VTsSPS? What's the VTsSPS anyway? All we have to do is spit on it and it will blow away! Article 75: "The rations are to be increased for heavier labor"? About face! Rations are to be reduced for easier work. Just like that, and the food allotment is intact.

The Corrective Labor Code with its hundreds of articles was swallowed up as if by a shark; and not only was it true that for twenty-five years afterward no one caught a glimpse of it, but even its name was unsuspected.

They shook up the Archipelago, and they became convinced that beginning back there with Solovki, and even more so during the period of the canals, the entire camp machinery had become intolerably loose. And now they got rid of all that weakness.

In the very first place, the whole *guard system* was no good. These weren't real camps at all; they had guards posted on the watchtowers only at night, and at the gatehouse there was just one unarmed guard, who could even be persuaded to let one out for a bit. They were still permitting kerosene lighting around the perimeter. And several dozen prisoners were being taken to work outside the camp by just a single rifleman. So now they wired the perimeter for electric light (using politically reliable electricians and motor mechanics). The riflemen of the guard were provided with battle statutes and military training. Attack-trained German shepherds were included in the required service staffs, with their own breeders and trainers, and their own separate statutes. The camps began to assume, at long last, a fully modern, contemporary appearance, which we know very well indeed.

This is not the place to list the many small details of daily life in which the camp regimen was made stricter and tightened up. And the many cracks that were discovered via which *freedom* could still observe the Archipelago. All those ties were now broken off, and the cracks were filled in, and the last few "observers' commissions" were expelled.[3] (At the same time the

3. There is not going to be any other place in this book for an explanation of what these were. So let this be a lengthy note for those curious about it.

Hypocritical bourgeois society thought up the idea of inspection of conditions in places of confinement and of the course of prisoner correction. In Tsarist Russia "the societies of guardianship over prisons"—"for the improvement of the physical and moral state of the prisoners"—were the charitable prison committees and the societies of prison patronage. In American prisons, commissions of observers, consisting of public representatives, already possessed broad rights in the twenties and thirties, including even the right of release ahead of term (not petitioning for it, but release itself, without action by a court). And indeed our dialectical legal experts pointedly protest: "One must not forget *what classes* the commissions represent. They reach decisions in accordance with their class interests."

It is quite a different thing here in our country. The very first "Temporary Instruction" of July 23, 1918, which created the first camps, provided for the creation of *"assignment commissions"* attached to Provincial Penal Departments. They assigned all sentenced prisoners one of *seven* different types of confinement, which had been established in the early Russian Soviet Federated Socialist Republic. This work (which apparently replaced that of the courts) was so important that the People's Commissariat of Justice in its report of 1920 called the activity of the assignment commissions "the nerve center of penal operations." Their makeup was very democratic; in 1922, for example, it was a *troika*: the Chief of the Provincial NKVD Administration, a member of the Presidium of the Provincial Court, and the Chief of Places of Confinement in the specific province. Later on one person was added from the Provincial Workers' and Peasants' Inspection and the Provincial Trade Union Council. But as early as 1929 there was great dissatisfaction with the commissions: they exercised their power to release prisoners before the end of term and to grant other benefits to hostile-class elements. "This was the rightist-opportunist practice of the NKVD leadership." For this reason, assignment commissions were abolished in that selfsame year of the Great Turning Point and in their place *observers'* commissions were created whose chairmen were *judges*, and whose members consisted of the chief of the camp, the prosecutor, and a representative of the *public*—from *workers in penal institutions*, the *police*, the district executive committee, or the Komsomol. And as our jurists pointedly declared: "One must not forget what classes—" Oh, excuse me, I have already quoted that. . . . And the observers' commissions were entrusted with these tasks: by the NKVD, to decide the question of time off sentences and release before the end of term, and by VTsIK (so to speak, by parliament), *to verify the fulfillment of the production and financial plans.*

And it was these observers' commissions which were abolished at the beginning of the Second Five-Year Plan. Speaking frankly, none of the prisoners sighed over the loss.

Another thing about classes now that we've mentioned them: one of the authors of that same collection we have cited so often before, Shestakova, on the basis of materials from the twenties and the beginning of the thirties, "reached a strange conclusion as to the similarity of the social origins of prisoners in bourgeois prisons and in our country." To her surprise it turned out

camp *phalanxes*—even though there seem to have been glimmerings of socialism in them—were renamed *columns* so as to distinguish them from Franco's.) The camp Security Section, which, up to this time, had had to make allowances for the goals of the general productive work and of the plan, now acquired its own self-contained dominating significance, to the detriment of all kinds of productive work and of any staff of specialists. True, they did not drive out the camp Cultural and Educational Sections, but this was partly because it was convenient to collect denunciations and summon stool pigeons through them.

And an iron curtain descended around the Archipelago. No one other than the officers and sergeants of the NKVD could enter and leave via the camp gatehouse. That harmonious order of things was established which the zeks themselves would soon come to consider the only conceivable one, the one we will describe in this part of this book—without the red ribbons by this time, and containing much more "labor" than "correction."

And that is when the wolf's fangs were bared! And that is when the bottomless pit of the Archipelago gaped wide!

"I'll shoe you in tin cans, but you're going to go out to work!"

"If there aren't enough railroad ties, I'll make one out of you!"

And that is when, sending freight trains through Siberia with a machine gun on the roof of every third car, they drove the 58's into excavation pits to guard them more securely. And that was when, even before the first shot of World War II, back when all Europe still danced fox trots, they could not manage to crush the lice in the Mariinsk *distributor* (the intercamp transit prison of the Mariinsk Camps) and brushed them off the clothes with whisk brooms. Typhus broke out, and in one short period fifteen thousand corpses were thrown into a ditch—curled up and naked, since even their underpants had been cut off them to be preserved for future use. (We have already recalled the typhus which raged at the Vladivostok Transit Camp.)

---

that both there and here those in prison were . . . workers. Well, of course, there has to be some kind of dialectical explanation here, but she couldn't find any. And we will add on our own behalf that this "strange resemblance" was violated only in a minor degree in 1937–1938 when high state officials flocked into the camps. But very soon the proportions evened out. All the multimillion waves of the war and the postwar period consisted only of waves of *the working classes.*

And there was only one of its new acquisitions of the recent past that Gulag did not part with: the encouragement of the hoodlums, the thieves (the blatnye). Even more consistently than before, the thieves were given all the "commanding heights" in camp. Even more consistently than before, the thieves were egged on against the 58's, permitted to plunder them without any obstacles, to beat, to choke. The thieves became just like an internal camp police, camp storm troopers. (During the war years in many camps the custodial staffs were cut back to almost nothing and their work was entrusted to the *commandant's headquarters*, meaning to "the thieves who had become bitches," to the *bitches* —and the bitches were more effective than any custodial staff: after all, there was no prohibition against their beating.)

They say that in February–March, 1938, a secret instruction was circulated in the NKVD: *Reduce the number of prisoners.* (And not by releasing them, of course.) I do not see anything in the least impossible here: this was a logical instruction because there was simply not enough housing, clothing, or food. Gulag was grinding to a halt from exhaustion.

And this was when the pellagra victims lay down and died en masse. This was when the chiefs of convoy began to test the accuracy of machine-gun fire by shooting at the stumbling zeks. And this was when every morning the orderlies hauled the corpses to the gatehouse, stacking them there.

In the Kolyma, that pole of cold and cruelty in the Archipelago, that very same about-face took place with a sharpness worthy of a pole.

According to the recollections of Ivan Semyonovich Karpunich-Braven (former commander of the 40th Division and of the XII Corps, who recently died with his notes incomplete and scattered), a most dreadfully cruel system of food, work, and punishment was established in the Kolyma. The prisoners were so famished that at Zarosshy Spring they ate the corpse of a horse which had been lying dead for more than a week and which not only stank but was covered with flies and maggots. At Utiny Goldfields the zeks ate half a barrel of lubricating grease, brought there to grease the wheelbarrows. At Mylga they ate Iceland moss, like the deer. And when the passes were shut by snowdrifts, they used to issue three and a half ounces of bread a day at the distant goldfields, without ever making up for previous deficiencies. Multitudes of "goners," unable to walk by themselves, were dragged to work on sledges by other "goners" who had not yet become quite so weak. Those who lagged behind were beaten with clubs and torn by dogs. Working in 50 degrees below zero Fahrenheit, they were forbidden to build fires and warm themselves. (The thieves were allowed this.) Karpunich himself also tried "cold drilling by hand" with a steel drill six and a half feet long, and hauling so-called "peat" (soil with broken stone and boulders) at 60 degrees below zero on sledges to which four men were hitched (the sledges were made of raw lumber, and the boxes on top were made of raw slab); a fifth accompanied them, a thief-*expediter*, "responsible for fulfillment of the plan," who kept beating them with a stave. Those who did not fulfill the norm (and what does it mean—those who did not fulfill?—because, after all, the production of the 58's was always "stolen" by the thieves) were punished by the chief of the camp, Zeldin, in this way: In winter he ordered them to strip naked in the mine shaft, poured cold water over them, and in this state they had to run to the compound; in summer they were forced to strip naked, their hands were tied behind them to a common pole, and they were left out, tied there, under a cloud of mosquitoes. (The guard was covered by a mosquito net.) Then, finally, they were simply beaten with a rifle butt and tossed into an isolator.

Some will object that there was nothing new in all this and no *development*—that this was a mere primitive return from the noisily educational canals to the directness of Solovki. Bah! But perhaps this was a Hegelian triad: Solovki-Belomor-Kolyma? Thesis, antithesis, synthesis? The negation of a negation, but enriched?

For example, here are *the death carriages*, which, so far as can be learned, did not exist on Solovki. This is according to the recollections of Karpunich at Marisny Spring (forty-one miles along the Srednekan trail). For an entire ten-day period the chief tolerated nonfulfillment of the norm. Only on the tenth day did he imprison in the isolator on a penalty ration those who had failed to fulfill and then had them taken out to work again. But whoever did not fulfill the norm, even in these circumstances, was given the *carriage*—a frame of sixteen by ten by six feet on a tractor sledge, made of rough beams, fastened together with construction staples. A small door, no windows, and inside nothing at all, not even any bed boards. In the evening those to be punished, sunk into a torpor and already indifferent, were taken from the penalty isolator and packed into the carriage, locked in there with an enormous lock, and hauled off by tractor to a vale two to three miles from the camp. Several of those inside cried out, but the tractor unhitched them and left them there for a day. After a day it was unlocked and the corpses were tossed out. The winter storms would bury them.

At Mylga (a subordinate camp of Elgen), under Chief Gavrik, the punishments for women who failed to fulfill the norm were lighter: simply an unheated tent in winter (but one was allowed to go outside and run around it), and at haying time under the mosquitoes—an unprotected wattle shack (the recollections of Sliozberg).

The intensification of the cruelty of the Kolyma regime was outwardly marked by the fact that Garanin was made the chief of USVitlag (the Administration of Northeastern Camps), and that the Divisional Commander of the Latvian Riflemen, E. Berzin, was replaced as head of Dalstroi by Pavlov. (Incidentally, this totally unnecessary reshuffle was due to Stalin's suspiciousness. What was there to make one think that the old Chekist Berzin could not just as well have satisfied the new demands of his associate? Would he have hesitated?)

At that point, they abolished the remaining days off for the 58's and lengthened the summer workday to fourteen hours, came to consider 50 and 60 degrees below zero Fahrenheit suitable for work; and allowed work to be canceled only on those days when the temperature was lower than 65 degrees below zero Fahrenheit. (And because of the caprices of individual chiefs some took the prisoners out for work even at 75 below.) At the Gorny Gold-fields (plagiarizing Solovki once more) those who refused to go out to work were tied to the sledges and hauled thus to the mine face. It was also accepted in the Kolyma that the convoy was not only present to guard the prisoners but was also answerable for their fulfillment of the plan, and therefore had to avoid dozing and continue slave-driving them eternally.

And then, too, the scurvy finished off many, without any help from the administration.

But all that was too little, insufficiently strict, and the number of prisoners wasn't being sufficiently reduced. And so the "Garanin shootings" began, which were outright murders. Sometimes to the roar of tractors, sometimes without. Many camp points were known for executions and mass graves: Orotukan, and Polyarny

Spring, and Svistoplyas, and Annushka, and even the agricultural camp Dukcha, but the most famous of all on this account were the Zolotisty Goldfields (Chief of Camp Petrov, Security Operations Officers Zelenkov and Anisimov, Chief of the Goldfields Barkalov, Chief of the District Branch of the NKVD Burov) and the Serpantinka. At Zolotisty they used to summon a brigade from the mine face in broad daylight and shoot the members down one after another. (And this was not a substitute for night executions; they took place too.) When the chief of Yuglag, Nikolai Andreyevich Aglanov, arrived, he liked at line-up to pick out some brigade or other which had been at fault for something or other and order it to be taken aside. And then he used to empty his pistol into the frightened, crowded mass of people, accompanying his shots with happy shouts. The corpses were left unburied. In May they used to decompose—and at that point the "goners" who had survived until then were summoned to cover them up, in return for a beefed-up ration, even including spirits. At the Serpantinka they used to shoot from thirty to fifty men every day under an overhanging roof near the isolator. Then they dragged the corpses off behind a hillock on tractor sledges. The tractor drivers, the stevedores, and the gravediggers lived in a separate barracks. After Garanin himself had been shot they shot all of them too. And another technique was used there: They led them up to a deep shaft blindfolded and shot them in the ear or the back of the head. (No one mentions any resistance whatsoever.) They shut down the Serpantinka and leveled both the isolator there and everything connected with the shootings, and filled in those shafts as well.[4] At those same goldfields where no executions were conducted, notices were read aloud or posted with the names in big letters and the alleged causes in small letters: "for counterrevolutionary propaganda," "for insulting the convoy," "for failure to fulfill the norm."

The executions were stopped temporarily because the plan for getting out the gold was not being fulfilled and because they could not send new groups of prisoners across the frozen Okhotsk Sea. (M. I. Kononenko waited more than half a year to be shot at the Serpantinka and survived.)

In addition, the regime hardened in respect to tacking on new

---

4. In 1954 they discovered commercial gold ores at the Serpantinka about which they had not known earlier. And they had to mine among human bones; the gold was more precious.

terms. Gavrik at Mylga used to organize this in a picturesque way: they used to ride ahead on horseback with torches (in the Arctic night), and behind them they pulled with ropes to the district NKVD (eighteen miles) those who faced new charges. At other camps it was all very routine: the Classification and Records Sections merely selected from the card file those whose unreasonably short terms were coming to an end, summoned them in groups of eighty to a hundred people, and prescribed for each a new *tenner*. (R. V. Rets.)

Actually, I almost left Kolyma out of this book. Kolyma was a whole separate continent of the Archipelago, and it deserves its own separate histories. Yes, and Kolyma was "fortunate": Varlam Shalamov survived there and has already written a lot: Yevgeniya Ginzburg survived there, and O. Sliozberg, N. Surovtseva, N. Grankina, and others—and all of them have written memoirs.[5] I only permit myself to cite here several lines of V. Shalamov on the Garanin executions:

For many months there day and night, at the morning and the evening checks, innumerable execution orders were read out. In a temperature of fifty below zero the musicians from among the non-political offenders played a flourish before and after each order was read. The smoking gasoline torches ripped apart the darkness. . . . The thin sheet on which the order was written was covered with hoarfrost, and some chief or other who was reading the order would brush the snowflakes from it with his sleeve so as to decipher and shout out the name of the next man on the list of those shot.

And so it was that the Archipelago completed the Second Five-Year Plan and, it would seem, entered socialism.

■

The beginning of the war shook the Archipelago chieftains: the course of the war at the very start was such that it might very likely have led to the breakdown of the entire Archipelago, and perhaps even to the employers having to answer to the workers.

5. How is it that there is such a concentration of Kolyma memoirs while the non-Kolyma memoirs are almost nonexistent? Was this because they really hauled off the cream of the crop to Kolyma? Or was it, no matter how strange this may seem, that in the "nearby" camps they died off more rapidly?

As far as one can judge from the impressions of the zeks from various camps, the course of events gave rise to two different kinds of conduct among the bosses. Some of them, those who were either more reasonable or perhaps more cowardly, relaxed their regime and began to talk with the prisoners almost gently, particularly during the weeks of military defeats. They were unable, of course, to improve the food or the maintenance. Others who were more stubborn and more vicious began, on the contrary, to be even stricter and more threatening with the 58's, as if to promise them death before liberation. In the majority of the camps they did not even announce the beginning of the war to the prisoners. Our implacable passion for lies and secrecy! And only on Monday did the zeks learn of it from those unescorted by convoy and from free personnel. Wherever radio existed (such as at Ust-Vym and many places in the Kolyma) it was silenced for the whole period of our military failures. In that very same Ust-Vym Camp they suddenly forbade the prisoners to *write* letters home (they could still receive them), and their kinfolk thereupon decided they had all been shot. And in some camps (sensing intuitively the direction of future policy) they began to isolate the 58's from the nonpolitical offenders in compounds guarded with particular strictness, put machine guns up on the watchtowers, and even spoke thus to the zeks who had formed up: "You are hostages! [Oh, how effervescent is this charge of carbonation, right from the Civil War! How hard it is to forget those words, and how easily they are remembered!] If Stalingrad falls, we are going to shoot the lot of you!" And that was the atmosphere in which the Archipelago natives asked about war communiqués: Is Stalingrad still holding out or has it already fallen? And in the Kolyma they hauled the Germans, Poles, and particularly notable prisoners from the 58's to such special compounds. But they immediately began to free the Poles in August, 1941.[6]

From the first days of the war, everywhere in the Archipelago (on opening the packages of mobilization instructions) they halted all releases of 58's. There were even cases of released prisoners being sent back to camp while on their way home. In

6. One hundred and eighty-six Poles were released from Zolotisty out of 2,100 brought there a year before. They went into Sikorski's army in the West. And there, evidently, they told all about Zolotisty. And in June, 1942, it was completely shut down.

Ukhta on June 23 a group released was already outside the perimeter waiting for a train when the convoy chased them back and even cursed them: "It's because of you the war began!" Karpunich received his release papers on the morning of June 23 but had not yet succeeded in getting through the gatehouse when they coaxed them out of him by fraud: "Show them to us!" He *showed* them and was kept in camp for another five years. This was considered to mean "until *special* orders." (When the war had already come to an end, in many camps they were forbidden even to go to the Classification and Records Section and ask when they would be freed. The point was that after the war there were not enough people for a while, and many local administrations, even if Moscow allowed them to release prisoners, issued their own "special orders" so as to hold on to manpower. And that was how Y. M. Orlova was held in Karlag—and why she did not manage to get home in time to see her dying mother.

From the very beginning of the war (in accordance, no doubt, with those same mobilization instructions) food norms were lowered in all camps. And the foodstuffs all got worse from year to year: vegetables were replaced by fodder turnips, grits by vetch and bran. (The Kolyma was supplied from America, and in some places there, in contrast, even white bread put in an appearance.) But as a result of the prisoners' growing weaker the fall-off in output in vital lines of production became so bad—from 80 to 90 percent—that they found it useful to return to prewar norms. Many camp production centers got orders for munitions, and the enterprising directors of such minifactories sometimes managed to feed the zeks with supplementary food from auxiliary gardens. Wherever they paid wages, these amounted in cash to thirty rubles monthly—and, in terms of wartime prices on the open market, to less than one kilogram of potatoes a month.

If one were to ask a wartime camp inmate his highest, supreme, and totally unattainable ambition, he would reply: "To eat just once a belly full of black bread—and then I could die." During the war they buried no fewer dead in the camps than at the front, except that they have not been eulogized by the poets. L. A. Komogor, in a team of "enfeebled prisoners," was engaged in the following light work for the entire winter of 1941–1942: packing coffin crates made of four boards, two naked corpses to each, head by feet, at the rate of thirty boxes a day. (Evidently the camp was close to the capital, which was why the corpses had to be packed into crates.)

The first months of the war passed and the country adapted to the wartime rhythm of life. Those who had to went off to the front, and those who had to went off to the rear, and those who had to engaged in leadership and wiped their brows after drinking. And so it was in the camps too. It turned out that all the scare had been for nothing, that everything was standing firm, that just as this particular spring had been wound up in 1937, so it would keep on working without stopping. Those jailers who at first had tried to curry favor among the zeks now became fierce and knew no moderation or letup. It turned out that the forms, the system, of camp life had been determined correctly once and for all and would continue so for all eternity.

Seven camp epochs will lay their cases before you, arguing as to which was worst for the human being. But pay attention to that of wartime. Zeks put it this way: Whoever didn't serve time in wartime didn't know what camp was really like.

Throughout the winter of 1941–1942 at Vyatlag only in the barracks of the Engineering and Technical Personnel and in the repair shops was any warmth of life flickering at all. And all the rest was frozen cemeteries (and Vyatlag was actually engaged in cutting firewood for the Perm Railroad).

Here's what the wartime camp was: more work and less food and less heat and worse clothes and ferocious discipline and more severe punishment—and that still wasn't all. The zeks had always been deprived of external, audible protest, but the war even did away with the protest inside the soul. Any scoundrel with shoulder boards who was hiding from the front could shake his finger and preach: "And how are people dying at the front? And how are they working in freedom? And how many have died in Leningrad?" And as a result the zeks had no protest left even inside themselves. Yes, people were dying at the front, some of them lying in the snow too. Yes, they were squeezing the life out of people in freedom, and the people were famished and starving. (Yes, and the free *Labor Front*, into which unmarried girls from the villages were mobilized and in which they worked at logging, had only twenty-four and a half ounces of bread and soup, which was dishwater and was as bad as any camp.) Yes, and in the Leningrad blockade they allotted even less than the camp punishment-cell ration. During the war the whole cancerous tumor of the Archipelago turned out to be (or in any case represented itself to be) an allegedly important and necessary organ of the Russian body. It, too, was allegedly working for the war! On it, too, victory depended! And all this shed a false and justifying light on the strands of barbed wire, on the citizen chief who was shaking his finger—and there you were dying as one of the tumor's rotting cells, and you were deprived even of the dying man's satisfaction of cursing it.

For the 58's the wartime camps were particularly unbearable because of their pasting on *second terms*, which hung over the prisoners' heads worse than any ax. The Security officers, busily engaged in saving themselves from the front, discovered in well-set-up backwaters and backwoods, in logging expeditions, plots involving the participation of the world bourgeoisie, plans for armed revolts and mass escapes. Such aces of Gulag as Y. M. Moroz, the chief of UkhtPechlag, particularly encouraged investigatory and interrogatory activity in his camps. In UkhtPechlag sentences poured as if from a sack—execution, twenty years—"for incitement to escape," "for sabotage." And how many there were for whom no trials at all were required, whose fates were determined by the movements of the stars: Sikorski displeased Stalin, and in one night they seized thirty Polish women at Elgen and took them off and shot them.

There were many zeks—and this is something which was not fabricated, it is quite true—who applied from the first days of the war to be sent to the front. They had tasted the most foully stinking camp dregs—and now they asked to be sent to the front in order to defend this camp system and to die for it in a penalty company! ("And if I come out of it alive, I will return to serve out the rest of my term!") The orthodox Communists now assure us that *they* were the ones who begged to be sent to the front. And some of them did (including those Trotskyites who had survived the executions), but not very many. For the most part they had got themselves set up in certain quiet spots in camp (not without the help of the Communist chiefs either), where they could spend their time in contemplation, discussion, recollection, and waiting, and, after all, in a penalty company you'd last no more than three days. This desire to enlist was an impulse not of ideological principle but of heart. That is what the Russian character was: It is better to die in an open field than in a rotten shed! To unwind, to become, even for just a short while, "like everyone else," an unrepressed citizen. To get away from the stagnant feeling of doom here, from the pasting on of new terms, from silent annihilation. And some of them took an even simpler view of it all, but one which was not in the least shameful: Out there you would still die eventually, but for the moment they would give you a uniform to wear, feed you up, give you something to drink, transport you, and you could look out of the window of the railroad car and you could flirt with the girls at the stations. And then, too, there was an attitude of good-natured forgiveness: You've wronged us, and here's how we answer you!

However, for the state there was no economic nor organizational sense in carrying out all this superfluous shifting about of some people from camp to the front, and some people to camp in their place. Everyone had had his own circle of life and death determined for him: Once you've been classified among the goats, then you have to die as a goat. Sometimes they did take non-political offenders with short terms for the front, and not in penalty companies, of course, just in the ordinary active army. It didn't happen at all often, but there were cases in which they took 58's as well. Vladimir Sergeyevich Gorshunov was taken from camp to the front in 1943, and at the end of the war he was returned to camp with an extended sentence. They were all marked men. And it was simple for the security chief in their unit *to paste* a new term on them, much simpler than on newcomers.

But the camp authorities did not entirely disregard this wave of patriotism. At the logging operations it had little impact. But slogans like "Let's give coal above plan—it's light for Leningrad!" or "Let us support the guard units with mortar ammunition!" caught on well, as eyewitnesses report. Arseny Farmakov, a venerable person with a well-adjusted personality, tells how their camp was *caught up* in work for the front; he intended to describe it. The zeks were unhappy when they were refused permission to collect money for a tank column ("the Dzhidinets").[7]

_____

7. This phenomenon requires elucidation on many different planes, as in fact does the entire Soviet-German War. The decades go by. We do not manage to sort things out and understand ourselves even on one plane before the

And as to rewards for this—as is universally known, soon after the end of the war an amnesty was proclaimed for deserters, swindlers, and thieves. And Special Camps for the 58's.

And the closer the war came to its end, the more and more cruel did the regimen for the 58's become. Nor did one have to go far away from Moscow, to the Dzhida or the Kolyma camps, to find this out. Right outside Moscow itself, almost within the boundaries of the city, in Khovrino, there was a shabby little factory to supply the internal needs of the NKVD itself, and attached to it a strict-regimen camp run by Mamulov, who was all-powerful because his own brother was the chief of Beria's secretariat. This Mamulov would pick out anyone he wanted from the Krasnaya Presnya Transit Prison, and he set up whatever regimen he pleased in his camplet. For example, he allowed visits with relatives (which were widely permitted almost everywhere in camps near Moscow) to be conducted only through two screens, as in prison. And he had the same kind of prison system in his barracks: many bright lights left on at night; constant observation of those who were sleeping to make sure that on cold nights they would not cover themselves with their padded jackets. (If they did, they were wakened.) In the punishment cells he had a clean cement floor and nothing else at all—just as in a regular efficient prison. But no punishment he had designated gave him any satisfaction unless along with it and before it he bloodied the nose of the culprit. In addition, late-night inspections by the (male) jailers of the women's barracks holding up to 450 prisoners were a regular practice in his camp. They rushed in with wild whoops and the command: "Stand next to your cots!" The half-dressed women jumped up, and the jailers searched both their persons and their beds with the minute thoroughness required to find a needle or a love note. If anything was discovered, the prisoner was sentenced to the punishment cell. Shklinik, chief of the Chief Mechanic's Section, went about the different factory sections on the night shift like a stooping gorilla; and no sooner had he noticed that someone had begun to doze, to nod his head, or shut his eyes, than with all his might he would hurl at him an iron block, a pair of pliers, a chunk of steel.

next one is deposited in a new layer of ash. There have not been freedom and purity of information in any decade—and from one blow to the next people have not been able to comprehend either themselves or others or events.

Such was the regimen the camp inmates of Khovrino earned with their work for the front: they produced mortar shells throughout the war. The little factory was adapted for this output by a prisoner engineer (alas, his name has not been remembered, but it won't get lost for good, of course). He created a design bureau also. He was serving time as a 58 and belonged to that category of human beings most repulsive to Mamulov because they refused to give up their own opinions and convictions. And yet for a time Mamulov had to tolerate this good-for-nothing! But no one is irreplaceable in our country! And when production was already sufficiently under way, one day in broad daylight, in the presence of the office personnel (intentionally in their presence— let everyone know, let them tell everyone! and we are telling it too, you see!), Mamulov and two of his assistants rushed in, grabbed the engineer by his beard, threw him to the floor, kicked him with their jackboots till the blood flowed, and then sent him off to the Butyrki to get a second term for his political declarations.

And this lovely little camplet was just fifteen minutes by electric train from the Leningrad Station. Not far, just sad!

(The newcomer zeks who got into the camps near Moscow tried to hold on to them tightly if they had relatives in Moscow, yes, and even without that: it seemed, all the same, that you were not being torn away into that far-distant abyss from which there was no return, that here despite everything you were on the edge of civilization. But this was self-deceit. They usually fed the prisoners there worse, calculating that the majority were receiving parcels, and they didn't even issue bedding. But the worst thing was the eternally nauseating *latrine rumors* which kept hovering over these camps about prisoner transports to far away: life was as chancy as on the point of a needle, and it was impossible to be certain even for a day that you would be able to live it out in one and the same place.)

Such are the forms into which the islands of the Archipelago hardened, but one need not think that as it hardened it ceased to exude more metastases from itself.

In 1939, before the Finnish War, Gulag's alma mater, Solovki, which had come too close to the West, was moved via the Northern Sea Route to the mouth of the Yeniseï River and there merged into the already created Norillag, which soon reached 75,000 in size. So malignant was Solovki that even in dying it threw off one last metastasis—and what a metastasis!

The Archipelago's conquest of the unpeopled deserts of Kazakhstan belongs to the prewar years. That was where the nest of Karaganda camps swelled like an octopus; and fertile metastases were propagated in Dzhezkazgan with its poisoned cuprous water, in Mointy and in Balkhash. And camps spread out over the north of Kazakhstan also.

New growths swelled in Novosibirsk Province (the Mariinsk Camps), in the Krasnoyarsk region (the Kansk Camps and Kraslag), in Khakassiya, in Buryat-Mongolia, in Uzbekistan, even in Gornaya Shoriya.

Nor did the Russian North, so beloved by the Archipelago, end its own growth (UstVymlag, Nyroblag, Usollag), nor the Urals (Ivdellag).

There are many omissions in this list. It was enough to write "Usollag" to remember that there was also a camp in Usolye in Irkutsk Province.

Yes, there was simply no province, be it Chelyabinsk or Kuibyshev, which did not give birth to its own camps.

A new method of creating camps was adopted after the exile of the Germans from the Volga: whole dispossessed villages were enclosed, just as they were, in a camp *compound*, and these were the Agricultural Camp Sectors (the Kamensky Agricultural Camps between Kamyshin and Engels).

We ask the reader's pardon for the many gaps and flaws in this chapter; we have cast only a frail bridge across the whole epoch of the Archipelago—simply because we did not have any more material available. We could not broadcast pleas for more on the radio.

Here once again the crimson star of Naftaly Frenkel describes an intricate loop in the heavens of the Archipelago.

The year 1937, which struck down its very own, did not spare his head either: chief of BAMlag, an NKVD general, he was once again, out of gratitude, imprisoned in the Lubyanka, with which he was already familiar. But Frenkel, nonetheless, did not weary of thirsting for the one true service, nor did the Wise Teacher weary of seeking out this service. The shameful and unsuccessful war with Finland began and Stalin saw that he was unprepared, that there were no supply lines to his army thrust out into the Karelian snows—and he remembered the inventive Frenkel and called him in: it was necessary right then, in the fierce winter, without any preparation whatsoever, without any existing plans even, or warehouses, or automobile roads, to build three railroads in Karelia—one "rocade" paralleling the border, and two more leading up to it—and to build them *in the course of three months*, because it was simply a disgrace for such a great power to mess about with that little pug dog Finland for such a long time. This was straight out of a fairy tale: the evil king ordered the evil sorcerer to do something totally impossible and unimaginable. And so the leader of socialism asked: "Can you?" And the joyous merchant and black-market currency speculator answered: "Yes!"

But this time he set his conditions:

1. That he be taken out of Gulag entirely and that a new zek empire be founded, a new autonomous archipelago called GULZhDS (pronounced "Gulzhedess")—the Chief Administration of Camps for Railroad Construction—and that as head of this archipelago there be named . . . Frenkel.

2. That all the national resources he selected would be put at his disposal (this was not going to be another Belomor).

3. That during the period of extreme emergency operation GULZhDS would also be removed from the socialist system with its exasperating accounting procedures. Frenkel would not be required to render accounts about anything. He did not set up tents and did not establish any camps. He had no rations, no system of differentiated dining facilities, and no system of differentiated food "pots"! (And it was he who had proposed the system of different levels of rations in the first place! Only a genius can repeal the laws of a genius!) He piled up in the snow heaps of the best food, together with sheepskin coats and felt boots, and every zek could put on whatever he pleased and eat as much as he wanted. Only the makhorka and the vodka were controlled by his assistants, and they were the only things which had to be "earned."

The Great Strategist was willing. And GULZhDS was created! Was the Archipelago split in two? No, the Archipelago only grew stronger, multiplied, and would proceed to take over the whole country even more swiftly.

Frenkel, however, did not succeed in completing his Karelian railroads; Stalin hurried to end the war in a draw. But GULZhDS hardened and grew. It received more and more new orders to carry out (but now with normal accounting procedures). There was the "rocade" railroad paralleling the Iranian border, then the "rocade" railroad paralleling the Volga from Syzran near Kuibyshev on down to Stalingrad, and then the "Railroad of Death" from Salekhard to Igarka, and then BAM proper—the Baikal-Amur Main Line, from Taishet to Bratsk and farther.

Further, Frenkel's idea enriched the development of Gulag itself; it came to be considered necessary to organize Gulag itself in terms of branch administrations. Just as the Sovnarkom—the Council of People's Commissars—consisted of Narkomats—People's Commissariats—so Gulag created its own ministries for its own empire: GlavLeslag—the Chief Administration of Logging Camps; GlavPromstroi—the Chief Administration of Camps for Industrial Construction; GULGMP—the Chief Administration of Camps for the Mining and Metallurgical Industry.

Then came the war. And all these Gulag ministries were evacuated to various cities. Gulag itself landed in Ufa; GULZhDS in Vyatka. The communications between provincial cities were by no means so reliable as the radial communications out of Moscow, and for the whole first half of the war it was as if Gulag had disintegrated: it no longer ran the whole Archipelago, and each surrounding area of the Archipelago was subordinate to the administration evacuated to it. Thus it was that it fell on Frenkel to run the entire Russian Northeast from Kirov (because other than the Archipelago there was almost nothing else there). But those who envisioned in this the fall of the Roman Empire were mistaken, for it would gather itself together again after the war in even greater majesty.

Frenkel remembered an old friendship; he summoned and named to an important position in GULZhDS a man named Bukhaltsev, who had been the editor of his yellow sheet, *The Kopeck*, in prerevolutionary Mariupol and whose colleagues had either been shot or scattered across the face of the earth.

Frenkel's talents were outstanding not only in commerce and organization. Taking in rows of figures at a glance, he could add them up in his head. He loved to brag that he could recognize forty thousand prisoners by face and that he knew the family name, given name and patronymic of each, their code article and their term (and it was required procedure in his camps to announce all this information at the approach of high-ranking chiefs). He always managed without a chief engineer. Looking at a plan for a railroad station that had been brought him, he was quick to note a mistake in it, and then he would crumple up the plan, throw it in his subordinate's face, and say: "It's time you understand that you are not a designer, just a jackass!" He had a nasal twang and his voice was ordinarily calm. He was short. He used to wear the high karakul hat—the papakha—of a railroad general, dark blue on top, with a red lining. And he always, through the varied years, wore a field jacket of military cut—a garment which simultaneously constituted a claim to being a leader of the state and a declaration of not belonging to the intelligentsia. Like Trotsky he always lived aboard trains, traveling around his scattered construction battlefields. And those summoned from the discomfort in which natives of the Archipelago lived to confer with him in his railroad car were astonished at his bentwood chairs, his upholstered furniture, and were all the more timid in confronting the reproaches and orders of their chief. He himself never entered a single barracks, never smelled all that stench—he asked and demanded only work. He particularly loved to telephone construction projects at night, helping to perpetuate the legend about himself that he never slept. (And in fact during Stalin's era many other big shots were accustomed to do the same.) He never married.

He was never again arrested. He became Kaganovich's deputy for railroad construction and died in Moscow in the fifties with the rank of lieutenant general, in old age, in honor, and in peace.

I have the feeling that he really hated this country!

Chapter 5

■

What the Archipelago Stands On

There used to be a city in the Far East with the loyal name of *Tsesarevich*—"Crown Prince." The Revolution saw it renamed *Svobodny*, meaning "Free." The Amur Cossacks who once inhabited the city were scattered—and the city was empty. They had to resettle it with someone. And they did: with prisoners and the Chekists guarding them. The whole city of Svobodny became a camp (BAMlag).

And so it is that symbols are spontaneously born of life.

The camps are not merely the "dark side" of our postrevolutionary life Their scale made them not an aspect, not just a side, but very nearly the very liver of events. It was rare for our half-century so to manifest itself so consistently, with such finality.

Just as every point is formed by the intersection of at least two lines, every event is formed by the intersection of at least two necessities—and so although on one hand our economic requirements led us to the system of camps, this by itself might have led us to labor armies, but it intersected with the theoretical justification for the camps, fortunately already formulated.

And so they met and grew together: like a thorn into a nest, or a protuberance into a hollow. And that is how the Archipelago was born.

The economic need manifested itself, as always, openly and greedily; for the state which had decided to strengthen itself in a very short period of time (and here three-quarters of the matter was in the *period* allotted, just as with Belomor!) and which did not require anything from outside, the need was manpower:

a. Cheap in the extreme, and better still—for free.
b. Undemanding, capable of being shifted about from place to place any day of the week, free of family ties, not requiring either established housing, or schools, or hospitals, or even, for a certain length of time, kitchens and baths.

It was possible to obtain such manpower only by swallowing up one's own sons.

The theoretical justification could not have been formulated with such conviction in the haste of those years had it not had its beginnings in the past century. Engels discovered that the human being had arisen not through the perception of a moral idea and not through the process of thought, but out of happenstance and meaningless work (an ape picked up a stone—and with this everything began). Marx, concerning himself with a less remote time ("Critique of the Gotha Program"), declared with equal conviction that the *one and only* means of correcting offenders (true, he referred here to criminals; he never even conceived that his pupils might consider politicals offenders) was not solitary contemplation, not moral soul-searching, not repentance, and not languishing (for all that was superstructure!)—but productive labor. He himself had never in his life taken a pick in hand. To the end of his days he never pushed a wheelbarrow, mined coal, felled timber, and we don't even know how his firewood was split—but he wrote that down on paper, and the paper did not resist.

And for his followers everything now fell into place: To compel a prisoner to labor every day (sometimes fourteen hours at a time, as at the Kolyma mine faces) was humane and would lead to his correction. On the contrary, to limit his confinement to a prison cell, courtyard, and vegetable garden, to give him the chance to read books, write, think, and argue during these years meant to treat him "like cattle." (This is from that same "Critique of the Gotha Program.")

True, in the heated times immediately following the October Revolution they paid little heed to these subtleties, and it seemed even more humane simply to shoot them. And those whom they did not shoot but imprisoned in the earliest camps were imprisoned there not for purposes of correction, but to render them harmless, purely for quarantine.

The point is that even then some minds were occupied with penal theory, for example, Pyotr Stuchka, and in the *Guiding Principles of the Criminal Law of the Russian Soviet Federated Socialist Republic* of 1919, the very concept of *punishment* was subjected to a new definition. Punishment, it was there very refreshingly affirmed, is *neither revenge* (the workers' and peasants' state was not taking vengeance on an offender) nor *expiation of guilt* (there is no such thing as individual *guilt*, merely class causation), but a defensive measure to protect the social structure—*a measure of social defense*.

Once it is accepted as a "measure of social defense," then it follows that war is war, and you either have to shoot ("the supreme measure of social defense") or else imprison. But in this the idea of *correction* had somehow gotten muddied—though in that very same 1919 the Eighth Congress of the Party had called for "correction." And, foremost, it had become incomprehensible: *What should one be corrected for if there had been no guilt?* It was hardly possible to be corrected for class causation!?

By then the Civil War had come to an end. In 1922 the first Soviet Codes were established. In 1923 the "congress of the penitentiary labor workers" took place. The new "basic principles of criminal legislation" were composed in 1924—the foundations of the new Criminal Code of 1926 (which hung around our necks for thirty-five years). And through all this the newly found concepts that there is no "guilt" and no "punishment," but that there is "social danger" and "social defense," remained intact.

Of course, this was more convenient. Such a theory made it possible to arrest anyone as a hostage, as a "doubtful person" (Lenin's telegram to Yevgeniya Bosh), even to exile entire peoples because they were dangerous (and the examples are well known), but, given all this, one had to be a first-class juggler in order still to construct and maintain in purified form the theory of *correction*.

However, there were jugglers, and the theory was there, and the camps were indeed called corrective. And we can bring many quotations to bear even now.

Vyshinsky: "All Soviet penal policy is based on a dialectical [!] combination of the principle of repression and compulsion with the principle of persuasion and re-education."[1] "All bourgeois penitentiary institutions try to 'harass' the criminal by subjecting him to physical and moral suffering." (They wish to "reform" him.) "In distinction from bourgeois punishment the sufferings of the prisoners in our country are not an end but a means. [Just as there, too, it would seem not an end but a means.—A.S.] The end in our country . . . is genuine reform, genuine correction, so conscientious laborers should emerge from the camps."

Now have you got it? Even though we use compulsion, we are nonetheless *correcting* (and also, as it turns out, via suffering!) —except it is not known exactly from *what*.

But right then and there, on a nearby page, we find:

"With the assistance of revolutionary violence the corrective-labor camps localize and render harmless the criminal elements of the old society."[2] (We are still talking about the old society! And even in 1952 we will still keep talking about the "old society." "Pile everything on the wolf's neck"—blame it all on the old society!)

So not a single word about correction? We are localizing and rendering harmless?

And then in that same 1934:

"The two-in-one task is suppression plus re-education of anyone who can be re-educated."

Of anyone who can be re-educated. It becomes clear that correction is not for everyone.

And now a ready-made phrase from somewhere already flits about among the small-time authors: "the correction of the corrigibles," "the correction of the corrigibles."

And what about the incorrigibles? Into a common grave? *To the Moon* (Kolyma)? *Below Shmidtikha** (Norilsk)?

Even the Corrective Labor Code of 1924 was criticized by Vyshinsky's jurists, from the heights of 1934, for "a false concept of universal correction." Because this code says nothing about *destruction*.

No one promised that they would *correct* the 58's.

And therefore I have called this Part "The *Destructive*-Labor Camps." That's how we felt them on our pelts.

---

1. A. Y. Vyshinsky, from his preface to I. L. Averbakh, *op. cit.*, p. vi.
2. *Ibid.*, p. vii.

And if some of the jurists' quotations fit together crookedly, so be it, just go raise up Stuchka from the grave, or drag out Vyshinsky, and let them make head or tail of it. I am not to blame.

It is only now, on sitting down to write my own book, that I decided to leaf through my predecessors' works; yes, good people had to help even here, because you'd not now be able to find their works anywhere. And as we dragged our soiled camp pea jackets about, we never even guessed at the existence of such books. That all our life there in camp was determined not by the will of the citizen chief but by some kind of legendary labor code for prisoners—that was not just an obscure *latrine rumor* for us alone; even the chief of the camp, a major, wouldn't have believed it for anything. Published in an edition "for official use only," never held in anyone's hands, and no one knew whether they were still kept in the Gulag safes or whether they had all been burned as wrecking activity. Neither were quotations from them hung up in the cultural and educational corners, nor were their miserable figures proclaimed from the wooden rostrums: How many hours long was the workday? How many rest days in a month? Is there payment for labor? Was there any provision for mutilation? Yes, and you would get a big horse laugh from your fellow zeks too if you even asked such questions.

Our diplomats were the ones who had seen and read these humane words. They had, it would seem, held up and brandished this booklet at international conferences. Indeed! I myself have only now obtained the quotations—and even now my tears flow:

• In the *Guiding Principles* of 1919: Given the fact that punishment is not vengeance, then it may include no elements of torture.

• In 1920: The use of the condescending familiar form of address is forbidden in speaking to the prisoners. (And, forgive my language, but what about "——— in the mouth"—is that permissible?)

• The Corrective Labor Code of 1924, Article 49: "The prison regime must be deprived of all elements of torture; handcuffs, punishment cells [!], strict solitary confinement, deprivation of food, visits through a grating only are under no circumstances permitted."

Well, that's enough. And there are no later instructions. That's enough even for the diplomats. And not even that is needed by Gulag.

And in the Criminal Code of 1926 there was an Article 9. I learned about it by chance and learned it by heart:

"Measures of social defense may not have as their purpose the infliction of physical suffering or the humiliation of human dignity and do not aim at exacting revenge and retribution."

Now that is clarity for you! Because I enjoyed catching our bosses out on *legal* grounds, I often rattled off this section to them. And all these protectors of ours only popped their eyes in astonishment and indignation. There were old veterans who had served for twenty years, who were nearing their pensions, who had never yet heard of any Article 9, and for that matter had never held the Code in their hands.

Oh, "what an intelligent, farsighted humane administration from top to bottom," as Supreme Court Judge Leibowitz of New York State wrote in *Life* magazine, after having visited Gulag. "In serving out his term of punishment the prisoner retains a feeling of dignity." That is what he comprehended and saw.

Oh, fortunate New York State, to have such a perspicacious jackass for a judge!

And oh, you well-fed, devil-may-care, nearsighted, irresponsible foreigners with your notebooks and your ball-point pens— beginning with those correspondents who back in Kem asked the zeks questions in the presence of the camp chiefs—how much you have harmed us in your vain passion to shine with understanding in areas where you did not grasp a lousy thing!

Human dignity! Of persons condemned without trial? Who are made to sit down beside Stolypin cars at stations with their rear ends in the mud? Who, at the whistle of the citizen jailer's lash, scrape up with their hands the urine-soaked earth and carry it away, so as not to be sentenced to the punishment block? Of those educated women who, as a great honor, have been found worthy of laundering the linen of the citizen chief of the camp and of feeding his privately owned pigs? And who, at his first drunken gesture, have to make themselves available, so as not to perish *on general work* the next day?

Fire, fire! The branches crackle and the night wind of late autumn blows the flame of the bonfire back and forth. The compound is dark; I am alone at the bonfire, and I can bring it still more carpenters' shavings. The compound here is a privileged one, so privileged that it is almost as if I were out in freedom —this is an Island of Paradise; this is the Marfino "sharashka"

—a scientific institute staffed with prisoners—in its most privileged period. No one is overseeing me, calling me to a cell, chasing me away from the bonfire. I am wrapped in a padded jacket, and even then it is chilly in the penetrating wind.

But *she*—who has already been standing in the wind for hours, her arms straight down, her head drooping, weeping, then growing numb and still. And then again she begs piteously: "Citizen Chief! Forgive me! Please forgive me! I won't do it again."

The wind carries her moan to me, just as if she were moaning next to my ear. The citizen chief at the gatehouse fires up his stove and does not answer.

This was the gatehouse of the camp next door to us, from which workers came into our compound to lay water pipes and to repair the old ramshackle seminary building. Across from me, beyond the artfully intertwined, many-stranded barbed-wire barricade and two steps away from the gatehouse, beneath a bright lantern, stood the punished girl, head hanging, the wind tugging at her gray work skirt, her feet growing numb from the cold, a thin scarf over her head. It had been warm during the day, when they had been digging a ditch on our territory. And another girl, slipping down into a ravine, had crawled her way to the Vladykino Highway and escaped. The guard had bungled. And Moscow city buses ran right along the highway. When they caught on, it was too late to catch her. They raised the alarm. A mean, dark major arrived and shouted that if they failed to catch the fugitive girl, the entire camp would be deprived of visits and parcels for a whole month because of her escape. And the women brigadiers went into a rage, and they were all shouting, one of them in particular, who kept viciously rolling her eyes: "Oh, I hope they catch her, the bitch! I hope they take scissors and—clip, clip—take off all her hair in front of the line-up!" (This wasn't something she had thought up herself. This was the way they punished women in Gulag.) But the girl who was now standing outside the gatehouse in the cold had sighed and said instead: "At least she can have a good time out in freedom for all of us!" The jailer overheard what she said, and now she was being punished; everyone else had been taken off to the camp, but she had been set outside there to stand "at attention" in front of the gatehouse. This had been at 6 P.M. and it was now 11 P.M. She tried to shift from one foot to another, but the guard stuck out his head and shouted: "Stand at attention, whore, or else it will be worse for you!" And now she was not moving, only weeping: "Forgive me, Citizen Chief! Let me into the camp, I won't do it any more!"

But even in the camp no one was about to say to her: *All right, idiot! Come on in!*

The reason they were keeping her out there so long was that the next day was Sunday and she would not be needed for work.

Such a straw-blond, naïve, uneducated slip of a girl! She had been imprisoned for some spool of thread. What a dangerous thought you expressed there, little sister! They want to teach you a lesson for the rest of your life.

Fire, fire! We fought the war—and we looked into the bonfires to see what kind of a Victory it would be. The wind wafted a glowing husk from the bonfire.

To that flame and to you, girl, I promise: the whole wide world will read about you.

This was happening at the end of 1947, a few days before the thirtieth anniversary of the October Revolution, in our capital city of Moscow, which had just celebrated eight hundred years of its cruelties. Little more than a mile away from the All-Union Agricultural Fair Grounds. And a half-mile away from the Ostankino Museum of Serf Arts and Handicrafts.

■

Serfs! This comparison occurred to many when they had the time to think about it, and not accidentally either. Not just individual features, but the whole central meaning of their existence was identical for serfdom and the Archipelago; they were forms of social organization for the forced and pitiless exploitation of the unpaid labor of millions of slaves. Six days a week, and often seven, the natives of the Archipelago went out to fatiguing "barshchina"*—forced labor—which did not bring them even the least little return. They were allowed neither a fifth day nor even a seventh in which to work for themselves, because their sustenance was a "mesyachina"—a monthly serf ration—a camp ration. They were divided just as precisely into the categories of those paying their dues in the form of forced labor—(Group "A") and the household serfs (Group "B"), who directly served the estate owner (chief of the camp) and the estate (the compound). Only those totally unable to get down from their peasant stoves (board bunks) were recognized as infirm (Group "C"). And similarly, there were punishments for offenders (Group "D"), except for the difference that the estate owner, acting in his own interests, punished with a lash in the stable and the loss of fewer workdays, and he had no punishment block, whereas, in accordance with state instructions, the chief of the camp placed the culprit in the ShIzo—the Penalty Isolator—or the BUR—the Strict Regimen Barracks. Like the estate owner, the chief of camp could take any slave to be his lackey, cook, barber, or jester (and he could also assemble a serf theater if he wished); he could take any slave woman as a housekeeper, a concubine, or a servant. Like an estate owner, he could play tricks and show his temper as much as he liked. (The chief of the Khimki Camp, Major Volkov, noticed that a girl prisoner was drying her long flaxen locks in the sun after washing them, and for some reason this made him angry and he shouted: "Cut off her hair." And they immediately cut all her hair off. That was in 1945.) And whenever the camp chief or the estate owner changed, all the slaves obediently awaited the new master, made guesses about his habits, and surrendered in advance to his power. Being incapable of foreseeing what the will of the master would be, the serf took little thought for the morrow, nor did the prisoner. The serf could not marry without the master's permission, and it was even more the case that a prisoner could acquire a camp wife only with the indulgence of the camp chief. Just as a serf had not chosen his slave's fate, since he was not to blame for his birth, neither did the prisoner choose his; he also got into the Archipelago by pure fate.

This similarity has long since been discerned by the Russian language: "Have you fed the people?" "Have you sent the people out to work?" "How many people do you have there?" "Send me one person!" *People, people,* whom do they mean? That's the way they talked about serfs. And that is how they speak about prisoners.[3] One cannot speak like that about officers or leaders, however—"How many people do you have?" No one would understand you.

3. And that is also the way they talk about collective farmers and unskilled laborers, but we are not going to carry this any further.

But there are some who will object that nonetheless there are really not so many similarities between serfs and prisoners. There are more differences.

And we agree with that: there are more differences. But what is surprising is that all the differences are to the credit of serfdom! All the differences are to the discredit of the Gulag Archipelago!

The serfs did not work longer than from sunrise to sunset. The zeks started work in darkness and ended in darkness (and they didn't always end either). For the serfs Sundays were sacred; and the twelve sacred Orthodox holidays as well, and local saints' days, and a certain number of the twelve days of Christmas (they went about in mummers' costumes). The prisoner was fearful on the eve of every Sunday: he didn't know whether they would get it off. And he never got holidays at all (just as the Volga didn't get any days off, remember?); those firsts of May and those sevenths of November involved more miseries, with searches and special regimen, than the holidays were worth (and a certain number were put into punishment blocks every year precisely on those very days). For the serfs Christmas and Easter were genuine holidays; and as for a *body search* either after work or in the morning or at night ("Stand next to your cots!"), the serfs knew not of these! The serfs lived in permanent huts, regarding them as their own, and when at night they lay down on top of their stoves, or on their sleeping platform between ceiling and stove—their "polaty"—or else on a bench, they knew: This is my own place, I have slept here forever and ever, and I always will. The prisoner did not know what barracks he would be in on the morrow (and even when he returned from work he could not be certain that he would sleep in that place that night). He did not have his "own" sleeping shelf or his "own" multiple bunk. He went wherever they drove him.

The serf on "barshchina," or forced labor, had his own horse, his own wooden plow, ax, scythe, spindle, chests, dishes, and clothes. Even the household serfs, as Herzen writes,[4] always had some clothes of their own which they could leave to their nearest and dearest and which were almost never taken away by the

---

4. A. I. Herzen, *Pismo Staromy Tovarishchu* (*Letter to an Old Comrade*), Academy Edition of Collected Works, Vol. XX, p. 585.

estate owner. In spring the zek was forced to turn in his winter clothing and in the autumn to turn in his summer clothing. At inventories they emptied his bag and took away for the government every extra piece of clothing. He was not permitted to have even a small penknife, or a bowl, and as far as livestock was concerned, only lice. One way or another a serf would cast his line and catch a fish. The zek caught fish only with a spoon and only in his gruel. The serf had a little cow named Brownie or at least a goat and chickens. The zek's lips never touched milk, and he'd never see hen's eggs for whole decades, and probably he'd not recognize them if he did.

Old Russia, which experienced Asiatic slavery for seven whole centuries, did not for the most part know *famine*. "In Russia no one has ever died of starvation," said the proverb. And a proverb is not made up out of lies and nonsense. The serfs were slaves, but they had full bellies.[5] The Archipelago lived for decades in the grip of cruel famine. The zeks would scuffle over a herring tail from the garbage pail. For Christmas and Easter even the thinnest serf peasant broke his fast with fat bacon. But even the best worker in camp could get fat bacon only in parcels from home.

The serfs lived in families. The sale or exchange of a serf away from his family was a universally recognized and proclaimed barbarism. Popular Russian literature waxed indignant over this. Hundreds of serfs, perhaps thousands (but this is unlikely), were torn from their families. But not millions. The zek was separated from his family on the first day of his arrest and, in 50 percent of all cases—forever. If a son was arrested with his father (as we heard from Vitkovsky) or a wife together with her husband, the greatest care was taken to see that they did not meet at the same camp. And if by some chance they

5. There is testimony on this for all the Russian centuries. In the seventeenth, Yuri Krizhanich wrote that the peasants and artisans of Muscovy lived more bountifully than those of the West, that the poorest inhabitants in Russia ate good bread, fish, meat. Even in the Time of Troubles "the long-preserved granaries had not been exhausted, there were stacks standing in the fields, threshing floors were filled full with specially stacked sheaves and stooks and haystacks—for from four to ten years" (Avraami Palitsyn). In the eighteenth century, Fonvizin, comparing the standard of living of the Russian peasants with that of the peasants of Languedoc, Provence, wrote: "I find, objectively judging things, that the state of our peasants is incomparably happier." In the nineteenth century, Pushkin wrote of the serf village:

"The evidence of abundance and work is everywhere."

did meet, they were separated as quickly as possible. Similarly, every time a man and a woman zek came together in camp for fleeting or real love, they hastened to penalize them with the punishment cell, to separate them and send them away from one another. And even the most sentimental of our writing ladies—Marietta Shaginyan or Tatyana Tess—never let fall a single silent tear into their kerchiefs about that. (Well, of course, *they didn't know*. Or else thought *it was necessary*.)

And even the herding of serfs from one place to another didn't occur in a frenzy of haste; they were permitted to pack their goods and chattels, to gather up their movables, and to move calmly a score or so of miles away. But a prisoner transport would hit the zek like a sudden squall: twenty minutes or ten, just time enough to turn in camp property, and his entire life would be turned upside down, and he would go off somewhere to the ends of the earth, maybe forever. In the life of one serf there was hardly ever more than one move, and most often they stayed put. But a native of the Archipelago unfamiliar with prisoner transports couldn't have been found. And many zeks were moved five, seven, eleven times.

Some serfs managed to escape to the freer "obrok" system*— a fixed money payment to the serf-owner—and the "obrok" serfs might travel far out of sight of the cursed master, go into trade, enrich themselves, and live like free people. But even the zeks privileged enough to go about without convoy lived inside that same camp compound and had to drag themselves early in the morning to the very same type of work to which the column of the other zeks was driven.

The household serfs were for the most part degenerate parasites ("Servants are a boorish spawn," as the saying goes): they lived off the labor of the "barshchina" serfs; but at least they themselves did not rule over the "barshchina" serfs. It was doubly nauseating for the zek: that, in addition to everything else, the degenerate trusties directed them and ordered them around.

And in general, the entire situation of the serfs was alleviated by the fact that the estate owner had necessarily to be merciful to them: they were worth money; their work brought him wealth. The camp chief was merciless to the prisoners: he had not bought them, and he would not be willing them to his children, and if they died, others would be sent him.

No, we got ourselves involved to no purpose in comparing our zeks with the serfs of the estate owners. The situation of the latter, one has to admit, was very much less harried and more humane. A closer comparison of the situation of the natives of the Archipelago would be with the *factory* serfs of the Urals, the Altai, and Nerchinsk. Or the inhabitants of the Arakcheyev* semimilitary settlements. (Some people object, however, even to this: they, too, had it good—in the Arakcheyev settlements there were also nature, family, and holidays. Only the slavery of the ancient East is a fair comparison.)

And there is only one, just one, plus which comes to mind on the side of the zeks as opposed to the serfs: the prisoner might land in the Archipelago even as a juvenile of twelve to fifteen but not from the very day of his birth! He did at least snatch a number of years in freedom before imprisonment! As for the advantage of a definite *sentence* in comparison with the lifetime of peasant serfdom, there are many qualifications: namely, if the term was not a "quarter"—twenty-five years; if the article was not 58; if it wasn't "until special orders"; if they didn't paste a second term on the prisoner in camp; if at the end of his term the prisoner was not automatically sent off into exile; if the prisoner after being released was not sent straight back to the Archipelago as a *repeater*. There is such a fence of qualifications, in fact, that, after all, it is only fair to recall that sometimes the nobleman master too might manumit his serf out of whimsy.

That is why, when the "Emperor Mikhail" informed us at the Lubyanka about the anecdotal deciphering of the initials of the Soviet Bolshevik Party (VKP-b) current among Moscow workers at that time as "Vtoroye Krepostnoye Pravo (Bolsheviks)"— "Second Serfdom (Bolsheviks)"—this did not seem to us so much funny as prophetic.

■

They sought a new stimulus for socially useful labor. They thought originally it would be found in conscientiousness and enthusiasm along with material disinterestedness. And that is why they seized so eagerly on the "great example" of the "sub-botniki"—voluntary Saturdays. But this turned out not to be the beginning of a new era, but a tremor of self-sacrifice on the part of one of the last generations of the Revolution. It can be seen, for example, from provincial materials in Tambov that in 1921 many members of the Party were already trying to get out of the "subbotniki"—and a mark was introduced in the Party record book for participation in "subbotniki." Yes, this outburst lasted another decade, enough for the Komsomols and us, the young Pioneers of those times. But then it came to an end for us too.

And what was next? Where was the stimulus to be sought? Money, piece rates, bonus payments? But all of that carried the acrid smell of recent capitalism, and a long period was required, another generation, for that smell to cease to irritate, so it could be peaceably accepted as "the socialist principle of material incentive."

They dug down deeper into the storage chest of history and dragged out what Marx had called "extraeconomic coercion." In camp and on collective farms this discovery was presented with bared fangs.

And then Frenkel came along and, like a devil sprinkling a poison potion into the boiling caldron, he poured in the *differentiated ration pot.*

There was a famous incantation repeated over and over again: "In the new social structure there can be no place for the discipline of the stick on which serfdom was based, nor the discipline of starvation on which capitalism is based."

And there you are—the Archipelago managed miraculously to combine the one and the other.

All in all, the particular techniques required for this totaled three: (1) *the differentiated ration pot;* (2) *the brigade;* and (3) *two sets of bosses.* (But the third of these was not absolutely necessary: at Vorkuta, for example, there was only one set of bosses, and things hummed.)

And so it was that the Archipelago rested on these three whales, these three pillars.

Or if one considers them *the driving belts,* they certainly made the wheels turn.

We have already explained about the differentiated ration pot. This was a redistribution of bread and cereals aimed at making our zek beat his head against the wall and break his back for the average prisoner's ration, which in parasitical societies is issued to an inactive prisoner. To fix it so that our zek could get his own lawful ration only in extra dollops of three and a half ounces and by being considered a shock worker. Percentages of output above 100 conferred the right to supplementary spoonfuls of kasha (those previously taken away). What a merciless knowledge of human nature! Neither those pieces of bread nor those cereal patties were comparable with the expenditure of strength that went into earning them. But as one of his eternal, disastrous traits the human being is incapable of grasping the ratio of an object to its price. For a cheap glass of vodka a soldier is roused to attack in a war not his own and lays down his life; in the same way the zek, for those pauper's handouts, slips off a log, gets dunked in the icy freshet of a northern river, or kneads clay for mud huts barefoot in icy water, and because of this those feet are never going to reach the land of *freedom*.

However, the satanical differentiated ration pot was not all-powerful. Not everyone took the bait. Just as serfs at one time or another grasped the truth that "You may have to eat less, but at least you won't have to break your back working," so the zeks, too, understood: in camp it was not the small ration that killed people but the big one. Lazy! Stupid! Insensible half-animals! They don't want that supplementary allotment of rations! They don't want a piece of that nourishing bread, made from a mix of potatoes, vetch, and water! They don't want to be released ahead of term! They don't even want to be posted on the Board of Honor! They don't want to rise to the interests of the construction project and the country; they don't want to fulfill the Five-Year Plans, even though the Five-Year Plans are in the interests of the workers! They wander about the nooks and crannies of the mines, on the floors of construction projects, and they are delighted to hide from the rain in a dark hole, just anything in order not to work.

Not often is it possible to arrange such mass labor projects as in the gravel pit near Yaroslavl: there hundreds of prisoners are clumped together in a small area visible to the naked eyes of the supervisors, and hardly has any one of them stopped moving than he is immediately conspicuous. These are ideal conditions: no one even dares to slow down, to straighten his back, to wipe off the sweat, until up on the hill the flag drops—the signal for a smoking period. How, then, is it to be managed in other cases?

Much thought was applied. And the *brigade* was invented.

Yes, and for that matter, how could we fail to invent it? In our country even the Narodniki—the populists—wanted to enter into socialism through the *obshchina*, the peasant commune, and the Marxists through the *collective*. And what do our newspapers write even nowadays? *"The main thing for a human being is work, and it must be work in a collective!"*

And in camp there is nothing but work and only in a collective! Does that mean that the Corrective Labor Camp is the highest goal of humanity? That the *main thing* . . . has been attained?

How the brigade serves the *psychological enrichment* of its members, the prodding, the surveillance, and the *heightened sense of dignity*, we have already had cause to explain (in Chapter 3). Consistent with the purposes of the brigade, worthy tasks and *brigadiers* (known in camp lingo as "*bugry*"—in other words, "lumps") are selected. Slave-driving the prisoners with club and ration, the brigadier has to cope with the brigade in the absence of the higher-ups, the supervisors, and the convoy. Shalamov cites examples in which the whole membership of the brigade died several times over in the course of one gold-washing season on the Kolyma but the brigadier remained the same. That was the kind of brigadier Perelomov was in Kemerlag. He did not use his tongue, merely his stave. The list of these names would take up many pages here, but I have not compiled it. It is of interest that this kind of brigadier most often came from the thieves, that is, from the lumpenproletariat.

However, what is there to which people cannot adapt? It would be crude on our part not to look closely and observe how the brigade sometimes became a natural constituent cell of the native society of the Archipelago, of the same kind that the family is in freedom. I myself knew such brigades—and more than one too. True, these were not brigades on general work—where someone had to die because otherwise the rest could not survive. These were usually special brigades: electricians, lathe operators, carpenters, painters. The fewer their members (some ten or twelve persons), the more clearly the principle of mutual protection and mutual support appeared in them.[6]

6. This was manifested, too, in big brigades made up of various trades, but only in the hard-labor camps and under special conditions. More about this in Part V.

For such a brigade and for such a role there also had to be a suitable brigadier: moderately hard, well acquainted with all the moral (immoral) laws of Gulag, perspicacious and fair within the brigade; with his own well-worked-out method of coping with the higher-ups, whether it be a hoarse bark or a quiet and underhanded approach; he had to be feared by all the trusties and let no opportunity go by to grab off for the brigade an extra three and a half ounces, padded trousers, a pair of shoes. But he also had to have connections among the influential trusties from whom he could learn all the camp news and impending changes. He needed this for correct leadership. He had to know the work well and the sectors which were advantageous and disadvantageous (and be adept at shoving the neighboring brigade —if there was a neighboring brigade—onto the disadvantageous sectors). With a sharp eye out for the chances for "tukhta" and sensing where best to grab it off within a particular five-day work period: whether through manipulating work norms or total volume. And defend this unwaveringly against the work assigner, when the latter was already waiting with splattering fountain pen to "cut back" the work sheets. And adroit at *greasing the paw* of the norm setter. And knowing who in his brigade was a stoolie (and if this stoolie was not very smart or malicious, then leaving him alone, since otherwise they'd send in a worse one). And he always had to know whom in the brigade he should encourage with a glance, and whom to curse out, and to whom to give a lighter job that particular day. And a brigade like that with a brigadier like that adapts itself to austerity and survives austerely. There is no tenderness here, but no one dies. I worked with brigadiers like that—with Sinebryukhov and Pavel Boronyuk. And if I were to compile a list of others like them, it would be many pages long. And on the basis of many different stories there is a consensus that such efficient and intelligent brigadiers most often originated from among the "kulak" sons.

But what was there to do? If they implacably forced the brigade on the zeks as a form of existence, then what was to be done? It was necessary somehow to adapt to it, was it not? We will die from the work, but we are able to survive only by working. (Of course, this is a questionable philosophy. A better answer would be: Don't teach me to die the way you want, but let me die the way I want. But they won't allow you to anyway, that's what. . . .)

And the choice facing the brigadier could be difficult also: if the logging brigade failed to fulfill the day's norm of seventy-two cubic yards, the brigadier went into the punishment block too. And if you don't want to go to the punishment block, then drive your brigade members to their deaths. Bow down to the stronger!

And the *two sets of bosses* were also convenient—in just the same way that pliers need both a right and left jaw. Two bosses —these were the hammer and the anvil, and they hammered out of the zek what the state required, and when he broke, they brushed him into the garbage bin. Even though the maintenance of a separate administration for the camp compound greatly increased the state's expenditures, and even if out of stupidity, caprice, and vigilance it often complicated the working process, nevertheless they put it there anyway, and this was no mistake. Two bosses—this was two tormenters instead of one, in shifts too, and placed in a situation of competition to see: who could squeeze more out of the prisoner and give him less.

Production, materials, tools, transportation were in the hands of one boss; all that was lacking was manpower. This manpower was brought in every morning by the convoy from the camp and taken away to the camp every evening (or in shifts). During those ten or twelve hours during which the zeks were in the hands of the production bosses there was no need to educate them or correct them, and even if they dropped dead during the course of the workday—this wouldn't disappoint either administration; corpses could be written off more easily than burned-up boards or stolen linseed oil. It was important for the production bosses to compel the prisoners to do more work in a day and to credit them with less in their work sheets, because it was necessary to make up somehow for all the fatal overexpenditures and shortages on the production side; because the trusts were engaged in stealing, and so were the Construction and Installation Administration, and the construction superintendents, and the foremen, and the work site superintendents, and the truck drivers, and the zeks least of all, and then not for themselves (for they had nowhere to take the stuff) but for their camp chiefs and their convoy. And still more than all of that put together was lost through careless and negligent management and also because the zeks didn't take good care of anything either—and there was just one way to make up for all these shortages: underpayment for manpower.

The camp administration, on the other hand, controlled the *work force* alone. ("Rabsila"*—and the tongue certainly knows how to abbreviate!) But this was the decisive factor. The camp chiefs, in fact, used to say: We can squeeze them (the production administration) because they can't find other workers anywhere else. (Where could you find manpower in the taiga and the desert?) Consequently they sought to squeeze more money out in return for their "rabsila," which in part was turned over to the government but in part went for the maintenance of the camp administration itself, in return for its guarding the zeks (from freedom), providing them with food and drink, dressing them, and morally harassing them.

Just as always in our well-thought-out social system, two different *plans* collided head on here too: the production plan, whose objective was to have the lowest possible expenditures for wages, and the MVD plan, whose objective was to extract the largest possible earnings from camp production. To an observer on the sidelines it seems strange: why set one's own plans in conflict with one another? Oh, but there is a profound meaning in it! Conflicting plans flatten the human being. This is a principle which far transcends the barbed wire of the Archipelago.

And what is also important is that these two sets of bosses are by no means hostile to each other, as one might think from their constant squabbles and mutual deceits. Where it is necessary to flatten someone thoroughly, they close ranks very tightly. And even though the camp chief is the zeks' dear father, yet he always willingly recognizes and signs an official affidavit that the zek himself was to blame for his own injury and not the contractor; he will not be very insistent on the zek's having work clothes nor demand ventilation in some section of a plant where there is none (well, if there isn't, there isn't, and what can you do; these are temporary difficulties, and what about the siege of Leningrad?). The camp chief will never refuse the production boss when he is asked to jail a brigadier in the punishment block for rudeness, or a worker for having lost a shovel, or an engineer who hasn't carried out an order the way he should have. Didn't both these chiefs constitute the cream of society in remote settlements—were they not the serf holders of taiga industry? And didn't their wives call on one another?

If nonetheless there is incessant "tukhta" in *padded* work

sheets; if there is a constant attestation to trenches dug and filled which never yawned in the earth's surface, repair of heating systems or lathes which were never out of order, replacement of perfectly sturdy posts which will still be standing there for another ten years—then this is done not at the instigation of the camp chiefs, who are quite calm and confident that the money will flow to the camp one way or another anyway, but by zeks themselves (brigadiers, norm setters, foremen), because all state work norms are the same: they are calculated not for real life on this earth, but for some kind of unearthly ideal on the moon. A human being dedicated, self-sacrificing, healthy, well nourished, and energetic is incapable of fulfilling those norms! And so what are you going to get out of a fagged-out, weak, hungry, and downtrodden convict? The state system of setting work norms prescribes an output impossible on this planet—and in this sense resembles socialist realism in belles-lettres. But if the unsold books are easily shredded later, it is more complicated to cover up industrial "tukhta." However, it is not impossible!

In their constant tail-chasing haste the director and the construction superintendent have, let's say, overlooked or missed noticing, failed to discover, the "tukhta." And the free foremen were either illiterate or drunk, or else well disposed to the zeks (with the expectation, of course, that in a difficult moment the zek brigadier would help them out). And by then the "percentage bonus had been eaten up," and you couldn't pull the bread back out of the belly. Accountants' inspections and audits are notorious for their clumsiness. They turn up "tukhta" after a delay of months or years, when the money paid out for the work has long since flitted away and all that can still be done is to bring charges against one of the free employees or else smudge it up and *write it off*.

Three pillars on which the Archipelago is propped were set there by the Leadership: the differentiated ration pot, the work brigade, and the two sets of bosses. And the fourth and main pillar was "tukhta," and it was put there by the Archipelago natives and by life itself.

For "tukhta" it is essential to have energetic, enterprising brigadiers, but production chiefs from among the zeks are even more necessary. No few of them were foremen, norm setters, planners, economists, because you just wouldn't drag free people off to those distant places. Some zeks in those positions forgot who they were, became more cruel than free workers, trampled on their brother prisoners, and made their way over dead bodies to their own release ahead of term. Others, on the contrary, retained a distinct consciousness of their motherland, the Archipelago, and introduced reasonable moderation in the management of production and a reasonable share of "tukhta" in their accounting. There was a risk for them in this: not the risk of getting a new *term*, because the terms were already piled high anyway and their Code articles were harsh, but the risk of losing their position, angering the chiefs, landing in a bad prisoner transport— and thus perishing silently. And therefore their staunchness and intelligence were all the more glorious in that they helped their brothers to survive.

Vasily Grigoryevich Vlasov, for example, whose acquaintance we have already made in connection with the Kady trial, was that kind of person. Throughout his whole long sentence (he served nineteen years without any interruption) he retained that same stubborn self-assurance which characterized his conduct during the trial and with which he had mocked Kalinin and the commutation of his death sentence. Through all these years, when he was dried up from starvation and breaking his back on general work, he perceived himself not as a scapegoat but as a genuine political prisoner and even as a "revolutionary," as he used to describe himself in heart-to-heart conversations. And when, thanks to his naturally sharp administrative grasp, which in his case substituted for his incomplete schooling in economics, he held jobs as a trusty in production posts, Vlasov sought not only to postpone his own death but also the chance to patch up the whole cart so it was easier for the rest of the fellows to pull it along.

In the forties, on one of the Ust-Vym logging camp sites (and UstVymlag was distinct from the general pattern in that it had only *one* unified set of bosses: the camp itself ran its logging, did its own auditing, and was responsible for plan fulfillment to the Ministry of the Timber Industry), Vlasov simultaneously combined the duties of norm setter and planner. He was the head of the whole thing there, and in winter, in order to provide support for the sloggers out logging, he credited their brigades with fictitious cubic yards of wood cut. One of the winters was particularly severe; and working just as hard as they could the zeks fulfilled the work norms by only 60 percent but received rations for having fulfilled 125 percent of norm; and with the help of these beefed-up rations they managed to last out the winter without halting work even one day. However, shipments of the "felled" (on paper) timber were far behind schedule, and the camp chief heard some evil rumors. In March he sent a commission of foremen into the woods—and they turned up a shortage of 10,500 cubic yards of timber! The enraged chief summoned Vlasov, who heard him out and then said to him: "Give 'em, chief, *five days* in the brig. They're all sluts. They were too lazy to get out into the woods because the snow is still deep. Set up a new commission with me as the chairman." And thereupon, with his own sensible troika, Vlasov, without leaving his office, drew up an official document and "found" all the missing timber. The chief was quieted down for the time being; but in May there was more trouble: they were still shipping out too little timber, and the higher-ups kept asking questions. So the chief called in Vlasov again. Vlasov was a short fellow, but he always retained his vigorous rooster-like bearing, and this time he didn't even pretend: the timber just didn't exist. "So how could you have drawn up a false document, blankety, blank, blank, blank!" Vlasov replied: "Do you think it would have been better for you to go to jail yourself? After all, ten and a half thousand cubic yards is a full *ten-ruble bill* for a free employee, and even for a Chekist it's a fiver." The chief cursed him out, but by this time it was too late to punish Vlasov; the whole thing depended on him. "Well, what's to be done now?" Vlasov answered: "Just wait till the roads have completely dissolved in mud." And the time came when the winter roads had all dissolved completely, and the summer logging trails were still impassable too. And at this point Vlasov brought the chief a detailed and watertight report for his signature, to be sent on to the administration higher-up. In it he proved that because of the highly successful timber-felling operations of the past winter it had been quite impossible to move 10,500 cubic yards out of the forests on the sledge trails. Neither could this timber be hauled out through the swampy forests. Next he gave estimates for the cost of a corduroy road to get the timber out, and he proved that the haulage would cost more than the timber was worth. So that in a year's time, because the logs were going to be lying there in the swamp for a whole summer and autumn, they would be unsuitable for lumber and acceptable to any possible customer only for firewood. And the administration agreed with these literate conclusions, which they were not ashamed to show any other commission—and therefore the whole 10,500 cubic yards of timber were written off.

And so it was that the trees were felled, and *eaten up*, and written off—and stood once again erect and proud in their green coniferous garb. And, in fact, the state paid very reasonably for these dead cubic yards: a few hundred extra loaves of black, gluey, watery bread. The thousands of trees and the hundreds of lives which were saved were of no account on the profit-and-loss sheet. Because this kind of wealth was never counted in the Archipelago.

In all probability Vlasov was not the only one who had been so perspicacious as to play the swindler, because from 1947 on they introduced a new system in all logging operations: complex work gangs and complex work brigades. And now the lumberjacks were combined with the teamsters in one work gang, and the brigade was only credited with timber hauled out to the "slide" on the river bank, to the site of the spring log drive.

And so what happened then? Did this burst the balloon of the "tukhta"? Hardly! It even flourished! It expanded out of necessity, and the mass of workers nourished on it grew larger and larger. For those among our readers who are not bored with this, let's go into it more deeply:

1. The zeks were not permitted to accompany the logs farther than the slide on the river bank. (Who would convoy them down the river? Vigilance!) Therefore an expediter of the log-rafting office, which was staffed with free lumberjacks, accepted the timber from the camp dispatcher (for all the brigades) at the river. Well, now, he, of course, was strict in his receipts? Not at all. The camp dispatcher would inflate the figures as much as he had to on behalf of the logging brigades, and the expediter of the log-rafting office was agreeable to the whole deal.

2. And here is why. The log-rafting office also had the problem of feeding its own free workers and their work norms were equally impossible. And the log-rafting office listed all

of this nonexistent, fictitious timber as having been rafted downriver.

3. At the general landing and sorting point downriver where the timber was collected from all the logging sectors, there was a *bourse*, which was a landing area for logs. Here again zeks were doing the work, attached to that selfsame UstVymlag (the fifty-two "islands" of UstVymlag were scattered over a territory 96 miles square—now that is what our Archipelago is like!). The dispatcher of the log-rafting office was quite at ease: the camp expediter would now accept back all the "tukhta"—in the second place so as not to betray his own camp, which had previously "delivered" it to the slide, and in the first place so as to feed *its own* prisoners working at the landing point with that same fictitious timber! (They, too, had their own fantastic work norms and they needed their *crust* too!) At this point, however, the camp expediter had to toil a bit for the sake of society: he not only had to accept the timber by total volume but also list it, existing and fictitious, by diameters and lengths, in a complete schedule. Now here was a benefactor for you! (Vlasov worked at this job too.)

4. After the "bourse" came the sawmill which processed the logs into cut lumber. Once more the workers were zeks. The brigades were given rations on the basis of their volume of raw timber processed, and the "extra" fictitious timber was just exactly what they needed in order to increase their own percentage output.

5. Next came the lumber yard for the completed product, which was required, according to state norms, to have 65 percent of the amount of raw timber received by the sawmill. Thus it was that 65 percent of the fictitious timber moved invisibly into the lumber yard (and the mythical lumber was likewise inventoried by sorts: wavy-edged slab, construction lumber; by thickness of board, edged, unedged). The lumberyard workers, too, got their food out of that same fictitious timber.

But what happened then? The fictitious lumber was shut up in the lumber yard, where it was guarded by the Camp Guard. And there could not be any more uncontrolled "losses." And who at this point was going to answer for the "tukhta"? And how?

At this point another great principle of the Archipelago came to the aid of the principle of "tukhta." This was the principle of *rubber*, in other words stretching things out with interminable delays. Once on the books, the fictitious production kept being carried over from one year to another. Whenever there was inventory-taking in this wild Archipelago backwoods, all those engaged in it were, after all, friends and all understood. You wouldn't go around moving every board in the place just for the sake of the audit. And fortunately a certain percentage of fictitious lumber could "spoil" from being kept too long and could be written off. And they would fire one manager of the lumber yard and then another and put them to work as work-norm setters. And how many people had been fed in the meanwhile!

Here is what they tried to do too: when they loaded lumber into railroad cars for shipment to buyers (there was no customer expediter up there, and the railroad cars would subsequently be scattered all over the country on the basis of bills of lading), they tried similarly to "ship" the fictitious lumber as well, in other words to inflate the amount shipped (and this fed the stevedore brigades, let's note). The railroad put a seal on the car. It couldn't care less. After a certain length of time somewhere in Armavir or Krivoi Rog they would break the seal on the car and open it up, and document the amount actually received. If the underweight was moderate, then all these differences in volume would be collected in some schedule or other and it would be up to the State Planning Commission to account for them. If the underweight was outrageous, the recipient would send a claim to UstVymlag, but these claims moved in a flood of millions of other papers and were stapled in a file somewhere and in time simply went out like a light. After all, they simply could not stand up against people's pressure *to live*. (And no one was going to send the carload of lumber back from Armavir: you took what you got—there was no timber in the South.)

Now let us note the fact that the state and the Ministry of the Timber Industry made serious use in their economic reports of these fictitiously inflated figures for the production of cut and processed timber. They were useful to the Ministry too.[7]

But probably the most surprising thing was this: it would seem

7. And this is how "tukhta," like many of the Archipelago's problems, could not be kept confined to it, but acquired a nationwide significance.

that there should have been *a shortage* of timber because of the fictitious inflation of quantities at every stage of its movement. However, the fact was that the expediter at the landing "bourse" managed to add so much fictitious timber to deliveries in the course of the summer season that by fall the timber-rafting office had *surpluses* waiting in the water! They had not been touched. And they must not be left in the river for the winter, because if they were, it would be necessary in the spring to call in a plane to bomb them loose. And therefore this *surplus* timber which no one needed was allowed in late autumn *to float downstream into the White Sea!*

Is that miraculous? Strange and wonderful? But it didn't just happen in one place. At the lumber yards in Unzhlag there was always *surplus* lumber left over which hadn't been loaded into railroad cars, and which was no longer listed as belonging to anyone anywhere! And for years after some lumber yard had been totally shut down people would subsequently journey to it from nearby camps for ownerless dry firewood, and burn in their stoves the stripped pit props which had taken so much suffering to produce.

And all this was a matter of attempting *to survive*, not to enrich oneself, and certainly not to plunder the state.

The state cannot be so excessively fierce—and force its subjects into deceit.

And here is what the prisoners used to say: *"Without 'tukhta' and ammonal, never could we have built the canal!"*

So all that is what the Archipelago stands on.

Chapter 6

■

"They've Brought the Fascists!"

"They've brought the Fascists! They've brought the Fascists!" the young zek lads and girls shouted excitedly, running through the camp when our two trucks, each loaded with thirty *Fascists*, entered the perimeter of the small rectangle of the Novy Iyerusalim* Camp.

We had just experienced one of the supreme hours of our life —the one hour's drive from Moscow's Krasnaya Presnya Prison—what is called a short-distance prisoner transport. Though we had spent the ride with our knees hunched up in the rear of the trucks, nonetheless all the air, the speed, the colors were ours. Oh, forgotten brightness of the world! The streetcars were red, the trolley-buses sky-blue, the crowd in white and many-colored. Do they themselves see these colors as they crowd onto the buses? And on top of this today, for some reason, all the buildings and the lampposts were decorated with banners and streamers, some sort of unexpected holiday—August 14, coinciding with the holiday of our liberation from prison. (On this day the capitulation of Japan had been announced, ending the seven-day war.) On the Volokolamsk Highway a whirlwind of scents of new-mown hay and of the early evening freshness of the meadows swirled around our shaven heads. This meadow breeze—who could breathe it in more greedily than prisoners? Real genuine green blinded our eyes, grown used to gray and more gray. I turned up on the transport with Gammerov and

Ingal, and we sat next to each other, and it seemed to us as if we were going to a gay dacha—a country house. The end of such a bewitching journey could not be something dismal.

And then we jumped from the trucks, stretched our numbed legs and backs, and looked around. We liked the compound of Novy Iyerusalim. It was even attractive: it was surrounded not by a solid fence but merely by an interwoven barbed-wire fence, and in every direction were visible the hilly, lively village and dacha countryside of the Zvenigorod land. It was as if we were part of that gay milieu; we could see the earth just like those who came here to rest and enjoy themselves, and we could even see it on a larger, deeper scale (for our eyes had grown used to flat walls, flat sleeping boards, and shallow cells), and to us it seemed even more succulent: the greenery which had faded by mid-August blinded us, and perhaps, too, it seemed to have so much succulence because the sun was setting.

"So you are the Fascists? Are all of you Fascists?" the approaching zeks asked us hopefully. And having confirmed that yes, we were the Fascists—they immediately scurried off and left the scene. There was nothing else about us that interested them.

(We already knew, of course, that "the Fascists" was a nickname for the 58's, introduced by the sharp-eyed thieves and very much approved of by the chiefs; previously they had well named the 58's—*KR's*. But then all that had grown stale, and a catchy label was needed.)

After our swift trip in the fresh air, here it seemed warmer, and because of that cozier. We were still looking around the tiny compound, with its two-story building of brick for men, and the women's building, which was wooden with an attic story, and some peasant-style tumble-down sheds for auxiliary services; and then at the long black shadows which lay everywhere in the fields, cast by the trees and the buildings, and at the high chimney of the brickyard, and at the already flaming windows of its two buildings.

"Well? Things aren't so bad here, it seems. . . ." We spoke to one another, trying to convince each other and ourselves.

One young fellow, with that sharply alert and hostile expression which we had already begun to notice in others, lingered near us longer than the rest, inspecting the Fascists with interest. His well-worn black cap sat crookedly forward on his forehead.

He kept his hands in his pockets, and he stood there just like that, listening to our chatter.

"Not bad!" His chest shook. Twisting his lips, he looked us over contemptuously once again and hurled out: "Star-va-tion station! You'll kick the bucket!"

And spitting under our feet, he went out. He found it unbearable to listen any longer to such idiots.

Our hearts fell.

The first night in camp! You are already being borne, borne along a slippery slide down, down—and somewhere there must be still a saving protruding ledge which you have to catch hold of, but you don't know where it is. Everything that was worst in your entire upbringing has come alive inside you—everything suspicious, gloomy, grasping, cruel, instilled there by hungry queues, by the blatant injustice of the strong. This worst in you has been even more aroused, even more stirred up inside you, by the preceding rumors about the camps: just don't get put on *general work!* The wolfish camp world! Here they tear you to pieces alive! Here they stomp on he who has stumbled! Just don't go on *general work!* But how can you avoid it? Which way is one to flee? One has to *give* something! One has to *give* to someone! But what in particular? And to whom? And how is it done?

Not an hour has gone by—and a fellow aboard our same transport comes up with a restrained smile: he has been named a construction engineer in the camp compound. And one more: he has been given permission to open a barbershop for the free workers at the factory. And yet another: he ran into an old acquaintance, and he is going to go to work in the planning section. Your heart winces: all this is skin off your back! They will survive in the offices and the barbershops. And you will perish. Perish.

The compound. Two hundred paces from barbed wire to barbed wire, and you can't go close to it either. Yes, all around you the Zvenigorod hills will gleam green, but in here is a starvation mess hall, and a stone dungeon for a penalty isolator, and a miserable lean-to over a burner for "individual cooking," a rotten shed of a bath, a gray booth of a tumble-down latrine with rotting seats, and—nowhere to hide from it. This was it. Perhaps this little island would be the last piece of earth in your life which your feet were destined to tromp on.

In all the rooms bare *multiple bunks*—"vagonki"—were installed. The multiple bunk was the invention of the Archipelago, an adaptation for the sleep of the natives never encountered anywhere else in the world: two stories of four wooden panels on two cross-shaped supports placed at the head and at the feet. When one sleeper stirred . . . three others rocked.

They did not issue mattresses in this camp, nor sacks to stuff with straw. The words "bed linen" were unknown to the natives of the Novy Iyerusalim island; no sheets or pillowcases existed here; and they did not issue or launder underwear. You had what you wore, and you had to look after it yourself. And the manager of camp property had never heard the word "pillow." The only pillows were those you owned, and were had only by women and thieves. In the evening, when you lay down on the naked panel, you could take off your shoes. But take into consideration that your shoes would be swiped. Better sleep with shoes on. Better not scatter your clothes about either—they'd swipe them too. On going out to work in the morning you must not leave anything in the barracks; whatever the thieves did not bother to take the jailers would, announcing, *"It's forbidden!"* In the morning you would go out to work just as nomads depart from a camp site, leaving it even cleaner: you would leave neither the ashes from your bonfires nor the bones of devoured animals; the room would be empty, totally bare, and you could even turn it over for others to occupy. And your own sleeping panel would have nothing to distinguish it from all the others: bare, greasy, polished by bodies.

But you couldn't cart anything off to work with you either. You would gather up your chattels in the morning, stand in line at the storeroom for personal belongings, and hide them in a bag or a suitcase. You'd return from work and stand in line again at the storeroom and take with you what you could foresee you would want overnight. Better not make a mistake, because you'd not get to the storeroom a second time.

And thus—for ten years! Hold your head high!

The morning shift returned to camp sometime after two. They washed up, had lunch, stood in line at the storeroom—and the bell rang for roll call. Everyone in the camp formed up in rows, and an illiterate jailer with a plywood board went around, slobbering on his pencil, wrinkling up his forehead wisely, and whispering over and over. He recounted the line-up several times, he went over all the buildings several times, leaving the line-up standing there. Either he was wrong in his arithmetic or he was confused as to how many were ill, and how many were imprisoned in the ShIzo under orders "not to be allowed out." This senseless expenditure of time kept dragging on for a long while—an hour, sometimes an hour and a half. And those to whom time was precious—even though this need is not very developed in our people and not at all among zeks—those who even in camp wanted to accomplish something, felt themselves particularly helpless and humiliated. It was forbidden to read "in line-up." My boys, Gammerov and Ingal, stood with closed eyes, composing either verses or prose or letters—but you were not permitted to stand like that in line-up because it looked as though you were sleeping and this was an insult to the roll call, and furthermore your ears were not closed, and the mother oaths and the stupid jokes and the dismal conversations—all kept swarming in. (The year was 1945 and Norbert Wiener would soon formulate cybernetics; the atom had already been split—and here pale-faced intellectuals were standing in a row waiting to hear the command, "Stand still, don't turn!"—while the stupid, red-mugged idiot lazily whispered his total!) The roll call was completed, and now, at 5:30, one could go and lie down and take a nap (because the night before had been short and the coming night might be even shorter). However, dinner would be in an hour. The time was all cut up into bits.

The camp administration was so lazy and so untalented it did not even have the desire and initiative to separate the workers on the three different shifts into different rooms. From seven to eight, after dinner, the first shift could have begun to rest, but those who were fed and fresh wanted no part of peace, and the thieves on their feather comforters were just beginning their card games, their yelling, and their little dramatic numbers. One thief of an Azerbaizanian type, creeping up in an exaggerated way, made the rounds of the room by jumping from bunk to bunk on the upper panels and roared out at the sloggers: "That's how Napoleon went to Moscow for tobacco." Having got himself tobacco he returned by the same route, stepping on and across people and shouting: "That's how Napoleon fled to Paris." Every escapade of the thieves was so astonishing and unusual that we could only gape at them. From nine in the evening, the night shift was shaking the bunks, tramping about, making preparations to leave, and taking their things off to the storeroom. They were marched out at 10 P.M.—at last it seemed we could sleep! But after ten the day shift returned. And now they were the ones tramping heavily about, shaking the bunks, washing up, going for things in the storeroom, and getting dinner. Only from perhaps half-past eleven on did the exhausted camp sleep.

But at a quarter after four the ring of singing metal was wafted over our small camp and across the sleepy collective farm around us, where the old folks still remember very well the chimes of the Istra church bells. Perhaps our silver-voiced camp bell came from the monastery also and had grown used, while there, to getting the monks up for prayer and work at the sound of the first cockcrow.

"Get up, first shift!" the jailer shouted into each room. Head dizzy from insufficient sleep, eyes still not unglued—no chance to wash! And you don't have to get dressed. That's how you slept. So straight off to the mess hall. You enter, still staggering with sleep. Everyone pushes ahead and is absolutely certain of what he wants. Some rush for their bread ration, others for gruel. You are the only one wandering about like a lunatic, beneath the dim lamps, unable in the steam of the gruel to see where to find either bread or gruel. Finally you receive nineteen and a quarter ounces of bread fit for a feast and an earthenware bowl with something hot and black. This is "black cabbage soup"—made from nettles. The black shreds of the boiled leaves lie in the blackish empty water. There is no fish, meat, nor fat. Not even salt: in cooking, the nettles soak up all the salt thrown in and therefore they don't put any in. If tobacco is camp gold, then salt is camp silver, and the cooks save it up. Unsalted nettle soup is a repulsive poison! You are hungry, but you can't pour it into yourself.

Lift up your eyes. Not to the heavens but to the ceiling. Your eyes have already grown accustomed to the dim lamps and you can now make out along the wall the long slogan written on wallpaper in the favorite red letters:

"WHOEVER DOES NOT WORK DOES NOT EAT!"

And goose pimples run up and down your chest. Oh, wise men from the Cultural and Educational Section! How satisfied you were when you sought out that great evangelical and Communist slogan—for the camp mess hall. But in the Gospel of St. Luke it says: "The labourer is worthy of his hire." And in the Book of Deuteronomy it says: "Thou shalt not muzzle the ox when he treadeth out the corn."

And what you have is an exclamation point! Thank you on behalf of the ox treading out the corn! And henceforth I will understand that you are not at all squeezing my emaciated neck because of shortages, that you are choking me not simply out of greed—but out of the bright principle of the onrushing society! Except that I do not see in camp those who work eating. And I do not see in camp those who don't work . . . starving.

Day is breaking. The predawn August heavens grow pale. Only the brightest of the stars are still visible in the sky. To the southeast, above the brickyard where we will now be taken, are Procyon and Sirius—the alpha stars of Canis Minor and Canis Major. Everything has abandoned us along with the jailers, even the heavens: the dogs in the heavens, like those on earth, are on the leashes of guards. The dogs bark madly, leap ahead, try to get at us. They are gloriously trained on human meat.

The first day in camp! I do not wish even my worst enemy that day! The folds of the brain are all mixed up because of the impossibility of absorbing the entire scope of the cruelty. How will it be? What will happen to me? My head keeps grinding it over and over. And the newcomers are all given the most meaningless work possible, just to keep them busy while things are sorted out. An endless day. You carry hand barrows or you push wheelbarrows along, and with each wheelbarrow load the day grows shorter by five or ten minutes only, and your mind remains free solely in order to keep turning over and over: How will it be? How will it be?

We see the absurdity of rolling this waste along, and we try to chat between wheelbarrows. It seems as if we have already become exhausted from those very first wheelbarrow loads, we have already given them our strength—and how are we going to go on pushing them for eight years? We try to talk about something in which we can feel our strength and our individuality. Ingal describes the funeral of Tynyanov, whose pupil he considers himself—and we argue about historical novels: Ought anyone dare write them? After all, an historical novel is a novel about things the author never saw. Burdened by distance and the maturity of his own era, the author can try as much as he pleases to convince himself that he has come to *comprehend*, but, after all, all the same he is unable to *live it*, and does this mean that an historical novel is first of all fantasy?

At this point they began to call into the office the zeks from the new prisoner transport, several at a time, for their assignments, and all of us left our wheelbarrows. The previous day Ingal had managed to get to know somebody—and as a result he, a literary person, was assigned to the factory bookkeeping office, even though he got figures ridiculously mixed up, and in all his born days had never done calculations on an abacus. Gammerov was incapable of begging and grabbing off a spot even to save his life. He was made an unskilled laborer. He came over, lay down on the grass, and during this last little hour in which he didn't have to be an unskilled laborer he told me about the persecuted poet Pavel Vasilyev, of whom I had never heard a word. When had these boys managed to read and learn so much?

I bit on a stalk of grass and wavered—which of my cards should I *play*—mathematics or my experience as an officer? I was unable to withdraw proudly like Boris. Once I had been brought up with other ideals, but from the thirties cruel life had rubbed us in only one direction: to go after and get.

And it happened quite naturally that when I crossed the threshold of the brickyard director's office I had tucked the stomach fold in my field shirt beneath my broad officer's belt along the sides. (And I had intentionally dressed up for this day too, disregarding the fact that I was to wheel a wheelbarrow.) My high collar was severely buttoned up.

"An officer?" the director immediately surmised.

"Yes, sir!"

"Do you have experience *working with people?*"[1]

"I do."

"What did you command?"

"An artillery battalion." (I lied on the wing—a battery seemed too small to me.) He looked at me with both trust and doubt.

"And will you manage here? It's hard here."

"I think I'll manage!" I replied. (After all, I didn't understand

---

1. Once more "with people," please note.

myself what a noose I was sticking my neck into. The main thing was to go after and get.) He squinted a bit and thought. (He was calculating how ready I was to remake myself into a dog and whether my jaw was firm.)

"All right. You will be a shift foreman in the clay pit."

And one other former officer, Nikolai Akimov, was also named a foreman in the clay pit. He and I went out of the office feeling kinship, gladness. We could not have understood then, even had we been told, that we had chosen the standard—for army men—servile beginning of a sentence. It was clear from Akimov's unintellectual and unassuming face that he was an open lad and a good soldier.

"What's the director scaring us with? Does he think we can't cope with twenty men? There's no mine field and no one is bombing us—what can't we cope with?"

We wanted to recreate inside ourselves our former front-line self-assurance. We were pups and we did not understand to what extent the Archipelago was unlike the front, to what degree its war of siege was more difficult than our war of explosives.

In the army even a fool and a nonentity can command, and, in fact, the higher the post he occupies, the greater will be his success. While a squad commander has to have a quick grasp of things, inexhaustible energy and courage, and understanding of the soldier's heart—it is quite enough for one marshal or another to be peevish, to curse, and to be able to sign his name. Everything else will be done for him, and the plan of operations will be brought him by the operations section of his staff, some bright officer with an unknown name. The soldiers will execute the orders not because they are convinced of their correctness (for often it is precisely the reverse), but because orders come from top to bottom through the hierarchy, and they are the orders of a machine, and whoever does not carry them out will have his head cut off.

But in the Archipelago it is not at all like that for the zek who has been appointed to command other zeks. The whole golden shoulder-board hierarchy is not towering behind your back and not at all supporting your orders; it will betray you and toss you out as soon as you're unable to carry out those orders with your own strength, your own skill. And the skill here is: either your fist, or pitiless destruction through starvation, or such a profound knowledge of the Archipelago that your order also appears to each prisoner as his own salvation.

A greenish Arctic moisture has to replace the warm blood inside you—only then can you command zeks.

And right then, during those very days, they started to bring from the ShIzo—the Penalty Isolator—to the clay pit, as the heaviest work of all, a penalty brigade—a group of thieves who just a bit earlier had almost cut the throat of the camp chief. (They had not wanted to cut his throat, because they were not such fools as that, but to frighten him so he would send them back to Krasnaya Presnya; they recognized Novy Iyerusalim as a deadly place where you'd never get enough to eat.) They were brought in at the end of my shift. They lay down in the clay pit in a sheltered spot, bared their short, thick arms and legs, their fat tattooed stomachs and chests, and lay there sunning themselves, content to be out of the wet cellar of the ShIzo. I went up to them in my military attire and precisely, properly, proposed that they set to work. The sun put them in a benign mood, and therefore they only laughed and sent me to the well-known mother. I was enraged and confused and departed empty-handed. In the army I would have begun with the order "Stand up!" But here it was quite clear that if any one of them did stand up—it would be solely to stick a knife in my ribs. And while I was cudgeling my brains over what to do (after all, the rest of the clay pit was watching and might also quit work)—my shift came to an end. Only thanks to this circumstance am I here today to write this study of the Archipelago.

I was replaced by Akimov. The thieves continued to lie there sunning themselves. He gave them one order, the second time he shouted a command at them (maybe even "Stand up!"), and the third time he threatened them with the camp chief—and they chased him, and in a low spot in the clay pit knocked him down and smashed him in the kidneys with a crowbar. He was taken directly from the factory to the provincial prison hospital, and this brought his career as a commander to an end and maybe his prison sentence and maybe his life. (In all probability, the director had appointed us as dummies to be beaten up by these thieves.)

My own short career at the clay pit lasted several days longer than Akimov's, but brought me not the satisfaction I had expected, only a constant spiritual depression. At 6 A.M. I entered the working compound more deeply despondent than if I had been going there to dig the clay myself. I wandered around the clay pit like one quite lost, hating both it and my own role in it.

From the wet pressing mill to the clay pit there was a trolley track. At the spot where the level area ended and its rails dipped into the workings, a windlass stood on a platform. This motor-driven windlass was one of the few miracles of mechanization in the whole brickyard. Along the entire line from clay pit to windlass and from the windlass to the pressing mill, the sloggers had to push the cars loaded with clay. Only on the rise out of the clay pit were the cars dragged up by the windlass. The clay pit occupied a distant corner of the brickyard compound, and it was a surface plowed up by cave-ins—the cave-ins branching off in all directions like ravines, leaving between them untouched prominences. The clay lay right up to the surface, and the stratum was not thin. One could probably have mined it deep down or else across its whole width continuously, but no one knew how it should be done, and no one made a plan for mining it, and it all was managed by the brigadier of the morning shift, Barinov—a cocky young Muscovite, a nonpolitical offender with a pretty face. Barinov worked the clay pit simply where it was most convenient; he excavated where the most clay could be dug for the least work. He never went too deep—so the cars wouldn't have to be pushed up too steep a slope. Properly speaking, Barinov was in charge of all eighteen to twenty men who worked during my shift in the clay pit. He was the only genuine boss of shift: he knew the lads, he *fed* them, in other words got for them big rations, and each day wisely decided himself how many cars of clay were to be delivered so that there would be neither too few nor too many. I liked Barinov, and if I had been somewhere in prison with him as a bunk neighbor, we would have got along very gaily. And we could have got along right here too. I should have gone to him and had a big laugh with him over the fact that the director had appointed me to the position of intermediate watchdog—while I understood nothing. But my officer's training did not permit this! And I tried to maintain a severe bearing with him and to get him to knuckle under, though not only I, and not only he, but the entire brigade, could see that I was as much of a useless meddler as a District Party instructor during crop sowing. It made Barinov angry that they had installed a stuffed shirt over him, and more than once he mocked me cleverly in front of the brigade. In the case of anything I considered necessary to do he immediately proved to me that it was impossible. On the other hand, loudly shouting, "Foreman! *Foreman!*" he would on occasion summon me to various corners of the clay pit and ask me for instructions: how to take up the old trolley tracks and lay new ones again; how a wheel that had jumped off the axle should be put back again; or what to do about the allegedly nonfunctioning windlass; or where the shovels should be taken to be sharpened. Already weakening from day to day in my impulse to command, in the face of his ridicule, I was by then quite happy if he simply ordered the fellows to dig that morning (he didn't always do it) and did not annoy me with his vexatious questions.

Thereupon I quietly kept out of the way and hid from my subordinates and my chiefs behind the high piles of earth that had been carted away, set myself down on the ground and sat stock-still with sinking heart. My spirit was numb from my first few days in camp. Oh, this was not prison! Prison has wings! Prison is a treasure house of thought. It was gay and easy to starve and argue in prison. And just try that here—ten years of starvation, work, and silence. Just try it! The iron caterpillar track was already dragging me to the grinder. I was helpless. I didn't know how, but I wanted to slip off to one side. To catch my breath. To come to myself. To lift my head and to see.

Over there, beyond the barbed wire, across a vale, was a knoll. On it was a little village—ten houses. The rising sun illuminated it with its peaceful rays. So close to us—and the very opposite of a camp! (For that matter, it, too, was a camp, but one forgets that.) For a long time there was no motion at all there, but then a woman walked by with a pail, and a tiny child ran across the weeds in the street. A cock crowed and a cow mooed. And there in the clay pit we could hear everything perfectly. And a mongrel barked—what a lovely voice that was too! It was not a convoy dog![2]

2. When there are discussions about universal disarmament, I am always quite concerned; after all, no one has included guard dogs in the lists of forbidden weapons. And yet they make life more insufferable for human beings than do rockets.

And from every sound there and from the very immobility itself a holy peace flooded into my soul. And I know for certain that if they should say to me at that very moment: That's your freedom! Just live in that village until your death! Renounce cities and the vanities of this world, your passing fancies, your convictions, the truth—renounce it all and live in that village (but not as a collective farmer!), look at the sun every morning and harken to the roosters! Are you willing? . . . Oh, not only willing, but, good Lord, please send me a life like that! I felt that I would be unable to last out in camp.

On the other side of the brickyard, invisible to me at the moment, a passenger train roared by on the Rzhev Line. In the clay pit they shouted: "The Trusties' Train!" Every train was familiar. They kept time by them. "The Trusties' Train" passed by at a quarter to nine, and at nine o'clock, separately, not at shift-changing time, they would conduct *the trusties* from the camp to the brickyard—the office employees and those in positions of responsibility. The favorite train was at half-past one, the "Provider," after which we soon went to line-up and to lunch.

My zek supervisor, Olga Petrovna Matronina, was brought to work along with the trusties, and sometimes, if her heart was anxious about the work, even earlier, by special convoy. I sighed, came out of my hiding place, and went along the clay pit trolley track to the wet pressing factory—to report.

The entire brickyard consisted of two plants—for wet pressing and dry pressing. Our clay pit worked only for the wet-pressing plant and the chief of the wet pressing was Matronina, an engineer-specialist in silicates. What kind of an engineer she was I do not know, but she was fussy and stubborn. She was one of those unshakable loyalists—an orthodox Communist—of whom I had already encountered a few in the cells (there were not many of them in general), on whose mountain peak, however, I myself could not cling. On the basis of the "letter" section, ChS, as a member of the family of one shot, she had received eight years from an OSO, and right now she was serving out her last months. True, they had not released any politicals throughout the war, and she, too, would be held until the notorious Special Decree. But even that did not cast any shadow on her state of mind; she served the Party, and it was unimportant whether in freedom or in camp. She was from a reserve for rare animals. In camp she tied a red scarf around her head and only a red scarf, even though she was already over forty. (Not one camp girl wore a scarf like that in the brickyard, and not one free Komsomol girl either.) She bore no grudge for her husband's execution, nor for her own eight years of imprisonment. All these injustices had been caused, in her opinion, by individual Yagoda or Yezhov henchmen, and under Comrade Beria the only arrests being made were just. Seeing me in the uniform of a Soviet officer, she said at our first meeting: "Those who arrested me can now see the proofs of my orthodoxy." Not long before she had written a letter to Kalinin, and she quoted from it to all who wished or were forced to listen: "My long sentence has not broken my will in the struggle for the Soviet government, for Soviet industry."

Meanwhile when Akimov had come and reported to her that the thieves refused to obey him, she herself did not go to explain to this socially friendly element that their conduct was harming industry, but she pulled him up short: "You have to *compel* them! That's why you were appointed!" Akimov was beaten up, and she made no effort to struggle further, but merely wrote the camp: "Don't send us that contingent any more." She also accepted very calmly the fact that in her factory young girls worked eight hours straight at automatic machines; they were confined uninterruptedly for the whole eight-hour period to monotonous motions at the conveyor belt. She said: "There is nothing to be done; there are more important sectors than that for mechanization." The day before, Saturday, there had been a rumor going the rounds that they would again not give us our Sunday off (and that's exactly what happened). The young girls at the automatic machines clustered around her and said to her bitterly: "Olga Petrovna! Are they really going to take our Sunday away from us again? After all, this is the third in a row! The war's over!" Wearing her red scarf, she indignantly tossed her dry, dark profile, which wasn't a woman's, nor a man's either: "Girls! What right have we to a Sunday? The construction project in Moscow is being held up because there are no bricks!" (In other words, of course, she didn't know anything about any particular construction project to which our bricks were being sent, but in her mind's eye she could see that big generalized construction project, and here were these young girls, so vile as to want to wash their things.)

I was necessary to Matronina in order to *double* the number of cars of clay in one shift. She took no account of the strength of the sloggers, the condition of the cars, or the capacity of the pressing plant, but merely demanded that it be doubled! (And how could an outsider unacquainted with the setup double the number of carloads except with his fist?) I did not double the output, and by and large the output did not change by one carload under me—and Matronina, merciless, scolded me in Barinov's presence and that of the workers, without being able to get through her woman's head that which the least sergeant knows: that one must not dress down even a corporal in the presence of a private. And then on one occasion, admitting my total defeat in the clay pit, and therefore my incapacity to *direct*, I went to Matronina and, as gently as I could, asked her:

"Olga Petrovna! I am a good mathematician; I do figures quickly. I have heard that you need an accountant in the plant. Take me!"

"An accountant?" she raged, and her cruel face grew even darker, and the ends of her red scarf wound about the back of her head. "I'll put any wisp of a girl to work as an accountant, but what we need are *commanders of production*. How many loads are you short for your shift? Be off with you!" And, like a new Pallas Athena, with outstretched arm she sent me back to the clay pit.

And a day later the position of foreman of the clay pit was abolished, and I was fired, not just straightforwardly but vengefully. Matronina summoned Barinov and gave him his orders:

"Put him to work with a crowbar and don't take your eyes off him! Make him load six cars a shift! Make him *sweat!*"

And right then, in my officer's uniform in which I took so much pride, I went forth to dig clay. Barinov was overjoyed. He had foreseen my fall.

If I had better understood the secret, alert connection between all camp events, I could have guessed at my fate the day before. In the Novy Iyerusalim mess hall there was a separate serving window for the ITR's—the Engineering and Technical Workers —from which the engineers, bookkeepers, and . . . shoemakers received their meals. After my appointment as foreman of the clay pit, catching on to the camp grasp of things, I had approached this window and demanded my meal. The cooks dragged their feet about it, saying that I wasn't on the list of

ITR's, but nonetheless they did each time issue me my meal, and even without protesting after a while, so that I myself came to believe that I was on their list. As I thought it over later—I was, for the kitchen, still a question mark: hardly had I arrived than I acted big; I had borne myself proudly and gone about in military uniform. Such a person might very easily in a week become a senior work assigner or the senior camp bookkeeper or a doctor. (In camp everything is possible!!) And then they would be in my hands. So even though in actual fact the plant was only trying me out and had not included me on any list at all—the kitchen kept on feeding me just in case. But one day before my fall, when even the plant didn't know, the camp kitchen already knew all about it, and slammed the door in my mug: I had turned out to be a *cheap sucker*. This tiny episode typifies the atmosphere of the camp world.

This so prevalent human desire to be set apart by clothes discloses us in fact, particularly to the keen eyes of camp. It seems to us that we're clothing ourselves, but in fact we're baring ourselves, we are showing what we're worth. I did not understand that my military uniform had the same price as Matronina's red scarf. But there was an unslumbering eye which had spied it all out from a hiding place. And one day an orderly was sent to get me. A lieutenant wanted to see me—over here, in a separate room.

The young lieutenant conversed with me very pleasantly. In the cozy, clean room he and I were alone. The sun was shining just before sinking in the west and the wind was blowing the curtain. He told me to be seated. For some reason he asked me to write my autobiography—and he could not have made a more pleasant proposal. After the protocols of interrogation in which I had only spat on myself, after the humiliation of the Black Marias and the transit prisons, after the convoy and the prison jailers, after the thieves and the trusties, who had refused to see in me a former captain of our glorious Red Army, here I sat behind a desk and without being pushed by anyone at all, and beneath the benign glance of a friendly lieutenant, I wrote at just the right length in thick ink on excellent smooth paper which did not exist in camp that I had been a captain, that I had commanded a battery, that I had been awarded some decorations. And thanks to the actual writing, it seemed that I had regained my own personality, my own "I." (Yes, my gnoseological subject, "I"! And yet I was, after all, a university man, a civilian, in the army by chance. Imagine how embedded it must be in a career officer—this insistence on being held in esteem!) And the lieutenant, on reading my autobiography, was quite satisfied with it. "So you are a Soviet person, right?" Well, to be sure, well, of course, why not? How pleasant it was to rise again from the mud and ashes, and once again become a Soviet person! It was one-half of freedom.

The lieutenant asked me to come see him in five days. During these five days, however, I was forced to say good-bye to my military uniform because it was bad to be digging clay in it. I hid my field shirt and my military britches in my suitcase, and at the camp storage room I received some patched and faded rag which appeared to have been washed after lying for a year in a trash bin. This was an important step, though I did not as yet recognize its significance: my soul had not yet become that of a zek, but my skin therewith became a zek's. With shaven head, tormented by hunger, and squeezed by enemies, I would soon acquire the glance of a zek too—insincere, suspicious, all-observant.

This was how I looked when in five days' time I went to see the security chief, still not understanding what he was getting at. But the security chief was not there. He had stopped coming there entirely. (He already knew, but we did not, that in another week we would all be dispersed and that they would be bringing Germans to Novy Iyerusalim to replace us.) And that is how I missed seeing the lieutenant.

I discussed with Gammerov and Ingal why it was that I wrote my autobiography, and we did not guess, innocents, that these were already the first claws of the beast of prey reaching into our nest. And yet meanwhile the picture was so clear: Three young men had arrived in the new prisoner transport, and they kept discussing something all the time, arguing among themselves, and one of them—swarthy, round, and gloomy, with little mustaches, the one who had gotten himself a place in the bookkeeping office—didn't sleep nights and kept writing something on the bunks, writing and hiding it. Of course, one could send someone and grab what he was hiding—but without causing an alarm it was simpler to find out about it all from the one of them who wore army britches. He, evidently, was an army man and a Soviet person, and he would assist in the spiritual surveillance.

Zhora Ingal, who was not exhausted by his work during the day, really did refuse to sleep the first half-nights—and thus defended the freedom of the creative spirit. He sat up on the upper panel of the multiple bunk, without mattress, pillow, or blanket, in his padded jacket (it was not warm in the rooms, for the nights were autumn nights), in his shoes, his feet stretched out on the panel, his back leaning against the wall, and sucking on his pencil, looked sternly at his sheet of paper. (One could not have dreamed up worse behavior for camp! But neither he nor we understood yet how all that stood out like a sore thumb and how they kept watch over such things.)

Sometimes he simply gave in to his frailties and wrote an ordinary letter. His twenty-three-year-old wife had not even worn out the shoes in which she'd gone with him that winter to the conservatory—and now she had left him: security questionnaires, a blot on one's record, yes, and a person wants to live. He wrote to another woman, whom he called a dear sister, concealing from himself and from her that he also loved her or was ready to love her (but that woman, too, soon got married). He could write like this:

"My dear little sister! Harken to the wonderful intimations of humanity: Handel, Tchaikovsky, Debussy! I, too, wanted to become an intimation, but the clock of my life has come to a stop. . . ."

Or simply: "You have become much closer to me during the course of these months. It has become clear that there are very many real, genuine people in the world, and I very much hope that your husband will also be a real human being."

Or like this:

"I have wandered through life, stumbling and in search of myself. . . . There is a bright light in the room, and I have never seen darkness that is blacker. But only here have I found myself and my own fate, and this time not in books either. And do you know, my little bird, I have never been such an optimist as I am right now. Now I know once and for all that there is nothing more precious in life than the idea one serves. And I also now know how and what I must write—that's the main thing."[3]

3. No, he did not yet know *how* to write. According to the account of Arkady Belinkov, later on in another camp Ingal kept on writing like that, keeping to himself on the bunks. The prisoners first asked, and then subse-

And for the time being, he wrote at night and hid during the day a story about El Campesino—the Spanish Republican with whom he had shared a cell and whose peasant common sense had delighted him. El Campesino's fate was a simple one: after having lost the war to Franco he came to the Soviet Union, and after a while he was imprisoned here.[4]

Ingal was not a warm person. He did not inspire one to open one's heart to him at the first impulse. (I have just written this and stopped to think: Was I called a warm person either?) But his steadfastness was a worthy model. To write in camp! I might someday be able to rise to it if I didn't perish. But for the time being I was tormented by my own restless search, depressed by my first days as a clay digger. On a serene September evening Boris Gammerov and I could find time only to sit awhile on a pile of cinders at the approach to the camp perimeter.

In the direction of Moscow thirty-seven miles away the heavens flamed with salutes—this was the "holiday of victory over Japan." But the lanterns of our camp compound burned with a dull tired light. A hostile reddish light emanated from the plant windows. And in a long and drawn-out string, as mysterious as the years and the months of our prison terms, the lanterns on the poles of the broad brickyard compound receded into the distance.

Arms around his knees, thin and coughing, Gammerov repeated:

> For thirty years I have nurtured
> My love for my native land,
> And I shall neither expect
> . . . your leniency . . .*

Nor desire it.

---

quently began to demand, that he show them *what* he was writing (denunciations, perhaps?). But regarding this only as one more act of violence against creative art—although from the opposite direction—he refused! And they . . . beat him up unmercifully.

I have quoted here these lines from his letters so that his grave may be marked with this tiny monument at least.

4. Ingal could never complete this short story about El Campesino because he never knew El Campesino's fate. El Campesino outlived his describer. I have heard that at the time of the great Ashkhabad earthquake he led a group of zeks out of a wrecked camp and shepherded them through the mountains into Iran. (Even the border guards had panicked.)

■

"They've brought the Fascists! They've brought the Fascists!" was a cry heard not only in Novy Iyerusalim. In the late summer and autumn of 1945, that's how it was on all the islands of the Archipelago. Our arrival—that of the *Fascists*—opened up the road to freedom for the nonpolitical offenders. They had learned of their amnesty back on July 7; since that time they had been photographed, and their release documents had been readied, and their accounts in the bookkeeping offices. But first for one month, then in places for two, and in some places for three months, the amnestied zeks had been languishing within the nauseating barbed-wire boundaries. There was no one to replace them!

There was *no one* to *replace* them!

And we, newborn blind innocents that we were, in our calked-up cells, had continued to hope all spring and summer for an amnesty! That Stalin would *take pity* on us! That he would "take account of the Victory"! . . . That, having passed us over in the first, the July, amnesty, he would subsequently declare a second amnesty, a special amnesty for political prisoners. (They used to report even one detail: this amnesty was already prepared; it was lying *on Stalin's desk*, and all that was left was for him to sign it; but he was off on vacation. The incorrigibles awaited a genuine amnesty, the incorrigibles believed! . . .) But if we had been pardoned, then who would have gone down into the mines? Who would have gone into the forests with saws? Who would have fired the bricks and laid them in walls? Stalin had managed to create a system under which—if it had manifested generosity or mercy—pestilence, famine, desolation, and ruin would have immediately embraced the entire country.

"They've brought the Fascists!" They had always hated us or at least disdained us, but now the nonpolitical offenders looked upon us almost with love because we had come to take their places. And those same prisoners who had learned, in German captivity, that there is no nation more despised, more abandoned, more alien and unneeded than the Russian, now learned, leaping down from red cattle cars and trucks onto the Russian earth, that even among this outcast people they were the most benighted and grievous of all.

Now that is what that great Stalinist amnesty turned out to be, one such as "the world had never seen." Where, indeed, had the world ever seen an amnesty which did not concern politicals?!?[5]

All those who had burglarized apartments, stolen the clothes off passers-by, raped girls, corrupted minors, given consumers short weight, played the hoodlum, disfigured the defenseless, been wantonly destructive in forests and waterways, committed bigamy, practiced blackmail or extortion, taken bribes, swindled, slandered, written false denunciations (but those particular people didn't actually even serve time at all—that's for the future!), peddled narcotics, pimped or forced women into prostitution, whose carelessness or ignorance had resulted in the loss of life, all went scot-free. (And I have merely listed here the articles of the Code covered by the amnesty; this is not a mere flourish of eloquence.)

And then they want morality from the people!

Half their terms were eliminated for: embezzlers, forgers of documents and ration cards, speculators, and thieves of state property. (Stalin still was touchy about the pockets of the state.)

But there was nothing so repugnant to the former front-line soldiers and POW's as the universal *blanket pardon of deserters* in wartime. Every man who, out of cowardice, ran away from his unit, left the front, did not show up at the conscription point, hid for many years in a pit in the vegetable garden of his mother's home, in cellars, behind the stove (always at the mother's! deserters, as a rule, did not trust their wives!), who for years had not pronounced one word aloud, who had turned into hunched-up hairy beasts—all of them, as long as they had been caught or had

5. It freed 58's who had sentences of up to *three* years, a sentence almost never given anyone, probably not as many as one-half of one percent of those to whom it applied. But even among that one-half percent of the cases, the implacable spirit of the amnesty proved stronger than its conciliatory wording. I knew one lad—his name, I believe, was Matyushin (he was an artist in the little camp at the Kaluga Gates)—who had been sentenced under 58-1b very early on, even before the end of 1941, for having been taken prisoner when it had not yet been decided how this was to be treated, or what term to give. They gave Matyushin just three years—an unbelievable happening! At the end of his term, he was of course not freed, but was told to await the Special Decree. But then came the amnesty! Matyushin began to ask (there was nowhere he could demand) for release. For almost five months—until December, 1945 —the frightened officials of the Classification and Records Section turned him down. Finally he was released to go back home to Kursk Province. There was a rumor (and it's quite impossible to believe in any other outcome!) that soon afterward he was raked in and given something up to a whole *tenner*. It was impermissible to allow him to take advantage of the absent-mindedness of the first court!

turned themselves in by the day of the amnesty, were proclaimed now unsullied, unjudged, equal Soviet citizens! (And that is when the perspicacity of the old proverb was justified: Flight is not beautiful, but it is healthy!)

And those who trembled not, who did not play the coward, who, for their Motherland, took the enemy's blow and then paid for it with captivity—there could be no forgiveness for them: that's how the Supreme Commander in Chief saw it.

Was it that something in the deserters struck a chord in Stalin? Did he remember his own aversion to serving as a rank-and-file soldier, his own pitiful service as a recruit in the winter of 1917? Or did he simply conclude that cowards represented no danger to his rule and that only the bold were dangerous? After all, it might seem that it was not at all reasonable to amnesty deserters even from Stalin's point of view: he himself had shown his people the surest and simplest way to save one's skin in any future war.[6]

In another book I have told the story of Dr. Zubov and his wife: An old woman in their house hid a wandering deserter, who later on turned them in for it; for this the Zubovs, husband and wife, got sentences of a *tenner* each under Article 58. The court determined that their guilt lay not so much in hiding a deserter as in the *absence of any self-serving motive* for this concealment: he was not a relative of theirs, which meant that it amounted to anti-Soviet intent! Under the Stalinist amnesty the deserter himself was liberated, without having served even three years, and he had already forgotten about that little episode of his life. But things went differently with the Zubovs! They each served out a full ten years in camp (four in Special Camps), and another four years, without any sentence, in exile. They were released only because exile in general was done away with, nor were their convictions annulled either when they were released, not even after *sixteen* years, nor even *nineteen* years, after the events, and because of them they could not return to their home near Moscow, and were prevented from quietly living out their lives.[7]

6. And very likely there was also an historical justice here: an old debt was paid to deserting from the front, without which our whole history would have gone quite differently.

7. In 1958 the Chief Military Prosecutor replied to them: Your guilt was proven and there are no bases for reconsidering the case. Only in 1962, after twenty years, was their case under Section 58-10 (anti-Soviet intent) and 58-11 (an "organization" of husband and wife) quashed. Under Article 193-17-7g (aiding a deserter) it was determined that their sentence was five years, and

Now that's what the rancorous, vengeful, unreasonable Law fears and what it does not fear!

After the amnesty, they began to smear and smear with the paintbrushes of the Cultural and Educational Sections, and the internal archways and walls of the camps were decorated with mocking slogans: "For the broadest amnesty we shall respond to our dear Party and government with doubled productivity."

The ones amnestied were the habitual criminals and nonpolitical offenders, and the ones to respond with doubled work productivity were the politicals. . . . When in history has our government shone with a sense of humor?

With our "Fascist" arrival, daily releases began immediately in Novy Iyerusalim. Just the day before, you had seen women in the camp compound, looking disgraceful, dressed in tatters, using profanity—and lo! they had suddenly been transformed, gotten washed, smoothed down their hair, and put on dresses with polka dots and stripes which they'd got hold of heaven knows where, and, with jackets over their arms, they went modestly to the station. Seeing them on the train, would you ever guess that they knew how to swear like troopers?

And there, leaving the gates, were thieves and *half-breeds* (who imitate the real thieves). They didn't drop their impudent bearing even there; they clowned and minced and waved to those left behind and shouted, and their friends shouted back to them from the windows. The guards didn't interfere—the thieves are permitted everything. One thief, not without imagination, stood his suitcase on end, climbed up on top of it lightly, and, cocking his cap and tossing back the flaps of his jacket, *copped off* at a transit prison somewhere or won at cards, played a farewell serenade to the camp on his mandolin, singing some sort of thieves' twaddle. Horse laughs.

Those released still had a long walk on the path circling the camp and on through the field, and the folds of the barbed wire did not shut off from us the open view. That night those thieves would be strolling on the boulevards of Moscow, and perhaps even in their first week they would make their *jump* (clean out an apart-

---

(! after twenty years!) the Stalinist amnesty was applied. And that's precisely the way in which the two old people whose lives had been smashed were notified in 1962: "As of July 7, 1945, *you are considered released* and your conviction annulled"!

ment), they'd take the clothes off your wife, or sister, or daughter on the night streets.

And as for you Fascists (and Matronina was also a Fascist!): Double your work productivity!

■

Because of the amnesty there was a shortage of manpower everywhere, and there were rearrangements. For a short time I was switched from the clay pit to a plant section. There I could take a look at Matronina's mechanization. Everyone had it bad here, but the most surprising of all was the work of one young girl—a real, genuine heroine of labor, though not suitable for the newspaper. Her place, her duty, in the shop had no name, but one could have called it the "upper distributor." Next to the conveyor belt emerging from the press with cut, wet bricks (just mixed from clay and very heavy) stood two girls, one of them the "lower distributor," and the other the "server-up." These did not have to bend down, but simply pivot, and not in a wide-angle turn either. But the "upper distributor," who stood on a pedestal like the queen of the shop, had incessantly to bend down, pick up a wet brick placed at her feet by the "server-up," and without crushing it raise it to the level of her waist or even shoulders, and, without changing the position of her feet, turn from the waist at a ninety-degree angle (sometimes to the right and sometimes to the left, depending on which receiving car was being loaded), and distribute the bricks on five wooden shelves, twelve on each. Her motion had no intermission, did not stop or change, and she moved at the speed of fast gymnastics—for the whole eight-hour shift, unless the press itself broke down. They kept handing and handing her half of all the bricks produced by the plant during a shift. Down below the girls switched duties, but she had no replacement for the entire eight hours. She ought to have grown dizzy from five minutes of such work, from those swings of her head and the bending and twisting of her torso. During the first half of her shift, however, the girl still kept her smile (she couldn't carry on a conversation because of the din of the press), and perhaps she liked being put up there on a pedestal like a beauty queen, where everyone could see her strong, bare legs below her hitched-up skirt and the ballet-like elasticity of her waist.

And for this work she got the highest ration in the camp: ten and a half extra ounces of bread (a total for the day of thirty ounces)—and for her dinner, besides the common black cabbage soup, *three Stakhanovite portions*—three pitiful portions of thin semolina cereal made with water. They gave her so little that she inhaled the full contents of the pottery bowl in one swallow.

"We work for money and you work for bread, no secret there," a grubby free mechanic who had come to fix the press said to me.

One-armed Punin from the Altai and I rolled away the loaded cars. These cars were like high towers—unsteady, because, thanks to ten shelves with twelve bricks each, their center of gravity was high up. Wobbling and tottering, like a bookcase overloaded with books, such a car had to be pulled by an iron handle along straight rails; then led up onto a supporting truck, halted there, and then this truck had to be pulled along another straight line past the drying chambers. Brought to a stop at the one required, the car then had to be taken off the truck and pushed ahead of one in still another direction into the drying chamber. Each chamber was a long, narrow corridor along whose walls stretched ten slots and ten shelf supports. One had to push the car right to the back, without letting it get out of line, and there release the lever, setting all ten shelves with the bricks on the ten supports, and release ten pairs of iron grips, and immediately roll the empty car back out. This whole scheme, it seems, was German, out of the nineteenth century (and the car had a German name), but the German scheme provided not only for rails to support the car but also for a floor laid beneath the pits to support the trucker. But for us the floor planks were rotten, broken, and I used to stumble and fall through. In addition, there was probably supposed to be ventilation in all the chambers, but there wasn't any, and while I struggled away at my mistakes in stacking (I often got things crooked, shelves got stuck, refused to set, and wet bricks tumbled down on my head), I gulped in carbon fumes and they burned my windpipe.

Therefore I was not very sorry to leave the plant when I was again driven out to the clay pit. There were not enough clay diggers—they were being released too. They sent Boris Gammerov to the clay pit too, and so we began to work together. The work norm there was well known: during one shift one worker was to dig, load up, and deliver to the windlass six cars full of clay—

eight cubic yards. For two persons the norm was sixteen. In dry weather the two of us together could manage six and a half. But an autumn drizzle began. For one day, two, three, without wind, it kept on, getting neither heavier nor stopping. It was not torrential, so no one was going to take the responsibility for halting the outdoor work. "It never rains on the canal" was a famous Gulag slogan. But in Novy Iyerusalim, for some reason, they did not even give us padded jackets, and there in the red clay pit beneath that monotonous drizzle we wallowed and smeared up our old front-line overcoats, which by the end of the third day had already absorbed a pail of water each. The camp also gave us no footwear, and we were rotting our last front-line boots in the wet clay.

The first day we still joked.

"And don't you find, Boris, that Baron Tuzenbakh would have envied us a good deal right now? After all, he dreamed of working in a brickyard. Do you remember? To work so hard that when he came home he would throw himself on his bed and instantly fall asleep. He evidently supposed that there would be a drier for wet clothes, that there would be a cot and a hot meal consisting of two courses."

But we rolled away a pair of cars, and angrily knocking our spades against the iron sides of the next car (the clay stuck to the shovels), this time I spoke with irritation:

"Just tell me, if you please, what devil made the sisters restless just sitting at home? No one forced them to go out on Sundays with young people to collect scrap. On Mondays no one required of them a précis of the Holy Scriptures. No one forced them to teach for nothing. No one drove them out into the blocks to put into effect universal education."

And after one more load:

"What empty, empty chatter they all indulged in: To work! To work! To work! Well, go ahead and work, the hell with you, who's stopping you? What a happy life it will be! So happy! So happy!! And what will it be like? You should have been accompanied by police dogs into that happy life. You'd have learned!"

Boris was weaker than I; he could hardly wield his spade, which the sticky clay made heavier and heavier, and he could hardly throw each shovelful up to the edge of the truck. Nonetheless, on the second day he tried to keep us up to the heights of

Vladimir Solovyev. He had outdistanced me there too! How much of Solovyev he had already read! And I had not read even one line because of my Bessel functions.

He told me whatever he remembered, and I kept trying to remember it, but I really couldn't; I didn't have the head for it at that moment.

No, how can one preserve one's life and at the same time arrive at the truth? And why is it necessary to be dropped into the depths of camp in order to understand one's own squalor?

He said: "Vladimir Solovyev taught that one must greet death with gladness. Worse than here . . . it won't be."

Quite true.

We loaded as much as we could. Penalty ration? So it would be a penalty ration! The hell with you! We wrote off the day and wound our way to camp. But there was nothing joyful awaiting us there: three times a day that same black, unsalted infusion of nettle leaves, and once a day a ladle of thin gruel, a third of a liter. And the bread had already been sliced—they gave fifteen and a quarter ounces in the morning, and not a crumb more during the day or in the evening. And then we were lined up for roll call out in the rain. And once again we slept on bare bunks in wet clothes, muddied with clay, and we shivered because they weren't heating the barracks.

And the next day that fine drizzle kept falling and falling. The clay pit had got drenched, and we were stuck in it but good. No matter how much clay you took on your spade, and no matter how much you banged it on the side of the truck, the clay would not drop off. And each time we had to reach over and push the clay off the spade into the car. And then we realized that we had been merely doing extra work. We put aside the spades and began simply to gather up the squelching clay from under our feet and toss it into the car.

Borya was coughing. There was still a fragment of German tank shell in his lungs. He was thin and yellow, and his nose, ears, and the bones of his face had grown deathly pointed. I looked at him closely, and I was not sure: would he make it through a winter in camp?

We still tried to divert our minds and conquer our situation—with thought. But by then neither philosophy nor literature was there. Even our hands became heavy, like spades, and hung down.

Boris suggested: "No, to talk . . . takes much strength. Let's be silent and think to some purpose. For example, compose verses. In our heads."

I shuddered. He could write verses here and now? The canopy of death hung over him, but the canopy of such a stubborn talent hung over his yellow forehead too.[8]

And so we kept silent and scooped up the clay with our hands. The rain kept coming. Yet they not only didn't take us out of the clay pit, but Matronina, brandishing the fiery sword of her gaze (her "red" head was covered with a dark shawl), pointed out to the brigadier from the edge the different ends of the clay pit. And we understood: they were not going to pull out the brigade at the end of its shift at 2 P.M., but would keep it in the clay pit until it fulfilled its norm. Only then would we get both lunch and dinner.

In Moscow the construction project was halted for lack of bricks.

But Matronina departed and the rain thickened. Light red puddles formed everywhere in the clay and in our car too. The tops of our boots turned red, and our coats were covered with red spots. Our hands had grown numb from the cold clay, and by this time they couldn't even throw anything into the car. And then we left this futile occupation, climbed up higher to the grass, sat down there, bent our heads, and pulled the collars of our coats up over the backs of our necks.

From the side we looked like two reddish stones in the field.

Somewhere young men of our age were studying at the Sorbonne or at Oxford, playing tennis during their ample hours of relaxation, arguing about the problems of the world in student cafés. They were already being published and were exhibiting their paintings. They were twisting and turning to find ways of distorting the insufficiently original world around them in some new way. They railed against the classics for exhausting all the subjects and themes. They railed at their own governments and their own reactionaries who did not want to comprehend and

8. That winter Boris Gammerov died in a hospital from exhaustion and tuberculosis. I revere in him a poet who was never even allowed to peep. His spiritual image was lofty, and his verses themselves seemed to me very powerful at the time. But I did not memorize even one of them, and I can find them nowhere now, so as to be able at least to make him a gravestone from those little stones.

adopt the advanced experience of the Soviet Union. They recorded interviews through the microphones of radio reporters, listening all the time to their own voices and coquettishly elucidating what they *wished to say* in their last or their first book. They judged everything in the world with self-assurance, but particularly the prosperity and higher justice of our country. Only at some point in their old age, in the course of compiling encyclopedias, would they notice with astonishment that they could not find any worthy Russian names for our letters—for all the letters of our alphabet.

The rain drummed on the back of our heads, and the chill crept up our wet backs.

We looked about us. The half-loaded cars had been overturned. Everyone had left. There was no one in the entire clay pit, nor in the entire field beyond the compound. Out in the gray curtain of rain lay the hidden village, and even the roosters had hidden in a dry place.

We, too, picked up our spades, so that no one would steal them —they were registered in our names. And dragging them behind us like heavy wheelbarrows, we went around Matronina's plant beneath the shed where empty galleries wound all around the Hoffmann kilns that fired the bricks. There were drafts here and it was cold, but it was also dry. We pushed ourselves down into the dust beneath the brick archway and sat there.

Not far away from us a big heap of coal was piled. Two zeks were digging into it, eagerly seeking something there. When they found it, they tried it in their teeth, then put it in their sack. Then they sat themselves down and each ate a similar black-gray lump.

"What are you eating there, fellows?"

"It's 'sea clay.' The doctor doesn't forbid it. It doesn't do any good, but it doesn't do any harm either. And if you add a kilo of it a day to your rations, it's as if you had really eaten. Go on, look for some; there's a lot of it among the coal."

And so it was that right up to nightfall the clay pit did not fulfill its work norm. Matronina gave orders that we should be left out all night. But . . . the electricity went out everywhere, and the work compound had no lights, so they called everyone in to the gatehouse. They ordered us to link arms, and with a beefed-up convoy, to the barking of the dogs and to curses, they took us to the camp compound. Everything was black. We moved along without seeing where it was wet and where the earth was firm, kneading it all up in succession, losing our footing and jerking one another.

And in the camp compound it was dark. Only a hellish glow came from beneath the burners for "individual cooking." And in the mess hall two kerosene lamps burned next to the serving window. And you could not read the slogan, nor see the double portion of nettle gruel in the bowl, and you sucked it down with your lips by feel.

And tomorrow would be the same and every day: six cars of red clay—three scoops of black gruel. In prison, too, we seemed to have grown weak, but here it went much faster. There was already a ringing in the head. That pleasant weakness, in which it is easier to give in than to fight back, kept coming closer.

And in the barracks—total darkness. We lay there dressed in everything wet on everything bare, and it seemed it was warmer not to take anything off—like a poultice.

Open eyes looked at the black ceiling, at the black heavens.

Good Lord! Good Lord! Beneath the shells and the bombs I begged you to preserve my life. And now I beg you, please send me death.

Chapter 7

■

The Way of Life and Customs of the Natives

To describe the native life in all its outward monotony would seem to be both very easy and very readily attainable. Yet it is very difficult at the same time. As with every different way of life, one has to describe the round of living from one morning until the next, from one winter to the next, from birth (arrival in one's first camp) until death (death). And simultaneously describe everything about all the many islands and islets that exist.

No one is capable of encompassing all this, of course, and it would merely be a bore to read whole volumes.

And the life of the natives consists of work, work, work; of starvation, cold, and cunning. This work, for those who are unable to push others out of the way and set themselves up in a soft spot, is that selfsame *general work* which raises socialism up out of the earth, and drives us down into the earth.

One cannot enumerate nor cover all the different aspects of this work, nor wrap your tongue about them. To push a wheelbarrow. ("Oh, the machine of the OSO, two handles and one wheel, so!") To carry hand barrows. To unload bricks barehanded (the skin quickly wears off the fingers). To haul bricks on one's own body by "goat" (in a shoulder barrow). To break up stone and coal in quarry and mine, to dig clay and sand. To hack out eight cubic yards of gold-bearing ore with a pick and haul them to the screening apparatus. Yes, and just to dig in the earth, just to "chew" up earth (flinty soil and in winter). To cut coal underground. And there are ores there too—lead and copper. Yes, and one can also . . . pulverize copper ore (a sweet taste in the mouth, and one waters at the nose). One can impregnate ties with creosote (and one's whole body at the same time too). One can carve out tunnels for railroads. And build roadbeds. One can dig peat in the bog, up to one's waist in the mud. One can smelt ores. One can cast metal. One can cut hay on hummocks in swampy meadows (sinking up to one's ankles in water). One can be a stableman or a drayman (yes, and steal oats from the horse's bag for one's own pot, but the horse is government-issue, the old grass-bag, and she'll last it out, most likely, but you can drop dead). Yes, and generally at the *"selkhozy"*—the Agricultural Camps—you can do every kind of peasant work (and there is no work better than that: you'll grab something from the ground for yourself).

But the father of all is our Russian forest with its genuinely golden tree trunks (gold is mined from them). And the oldest of all the kinds of work in the Archipelago is logging. It summons everyone to itself and has room for everyone, and it is not even out of bounds for cripples (they will send out a three-man gang of armless men to stamp down the foot-and-a-half snow). Snow comes up to your chest. You are a lumberjack. First you yourself stamp it down next to the tree trunk. You cut down the tree. Then, hardly able to make your way through the snow, you cut off all the branches (and you have to feel them out in the snow and get to them with your ax). Still dragging your way through the same loose snow, you have to carry off all the branches and make piles of them and burn them. (They smoke. They don't burn.) And now you have to saw up the wood to size and stack it. And the work norm for you and your brother for the day is six and a half cubic yards each, or thirteen cubic yards for two men working together. (In Burepolom the norm was nine cubic yards, but the thick pieces also had to be split into blocks.) By then your arms would not be capable of lifting an ax nor your feet of moving.

During the war years (on war rations), the camp inmates called three weeks at logging *"dry execution."*

You come to hate this forest, this beauty of the earth, whose praises have been sung in verse and prose. You come to walk beneath the arches of pine and birch with a shudder of revulsion! For decades in the future, you only have to shut your eyes to see those same fir and aspen trunks which you have hauled on your back to the freight car, sinking into the snow and falling down and hanging on to them tight, afraid to let go lest you prove unable to lift them out of the snowy mash.

Work at hard labor in Tsarist Russia was limited for decades by the Normative Statutes of 1869, which were actually issued for free persons. In assigning work, the physical strength of the worker and the degree to which he was accustomed to it were taken into consideration. (Can one nowadays really believe this?) The workday was set at seven hours (!) in winter and at twelve and a half hours in summer. At the ferocious Akatui hard-labor center (Yakubovich, in the 1890's) the work norms were *easily fulfilled* by everyone except him. The summer workday there amounted to eight hours, including *walking to and from work.* And from October on it was seven hours, and in winter only six. (And this was even before any struggle for the universal eight-hour workday!) As for Dostoyevsky's hard labor in Omsk, it is clear that in general they simply loafed about, as any reader can establish. The work there was agreeable and went with a swing, and the prison administration there even dressed them up in *white* linen jackets and trousers! Now, how much further could they have gone? In our camps they used to say: "You could even put on a white collar"—which meant things were very, very easy and there was absolutely nothing to do. And they had . . . even white jackets! After work the hard-labor convicts of the "House of the Dead" used to spend a long time *strolling* around the prison courtyard. That means that they were *not* totally fagged out! Indeed, the Tsarist censor did not want to pass the manuscript of *The House of the Dead* for fear that the *easiness* of the life depicted by Dostoyevsky would fail to deter people from crime. And so Dostoyevsky added new pages for the censor which demonstrated that life in hard labor was *nonetheless* hard![1] In our camps only the trusties went strolling around on Sundays, yes, and even they hesitated to. And Shalamov remarks with respect to the *Notes of Mariya Volkonskaya* that the Decembrist prisoners in Ner-

---

1. Letter of I. A. Gruzdev to Gorky. Gorky Archives, Vol. XI, Moscow, 1966, p. 157.

chinsk had a norm of 118 pounds of ore to mine and load each day. (One hundred and eighteen pounds! One could lift that all at once!) Whereas Shalamov on the Kolyma had a work norm per day of 28,800 pounds. And Shalamov writes that in addition their summer workday was sometimes sixteen hours long! I don't know how it was with sixteen, but for many it was thirteen hours long—on earth-moving work in Karlag and at the northern logging operations—and these were hours on the job itself, over and above the three miles' walk to the forest and three back. And anyway, why should we argue about the length of the day? After all, the *work norm* was senior in rank to the length of the workday, and when the brigade didn't fulfill the norm, the only thing that was changed at the end of the shift was the convoy, and the work sloggers were left in the woods by the light of searchlights until midnight—so that they got back to the camp just before morning in time to eat their dinner along with their breakfast and go out into the woods again.[2]

There is no one to tell about it either. They all died.

And then here's another way they raised the norms and proved it was possible to fulfill them: In cold lower than 60 degrees below zero, workdays were written off; in other words, on such days the records showed that the workers had not gone out to work; but they chased them out anyway, and whatever they squeezed out of them on those days was added to the other days, thereby raising the percentages. (And the servile Medical Section wrote off those who froze to death on such cold days on some other basis. And the ones who were left who could no longer walk and were straining every sinew to crawl along on all fours on the way back to camp, the convoy simply shot, so that they wouldn't escape before they could come back to get them.)

And how did they feed them in return? They poured water into a pot, and the best one might expect was that they would drop unscrubbed small potatoes into it, but otherwise black cabbage, beet tops, all kinds of trash. Or else vetch or bran, they didn't

2. Those who increase work norms in industry can still deceive themselves into thinking that such are the successes of the technology of production. But those who increase the norms of *physical labor* are executioners *par excellence!* They cannot seriously believe that under socialism the human being is twice as big and twice as muscular. They are the ones . . . who should be tried! They are the ones who should be sent out to fulfill those work norms!

begrudge these. (And wherever there was a water shortage, as there was at the Samarka Camp near Karaganda, only one bowl of gruel was cooked a day, and they also gave out a ration of two cups of turbid salty water.) Everything any good was always and without fail stolen for the chiefs (see Chapter 9), for the trusties, and for the thieves—the cooks were all terrorized, and it was only by submissiveness that they kept their jobs. Certain amounts of fat and meat "subproducts" (in other words, not real food) were signed out from the warehouses, as were fish, peas, and cereals. But not much of that ever found its way into the mouth of the pot. And in remote places the chiefs even took all the *salt* for themselves for their own pickling. (In 1940, on the Kotlas-Vorkuta Railroad, both the bread and the gruel were unsalted.) The worse the food, the more of it they gave the zeks. They used to give them horse meat from exhausted horses driven to death at work, and, even though it was quite impossible to chew it, it was a feast. Ivan Dobryak recalls today: "In my own time I have pushed no small amount of dolphin meat into my mouth, also walrus, seal, sea bear, and all kinds of other sea animal trash. [I interrupt: we ate whale meat in Moscow, at the Kaluga Gates.] I was not even afraid of animal feces. And as for willow herbs, lichens, wild camomile—they were the very best of dishes." (This means he himself *went out and added to* his rations.)

It was impossible to try to keep nourished on Gulag norms anyone who worked out in the bitter cold for thirteen or even ten hours. And it was completely impossible once the basic ration had been plundered. And this was where Frenkel's satanic mixing paddle was put into the boiling pot: some sloggers would be fed at the expense of others. The *pots* were divvied up; if less than 30 percent of the norm (and in each different camp this was calculated in a different way) was fulfilled, the ration issued you was a punishment block ration: 10½ ounces of bread and a bowl of gruel a day; for from 30 to 80 percent of norm they issued a penalty ration of 14 ounces of bread a day and two bowls of gruel; for from 81 to 100 percent you got a work ration of from 17½ to 21 ounces of bread and three bowls of gruel; and after that came the shock workers' pots, and they differed among themselves, running from 24½ to 31½ ounces of bread a day and supplementary kasha portions—two portions—and the *bonus dish*, which was some kind of dark, bitterish, rye-dough fingers stuffed with peas.

And for all this watery food which could not possibly cover what the body expended, the muscles burned up at body-rending toil, the shock workers and Stakhanovites went into the ground sooner than did the malingerers. This was something the old camp veterans understood very well, and it was covered by their own saying: *Better not to give me an extra kasha—and not to wake me up for work!* If such a happy stroke of fortune befalls you . . . as to be allowed to stay on your bunk for lack of clothing, you'll get the "guaranteed" twenty-one ounces. If they have dressed you up *for the season* (and this is a famous Gulag expression!) and taken you out to work on the canal—even if you wear your sledge hammer down to a chisel, you'll never get more than ten and a half ounces out of the frozen soil.

But the zek was not at liberty to stay on his bunk.

Of course, they did not feed the zeks so badly everywhere and always, but these are typical figures for Kraslag in wartime. At Vorkuta in that same period the miner's ration was in all likelihood the highest in all of Gulag (because heroic Moscow was being heated with that coal): it was 45½ ounces for 80 percent of norm underground or 100 percent on the surface. And in that most horribly murderous Tsarist hard-labor Akatui on a *nonworking* day (spent "on the bunk") they used to give out 2½ Russian pounds of bread (35 ounces) as well as 32 zolotniks (in other words, 4.65 ounces) of meat. And on a working day there they gave out 3 Russian pounds (43 ounces) of bread and 48 zolotniks (7 ounces) of meat. Was that not maybe higher than the front-line ration in the Red Army? And the Akatui prisoners carted off their gruel and their kasha by the tubful to the jailers' pigs. And P. Yakubovich found their thin porridge made from buckwheat kasha (! Gulag never ever saw that!) "inexpressibly repulsive to the taste." Danger of death from malnutrition is something else that never hung over the hard-labor convicts of Dostoyevsky's book. And what can you say if geese went wandering around (!!) in their prison yard ("in the camp compound") and the prisoners didn't wring their necks?[3] The bread at Tsarist

3. On the basis of the standards of many harsh camps Shalamov justly reproached me: "And what kind of a hospital *cat* was it that was walking around where you were? Why hadn't they killed it and eaten it long before?

Akatui was set out on their tables *unrestricted*, and at Christmas they were given a *pound* of beef and unlimited butter for their cereal. On Sakhalin the Tsarist prisoners working on roads and in mines during the months of the most work received each day 56 ounces of bread, 14 ounces of meat, 8¾ ounces of cereal! And the conscientious Chekhov investigated whether these norms were really enough, or whether, in view of the inferior quality of the baking and cooking, they fell short. And if he had looked into the bowl of our Soviet slogger, he would have given up the ghost right then and there.

What imagination at the beginning of our century could have pictured that "after thirty or forty years," not just on Sakhalin alone, but throughout the entire Archipelago, prisoners would be glad to get even more soggy, dirty, slack-baked bread, with ad-mixtures of the devil only knew what—and that 24½ ounces of it would be an enviable *shock-worker* ration?

No, even more! That throughout all Russia the collective farmers would even envy that prisoners' ration! "We don't get even that, after all!"

Even at the Tsar's Nerchinsk mines they gave a supplementary "gold prospectors' " payment for everything over the government norm (which was always moderate). In our camps, for most of the years of the Archipelago, they either paid nothing for labor or just as much as was required for soap and tooth powder. Only in those rare camps and in those short periods when for some reason they introduced *cost accounting* (and only from one-eighth to one-fourth of the genuine wage was credited to the prisoner) could the zeks buy bread, meat, and sugar. And all of a sudden—oh, astonishment!—a crust would be left on the mess hall table, and it might be there for all of five minutes without anyone reach-ing out a hand to grab it.

And how were our natives dressed and shod?

All archipelagoes are like all archipelagoes: the blue ocean rolls about them, coconut palms grow on them, and the adminis-tration of the islands does not assume the expense of clothing the

And why does Ivan Denisovich in your story carry a *spoon* with him, even though it is well known that everything cooked in camp can easily be drunk down as a liquid by *tipping up the bowl?*"

natives—they go about barefoot and almost naked. But as for our cursed Archipelago, it would have been quite impossible to picture it beneath the hot sun; it was eternally covered with snow and the blizzards eternally raged over it. And in addition to everything else it was necessary to clothe and to shoe all that horde of ten to fifteen million prisoners.[4]

Fortunately, born outside the bounds of the Archipelago, the zeks arrived here not altogether naked. They wore what they came in—more accurately, what the *socially friendly* elements might leave of it—except that as a brand of the Archipelago, a piece had to be torn off, just as they clip one ear of the ram; greatcoats have their flaps cut off diagonally, Budenny helmets have the high peak cut off so as to leave a draft through the top. But alas, the clothing of free men is not eternal, and footgear can be in shreds in a week from the stumps and hummocks of the Archipelago. And therefore it is necessary to clothe the natives, even though they have nothing with which to pay for the clothing.

Someday the Russian stage will yet see this sight! And the Russian cinema screen! The pea jackets one color and their sleeves another. Or so many patches on the pea jacket that its original cloth is totally invisible. Or a *flaming* pea jacket—with tatters on it like tongues of flame. Or patches on britches made from the wrappings of someone's food parcel from home, and for a long while to come one can still read the address written in the corner with an indelible pencil.[5]

And on their feet the tried and true Russian "lapti"—bast sandals—except that they had no decent "onuchi"—footcloths—to go with them. Or else they might have a piece of old automobile tire, tied right on the bare foot with a wire, an electric cord. (Grief has its own inventiveness. . . .) Or else there were "felt boots"— "burki"—put together from pieces of old, torn-up padded jackets, with soles made of a layer of thick felt and a layer of rubber.[6] In the morning at the gatehouse, hearing complaints about the

---

4. According to the estimates of the encyclopedia *Rossiya-SSSR*, there were up to fifteen million prisoners at a time. This figure agrees with the estimate made by prisoners inside the U.S.S.R., as we ourselves have added it up. Whenever they publish more proven figures, we will accept them.

5. In Tsarist Akatui the prisoners were given fur overcoats.

6. Neither Dostoyevsky, nor Chekhov, nor Yakubovich tells us what the prisoners of their own Tsarist times wore on their feet. But of course they were doubtless shod, otherwise they would have written about it.

cold, the chief of the camp would reply with his Gulag sense of humor:

"My goose out there goes around barefoot all winter long and doesn't complain, although it's true her feet are red. And all of you have got rubber overshoes."

And then, in addition, bronze-gray camp faces will appear on the screen. Eyes oozing with tears, red eyelids. White cracked lips, covered with sores. Skewbald, unshaven bristles on the faces. In winter . . . a summer cap with earflaps sewn on.

I recognize you! It is you, the inhabitants of my Archipelago!

But no matter how many hours there are in the working day—sooner or later sloggers will return to the barracks.

Their barracks? Sometimes it is a dugout, dug into the ground. And in the North more often . . . *a tent*—true, with earth banked and reinforced hit or miss with boards. Often there are kerosene lamps in place of electricity, but sometimes there are the ancient Russian "splinter lamps" or else cotton-wool wicks. (In Ust-Vym for two years they saw no kerosene, and even in headquarters barracks they got light from oil from the food store.) It is by this pitiful light that we will survey this ruined world.

Sleeping shelves in two stories, sleeping shelves in three stories, or, as a sign of luxury, "vagonki"—multiple bunks—the boards most often bare and nothing at all on them; on some of the work parties they steal so thoroughly (and then sell the spoils through the free employees) that nothing government-issue is given out and no one keeps anything of his own in the barracks; they take both their mess tins and their mugs to work with them (and even tote the bags containing their belongings—and thus laden they dig in the earth); those who have them put their blankets around their necks (a film scene!), or else lug their things to trusty friends in a guarded barracks. During the day the barracks are as empty as if uninhabited. At night they might turn over their wet work clothes to be dried in the drier (if there is a drier!)—but undressed like that you are going to freeze on the bare boards! And so they dry their clothes on themselves. At night their caps may freeze to the wall of the tent—or, in a woman's case, her hair. They even hide their bast sandals under their heads so they won't be stolen off their feet. (Burepolom during the war.) In the middle of the barracks there is an oil drum with holes in it which has been converted into a stove, and it is good when it gets red-hot—then the steamy odor of drying footcloths permeates the entire barracks—but it sometimes happens that the wet firewood in it doesn't burn. Some of the barracks are so infested with insects that even four days' fumigation with burning sulphur doesn't help and when in the summer the zeks go out to sleep on the ground in the camp compound the bedbugs crawl after them and find them even there. And the zeks boil the lice off their underwear in their mess tins after dining from them.

All this became possible only in the twentieth century, and comparison here with the prison chroniclers of the past century is to no avail; they didn't write of anything like this.

It is necessary to add to all this the picture of the way the brigade's bread is brought on a tray from the bread-cutting room into the mess hall under guard of the huskiest brigade members carrying staves—otherwise other prisoners will grab it, tear it apart, and run off with it. And the picture should also be added of the way food parcels from home are knocked out of the zeks' hands at the very moment they leave the parcel office. And also the constant alarm whether the camp administration is going to take away the rest day (and why talk about the war if for a whole year before the war they had not had one day off on the "Ukhta State Farm," and no one in Karlag could remember any rest days from 1937 right through 1945?). Then on top of everything one has to add the eternal impermanence of camp life, the fear of change: rumors about a prisoner transport; the prisoner transport itself (the hard labor of Dostoyevsky's time knew no prisoner transports, and for ten or even twenty years people served out their term in one prison, and that was a totally different kind of life); then some sort of dark and sudden shuffling of "contingents"—either a transfer "in the interests of production," or a "*commissioning*" by a medical review board, or inventory of property, or sudden night searches that involve undressing and the tearing apart of all the prisoners' meager rags—and then beyond that the thorough individual searches before the big holidays of May 1 and November 7 (the Christmas and Easter of hard labor in the past century knew nothing like this). And three times a month there were the fatal, ruinous baths. (To avoid repetition, I will not write about them here; there is a detailed story-investigation in Shalamov, and a story by Dombrovsky.)

And later there was that constant, clinging (and, for an intellectual, torturing) *lack of privacy*, the condition of not being an individual but a member of a brigade instead, and the necessity of acting for whole days and whole years not as you yourself have decided but as the brigade requires.

And one must remember as well that everything that has been said refers to the established camp in operation for some time. But that camp had to be *started* at some time and by someone (and by whom if not by our unhappy brother zeks, of course?): they came to a cold, snowy woods, they stretched wire on the trees, and whoever managed to survive until the first barracks knew those barracks would be for the guard anyway. In November, 1941, near the station of Reshoty, Camp No. 1 of Kraslag was opened (over a ten-year period they increased to seventeen). They drove 250 soldiers there, removed from the army to strengthen it morally. They cut timber, they built log frames, but there was nothing to cover the roofs with, and so they lived with iron stoves beneath the sky. The bread brought them was frozen, and they chopped it up with an ax, and gave it out in handfuls—broken up, crushed up, crumby. Their other food was heavily salted humpback salmon. It burned their mouths, and they eased the burning with snow.

(When you remember the heroes of the War of the Fatherland, do not forget these!)

Now that is the way of life of my Archipelago.

■

Philosophers, psychologists, medical men, and writers could have observed in our camps, as nowhere else, in detail and on a large scale the special process of the narrowing of the intellectual and spiritual horizons of a human being, the reduction of the human being to an animal and the process of dying alive. But the psychologists who got into our camps were for the most part not up to observing; they themselves had fallen into that very same stream that was dissolving the personality into feces and ash.

Just as nothing that contains life can exist without getting rid of its wastes, so the Archipelago could not keep swirling about without precipitating to the bottom its principal form of waste—the *last-leggers*. And everything built by the Archipelago had been squeezed out of the muscles of the last-leggers (before they became last-leggers). And those who survived, who reproach *the*

7. See Chapter 22.

last-leggers with being themselves to blame, must take upon themselves the disgrace of their own preserved lives.

And among the surviving, the orthodox Communists now write me lofty protests: How base are the thoughts and feelings of the heroes of your story *One Day in the Life of Ivan Denisovich!* Where are their anguished cogitations about the course of history? Everything is about bread rations and gruel, and yet there are sufferings much more unbearable than hunger.

Oh—so there are! Oh—so there are indeed much more unbearable sufferings (the sufferings of orthodox thought)? You in your medical sections and your storerooms, you never knew hunger there, orthodox loyalist gentlemen!

It has been known for centuries that Hunger . . . rules the world! (And all your Progressive Doctrine is, incidentally, built on Hunger, on the thesis that hungry people will inevitably revolt against the well-fed.) Hunger rules every hungry human being, unless he has himself consciously decided to die. Hunger, which forces an honest person to reach out and steal ("When the belly rumbles, conscience flees"). Hunger, which compels the most unselfish person to look with envy into someone else's bowl, and to try painfully to estimate what weight of ration his neighbor is receiving. Hunger, which darkens the brain and refuses to allow it to be distracted by anything else at all, or to think about anything else at all, or to speak about anything else at all except food, food, and food. Hunger, from which it is impossible to escape even in dreams—dreams are about food, and insomnia is over food. And soon—just insomnia. Hunger, after which one cannot even eat up; the man has by then turned into a one-way pipe and everything emerges from him in exactly the same state in which it was swallowed.

And this, too, the Russian cinema screen must see: how the last-leggers, jealously watching their competitors out of the corners of their eyes, stand duty at the kitchen porch waiting for them to bring out the slops in the dishwater. How they throw themselves on it, and fight with one another, seeking a fish head, a bone, vegetable parings. And how one last-legger dies, killed in that scrimmage. And how immediately afterward they wash off this waste and boil it and eat it. (And inquisitive cameramen can continue with their shooting and show us how, in 1947 in Dolinka, Bessarabian peasant women who had been brought in from *freedom* hurled themselves with that very same intent on slops which the last-leggers had *already checked over.*) The screen will show bags of bones which are still joined together lying under blankets at the hospital, dying almost without movement—and then being carried out. And on the whole . . . how simply a human being dies: he was speaking—and he fell silent; he was walking along the road—and he fell down. "Shudder and it's over." How (in camp at Unzha and Nuksha) the fat-faced, socially friendly work assigner jerks a zek by the legs to get him out to line-up—and he turns out to be dead, and the corpse falls on its head on the floor. "Croaked, the scum!" And he gaily gives him a kick for good measure. (At those camps during the war there was no doctor's aide, not even an orderly, and as a result there were no sick, and anyone who pretended to be sick was taken out to the woods in his comrades' arms, and they also took a board and rope along so they could drag the corpse back the more easily. At work they laid the sick person down next to the bonfire, and it was to the interest of both the zeks and the convoy to have him die the sooner.)

What the screen cannot catch will be described to us in slow, meticulous prose, which will distinguish between the nuances of the various paths to death, which are sometimes called scurvy, sometimes pellagra, sometimes alimentary dystrophy. For instance, if there is blood on your bread after you have taken a bite —that is scurvy. From then on your teeth begin to fall out, your gums rot, ulcers appear on your legs, your flesh will begin to fall off in whole chunks, and you will begin to smell like a corpse. Your bloated legs collapse. They refuse to take such cases into the hospital, and they crawl on all fours around the camp compound. But if your face grows dark and your skin begins to peel and your entire organism is racked by diarrhea, this is pellagra. It is necessary to halt the diarrhea somehow—so they take three spoons of chalk a day, and they say that in this case if you can get and eat a lot of herring the food will begin to hold. But where are you going to get herring? The man grows weaker, weaker, and the bigger he is, the faster it goes. He has already become so weak that he cannot climb to the top bunks, he cannot step across a log in his path; he has to lift his leg with his two hands or else crawl on all fours. The diarrhea takes out of a man both strength and all interest—in other people, in life, in himself. He grows deaf and stupid, and he loses all capacity to weep, even when he is being dragged along the ground behind a sledge. He is no longer afraid of death; he is wrapped in a submissive, rosy glow. He has crossed all boundaries and has forgotten the name of his wife, of his children, and finally his own name too. Sometimes the entire body of a man dying of starvation is covered with blue-black pimples like peas, with pus-filled heads smaller than a pinhead—his face, arms, legs, his trunk, even his scrotum. It is so painful he cannot be touched. The tiny boils come to a head and burst and a thick wormlike string of pus is forced out of them. The man is rotting alive.

If black astonished head lice are crawling on the face of your neighbor on the bunks, it is a sure sign of death.

Fie! What naturalism. Why keep talking about all that?

And that is what they usually say today, those who did not themselves suffer, who were themselves the executioners, or who have washed their hands of it, or who put on an innocent expression: Why remember all that? Why rake over old wounds? (*Their* wounds!!)

Lev Tolstoi had an answer for that—to Biryukov: "What do you mean, why remember? If I have had a terrible illness, and I have succeeded in recovering from it and been cleansed of it, I will always remember gladly. The only time I will refuse to remember is when I am still ill and have got worse, and when I wish to deceive myself. If we remember the old and look it straight in the face, then our new and present violence will also disclose itself."[8]

I want to conclude these pages about last-leggers with N.K.G.'s story about the engineer Lev Nikolayevich Y. (! indeed, this must, in view of the first name and patronymic, be in honor of Tolstoi!)—a last-legger theoretician who found the last-legger's pattern of existence to be the most convenient method of preserving his life.

Here is how the engineer Y. occupies himself in a remote corner of the camp compound on a hot Sunday: Something with a resemblance to a human being sits in a declivity above a pit in which brown peaty water has collected. Set out around the pit are sardine heads, fish bones, pieces of gristle, crusts of bread, lumps of cooked cereal, wet washed potato peelings, and something in addition which it is difficult even to name. A tiny bonfire has been built on a piece of tin, and above it hangs a soot-black-

8. Biryukov, *Razgovory s Tolstym* (*Conversations with Tolstoi*), Vol. 3–4, p. 48.

ened soldier's mess tin containing a broth. It seems to be ready! The last-legger begins to dip out the dark slops from the mess tin with a wooden spoon and to wash down with them one after another the potato peelings, the gristle, then the sardine heads. He keeps chewing away very, very slowly and deliberately (it's the common misfortune of last-leggers to gulp things down hastily without chewing). His nose can hardly be seen in the midst of the dark gray wool that covers his neck, his chin, his cheeks. His nose and his forehead are a waxy brown color and in places the skin is peeling. His eyes are teary and blink frequently.

Noticing the approach of an outsider, the last-legger quickly gathers up everything set out there which he has not yet eaten, presses his mess tin to his chest, falls to the ground, and curls up in a ball like a hedgehog. And now he can be beaten, shoved—but he is firmly on the ground, he won't stir, and he won't give up his mess tin.

N.K.G. speaks to him in a friendly voice—and the hedgehog uncurls a bit. He sees his visitor does not intend to beat him or take away his mess tin. A conversation ensues. They are both engineers (N.G. a geologist, and Y. a chemist), and now Y. discloses to G. his own faith. Basing himself on his still-remembered formulas for the chemical composition of substances, he demonstrates that one can get everything nutritionally necessary from refuse; one merely has to overcome one's squeamishness and direct all one's efforts to extracting nourishment from this source.

Notwithstanding the heat, Y. is dressed in several layers of clothes, all dirty. (And he had a basis for this too: Y. had established experimentally that lice and fleas will not multiply in *extremely* dirty clothing, as though they themselves were squeamish. Therefore he had even picked out for one of his undergarments a piece of wiping in the repair shop.)

Here was how he looked: He wore a Budenny helmet with a black candle stump in place of the spiked peak; the helmet was covered with scorch marks. In some places hay and in some places oakum adhered to the greasy elephant ears of the helmet. From his outer clothing torn pieces and tatters stuck out like tongues on his back and sides. Patches and patches. A layer of tar on one side. The cotton-wool lining was hanging out in a fringe along the hem. Both outer sleeves were torn to the elbows, and when the last-legger raised his arms—he looked like a bat shaking its wings. And on his feet were boatlike rubber overshoes glued together from red automobile tires.

Why was he dressed so warmly? In the first place, the summer was short and the winter long, and it was necessary to keep everything he had for the winter, and where else could he keep it except on himself? In the second place, the principal reason, he created by this means a soft and well-padded exterior, and thus did not feel pain when he was struck. He could be kicked and beaten with sticks without getting bruised. This was his one defense. All he had to do was be quick enough to see who was about to strike him, drop to the ground in time, pull his knees up to his stomach, thus covering it, press his head down to his chest and embrace it with his thickly padded arms. Then the only places they could hit him were padded. And so that no one should beat him for too long at a time—it was necessary quickly to give the person beating him a feeling of triumph. And to this end Y. had learned to howl hideously, like a piglet, from the very first blow, even though he wasn't hurting in the least. (For in camp they are very fond of beating up the weak—not only the work assigners and the brigadiers, but the ordinary zeks as well—so as not to feel completely weak themselves. And what was to be done if people simply could not believe in their own strength unless they subjected others to cruelty?)

And to Y. this seemed a fully endurable and reasonably chosen way of life—and one, in addition, which did not require him to soil his conscience! He did nobody harm!

He hoped to survive his term.

The interview with the last-legger is over.

■

In our glorious Fatherland, which was capable *for more than a hundred years* of not publishing the work of Chaadayev because of his reactionary views, you see, you are not likely to surprise anyone with the fact that the most important and boldest books are never read by contemporaries, never exercise an influence on popular thought in good time. And thus it is that I am writing this book solely from a sense of obligation—because too many stories and recollections have accumulated in my hands and I cannot allow them to perish. I do not expect to see it in print anywhere with my own eyes; and I have little hope that those who managed to drag their bones out of the Archipelago will ever read it; and I do not at all believe that it will explain the truth of our history in time for anything to be corrected. In the very heat of working on this book I was struck by the greatest shock of my life: The dragon emerged for one minute, licked up my novel with his wicked rough red tongue, and several other old works*— and retired behind the curtain for the time. But I can hear his breathing, and I know that his teeth are aimed at my neck, that it is just that my time is not up yet. And with devastated soul I am going to gather my strength to complete this investigation, so that it at least may escape the dragon's teeth. In the days when Sholokhov, who has long since ceased to be a writer, journeyed from this country of harried and arrested writers to receive a Nobel prize, I was trying to duck the dicks, seeking a hiding place and trying to win time for my clandestine, panting pen to complete this very book.

I have digressed, but what I wanted to say was that in our country the best books remain unknown to their contemporaries, and it is very possible that I am therefore vainly repeating the secret work of someone else, when, had I known of it, I could have made my own work shorter. But during the seven years of our frail and pale freedom some things did nevertheless emerge, despite everything, and one swimmer in the dawn-lit ocean has spied another head and cried out in a wheezy voice to him. And it was in this way that I learned of Shalamov's sixty camp stories and of his study of the thieves.

I want to declare here that, apart from several individual points on which we disagree, no difference of interpretation has ever arisen between us in explaining the Archipelago. He and I evaluate the whole native life in the same way. Shalamov's camp experience was more bitter and longer than mine, and I acknowledge with esteem that it fell to him rather than to me to plumb those depths of beastliness and despair to which the whole camp way of life was dragging us all down.

This, however, does not prohibit my raising objections to specific points on which we disagree. One such point is the evaluation of the camp Medical Section. Shalamov speaks with hate and gall (and rightly too!) of every camp establishment, but he always makes a biased exception solely for the Medical Section. He supports, if he does not create, a legend about the benign camp Medical Section. He affirms that everything in the camp was against the camp inmate except the doctor—he alone could help him.

That he *can* help still doesn't mean that he does. He *can* help, if he so desires, just as the construction superintendent, the norm setter, the bookkeeper, the storeroom clerk, the cook, the orderly, and the work assigner can too—but do many of them actually help?

Perhaps up to 1932, when the camp Medical Sections were still subordinate to the People's Commissariat of Health, the doctors could still be doctors. But in 1932 the Medical Sections were turned over in toto to Gulag—and it became their goal to help the oppressors and to be gravediggers. So, leaving aside the good cases with good doctors—just who would have kept those Medical Sections in the Archipelago at all if they had not served the common purpose?

When the commandant and the brigadier beat up on a last-legger because he refused to go out to work—so badly that he was left licking his wounds like a dog and lay unconscious for two days in a punishment cell (Babich), and for two months afterward could not even crawl down from the bunks—was it not the Medical Section (at Camp No. 1 of the Dzhida group of camps) that refused to draw up official certification of the beating and subsequently to treat him?

And who was it if not the Medical Section that signed every decree for imprisonment in the punishment block? (Incidentally, let us not lose sight of the fact that the chiefs did not have all that great a need for that doctor's signature. In the camp near the Indigirka, S. A. Chebotaryov was a free "*plasterer*" [a medical assistant—this term being, not by chance, a piece of camp slang too]. He did not sign a single one of the camp chief's decrees for imprisonment in the punishment block, since he considered that even a dog shouldn't be put in such a punishment block, let alone people; the stove only warmed the jailer out in the corridor. That was all right; incarcerations took place there without his signature.)

When, through the fault of the construction superintendent or the foreman, or because of the absence of fencing or safety precautions, a zek died at work, who was it if not the medical assistant and the Medical Section that signed the certificate attesting that he had died of a heart attack? (And what that meant was that everything could be left just as it was and tomorrow others would die. Otherwise, the medical assistant would soon be working at the mine face himself! And the doctor too!)

When quarterly *commissioning* took place—that comedy of general medical examination of the camp population with assignment to categories: TFT (Heavy Physical Labor), SFT (Average Physical Labor), LFT (Light Physical Labor), and IFT (Individual Physical Labor)—were there many good doctors who opposed the evil chief of the Medical Section, who was kept in his job only because he supplied columns for heavy labor?

Or perhaps the Medical Section was at least merciful to those willing to sacrifice a part of their own bodies in order to save the rest? Everyone knows the law, not just in one camp or another: Self-mutilators, self-maimers, and *self-incapacitators* were *refused* all medical help! This was an administration order, but who actually *refused* the help? The doctors . . . Let's say you've blown off four of your fingers with a dynamite cap, and you've come to the infirmary—they give you no bandage: Drop dead, dog! And back at the Moscow-Volga Canal during the wave of universal competition, for some reason (?) too many cases of self-maiming suddenly appeared. And there was an immediate explanation: this was a sally of the class enemy. And was one then to treat them? (Of course, much depended here on the cleverness of the zek who had maimed himself: it was possible to do it in such a way that it could not be proved. And Bernshtein scalded his hand adroitly with boiling water poured through a cloth—and thus saved his life. Another might adroitly freeze his hand by not wearing a mitten or else urinate in his felt boots and go out into the bitter cold. But you couldn't take everything into account: gangrene could set in and death would follow. Sometimes there were cases of unforeseen self-incapacitation: Babich's unhealing scurvy ulcers were diagnosed as syphilis and there was nowhere to make a blood test; he thereupon cheerfully lied that he and his entire family had syphilis. He was moved into the venereal-disease zone of the camp and by this means he postponed his death.)

Was there ever a time when the Medical Section excused from work all the prisoners genuinely ill on a given day? Or when it didn't drive a given number of seriously ill people out of the camp compound to work? Dr. Suleimanov refused to put Pyotr

Kishkin, the hero and comedian of the zek people, into the hospital because his diarrhea did not satisfy the norm: every half-hour, and it had to be bleeding. So when the column formed up to go to the work site, Kishkin *sat down*, running the risk of getting shot. But the convoy turned out to be more merciful than the doctor: they stopped a passing car and sent Kishkin to the hospital. People will object that the Medical Section was held to a strictly limited percentage of Group "C"—inpatients and ambulatory cases.[9] So there was an explanation in every case, but in every case there also remained a cruelty in no wise outweighed by the consideration that "on the other hand" they were doing good to "someone else."

And then we have to bring in here the horrible camp hospitals, like the one at Camp No. 2 of Krivoshchekovo: a small reception room, a toilet, and a hospital room. The toilet stank and filled the hospital air, but was that the worst of it? In each hospital cot lay *two* diarrhea patients, and others were lying on the floor between cots. Those who had grown weak evacuated in their cots. There were no linens or medicines (1948–1949). The hospital was run by a third-year medical student (a 58 himself). He was desperate, but there was nothing he could do. The hospital orderlies who were supposed to feed the patients were strong, fat young fellows. They ate the patients' food, stealing from their hospital ration. Who had put them in their cushy spots? The *godfather*, no doubt. The student didn't have the strength to get rid of them or defend the patients' rations. But would any doctor have had it either?[10]

Or could it possibly be contended that the Medical Section in every camp was able to insist on really human nutrition? Well, at least to the extent of not having those "night-blind brigades"

9. Doctors got around that as best they could. In Sym Camp they organized a semihospital; the last-leggers lay there on their pea jackets and went out to shovel snow, but were fed from the hospital rations. The free chief of the Medical Department, A. M. Statnikov, got around the Group "C" quota in the following way: he cut back on the hospitals in the working compounds but in turn expanded the hospital camps, i.e., camps entirely for the sick. In the official Gulag documents they sometimes even wrote: "Raise the *physical fitness* of the zeks"—but they refused to give any funds for this purpose. In fact, the very complexity of these subterfuges of honest physicians proves that the Medical Sections were not allowed to interfere with the death process.

10. Dostoyevsky entered the hospital without any hindrance. And the Medical Section in his prison was the same for both prisoners and convoy. What immaturity!

returning from work in the evenings in a line of the night-blind, clinging to one another? No. If by some miracle some intervention did secure an improvement in nutrition, it would only have been the work administration, so as to have strong sloggers. And certainly never the Medical Section.

No one is blaming the physicians for all this (though their courage to resist was often weak because they were afraid of being sent to general work), but the legends about the saviors from the Medical Sections aren't needed either. Like every branch of the camp administration, the Medical Section, too, was born of the devil and filled with the devil's blood.

Continuing his thought, Shalamov says that the prisoner in camp could count only on the Medical Section and that he could not count on the work of his own hands, that he did not dare: this led to the grave. "In camp it is not the small ration that kills but the big one."

The saying is true: The big ration is the one that kills. In one season of hauling timber the strongest slogger would end up a hopeless last-legger himself. At that point he would be certified a temporary invalid: fourteen ounces of bread and gruel from the bottom-ranking "pot." During the winter, a number of such people died (well, say 725 out of 800). The rest of them went onto "light physical" work and died on that.

So what other way out can we offer Ivan Denisovich if they are unwilling to take him on as a medical assistant or a hospital attendant, and also won't fake him a release from work for even one day? If he is too short on schooling and too long on conscience—to get himself fixed up with a job as trusty in the camp compound? Is there any other course left him than to put his trust in his own two hands? What about the Rest Point (the OP)? What about maiming himself? And what about early release on medical grounds—"aktirovka"?

Let Ivan Denisovich talk about them in his own words. For he has given them plenty of thought. He had the time.

"The Rest Point—the OP—that's like a camp rest home. Tens of years the zeks bend their backs, don't get vacations, so they have Rest Points—for two weeks. They feed much better there and they're not driven outside the camp compound to work, and in the compound they only put in three, four hours of real easy work: pounding rocks to pave roads, cleaning up the compound, or making repairs. And if there were half a thousand people in the camp—they'd open a Rest Point for fifteen. And then if everything had been divided up honestly, everyone would have gotten Rest Point once in just over a year. But just as there was no justice in anything in camp, there was especially none with Rest Points. They would open up a Rest Point sneakily, the way a dog snaps, and right off there would be lists ready for three whole shifts there. Then they would shut it down quick as a wink too—it wouldn't last half a year. The types who pushed in would be the bookkeepers, barbers, shoemakers, tailors—the whole aristocracy, with just a few real sloggers thrown in for the look of the thing—the best workers, they said. And then the tailor Beremblyum would shove under your nose, 'I made a fur coat for somebody outside and a thousand rubles was paid the camp cashier for it, and you, idiot, haul beams a whole month and the camp doesn't even get a hundred rubles for you, so who's the best worker? Who should get Rest Point?' And so there you go around, your heart bleeding, trying to figure how to get into Rest Point just to catch your breath a little bit, and before you look around it has already been shut down, and that's the end of it. And the sorest point of all is that at least they could enter in your prison file that you had been at a Rest Point in such and such a year—it wasn't that they didn't have enough bookkeepers in camp. No, they wouldn't. Because it was no good to them. The next year they'd open up a Rest Point again—and again Beremblyum would be in the first shift, and again you'd be bypassed. In the course of ten years they'd roll you sideways through ten camps and in the tenth you'd beg them just to let you poke your nose in the OP to see what it was like, whether the walls were painted decently and so on, because after all you'd never been in one your whole term—but how could you prove it?

"No, no point in getting worked up about the Rest Points.

"But maiming yourself was another matter. To cripple yourself but still stay alive and become an invalid. As they say: one minute's endurance—and a year of loafing. Break your leg, and then stop the bone from knitting right. Drink salt water and swell up. And smoke tea—spoil your heart. Or drink stewed tobacco —good for wrecking the lungs. But you had to be careful not to overdo, hurting yourself so badly that you leapfrogged invalidism into the grave. And who knew just how far to go?

"In many ways, an invalid didn't have things too bad: he might be able to get himself a spot in the cookhouse, or the bast-sandal shop. But the main thing smart people were looking for in making themselves invalids was early release on health grounds— 'aktirovka.' Except that 'aktirovka,' especially in waves, was even harder than getting into Rest Points. They got together a commission, inspected the invalids, and for the very worst of them wrote up an 'act'—a certificate: from such and such a date, because of state of health, so-and-so is classified as unsuited to serve out his term further, and we petition for his release.

"We only *petition!* And while this certificate proceeded upward to the higher-ups and then back down again you could cash in your chips. That happened often. After all, the higher-ups were sly bastards. They released ahead of time on health grounds those who were going to kick the bucket in a month anyway.[11] And also the ones who could pay well. There was a confederate of Kalikman who had got away with half a million—she paid a hundred thousand—and went free. Not like us fools.

"There used to be a book* going around the barracks, and the students read it aloud in their corner. In it there was one fellow who got himself a million and didn't know what to do with his million under Soviet power—there wasn't supposed to be anything to buy, and you could die of starvation with it, with that million. We used to laugh: Tell that bull to someone else. As for us, we've seen quite a few of those millionaires walk out of camp too. You can't buy God's health back for a million, but you can buy freedom, and buy power, and buy people too, lock, stock, and barrel. And there are oh, oh, oh, so many of those who have piled up millions out in freedom too; only they just don't shout it from the housetops or wave their arms about when they have it.

"But for the 58's early release for health is a closed door. During all the time the camps have existed, they say that maybe three times, for a month apiece, prisoners sentenced under Section 10 were released early for health, and then that door, too,

---

11. In O. Volkov's story "Grandfathers," those old men released for bad health were driven out of camp, but they had nowhere to go, and hung on right in the vicinity to die—without the bread ration and shelter they had in camp.

was slammed shut. And no one will take money from them, from the enemies of the people. If you did, you'd be putting your own head on the block in place of theirs. Yes, and they don't have any money, those 'politicians.' "

"What do you mean, Ivan Denisych, *they* don't have any?"

"Well, all right, we don't have any. . . ."

■

But there is one form of *early release* that no bluecap can take away from the prisoner. This release is—death.

And this is the most basic, the steadiest form of Archipelago output there is—with no norms.

From the fall of 1938 to February, 1939, at one of the Ust-Vym camps, 385 out of 550 prisoners died. Certain work brigades (Ogurtsov) died off totally, including the brigadiers. In the autumn of 1941, Pechorlag (the railroad camp) had a listed population of fifty thousand prisoners, and in the spring of 1942, ten thousand. *During this period not one prisoner transport was sent out of Pechorlag anywhere*—so *where* did the *forty thousand* prisoners go? I have written *thousand* here in italics—why? Because I learned these figures accidentally from a zek who had access to them. But you would not be able to get them for all camps in all periods nor to total them up. In the central sector of Burepolom Camp, in the barracks housing the last-leggers, in February, 1943, out of fifty people there were never fewer than four deaths a night, and one night there were twelve. In the morning their places were taken by new last-leggers who dreamed of recuperating on a diet of thin *magara** gruel and fourteen ounces of bread.

Corpses withered from pellagra (no buttocks, and women with no breasts), or rotting from scurvy, were checked out in the morgue cabin and sometimes in the open air. This was seldom like an autopsy—a long vertical cut from neck to crotch, breaking leg bones, pulling the skull apart at its seam. Mostly it was not a surgeon but a convoy guard who *verified* the corpse —to be certain the zek was really dead and not pretending. And for this they ran the corpse through with a bayonet or smashed the skull with a big mallet. And right there they tied to the big toe of the corpse's right foot a tag with his prison file number, under which he was identified in the prison lists.

At one time they used to bury them in their underwear but later on in the very worst, lowest-grade, which was dirty gray. And then came an across-the-board regulation not to waste any underwear on them at all (it could still be used for the living) but to bury them naked.

At one time in Old Russia it was thought that a corpse could not get along without a coffin. Even the lowliest serfs, beggars, and tramps were buried in coffins. Even the Sakhalin and the Akatui hard-labor prisoners were buried in coffins. But in the Archipelago this would have amounted to the unproductive expenditure of millions on labor and lumber. When at Inta after the war one honored foreman of the woodworking plant was actually buried in a coffin, the Cultural and Educational Section was instructed to make propaganda: Work well *and you, too, will be buried in a wooden coffin.*

The corpses were hauled away on sledges or on carts, depending on the time of year. Sometimes, for convenience, they used one box for six corpses, and if there were no boxes, then they tied the hands and legs with cord so they didn't flop about. After this they piled them up like logs and covered them with bast matting. If there was ammonal available, a special brigade of gravediggers would dynamite pits for them. Otherwise they had to dig the graves, always common graves, in the ground: either big ones for a large number or shallow ones for four at a time. (In the springtime, a stink used to waft into the camp from the shallower graves, and they would then send last-leggers to deepen them.)

On the other hand, no one can accuse us of gas chambers.

Where there was more time to spare on such things—as, for example, in Kengir—they would set out little posts on the hillocks, and a representative of the Records and Classification Section, no less, would personally inscribe on them the inventory numbers of those buried there. However, in Kengir someone also did some wrecking: Mothers and wives who came there were shown the cemetery and they went there to mourn and weep. Thereupon the chief of Steplag, Comrade Colonel Chechev, ordered the bulldozers to bulldoze down the little grave posts and level off the hillocks—because of this lack of gratitude.

Now that, fair reader, is how your father, your husband, your brother, was buried.

And that is how the path of the native and his way of life . . . come to an end.

But as a matter of fact it was Pavel Bykov who said: "Until twenty-four hours have passed after death, don't be so sure that it's all over."

■

"Well, Ivan Denisovich, what is there left that we haven't yet recounted? From the routine of our daily lives?"

"Whooo! You haven't even begun. It would take as many years as you served to tell it all. Like about the zek who broke formation to chase a cigarette butt and the convoy guard shot him.[12] How the invalid zeks in the kitchen gulped down raw potatoes: once cooked they'd not get any. How tea was used in place of money in camps. How they used to *brew up a superstrong tea mix*—1¾ ounces to a glass—and get a high. But that was mostly the thieves. They used to buy tea from the free employees with stolen money.

"And how did a zek manage to live on the whole? If he couldn't manage to weave string from sand—if he wasn't both tight-fisted and ingenious—he couldn't survive. Even in his sleep the zek had to keep thinking how to dodge and twist his way through the next day. And if you got your hands on something, or sniffed out some loophole—then keep your mouth shut! Keep it shut, or else the guys next to you would find out—and mess it all up. That's how it is in camp: there just isn't enough for everyone anyway, so see to it there's enough for you.

"Well that's as may be, but still—even in camp you have the old human custom of making friends. Not only old friendships—codefendants or comrades from out in freedom—but new ones made here. People's hearts went out to each other and they confided in each other. Buddies! Whatever we have we—share, and whatever we don't—fifty-fifty. It's true that we keep our precious bread ration separate, but everything gotten hold of otherwise is cooked in one mess tin and ladled from the same one.[13]

12. In Dostoyevsky's time a prisoner could leave formation to beg alms. And in formation the prisoners used to chat and sing.
13. For some reason, in the hard-labor regime described by Dostoyevsky friendship did not flourish and no one paired off even to eat.

"There were buddies who stayed together a short time and others who stayed together a long time. Some pairings were based . . . on conscience and others . . . on deceit. Like a snake, the 'godfather' used to like to crawl in between such friendships. Over a common mess tin and in a whisper you'd talk about everything.

"The old zeks admit and the former POW's will tell you too: The one who sells you down the river is the one who ate from the mess tin with you.

"And that's also a partial truth.

"But the best deal is not to have a buddy but a girl buddy. A camp wife, a zechka.* As they used to say, to get *submarried*. What was good if you were young was to ———— her somewhere in a one-night shack-up, and that would do your soul good. And even for an old, weak guy it was still good. You could get something anyway, earn a favor, maybe she would do your washing for you, bring it to your barracks, put your shirt under your pillow, and no one would laugh—it was *in the law*. She would cook for you too, you would sit down on your cot next to each other and eat. And that kind of camp espousal would suit even an old chap particularly well, just barely warm with a little touch of bitter flavor. You'd look at her through the steam from the mess pot—and there were wrinkles on her face, yes, and on your own too. You were both in gray camp rags, your padded jackets were all stained with rust and clay and lime and alabaster and lubricating grease. You never knew her before, and you had never set foot on her native soil, and she didn't talk like one of 'ours' either. And out in freedom her children were growing up, and yours too. And she had left a husband there too— who was skirt-chasing. And your own wife had been left alone too, and she wasn't letting the grass grow under her feet either: after all, eight years, ten years, everyone wants to live. And this, your camp wife, drags the same chain as you do and doesn't complain.

"And we live—not like people. And we die—not like parents.

"Some zeks got visits from their real wives. In various camps under various chiefs they were allowed to sit together for twenty minutes in the gatehouse. And there were even cases where they spent a night or two together in a separate shack. If you were a 150 percenter. But these visits were nothing more than poison. Why touch her with your hands and talk with her about something if you still had years and years to go before living with her again? It split the men in two. With a camp wife everything is clearer: Between us we have one cup of grits left; they say we're going to get burnt sugar this coming week. It won't be white, of course, the rats . . . Lathe operator Rodichev's wife came to visit him, and just before she arrived his shack-up bit him on the neck while making love. Rodichev swore a blue streak because his wife was coming, and off he went to the Medical Section to get a bandage put on his bruise: I can say I caught cold.

"And what kind of women were there in camp? There were women thieves and there were loose women and there were politicals, but most of all there were lowly and humble women sent there under the decree. They were all sent up under the decree for theft of state property. During and after the war, who crowded all the factories full? Women and girls. And who had to feed the family? They. And what were they to feed the family with? Need knows no law. And so they would pilfer: they used to put sour cream in their pockets, sneak out rolls between their legs, wind stockings around their waists, and the likeliest way was to go to work barefoot and grab new stockings there at work, put them on and wash them at home and take them to the open market to sell. Whoever produced something would swipe that. They would stick a spool of thread between their breasts. All the watchmen had been bribed, for they had to live too, and they only picked off a few, hit or miss. And then the guard would jump in and there would be a body search—and it was ten years for that shitty spool! The same as for treason! And thousands got caught with those spools.

"Everyone was on the take to the extent that her work permitted it. Nastya Gurkina had it good—she used to work in the baggage cars. And she reasoned things out quite correctly: Our own Soviet people are persistent bastards and they'll jump at your throat just for a lousy towel. Therefore she never touched Soviet suitcases and cleaned out only foreigners'. The foreigner, she said, wouldn't even think to check up on his things in time, and by the time he found out about it, he wouldn't bother to write a complaint, and all he would do was spit out: "Russian thieves!" And he would go back to his own country.

"Shitarev, an old bookkeeper, used to reproach Nastya: 'You ought to be ashamed of yourself, you're just a piece of meat!

Why didn't you think about the honor of Russia?' And she would tell him off: 'Up yours, and stand still for it too! Why didn't *you* worry about Victory? You used to let all those gentlemen officers go home to play stud dog.' (Shitarev had been a hospital bookkeeper during the war, and the officers used to grease his palm so that he would extend their period of sick leave by forging their travel documents, and they could go home before returning to the front. This was very serious. Shitarev had been sentenced to be shot, and only later was his sentence commuted to a 'tenner.')

"Of course, there were all kinds of unfortunates serving time as well. One woman got a 'fiver' for fraud: her husband had died in the middle of the month and she went on collecting his bread rations till the end of the month without turning the card in, using it for herself and for her two children. Her neighbors informed on her out of jealousy. She served four years too—and one year was knocked off by the amnesty.

"And this could happen too: A house was bombed out, the wife and children were killed and the husband was left. All the ration cards were burned, but the husband was out of his mind and lived through the whole thirteen days until the end of the month without bread rations and did not ask for a ration card for himself. Therefore they suspected that all his ration cards were intact. They gave him three years. And he served one and a half of the three."

Now just a minute there, just a minute, Ivan Denisych, that's all for another time. And so you are telling us about a girl buddy, right? About "submarriage"? She drags the same chain you do —and doesn't complain?

Chapter 8

∎

Women in Camp

And how could one not think of them, even back during interrogation? After all, they were somewhere here in neighboring cells! In this very same prison, under this very same regimen, enduring this unbearable interrogation—and how could they bear it, such weak beings?

The corridors were soundless, and you could not distinguish their walk or the rustle of their dresses. But one day, one of the Butyrki jailers was fussing with a lock, and left our men's cell to stand half a minute at the windows in the well-lit upper corridor, and, peering underneath the "muzzle" of a corridor window, we suddenly saw down below, in the little green garden on a corner of asphalt, standing in line in pairs like us—and also waiting for a door to be opened—women's shoes and ankles! All we could see were just ankles and shoes, but on high heels! And it was like a Wagnerian blast from *Tristan and Isolde*. We could see no higher than that and the jailer was already driving us into the cell, and once inside we raved there, illumined and at the same time beclouded, and we pictured all the rest to ourselves, imagining them as heavenly beings dying of despondency. What were they like? What were they like!

But it seems that things were no harder for them and maybe even easier. I have so far found nothing in women's recollections of interrogation which could lead me to conclude that they were any more disheartened than we were or that they became any more deeply depressed. The gynecologist N. I. Zubov, who served ten years himself and who in camp was constantly engaged in treating and observing women, says, to be sure, that statistically women react more swiftly and more sharply to arrest than men and to its principal effect—the loss of the family. The woman arrested is spiritually wounded and this expresses itself most often in the cessation of the vulnerable female functions.

But what particularly surprised me in the women's recollections of interrogation was what "trifles" from a prisoner's point of view (but not at all from a woman's) they could be thinking about there. Nadya Surovtseva, pretty and still young, hastily pulled on stockings that didn't match to go to her interrogation, and there in the interrogator's office she was embarrassed because the interrogator kept looking at her legs. You would think she should be saying: The hell with him! Horseradish on his snoot! It wasn't as if she were going to the theater with him, and besides she was almost a doctor of philosophy—in the Western sense— and a fervid political partisan—so who would have thought it! And Aleksandra Ostretsova, imprisoned in the Big Lubyanka in 1943, told me later on in camp that they used to kid around in there: they would hide under the table and the scared jailer would come in to look for the one who was missing; or they would paint themselves red with beet juice and go out like that for their walk. Or already summoned to interrogation, she would have an animated discussion with her cellmates whether she should dress simply that day or put on her evening dress. True, Ostretsova was at that time a spoiled, naughty young girl and was imprisoned with young Mira Uborevich. But another prisoner, N. I. P——va, older and a scientist, used to sharpen her aluminum spoon in her cell. And why do you think—to cut her throat? No, to cut off her braids (and she did cut them off)!

Subsequently, in the yard at Krasnaya Presnya I happened to be next to a prisoner transport of women who like us had been recently sentenced. And with astonishment I saw that they were not so thin, not so emaciated and pale as we were. Equal prison rations for all and equal prison torments turn out on the average to be easier for women. They do not weaken so quickly from hunger.

But of course for all of us, and for women in particular, prison was just the flower. The berries came later—camp. And it was precisely in camp that the women would either be broken or else, by bending and degenerating, adapt themselves.

In camp it was the opposite—everything was harder for the women than for us men. Beginning with the camp filth. Having already suffered from the dirt in the transit prisons and on the prisoner transports themselves, the woman would then find no cleanliness in camp either. In the average camp, in the women's work brigades, and also, it goes without saying, in the common barracks, it was almost never possible for her to feel really clean, to get warm water (and sometimes there was no water at all: in winter at Krivoshchekovo Camp No. 1 it was impossible to wash anywhere in the whole place. The only water was frozen and there was nowhere to thaw it). There was no lawful way a woman could lay hands on either cheesecloth or rags. No place there, of course, to do laundry!

A bath? Well! The initial arrival in camp began with a bath— if one doesn't take into account the unloading of the zeks from the cattle car onto the snow, and the march across with one's things on one's back surrounded by convoy and dogs. In the camp bath the naked women were examined like merchandise. Whether there was water in the bath or not, the inspection for lice, the shaving of armpits and pubic hair, gave the barbers, by no means the lowest-ranking aristocrats in the camp, the opportunity to look over the new women. And immediately after that they would be inspected by the other trusties. This was a tradition going right back to the Solovetsky Islands. Except that there, at the dawn of the Archipelago, a shyness still existed, not typical of the natives—and they were inspected clothed, during auxiliary work. But the Archipelago hardened, and the procedure became more brazen. Fedot S. and his wife (it was their fate to be united!) now recollect with amusement how the male trusties stood on either side of a narrow corridor and passed the newly arrived women through the corridor naked, not all at once, but one at a time. And then the trusties decided among themselves who got whom. (According to the statistics of the twenties there was one woman serving time for every six or seven men.[1] After the decrees of the thirties and forties the proportion of women to men rose substantially—but still not sufficiently for women not to be valued, particularly the attractive ones.) In certain camps a polite procedure was preserved: The women were conducted to

1. Vyshinsky, *op. cit.*, p. 358.

their barracks—and then the well-fed, self-confident, and impudent trusties entered the barracks, dressed in new padded jackets (any clothing in camp which was not in tatters and soiled seemed mad foppery). Slowly and deliberately they strolled between the bunks and made their choices. They sat down and chatted. They invited their choices to "visit" them. And they were living, too, not in a common-barracks situation, but in cabins occupied by several men. And there they had hot plates and frying pans. And they had fried potatoes too! An unbelievable dream! The first time, the chosen women were simply feasted and given the chance to make comparisons and to discover the whole spectrum of camp life. Impatient trusties demanded "payment" right after the potatoes, while those more restrained escorted their dates home and explained the future. You'd better make your arrangements, make your arrangements, inside *the camp compound*, darling, while it is being proposed in a gentlemanly way. There's cleanliness here, and laundry facilities, and decent clothes and unfatiguing work—and it's all yours.

And in this sense it is considered to have been "easier" for women in camp. It was "easier" for women to preserve life itself. And with that "sexual hatred" with which certain of the lastleggers looked on those women in camp who had not descended to pickings from the slops, it was natural to reason that it was easier for women in camp, since they could get along on a lesser ration, and had a way to avoid starvation and remain alive. For the man crazed by hunger the entire world is overshadowed by the wings of hunger, and nothing else in the world is of any importance.

And it is true there are women who by their own nature, out in freedom too, by and large, get together with men easily, without being choosy. Such women, of course, always had open to them easy ways out. Personal characteristics do not get distributed simply on the basis of the *articles* of the Criminal Code, yet we are not likely to be in error if we say that the majority of women among the 58's were not of this kind. For some of them, from the beginning to the end, this step was less bearable than death. Others would bridle, hesitate, be embarrassed (and they were held back by shame before their girl friends too), and when they had finally decided, when they had reconciled themselves—it might be too late, they might not find a camp taker any longer.

Because not every one was lucky enough *to get propositioned*.

Thus many of them gave in during the first few days. The future looked too cruel—and there was no hope at all. And this choice was made by those who were almost little girls, along with solidly married women and mothers of families. And it was the little girls in particular, stifled by the crudity of camp life, who quickly became the most reckless of all.

What if you said . . . no? All right, that's your lookout! Put on britches and pea jacket. And go marching off to the woods, with your formless, fat exterior, and your frail inner being. You'll come crawling yet. You'll go down on bended knees.

If you have arrived in camp in good physical shape, and if you have made a *wise* decision at the very beginning—then you are all set for a long stay, in the Medical Section, in the kitchen, in the bookkeeping office, in the sewing shop or in the laundry, and the years will flow past comfortably enough, quite like out in freedom. And if a prisoner transport comes your way, you will arrive in your new place, too, in full flower, and you will already know how to act there from the very start. One of the most successful moves you can make . . . is to become a servant to one of the chiefs. When I.N. arrived in camp on a new prisoner transport, she was a portly, well-preserved woman, who for many years had been the prosperous wife of a high army commander. The chief of the Records and Classification Section immediately spotted her and gave her the post of honor of washing floors in the chief's office. And that is how she began serving out her term in a soft spot, fully aware that this was a piece of luck.

And what of it if you loved someone out in freedom and wanted to remain true to him? What profit is there in the fidelity of a female corpse? *"When you get back to freedom—who is going to need you?"* Those were the words which kept ringing eternally through the women's barracks. You grow coarse and old and your last years as a woman are cheerless and empty. Isn't it smarter to hurry up and grab something too, even from this savage life?

And it was all made easier by the fact that no one here condemned anyone else. "Everyone lives like that here."

And hands were also untied by the fact that there was no meaning, no purpose, left in life.

Those who did not give in right off . . . either changed their minds or else were compelled to anyway. And even the most stubborn of all, if she was good-looking, would give in, give in and go to bed under duress: give in!

In our minicamp at the Kaluga Gates in Moscow there was a proud wench, M., a former lieutenant and a sniper. She was like a princess in a fairy tale: crimson lips, the bearing of a swan, jet-black locks.[2] And the fat, dirty old stock clerk, Isaak Bershader, decided to buy her. He was nauseating in appearance —and to her, in view of her own resilient beauty, her own recent heroic life, he was particularly repulsive. He was a rotten snag and she was a tall beautiful poplar. But he besieged her so persistently and hard she could hardly breathe. He not only condemned her to general work. (All the trusties acted in concert and helped him in his entrapment.) She was subjected to harassment by the jailers. (He also had the jailers on his *hook*.) And he even threatened her with an assuredly bad prisoner transport to far away. And one evening, when the lights had gone out in the camp, I myself saw how, in a twilight pale because of snow and sky, M. went like a shadow from the women's barracks and knocked with bent head at this greedy Bershader's storeroom. After that she was well taken care of inside the camp compound.

M.N., who was already middle-aged, and a draftsman out in freedom, the mother of two children, who had lost her husband in prison, had already gone far along the path of a last-legger in the women's logging brigade—and still kept on being stubborn, and was close to the point of no return. Her legs swelled up. She stumbled back from work at the tail end of the column, and the convoy would drive her along with blows of their gunstocks. One day she somehow stayed behind in the compound. The cook *played up to her*: Come on over to my cabin. I will feed you a bellyful. She went. He put a big frying pan of fried potatoes and pork in front of her. She ate it all up. But after she had paid for it she threw up—and the potatoes were all lost. The cook swore at her: "Just think! What a princess!" And from then on she got used to it gradually. She got in a better position. And later, sitting at a camp film showing, she would pick out a man for the night.

And anyone who went on waiting longer . . . would have to drag herself to the men's common barracks on her own—not

2. In my play* I portrayed her under the name Granya Zybina, but there I endowed her with a better fate than the one she actually had.

to the trusties by this time—and walk down the aisles between the bunks repeating monotonously, "Half a kilo, half a kilo." And if a rescuer would go with her for a bread ration, then she would curtain off her bunk with sheets on three sides and in this tent, this shack (hence "shack-up"), earn her bread. If the jailer didn't catch her first.

A multiple bunk curtained off with rags from the neighboring women was a classic camp scene. But things could be a great deal simpler than that too. This again refers to the Krivoshchekovo Camp No. 1, 1947–1949. (We know of this No. 1, but how many were there?) At this camp there were thieves, nonpolitical offenders, juveniles, invalids, women and nursing mothers, all mixed up together. There was just one women's barracks—but it held five hundred people. It was indescribably filthy, incomparably filthy and rundown, and there was an oppressive smell in it and the bunks were without bedding. There was an official prohibition against men entering it, but this prohibition was ignored and no one enforced it. Not only men went there, but juveniles too, boys from twelve to thirteen, who flocked in to learn. First they began with simple observation of what was going on; there was no false modesty there, whether because there were no rags or perhaps not enough time; at any rate *the bunks were not curtained off*. And, of course, the light was never doused either. Everything took place very naturally as in nature in full view, and in several places at once. Obvious old age and obvious ugliness were the only defenses for a woman there—nothing else. Attractiveness was a curse. Such a woman had a constant stream of visitors on her bunk and was constantly surrounded. They propositioned her and threatened her with beatings and knives— and she had no hope of being able to stand up against it but only to be smart about whom she gave in to—to pick the kind of man to defend her with his name and his knife from all the rest, from the next in line, from the whole greedy queue, from those crazy juveniles gone berserk, aroused by everything they could see and breathe in there. And it wasn't only men that she had to be defended against either. Nor only the juveniles who were aroused. What about the women next to them, who day after day had to see all that but were not themselves invited by the men? In the end those women, too, would explode in an uncontrollable rage and hurl themselves on their successful neighbors and beat them up.

And then, too, venereal diseases were nearly epidemic at

Krivoshchekovo. There was a rumor that nearly half the women were infected, but there was no way out, and on and on both the sovereigns and the suppliants kept crossing the same threshold. And only those who were very foresighted, like the accordionist K., who had his own connections in the Medical Section, could each time check the secret list of the venereal-disease patients for himself and his friends in order not to get caught.

And what about the women in the Kolyma? After all, women were extremely rare there and in desperate demand. It was better for a woman not to get caught on the work sites there—by a convoy guard, a free employee, or a prisoner. The Kolyma was where the expression *streetcar* for a gang rape arose. K.O. tells how a truck driver lost at cards a whole truckload of women, including K.O. herself, being transported to Elgen. And, turning off the road, he delivered them for the night to a gang of unconvoyed construction workers.

And what about the *work?* In any mixed brigade there was some kind of indulgence for a woman, some kind of work which was a bit easier. But if the entire brigade consisted of women— then there was no mercy shown, then they demanded *the same cubic yards!* And there were camps populated entirely by women, and in such camps the women were lumberjacks, and ditch-diggers, and adobe bricklayers. And it was only to the copper and tungsten mines that women were not assigned. Take Karlag "Camp 29"—how many women were there at that *point?* No more, no less than six thousand![3] What kind of work did these women do? Yelena O. worked as a loader. She used to haul bags weighing 175 to 200 pounds each! True, she was given help in getting them up on her shoulders, yes, and in her youth she had been a gymnast too. (Yelena Prokofyevna Chebotaryeva worked as a loader throughout her ten-year sentence.)

At the women's camps the established pattern of conduct was

---

3. This is relevant to the question of *the total number* of zeks in the Archipelago. Who knew this Camp 29? And was it the last one in Karlag? And how many people were there in each of the remaining camps? Anyone with the time to spare can multiply it for himself! And who knew a certain Fifth Construction Sector of the Rybinsk hydro project? In fact, there were more than a hundred barracks there and, given even the least possible crowding, a good six thousand were to be found there too. Loshchilin recollects that there were more than ten thousand.

generally unfeminine and cruel, incessant cursing, incessant fights, misbehavior. Otherwise you'd not survive. (But, as the unconvoyed engineer Prokhorov-Pustover reports: women taken from a women's unit such as that and assigned as servants or to decent work immediately changed into quiet and hard-working women. He had occasion to observe such units in the thirties, on the Baikal-Amur Main Line working on second-tracking the Trans-Siberian Railroad. Here is a picture: On a hot day three hundred women asked the convoy to permit them to bathe in a flooded ravine. The convoy refused permission. At that point the women undressed to their bare skins and lay down to sun themselves—right along the railroad track in sight of all the passing trains. While local trains carrying Soviet citizens were passing by, this was no disaster, but they were expecting the international express, in which there were foreigners. The women refused to obey orders to put their clothes on. So then the authorities summoned the local fire department and frightened them off with hoses.)

Here is what *women's* work was like in Krivoshchekovo. At the brickyard, when they had completed working one section of the clay pit, they used to take down the overhead shelter (before they had mined there, it had been laid out on the surface of the earth). And now it was necessary to hoist wet beams ten to twelve yards up out of a big pit. How was it done? The reader will say: with machines. Of course. A women's brigade looped a cable around each end of a beam, and in two rows like barge haulers, keeping even so as not to let the beam drop and then have to begin over again, pulled one side of each cable and . . . out came the beam. And then a score of them would hoist up one beam on their shoulders to the accompaniment of command oaths from their out-and-out slave driver of a woman brigadier and would carry the beam to its new place and dump it there. A tractor, did you say? But, for pity's sakes, where would you get a tractor in 1948? A crane, you say? But you have forgotten Vyshinsky: "work, the miracle worker which transforms people from nonexistence and insignificance into heroes"? If there were a crane . . . then what about the miracle worker? If there were a crane . . . then these women would simply wallow in insignificance!

The body becomes worn out at that kind of work, and everything that is feminine in a woman, whether it be constant or whether it be monthly, ceases to be. If she manages to last to the next "commissioning," the person who undresses before the physicians will be not at all like the one whom the trusties smacked their lips over in the bath corridor: she has become ageless; her shoulders stick out at sharp angles, her breasts hang down in little dried-out sacs; superfluous folds of skin form wrinkles on her flat buttocks; there is so little flesh above her knees that a big enough gap has opened up for a sheep's head to stick through or even a soccer ball; her voice has become hoarse and rough and her face is tanned by pellagra. (And, as a gynecologist will tell you, several months of logging will suffice for the prolapse and falling out of a more important organ.)

Work—*the miracle worker!*

Nothing is ever equal, by and large, in life, and this is all the more true in camp. And not everyone had the same hopeless fate at work. And the younger they were sometimes, the easier things were for them. I can just see the sturdy nineteen-year-old Napolnaya, her peasant cheeks ruddy all over. In the minicamp at the Kaluga Gates she was crane operator on the turret crane. She used to climb up like a monkey to her seat in the crane, and sometimes she would crawl out on its swinging arm without any need to, and shout to the whole construction yard "Hi-ho!" And from the cabin she would shout back and forth with the free construction superintendent, with the foremen—she had no telephone. Everything was amusing to her, gay, as if she weren't in camp: Go join the Komsomol. She smiled at everyone with some sort of good nature untypical of camp. She always was given 140 percent—the highest ration in camp. And no enemy was fearsome to her (well, other than the *godfather*). Her construction superintendent would not have allowed anyone to offend her. The only thing I don't know was how she managed to learn to be a crane operator. Did she get into that work without some self-interest somewhere? She was in for one of the inoffensive nonpolitical articles. Strength blazed out all over her. And the position she had won for herself permitted her to give her love not out of need but from her own heart's desire.

Sachkova, who was imprisoned at nineteen, describes her own position in the same light. She got into an agricultural penal colony, where, incidentally, there is always more to eat and where things are therefore easier. "I used to run from reaping machine to reaping machine with a song on my lips, and learned to tie up sheaves." If one has no other youth but youth in camp then . . . one has to be gay there too, where else? And then she was taken to the tundra near Norilsk, and Norilsk, too, "seemed like some sort of fairy-tale city I had dreamed about in childhood." Having served out her term, she stayed there as a free employee. "I remember I was walking in a blizzard, and all of a sudden I was seized by a mood of exaltation and I walked along, waving my arms, fighting with the blizzard, singing the song 'The Heart Is Joyful from a Gay Song.' I looked at the iridescent curtain of the northern lights, threw myself down on the snow, and looked up into the sky. I wanted to sing so loudly that Norilsk could hear me: that it was not the five years that had conquered me but I them, that all those barbed wires and sleeping shelves and convoys had come to an end. I wanted to love! I wanted to do something for people so there would be no more evil in the world."

Well, yes, many others wanted that too.

Sachkova, nonetheless, did not manage to free us from evil: the camps still stand. But she herself had good luck: after all, not five years but five weeks are enough to destroy both the woman and the human being.

And only these two cases contrast in my investigation with thousands that were joyless or unconscionable.

But, of course, where else but in camp would you experience your first love if they had imprisoned you *for fifteen years* (on a political charge) as an eighth-grader, like Nina Peregud? How could you fail to fall in love with the handsome jazz musician Vasily Kozmin, who not long before, out in freedom, had been adored by the whole city, and in his aura of fame and glory had seemed unattainable? And Nina wrote her verses "A Twig of White Lilac," and he set them to music and sang them to her over the perimeter barrier separating the compounds. (They had already separated them, and again he was unattainable.)

The girls of the Krivoshchekovo barracks also pinned flowers in their hair—a sign they had . . . a camp marriage, but also, perhaps . . . that they were in love?

External legislation (for outside Gulag) seemingly abetted

camp love. An All-Union Decree of July 8, 1944, on the strengthening of marriage ties was accompanied by an unpublished decree of the Council of People's Commissars and an instruction of the People's Commissariat of Justice dated November 27, 1944, in which it was stated that the court was required to dissolve unconditionally a marriage with a spouse in prison (or in an insane asylum) at the first indication of desire on the part of a free Soviet person, and even to encourage this by freeing such a person from the fee for issuance of a divorce decree. (And at the same time no one was obliged legally to inform the other spouse of the accomplished divorce!) By this token, citizenesses and citizens were called on to abandon their imprisoned wives and husbands all the more speedily in misfortune. And prisoners were correspondingly invited . . . to forget about their marriages all the more thoroughly. Now it became not only silly and nonsocialist but also illicit for a woman to languish for a husband from whom she had been separated if he remained out in freedom. Zoya Yakusheva was imprisoned as a ChS— Family Member—because of her husband, and here's how it went with her. After three years, her husband was liberated as an important specialist, but he did not make his wife's release an obligatory condition of his own. And she had to drag out her *eight* full years because of him.

Yes, the zeks were to forget about their marriages, but Gulag instructions also forbade indulgence in love affairs as a diversionary action against the production plan. After all, these unscrupulous women who wandered about the work sites, forgetting their obligations to the state and the Archipelago, were ready to lie down on their backs anywhere at all—on the damp ground, on wood chips, on road stone, on slag, on iron shavings—and the plan would collapse! And the Five-Year Plan would mark time! And there would be no prize money for the Gulag chiefs! And besides some of those *zechkas* secretly nurtured a desire to get pregnant and, on the strength of this pregnancy, exploiting the humanitarianism of our laws, to snatch several months off their terms, which were often a short three or five years anyway, and not work at all those months. That was why Gulag instructions required that any prisoners caught cohabiting should be immediately separated, and that the less useful of the two should be sent off on a prisoner transport. (Now this, of course, had nothing in common with those cruel Saltychikhas in serf times who used to send girl serfs off to distant villages.)

All that lyrical love beneath pea jackets was also vexatious for the custodial staff. At nights when the citizen jailer might otherwise have snored away in his duty room, he had to go about with a flashlight and catch all those brazen naked-legged women in bunks in the men's barracks and those men over in the women's barracks. Not to mention his own possible lusts (for, after all, the citizen jailer was not made of stone either), he had furthermore the labor of hauling the offender off to the punishment block or perhaps spending the whole long night remonstrating with her, explaining to her in what way her conduct had been improper, and then writing a complete report on the subject (which, given lack of higher education, was even a torment).

Plundered of everything that fulfills female life and indeed human life in general—of family, motherhood, the company of friends, familiar and perhaps even interesting work, in some cases perhaps in art or among books, and crushed by fear, hunger, abandonment, and savagery—what else could the women camp inmates turn to except love? With God's blessing the love which came might also be almost not of the flesh, because to do it in the bushes was shameful, to do it in the barracks in everyone's presence was impossible, and the man was not always up to it, and then the jailers would drag the culprits out of every *hideout* (seclusion) and put them in the punishment block. But from its unfleshly character, as the women remember today, the spirituality of camp love became even more profound. And it was particularly because of the absence of the flesh that this love became more poignant than out in freedom! Women who were already elderly could not sleep nights because of a chance smile, because of some fleeting mark of attention they had received. So sharply did the light of love stand out against the dirty, murky camp existence!

N. Stolyarova saw the "conspiracy of happiness" on the face of her girl friend, a Moscow actress, and on that of the latter's illiterate partner at hay-hauling, Osman. The actress revealed that no one had ever loved her that way before—neither her film-director husband nor all her former admirers. And only because of this did she decline to be taken off hay-hauling, from the general work.

Then there was the risk—almost like war, almost fatal: as punishment for one discovered rendezvous, you might be sent away from a place grown habitable—in other words, pay with your life. Love on the knife edge of danger, where personalities deepen so and unfold, where every inch is paid for with sacrifices —that is heroic love! (In Ortau, Anya Lekhtonen stopped loving—fell out of love with—her sweetheart in the course of those twenty minutes when the guard was leading them to the punishment block and her sweetheart was humiliatingly begging the guard to let him go.) Some became the kept women of trusties without love—in order to save themselves, and others went on *general work*—and perished—for love.

And women who were not at all young turned out to be involved in this too, even placing the jailers in a quandary: out in freedom no one would ever have considered such a woman! And these women did not seek passion, but to satisfy their need to look after someone, to keep him warm, to sacrifice their own rations in order to feed him up, to wash and darn for him. The common bowl out of which they ate was their sacred wedding ring. "I do not need to sleep with him, but in our beastly life, in which we curse each other in the barracks the whole day long over the bread ration and over rags, I keep thinking to myself: Today I must mend his shirt, and boil his potatoes," one woman explained to Dr. Zubov. But the man at times wanted more, and it was necessary to yield, and *right then* the supervisors would catch them. . . . And that was how, in Unzhlag, the hospital laundress Auntie Polya, who had been widowed very early, who had subsequently been alone all her life, and who had later helped out in a church, was caught at night with a man at the very tail end of her camp term. "How did that happen, Auntie Polya?" The doctors were astonished. "We were counting on you. And now they are going to send you out to *general work*." "Yes, I'm to blame," the old woman nodded, crushed. "In the Gospel sense I'm a sinner, and in the camp sense a ———."

But in the punishment of lovers who had been caught, as in the entire structure of Gulag, there was no fairness. If one of the pair was a trusty, close to the chiefs, or very much needed at work, then they might for years look through their fingers at this liaison. (When an unconvoyed electrical repairman appeared at the Women's Hospital Camp of Unzhlag, all the free employees were interested in his services, and the chief doctor, a free woman, summoned the nurse housekeeper, a zechka, and gave instructions: "Create suitable conditions for Musa Butenko." Musa was the nurse because of whom the repairman had come.) But if the zeks involved were insignificant or in disfavor, they were punished swiftly and cruelly.

In Mongolia, in the GULZhDS Camp (our zeks built a railroad there from 1947 to 1950), two unconvoyed girls were caught running to see friends in the men's column. The guard tied them behind his horse and, mounting the horse, *dragged them across the steppe.*[4] None of your serf-owning Saltychikhas did that! But they used to do it at Solovki.

Eternally persecuted, exposed, and separated, these native couples could not, it would seem, be long-lasting or stable. At the same time, however, cases are known in which they managed to keep up a correspondence and got together again after their release. One such case is known, for example: One doctor, B.Y.S., an assistant professor at a provincial medical institute, lost count of his liaisons in camp—he had not let even one nurse get by, and there were others too! But in this long line he encountered Z., and the line stopped. Z. did not cut short her pregnancy and gave birth to a child. B.S. was released shortly afterward and, having no limitations on him, could have gone to his own native city. But he remained in the camp as a free employee so as to be near Z. and the child. His own wife, losing patience, came to him there. At this point he hid from her inside *the camp compound.* (Where, of course, his wife could not get to him!) He lived there with Z. and communicated to his wife by every possible means that he had divorced her and that she should go away.

But it was not only the custodial staff and camp chiefs who would break up camp marriages. The Archipelago was such an upside-down land that in it a man and a woman could be split up by what ought to have united them even more firmly: the birth of a child. A month before giving birth a pregnant woman was transported to another camp, where there was a camp

4. Who today will seek out his name? And him? Yes, and if one were even to speak to him about it, he would be astonished: What's he guilty of? He was ordered to do it! So why did they have to go to the men anyway, the bitches?

hospital with a maternity ward and where husky little voices shouted that they did not want to be zeks because of the sins of their parents. After giving birth the mother was sent to a special nearby camp for *mamki*—nursing mothers.

And right here we have to interrupt! Right here it is impossible not to interrupt! How much self-ridicule there is in this world! "We are . . . not the real thing!" The zek language dearly loves and makes stubborn use of all these disparaging diminutive Russian suffixes: not "mat"—mother—but *mamka*; not "bolnitsa"—hospital—but bol*nichka*; not "svidaniye"—a rendezvous—but svidan*ka*; not "pomilovaniye"—pardon—but pomilov*ka*; not "volny"—a free person—but volny*ashka*; not "zhenitsa"—to marry a woman—but pod*zhenitsa*—to "submarry," this being the same derisiveness even though not in the suffix. And even chetvertnaya (a twenty-five-year term) is demoted to chetver*taka* —from twenty-five rubles to twenty-five kopecks!

By this insistent bias of the language, the zeks demonstrate also that nothing in the Archipelago is genuine, everything is a forgery, everything is of the lowest grade. And that they themselves do not set any value on the things ordinary people value. They show awareness of the fake nature of the medical treatment they get, the fake character of the petitions for pardon which they write out of compulsion and without faith. And by demoting the slang term for a twenty-five-year sentence from twenty-five rubles to twenty-five kopecks the zek wants to demonstrate his own superiority even to what is almost a life term!

And so it is that the "mamki" live and work at their own camp, being taken from there at intervals under convoy to breast-feed the newly born natives. The child meanwhile is no longer in the hospital, but in a "children's village" or "infants' home," as it is called in different places. After the end of the breast-feeding period the mothers are no longer allowed visits to their babies—except perhaps as an exception to the general rule because of "model labor and discipline." (The point, of course, was not to have to keep the mothers close by because of the baby but to be able to send them off to work wherever they were required.) But most often the woman doesn't return to her old camp and her camp "husband" either. And the father will not see his child at all, by and large, as long as he is in camp. After being weaned the children are kept a year in the children's village. (They are fed on norms for free children, and therefore the medical and house-keeping personnel around them get well fed too.) Some children cannot adjust to artificial feeding without their mothers and die. The survivors are sent after a year to a general orphanage. And thus it is that the son of two natives may depart from the Archipelago for the time being, though not without hope of returning as a *juvenile offender*.

Those who kept track of this said it was infrequent for a mother to take her child from an orphanage after release (and the women thieves . . . never did). So that many of these children who had breathed in the infected air of the Archipelago with the first breath of their tiny lungs were thus damned from the start. Others . . . did take them or, even before their own release, sent some ignorant old women for them (perhaps religious women). And despite the harm thereby done the government's upbringing and the irreparable loss to Gulag of funds allotted for the maternity home, for the mother's maternity leave, and for maintenance of the infants' home, Gulag released these children.

During all those years, prewar and war, when pregnancy separated camp spouses and broke up those hard-won, doggedly concealed, constantly threatened and in any case fragile unions . . . women tried not to have children. And again the Archipelago was not like freedom: in the years when abortions were prohibited and prosecuted out in freedom, and were very difficult to obtain . . . the camp chiefs here took an indulgent attitude toward abortions, which were often carried out in hospitals: after all, it was best for the camp.

And these issues of whether to give birth or not, which were difficult enough for any woman at all, were still more confused for a woman camp inmate. And what would happen to the child subsequently? And if such a fickle camp fate gave one the chance to become pregnant by one's loved one, then how could one go ahead and have an abortion? Should you have the child? That meant certain separation immediately, and when you left would he not pair off with some other woman in the same camp? And what kind of child would it be? (Because of the malnutrition of the parents it was often defective.) And when you stopped nursing the child and were sent away (you still had many years left to serve), would they keep an eye out so as not to do him in? And would you be able to take the child into your own

34. The Glebovs

family? (For some this was excluded.) And if you didn't take him, would your conscience then torment you all your life? (For some—not at all.)

Those who counted on being united with the father of their child after release went into motherhood in camp with self-assurance and confidence. (And sometimes these expectations worked out. Here is A. Glebov with his camp wife twenty years afterward: with them is their daughter born back in Unzhlag, who is now nineteen; what a lovely girl she is too; and another daughter, born out in freedom ten years later, when the parents *had served out* their terms. [Illustration No. 34.]) There were those who went into it who passionately desired to experience motherhood—in camp, since that was the only life they had. After all, this is a living thing sucking at your breast—not fake or ersatz, and not second-grade either. (The Harbin girl Lyalya had a second child only in order to be able to return to the children's village and see her first there! And then she had a third so as to return to see the first two. And having served out her five-year sentence she managed to keep all three of them and was released with them.) Irreparably humiliated, the camp women were reconfirmed in their human dignity through motherhood and for a short time felt as though they had attained equality with free women. Or else: "So I am a prisoner, but my child is free!" And they jealously demanded maintenance and care for the child on the same level as for a genuinely free child. Others, usually from among the veteran camp women and the thieves, looked upon motherhood as a year of *loafing*, sometimes as a way of *early release*. They did not even consider their own child to be their own, and did not even want to see it, and did not even try to find out whether it was alive.

The mothers from the *zakhidnitsy*—Western Ukrainians— and sometimes from among the Russians too—the more simple folk in origin—sought persistently to have their children christened. (This was in the postwar years.) The crucifix was either sent carefully hidden in a parcel (the jailers would never have permitted such counterrevolution to get through) or else was ordered from some clever fellow in camp in return for bread. They also used to get a ribbon for the cross, and managed to make a fancy baby's vest, and a cap. By saving up sugar from their ration they managed to bake a tiny christening cake out of something or other—and their closest women friends were invited. There was always a woman who could pronounce a prayer—any prayer would do—and the child was dipped in warm water and baptized, and the glowing mother invited everyone to the table.

For "mamki" with nursing children (though not, of course, for the 58's among them) special amnesties were sometimes issued, or else simply orders for release ahead of term.

Those most often affected by these orders were habitual criminals involved in lesser crimes and women thieves—and they were the ones who had, in fact, been partly counting on these benefits. And just as soon as these "mamki" had received their passport and their railway ticket in the nearest provincial center, they often left their child, who was no longer needed, right there on the station bench or on the first porch they came to. (But one does have to realize that not all of them could expect to find housing, or a sympathetic greeting from the police, or passport registration, or work, and there would not be a camp ration ready and waiting for them the next morning either. It was easier to begin to live without the child.)

In 1954 at the Tashkent Station I happened to be spending the night not far from a group of zeks who were on their way from camp and who had been released on the basis of some special order. There were about three dozen of them, and they took up a whole corner of the hall, behaving very noisily, with a semi-underworld insolence, like genuine children of Gulag, knowing what life was worth and holding in contempt all the free people there. The men played cards and the "mamki" argued loudly about something. And all of a sudden one mother screamed something more shrilly than the rest, jumped up, swung her child by the legs and audibly banged his head on the cement floor. The hallful of *free* people gasped: A mother! How could a *mother* do that!

. . . They just didn't understand that it was not a mother—but a *mamka*.

■

Everything said so far refers to *joint*, coeducational, camps, such as existed from the first years of the Revolution right up to the end of World War II. In those years in the Russian Republic there was only the Novinsky House of Detention (converted from a former Moscow women's prison) where women only were imprisoned. This experiment did not spread, and did not even last very long itself.

But having risen, safe and sound, from beneath the ruins of the war, which he had nearly lost, the Teacher and Founder took thought as to the welfare of his subjects. His thoughts were now freed to look to the ordering of their lives, and much that he devised at this time was useful, much was moral, and, among other things, the male sex and the female sex were separated—first in schools and camps. (And then, perhaps, he hoped to extend this to all *freedom* as well—and in China there was such an experiment, even more extensive.)

And in 1946 the great and complete separation of women from men began in the Archipelago, and in 1948 it was completed. They sent them to different islands, and within any one island they stretched that well-tried friend, barbed wire, between the women's and the men's camp compounds.[5]

But like many other scientifically forecast and scientifically

---

5. Many of the initiatives of the great Coryphaeus have by now been admitted to be not altogether so perfect, and many of them have been abolished. But the separation of the sexes in the Archipelago has remained hard and fast right to this very day. For here the basis is a profoundly moral one.

thought-out actions, this measure, too, had unexpected consequences which were the exact opposite of those intended.

With the separation of women from men, the women's general situation at work worsened sharply. Previously, at mixed camps many women had worked as laundresses, hospital attendants, cooks and kitchen attendants, storeroom attendants and accountants. And now they had to yield all these positions, and there were far fewer of them in the women's camps. And the women were driven out to general work, driven into brigades exclusively of women, where things were particularly hard for them. To get off general work for at least a while became a question of life and death. And the women began to pursue pregnancy, trying to catch it from any passing encounter, any contact. Pregnancy did not, as before, carry the threat of being parted from a spouse—all partings had already been bestowed in one single Wise Decree.

And now the number of children who entered the infants' homes *doubled* in one year! (Unzhlag, 1948: three hundred compared with one hundred and fifty.) Even though the number of imprisoned women did not increase during this period.

"What are you going to call the little girl?" "Olympiada. I got pregnant at the Olympiad of amateur stage performances." Out of inertia such forms of cultural activity were retained: Olympiads, visits by male cultural brigades to women's camps, joint rallies of shock workers. Common hospitals were likewise retained—and they, too, became houses of assignation. They say that in Solikamsk Camp in 1946 the wires separating the men from the women were few in number and strung on one set of posts (and, of course, no armed guard there). And the insatiable natives thronged to this wire from both sides, with the women in the position they would have been in had they been washing floors, and the men took them without crossing the forbidden line.

After all, immortal Eros is worth something! It was not just a reasoned calculation for getting out of general work. The zeks sensed that this line was being drawn there for a long time to come and that it would, like everything else in Gulag, only harden, become more rigid.

If before the separation of the sexes there was amicable cohabitation, camp marriage, even love, now it had become merely plain lechery.

Of course, the chiefs were not dozing, and corrected their scientific predictions as they went along. To the one row of barbed wire they added forbidden zones on either side. And then, recognizing these barriers to be insufficient, they replaced them with a six-foot-high fence—also with prohibited zones on either side.

In Kengir even that barrier did not help; the intending lovers leaped over it. Then on Sundays (for it was impossible to spend workdays on this! Yes, and it was natural that people should occupy themselves with their living arrangements on their days off) they began to hand out special Sunday jobs on either side of the barricade, and compelled them to raise the height of the wall to twelve feet. And here's what's funny: the zeks really went out to those Sunday work assignments gaily! Before their final farewells they might at least make someone's acquaintance on the other side of the wall, chat a bit, arrange to correspond!

Later in Kengir they increased the height of the dividing wall to fifteen feet, and stretched barbed wire, too, along the top. And then they added a high-voltage wire as well. (How strong that cursed Cupid is!) And in addition to everything else they put watchtowers at both ends as well. This Kengir wall had its own special destiny in the history of the whole Archipelago (see Part V, Chapter 12). But they built others like it, too, in other Special Camps (for example, in Spassk).

One has to picture to oneself the well-reasoned methodology of these employers who thought it entirely natural to divide the slave men from the slave women with barbed wire but would have been astonished if anyone had proposed that the same be done to themselves and their families.

The walls grew—and Eros dashed back and forth. Finding no other sphere, he either flew too high—into platonic correspondence—or else too low—into homosexual love.

Notes were thrown over the fence, or else left at the factory in prearranged hiding places. The addresses on the notes were coded, so the jailer, if he found them, couldn't work out who was writing whom. (By now, the punishment for notes was the camp prison.)

Galya Venediktova recalls that sometimes people even made one another's acquaintance blindly, corresponded without seeing each other, and said farewell to one another blindly too, without seeing each other. (Anyone who has ever conducted such a correspondence knows both its desperate sweetness and its hopelessness and blindness.) In that very same Kengir, Lithuanian women were *married* across the wall to Lithuanian men whom they had never seen or met; and the Lithuanian Roman Catholic priest (also, of course, a prisoner in the standard pea jacket) would provide written documentation that so-and-so and so-and-so had been joined for eternity in holy matrimony in the eyes of God. In this marriage with an unknown prisoner on the other side of a wall—and for Roman Catholic women such a marriage was irreversible and sacred—I hear a choir of angels. It is like the unselfish, pure contemplation of the heavenly bodies. It is too lofty for this age of self-interested calculation and hopping-up-and-down jazz.

The Kengir marriages also had an unexpected outcome. The heavens heard the prayers and intervened. (Part V, Chapter 12.)

And the women themselves and the doctors who treated them in the divided compounds confirm that the women suffered worse than the men from the separation. They were particularly excited and nervous. Lesbian love developed swiftly. The gentle and the young went about looking sallow, with dark circles under their eyes. The women of a cruder type became the "men." No matter how the jailers tried to break up such pairs they turned up again in the same bunks. They sent one or the other of these "spouses" away from the camp. Stormy dramas burst out, with people leaping onto the barbed wire under fire from the sentries.

In the Karaganda division of Steplag, where women solely from Article 58 were assembled, many of them, N.V. recounts, awaited a summons to the security chief with palpitations—not with fear or hatred for that loathsome political interrogation, but with heart palpitating because this man would lock you up alone in the room with him.

The separate women's camps bore the same full burden of general work. True, in 1951, logging by women was formally forbidden—hardly because it was the beginning of the second half of the twentieth century. But in Unzhlag, for example, the men's camps could not fulfill the plans at all. And then a method was devised to spur them on—to compel the natives to pay with their own work for what is provided without payment to every living thing in the whole wide world. They began to drive the women out to logging too, in a single convoy cordon with the men, with only a ski track separating them. All the timber cut here was subsequently to be registered as the output of the men's camp, but the norm was demanded from both men and women. Here is what a chief with two stripes on his shoulder boards said to Lyuba Beryozina, the "timber foreman": "If you and your broads fulfill the norm, Belenky will be in your cabin!" But now both the strongest men sloggers, and especially the work trusties who had money, shoved it at the convoy guards (who couldn't exactly go out on the town on their wages either), and for an hour and a half (until the bribed guard changed) they rushed across into the women's cordon.

In the space of this hour and a half in the snowy frigid woods, a man had to pick one out, get acquainted with her (if they hadn't corresponded before), find a place, and do it.

But why rake up all that past? Why reopen the old wounds of those who were living in Moscow and in country houses at the time, writing for the newspapers, speaking from rostrums, going off to resorts and abroad?

Why recall all that when it is still the same even today? After all, you can only write about whatever "will not be repeated."

Chapter 9

■

The Trusties

One of the first native concepts a newcomer coming to a camp learns is that of the *trusty*.* That is what the natives rudely called everyone who managed not to share the common, foredoomed lot—who either got out of *general work* or never ever got into it.

There was no lack of trusties in the Archipelago. Limited in the living zone to a strict percentage of registration Group "B," and at work by staff tables, they nonetheless always managed to surge over that percentage—partly because of the pressure from those desiring to save their skins, partly because of the ineptitude of the camp bosses, who were incapable of managing and administering with a small staff.

According to 1933 statistics of the People's Commissariat of Justice, the personnel at places of detention, including economic managers and, it's true, *trusty guards*, constituted 22 percent of the total number of natives. If we reduce this figure to 17 or 18 percent (taking out the trusty guards), this still amounts to one-sixth. So it is already clear that we are speaking in this chapter of a very significant camp phenomenon. But the total percentage of trusties was much higher than one-sixth; after all, these were only the *compound* trusties, and in addition there were all the *work* trusties. And then there was also a turnover among the trusties, and many more prisoners at one time or another during their camp career were apparently trusties for a time. And the main thing was that among those who survived, those released, the trusties constituted a very high proportion—I would say nine-tenths of the long-termers from the 58's.

Almost every long-term zek you congratulate on having survived was a trusty. Or had been one for a large part of his term.

Because the camps were destructive, and this must not be forgotten.

All classifications in this world lack sharp boundaries, and all transitions are gradual. So it is here: the edges are blurred. By and large, everyone who did not leave the camp compound during the working day could be considered a compound trusty. A worker in the camp workshops lived much more easily and better than the slogger on general work: he did not have to go out for line-up, and this meant he could rise and breakfast much later; he did not have to march under convoy to the work site and back; there were fewer severities, less cold, less strength spent; also his workday ended earlier; either his work was in a warm place or else a place to warm up was always handy. And he usually worked not in a brigade, but as an individual craftsman, which meant he did not have to put up with nagging from his comrades but only from the chiefs. And since he was often enough engaged in making something on personal orders of those same chiefs, instead of being nagged at, he even got handouts, favors, and permission to have first call on clothes and footwear. He had a good chance of earning something on orders from other zeks too. To make things more clear: the "khozdvor" was like the working part of an establishment of servants in the manor of a serf-owner. If within this category a lathe operator, a carpenter, a stovemaker, was not yet a full-fledged trusty, a shoemaker, however, and a tailor even more so, was already a high-class trusty. "Tailor" in camp sounds and means something like "Assistant Professor" out in freedom. (And the reverse side is that in camp the genuine title "Assistant Professor" sounds derisive, and it is best not to call yourself that and become a laughingstock. The camp scale of the significance of professions is quite the reverse of the scale out in freedom.)

A laundress, a hospital attendant, a dishwasher, a stoker, bath workers, a cook's helper, simple bakers, and barracks orderlies were also trusties, but of a lower class. They had to work with their hands, and sometimes hard. All, however, were well fed.

The genuine compound trusties were: cooks, bread cutters, stock clerks, doctors, medical assistants, barbers, instructors of the Cultural and Educational Section, bath managers, bakery managers, storeroom managers, parcel room managers, senior barracks orderlies, superintendents of quarters, work assigners, accountants, clerks of the headquarters barracks, engineers of the camp compound and of the camp workshops. Not only were they all well fed, clad in clean clothes, and exempt from lifting heavy weights and from crooks in their backs, but they had great power over what was most needed by a human being, and consequently power over people. Sometimes they fought, group against group, conducted intrigues, overthrew each other, or raised each other up, or quarreled over "broads," but more often they lived in a state of joint mutual defense against the rabble, as a satisfied establishment, which had no reason to divvy things up with others since everything had long since been divvied up once and for all, and each had his own sphere. And the stronger this clique of compound trusties was, the more the camp chief depended on it, sparing himself worry. The fates of all arriving and sent off on prisoner transports, the fates of all the ordinary sloggers, were decided by these trusties.

Because of the human race's customary narrow-minded attachment to caste, it very soon became inconvenient for trusties to sleep in the same barracks as ordinary sloggers, on the same multiple bunks, or even, for that matter, on any multiple bunk at all, or anywhere else except a bed, or to eat at the same table, to undress in the same bath, or to put on the same underwear in which the sloggers had sweated and which they had torn. And so the trusties set themselves apart in small rooms with two, four, or eight persons in each, and ate there food of their choice, supplementing it illegally, discussed all camp appointments and business, including the fates of people and of brigades, without the risk of running into insults from the sloggers or brigadiers. They spent their leisure separately (and they had leisure). They had their "individual" bed linen changed on a separate schedule. By virtue of the same caste foolishness they tried to be distinctive from the camp masses in clothing too, but these possibilities were not great. If in a particular camp black padded jackets or ordinary jackets predominated, they would try to get dark blue ones from the storeroom, and if dark blue ones predominated, they put on black ones. In addition, they got the narrow camp britches broadened into bell bottoms in the tailors' shop—through use of triangular inserts.

The work trusties properly speaking consisted of the engineers, technicians, construction superintendents, foremen, heads of shops, planners, norm setters, and, in addition, accountants, secretaries, typists. They differed from the compound trusties in that they had to go out to line-up and were marched to work in a convoyed column (though sometimes they were not convoyed). But their situation on the site was privileged—they did not have to endure physical torments and were not utterly exhausted. On the contrary, the work, the feeding, the life of the sloggers was dependent in great degree on them. Even though less connected with the camp compound, they tried to defend their positions there too and to receive a significant number of the same privileges as the compound trusties, though they could never manage to catch up with them.

There were no precise boundaries here either. Also in this category were designers, technologists, geodesists, motor mechanics, machinery maintenance personnel. They were by no means "commanders of production"; they did not share the fatal power, and they had no responsibility for people's deaths (as long as these deaths were not caused by the technology of production selected or serviced by them). They were simply intelligent or even semieducated sloggers. Like every zek at work, they *faked*, deceived the chiefs, tried to drag out for a week what could be done in half a day. Customarily they lived in camp almost like sloggers, were often members of work brigades, and only in the work compound did they have it warm and peaceful. There, alone in their offices and cabins, with no free people about, they would drop the subject of government work and gossip about life, about prison terms, about the past and the future, and, most of all, about rumors that 58's (they themselves were most often recruited from the 58's) would soon be sent off to *general work*.

And for this there was a profound, uniquely scientific foundation: after all, it was virtually impossible *to correct* socially hostile prisoners, so rooted were they in their class corruption. The majority could be corrected only by the grave. And even if, nonetheless, a certain minority was indeed capable of being corrected, then, of course, it could only be by *labor*, physical labor, heavy labor (replacing machines), the sort of labor which would have been degrading for a *camp* officer or jailer, but which nonetheless once created the human being from the ape (and in camp inexplicably transforms him back into an ape again). And that is why it is not at all out of vengeance but only in the faint hope of correcting the 58's that it is strictly stated in the Gulag regulations (and this regulation is continually being renewed) that persons condemned under Article 58 cannot occupy any privileged positions either in the camp compound or at work. (The only prisoners able to occupy positions having to do with material values are ones who out in freedom have already distinguished themselves by stealing.) And that is how it would have been—for, after all, the camp chiefs hardly harbored any love for the 58's. But they did know: that there were not even one-fifth as many specialists under all the other articles combined as under 58. The physicians and engineers were almost entirely 58's. And you'd not find better workers or more straightforwardly honest people even among the free employees. And so in covert opposition to the One-and-Only Scientific Theory, the employers began surreptitiously assigning 58's to trusty positions. Meanwhile the most lucrative ones always remained in the hands of the nonpolitical offenders, with whom the chiefs found it easier to make deals—and too much honesty would have even been a hindrance. So they used to put the 58's in trusty positions, but with each renewal of this regulation (and it kept being renewed), and before the arrival of any verification commission (and they kept arriving), a wave of the chief's white hand would send off the 58's to *general work* without hesitation or regrets. Temporary well-being painstakingly built up over months was shattered to bits in one fell day. But this expulsion was not so ruinous in itself as were the eternal rumors of its approach, which ground down and wore out the political trusties. These rumors poisoned the trusty's whole existence. Only the nonpolitical offenders could enjoy their trusty situation serenely. (However, the commission would come and go, the work would quietly fall apart again, and the engineers would once again be quietly hauled in to fill trusty positions, only to be driven out when the next commission was due.)

And other than the plain, ordinary 58's, there were also those whose prison files had been branded with a separate curse from Moscow: "To be used only on general work!" Many of the Kolyma prisoners in 1938 carried this brand. And for them to get work as a laundress or a drier of felt boots was an unattainable dream.

How does the *Communist Manifesto* go? "The bourgeoisie has stripped of its halo every occupation hitherto honored and looked up to with reverent awe." (A certain resemblance here!) "It has converted the physician, the lawyer, the priest, the poet, the man of science, into its paid wage laborers."[1]* Well, at least they were paid! And at least they were left to work in their own "field of professional specialization"! And what if they had been sent out to *general work?* To logging? And unpaid! And unfed! True, physicians were sent out on general work only rarely: after all, they were called upon to cure the chiefs' families as well. But as for lawyers, priests, poets, and men of science—they were only fit to rot doing general work. There was no place for them among the trusties.

The *brigadiers* occupied a special position in the camp. In camp terms they were not considered trusties, but you couldn't call them sloggers either. Therefore the arguments advanced in this chapter apply to them as well.

■

Just as in battle, so in camp life there is no time for discussion; a position as trusty becomes available—so you grab it.

But years and decades have passed. We have survived and our comrades have perished. To astounded *free people* and our indifferent heirs we are beginning to disclose bit by bit the world of then and there, which had almost nothing human in it—and we must evaluate it in the light of the human conscience.

And one of the principal moral questions here concerns the trusties.

In choosing the hero of my story about the camps I chose a slogger, and I could not have chosen anyone else, for only he could perceive the true interrelationships of camp life. (Just as it is only the infantryman who can weigh a whole war in the balance, though for some reason it is not he who writes the war memoirs.) This choice of a hero and certain sharp remarks in my story perplexed and offended some former trusties—and, as I have already said, nine-tenths of the survivors are indeed trusties. Thereupon

1. Marx and Engels, *Sobrannye Sochineniya* (*Collected Works*), 1928 edition, Vol. IV, p. 427.

"Memoirs of a Trusty," by Dyakov, appeared (*Memoirs of Survival*),* complacently confirming their resourcefulness in getting well fixed and cleverness in surviving at any cost. (And this is precisely the sort of book that should have appeared before my own.)

In those few short months when it seemed possible to *discuss*, a certain amount of debate flared up about the role of the trusties, and a certain general question was raised of the moral position of the trusty in camp. But in our country they do not permit any information to be X-rayed through and through, nor any discussion to encompass all the facets of a subject. All this is invariably suppressed at the very beginning—so no ray of light should fall on the naked body of truth. And then all this is piled up in one formless heap covering many years, where it languishes for whole decades—until all interest and all means of sorting out the rusty blocks from all this trash are lost. And so it was that all discussion of the trusties was dampened down at the very beginning, and passed out of the pages of the public press into private letters.

And the distinction between a trusty and a slogger in camp (though no sharper than that which existed in reality) had to be made, and it was very good that it was made right at the very birth of the camp theme in literature. But in V. Lakshin's censored article[2] there was a certain excessiveness of expression on the subject of camp labor (seeming to glorify that very thing which replaced machines and created us from the apes), and the generally correct direction of the article and to a certain extent my own novella as well were met with a counterwave of indignation —both from former trusties and from their never-imprisoned intellectual friends: What's going on here . . . is slave labor being glorified (the cinder-block-laying scene in *One Day in the Life of Ivan Denisovich*)?! What's going on here . . . since when does "earn your bread by the sweat of your brow" mean do what the Gulag chiefs want you to? *We* trusties are particularly proud that we avoided work and didn't drag out our existence at it.

In answering these objections right now, I only regret that they will not be read for some time.

In my opinion, it is unworthy of an intellectual to be proud of the fact that he didn't descend to physical slave labor, you see, because he was able to get into office work. In this situation the Russian intellectuals of the past century would have presumed to boast *only* if, at the same time, they could have *liberated their younger brother from slave labor* as well. After all, Ivan Denisovich didn't have that way out—fixing himself up with an office job! So what should we do about our *younger brother?* Is it all right to let our younger brother drag out his existence at slave labor? (Well, why not? After all, we've been letting him do it long enough on the collective farms! We even fixed him up with it there!) But if we let him do this, then maybe, at least once in a while, for at least an hour or so on occasion, before knocking off, when the masonry work has gone well, we can let him take an interest in his work? *We*, after all, even in camp, find a certain enjoyment in sliding the pen along the paper, in drawing a black line on tracing paper with a drawing pen. How could Ivan Denisovich get through ten years if all he could do was curse his work day and night? After all, in that case he would have had to hang himself on the first handy hook!

And what, then, can one say about such an unlikely story as this: Pavel Chulpenyov, who had worked at logging for seven years in a row (and at a penalty camp at that), could hardly have survived and kept working if he had not found meaning and interest in that logging. Here is how he stood it: The camp chief, who took an interest in his few permanent workers (a surprising camp chief), in the first place fed them "belly full" with gruel, and in the second place permitted only his record-holding shock workers to work nights in the kitchen. This was their bonus! After a whole day of logging Chulpenyov went to wash and fill the food pots, stoke the oven, and clean potatoes until 2 A.M., and after that ate his fill and went off to sleep for three hours without taking off his pea jacket. Once, also as a bonus, he was allowed to work for one month in the bread-cutting room. And he rested up another month by self-mutilation (because he was a record holder no one suspected him). And that is all. (But, of course, explanations are required here too. In their work gang was a woman thief, a veteran bazaar swindler who worked for a year as their draywoman, and she was living with two trusties at the same time: the weighing-in checker and the warehouse manager. As a result, their work gang always overfulfilled its norm, and, more important, their horse, Gerchik, ate all the

oats he wanted and hauled well. Other horses were rationed according to the work gang's norm fulfillment! I am sick of saying, *"Poor people!"* At least here I can interject, "Poor horses!")
But nonetheless *seven years on logging without interruption*—it is almost a legend! But how could you work for seven years if you didn't work well, if you didn't find some meaning in it, if you didn't become absorbed in the work? All they had to do, said Chulpenyov, was to feed me and I would have kept working and working. That's the Russian character. . . . He mastered the technique of "continuous felling"—felling in such a way that the first branch supported the trunk so it didn't sag, and was easy to trim. And all the subsequent trunks were dropped atop one another crisscross so the branches fell neatly into one or two bonfires, without having to be hauled away. He knew how to "pull" a falling tree in exactly the required direction. And when he heard from the Lithuanians about Canadian lumberjacks who for a wager would put a stake in the ground and then drive it down into the ground with a falling tree, he was filled with enthusiasm: "All right, we'll try the same thing!" And it worked.

And that is how it turns out: such is man's nature that even bitter, detested work is sometimes performed with an incomprehensible wild excitement. Having worked for two years with my hands, I encountered this strange phenomenon myself: suddenly you become absorbed in the work itself, irrespective of whether it is slave labor and offers you nothing. I experienced those strange moments at bricklaying (otherwise I wouldn't have written about it), at foundry work, carpentry, even in the fervor of breaking up old pig iron with a sledge. And so surely we can allow Ivan Denisovich not to feel his inescapable labor as a terrible burden forever, not to hate it perpetually?

Well, as I see it, they will yield on this point. They will yield to us, but with the obligatory condition that no reproaches should be implied for those trusties who never spent even a minute earning their daily bread by the sweat of their brow.

Whether by the sweat of their brow or not, they at any rate carried out the commands of the Gulag bosses diligently. (Otherwise off to *general work!*) And painstakingly, using their special skills! After all, all the significant trusty positions were essential links in the camp administration and in camp production. These were precisely those specially forged ("skilled") links in the chain without which (if every last one of the zeks had refused to accept trusty positions!) *the whole chain of exploitation would have broken*, the entire camp system! Because society *outside* could never have supplied such a quantity of highly skilled specialists who were willing in addition to live for years in conditions unfit for dogs.

So why didn't they refuse? Why didn't they break the magic chain?*

The trusties' positions were the key positions for exploitation. Norm setters! And were their bookkeeper helpers much less guilty? The construction superintendents! And were the technicians so guiltless themselves? What trusty position did not in fact involve playing up to the bosses and participating in the general system of compulsion? Was it only as Cultural and Educational Section instructors or as *godfather's* orderlies, who did the devil's work? And if N. worked as a typist—solely as a typist —yet typed out requisitions for the Administrative Section of the camp, did this mean nothing? Let us think about that. And if she ran off copies of orders? This was not for the good of the zeks. . . . Let's suppose the security officer had no typist of his own. That he himself had to type out his formal charges and the final version of the denunciations—of free persons and zeks he was going to imprison the next day. But, you see, he could give this material to the typist—and she would type it up and keep silent, without warning the endangered person. Yes, for that matter, would not a low-ranking trusty, the locksmith of the camp workshops, have to fill a requisition for handcuffs? Or strengthen the grids of iron bars in the punishment block? Or let us stay among written materials: what about the planner? Would not an innocent planner aid and abet planned exploitation?

I do not understand—in what way was this intellectual slave labor purer and nobler than physical slave labor?

So it is not Ivan Denisovich's sweat we should be getting most upset about, but the peaceful pen scratching in the camp office!

For half my term I myself worked at a *sharashka*,* one of those Islands of Paradise. We were torn away from the rest of the Archipelago, we did not see its slave existence. But were we not exactly the same sort of trusties? And did we not, in the very broadest sense, by our scientific work, strengthen that same Ministry of Internal Affairs and the overall system of repression?[3]

And is not everything bad that goes on in the Archipelago or on the entire earth . . . accomplished through us? Yet we attacked Ivan Denisovich—for laying bricks? More of our bricks are there than his!

In camp they more often expressed the contrary insults and reproaches: that the trusties rode on the sloggers' backs, devoured their food, survived at their expense. These charges were made against the compound trusties in particular, frequently not without grounds. Who short-weighed Ivan Denisovich's bread? Who stole his sugar by dampening it with water? Who kept fats, meat, or good cereals from the common pot?

Those camp compound trusties on whom food and clothing depended were chosen on a special basis. To get those positions impudence, slyness, bribery were required; to hold such jobs ruthlessness and a deaf ear to conscience were required (and, in most cases, to be a stool pigeon as well). Of course, all generalizations overstate their case; and from my own recollections I can undertake to name opposite examples of uncorrupted, honest compound trusties—but they didn't last long in their posts. As far as the bulk of well-fixed camp compound trusties are concerned, however, one can say without fear of being wrong that on the average more depravity and malice were concentrated among them than in the average native population. It was not a matter of chance that these were the very jobs the camp bosses gave to their former cronies—imprisoned former Security people. When the MVD chief of Shakhty District was imprisoned, he wasn't sent to cut timber but popped up as work assigner at the headquarters camp of Usollag. And when MVD man Boris Guganava was imprisoned ("Because I once took a cross off a church, I have never since known any happiness in life"), he would be the manager of the camp kitchen at Reshoty Station. But another

---

3. And this problem goes beyond the bounds of the Archipelago. Its scale is that of our whole society. Have not all our educated strata—technologists and those trained in the humanities—been for all these decades precisely the same kind of links in the magic chain, the same kind of "trusties"? Can anyone point out to us scholars or composers or cultural historians among even the most honest of those who have survived safe, sound, and whole and who flourish, who have sacrificed themselves to establish a common life in disregard of their own?

seemingly quite different breed latched on to this group too. The Russian interrogator from Krasnodon who under the Germans had conducted the case against the Young Guard* partisans[4] was an honored work assigner in one of the divisions of Ozerlag. Sasha Sidorenko, a former intelligence agent who had fallen into German hands right off, and who had gone to work for them right off, was now storeroom manager in Kengir and loved getting back at the Germans there for his own fate. Hardly had they gone to sleep after roll call, tired from the day's work, than he would come to them pretending to be drunk and raise a heart-rending cry: "Germans! Achtung! I'm . . . your God! Sing to me!" (And the frightened Germans, rising up on their bunks half asleep, began to sing "Lilli Marlene" for him. And what kind of people were those bookkeepers who released Loshchilin[5] from camp in late autumn wearing just his shirt? Or that shoemaker in Burepolom who, without even a twinge of remorse, took Ans Bernshtein's new army boots in return for a bread ration?

When they got together on their porch for a friendly smoke and a chat about camp affairs, it was hard to picture just who among them might be different.

True, they, too, have something to say in justification of themselves. For example, I. F. Lipai wrote a passionate letter:

The prisoner's ration was outrageously and pitilessly plundered on all sides. The thievery of the trusties for their own sake . . . was petty thievery. While those trusties who engaged in larger-scale thievery were forced [?] into it. The Administration officials, both free workers and prisoners, particularly during wartime, squeezed the paw of the division officials, and the division officials did the same to the camp officials, and the latter did the same to the storeroom and kitchen personnel—and all at the expense of the zek's ration. The most fearful sharks of all were not the trusties but the nonprisoner chiefs (Kuragin, Poisui-Shapka, Ignatchenko from SevDvinlag). They did not just steal but "removed" from the storerooms, and not just by the pound, but in sacks and barrels. And again it wasn't only for themselves—they had to divvy up. And the trusties had somehow to cover all this up and forge the records. And anyone who refused to do it was not

---

4. The genuine content of this case, it seems, was vastly different from *even* the first version of Fadeyev. But we will not put our faith solely in camp rumors.

5. For his surprising—or too ordinary—fate, see below, Part IV, Chapter 4.

only sacked from his job but sent to a penalty or strict-regimen camp. And so the trusty staffs, by the will of the chiefs, were riddled with cowards afraid of physical work, and scoundrels and thieves. And the only ones ever prosecuted were storekeepers and bookkeepers, while the chiefs kept out of it—after all, it wasn't they who signed the receipts. And the interrogators considered it a provocation for storekeepers to testify against bosses.

The picture is quite vertical. . . .

It so fell out that a woman of my acquaintance, Natalya Milevna Anichkova, who was honest in the extreme, was once assigned to manage the camp bakery. At the very beginning she ascertained that it was customary to send a certain amount of baked bread (from the prisoners' bread rations) outside the camp compound daily (without any documents, of course), in return for which the bakers received a small amount of preserves and butter from the shop for the free employees. She forbade this system, stopped the bread leaving the camp compound—and immediately the bread began to turn out underbaked or rock hard, and then the batch would be late (this from the bakers), and then they began to withhold flour from the warehouse—and the camp chief (he had been getting more out of this than anyone!) refused a horse to fetch and deliver. Anichkova struggled for so many days and then surrendered—and at once the work went smoothly again.

Even if a compound trusty was able to keep out of this universal thievery, it was nonetheless nearly impossible for him to desist from using his privileged position to get himself other benefits—such as Rest Point out of turn, hospital food, the best clothing, bed linen, or the best place in the barracks. I do not know and cannot picture a trusty so saintly that he never grabbed the least tiny bit of something for himself from all those benefits strewn about. And his fellow trusties would have been afraid of him. They would have forced him out! Everyone, even though indirectly, or in a roundabout way, even though almost not knowing, nonetheless made use of these benefits—and in some degree lived off the sloggers.

It is hard, very hard, for a compound trusty to have an unsullied conscience.

And then there is another question—about the means with which he got his position. Very rarely was it a clear-cut question of qualifications (as for a physician or for many work trusties). The unobjectionable path was to be an invalid. But frequently it was the protection of the "godfather." Of course, there were apparently neutral ways to get there: people got positions because of old prison connections; or thanks to collective group support (often based on ties of nationality—certain of the smaller nationalities were successful at this and used traditionally to cluster in trusty jobs; and then the Communists used to help each other out privately).

And there was another question too. When you were raised up, how did you conduct yourself toward the rest, toward the common herd? How much arrogance was here, how much rudeness, how much forgetfulness that we were all natives and that our power was transient?

And finally the highest question of all: If you were in no way harmful to your brother prisoners, were you at least in any way useful to them? Did you ever use your position, even once, to defend the general welfare—or only and always on your own?

As far as the work trusties were concerned, it would be quite unjust to accuse them of "eating the sloggers' food," or "riding on their backs"; the sloggers weren't paid for their labor, true, but not because they fed the trusties. The trusties weren't paid for their work either—everything went into the same abyss. But the other moral doubts still remain: the virtual inevitability of exploiting advantages in living conditions; the not always clean ways of getting the right assignment; arrogance. And then always that same question at the top: What did you do for the general good? Anything at all? Ever?

Yet there were some who could, like Vasily Vlasov, look back on deeds on behalf of the universal good. Yes, such clearheaded, smart fellows who managed to get around the arbitrary camp rules, who helped to organize the common life so not all would die, and so as to deceive both the trust and the camp. Those heroes of the Archipelago, who understood their duty not in terms of feeding their own persons but as a burden and an obligation to the whole prison herd. The tongue simply cannot be twisted to call such as these "trusties." And most came from the engineers. And . . . glory to them!

But for the rest no glory. There is no reason to put them on a pedestal. And there is also no reason for the former trusties to be contemptuous of Ivan Denisovich because they succeeded in sidestepping all kinds of slave labor and did not lay bricks by the sweat of their brow. Nor is it worth arguing that we intellectuals expend twice as much energy on general work—on the work itself, and then by a sort of psychic combustion, on all the mental activity and suffering which we simply cannot stop, and as a result of which it is fair for us to avoid the general work; and let cruder types *slog away*. (It is still not clear whether we do in fact expend twice as much energy.)

Yes, in order to abstain from coming to some sort of an "arrangement" in camp and let the force of gravity take over and drag you down to the bottom, one must have a very stable soul, a very illumined consciousness, a large part of one's term behind one, and, probably, in addition regular parcels from home—otherwise it is straight suicide.

As the gratefully guilty old camp veteran D. S. L——v put it: If I am alive today, that means someone else was on the list for execution in my place that night; if I am alive today, it means that someone else suffocated in the lower hold in my place; if I am alive today, it means that I got those extra seven ounces of bread which the dying man went without.

All this is written . . . not in reproach. The basic viewpoint of this book has already been set forth and will be held to until the end: all who suffered, all who were squeezed, all who were forced to make a cruel choice ought rather to be vindicated than accused. The more correct thing will be . . . to vindicate them.

But in forgiving oneself the choice between dying and being saved—do not forgetfully cast a stone at the one whose choice was even harder. We have already met such people in this book. And there will be more.

■

The Archipelago was a world without diplomas, a world in which the only credentials were one's own claims. The zek was not supposed to have documents with him, including educational records. In arriving at a new camp you yourself would invent who you would make yourself out to be this time.

In camp it was advantageous to be a medical assistant, a barber, an accordion player—I daren't go any higher. You would get along all right if you were a tinsmith, a glass blower, or an automobile mechanic. But woe on you if you were a geneticist or, God help you, a philosopher, a linguist, an art historian—then you had had it! You would *kick the bucket* on general work in two weeks.

More than once I dreamed of declaring myself a medical assistant! How many writers and philologists saved themselves in the Archipelago this way! But each time I could not make up my mind to it—not even because of the superficial examination (knowing medicine within the limits of a literate layman, yes, and having a smattering of Latin, somehow or other I would have *bluffed my way through*), but I found it awful to picture myself giving shots without knowing how. If there had been only powders, syrups, poultices, and cupping, I would have tried it.

Having learned from my experience at Novy Iyerusalim that being a "commander of production" was repulsive, when I was shifted to my next camp, at Kaluga Gates, in Moscow itself—right at the threshold, at the gatehouse, I lied, saying that I was a norm setter (I had heard that term in camp for the first time in my life, and I had not the faintest idea what norm setting was, but I hoped it was along mathematical lines).

The reason I had to tell my lie right there at the gatehouse, on the threshold, was that the site chief, Junior Lieutenant Nevezhin, a tall, gloomy hunchback, came to question the new prisoner transport right away then and there at the gatehouse despite our arrival at night; he had to decide by morning who was to be sent where, he was that businesslike. With a distrustful stare he sized up my officer's britches stuffed into my boots, my long-skirted overcoat, my face lit up with eagerness to serve, and asked me a couple of questions about norm setting. (I felt I had replied skillfully, but I realized afterward that my first two words had exposed me to Nevezhin.) And in the morning I was not taken out to work—I had been victorious. Two days passed and he appointed me—not a norm setter, but much higher—"works manager." In other words, I was senior to the work assigner—chief of all the brigadiers! I had got out of the frying pan into the fire! There had been no such post before I came there. That showed what a loyal dog I had looked to him to be! And what a one Nevezhin would have made of me too!

But once again my career fell through. God saved me: that

same week Nevezhin was removed from his post for stealing building materials. He had a very powerful personality, possessed an almost hypnotic stare, and he did not even have to raise his voice for the whole line-up to listen to him in trepidation. On grounds both of age—he was over fifty—and of camp experience and his own cruelty he ought long since to have been an NKVD general, and they said he had in fact already been a lieutenant colonel; however, he could not overcome his passion for stealing. He was never arrested because he was *one of their own*, but instead was merely removed from duty for a time and each time reduced in rank. And now he hadn't even been able to hold on to the rank of junior lieutenant either. Lieutenant Mironov, who replaced him, didn't have the patience to train anyone, and I myself could not get it into my head that what they wanted was for me to be a crushing hammer. Mironov turned out to be dissatisfied with me in every way, and he was even annoyed with and rejected my energetic reports:

"You don't even know how to write, you have a clumsy style." And he held out to me the report by Pavlov, the foreman: "Here's a man who knows how to write."

"On analyzation of certain facts of reduction of fulfillment of plan there is:

1. insufficient quantity of construction materials
2. because of incomplete supply with tools of the brigades
3. upon insufficient organization of work on the side of technical personnel
4. and also safety precautions are not being observed."

The value of this style was that the work management was to blame for everything and the camp administration . . . for nothing.

Incidentally, this Pavlov, a former tank officer (who still went around in his helmet), had a similar way of talking: "If you understand about love, then prove to me what's love."

(He was discussing a familiar subject: he was unanimously praised by the women who had been intimate with him. In camp this sort of thing is not kept very secret.)

The second week there I was demoted in disgrace to general work, and in my place they appointed that same Vasya Pavlov. Since I had not contested with him for the place and had not resisted my ouster, he sent me out not with a shovel but with a painters' brigade.

The whole brief history of my leadership did, however, secure me an advantage in living conditions: as works manager I was housed in a special trusties' room, one of the two privileged rooms in the camp. And Pavlov was already living in the other such room, and when I was dismissed no worthy claimant turned up for my cot, and for several months I continued to live on there.

And at the time I valued only the better living conditions in this room: Instead of multiple bunks there were ordinary cots and one bed table for every two persons, not for a whole brigade. During the day the door was locked and you could leave your things there. Last, there was a half-legal electric hot plate, and it was not necessary to go and crowd around the big common stove in the yard. Slave of my oppressed and frightened body, I valued only this at the time.

But now, when I have an urge to write about my neighbors in that room, I realize what its principal advantage was: never again in my life, either through personal inclination or in the social labyrinth, would I get close to such people as Air Force General Belyayev and the MVD man Zinovyev, who, if not a general, was close to it.

I now know that a writer cannot afford to give in to feelings of rage, disgust, or contempt. Did you answer someone in a temper? If so, you didn't hear him out and lost track of his system of opinions. You avoided someone out of disgust—and a completely unknown personality slipped out of your ken—precisely the type you would have needed someday. But, however tardily, I nonetheless caught myself and realized I had always devoted my time and attention to people who fascinated me and were pleasant, who engaged my sympathy, and that as a result I was seeing society like the Moon, always from one side.

But just as the Moon, as it swings slightly back and forth ("libration"), shows us a portion of its dark side too—so that chamber of monstrosities disclosed people unknown to me.

Air Force Major General Aleksandr Ivanovich Belyayev (everyone in camp still called him "general") was invariably noticed by every new arrival on the first day in the first line-up. He stood out from the whole blackish-gray, lousy camp column, not only in height and bearing, but because of his excellent leather coat, no doubt foreign-made, of a kind you would not see on the street in Moscow (the people who wore them ride about in automobiles) and even more because of his particular air of *nonpresence*. Even without stirring in the camp column he was able to demonstrate that he had no relationship whatever to all that camp rabble swarming about him, that he would even die without realizing how he had come to be there. Stretched to his full height he looked over the heads of the mob, just as if he were reviewing a completely different parade which we could not see. And when the trooping out began and the guard at the gatehouse whacked a board across the backs of the zeks on the outside in the departing fives, Belyayev (in his brigade of work trusties) tried never to be the one on the end. If he did happen to get there, then he squeamishly shuddered and bent down as he went past the gatehouse, showing by his whole back how he held the gatehouse sentry in contempt. And the latter did not dare to touch him.

While I was still works manager, in other words an important chief, I became acquainted with the general in the following way: In the construction office where he was working as assistant norm setter I noticed that he was smoking, and I approached him to get a light from his cigarette. I politely asked his permission and had already bent over his desk in readiness. With a sharp gesture Belyayev jerked his cigarette from in front of mine, as though fearing I might infect it, got out an expensive chrome-plated lighter, and placed it down before me. It was easier for him to let me soil and spoil his lighter than to lower himself by holding his cigarette for me! I was embarrassed. And whenever anyone was impudent enough to ask him for a light from his cigarette he always placed his expensive lighter in front of him the same way, thus crushing him completely and dispelling any desire to approach him a second time. And if anyone managed to catch him at the very moment when he himself was lighting up with his lighter, and hastened to shove a cigarette toward him —he calmly blew out the lighter, closed its top, and placed it, like that, in front of the person approaching. This gave them to understand the whole magnitude of his sacrifice. And if there was no one else from whom to get a light, all the free foremen and prisoner brigadiers who swarmed in the office went outdoors in the courtyard to get one rather than to him.

Housed in the same room with him now, and with our cots in fact side by side, I was able to discover that squeamishness, disdain, and irritation were the principal feelings possessing him in his situation as a prisoner. Not only did he never go to the camp mess hall ("I don't even know where the door to it is!"), but he wouldn't let our neighbor Prokhorov bring him anything from the camp slops—except his bread ration. Was there any other zek in the Archipelago who could have so mocked his poor bread ration? Belyayev took it gingerly like a dirty toad—for, you see, it had been touched by hands and carried on wooden trays—and trimmed it with his knife on all *six* sides—cutting off both the crust and the dough as well. These six cut-off pieces he never gave to those who asked for them—to Prokhorov or the old-man orderly—but threw them in the slop bucket. Once I was even so bold as to ask him why he did not give them to Prokhorov. He proudly threw back his head, his white hair cropped very short (he wore his hair so short so that it would seem both a hair style and a camp haircut): "My cellmate at the Lubyanka once asked me: 'Please let me finish your soup!' I was nearly sick to my stomach! I . . . react very painfully to human humiliation!" He refused bread to the hungry so as not to humiliate them!

The general was able to preserve all this haughtiness with such ease because there was a trolleybus No. 4 stop near the gatehouse. Every day at 1 P.M. when we returned from the work compound to the residence compound for lunch, the general's wife would descend from a trolleybus at the outer gatehouse, bringing a hot meal in thermoses, cooked just an hour before in the general's kitchen at home. On weekdays they were not permitted to meet, and the thermoses were handed over by the turnkey. But on Sundays they spent half an hour together at the gatehouse. They said his wife always left in tears; Aleksandr Ivanovich took out on her everything that had accumulated in his proud and suffering soul in the course of a week.

Belyayev made one accurate observation: "In camp it is impossible to keep things or foodstuffs simply in a box or simply under lock and key. The box has to be a steel box and bolted to the floor." But from this there followed the conclusion: "Out of a hundred people in camp eighty are scoundrels!" (He didn't say ninety-five so as not to lose all his listeners.) "If I should ever meet anyone from in here out in freedom and that person should rush up to me, I would say: 'You are insane! I have never met you before!' "

"How I suffer from barracks living!" he said. (This with only six people there!) "If only I could eat by myself, locked in alone!" Was he hinting that we ought to go out while he ate? He especially wanted to *eat* alone! Was it because what he ate today was incomparable with what others ate, or was it simply out of his own circle's established custom of hiding their bounty from the hungry?

On the other hand, he loved to talk with us, and it is highly unlikely that he would really have liked to be in a separate room. But the way he liked to talk was one-sided—loudly, self-confidently, and only about himself: "They offered *me* another camp with more comfortable conditions. . . ." (I can quite well picture that they do offer such as him a choice.) "That never happens to *me*." "Do you know, I . . ." "When I was in the Anglo-Egyptian Sudan . . ." But nothing of any interest at all came after that, just some sort of nonsense to provide some kind of justification for that resounding introduction: "When I was in the Anglo-Egyptian Sudan . . ."

He had really been around and seen sights. He was less than fifty and was still good and strong. There was just one strange thing: he was an Air Force major general, but he never talked about a single battle flight, not even one single flight. And yet, judging by his own account, he was the head of our Air Force purchasing mission in the United States during the war. America had evidently astonished him. And he managed to buy a lot there too. He never lowered himself to explain to us what precisely he had been arrested for, but evidently it was in connection with this American trip or his stories about it. "Otsep[6] proposed the path of complete confession.[7] But I said, 'I would rather have my term doubled, but I am guilty of nothing!' " One can readily believe that as far as the government was concerned he *was* innocent of any guilt; they gave him not a double but a half-term —five years, when even sixteen-year-old chatterboxes got more than that.

Looking at him and listening to him, I used to think: This is

6. A well-known Soviet lawyer.
7. In other words, he seconded the interrogator.

what he is like now! *After* the rough fingers had torn his shoulder boards off (I can just picture how he had cringed!), after the body searches, after the boxes, after the Black Marias, after "Hands behind your backs!"—he did not allow himself to be contradicted even in petty things, let alone in big things. (Big things he would not even have discussed with us, since we were unworthy, except for Zinovyev.) But not once did I ever see him absorb any thought he himself had not expressed. He was simply *incapable* of accepting any argument! He knew everything *before* we spoke! What had he been like earlier as head of the purchasing mission, a Soviet envoy to the West? A polished, white-faced, impenetrable sphinx, a symbol of the "New Russia," as they understood it in the West. What would it have been like to approach him with a request? Or to shove your head into his office with a request? How he would have barked! How he'd come down on you! It would have explained a lot if he had come from a long line of military men—but he hadn't. These Himalayas of self-assurance had been mastered by a Soviet general of the first generation. During the Civil War in the Red Army he was probably a young fellow in bast sandals who couldn't sign his name. How had all this come into being so swiftly? . . . He had always been in an elite circle—even aboard trains, even at resorts, always with those of his own group, behind the iron gates where entrance was permitted only with passes.

And what about the others? More likely to be like him than different. And what would happen if the truth that the "sum of the angles of a triangle is equal to 180 degrees" were to threaten their private residences, their ranks, their assignments abroad? In that case they would cut off your head for drawing a triangle! Triangular pediments would be knocked off all houses! A decree would be issued that angles henceforth were to be measured in radians!

And once again I thought: What about me? Why couldn't they have made the same sort of general out of me in the course of twenty years? Of course they could have.

And once again I looked closely: Aleksandr Ivanovich was not at all a bad chap. When he read Gogol he laughed warmly. And he used to make us all laugh when he was in a good mood. He had an intelligent laugh. If I had wanted to nourish hatred for him in myself—there when we were lying next to one another on our cots—I could not have done it. The way was not closed for him to become a fully good person. But—only through suffering. Through suffering.

Pavel Nikolayevich Zinovyev didn't go to the camp mess hall either, and also would have liked to arrange things so that he had his meals brought to him in thermos jugs. It was a bitter pill to swallow to be left behind Belyayev, to turn out to be on a lower rung. But his circumstances were more difficult. Belyayev had not been punished by confiscation of his property, whereas Zinovyev had been subjected to partial confiscation. His money, his savings accounts had evidently all been hauled in and taken from him, and all that was left him was a good rich apartment. And how he used to love to talk about that apartment—time and time again, at great length, smacking his lips over every detail of the bath, realizing what enjoyment we must be getting from his story. He even had a saying of his own: After forty a man's value is determined by his apartment! (He used to recount all this in Belyayev's absence because Belyayev would not even have listened to him but would have started telling stories about himself instead, although not about his apartment, for he considered himself an intellectual, but perhaps about the Sudan again.) But according to Pavel Nikolayevich, his wife was ill and his daughter was obliged to work—and there was no one to bring him any thermoses. However, even the food parcels he received on Sundays were modest. And he was forced to bear his situation with the pride of an impoverished nobleman. Nonetheless he did not go to the mess hall, disdaining the filth there and the mass of chomping rabble, but he used to ask Prokhorov to bring both the gruel and the cereal to the room, where he warmed them up on the hot plate. He would willingly have cut six sides off the bread ration too, but he had no other bread, and he therefore limited himself to holding his bread ration over the hot plate, burning from all six sides the microbes implanted there by the hands of the bread-cutters and Prokhorov. He did not go to the mess hall and could even on occasion renounce his gruel, but he didn't have enough blue-blooded pride to restrain himself from petty begging in the room: "Could I just try a tiny piece? I haven't eaten any of that for a long time. . . ."

On the whole he was exaggeratedly gentle and polite—till

something rubbed him the wrong way. His politeness was particularly notable beside Belyayev's unnecessary rudeness. Inwardly restrained, outwardly restrained, with a deliberate way of chewing and cautious movements—he was the genuine Chekhov character "The Man in the Case." So true to life that there is no need to describe the rest of it, he was just as in Chekhov, except that he was not a schoolteacher, but an MVD general. It was impossible to use the electric hot plate even for a second during those minutes Pavel Nikolayevich had set aside for himself; beneath his snakelike stare you just jerked your mess tin off the hot plate immediately, and if you hadn't . . . he would have ticked you off pronto. During the lengthy Sunday daytime roll calls in the courtyard I used to try to take a book out with me (always about physics, keeping as far from literature as possible), and I hid behind the backs of those in front and read. Oh, what torments this violation of discipline gave Pavel Nikolayevich! You see, I was reading *in formation*, in sacred formation! And by doing this I was stressing my own challenge, flaunting my insolence. He didn't attack me directly, but stared at me in such a way, and squirmed in such torment, so groaned and grunted, that all the other trusties were sick of my reading too, so in the end I had to renounce my book, and stand there like an idiot for an hour at a time. (And you couldn't read in the room, you had to listen to the stories.) Once one of the girl bookkeepers from the construction office was late at line-up and thereby held up the departure of the trusty brigade to the work compound five minutes. And so, instead of being led out at the head of the column, our brigade was put at the end. There was nothing unusual about this and neither the work assigner nor the jailer even paid any attention, but Zinovyev in his special bluish-gray fine woolen overcoat, in his severely cocked visored cap, long since without its star, in spectacles, greeted the tardy woman with an angry snarl: "Why the devil are you late? We're standing here because of you!" (He just could not hold his tongue! He had grown utterly exasperated in the course of those five minutes! He had grown ill!) The girl turned on him sharply and with eyes glistening with pleasure told him off: "Apple polisher! Big nothing! Chichikov!" (Why Chichikov? She probably mixed him up with Belikov.) "Shut your trap!" And more and more and more, right to the borderline of the mother oaths. She managed everything with just her sharp agile tongue. She didn't lift a finger.

But it seemed as if she were invisibly whipping him across the cheeks, because spots, spots of red, flamed on his lusterless womanlike skin, and his ears blushed crimson and his lips twitched. He ruffled up but said nary another word and did not attempt to raise his hand in self-defense. That same day he complained to me: "What can I do with the *incorrigible directness* of my personality! It is my misfortune that even *here* I can't get away from discipline. I am *compelled* to utter reprimands; it disciplines those nearby."

He was always nervous at the morning line-up—he wanted to rush to work as quickly as possible. And hardly had the trusty brigade been let into the work compound than he very demonstratively overtook all those who were not hurrying, whose pace was leisurely, and almost ran into the office. Did he want the chiefs to observe him? Not very important. Was it so the zeks would see how intensely busy he was at his work? In part, yes. But the most important thing, the most sincere part, was to separate himself from the crowd as swiftly as possible, to get out of the camp compound, to hide himself in the quiet little planning section and once there . . . once there, certainly not to do the kind of work Vasily Vlasov did, trying to figure out how to rescue the working brigades, but instead, for whole hours at a time, to loaf, to smoke, to dream about one more amnesty, and to imagine another desk for himself, another office, with a buzzer to summon people, with several telephones, with servile secretaries, with visitors stiffly at attention.

Little we knew about him! He didn't like to speak of his MVD past—nor about his rank, his positions, or the nature of his work—the customary "reticence" of the former MVD men. But his greatcoat was, as it happens, that same sort of dark bluish-gray that is described by the authors of the book about the White Sea–Baltic Canal. And not even in camp did it occur to him to rip the sky-blue edgings off his tunic and his britches. During his two years' imprisonment he had evidently not had to encounter the real gaping maw of camp, to sniff the abyss of the Archipelago. Our camp had of course been assigned him by his choice: his apartment was just a few trolleybus stops from the camp, somewhere on Kaluga Square. And, not realizing the depths to which he had fallen, or just how hostile he was being to his present company, he sometimes let something drop in the room: One day he disclosed a close acquaintanceship with Kruglov (who at that time was not yet Minister of Internal Affairs), another with Frenkel, or with Zavenyagin, all big shots in Gulag. Once he recalled that during the war he had been in charge of construction on a large section of the Syzran-Saratov Railroad, and this meant he had been in Frenkel's GULZhDS. What did he mean—in charge? He was no engineer. Had he been chief of camp administration? Another darling Kleinmikhel?* And then, from those heights, he had painfully fallen almost to the level of an ordinary prisoner. He had been sentenced under Article 109, and in the MVD that meant that he had *taken* more than his rank permitted. They gave him seven years—*as one of their own*. That meant that he had grabbed off enough for a whole twenty. Under Stalin's amnesty they had already knocked off half of what remained, and he was therefore left with two years and a fraction. But he suffered—just as much as if he'd had the whole tenner.

The one and only window in our room looked out on the Neskuchny Park. Quite close to the window and just a bit below us the treetops rustled. Everything kept changing there: snow-storms, thaws, the first foliage. When Pavel Nikolayevich was not being irritated by anything inside and was only moderately sad, he would stand at the window, looking out at the park, and croon softly and pleasantly:

> Sleep deep, my heart!
> Don't awaken, don't arouse what used to be.

And there he was—a most agreeable person in a drawing room! But how many mass graves had he left along his section of the track!

The corner of the Neskuchny Park facing our compound was set off by hillocks from people strolling in the park and was secluded, or would have been, if you did not count our shaven heads peering out of windows. On May 1 some lieutenant brought to this hiding place his girl, who was wearing a bright-colored dress. Here they were concealed from the rest of the park, but they paid no more heed to us than to the stare of a dog or a cat. The officer laid his girl right there on the grass, and she was not shy either.

> Do not call back what has dashed off afar,
> Do not love what you used to love.

On the whole our room was a model room. The MVD man and the general ran us. We could make use of the hot plate only with their permission (it was a *people's* hot plate) when they were not using it themselves. They alone decided whether the room should be ventilated or not, where to put our shoes, where to hang trousers, when to stop talking, when to go to sleep, when to wake up. Several steps down the corridor was the door to the big barracks room where a republic led its stormy life, where they kept sending all authorities "up the mouth," "up the nose," etc. But here we had privileges, and in clinging to them, we also had to observe all the legalities. Having been booted into the insignificant painters' brigade I had no say: I had become a proletarian and at any moment they might cast me out into the common barracks. The peasant Prokhorov, even though he was considered the "brigadier" of the work trusties, had been appointed to that position chiefly to act as servant—to carry bread and mess tins, to communicate with the jailers and the barracks orderlies, in a word to perform all the dirty work (it was this very same peasant who had fed the two generals).* And so it was that we were compelled to submit to our dictators. But where was the great Russian intelligentsia and what was it looking at?

Dr. Pravdin*·(and I did not invent the name either) was a neuropathologist and the camp physician. He was seventy. This meant that the Revolution had arrived when he was already in his forties, that he had come to full maturity during the best period of Russian thought, in the spirit of conscientiousness, honor, and reverence for the common people. And what an appearance! An enormous venerable head with silvery flopping gray hair which the camp clippers did not dare to touch (a special privilege from the chief of the Medical Section). His portrait would have embellished the finest medical journal in the world! Any country would have been honored to have such a minister of health! His big nose, which knew its own value, inspired total confidence in his diagnoses. His movements were all dignified. He was so capacious a doctor that he hardly fitted on a single metal cot and hung over the sides.

I don't know how good a neuropathologist he was. It is quite possible he could have been a good one, but only in a mellow, well-mannered epoch, and most certainly not in a government hospital, but at his own house, behind his brass nameplate on an oaken door, to the melodic chiming of a grandfather clock against the wall, and not subordinate to anything except his own conscience. However, he had been thoroughly frightened since then —frightened enough to last the rest of his life. I don't know whether he had ever been imprisoned before, whether perhaps he had been hauled out to be shot during the Civil War (this would not have been surprising). But even without a revolver at his head he had been frightened enough. It was enough to have had to work in outpatient departments where they had demanded he see nine patients an hour, where there was only enough time to tap for a knee jerk with a rubber mallet; and to have been a member of an Experts' Commission on Workmen's Disabilities (VTEK), and a member of a Health Resort Commission, and a member of a military conscription board, with papers everywhere to sign, sign, sign, and to know that your head was at stake with every signature, that some doctors had already been arrested, others threatened, and you still had to keep signing medical certificates, and diagnoses and expert testimony, and medical attestations and histories of illnesses, and every single signature involved a Hamlet-like soul-searching as to whether a given patient should be freed from work or not, whether he was suitable for service or not, whether he was sick or healthy. Sick people implored you in one direction and the bosses pulled you in the other, and the frightened doctor would lose his presence of mind, become a prey to doubt and trepidation, and then remorse.

But all that was out in freedom, those were sweet nothings! In here, arrested as an enemy of the people, so terrified by the interrogator that he was ready to die of a heart attack (I can imagine how many people, a whole medical institute, no doubt, he may have dragged there with him in such a state of terror!) —what was he now? An ordinary scheduled visit of the free chief of the Medical Section of the camp, an old toper with no medical education, put Pravdin into such a condition of nervousness and total confusion that he was quite incapable of reading the Russian texts on the hospital cards. His doubts now multiplied by ten. In camp he was simply in such a state he didn't know whether a prisoner could be freed from work with a temperature of 99.86 degrees or not. What if they dressed him down? And he would come to our room to get our advice. He could maintain a calm equilibrium no longer than a day at a time—

one day after he had been praised by the camp chief or even a junior jailer. As a result of this praise he somehow felt himself safe for the next twenty-four hours. But the next morning he was again overtaken by a sense of implacable alarm. One day an extremely urgent prisoner transport was dispatched from the camp and they were in such a hurry that there was no time to arrange for baths. (It was fortunate they didn't simply drive them naked into the icy spray.) The senior jailer came to Pravdin and ordered him to sign a certificate to the effect that the transported prisoners had undergone hygienic processing. Pravdin, as always, obeyed the orders—but you should have seen him afterward! Coming to the room, he sank onto his cot like someone in a state of collapse. He clutched at his heart, he groaned, and would not listen to our reassurances. We went to sleep. He smoked one cigarette after another, ran back and forth to the toilet, and finally, after midnight, dressed himself, and with the look of a madman went to the duty jailer whose nickname was Shorty—an illiterate pithecanthropus, but with a star on his forage cap—to ask his advice: What would happen to him now? Would they or would they not give him a second term under Article 58 for this crime? Or would they only send him away from his Moscow camp to a far-distant one? (His family was in Moscow and used to bring him rich parcels, so he clung to our minicamp for all he was worth.)

Intimidated and frightened, Pravdin lost his will to do anything, even in preventive hygiene. He was totally unable to make demands on the cooks or the barracks orderlies or even his own Medical Section. It was dirty in the mess hall, in the kitchen the bowls were badly washed, and in the Medical Section itself it was never clear whether the blankets were ever shaken out. He knew all this, but was incapable of insisting on cleanliness. There was only one fetish which he shared with the whole camp administration (it was a whim known to many camps)—the daily washing down of the floors in the residence quarters. This was carried out without fail. The air and the cots never dried out because of the eternally wet and rotting floors. Pravdin was regarded without respect by even the lowliest last-legger in the camp. Throughout his prison career he was left unplundered and uncheated only by those who didn't feel like bothering. Only because our room was locked up all night did his things, scattered about his bed, remain intact, and his night table, the most disorderly in the camp, from which everything kept falling onto the floor, remain unplundered.

Pravdin had been imprisoned for eight years under Articles 58-10 and 58-11, in other words as a political propagandist and organizer, but I discovered in him the naiveté of a backward child! Even in his third year of imprisonment he had still not matured to the level of the thoughts he had confessed to at his interrogation. He believed we had all been imprisoned only temporarily, as a kind of joke, and that a magnificent and generous amnesty was being prepared so that we would value freedom all the more and be eternally grateful to the Organs for this lesson. He believed in the prosperity of the collective farms, in the infamous perfidy of the Marshall Plan for enslaving Europe, and in the intrigues of the Allies striving to start a third world war.

I remember that he came in radiant one day, shining with that quiet, benevolent happiness that believers return with after a good vespers. Set in his large, good-natured, open face, his always prominent eyes, with sagging lower lids, were all aglow with an unearthly meekness. It turned out that a meeting of the camp compound trusties had just taken place. The camp chief had first shouted at them and banged his fist, but then all of a sudden had calmed down and said that he trusted them *as his loyal assistants!* And Pravdin touchingly confided in us: "I got back all my enthusiasm for our work after those words!" (To give the general his due, he made a contemptuous grimace.)

The doctor's name did not lie: he was truth-loving and loved truth. He loved it, but he was unworthy of it!

In our tiny model he was merely amusing. But if one moves from this tiny model to the larger scale, it's enough to make your blood run cold. What proportion, what percentage, of our *spiritual* Russia has come to this? Purely as a result of fear . . .

Pravdin had grown up in a cultured milieu, and all his life he had been occupied with mental work; he had been surrounded by intellectually sophisticated people—but was he really an *intellectual*, in other words a person with an individual *intellect* of his own?

Over the years I have had much occasion to ponder this word, the *intelligentsia*. We are all very fond of including ourselves in it—but you see not all of us belong. In the Soviet Union this word has acquired a completely distorted meaning. They began to classify among the intelligentsia all those who don't work (and are afraid to) with their hands. All the Party, government, military, and trade-union bureaucrats have been included. All bookkeepers and accountants—the mechanical slaves of Debit. All office employees. And with even greater ease we include here *all* teachers (even those who are no more than talking textbooks and have neither independent knowledge nor an independent view of education). *All* physicians, including those capable only of making doodles on the patients' case histories. And without the slightest hesitation all those who are only in the vicinity of editorial offices, publishing houses, cinema studios, and philharmonic orchestras are included here, not even to mention those who actually get published, make films, or pull a fiddle bow.

And yet the truth is that not one of these criteria permits a person to be classified in the intelligentsia. If we do not want to lose this concept, we must not devalue it. The intellectual is not defined by professional pursuit and type of occupation. Nor are good upbringing and a good family enough in themselves to produce an intellectual. An intellectual is a person whose interests in and preoccupation with the spiritual side of life are insistent and constant and not forced by external circumstances, even flying in the face of them. An intellectual is a person whose thought is nonimitative.

In our chamber of monstrosities the leading intellectuals were considered to be Belyayev and Zinovyev; and as for the foreman Orachevsky and the stock clerk and toolmaker, the coarse, uncultured fellow Prokhorov, their presence offended the feelings of these highly placed people; and during the period when I was prime minister, the general and the MVD man both managed to appeal to me, trying to persuade me to toss both these peasants out of our room—because of their slovenliness, their way of lying down on their cots in their boots, and in general for their lack of intellectual qualities. (The generals were giving thought to getting rid of the peasant who fed them!) But, in fact, I liked them both—I myself am a peasant at heart. And so a balance was established in the room. (And very soon no doubt the generals spoke to someone about me—trying to have me thrown out as well.)

Orachevsky really did have a coarse exterior and there was

nothing "intellectual" about him. In music he understood nothing but Ukrainian songs. He had never heard anything at all of ancient Italian painting nor of modern French painting. Whether he loved books I couldn't say because we had none in the camp. He never intervened in the abstract arguments which used to start up in the room. He seemed not even to hear Belyayev's best monologues on the subject of the Anglo-Egyptian Sudan and Zinovyev's on his apartment. During his free time he preferred to brood for long periods in gloomy silence, with his feet placed on the rail at the foot of the cot, the heels of his boots on the rail itself, their soles aimed at the generals. (Not out of a desire to taunt, but because in getting ready for line-up, or in the lunch interval or in the evening, if one expects to go out again, how could any reasonable person renounce the satisfaction of lying down for a moment? And it was a lot of fuss to take boots off— they had been pulled tightly over two sets of footcloths.) Orachevsky also failed to react to the doctor's self-torments and doubts. And then suddenly, after having been silent an hour or two, he might, quite regardless of what was going on in the room at that time, declare tragically: "Yes! It is easier for a camel to pass through the eye of a needle than for a 58 to get out of jail." On the other hand, in practical arguments, on the attributes of everyday objects, or on correct conduct in everyday life, he might mobilize all his Ukrainian stubbornness to assert and prove with great passion that felt boots—valenki—spoil from being dried out on the stove, and that it was better and pleasanter to wear them the whole winter without drying them out. So, of course, what kind of intellectual could he be!

But he alone of all of us was sincerely devoted to the construction project, he alone could speak with interest about it in nonworking time. Learning that the zeks had managed to break down the partitions between rooms that were already completely installed and use them for firewood, he seized his rough head with his rude hands and rocked back and forth as if in pain. He could not comprehend the natives' barbarity! Perhaps because he had been in prison for only one year. Someone came and said that they had dropped a concrete block from the eighth floor. Everyone exclaimed: "Did it kill anyone?" But Orachevsky said: "Did you see *how* it broke? What directions did the cracks run in?" (The slabs had been cast according to his drawings, and what he wanted to know was whether he had put the reinforcing rods in the right places.) In the severe December cold the brigadiers and the foremen had gathered in the office one day to warm themselves and recount assorted camp gossip. Orachevsky came in, took off a mitten, and triumphantly and with great care emptied from it onto the desk an unmoving but still living orange and black beauty of a butterfly. "Now that's a butterfly for you—to survive a frost like that at five below! She was sitting on one of the rafters."

Everyone gathered around the butterfly and all fell silent. Those of us who proved fortunate enough to survive would be unlikely to end our terms with any more liveliness in them than that butterfly.

Orachevsky had been given only five years. He had been imprisoned for a *facial crime* (really out of Orwell)—for a *smile!* He had been an instructor in a field engineers' school. While showing another teacher in the classroom something in *Pravda*, he had smiled! The other teacher was killed soon after, so no one ever found out *what* Orachevsky had been smiling at. But the smile *had been observed*, and the fact of smiling at the central organ of the Party was in itself sacrilege! Then Orachevsky was invited to make a political report. He replied that he would carry out the order but he would be making the report without enthusiasm. This had filled the cup to overflowing!

Now which of the two—Pravdin or Orachevsky—was the closer to being an *intellectual?*

And there is no getting around speaking of Prokhorov here. He was a portly peasant, heavy-footed, with a heavy stare, and not much friendliness in his face, for he only smiled after thinking something through. In the Archipelago men like that are called "gray wolf." He had no inclination to make any concessions of his own or to do good to anyone. But what I liked about him right off was this: In bringing Zinovyev his mess tins and Belyayev his bread Prokhorov was not servile, with a false smile or even an empty word. Somehow he delivered these things majestically and with reserve, showing thereby that service was service but that he was no mere boy. To feed his big worker's body he had to have a lot to eat. For the sake of the general's gruel and grits he was willing to suffer his humiliating position in silence; knowing that they despised him there, he did not answer them rudely, but neither did he go running off in a flurry of haste for them "on tiptoe."[8] He could see through all of us, every last one of us he could see through, as if we were naked, but the occasion never did arise for him to speak his mind. I felt about Prokhorov that he was founded on bedrock, that much in our people rests on shoulders like his. He was in no hurry to smile at anyone; his gaze was sullen; but he never snapped at anyone's heels either.

He had not been imprisoned under Article 58, but he understood the facts of life from beginning to end. For many years he had been the chairman of a village soviet near Naro-Fominsk. In that kind of job one also had to know how to twist and turn, and be cruel, and stand one's ground against the higher-ups. Here is how he described his work as chairman:

"To be a patriot means always to be out in the lead. And it is obvious that you are going to be the first to run into all kinds of trouble. You make a report to the village soviet, and even though village talk for the most part *comes down to material things*, nonetheless some long-beard lets fly: 'What's permanent revolution?' The devil take it, whatever it is, I know that city women wear permanents, and if you don't answer him, they'll say: 'You've stuck your pig's snout where it doesn't belong.' And so I say that it is a kind of revolution that twists and turns and can't be held in the hand—go to the city and look at the women's curls, or on a sheep. And when our people started cursing out MacDonald, I corrected the authorities in my report: 'And you, comrades,' I said, 'would do better to step less on other dogs' tails!' "

Over the years he had become familiar with all the window dressing of our life, and had himself participated. He summoned the collective farm chairman one day and said: "Get one milkmaid ready for a gold medal at the agricultural fair—with a daily milking record of sixty liters!" And in the whole collective they collaborated to turn out such a milkmaid, they filled her cow's manger with high-protein feeds and even sugar. And the whole village and the whole collective farm knew what that agricultural fair was worth. But up above they were playacting, kidding themselves—which means this was what they wanted.

When the front approached Naro-Fominsk, Prokhorov was

8. This expression "on tiptoe"—"na tsyrlakh"—is explained in Chapter 19.

entrusted with evacuating the village soviet's cattle. But this measure, when you get down to it, was aimed not at the Germans but against the peasants themselves; they were the ones left behind on the bare earth without cattle or tractors. The peasants didn't want to hand their cattle over and fought back. (They were hoping the collective farms would fall apart and the cattle would then come to them.) And they nearly killed Prokhorov.

The front rolled past their village—and settled down for the whole winter. An artilleryman from way back in 1914, Prokhorov, without cattle and as a last resort, joined up with a Soviet artillery battery and carried shells until they drove him away. In the spring of 1942 Soviet power returned to their district and Prokhorov again became the chairman of the village soviet. By now he had acquired the full power to settle accounts with his enemies and to become a worse cur than before. And he would have prospered to this day. But—strangely—he did not. His heart had been shaken.

Their locality was desolated, and they gave the chairman bread coupons: to provide a bit from the bakery for those whose homes had burned down and those who were close to starvation. Prokhorov, however, began to take pity on the people, and disobeyed orders by overspending coupons, and got imprisoned under the law of "Seven-eighths"—for ten years. They had forgiven him MacDonald because of his lack of learning, but they did not forgive him human mercy.

Prokhorov, too, liked to lie there in the room for hours at a time, just like Orachevsky, with his boots on the foot rail of his cot, looking at the peeling ceiling. He only spoke up when the generals weren't present. I was fascinated by some of his judgments and expressions:

"What kind of line is harder to draw—one straight or one crooked? For a straight line you have to have instruments, while even a drunk can draw a crooked line with his foot. So it is with the line of life."

"Money—nowadays has *two stories*." (How apt that was! Prokhorov was referring to the way foodstuffs were bought from the collective farm at one price and sold to people at quite a different price. But he saw this on a broader plane too. The "two stories" of money are apparent in many areas; this permeates our whole life. The state pays us money on the first floor, and we have to pay out money everywhere on the second floor, and what that means is that we ourselves also have to collect somewhere on the second floor, since otherwise you'd go quickly bust.)

"A human being is not a devil, but he won't let you live," was another of his proverbs.

And there was much else in the same spirit, and I very much regret that I failed to preserve it all.

I called this room a chamber of monstrosities, but I could not have classified either Prokhorov or Orachevsky as a monstrosity. However, out of six there was a majority of monstrosities because what was I myself if not a monstrosity? Scraps and snatches of tangled-up beliefs, false hopes, and imaginary convictions still floated about in my head, even though they were already tattered and torn. And though I was already entering on the second year of my term, I still did not understand the finger of fate, nor what it was pointing out to me, thrust out there onto the Archipelago. I was still under the influence of the first superficial and corrupting thought instilled in me by that special-assignment prisoner at Krasnaya Presnya: "Just don't get into general work! Survive!" Inward development in the direction of general work came to me with great difficulty.

One night a passenger car came to the gatehouse, and a jailer entered our room, shook General Belyayev by the shoulder, and ordered him to accompany him "with his things." They led out the general, who was still dazed from having been suddenly awakened. He managed to send us a note from the Butyrki: "Don't lose heart!" (Evidently he meant because of his departure.) "If I am alive, I will write." (He did not write, but we found out about him elsewhere. They evidently considered him dangerous in a Moscow camp. He was sent to Potma. There were no thermos jugs with homemade soup there, and I rather imagine he no longer cut off the outside of his bread ration on six sides. And half a year later we heard rumors that he had sunk very low in Potma, that he was distributing gruel so as to get a sip now and then. I do not know whether this is true. As they say in camp: I sell it to you for what I paid for it.)

And so, losing no time, the very next morning I got myself the job of assistant norm setter in the general's place, still without having learned painting. But I didn't learn norm setting either, but only multiplied and divided to my heart's content. In the course of my new work I had occasion to go roaming about the whole construction site and time to sit on the ceiling of the eighth floor of our building, in other words, as if on the roof. And from there we prisoners had a panoramic view of Moscow.

On one side were the Sparrow Hills,* still open and clear. The future Lenin Prospekt had just been projected and outlined but did not exist. The insane asylum—"Kanatchikova dacha"—could be seen in its pristine, original state. In the opposite direction were the cupola of the Novodevichi Monastery, the carcass of the Frunze Academy, and in a violet haze far, far ahead, beyond the bustling streets, was the Kremlin, where all they had to do was merely sign that amnesty which had already been prepared for us. We, the doomed, were tempted by the sight of this world which in its riches and glory was virtually at our feet, yet at the same time forever unattainable.

But no matter how much of a greenhorn I was in champing at the bit to be out "in freedom," this city did not arouse in me envy or the wish to soar down onto its streets. All the evil holding us prisoner had been woven here. This arrogant city had never before provided such a justification as it did now after the war for the saying:

"Moscow turns its back on tears!"[9]

9. And now, from time to time, I take advantage of this opportunity—so rare for a former zek—to visit *his own* camp. Each time I am excited and nervous. It is so useful for measuring the relative dimensions of life—to immerse oneself in the inescapable past, to feel again *what one was before*. Where the mess hall, the stage, and the Cultural and Educational Section were before, the "Spartak Store" is now. Right there at the surviving trolleybus stop was the external gatehouse. Right there on the third floor is the window of our chamber of monstrosities. Right there was the line-up line. Right there Napolnaya's turret crane used to rise. Over there was where M. flitted over to Bershader. Along the asphalt courtyard people walk, promenade, talk about petty things. They do not know they are walking on corpses, on our recollections. They could not imagine that this courtyard might once have not been part of Moscow, twenty minutes' drive from the center, but a tiny islet of the savage Archipelago, more closely tied to Norilsk and the Kolyma than to Moscow. But I cannot now go up on the roof where we used to go freely and I cannot now enter those apartments in which I used to putty doors and lay floors. I put my hands behind my back as I used to do and I pace back and forth in the compound, imagining that I cannot leave here, that I can pace only from here to there and back again, and that I do not know where they will send me tomorrow. And those same trees in the Neskuchny Park, no longer fenced off by the compound fence, testify to me that they remember it all, that they remember me too, and that that is really how it was.

I pace in a prisoner's straight back-and-forth, with turns at each end, and as I do so all the complexities of life today gradually begin to melt away like wax.

I cannot restrain myself, I play the hooligan: I climb up the stairs and on a white windowsill, half a flight below the office of the camp chief, I write in black: "Camp Sector 121." People will pass this way and read it—and perhaps they will ponder it.

■

Although we were trusties, we were work trusties and our room wasn't the main room—up above us there was another one just like it where the compound trusties lived, and whence the triumvirate of the bookkeeper Solomonov, the stock clerk Bershader, and the work assigner Burshtein ruled our camp. Right there the reorganization was decided on: Pavlov to be removed from his position as works manager and replaced by K. And so one day this new prime minister came to live in our room. (And just before that Pravdin, despite all his attempts to curry favor, had been *hauled off* on a prisoner transport.) They didn't suffer me around much longer; they kicked me out of norm-setting work and out of that room as well. (In camp when you fall in social position, you rise to the upper level on a multiple bunk.) But while I was still there I had time to observe K., who filled out our small "model" not at all badly with one additional important postrevolutionary variety of the intellectual.

Aleksandr Fyodorovich K., a thirty-five-year-old calculating and grasping businessman (in other words, "a brilliant organizer"), was a construction engineer by profession. (But somehow he showed very little professional skill and merely fussed about with a slide rule.) He had received ten years under the terms of the law of August 7, had already served three years, had thoroughly oriented himself in camp, and felt himself as free and easy here as out in freedom. It was as if general work did not threaten him in the least. All the less, therefore, was he inclined to take pity on the untalented masses doomed precisely to this general work. He was one of those prisoners whose actions put more fear into the zeks than the actions of the Archipelago's inveterate bosses; once he had grabbed you by the throat he would never let go or relax his grip. He got reduction of rations (by increasing the differentials), deprivation of visits from relatives, and dispatch of more prisoners out on transports—anything to squeeze more out of the prisoners. Both the camp and the construction were equally delighted with him.

But here was what was interesting: All those devices were clearly and obviously methods predating camp. That is how he had learned *to lead* out in freedom, and it turned out that his method of leadership was exactly what was wanted in the camps.

Similarities aid cognition. I soon noticed that K. reminded me very much of someone else. Of whom? Of Leonid Z——v, my Lubyanka cellmate! Not at all primarily in external appearance, not at all, for Z. had been boarlike, and K. was tall, slim, and gentlemanly. But, juxtaposed, they enabled me to perceive through them a whole generation—that first wave of the *new* engineers who had been awaited impatiently so that the old "spetsy"—specialists—could be thrown out of their jobs and be, many of them, repressed. And they had arrived, first graduates of the new Soviet higher technical education institutions! As engineers they could not hold a candle to the engineers of the older generation—either in the breadth of their technical education or in their artistic sensitivity and love for their work. (Even in comparison with the bear Orachevsky, evicted from the room right off, the resplendent K. immediately turned out to be an empty chatterbox.) As claimants to a general culture they were comic. (K. said: "My favorite work is *Three Colors of Time* by Stendhal."* Though dealing hesitantly with the integral $x^2 dx$, he plunged right into arguments with me on any question of higher mathematics. He had memorized five to ten school phrases in German, and used them whether they were appropriate or not. He did not know English at all, but stubbornly argued about correct English pronunciation, which he had once heard in a restaurant. He had a notebook with aphorisms. He often used to browse through it and learn phrases by heart, so as to be able to shine on the right occasion.)

But despite all this, one would have expected from them, who had never seen the capitalist past, who had been in no possible way infected by its ulcers, a republican purity, *our own* Soviet fidelity to principles. Many of them had received high positions and very high salaries straight from the school desk; and during the war the Motherland had excused them from the front and had demanded nothing in return beyond the use of their professional skills. And because of this they were patriots, though they joined the Party with no enthusiasm. What they had never experienced was the fear of class-based accusations, and therefore they were not afraid of overstepping in their decisions, and on occasion they defended these decisions by shouting. For the same reason they were not shy in the face of the working masses and, on the contrary, they kept a common cruel, resolute grip on them.

And that was all. And in accordance with their possibilities they tried to keep their working day limited to eight hours. And afterward the cup of life began: actresses, the Hotel Metropole, the Hotel Savoy. And from here on the stories of K. and Z. were astonishingly alike. Here is K's account of an ordinary Sunday in the summer of 1943 (not without exaggeration, but in the main correct, and you believed him right off too!). Telling us about it he grew quite radiant.

"Saturday evening we used to roll off to the Prague Restaurant. Dinner! Do you understand what *dinner* is for a woman? For a woman it is absolutely unimportant what she had for breakfast or luncheon or what kind of work she does during the day. What's important for her is: her dress, her shoes, and her dinner! At the Prague there was a blackout, but you could go up on the roof anyway. There was a balustrade! The aromatic summer air! The Arbat down below, sleepy and blacked out. Next to you a woman in a *silk* [he would always stress that word] dress. We have caroused the whole night long. And now we are drinking only champagne! From behind the spires of the Defense Ministry a crimson sun floats up! Sunlight, windowpanes, roofs! We pay the bill. My personal car waits at the exit. It had been summoned by phone! The wind pours through the open car windows and refreshes us. At the dacha, the pine woods! Do you understand what a pine forest is like in the morning? Several hours of sleep behind closed shutters. We wake about ten—with the sun trying to break in through the Venetian blinds. All around the room is the lovely disorder of women's clothes. A light breakfast (do you understand what *light* means?) with red wine on the veranda. And then friends drop in—the river, sunning, bathing. And in the evening off by car to our respective homes. If it is a working Sunday, then after breakfast round about eleven you have to go off to give a few orders."

Now can the two of us ever, *ever* understand each other?

He sits there on my cot and tells his story, waving his hands for greater accuracy in the entrancing details, twisting his head in the burning voluptuousness of recollection. And I remember one after another those fearsome Sundays of the summer of 1943.

July 4. At dawn the whole earth shook to the left of us on the Kursk arc. And the crimson sun provided the light for us to read the falling leaflets: "Surrender! You have more than once experienced the crushing strength of the German attacks."

July 11. At dawn thousands of whistles cut through the air above us—our own attack on Orel has begun.

"A light breakfast?" Of course I understand. It is still dark in the trenches, and one can of American pork stew for eight men, and then—"Hurrah! For the Motherland! For Stalin!" and over the top.

Chapter 10

■

In Place of Politicals

But in that grim world where everyone gnawed up whomever he could, where a human's life and conscience were bought for a ration of soggy bread—in that world who and where were *the politicals*, bearers of the honor and the torch of all the prison populations of history?

We have already traced how the original "politicals" were divided, stifled, and exterminated.

And in their place?

Well—what did take their place? Since then we have had no politicals. And we could not possibly have any. What kind of "politicals" could we have if universal justice had been established? Once upon a time in the Tsarist prisons we put to good use the special privileges of the politicals, and, as a result, came to realize all the more clearly that they had to be abolished. They simply . . . abolished the politicals. There are none, and there won't be any.

And as for those who were imprisoned, well, they were *KR*'s, enemies of the Revolution. As the years passed, the word "revolution" itself faded. Very well then, let them be "enemies of the people." That sounded even better. (If, basing ourselves on our review of the Waves, we count the numbers imprisoned under this article, and add three times that number for the members of their families—banished, suspected, humiliated, and persecuted—then we shall be forced to admit to our astonishment that for the first time in history the *people* had become *its own enemy*, though in return it acquired the best of friends—the secret police.)

There is a famous camp anecdote about a sentenced woman who for a long time could not get through her head why the prosecutor and judge at her trial had kept calling her "konny militsioner" (a mounted policeman), which was what she understood of "kontr-revolyutsioner" (a counterrevolutionary)! As one who has served time in camps and looked about, I can see this anecdote as fact.

A tailor laying aside his needle stuck it into a newspaper on the wall so it wouldn't get lost and happened to stick it in the eye of a portrait of Kaganovich. A customer observed this: Article 58, ten years (terrorism).

A saleswoman accepting merchandise from a forwarder noted it down on a sheet of newspaper. There was no other paper. The number of pieces of soap happened to fall on the forehead of Comrade Stalin. Article 58, ten years.

A tractor driver of the Znamenka Machinery and Tractor Station lined his thin shoes for warmth with a pamphlet about the candidate for elections to the Supreme Soviet, but a charwoman noticed it was missing (she was responsible for the leaflets) and found out who had it. KRA—Counter-Revolutionary Agitation—ten years.

The village club manager went with his watchman to buy a bust of Comrade Stalin. They bought it. The bust was big and heavy. They ought to have carried it in a hand barrow, both of them together, but the manager's status did not allow him to. "All right, you'll manage it if you take it slowly." And he went off ahead. The old watchman couldn't work out how to do it for a long time. If he tried to carry it at his side, he couldn't get his arm around it. If he tried to carry it in front of him, his back hurt and he was thrown off balance backward. Finally he figured out how to do it. He took off his belt, made a noose for Comrade Stalin, put it around his neck, and in this way carried it over his shoulder through the village. Well, there was nothing here to argue about. It was an open-and-shut case. Article 58-8, terrorism, ten years.

A sailor sold an Englishman a "Katyusha" cigarette lighter—a wick in a piece of pipe with a striking wheel—as a souvenir for one pound sterling. Subversion of the Motherland's dignity—58, ten years.

A shepherd in a fit of anger swore at a cow for not obeying: "You collective-farm wh——!" And he got 58, and a term.

Ellochka Svirskaya sang a ditty at an amateur concert which just barely *touched on* something sensitive. And this was open rebellion! 58, ten years.

A *deaf and dumb* carpenter got a term for counterrevolutionary *agitation!* How? He was laying floors in a club. Everything had been removed from a big hall, and there was no nail or hook anywhere. While he was working, he hung his jacket and his service cap on a bust of Lenin. Someone came in and saw it. 58, ten years.

How many of them there were in Volgolag before the war—illiterate old villagers from Tula, Kaluga, and Smolensk provinces. They all had Article 58-10, in other words, anti-Soviet propaganda. Because, when they had to sign, they made their mark with a cross. (This is Loshchilin's story.)

After the war I did time in camp with a man from Vetluga named Maksimov. He had served from the beginning of the war in an antiaircraft battery. During the winter their political commissar had assembled them to discuss with them the *Pravda* lead editorial of January 16, 1942: "During the winter we must smash the German so badly that in the spring he will not be able to rise again." He assigned Maksimov to speak on this topic too. The latter said: "That's right! We have to drive him out, the bastard, while the storms are raging, while he has no felt boots, even though we ourselves have ordinary shoes on now and then. But in the spring it's going to be worse because of his equipment." And the political commissar applauded as if everything was all right. But then Maksimov was summoned to SMERSH and had eight years tied on him for . . . "praising German equipment," 58. (And Maksimov's education had been one year at a village school. His son, a Komsomol member, came to camp from the army, and ordered him: "Don't write Mother you're arrested. Say you're in the army and they won't let you go." His wife wrote back to the P.O. box address: "Your class has all been released; why don't they let you go?" And the convoy guard looked at Maksimov, who was always unshaven and crestfallen, and a bit deaf in addition, and advised him: "So write that you've become an officer and that's why they are keeping you." Someone at the construction site once got angry at Maksimov for his deafness and stupidity, and cursed him out: "*They spoiled Article 58 with you!*")

The children in a collective farm club got out of hand, had a fight, and accidentally knocked some poster or other off the wall with their backs. The two eldest were sentenced under Article 58.

(On the basis of the Decree of 1935, children from the age of twelve on had full criminal responsibility for all crimes!) They also sentenced the parents for having allegedly told them to and sent them to do it.

A sixteen-year-old Chuvash schoolboy made a mistake in Russian in a slogan in the wall newspaper; it was not his native language. Article 58, five years.

And in a state farm bookkeeping office the slogan hung: "Life has become better; life has become more gay. (Stalin)" And someone added a letter in red pencil to Stalin's name, making the slogan read as though life had become more gay *for* Stalin. They didn't look for the guilty party—but sentenced the entire bookkeeping office.

Gesel Bernshtein and his wife, Besschastnaya, were sentenced to five years under 58-10 for holding . . . a spiritualist séance at home! The interrogator kept asking: *"Who else was in on it?"*[1]

Nonsensical? Fantastic? Senseless? It's not at all meaningless. For that is just exactly what "terror as a means of persuasion" is. There is a proverb: "Beat the crow and beat the raven—and in the end you'll get to the white swan!" Just keep beating one after another—and in the end you'll hit the one you need. The primary meaning of mass terror lies precisely in this: even the strong and well hidden who could never be ferreted out simply will be caught and perish.

And what absurd accusations weren't manufactured in order to provide a foundation for the arrest of random or marked individuals!

The charge against Grigory Yefimovich Generalov, from Smolensk Province, was that he "used to drink heavily because he hated the Soviet government." (And actually he used to drink heavily because he and his wife got along badly.) He got eight years.

Irina Tuchinskaya (the fiancée of Sofronitsky's son) was arrested while leaving church. (The intention was to arrest their whole family.) And she was charged with having "prayed in church for the death of Stalin." (Who could have heard that prayer?!) Terrorism! Twenty-five years!

Aleksandr Babich was accused of "having in 1916 acted

---

1. There was a rumor in camp that Gesel had been imprisoned for "fortune-telling"—and the trusties used to bring him bread and tobacco and say: "Tell my fortune too!"

against the Soviet government [!!] while serving in the Turkish army." (In actual fact he had been a Russian volunteer on the Turkish front.) And he was additionally charged with the intent of turning over to the Germans in 1941 the icebreaker *Sadko*—on which he was a passenger. And the sentence was: to be shot! (They replaced it with a ten-ruble bill and he died in camp.)

Sergei Stepanovich Fyodorov, an artillery engineer, was charged with "wrecking by slowing down the projects of young engineers." (You see, these Komsomol activists do not have any leisure time in which to complete their drawings.)[2]

Corresponding Member of the Academy of Sciences Ignatovsky was arrested in Leningrad in 1941 and accused of having been recruited by the German intelligence service when he was working for Zeiss in 1908! And he was supposed to have had a very strange assignment too: *not* to engage in espionage in the coming war (which was of course the center of interest of *that* generation of the intelligence services) but only in the *next* one! And therefore he had loyally served the Tsar in World War I, and then the Soviet government also, and had put into operation the only optical factory in the country (GOMZ), and been elected to the Academy of Sciences, and then at the beginning of World War II he had been caught, rendered harmless, and shot!

However, for the most part fantastic accusations were not really required. There existed a very simple standardized collection of charges from which it was enough for the interrogator to pick one or two and stick them like postage stamps on an envelope:

- Discrediting the Leader
- A negative attitude toward the collective-farm structure
- A negative attitude toward state loans (and what normal person could have had a positive attitude!)
- A negative attitude toward the Stalinist constitution
- A negative attitude toward whatever was the immediate, particular measure being carried out by the Party
- Sympathy for Trotsky
- Friendliness toward the United States
- Etc., etc., etc.

---

2. And nonetheless this desperate wrecker was taken straight from the Kresty Prison . . . to war factories as a consultant.

The pasting on of these stamps of varying value was monotonous work requiring no artistry whatsoever. All the interrogator needed was the next victim in line, so as not to lose time. Such victims were selected on the basis of arrest quotas by Security chiefs of local administrative districts, military units, transportation departments, and educational institutions. And so that the Security chiefs did not have to strain their brains, denunciations from informers came in very handy.

In the conflicts between people in freedom, denunciations were the superweapon, the X-rays: it was sufficient to direct an invisible little ray at your enemy—and he fell. And it always worked. For these cases I have not recollected the names of the individuals involved, but I can affirm that I heard *many* stories in imprisonment about the use of denunciations in lovers' quarrels: a man would remove an unwanted husband; a wife would dispose of a mistress, or a mistress would dispose of a wife; or a mistress would take revenge on her lover because she had failed to separate him from his wife.

The most frequently used postage stamp was *Section 10*— counterrevolutionary (subsequently renamed anti-Soviet) agitation. If our descendants should someday read the interrogation and trial records of Stalin's times, they will be utterly astounded to find what indefatigable and adroit operators those anti-Soviet propagandists were. They were quite capable of using a needle or a tattered service cap for propaganda purposes, washed floors (see below) or unwashed linens, a smile or its absence, too expressive or too impenetrable a look, soundless thoughts inside the skull, notes in an intimate diary, love letters, graffiti in toilets. They propagandized on the highways and byways, at a fire, at the collective-farm market, in the kitchen, behind the domestic tea table, and in bed whispering in the ear. And only the invincible social structure of socialism could withstand such a propaganda assault!

In the Archipelago they used to love to joke that not all the articles of the Criminal Code were *accessible*. One or another person might wish to violate the law on protection of socialist property, but was not allowed near it. Some other person wouldn't hesitate to commit embezzlement—but could not manage to get a job as a cashier. To murder one had to have at least a knife; to possess a weapon unlawfully one first of all had to acquire a weapon. To have carnal knowledge of animals one had to have livestock. Even Article 58 was not so easily accessible: just how can you betray the Motherland under the heading of Section 1b if you don't serve in the army? How can you establish contact with the world bourgeoisie, under Section 4, if you live in Khanty-Mansiisk? And how can you subvert state industry and transportation, under Section 7, if you work as a barber? If you don't have at least a stinking old sterilizer so it can explode (chemical engineer Chudakov, arrested in 1948 for "diversionary activities")?

But Section 10 of Article 58 was *universally accessible*. To aged old women and twelve-year-old schoolboys. To married and single, to pregnant women and virgins, to athletes and cripples, to drunk and sober, to those who can see and to the blind too, to owners of automobiles and beggars of alms. One can earn one's sentence via Section 10 just as readily in the winter as in the summer, on a weekday as on a Sunday, early morning and late at night, at work or at home, on a stair landing, at a Metro station, in a dense forest, in an intermission at the theater, or during the course of a solar eclipse.

The only other section which could rival Section 10 in its accessibility was Section 12—*failure to make a denunciation*, or "He knew but he didn't tell." All those same people listed above could receive this section and in all the same conditions, but the special advantage in this case was that one did not even have to open one's mouth, nor take pen in hand. The whole point of this section was failure to act! And the sentence was the same: ten years of imprisonment and five years "muzzled."

Of course, after the war Section 1 of Article 58—"treason to the Motherland"—no longer seemed difficult to attain either. Not only all the POW's, not only all those who had been in occupied territories had a right to it, but even those who had dallied over being evacuated from threatened areas and who thereby disclosed their *intent* to betray the Motherland. (Professor of mathematics Zhuravsky asked for three plane seats out of Leningrad: for his wife, his sick sister-in-law, and himself. They gave him two, none for the sister-in-law. He sent off his wife and sister-in-law and stayed behind. The authorities could only interpret this act to mean that the professor was waiting for the Germans. Article 58-1a, via 19, ten years.)

In comparison with those unfortunates described earlier—the tailor, the club watchman, the deaf and dumb man, the sailor, or the man from Vetluga—here are some others whose sentences will seem fully justified:

• The Estonian Enseld, who arrived in Leningrad from still independent Estonia, had a letter taken from him written in Russian. To whom? From whom? "I am an honorable man and I cannot tell you." (The letter was from V. Chernov to his relatives.) Aha, bastard! So you are an honorable man? So off to Solovki with you! At least he actually did have a letter.

• Girichevsky, the father of two front-line soldiers, got conscripted into peat digging during the wartime labor mobilization, and he criticized the watery oversalted soup there. (He actually did criticize! He did open his mouth!) And quite deservedly he got 58-10 for this—ten years. (He died picking potato peelings out of the camp slops. In his dirty pocket was a photograph of his son, his chest covered with medals.)

• Nesterovsky was an English-language teacher who in his own *home*, over the tea table, told his wife and her best friend (he really did tell them!) how impoverished and hungry were the rear areas on the right bank of the Volga River. Her best friend *did in* both the Nesterovskys: he got ten years under Section 10, and she got the same under Section 12. (And what about their apartment? I don't know, perhaps it went to the best friend?)

• N. I. Ryabinin, in 1941, said during our retreat, said aloud where everyone could hear, "We should have sung fewer songs like 'Don't touch us and we won't touch you! We'll give no quarter if you do!'" Well, now, a scoundrel like that certainly ought to have been shot at the very least, but they only gave him ten years.

• Reunov and Tretyukhin, both Communists, got as hot and bothered as if a wasp had stung them on the neck because the Party Congress was long overdue, and this was a violation of the statutes. (As if it were any of their lousy business!) They got ten each!

• Faina Yefimovna Epshtein, astounded at Trotsky's criminal activity, asked at a Party meeting: "Why was he allowed to leave the U.S.S.R.?" (As if the Party was answerable to her! And maybe Iosif Vissarionovich was kicking himself about that!) For this awkward question she deservedly got and served out *three terms* one after another. (Even though not one of the interrogators or prosecutors could explain to her where her guilt lay.)

• And Grusha-the-Proletarian committed a crime of simply astounding gravity. She worked at a glass factory for twenty-three years and her neighbors had never seen an icon in her home. But just before the Germans got to her district she did put up some icons. (She had simply stopped being afraid; after all they *used to* persecute people who had icons!) And what the interrogation particularly noted on the basis of the denunciation of her neighbors was that she had also washed her floors! (But the Germans never did get there.) Then, too, she had picked up near her house a pretty German leaflet with a picture and pushed it into the vase on her dresser. And despite all this our humane court, taking into consideration her proletarian origins, gave Grusha *only* eight years of camp and three years of disenfranchisement. Meanwhile her husband perished at the front. And her daughter was a student in the technological institute, but the *cadres* kept tormenting her: "Where is your mother?" And the girl *poisoned herself*. (Grusha could never get past the point of her daughter's death in telling her story. She sobbed and went out.)

And what was Gennady Sorokin, a student in the third year at the Chelyabinsk Pedagogical Institute, to be given for having published two of his own essays in a students' literary journal (1946)? Small change, of course: ten years.

And what about reading the poet Sergei Yesenin? After all, we keep forgetting everything. Soon they will be telling us that "this was not so; Yesenin was always a revered poet of the people." But Yesenin was a counterrevolutionary poet. His verses were forbidden literature. M. Y. Potapova was charged as follows in the Ryazan State Security: "How did you dare admire Yesenin [before the war], if Iosif Vissarionovich said that the best and the most talented was Mayakovsky? That's how your anti-Soviet nature showed itself."

And that civil aviation flier, assistant pilot of a "Douglas," looks like a dyed-in-the-wool anti-Soviet. Not only did they find a complete collection of Yesenin in his possession, not only did he talk about how well-to-do and well fed people were in East Prussia until we got there—but during the course of *a public debate* in an aviation unit, he got into a public argument with Ilya Ehrenburg about Gemany. (In view of Ehrenburg's position at that time one may conclude that the pilot was proposing gentler treatment of the Germans.)³ At a debate—a public argument! Court-martial: ten years' imprisonment and five of disenfranchisement.

I. F. Lipai created a collective farm in his own local district a year before the bosses gave orders to create them—a completely voluntary collective farm! And could GPU Commissioner Ovsyannikov allow that hostile sally to go unchallenged? I don't need your good one. Give me my bad one! The collective farm was proclaimed to be kulak, and Lipai himself an ally of the kulaks—and they dragged him through the hummocks. . . .

F. V. Shavirin, a worker, spoke *out loud* (!) at a Party meeting about Lenin's testament! Well! Nothing could be worse than that—he had to be a sworn enemy! Whatever teeth he had managed to keep through the interrogation he lost in his first year in the Kolyma.

See what awful criminals were to be encountered among the 58's! And indeed some were really venomous, with a touch of the underground. For example, there was Perets Gertsenberg, an inhabitant of Riga. All of a sudden he moved to the Lithuanian Socialist Republic and registered himself as being of *Polish* origin. And in fact he was a Latvian Jew. What was particularly outrageous about this was the desire to deceive his own native state. It meant he was counting on our letting him go to Poland and from there he would slip off to Israel. Nothing doing, darling, you didn't want to stay in Riga, so off to Gulag. Betrayal of the Motherland via intention: ten years.

And what secretive people there were about too! In 1937 among the workers of the "Bolshevik" Factory (Leningrad) some former pupils of the trade schools were discovered who had been present, in 1929, at a meeting addressed by Zinoviev. (A list of those present had been found attached to the minutes.)

3. In Ehrenburg's memoirs you will find no trace of such trivial incidents. Anyway, he might not have known that the man arguing with him had been arrested. He merely offered a fairly standard Party-line reply at that particular moment and then forgot about it. Ehrenburg writes that he himself "survived by lottery." Well, that little lottery had marked numbers. If *they* were *rounding up* your friends, you had to stop phoning them in time. If the wagon shaft turned, it was necessary to turn too. Ehrenburg heated up hatred for the Germans so insanely that Stalin had to pull him up short. If you feel toward the end of your life that you helped establish a lie, then what is required to justify yourself is not memoirs but an immediate bold self-sacrifice.

For eight years these people had concealed themselves by sneaking into the ranks of the proletariat. Now all of them were arrested and shot.

Said Marx: "The state cripples itself by turning a citizen into a criminal."[4] And very touchingly he explained how in every violator of the law the state must see a warm-blooded human being as well, and a soldier who defends the Fatherland, and a member of the community, and a father of a family, "whose existence is sacred," and—most importantly—a citizen. But our jurists have no time to read Marx, particularly such unthought-out parts as these. Let Marx read our instructions if he feels like it.

People will exclaim that this whole list is what—monstrous? Ridiculous. That it is beyond belief? That Europe won't believe it?

Europe, of course, won't believe it. Not until Europe itself *serves time* will she believe it. Europe has believed our glossy magazines and can't get anything else into her head.

But what about us? Fifty years ago we would not have believed it either for anything. And one hundred years ago we would not have believed it. Belinsky, Chernyshevsky—they would not have believed it. But if we dig down three or four spades deep, back to Peter the Great and before—why shouldn't we believe it? What's so bad about that? It has been going on since time immemorial:

• The prison watchman Senka spoke: "Don't pull my beard! I'm a peasant who belongs to the state—but does that mean my beard belongs to the state too?" (Article 58—to be flogged with cudgels without mercy.)

• The Streltsy junior officer Ivashko Raspopin gestured with his finger and announced: "That's what you can do with your sovereign." (58—to be flogged with cudgels without mercy.)

• The tradesman Blestin, cursing out the Cossacks, said: "The great prince is stupid to give food and drink to you Cossacks." (Article 58—to be flogged with cudgels without mercy.)

• The knight Ivan Pashkov said: "The Sovereign-Tsar is higher than Saint Athanasius." And the sacristan of the Church of Saint Athanasius, Nezhdan, said: "Then why does the Tsar pray to Athanasius?" This was in Holy Week and both were

4. Marx and Engels, *op. cit.*, Vol. 1, p. 233.

drunk. Moscow delivered its verdict without prejudice: the boyar's son must be flogged with cudgels without mercy, and the sacristan flogged for the same reason.[5]

At the very least everyone keeps his mouth shut. And that is what is needed.

■

In the former Russia the *politicals* and the philistines were—two opposite extremes in the population. It was impossible to find more mutually exclusive ways of life and ways of thinking.

In the U.S.S.R. they began to rake in the philistines as "politicals."

And as a result the politicals were equated with the philistines.

Half the Archipelago consisted of the 58's. And there weren't any . . . politicals. (If there had been that many real *politicals*, the government would long since have been sitting on a different bench in the courtroom!)

Into this Article 58 were thrown all those for whom no criminal article had been chosen right off. It contained an unimaginable medley and motley.[6] To put a person into 58 was the simplest of all methods of getting rid of him, to remove him quickly and forever.

And in addition just plain *family members* went into this classification, especially the ChS wives. Today it is well known that the wives of important Party leaders were arrested as ChS's —members of families. But this custom had been established earlier. That was how they purged the families of the nobility as

5. These examples are taken from Plekhanov's book *Istoriya Russkoi Obshchestvennoi Mysli (A History of Russian Social Thought)*.

6. For example, a young American who married a Soviet girl and was arrested the first night spent outside the American Embassy (Morris Gershman). Or a former Siberian partisan, Muravyov, famous for his reprisals against the Whites (vengeance for his brother), never got out of the GPU from 1930 on (it had begun because of gold) and in the end he lost his health, his teeth, his mind, and even his name (he became Foks). Or the Soviet quartermaster caught embezzling who fled from criminal prosecution into the Western zone of Austria. But when he got there—and here's a laugh!—he could not find employment. Stupid bureaucrat that he was, he wanted a high-ranking position there, but how could he get one in a society in which talents compete? So he decided to return to the Motherland. Here he received twenty-five years for the combined offenses of theft and suspected espionage. And glad was he: here he could breathe more freely!

Such examples are innumerable.

well, and the families of prominent intellectuals, and clerics. (And even in the fifties: the historian Kh——tsev received twenty-five years for committing ideological errors in his book. But shouldn't his wife get her sentence too? Ten years. But why leave out his old mother, aged seventy-five, and his sixteen-year-old daughter? Both got sentences for failure to inform on him. And all four were sent off to different camps without the right to correspond with one another.)

And the more peaceful, quiet, and even illiterate people, remote from politics, the more people occupied only with their own daily round before their arrest who were drawn into the maelstrom of undeserved punishment and death, the more gray and timid became Article 58. Stripped gradually of its last political sense, it turned into a lost herd of lost people.

But it isn't enough to say *who* made up Article 58. It is more important to know *how the 58's were treated* in camp.

From the first years of the Revolution on, this group was cut off on all sides: by the prison regimen and by juridical formulations.

If we take Cheka Order No. 10 of January 8, 1921, we learn there that only a worker or a peasant could not be arrested without convincing proofs—which means that an intellectual could be, say, just out of antipathy. Or if we listen to Krylenko at the Fifth Congress of Justice Workers in 1924, we learn that "in regard to convicted hostile-class elements . . . correction is impotent and *purposeless*." At the beginning of the thirties they remind us once more that shortening the terms of hostile-class elements is a right-opportunist practice. And it is also "an opportunist directive that held that 'in prison all are equal,' that from the moment of sentencing the class struggle somehow ceases to exist," that "the class enemy is beginning to 'be. corrected.' "[7]

If we pull all of that together, then here's what: you can be arrested for *nothing:* and it is purposeless to try to correct you; and in camp we will put you in an oppressed position and finish you off there with class struggle.

But how are we to understand that the class struggle continues even in camp? After all, it's true, isn't it, that all prisoners are sort of equal. But no, don't be in such a hurry, that's a

7. Vyshinsky, *op. cit.*, p. 384.

bourgeois concept! The whole reason they deprived the politicals of the right to be held apart from the nonpolitical criminals was so as to have the criminals on their backs! (This was devised, too, by people who had come to understand in Tsarist prisons the strength of possible political unity, of political protest, and its dangers for the regime.)

Yes, here is Averbakh, Johnny-on-the-spot again, to explain to us: "The tactic of re-education is based on class differentiation . . . is based on the strata friendliest to the proletariat"[8] (and who are these friendly prisoners? They are "former workers," i.e., *thieves*, and they are the ones to be sicked on the 58's). "Re-education *is impossible without kindling political passions*" (and this is a literal quotation!).

And so when our lives were put wholly in the power of the thieves, this was no simple caprice on the part of lazy chiefs in remote camps, it was the exalted Theory!

"The class-differentiated approach to the regimen . . . incessant administrative pressure on hostile-class elements." Yes, dragging out your endless sentence, in your tattered padded jacket, with head bowed—can you even imagine this: *incessant administrative pressure on you?!*

And we can even read in that same remarkable book a list of methods for creating unbearable conditions for the 58's in camp. All you have to do, it says, is reduce the number of visits, parcels, correspondence, the right to complain, the right to move about within (!) the camp. And, it says, you have to create separate brigades of the hostile-class elements and *put them in more difficult situations* (I elucidate on my own: this means cheat them in measuring the work performed)—and then when they fail to fulfill the norm, declare this to be a sally of the class enemy. (Hence the Kolyma executions of entire brigades!) And then it gives frequent creative advice: The kulaks and their supporters (i.e., the best peasants imprisoned in the camps, those who even in their dreams used to yearn for peasants' work) were not to be assigned to agricultural work! And it also says: the highly skilled hostile-class element (in other words, the engineers) were not to be entrusted with any responsible work "without a preliminary verification." (But who is there in camp suf-

8. Averbakh, *op. cit.*, p. 35.

ficiently qualified to verify the engineers? Evidently the thieves' light cavalry from the Cultural and Educational Section, something like the Chinese Communist Red Guards.) It was difficult to act on this advice on the canals; after all, locks do not design themselves, the canal doesn't dig itself; so then Averbakh simply begged: let the specialists spend their first six months in camp at least on *general work*. (That's all it took to die!) In that case, presumably, through not living in a privileged intellectual barracks, "they will experience the pressure of the collective"; "the counterrevolutionaries will see that the masses are against them and despise them."

And how convenient it is, having mastered class ideology, to turn everything that takes place inside out. What if someone fixes up "former" top people and intellectuals with trusty jobs? Then it goes without saying that he "is giving the heaviest work to inmates from among the working class." What if a former officer is working in the storeroom, and there isn't enough clothing? Then it goes without saying that he is "deliberately holding it back." What if someone says to the shock-work record holders: "The others are not keeping pace with you"? Then it goes without saying that he is a class enemy! What if a thief gets drunk, or escapes, or steals? Then explain to him that it was not he who was guilty, that it was the class enemy who made him drunk, or taught him to escape, or taught him to steal (an intellectual teaching *a thief how to steal!*—and this was written quite seriously in 1936!). And if "the hostile element itself is turning in good work performances," he is "doing this for purposes of camouflage."

The circle is closed! Whether you work or whether you don't. Whether you love us or whether you don't. We hate you and will annihilate you with the hands of the thieves!

And so it is that Pyotr Nikolayevich Ptitsyn (imprisoned as a 58) sighs: "Well, you see the real criminals are incapable of genuine labor. It is actually the innocent person who sacrifices himself totally, to the last breath. There is the drama: the enemy of the people is the friend of the people."

But—nobody needs your sacrifice.

"An innocent person!" That is the main sensation of those ersatz politicals rounded up and put into camps. In all probability this was an unprecedented event in world prison history: when *millions* of prisoners realize that they are right, all of them

right, and that *no one* is guilty. (Only *one* innocent was imprisoned at hard labor with Dostoyevsky.)

However, these crowds of chance people, chased behind barbed
wire not in conformity with their convictions but by a thrust of
fate, were by no means strengthened by the consciousness of
their own rightness. Perhaps it even oppressed them more by
emphasizing the absurdity of their situation. Clinging more to
their former way of life than to any convictions whatever, they
in no way manifested readiness for sacrifice, unity, or fighting
spirit. While still in prison, entire cells allowed themselves to be
plundered by two or three snotty thieves. By the time they got to
the camps they were already totally demoralized. All they were
prepared to do was to bend their backs beneath the cudgels of
the work assigner and the thief, beneath the fist of the brigadier,
and all they remained capable of was mastering the camp philosophy (disunity, everyone for himself, and mutual deceit) and
the camp language.

When she arrived in a general camp in 1938, Y. Olitskaya
looked on all those 58's with astonishment, with the eyes of a
socialist who had known Solovki and the isolators. Once, in her
own recollection, the politicals shared everything, but now each
one lived and chewed only for himself, and even the "politicals"
traded clothes and rations!

Political riffraff—that's what Anna Skripnikova called them
(us). Back in 1925 she herself had learned that lesson: she complained to the interrogator that her cellmates were being dragged
by their hair by the Lubyanka Prison chief. The interrogator
laughed and asked her: "Is he dragging you too?" "No, but my
comrades!" And he exclaimed in deadly earnest: "Aha, how
frightening it is that you protest! Drop all those *useless airs of
the Russian intelligentsia! They are *out of date!* Worry *about
yourself only!* Otherwise, you're in for a hard time."

And this is exactly the thieves' principle: If they're not raking
you in, then don't lie down and ask for it.* The Lubyanka interrogator in 1925 *already* possessed the thieves' philosophy.

And so to the question which sounds so outlandish to the educated public: "Can a *political* steal?" we simply have to counter
with astonishment: "And why not?"

"Is he capable of *informing?*" "What makes him any worse
than the others?"

And when people naïvely protest to me about *Ivan Denisovich*:

"How is it that the politicals in your book express themselves in thieves' jargon?" I have to reply: "And what if there is no other language in the Archipelago? Do you really expect political riff-raff to counterpose a language of their own to that of the criminal riffraff?"

They drum into them day and night that they are criminals, and the most heinous of all criminals, and that those who are *not* criminals are not imprisoned in our country!

They broke the back of the 58's—and there were *no* politicals. Having poured them into the pigs' trough of the Archipelago, they drove them to die at work and shouted into their ears the camp lie that each was an enemy of the other.

The proverb says: "When hunger takes hold, the voice will appear." But among us, among our natives, it did not. Even from hunger.

And yet how little, how very little, they needed to be saved! Just one thing: not to cling to life, which was already lost anyway, and . . . to rally together.

This took place with success sometimes among entire foreign groups, for example, the Japanese. In 1947, at Revuchi, the penalty camp for the Krasnoyarsk camps, they brought in about forty Japanese officers, so-called "war criminals." (Though one could not even imagine what they were guilty of in relation to us.) It was bitterly cold. There was logging, unbearable even for Russians. The *otritsalovka*—"the band of rejecters"[9]—swiftly stole the clothes from some of them and swiped the whole tray with their bread several times. The Japanese, in dismay, waited for the chiefs to intervene, but the chiefs, of course, paid no attention. Then their brigadier, Colonel Kondo, accompanied by two senior officers, went one evening to the office of the camp chief and warned him (they knew Russian very well) that if the violence against them did not stop, two officers who had announced their desire to do so would commit hara-kiri at dawn the next morning. And this would be only the beginning. The chief of the camp (the blockhead Yegorov, former political commissar of a regiment) immediately sensed that he could very easily come to a bad end because of this. For two days the Japanese

---

9. The members of the "otritsalovka" took the position: "I reject everything the chiefs demand of me—both the regimen and the work." Customarily this was a powerful nucleus of thieves.

brigade was not taken out to work, was fed normally, and then taken off the penalty regimen.

How little was required for struggle and victory—*merely* not to cling to life! A life that was in any case already lost.

But our 58's were kept constantly mixed with the thieves and the nonpolitical offenders and were never allowed to be alone together—so they wouldn't look into one another's eyes and realize: *who we are.* And those bright heads, hot tongues, and firm hearts who might have become prison and camp leaders—had all, on the basis of special notations in their *files,* been culled out, gagged, and hidden away in special isolators and shot in cellars.

■

However, in accordance with that important phenomenon of life noted already in the teachings of Taoism, we were bound to expect that the moment the politicals ceased to exist was also the very moment when they appeared.

I will risk declaring that in the Soviet period not only were there genuine politicals, but also that:

1. There were *more* of them than in Tsarist times, and
2. They manifested *more* steadfastness and courage than did the earlier revolutionaries.

This seems to contradict the preceding, but it does not. The politicals in Tsarist Russia were in a very favorable situation, very much in the public eye—producing immediate repercussions in society and the press. And we have already seen (in Part I, Chapter 12) that in Soviet Russia the socialists had things incomparably more difficult.

And not only socialists were now politicals. The politicals were splashed in tubfuls into the fifteen-million-criminal ocean, and they were invisible and inaudible to us. They were mute. They were muter than all the rest. Their image was the fish.

The fish, symbol of the early Christians. And the Christians were their principal contingent. Clumsy, semiliterate, unable to deliver speeches from the rostrum or compose an underground proclamation (which their faith made unnecessary anyway), they went off to camp to face tortures and death—only so as not to renounce their faith! They knew very well *for what* they were serving time, and they were unwavering in their convictions! They were the only ones, perhaps, to whom the camp philosophy and even the camp language did not stick. And were these not politicals? Well, you'd certainly not call them riffraff.

And women among them were particularly numerous. The Tao says: When faith collapses, that is when the true believers appear. Because of our enlightened scoffing at Orthodox priests, the squalling of the Komsomol members on Easter night,* and the whistles of the thieves at the transit prisons, we overlooked the fact that the sinful Orthodox Church had nonetheless nurtured daughters worthy of the first centuries of Christianity—sisters of those thrown to the lions in the arenas.

There was a multitude of Christians: prisoner transports and graveyards, prisoner transports and graveyards. Who will count those millions? They died unknown, casting only in their immediate vicinity a light like a candle. They were the best of Russia's Christians. The worst had all . . . trembled, recanted, and gone into hiding.

Is this not *more?* Was there ever a time when Tsarist Russia had known that many politicals? Tsarist Russia could not even count them in tens of thousands.

But so cleanly, so unwitnessed was the strangling of our politicals, that it is only rarely that the story of one or another surfaces for us.

Archpriest Preobrazhensky (the face of a Tolstoi, a gray beard). Prison, exile, camp, prison, exile, camp (the Big Solitaire). After being worn down in this way for many, many years, in 1943 he was summoned to the Lubyanka—and on the way there the thieves stole his tall cylindrical priest's hat. It was proposed to him that he become a member of the Synod. It would seem that after so many years he might have allowed himself some respite from prison? But no, he refused: it was not a pure synod, not a pure church. And—back to camp.

And what about Valentin Feliksovich Voino-Yasenetsky (1877–1961), Archbishop Luke, and author of the famous work *Purulent Surgery?* His biography will, of course, be compiled, and it is not for us to write about him here. This man abounded in talent. Before the Revolution he had already successfully competed for entry into the Academy of Arts, but had left it in order to serve humanity better—as a physician. In the hospitals of World War I he emerged as an expert eye surgeon, and after the Revolution he headed a Tashkent clinic, extremely popular in all Central Asia. A smooth and untroubled career was spread out before him, like the paths trod by our highly successful contemporaries. But Voino-Yasenetsky sensed that his service was insufficient, and he put on the robes of a priest. He hung an icon in his operating room and delivered his lectures to his students wearing clerical robes and with a cross around his neck (1921). Patriarch Tikhon managed to appoint him Bishop of Tashkent. In the twenties Voino-Yasenetsky was exiled to the Turukhansky region, but was then brought back thanks to the exertions of many, but his chair and his diocese had already been taken. He had a private practice (the sign on his door reading "Bishop Luke"), and masses of the sick poured in to see him (the "leather coats," too, in secret), and he gave what he did not need of his money to the poor.

It is worth noting how they got rid of him. He had been sent to his second exile (in Archangel in 1930) not as a 58, but "for inciting to murder." (This was a nonsensical story, according to which he had brought influence to bear on the wife and mother-in-law of the physiologist Mikhailovsky who committed suicide —and who, when already insane, had been engaged in injecting into corpses solutions which had allegedly stopped the disintegration of tissue, about which the newspapers had made a big to-do as a "triumph of Soviet science" and artificial "resurrection.") This administrative method compels us to take an even more informal approach to the question of who the real politicals were. If not struggle with the regime, then moral or energetic resistance to it— that is the chief criterion. And the matter of which "article" was pasted on didn't mean a thing. (Many sons of the liquidated "kulaks" were given thieves' articles, but in camp showed themselves to be genuine politicals.)

In exile in Archangel, Voino-Yasenetsky worked out a new method of healing purulent wounds. He was summoned to Leningrad, and Kirov himself tried to persuade him to lay aside his priest's robes and immediately offered him his own institute. But the stubborn bishop would not even consent to have his book published without an indication, in parentheses, of his clerical rank. And thus it was that without an institute and without his book he completed his exile in 1933, returned to Tashkent, and there was sentenced to a third term of exile, in the Krasnoyarsk region. From the beginning of the war, he worked in Siberian hospitals, where he applied his technique of healing purulent wounds—and this led him to a Stalin Prize. And he only agreed to accept it dressed in his full bishop's regalia.[10]

And the engineers? How many of them refused to sign stupid, disgusting confessions of wrecking and were scattered to the four winds and shot? And how Pyotr Akimovich (Ioakimovich) Palchinsky (1875–1929) gleams like a bright star among them! He was an engineer and scholar with an astonishing breadth of interests. A graduate (in 1900) of the Mining Institute, an outstanding authority on mining, he studied and, as can be seen from the list of his books, left behind him works on general questions of economic development, on the fluctuations of industrial prices, on the export of coal, on the equipment and operation of Europe's trading ports, on the economic problems of port management, on industrial-safety techniques in Germany, on concentration in the German and English mining industries, on the economics of mining, on the reconstruction and development of the building materials industry in the U.S.S.R., on the general training of engineers in higher education—and, in addition, works on purely mining subjects, such as descriptions of individual areas and individual ore deposits (and not all his works are yet known to us today). Like Voino-Yasenetsky in medicine, Palchinsky would never have come to grief in his own engineering work; but just as the former could not stop propagating the faith, so he could not stop meddling in politics. Even as a student in the Mining Institute, Palchinsky had been listed by the Tsarist gendarmes as a "leader of the movement." In 1900 he had been the chairman of a students' assembly. As an engineer in 1905 in Irkutsk he had already been prominently involved in the revolutionary uprisings, and in the "case of the Irkutsk Republic" he was sentenced to hard labor. He escaped and went off to Europe. Having already before this been in sympathy with the Anarchists, he became friendly with Kropotkin. He used his émigré years to perfect his knowledge in several engineering areas and studied European

---

10. When medical students today ask about his biography, they receive the reply: "There is no literature on him."

technology and economics, but at the same time he never lost sight of the program of popular publications "for disseminating Anarchist ideas among the masses." In 1913, amnestied, he returned to Russia and wrote to Kropotkin: "In view of the program of my own activities in Russia, I aim to take part . . . wherever I am able in the general development of the productive forces of the country and in the development of spontaneous social and public activity in the broadest sense of this word."[11] During his first trip through the main Russian centers, he was snowed under with suggestions to stand for such positions as business manager of the Council of the Congress of the Mining Industry, offered "brilliant positions in directorships in the Donbas," consultancies to banks, lecturer in the Mining Institute, the post of director of the Department of Mines. There were few men in Russia with such energy and such broad knowledge!

And what was his further fate? We have already reported above (Part I, Chapter 10) how in World War I he became a Deputy Chairman of the War Industry Committee and, after the February Revolution, Deputy Minister of Trade and Industry. As evidently the most energetic of the members of the weak-willed Provisional Government, Palchinsky was successively Governor-General of Petrograd during the Kornilov days[12] and Chief of Defense of the Winter Palace during the October Revolution. Immediately afterward he was imprisoned in the Peter and Paul Fortress and served four months there. Then, it's true, he was released. In June, 1918, he was arrested without any charges being made against him. On September 6, 1918, he was included in a list of 122 prominent hostages. ("If even one Soviet official is killed, the hostages listed below will be shot. Signed: Petrograd Cheka; G. Boky, Chairman; A. Ioselevich, Secretary.")[13] However, he was not shot, and at the end of 1918 he was even released because of the inappropriate intervention of the German Social-Democrat Karl Moor (who was astounded at the kind of people we were leaving to rot in prison). From 1920 on he was a professor at the Mining Institute, visited Kropotkin in Dmitrov, and after Kropotkin's death not long afterward created a committee

11. Letter to Kropotkin, February 20, 1913, TsGAOR, collection 1129, shelf 2, unit 1936.

12. *Birzhevyye Vedomosti* (*Stock Exchange News*), August 31, 1917, and September 2, 1917.

13. *Petrogradskaya Pravda*, September 6, 1918, No. 193.

for the (unsuccessful) perpetuation of Kropotkin's memory—and soon, either because of or notwithstanding this, was again arrested. A curious document on the release of Palchinsky from this third Soviet imprisonment has been preserved in the archives— a letter to the Moscow Revtribunal, dated January 16, 1922:

Considering that the permanent consultant of the State Planning Commission, Engineer P. A. Palchinsky, is to deliver a report in the Southern Bureau on Jan. 18 of this year at 3 P.M. on the question of restoring Southern Metallurgy, which is of particularly important significance at the present moment, the Presidium of the State Planning Commission requests the Revtribunal to release Comrade Palchinsky by the above-named hour in order that he may carry out the assignment given him.

Chairman of the State Planning Commission
KRZHIZHANOVSKY[14]

Krzhizhanovsky *asked*—and without much authority either. And only because southern metallurgy was of "particularly important significance at the present moment," and only "in order that [Palchinsky] may carry out the assignment given him"—otherwise you can do whatever you want with him, or put him back in his cell if you please.

No, Palchinsky was permitted to go on working for a while, reconstructing the mining industry of the U.S.S.R. After showing heroic steadfastness in prison, he was shot without trial—in 1929.

You would have to have no love whatever for your country, you would have to be hostile to it, to shoot the pride of the nation —its concentrated knowledge, energy, and talent!

And wasn't it exactly the same twelve years later in the case of Nikolai Ivanovich Vavilov? Was not Vavilov a genuine political (out of bitter necessity)? In the course of eleven months of interrogation he endured four hundred interrogation sessions. And at his trial (July 9, 1941) he refused to confess to the charges against him!

And without any world fame whatever, the hydraulic engineer Professor Rodionov (Vitkovsky has told us about him) *refused* to work at his profession when he was imprisoned—though that would have been the easy path for him. He cobbled boots. Was he not a genuine political? He was a peaceful hydraulic engineer. He had never prepared for struggle. But if despite his prison keepers, he held fast to his convictions—was he not a genuine

14. TsGAOR, collection 3348, unit 167, sheet 32.

political? What need had he for some Party membership card for that?

Just as a star suddenly flares to a hundred times its previous brightness—and then fades away, so, too, a human being not disposed to be a political may nonetheless flare up briefly and intensely in prison and perish as a result. Ordinarily we do not learn about these cases. Sometimes there is a witness to tell about them. Sometimes there is merely a faded piece of paper in front of us on which we can only build hypotheses:

Yakov Yefimovich Pochtar, 1887, non-Party, physician. From the beginning of the war he was at the 45th Air Force Base of the Black Sea Fleet. His first sentence from a court-martial at the Sevastopol base (November 17, 1941) was five years of corrective-labor camp. This would seem to be not too bad. But what's this? There was a second sentence on November 22: to be shot. And on November 27 he was shot. What happened in those fateful five days between the seventeenth and the twenty-second? Did he explode like a star? Or was it merely that the judges suddenly realized they had given him too little?[15]

What about the Trotskyites? They were pure-blooded politicals. That's something you cannot deny them.

(Someone is shouting at me! A little bell is being jingled at me: Stop right there! Speak about the one-and-only politicals! About the uncrushable Communists who even in the camps continued to keep the sacred faith . . . All right, we will set aside the next chapter separately for them.)

Someday historians will study the question: At what moment did a trickle of *political young people* begin to flow in our country? It seems to me that it began in 1943 and 1944. (I am not referring here to the socialist and Trotskyite young people.) While still practically schoolboys, they suddenly began to seek out their own platform (remember the "Democratic Party" of 1944), different from the one that was being intensely urged on them and shoved under their feet. Well, what else can we call them?

Only that we know nothing of them and never will.

But if twenty-two-year-old Arkady Belinkov was imprisoned for his first novel, *A Rough Draft of Feelings* (1943), never published, of course, and continued to write in camp (but at death's

---

15. He has now been rehabilitated on the initial charges. And that means that if it had not been for the second case against him . . . ?

door trusted the stool pigeon Kermaier and was handed another sentence), can we really deny him the title of political?

In 1950 the students of the Leningrad School of Mechanics created their own party with a program and statutes. Many were shot. Aron Levin, who got twenty-five years for it, told us. And that is all: a roadside marker.

And it goes without saying that our contemporary politicals need incomparably greater steadfastness and heroism than the earlier revolutionaries. In those days the punishments given for far more serious actions were quite light and revolutionaries didn't have to be so very bold: in case of failure they risked only themselves (not their families!), and not even their heads—but a short term only.

What did posting leaflets amount to before the Revolution? It was an amusement, like scaring pigeons, and you wouldn't even get three months for it. But five boys in Vladimir Gershuni's group prepared leaflets declaring that "Our government has compromised itself!" This required approximately the same determination as the five boys in Aleksandr Ulyanov's group needed in their attempt to assassinate the Tsar.

And how the following story blazes up through spontaneous combustion, how it comes awake on its own somewhere inside! In the city of Leninsk-Kuznetskiy was one boys' school. Starting in the ninth grade, five boys (Misha Bakst, their Komsomol organizer; Tolya Tarantin, also a Komsomol activist; Velvel Reikhtman, Nikolai Konev, and Yuri Anikanov) lost their peace of mind. Not over the girls nor over the latest dances—they looked around them at the savagery and drunkenness in their own city and pored over their history textbooks, trying to make connections and compare. As they entered the tenth grade in 1950, just before the elections to the local soviets, they produced their first (and last) naïve leaflet, in printed characters:

Listen, worker! Are we really living the kind of life for which our grandfathers, fathers, and brothers fought? We work—and get only a pitiful pittance in return, and they even cut down on that too. Read this and think about your life.

They themselves were only thinking—and therefore they did not summon to any particular action. (Their plan was to issue a series of such leaflets and to make their own hectograph.)

Here is how they posted the leaflets: They went around together at night. One of them would plaster four pieces of wet bread on the wall, and another would paste a leaflet on them.

In early spring some new pedagogue came to them in class and asked them . . . to fill out a questionnaire, printing the letters.[16] The principal pleaded that they not be arrested before the end of the school year. Imprisoned and under interrogation, the boys regretted most of all not being at their own graduation party. "Who was directing you? Confess!" (The gaybisty simply couldn't believe that the boys had been guided simply by their own consciences. After all, it was an extraordinary occurrence. After all, you only live once. Why *think about things?*) Punishment blocks, night interrogations, long hours of standing. A session of the Provincial Court closed to the public (of course).[17] Pitiable defense lawyers, confused judicial assessors, a threatening prosecutor named Trutnev(!).* And all of them given eight- and ten-year sentences, and all of them, seventeen-year-olds, sent to Special Camps.

No, the old proverb does not lie: Look for the brave in prison, and the stupid among the political leaders!

I am writing for mute Russia and therefore I have but little to say about the Trotskyites; they are all people who write, and any who have succeeded in surviving have in all probability prepared detailed memoirs and will write their dramatic epics more completely and more accurately than I could.

But here are a few words for the sake of the overall picture.

They conducted a regular underground struggle in the late twenties, deploying all their experience as former revolutionaries, except that the GPU arrayed against them was not as stupid as the Tsarist Okhrana. I do not know whether they were prepared for that total annihilation which Stalin had allotted them, or whether they still thought that it would all end with jokes and reconciliation. In any case, they were heroic people. (I fear, however, that if they had come to power, they would have brought us a madness no better than Stalin's.) Let us note that even in

16. The boys were sold down the river by Fyodor Polotnyanshchikov, later Party organizer at the Polysayev mine. The country must know its stool pigeons.
17. The judge's name was Pushkin. He was soon afterward convicted of accepting bribes.

the thirties, when their end was near, they still considered any kind of contact with the socialists to be a betrayal and a disgrace, and therefore kept to themselves in the isolators and would not even pass on the prison mail of the socialists. (You see, they considered themselves Leninists.) The wife of I. N. Smirnov (even after his execution) avoided contact with the socialists "so that the jailers would not see it" (i.e., so to say, the eyes of the Communist Party)!

One gets the impression (though I will not insist on it) that there was too much vanity in their political "struggle" in camp conditions, which gave it a touch of tragicomedy. In the cattle trains from Moscow to the Kolyma they used to agree "on underground contacts, passwords"—and they were scattered among various camps and various brigades.

For instance, a brigade of prisoners sent up for Counter-Revolutionary Trotskyite Activity which had honestly earned its work ration was suddenly put on penalty rations. What was to be done? "The well-hidden underground Communist Party cell" discussed the question. Should they strike? But this would have meant to nibble the bait of the provocation. They want us to fall for their provocation, but we—we will go proudly to work even without our ration! We will go to work, but we will work on a penalty-norm basis.[18]

At Utiny Goldfield they were making preparations for the twentieth anniversary of the October Revolution. They collected black rags and they blackened white ones with charcoal. On the morning of November 7 they intended to hang black mourning flags on all the tents and to sing the "Internationale" at line-up, locking arms firmly so as not to allow the jailers or the convoy guards into their ranks. They were determined to sing it through, no matter what! And then not under any circumstances to leave the camp compound to work! And to shout slogans: "Down with Fascism!" "Hail Leninism!" "Hail the Great October Socialist Revolution!"

---

18. This was 1937, and the brigade included not only "pure" Trotskyites but also "pure" orthodox Stalinists sentenced as Trotskyites. They had sent petitions to the Central Committee addressed to Comrade Stalin, to the NKVD addressed to Comrade Yezhov, to the Central Executive Committee addressed to Comrade Kalinin, and to the Prosecutor General also, and at the time they were anxious to avoid a falling-out with the camp chiefs, on whom would depend the accompanying recommendations.

In this plan we find a sort of hysterical enthusiasm mixed with futility, bordering on the ridiculous.

However, someone, or one of themselves, *turned them in* ahead of time, and on November 6 they were taken to Yubileiny Gold-field and locked in for the holidays. In closed tents (which they were forbidden to leave) they sang the "Internationale," just as the Yubileiny sloggers were going out to work. (But even among those singing there was a division: present were unjustly imprisoned Communists who stood aside, who did not sing the "Internationale," but showed their orthodoxy by their silence.)

"If we are being kept behind bars that means we are still worth something," Aleksandr Boyarchikov consoled himself. A false consolation. Who didn't they keep there?

The greatest achievement of the Trotskyites in the camp struggle was their hunger strike and work stoppage throughout the entire Vorkuta system of camps. (Before that also there had been a hundred-day strike somewhere in the Kolyma, it seems: they demanded a free settlement instead of camps, and they *won:* they were promised satisfaction, and the hunger strike was lifted, they were scattered among various camps, where they were gradually annihilated.) The information I have on the Vorkuta hunger strike is contradictory. Here is approximately how it went:

It began on October 27, 1936, and continued for 132 days. (They were fed artificially, but did not lift the hunger strike.) Several died of starvation. Their demands were:

- Separation of the politicals from the criminals[19]
- An eight-hour workday
- The restoration of the special ration for politicals[20] and the issuing of rations independently of work performance
- Destruction of the OSO—the Special Board—and annulment of its verdicts

They were fed through a tube, and thereupon a rumor spread through the camps that there was a shortage of sugar and butter "because it had all been fed to the Trotskyites"—a trick worthy of

19. Did they include among those politicals the 58's other than themselves? Probably not; if they had rejected even the socialists, they were unable to recognize the KR's as their brothers.
20. This, of course, was solely for themselves.

the bluecaps! In March, 1937, a telegram came from Moscow: The demands of the hunger strikers are to be accepted in toto! The hunger strike was lifted. Helpless prisoners, how could they enforce the fulfillment of those promises? They were just lied to— not one of their demands was met. (No Westerner will ever believe or comprehend that it was possible to act like this. But that's the whole story of our country.) On the contrary, all the hunger strikers were processed through the security·chief's office and charged with continuing their counterrevolutionary activity.

The great hoot owl in the Kremlin had already thought up his short shrift for them.

A bit later at Vorkuta Mine No. 8 there was one more big hunger strike. (Which may have been part of the preceding one.) One hundred and seventy persons participated in it, certain of them known by name: the strikers' spokesman was Mikhail Shapiro, a former worker of the Kharkov VEF; Dmitri Kurinevsky from the Kiev Province Komsomol Committee; Ivanov, former commander of a squadron of patrol boats in the Baltic Fleet; Orlov-Kamenetsky; Mikhail Andreyevich; Polevoi-Genkin; V. V. Verap, the editor of the Tbilisi newspaper *Zarya Vostoka (Dawn of the East)*; Sokrat Gevorkyan, Secretary of the Central Committee of the Party in Armenia; Grigory Zolotnikov, a history professor; and his wife.

The nucleus of the hunger strike consisted of sixty persons imprisoned together in 1927–1928 in the Verkhne-Uralsk Isolator. It was a big surprise—gratifying to the strikers and unpleasant for the chiefs—that twenty thieves also joined in the strike, headed by their ringleader, who was known by the nickname of *Moscow*. (In that camp he was famous for one nighttime escapade: he had made his way to the camp chief's office and there relieved himself on the desk. Any of our politicals would have been shot for that, but all he got was a reprimand: It must have been the class enemy who taught you that.) These twenty thieves truly irritated the chiefs, whereas the security officer of Vorkutlag, Uzkov, taunted the "hunger-strike leadership" of hostile prisoners by saying: "Do you think that Europe knows about your strike? We don't give a damn about Europe!"

And he was right. But the socially friendly bandits could be neither beaten up nor allowed to die. However, halfway through the strike things got through to their lumpenproletariat consciousness, and the thieves broke off, and their ringleader, Moscow, explained on the camp radio that the Trotskyites had deceived him.

After this the fate of the rest was to be shot. Their hunger strike had provided both their applications and the list of those executed.

No, there were genuine politicals. There were many of them. And they sacrificed themselves.

But why were the results of their opposition so insignificant? Why did they not leave even the scantiest bubbles on the surface?

We will analyze this too. Later on.[21]

---

21. Part V, Chapter 4.

Chapter 11

■

The Loyalists

But I hear an angry roar of voices. The *comrades'* patience has run out! They will slam my book shut, toss it away, and spit on it:

"In the last analysis, this is brazen impudence! It's slander! Where is he looking for genuine politicals? Whom is he writing about? About some priests, technocrats, sniveling schoolboys . . .? The real politicals are us! Us, the unshakable! Us, the ortho-dox, crystal-clear people." (And Orwell called them *Goodthink-ers.*) Us, who even in the camps stayed faithful to the very end to the one-and-only-true . . .

Yes, judging by our press and publishers—you were the only ones imprisoned, by and large. Only you suffered. You are the only ones we are allowed to write about. All right, let's do it.

Will the reader agree with this criterion: that political prisoners are those who know *what* they are serving time *for* and are firm n their convictions?

If you agree, then here is the answer: Our unshakable Com-munists, who despite their personal arrest remained devoted to :he one-and-only-true, etc., were firm in their convictions *but did not know what they were serving time for!* And therefore they cannot be considered political prisoners.

If my criterion is no good, then let us take the criterion of Anna Skripnikova, who, in the course of her five terms, had time enough to think the matter over. Here it is:

A political prisoner is one with beliefs whose renunciation could could secure his release. People without such beliefs are political riffraff.

In my opinion this is not a bad criterion. All those who at any time have been persecuted for ideology fit into it. All revolutionaries fit into it. All the so-called "nuns" and the Archpriest Preobrazhensky fit into it, and Engineer Palchinsky. But the orthodox Communists . . . do not: Which beliefs are they being required to renounce?

None. And that means that the orthodox Communists, even though it is insulting to put it this way, are like that tailor and the deaf-and-dumb man and the club watchman, who fitted into the category of helpless, uncomprehending victims. But—with arrogance.

Let us be precise and define our subject. Who are we going to be dealing with in this chapter?

With all those who, despite their imprisonment, the mockery of an interrogation, their undeserved sentence, and the subsequent searing camp experiences, retained their Communist convictions?

No, not about all of them. Among them were people for whom this Communist faith was an inner thing, sometimes the sole meaning of the lives remaining to them, but:

- They did not let it lead them into taking a "party" attitude toward their imprisoned comrades, and in cell and barracks arguments they did not shout at others that these latter had been justly imprisoned. (Meaning that "I" was imprisoned unjustly.)
- They did not rush to declare to the citizen camp chief (and to the security chief), "I am a Communist," and did not use this formula to survive in camp.
- And now, when speaking of the past, they do not see the principal and only violence of the camps to have consisted in the fact that Communists were imprisoned—and spit on all the rest.

In a word, they were those whose Communist convictions were inward and not constantly on the tips of their tongues. It was as if this were an individualist trait, but in fact such individuals did not ordinarily hold big jobs in freedom, and in camp they worked as ordinary sloggers.

Take, for example, Avenir Borisov, a village schoolteacher:

"Do you remember our youth—I myself was born in 1912—when our supreme happiness was the green 'Jungsturm' uniform made out of homespun cloth, with a waist belt and a shoulder strap, when we despised money and everything private and personal and *were ready to march in any cause, as soon as the summons came?*[1] I joined the Komsomol at the age of thirteen. And when I was all of twenty-four years old the NKVD organs charged me with nearly every section in Article 58." (We will see later how he conducted himself after his release; he is a decent person.)

Or Boris Mikhailovich Vinogradov, with whom I served time in prison. In his youth he had been a locomotive engineer (not just for one year either, in the way that certain deputies were shepherds for a year). After the workers' school and an institute, he became a railway transport engineer (and was not put immediately on Party work, as often happens too), and he was a good engineer (in the sharashka he carried out complex calculations in gas dynamics for jet turbines). But by 1941, it's true, he had become the Party organizer of the Moscow Institute for Railroad Engineering. In the bitter Moscow days of October 16 and 17, 1941, seeking instructions, he telephoned but no one replied. He went to the District Party Committee, the City Party Committee, the Provincial Party Committee, and found no one there; everyone had scattered to the winds; their chambers were empty. And it seems he didn't go any higher than that. He returned to his own people in the Institute and declared: "Comrades! All the leaders have run away. But we are Communists, we will join the defense." And they did just that. But for that remark of his, "They have all run away," those who had run away sent him who had not run away to prison for eight years—for Anti-Soviet Propaganda. He was a quiet worker, a dedicated friend, and only in heart-to-heart conversation would he disclose that he believed, believes, and will go on believing. And he never wore it on his sleeve.

Or take the geologist Nikolai Kalistratovich Govorko, who, when he was a Vorkuta last-legger, composed his "Ode to Stalin" (which has been preserved). But he did not write it for publication, nor in order to receive privileges in return, but because it poured straight from his heart. And he hid that ode in the mine! (Though what was there to hide?)

1. The italics, to be sure, are mine.

Sometimes such people kept their faith to the end. Sometimes (like Kovacs, a Hungarian from Philadelphia arrested in 1937, who belonged to one of the thirty-nine families who had come to found a commune near Kakhovka) they refused after rehabilitation to take back their Party card. Certain others broke away even earlier, like another Hungarian named Szabo, who had been commander of a Siberian partisan detachment in the Civil War. Back in 1937 he had declared in prison, "If I were free right now, I'd collect my partisans together, raise Siberia, and march on Moscow and chase all those bastards out."

So we are not going to deal in this chapter with Communists of either the first or the second kind. (And the orthodox Communists themselves have eliminated all those who broke with the Party, like the two Hungarians.)

Nor will we be concerned with such anecdotal individuals— as those who in prison only pretended to be orthodox Communists, so that the *cell stoolie* would give the interrogator a good report: like the young Podvarkov, who when free had pasted up leaflets, but in the Spassk Camp used to argue loudly with all opponents of the regime, including his own father, counting on lightening his own fate by this means.

Here we shall concern ourselves particularly with those orthodox Communists who made a display of their ideological orthodoxy first to the interrogator, then in the prison cells, and then in camp to all and everyone, and now recall their camp past in this light.

By a strange selective process none of them will be sloggers. Such people ordinarily had held big jobs before their arrest, and had had an enviable situation; and in camp they found it hardest of all to reconcile themselves to extinction, and they fought fiercest of all to rise above the universal zero. In this category were all the interrogators, prosecutors, judges, and camp officials who had landed behind bars. And all the theoreticians, dogmatists, and loud-mouths (the writers G. Serebryakova, B. Dyakov, and Aldan-Semyonov belong here, and nowhere else).

We have to understand them, and we won't scoff at them. It was painful for them to fall. "When you cut down trees, the chips will fly!" was the cheerful proverb of justification. And then suddenly they themselves were chopped off with all the other chips.

Prokhorov-Pustover describes a scene at Manzovka, a special

camp of BAMlag, at the beginning of 1938. To the surprise of all the natives, they brought in some sort of unprecedented "special contingent" and separated it from the others with great secretiveness. No one had ever yet observed such an arrival: the newcomers wore leather coats, fur caps, woolen and cheviot suits, fashionable shoes and oxfords (by the twentieth anniversary of the Revolution this select group had already discovered a standard of taste in clothes which was not available to working people). Because of bad management or out of mockery the camp authorities didn't give them work clothes and drove them out just as they were, in their cheviots and chrome leather, to dig ditches in liquid clay up to their knees. At the junction of the wheelbarrow run one zek upset a wheelbarrow with cement, and the cement poured out. A thief brigadier ran up, cursed the zek at fault, and pushed him in the back: "Pick it up with your hands, stupid!" And the zek shouted hysterically: "How dare you taunt me! I am a former prosecutor of the Republic!" And big tears rolled down his face. "What the ——— do I care if you're a prosecutor of the Republic, scum! I'll push your snoot in that cement, then you'll be a prosecutor! Now you're an enemy of the people and you've got to put your nose to the grindstone!" (However, it appears that the work supervisor intervened on behalf of the prosecutor.)

Now just tell us of a scene like that involving a Tsarist prosecutor in a concentration camp in 1918—no one would have dreamed of taking pity on him; it was unanimously recognized that they were not people. (And the sentences they had sought for the defendants they had prosecuted had been one year, three years, five.) But how was it possible—*not* to take pity on one's own Soviet proletarian prosecutor, even if he was dressed in a woolen suit? (The sentences he had demanded were . . . a *ten-ruble bill* and the *super.*)

To say that things were *painful* for them is to say almost nothing. They were incapable of assimilating such a blow, such a downfall, and from their *own people* too, from their dear Party, and, from all appearances, for nothing at all. After all, they had been guilty of nothing as far as the Party was concerned—nothing at all.

It was painful for them to such a degree that it was considered taboo among them, uncomradely, to ask: "What were you imprisoned for?" The only squeamish generation of prisoners! The rest of us, in 1945, with tongues hanging out, used to recount our arrests, couldn't wait to tell the story to every chance newcomer we met and to the whole cell, as if it were an anecdote.

Here's the sort of people they were. Olga Sliozberg's husband had already been arrested, and they had come to carry out a search and arrest her too. The search lasted four hours—and she spent those four hours sorting out the minutes of the congress of Stakhanovites of the bristle and brush industry, of which she had been the secretary until the previous day. The incomplete state of the minutes troubled her more than her children, whom she was leaving forever! Even the interrogator conducting the search could not resist telling her: "Come on now, say farewell to your children!"

Here's the sort of people they were. A letter from her fifteen-year-old daughter came to Yelizaveta Tsvetkova in the Kazan Prison for long-term prisoners: "Mama! Tell me, write to me—are you guilty or not? I hope you weren't guilty, because then I won't join the Komsomol, and I won't forgive them because of you. But if you are guilty—I won't write you any more and will hate you." And the mother was stricken by remorse in her damp gravelike cell with its dim little lamp: How could her daughter live without the Komsomol? How could she be permitted to hate Soviet power? Better that she should hate me. And she wrote: "I am guilty. . . . Enter the Komsomol!"

How could it be anything but hard! It was more than the human heart could bear: to fall beneath the beloved ax—then to have to justify its wisdom.

But that is the price a man pays for entrusting his God-given soul to human dogma.

Even today any orthodox Communist will affirm that Tsvetkova acted correctly. Even today they cannot be convinced that this is precisely the "perversion of small forces," that the mother perverted her daughter and harmed her soul.

Here's the sort of people they were: Y.T. gave sincere testimony against her husband—anything to aid the Party!

Oh, how one could pity them if at least now they had come to comprehend their former wretchedness!

This whole chapter could have been written quite differently if today at least they had forsaken their earlier views!

But it happened the way Mariya Danielyan had dreamed it would: "If I leave here someday, I am going to live as if nothing had taken place."

Loyalty? And in our view it is just plain pigheadedness. These devotees of the theory of development construed loyalty to that development to mean renunciation of any personal development whatsoever. As Nikolai Adamovich Vilenchik said, after serving seventeen years: "We believed in the Party—and we were *not mistaken!*" Is this loyalty or pigheadedness?

No, it was not for show and not out of hypocrisy that they argued in the cells in defense of all the government's actions. They needed ideological arguments in order to hold on to a sense of their own rightness—otherwise insanity was not far off.

How easily one could sympathize with them all! But they all see so clearly what their sufferings were—and they don't see wherein lies their own guilt.

This sort of person was not arrested before 1937. And after 1938 very few such people were arrested. And that is why they were named the "call-up of 1937," and this would be permissible but shouldn't be allowed to blur the overall picture: even at the peak they were not the only ones being arrested, and those same peasants, and workers, and young people, and engineers, and technicians, and agronomists, and economists, and ordinary believers continued to stream in as well.

The "call-up of 1937" was very loquacious, and having access to the press and radio created the "legend of 1937," a legend consisting of two points:

1. If they arrested people at all under the Soviet government, it was only in 1937, and it is necessary to speak out and be indignant only about 1937.
2. In 1937 they were . . . the only ones arrested.

Here's what they write: that terrible year when they arrested the most devoted Communist executives: secretaries of the Central Committees of the Union Republics, secretaries of the Provincial Party Committees; chairmen of the Provincial Executive Committees; all the commanders of the military districts, of corps and divisions, marshals and generals, provincial prosecutors, secretaries of District Party Committees, chairmen of District Executive Committees . . .

At the very beginning of our book we gave a conspectus of the *waves* pouring into the Archipelago during the two decades up to 1937. How long all that dragged on! And how many millions there were! But the future call-up of 1937 didn't bat an eyelid and found it all normal. We do not know what expressions they used in discussing it among themselves, but P. P. Postyshev, unaware that he himself was destined to go the same way, spoke like this:

In 1931, at a conference of justice officials: ". . . while retaining our penal policy in all its severity and cruelty in relation to the class enemy and to déclassé offshoots . . ." (*"Déclassé offshoots"* —how priceless! Just about anybody could be classified as a "déclassé offshoot"!)

In 1932: "It is understandable that . . . in putting them through the crucible of dekulakization . . . we must never lost sight of the fact that this kulak of yesterday has not morally disarmed . . ."

And again: "In no case must the sharp blade of penal policy become dull."

And that blade, Pavel Petrovich, was so sharp! And that crucible so very hot!

R. M. Ger explained it like this: "So long as the arrests involved people who were unknown or scarcely known to me, I and my acquaintances had no doubts about the well-foundedness [!] of those arrests. But when people close to me were arrested and I myself was arrested, and when I encountered dozens of the most loyal Communists in prison, then . . ."

In a word, they remained calm while *society* was being imprisoned. Their "outraged reason boiled" when *their own fellowship* began to be imprisoned. Stalin violated a taboo that appeared firmly established, and that was why they had led such a gay life.

Of course, they were stunned! Of course, it was a fantastic thing to have to grasp! And in the cells they asked heatedly: "Comrades! Do you know whose coup this was? Who seized power in our city?"

And for a long time after, as they became convinced of the irrevocability of their fate, they sighed and groaned: "If only Lenin were alive, this never would have happened!"

(What did they mean by *this?* Was it not precisely *this* that had happened to the others before them? See Part I, Chapters 8 and 9.)

But nonetheless—they were government people! Enlightened Marxists! Theoreticians! And how did they cope with this ordeal? How did they reprocess and make sense of an historical event not previously digested nor explained in the newspapers? (And historical events always swoop down unexpectedly.)

Dragged roughly for years down a false trail, they offered explanations astonishing in their profundity:

1. It is the very cunning work of foreign intelligence services.

2. It is wrecking on an enormous scale! Wreckers have taken over the NKVD! (A variation on this was: German agents had taken over the NKVD!)

3. It is a plot by local NKVD men.

And in all three cases the message was: that we ourselves were to blame for relaxing our vigilance! Stalin doesn't know anything! Stalin doesn't know about these arrests!! When he finds out, he will destroy them all and free us!!

4. In the ranks of the Party there was terrible treason (but why??); and the entire country is teeming with enemies, and the majority of the people here have been correctly arrested; they aren't Communists but . . . Counter-Revolutionaries— and in the cells you have to take precautions and be careful not to speak in their presence. "I am the only one here who is completely innocent. Well, you too maybe." (This was the variation which was adopted by Mekhanoshin, a former member of the Revolutionary War Council. In other words, let him out, give him his way—and see how many he arrests.)

5. These repressions are an historical necessity for the development of our society. (This was how a few of the theoreticians talked who had not lost their self-possession, as, for example, a professor from the Plekhanov Institute of National Economy. The explanation was a sure one, and one had to admire how quickly and correctly he had understood it—but none of them ever explained what laws they had in mind and they just kept blowing on the same flute from their permanent selection: "the historical necessity of development"—you can spout that nonsense about anything and you'll always be right.)

And in all five variations no one, of course, accused Stalin —he remained an uneclipsed sun![2]

And if one day one of the old Party members, like, for example, Aleksandr Ivanovich Yashkevich, the Byelorussian censor, wheezed from the corner of the cell that Stalin was no right hand of Lenin but a dog, and until he croaked, nothing good would happen—they would hurl themselves on such a person with fists, and hurry to denounce him to their interrogator!

It is impossible to imagine to oneself a Goodthinker who for one moment in a daydream would let out a peep about the death of Stalin.

Right on that level of inquisitive thought is where the year 1937 caught up with the loyalist orthodox Communists! And what kind of an attitude to their trial were they left with? Evidently like Parsons in Orwell's *1984:* "You don't think the Party would arrest an innocent man? . . . 'Thank you,' I'm going to say [to the tribunal], 'thank you for saving me before it was too late!' "

And what way out did they find for themselves? What active decision did their revolutionary theory indicate? Their decision is just as priceless as their explanations! Here is what it is:

The more people that are arrested, the quicker those at the top are going to *understand their mistake!* And therefore . . . one has to try *to name as many names as possible!* One has to give as much fantastic testimony as possible against innocents! *They won't arrest the entire Party!*

(But Stalin didn't need the whole Party. All he needed was its leadership and the members with seniority.)

Just as out of the members of all the Russian parties it was the Communists who turned out to be the *first* to give *false testimony against themselves*[3]—so, too, they were the first to make the merry-go-round discovery: that you should name as many names as possible! Russian revolutionaries had never heard of anything like that!

2. And against the background of these astonishing explanations, that particular one which Narokov (Marchenko) in his novel *Mnimyye Velichiny* (*Imaginary Values*) ascribes to his characters seems psychologically very possible: that all these arrests were simply a show put on to test the true Stalinists. You had to do everything demanded of you and whoever would sign everything without becoming embittered would be promoted substantially later on.

3. Well, perhaps the "Union Bureau of Mensheviks" preceded them, but they, on the basis of their convictions, were almost Bolsheviks.

Was it their shortsightedness that showed itself in this theory? The poverty of their ideas? I sense instinctively that this was not the case, that what moved them here was fear. And that this theory was only a handy camouflage to cover up their weakness. For, after all, they called themselves (long since unlawfully) revolutionaries, but when they looked inside themselves they shuddered: it turned out that they were incapable of standing up to the interrogator. And this "theory" freed them from the necessity of struggling against the interrogator.

They ought to have been able to understand at least this— that for Stalin this purge of the Party was necessary in order to downgrade the Party in comparison with himself (for he himself did not have the genius to rise in comparison with the Party, even such as it was).

Of course, they did not remember how very recently they themselves had helped Stalin destroy the opposition, yes, and even themselves too. After all, Stalin gave his own weak-willed victims the opportunity of taking a chance and rebelling, for this game was not without its satisfactions for him. To arrest each member of the Central Committee required the sanction of all the others! That is something the playful tiger thought up. And while the sham plenums and conferences proceeded, a paper was passed along the rows which stated impersonally that materials had been received compromising a certain individual; and it was requested that consent be given (or refused!) to his expulsion from the Central Committee. (And someone else watched to see whether the person reading this paper held it for a long time.) And they all . . . signed their names. And that was how the Central Committee of the All-Union Communist Party (Bolsheviks) shot itself. (Stalin had calculated and verified their weakness even earlier than that: once the top level of the Party had accepted as their due high wages, secret provisioning facilities, private sanatoriums, it was already in the trap and there was no way to backtrack.) And *who* made up the Special Assizes that tried Tukhachevsky and Yakir? Blücher! Yegorov! (And S. A. Turovsky.)

And they had forgotten even more (yes, and had never read it anyway) such ancient history as the message of the Patriarch Tikhon to the Council of People's Commissars on October 26, 1918. Appealing for mercy and for the release of the innocent, the staunch Patriarch warned them: "That the blood of all the prophets which was shed from the foundation of the world may be required of this generation." (St. Luke, 11:50.)* And: ". . . for all they that take the sword shall perish with the sword." (Matthew, 26:52)* But at that time it seemed absurd, impossible! How could they imagine at that time that History sometimes does know revenge, a sort of voluptuous and delayed justice, but chooses strange forms for it and unexpected executors of its will.

And though, when the young Tukhachevsky returned victorious from suppressing the devastated Tambov peasants, there was no Mariya Spiridonova waiting at the station to put a bullet through his head, it was done sixteen years later by the Georgian priest who never graduated.

And though the curses of the women and children shot in the Crimean spring of 1921, as Voloshin has told us, were incapable of piercing the breast of Bela Kun, this was done by his own comrade in the Third International.

And so it was with Peters, Latsis, Berzin, Agranov, Prokofyev, Balitsky, Artuzov, Chudnovsky, Dybenko, Uborevich, Bubnov, Alafuzo, Alksnis, Arenshtam, Gekker, Gettis, Yegorov, Zhloba, Kovtyukh, Kork, Kutyakov, Primakov, Putna, Y. Sablin, Feldman, R. Eideman; and Unshlickt, Yenukidze, Nevsky, Steklov, Lomov, Kaktyn, Kosior, Rudzutak, Gikalo, Goloded, Shlikhter, Beloborodov, Pyatakov, and Zinoviev. All were executed by the little redheaded butcher. And it would take a patient search on our part to track down now what they had set their hands and signatures to over the fifteen or twenty preceding years.

Fight back? Not one of them tried to fight back. If they say it was difficult to fight back in Yezhov's cells, why didn't they begin to fight the day before their arrest? Was it really unclear where things were going? That means their whole prayer was that they themselves should be bypassed! Why did Ordzhonikidze commit suicide so cravenly? (Or, if he was killed, why did he wait for it?) Why didn't Lenin's faithful companion, Krupskaya, fight back? Why didn't she speak out even once with a public exposé, like the old worker in the Rostov Flax Works? Was she really so afraid of losing her old woman's life? The members of the first Ivanovo-Voznesensk 1905 Soviet of Deputies—Alalykin and Spiridonov—why did they now sign* shameful charges against themselves? And why did Shubin, the representative of that same Soviet of Deputies, sign even more than that—that there had been no Ivanovo-Voznesensk Soviet of Deputies in 1905? How was it possible to spit on one's whole life like that?

The Goodthinkers themselves, remembering 1937 now, groan over the injustices and horrors—but no one recalls the possibilities of *fighting back* which existed and which they physically possessed—and which no one made use of. And of course they never will explain it either. Will Yevgeny Yevtushenko, full of energy, take up that task—the true grandson of his grandfather* with precisely the same set of concepts (in his *Autobiography* and in *The Bratsk Power Station*) as those of the call-up of 1937? No, the time for such arguments has passed.

All the wisdom of the imprisoned true believers was merely enough to destroy the traditions of our political prisoners. They avoided their cellmates who thought differently, hid from them, whispered about the horrors of the interrogation in such a way that the non-Party people or, God help us, the SR's, could not hear—"so as not to give them material against the Party."

Yevgeniya Goltsman in the Kazan Prison (1938) was opposed to knocking out signals between cells; as a Communist she was against violating Soviet laws! And when they brought a newspaper, Goltsman insisted that her cellmates read it in full detail, not just superficially!

The prison portion of Y. Ginzburg's memoirs gives us frank testimony on the call-up of 1937. The hard-head Yuliya Annenkova demanded of the cell: "Don't dare make fun of the jailer! *He is the representative here of Soviet power!*" (Well? Everything had turned upside down! Show that little scene in that fairy-tale crystal ball to the unruly revolutionary women in a Tsarist prison!) And the Komsomol member Katya Shirokova asked Ginzburg in the frisking room: "That German Communist woman over there has gold hidden in her hair, but it's our Soviet prison, so shouldn't we tell the jailer?"

And Yekaterina Olitskaya, who traveled to the Kolyma in the same railroad car as Ginzburg, No. 7—this car consisted almost entirely of women Communists—supplements her rich recollections with two astonishing details.

Those who had money gave some of it to buy scallions, and Olitskaya was the person in the car to whom they were handed. With her SR traditions, it never entered her head to do otherwise than divide them up among all forty prisoners. But she was immediately brought up short: "Divide them among the people who gave the money!" "We can't feed paupers!" "We don't have enough ourselves!" Olitskaya was stupefied: were these politicals? They were women Communists of the 1937 call-up!

And a second episode. In the Sverdlovsk Transit Prison baths these women were driven naked between formations of jailers. Nothing happened, and they were reassured. And in the ensuing stages of their journey they sang in their car:

> I know no other country
> Where a person breathes so freely!

Now it's with that sort of complex of world outlook, it's on that level of consciousness, that the Goodthinkers started on their long camp road. Having understood nothing from the very beginning, neither about their arrest, nor interrogation, nor events in general, out of stubbornness, out of loyalty (or out of desperation?), they would henceforth, throughout the journey, regard themselves as bearers of light, and proclaim themselves as the only ones who understood the essence of things.

Having once made the decision not to notice anything around them and not to draw conclusions, they would then try all the more not to notice what was worst of all for them: how they looked, this newly arrived call-up of 1937, still very decent in clothes, manners, and conversation, to the camp inmates, to the nonpolitical offenders, and to the 58's too. (Any of the dispossessed "kulaks" who had survived was, right then, finishing his first *tenner*.) Here they came, those who used to carry briefcases and look important! Here came those who had gone about in personally assigned automobiles! Here came those who, at the time of ration cards, used to receive provisions from special closed stores! Here came those who got fat at sanatoriums and womanized at resorts! While the rest of us, under the law of "Seveneighths," were being given ten years in camp for a head of cabbage, for an ear of corn. And so they were hated and told: "Out there in freedom, *you* did *us* in, but here *we* are going to do *you* in!" (But this won't happen. All the orthodox Communists are soon going to get themselves well fixed up.)[4]

4. Y. Ginzburg cites a completely contrary scene. The prison nurse asks: "Is it true that you tried to help the poor people, that you are imprisoned because of the collective farmers?" It is an almost unbelievable question. Perhaps the prison nurse, behind bars, saw nothing at all, and therefore asked such a stupid question. But the collective farmers and the ordinary camp inmates had eyes and they immediately recognized the people who had carried out the monstrous cattle drive of "collectivization."

What does the loyalists' lofty truth consist of? Simply that they do not want to renounce a single one of their former values or accept a single new one. Let life gush over them, surge over them, and even roll over them with wheels—still they won't let it into their heads! They won't accept it, as though it weren't happening at all! This reluctance to change anything inside their own brains, this simple inability to make a critical assessment of their life's experience, is what they pride themselves on! Prison must not influence their world outlook! Camp must not influence it! What they stood upon before, they will continue to stand by now! We . . . are Marxists! We . . . are materialists! How can we possibly change because we landed in prison by sheer chance? (How can our consciousness change if existence changes, if it manifests new aspects of itself? Not for anything! Even if that existence falls through the floor and disappears, it won't determine our consciousness! For, after all, we are materialists! . . .)

That is the extent of their perception of what has happened to them. V. M. Zarin: "I always used to say to myself in camp: just because of fools [i.e., those who had arrested him] I do not intend to quarrel with Soviet power!"

Here is their inevitable moral: I have been imprisoned for nothing and that means I am good, and that all these people around me are enemies and have been imprisoned for good cause.

And here is how their energy is spent: Six and twelve times a year they send off complaints, declarations, and petitions. And what do they write about? What do they scrawl in them? Of course, they swear loyalty to the Great Genius (and without that they won't be released). Of course, they dissociate themselves from those already shot in their case. Of course, they beg to be forgiven and permitted to return to their old jobs at the top. And tomorrow they will gladly accept any Party assignment whatever —even to run this camp! (And the fact that all the complaints and petitions were met with just as thick a shoal of rejections —well, that was because they didn't reach Stalin! He would have understood! He would have forgiven, the benefactor!)

Fine "politicals" they were if they begged the government for . . . forgiveness! Here was the level of their consciousness— General Gorbatov in his memoirs: "The court? What had it done wrong? Someone had given it orders. . . ." Oh, what a profound analysis! And what angelic Bolshevik meekness! The thieves asked Gorbatov: "Why did you get here?" (Incidentally,

Gorbatov has them asking politely, which they would never do!) And Gorbatov replied: "Bad people slandered me." No, what an analysis, really, what an analysis! And the general behaved not like Ivan Denisovich Shukhov, but like Fetyukov instead: he went to clean up the office in the hope of receiving an extra crust of bread for it. "Brushing the crumbs and crusts from the table, and sometimes pieces of bread, I began to satisfy my hunger somewhat better." All right, go on and satisfy it! But Ivan Denisovich is charged with heavy guilt because he thinks about porridge and has no social consciousness, while General Gorbatov can get away with anything because he *thinks* . . . about bad people! (Nonetheless Ivan Denisovich did not go wrong, and he has bolder opinions about what goes on in the country than the general.)

And here is V. P. Golitsyn, son of a district physician, a road engineer; he was imprisoned for 140 (one hundred forty!) days in a death cell (plenty of time to think!). And then he got fifteen years, and after that external exile. "In my mind nothing changed. I was the same non-Party Bolshevik as before. My faith in the Party helped me, the fact that the evil was being done not by the Party and government but by the evil will of *certain people* [what an analysis!] who came and went [but somehow they never seemed to go . . .], but all the rest [!!] remained. . . . And ordinary Soviet people also helped me endure it, of whom in 1937–1938 there were *very many*, both in the NKVD [i.e., in its apparatus!], and in the prisons, and in the camps. Not the 'godfathers' but the real Dzerzhinsky men." (This surpasses all understanding: those Dzerzhinsky men, of whom there were so many—what were they doing there, just looking on at the crimes of *certain people?* Yet they did not get involved in these crimes themselves? Though at the same time they survived? Miracles . . . !)

Or Boris Dyakov: "I suffered Stalin's death with acute pain." (Was he alone? All the orthodox Communists felt the same.) It seemed to him as if all hopes for release had faded! . . . [5]

But people are shouting at me: "That's dishonest! Dishonest! You must argue with real theoreticians! From the Institute of Red Professors!"

All right; as you will! As if I'd not done it before! What else was I doing in prison? And on prison transports? And at transit prisons? At first I argued alongside them, taking their side. But somehow our arguments seemed to me too thin. And at that point I began to keep silent and just listen. And then I argued against them. Yes, even Zakharov himself, the teacher of Malenkov (and he was very proud—of having been Malenkov's teacher too), even he condescended to debate with me.

And here's what: All those arguments seem in retrospect to have coalesced into one argument in my head. It is as if all these dogmatists taken together had been rolled into . . . one person. Time after time he would advance the very same argument in the same words at the same point. And would be equally impenetrable—impenetrability, that was their chief trait! Armor-piercing shells for iron-heads have not yet been invented! In arguing with them, you wear yourself out, unless you accept in advance that the argument is simply a game, a jolly pastime.

My friend Panin* and I are lying on the middle shelf of a Stolypin compartment and have set ourselves up comfortably, tucked our salt herring in our pockets so we don't need water and can go to sleep. But at some station or other they shove into our compartment . . . a Marxist scholar! We can even tell this from his goatee and spectacles. He doesn't hide the fact: he is a former professor of the Communist Academy. We hang head down in the square cutout—and from his very first words we see that he is: impenetrable. But we have been serving time for a long while and have a long time left to serve, and we value a merry joke. We must climb down to have a bit of fun! There is ample space in the compartment, and so we exchange places with someone and crowd in:

"Hello."

"Hello."

"You're not too crowded?"

"No, it's all right."

"Have you been in the jug a long time?"

"Long enough."

"Are you past the halfway mark?"

"Just."

"Look over there: how poverty-stricken our villages are—straw thatch, crooked huts."

"An inheritance from the Tsarist regime."

"Well, but we've already had thirty Soviet years."

"That's an insignificant period historically."

"It's terrible that the collective farmers are starving."

"But have you looked in *all* their ovens?"

"Just ask any collective farmer in our compartment."

"Everyone in jail is embittered and prejudiced."

"But I've seen collective farms myself."

"That means they were uncharacteristic."

(The goatee had never been in any of them—that way it was simpler.)

"Just ask the old folks: under the Tsar they were well fed, well clothed, and they used to have so many holidays."

"I'm not even going to ask. It's a subjective trait of human memory to praise everything about the past. The cow that died is the one that gave twice the milk. [Sometimes he even cited proverbs!] And our people don't like holidays. They like to work."

"But why is there a shortage of bread in many cities?"

"When?"

"Right before the war, for example."

"Not true! Before the war, in fact, everything had been worked out."

"Listen, at that time in all the cities on the Volga there were queues of thousands of people. . . ."

"Some local failure in supply. But more likely your memory is failing you."

"But there's a shortage now!"

"Old wives' tales. We have from seven to eight billion poods of grain."[6]

"And the grain itself is rotten."

"Not at all. We have been successful in developing new varieties of grain."

"But in many shops the shelves are empty."

"Inefficient distribution in local areas."

"Yes, and the prices are high. The workers have to do without many things."

"Our prices are more scientifically based than anywhere else."

"That means wages are low."

6. And not so soon afterward Khrushchev would discover that in 1952 less breadgrain was being harvested than in 1913.

"And the wages, too, are scientifically based."

"That means they're based in such a way that the worker works for the state for free the greater part of his time."

"You don't know anything about economics. What is your profession?"

"Engineer."

"And I am an economist. Don't argue. Surplus value is even impossible here."

"But why is it that the father of a family used to be able to feed his family by his own labor, and that now two or three in the family have to work?"

"Because there was unemployment previously, and the wife couldn't get work. And the family went hungry. Furthermore, the wife's working is important for her equality."

"What the devil do you mean by equality? And who does all the household work?"

"The husband has to help."

"And how about you—did you help your wife?"

"I am not married."

"So each of them used to work during the day, and now both of them have to work in the evenings too. And the woman has no time for the main thing—for bringing up the children."

"She has quite enough. They are mainly brought up by the kindergarten, school, and Komsomol."

"Well, and how are they bringing them up? They grow up to be hooligans and petty thieves and the girls . . . run free and loose."

"Not at all. Our youth have lofty principles."

"That's what the papers say. But our papers tell lies!"

"They are much more honest than the bourgeois newspapers! You ought to read the bourgeois newspapers."

"Just give me the chance!"

"That's not necessary at all."

"And our newspapers still tell lies!"

"They are openly bound to the proletariat."

"That's the kind of bringing up that makes the crime rate grow."

"On the contrary, it's falling. Give me the statistics."

(This in a country where even the number of sheep tails is classified as a secret!)

"And another reason our crime rate is rising is that our laws themselves give rise to crime. They are ferocious and ridiculous."

"On the contrary, they are fine laws. The finest in the history of humanity."

"Especially Article 58."

"Without it our young state would not have been able to hold out."

"It's no longer so very young!"

"Historically speaking it is very young."

"But look around at the number of people imprisoned."

"They got what they deserved."

"And what about you?"

"I was jailed by mistake. They will sort things out and release me."

(They all leave themselves this loophole.)

"By mistake? Then what kind of laws do we have?"

"The laws are excellent, it is the deviations from them that are unfortunate."

"Everywhere there is graft, bribes, corruption."

"We have to intensify our Communist upbringing."

And so forth. He is imperturbable. He speaks in a language which requires no effort of the mind. And arguing with him is like walking through a desert.

It's about people like that that they say: "He made the rounds of all the smithies and came home unshod."

And when they write in their obituaries: "perished tragically during the period of the cult," this should be corrected to read: "perished comically."

But if his fate had worked out differently, we would never have learned what a dry, insignificant little man he was. We would have respectfully read his name in the newspaper. He would have become a people's commissar or even ventured to represent all Russia abroad.

To argue with him was useless. It was much more interesting to play with him . . . no, not at chess, but at the game of "comrades." There really is such a game. It is a very simple game. Just play up to him a couple of times or so, use some of his own pet words and phrases. He will like it. For he has grown accustomed to find that all around him . . . are enemies. He has become weary of snarling and doesn't like to tell his stories because all those stories will be twisted around and thrown right back in his face. But if he takes you for one of his own, he will quite humanly disclose to you what he has just seen at the station: People are passing by, talking, laughing, life goes on. The Party is providing leadership, people are being moved from job to job. Yet you and I are languishing here in prison, there are a handful of us, and we must *write* and write petitions, begging a review of our cases, begging for a pardon. . . .

Or else he will tell you something interesting: In the Communist Academy they decided to *devour* one comrade; they felt he wasn't quite genuine, *not one of our own;* but somehow they couldn't manage it: there were no errors in his essays, and his biography was clean. Then all of a sudden, going through the archives, what a find! They ran across an old brochure written by this comrade which Vladimir Ilyich Lenin himself had held in his hands and in the margin of which he had written in his own handwriting the notation: "As an economist he is shit." "Well, now, you understand," our companion smiled confidentially, "that after *that* it was no trouble at all to make short work of that muddlehead and impostor. He was expelled from the Academy and deprived of his scholarly rank."

The railroad cars go clicking along. Everyone is already asleep, some lying down, some sitting up. Sometimes a convoy guard passes along the corridor, yawning.

And one more unrecorded episode from Lenin's biography is lost from *view*. . . .

■

For a complete picture of the loyalists we must inquire into their conduct in all the basic areas of camp life.

A. *Attitude toward the Camp Regimen and toward the Prisoners' Struggle for Their Rights.* Inasmuch as the camp regimen has been established *by us*, the Soviet government, it must be observed not only willingly but conscientiously. The *spirit* of the regimen has to be observed even before this is demanded or requested by the supervisors.

There are some astonishing observations in the work of that

same Y. Ginzburg: The women *justify* the cropping of their own hair (with clippers)! (Since the prison regimen requires it.) From a closed prison they were sent to die in the Kolyma. And they had their own explanation already prepared: "That means they *trust* us, that we will work there conscientiously!"

And what the devil is the point of talking about any kind of *struggle?* Struggle against whom? Against *our own people?* Struggle—for what? For our personal release? For that you don't need to struggle, you have to ask according to rules. A struggle for the overthrow of the Soviet government? Shut your mouth!

Among the camp inmates were those who wanted to struggle but could not, those who could but didn't want to, those who both could and wanted to (and did! when the time comes, we will tell about them too!). The orthodox Communists represented a fourth group: those who didn't want to and *couldn't* even if they had wanted to. All their preceding life had prepared them only for an artificially conditioned environment. Their "struggle" out in freedom had consisted in adopting and transmitting resolutions and instructions already approved by their higher-ups with the help of the telephone and the electric bell. In camp conditions where the struggle most frequently was hand-to-hand, with unarmed prisoners marching against machine pistols, crawling on their bellies under fire, they were the "Sidor Polikarpoviches" or the "Dill Tomatoviches," frightening no one and good for nothing.

And even less did these principled warriors for universal human happiness offer any hindrance to the depredations of the thieves, nor did they object to the dominance of the thieves in the kitchens and among the trusties. (Just read General Gorbatov. You can find it there.) For it was on the basis of *their* theory that the socially friendly thieves got such vast power in camp. They didn't prevent the thieves from plundering weak zeks in their presence, and they themselves did not resist being plundered by them.

And all this was completely logical, there were no loose ends lying about, and no one disputed it. But then the time came to write our history, and the first half-stifled voices were raised about life in the camps, and the Goodthinkers looked back and were pained: how could that be? They who were so progressive, so conscientious—and they had not struggled! And they had not even known that there was a personality cult of Stalin![7] And they certainly hadn't supposed that dear Lavrenti Pavlovich Beria was an inveterate enemy of the people!

And they had to hasten to spread some kind of muddied version to the effect that *they had struggled*. And all the snarling dogs on magazines who felt up to it blamed my Ivan Denisovich, the son-of-a-bitch, for not waging a struggle. *Moskovskaya Pravda* (December 8, 1962) even reproached Ivan Denisovich for not going to the underground meetings arranged by the Communists in camp, claiming he was unwilling to learn from thinking people.

But what kind of delirium is this? What underground meetings? And why? To show the finger inside their pockets? And at whom would they have shown that finger—if from the junior jailer right on up to Stalin himself, one and all were that same Soviet power? So when and *with what methods* did they struggle?

No one can tell us that.

And *what were they thinking about* then—if all they allowed themselves to do was keep repeating that "everything that is real is rational"? What were they thinking of if their entire prayer was: "Do not beat me, please, O whip of the Tsar!"

B. *Relationship to the Camp Administration.* What kind of attitude other than the most respectful and friendly could the *Goodthinkers* have toward the camp chiefs? After all, the camp chiefs were all Party members and were carrying out the Party's directives, and it was not their fault that "I" ("I" = the one and only innocent) had been sentenced and sent here. The orthodox Communists understood quite well that if they themselves had suddenly turned up in the position of the camp chief they would have done everything just as he did.

Todorsky, whom today our whole press has proclaimed a camp hero (he is a former seminarist who became a journalist, singled out by Lenin, and by the thirties for some reason installed as the Chief of the Air Force [?] Academy, though he was not a flier), would even, according to Dyakov's account, talk to the

7. In 1957 the head of the personnel department of the Ryazan Province Education Department asked me: "What were you arrested for in 1945?" "For speaking out against the cult of personality," I replied. "How can that be?" She was astonished. "Was there a cult of personality *then?*" (She was seriously under the impression that the cult of personality had been proclaimed only in 1956. So how could it have been there in 1945?)

supply chief (whom a slogger would pass without a glance) like this: "How can I serve you, Citizen Chief?"

For the chief of the Medical Section Todorsky composed a synopsis of the *Short Course* of Party history. If Todorsky ever had any *thoughts* in the least unlike those in the *Short Course*, then where were his principles, how could he compose a synopsis exactly according to Stalin?[8] And if he really thought *precisely like that*, then that's what is called "perished comically."

But it is too little to love one's camp bosses! What is required is that the bosses love you. It is necessary to explain to the chiefs that we are of the same stuff as you, and you have to take care of us somehow. And this is why the heroes of Serebryakova, Shelest, Dyakov, Aldan-Semyonov on every occasion, whether necessary or not, whether convenient or not, when the prisoner transport is being received, when the names are read out from the lists, declare themselves Communists. That is their application for a cozy spot!

Shelest even thinks up a scene like this. At the Kotlas Transit Prison the roll is being called. "Party member?" asks the chief. (What fools is he writing this for? Where in a prison list is there a column for Party membership?) "Member of the Communist Party of Bolsheviks," replies Shelest to the faked question.

And one has to give the chiefs their due, Dzerzhinsky men or Beria men: they *heard*. And . . . they arranged things for them. Yes, and were there not perhaps some written or at least oral directives: to make things easier for the Communists? For even in periods of the sharpest persecutions of the 58's, when they were being ousted from all jobs as trusties, former big-shot Communists for some reason kept their places. (For example, in Kraslag. Former member of the Military Council of the North Caucasus Military District Aralov remained as brigadier of the vegetable gardeners, and former General Ivanchik remained as a brigadier for cottages, and former secretary of the Moscow Committee Dedkov also kept a soft spot.) But even without any directive, plain solidarity and plain self-interest—"You today, me tomorrow"—were bound to compel the MVD men to look after the true believers.

---

8. They will object: Principles are principles, but sometimes it is necessary to be elastic. There was a period when Ulbricht and Dimitrov instructed their Communist Parties to make peace with the Nazis and even support them. Well, we have nothing to top that: that's *dialectics!*

And the way it turned out was that the chiefs kept the orthodox Communists at their right hand so that they constituted a firmly established privileged stratum in camp. (But this did not extend to the quiet rank-and-file Communists who did not go to the chiefs to trumpet their faith.)

Aldan-Semyonov writes quite straightforwardly that the Communist camp chiefs tried to transfer Communist prisoners to lighter work. And Dyakov doesn't conceal it either: The newcomer Rom announced to the chief of the hospital that he was an Old Bolshevik. And right away he was assigned as a Medical Section clerk—an enviable post! And the camp chief also gave orders that Todorsky was not to be removed from his post as a medical orderly.

But the most remarkable case of all is recounted by G. Shelest in his *Kolyma Notes*:[9] A new MVD big shot arrived there and recognized the prisoner Zaborsky as his former corps commander from the Civil War. They wept on meeting. Go ahead, ask half my kingdom! And Zaborsky agreed to accept "special food from the kitchen and to take as much bread as he needed" (in other words, to eat the bread of the sloggers, since no one was going to prescribe a new ration norm for him), and asked only to be given a six-volume set of Lenin to read in the evening by the light of the kerosene lamp! And that is how everything was arranged; during the day he was fed with stolen rations; in the evening he read Lenin! And that is how openly and with enjoyment vileness is glorified!

Shelest writes about some kind of mythical "underground politburo" of the work brigade (a bit too big a deal, wasn't it, for a work brigade?), which managed to get hold of a loaf of bread from the bread-cutting room after hours, as well as a bowl of oatmeal. And what that means is that we have our own trusties everywhere. And also: Let's swipe what we can, Goodthinkers?

That very same Shelest gives us his final conclusion:

"Some survived thanks to *their strength of spirit* [those were those orthodox Communists swiping bread and cereal—A.S.], while others survived thanks to an extra bowl of oatmeal [that was Ivan Denisovich]."[10]

9. *Znamya* (*The Banner*), 1964, No. 9.
10. *Zabaikalsky Rabochi* (*Trans-Baikal Worker*), August 27, 1964.

Well, so be it. Ivan Denisovich had no friends among the trusties. Just tell us one thing: Who laid the bricks, who laid the bricks in the wall? Was it you, you hard-heads?

C. *Attitude toward Labor.* It appears that on the whole the orthodox Communists were devoted to work. (Eikhe's deputy, even in a typhoid delirium, could calm down only when the nurse assured him that, yes, the telegrams on grain procurements had already been sent.) It appears that on the whole they approved of camp labor also; it was necessary to the building of Communism, and without it the issuing of gruel to the whole horde of prisoners would have been undeserved. Therefore they considered it quite rational that persons refusing to go out to work should be beaten and imprisoned in the punishment block and shot in wartime. They considered it quite moral to be a work assigner, a brigadier, any kind of cattle driver or whip cracker. (And in this regard they disagreed with the so-called "honest thieves" and were in agreement with the "bitches.")

Take, for example, the brigadier of the logging brigade Yelena Nikitina, a former secretary of the Kiev Komsomol Committee. Here is what they say about her: She stole from the output of her own brigade (of 58's) and traded it with the thieves. Lyusya Dzhaparidze (daughter of a Baku Commissar) bought her way out of work from Nikitina with chocolate received in a food parcel. On the other hand, this woman brigadier refused to let the Anarchist Tatyana Garasyeva leave the woods for three days—until she had frostbite.

Take Prokhorov-Pustover, also a Bolshevik, though not a Party member, who turned in zeks for deliberately failing to fulfill norms. (He used to report this to the chiefs, and the zeks got punished.) To the zeks' reproaches that he must realize it was slave labor, Pustover replied: "That's a strange philosophy! In capitalist countries the workers struggle against slave labor; but we, even if we are slaves, work for a socialist state, not for private persons. These officials are only temporarily [?] in power. One blow from the people . . . and they will disappear, but the people's state will remain."

It's . . . a jungle, the consciousness of an orthodox Communist. It's impossible to make sense of it.

And the only exception the Goodthinkers make is this reservation for themselves: It would be wrong to use them on general camp work, since it would then be difficult for them to preserve themselves for the future fertile leadership of the Soviet people. And anyway it would also be difficult for them *to think* during those years in camp, in other words to repeat in turn, one after another while gathered in a circle, that Comrade Stalin, Comrade Molotov, Comrade Beria, and all the rest of the Party were right.

And therefore, using all their efforts under the protection of the camp chiefs and with each other's secret help, they tried to get themselves places as trusties—in jobs where no knowledge or skills were required (none of them was a specialist), in calm and quiet places farther from the main hand-to-hand camp struggle. And so they grabbed hold: Zakharov (Malenkov's teacher)—as storage room clerk for personal property; the above-mentioned Zaborsky (Shelest himself?)—at the clothing-issue desk; the notorious Todorsky—in the Medical Section; Konokotin—as a medical assistant (though he was not a medical assistant at all); Serebryakova—as a nurse (though she was no nurse at all). And Aldan-Semyonov was also a trusty.

The camp biography of Dyakov—the biggest loud-mouth of all the loyalists—has been depicted by his own pen and is truly astonishing. During the five years of his sentence he contrived to leave the camp compound *just once*—and then for only half a day, and during that half-day he worked for half an hour, cutting branches, and then the jailer said to him: "You're fagged out, take a rest!" Half an hour in five years—not everyone gets away with that! For a certain length of time he *malingered* on the pretext of a rupture, and subsequently a fistula resulting from the rupture—but listen here, not for five years! To receive such golden jobs as medical statistician, librarian of the Cultural and Educational Section, and storage room clerk for personal possessions, and to stay in such jobs for your *entire term*—a bribe of fat bacon wasn't enough; most likely you had to sell your soul to the "godfather" as well. Let the old camp veterans be the judge of this. And Dyakov was not merely a trusty but an aggressive trusty; in the first version of his story,[11] before he was publicly shamed for it,[12] he elegantly explained why an intelligent person

11. *Zvezda*, 1963, No. 3.
12. Lakshin in *Novy Mir*, 1964, No. 1.

ought to avoid the crude lot of the people ("a chess tactic," "castling"—i.e., setting someone else in the forefront of the battle). And this is the person who has now taken it upon himself to become the principal interpreter of camp life!

G. Serebryakova reports to us on her own camp biography with careful omissions. There are said to be serious witnesses against her. I did not have the opportunity of checking this.

Not only the authors themselves, but *all the rest* of the loyalists are also portrayed by this chorus of authors as being *outside manual labor*—either in the hospital or in trusty jobs where they carry on their obscurantist (although somewhat updated) conversations. These writers are not telling lies; they simply didn't have enough imagination to show those hard-heads engaged in labor useful to society. (How can you portray it if you never worked yourself?!)

D. *Attitude toward Escapes.* The hard-heads themselves never attempted to escape; you see, that would have been an act of struggle against the regime, a dislocation of the MVD, in other words an act of subversion of Soviet power. Furthermore, every orthodox Communist always had two or three petitions for pardon traveling around in the highest appeals jurisdictions. And an escape might be interpreted there, at the top, as lack of patience, even as lack of confidence, in the highest jurisdictions.

Anyway, the Goodthinkers *didn't need* "freedom in general." They didn't need the ordinary common freedom of humans and birds. Every truth is concrete! And the only freedom they needed was freedom given them by the state, lawful freedom, duly signed and sealed, with a return to their prearrest situation and privileges! Without that what use was freedom?

Well, and if they themselves didn't try to escape, then all the more did they condemn the escapes of others as pure subversion of the MVD system and of economic construction.

And if escapes were so detrimental, then it was probably the civic duty of a loyal Communist, on learning of an escape attempt, to denounce it to the comrade security chief? Was it not logical?

True, there were one-time members of the underground among them, and bold people from the Civil War! But their dogma had transformed them into . . . political riffraff.

E. *Attitude toward the Rest of the 58's.* They never mingled with their comrades in distress. This would have been non-Party conduct. Sometimes in secret among themselves, and sometimes quite openly too (for there was no risk in it for them), they opposed themselves to the dirty 58's and attempted to regain purity by holding themselves apart. It was precisely this simple-hearted mass that they had led out in freedom—where they never allowed it to utter a free word. And now when they turned out to be in the same cells with them, on equal terms, they still weren't in the least depressed by it and shouted as much as they pleased: "That's what you deserve, scoundrels! You were all pretending out there in freedom! You are all enemies and they were right to arrest you! Everything is in order. And everything is progressing toward the great victory!" (*I* am the only one unjustly imprisoned.)

And the loyalists seriously ascribed to the strength of the all-conquering teaching the absence of any resistance to the path of their prison monologues (because the administration was always on the side of the orthodox Communists, and the KR's did not even dare raise an objection since otherwise they would get second terms), to the strength of the all-conquering doctrine.[13]

It was with frank contempt, with commanding class hatred, that the orthodox Communists gazed around them at all the 58's except themselves. Dyakov: "I thought with horror, 'Who are we among here?'" Konokotin didn't want to give an injection to a sick Vlasov man (though as a medical assistant it was his duty). But he self-sacrificingly contributed blood for a sick convoy guard. (Just like their free doctor Barinov: "First of all I am a Chekist, and *then* I am a physician." Now that is medicine!) Now we understand why "honest people are required" in the hospital (Dyakov)—so as to know who to inject and who not.

And they transformed this hatred into action (how could they and why should they keep this class hatred to themselves?). In Shelest's account, Samuil Gendal, a professor—probably of Communist jurisprudence—provided the ammunition when the lack

---

13. Well, it could happen now and then that there was a different relationship of forces. A certain prosecutor, imprisoned in Unzhlag, had to pretend to be an idiot, and for more than a year too. That was his only means of saving himself from reprisals (he was imprisoned along with his "godchildren").

of any desire to go out to work on the part of the Caucasian nationalities became apparent: the Moslem mullah must be suspected of sabotage.

F. *Attitude toward Stool Pigeons.* Just as all roads lead to Rome, so all the preceding points lead us to this one: it was impossible for the hard-heads not to cooperate with the best and most sincere of the camp chiefs—the security chief. In their situation this was the most reliable method of helping the NKVD, the state, and the Party.

In addition it was very profitable. It was the best way of getting together with the higher-ups. Services rendered to the "godfather" did not go unrewarded. The only means of sticking for years on end in the best trusty soft spots inside the camp compound was with the help of the "godfather."

In one of the books about camp from this same orthodox Communist wave[14] here is the camp system of values of the positive Communist Kratov, who is the author's favorite: (1) Survive at any price, adapting to everything. (2) It is better for decent people to become stool pigeons—because it's better than to leave it to scoundrels.

But even if some orthodox Communist got stubborn and chose not to work for the "godfather," it was still hard for him to avoid that door. The security chief would certainly not omit to offer an affectionate invitation to all true believers, who loudly proclaimed their faith, asking in a fatherly tone: "Are you a Soviet person?" And the loyalist could not answer "No," and that meant "Yes."

And if the answer was "Yes," then come and collaborate, comrade. There is nothing to hinder you.[15]

Only now, when distorting the entire history of the camps, are they ashamed to admit their collaboration. Not all of them got caught red-handed, like Liza Kotik, who dropped a written denunciation. But now someone has blurted out that security officer Sokovikov used to send off Dyakov's letters for him, bypassing the camp censor, and the only thing unsaid is: *In exchange for what* did he send them? That kind of friendship—

---

14. Viktor Vyatkin, *Chelovek Rozhdayetsya Dyazhdy (Man Is Born Twice)*, Part II, Magadan, 1964.

15. Ivanov-Razumnik recalls that they managed to expose three stoolies in their Butyrki cell, and all three turned out to be Communists.

whence came it? They remember to report that the security officer Yakovlev advised Todorsky not to declare himself a Communist openly, but they don't go on to explain why he was concerned about this.

But this is only temporary. Already at hand is that glorious time when people will be able to fling restraint to the winds and admit loudly: "Yes! We . . . were *stoolies* and we are proud of it!"[16]

However—why this whole chapter? Why this whole lengthy survey and analysis of the loyalists? Instead we shall just write in letters a yard high:

JANOS KADAR and **WLADYSLAW GOMULKA**[17]

They both underwent unjust arrest and interrogation with torture, and both of them served time so-and-so many years.

And the whole world sees how much they learned. The whole world has learned what they are worth.

16. I wrote this at the beginning of 1966, and at the end of that same year I read Bukovsky's essay in *Oktyabr* magazine, No. 9. Just as I predicted—they are already bragging openly.

17. And now we can add also **Gustav Husak.** (1972 footnote.)

Chapter 12

■

Knock, Knock, Knock . . .

The Cheka-GB (no doubt a resonant, convenient, and concise name for this organization and one which also preserves its continuity in time) would be an insensate log incapable of carrying out surveillance over its people if it did not have a constant eye and a constant ear. In our technological years cameras and photoelectric elements often work in place of eyes, and microphones, tape recorders, and laser listening devices often replace ears. But for the entire epoch covered by this book almost the only eyes and almost the only ears of the Cheka-GB were *stool pigeons*.

In the early years of the Cheka they were called, in a businesslike manner, secret collaborators (in contrast to staff employees who were in the open). In the manner of those years this was abbreviated to the term *seksoty*,* and that is how it passed into general usage. Whoever thought up this word (not supposing it would become so widely disseminated—and not taking due care) did not have the gift of perceiving it with unprejudiced ear and hearing even in its mere sound the loathsomeness woven into it —something more disreputable even than sodomy. And over the years it became colored with the yellowish-brown blood of betrayal—and there was no nastier word in the whole Russian language.

But this word was used only in freedom. In the Archipelago they had their own words: in prison it was a "nasedka"—a "sitting hen"—and in camp it was a "stukach"—a "knocker"—stool pigeons all. However, just as many words of the Archipelago subsequently moved out into the whole range of the Russian language and took over the entire country, so too the word "knocker" became in time a common concept. This reflected both the unity and the universality of the phenomenon itself.

Without having the experience and without having thought the matter over sufficiently, it is difficult to evaluate the extent to which we are permeated and enveloped by stool-pigeoning. Just as, without a transistor in hand, we do not sense in a field, in a forest, or on a lake that multitudes of radio waves are constantly pouring through us.

It is difficult to school oneself to ask that constant question: *Who is the stool pigeon among us?* In our apartment, in our courtyard, in our watch-repair shop, in our school, in our editorial office, in our workshop, in our design bureau, and even in our police. It is difficult to school oneself, and it is repulsive to become schooled—but for safety one must. It is impossible to expel the stoolies or to fire them—they will recruit new ones. But you have to *know* them—sometimes in order to beware of them; sometimes to put on an act in their presence, to pretend to be something you aren't; sometimes in order to quarrel openly with the informer and by this means devalue his testimony against you.

We will speak in a special chapter on *freedom* about the density of the network of informers. Many sense this density, but they do not make the effort to imagine the informer's face—his simple human face. And for this reason the network seems more enigmatic and more fearsome than in actual fact it is. And yet the informer is that very same pleasant Anna Fyodorovna who lives next door and came in to ask you for some yeast and then ran to report at a prearranged contact point (perhaps a shop or a drugstore) that an unregistered visitor is in your apartment. It is that very same Ivan Nikiforovich whom you like so much, with whom you drank a glass of vodka, and he reported that you cursed because there was nothing in the store to buy and said the higher-ups were getting it all under the counter. You don't know informers face to face, and then you are surprised that the omnipresent Organs could know that during the mass singing of the "Song on Stalin" you merely opened your mouth and didn't waste your voice? Or that you didn't enjoy yourself at the November 7 demonstration? Well, where were they, those penetrating and burning informer's eyes? But the informer's eyes can be a languid blue or hold a senile tear. It is not at all necessary for them to gleam wickedly. Do not expect that he will always be a villain who looks repulsive. He is an ordinary human being like you and me with a measure of good feelings, a measure of malice and envy, and with all the weaknesses which make us vulnerable to spiders. If the recruitment of stool pigeons were entirely voluntary and based on enthusiasm, there would be few of them (as it was perhaps in the twenties). But the recruitment proceeds by means of entanglement and capture, and his weaknesses are what betray a person into this shameful service. And even those who honestly want to rid themselves of this sticky spiderweb, this second skin . . . just can't, just can't.

Recruitment is in the very air of our country. In the fact that what belongs to the state is higher than what belongs to the individual. That Pavlik Morozov is a hero. That a denunciation is not a denunciation but *a help* to the person denounced. Recruitment is interlaced with ideology: for if the Organs wish it, then the recruited person must also wish for one and the same thing: our country's successful advance to socialism.

The technical side of recruitment is beyond praise. Alas, our detective comics do not describe these methods. The recruiters work at propaganda centers before elections. The recruiters work on the faculties of Marxism-Leninism. They call you in—"There's some kind of commission there, go on in." The recruiters work in army units barely back from the front lines; a SMERSH man comes, and *jerks in* half your company one at a time; with some he merely talks about the grits and the weather, but some he assigns to keep watch on each other and on their commanders. A craftsman is sitting in his den repairing leather goods. A friendly man enters: "Could you fix this buckle for me?" And quietly he adds: "You are to shut down your shop right now and go out on the street. There is an automobile there with license number 37–48. Open the door without hesitation and get in. It will take you where you are to go." (And when you get there, the whole thing is routine: "Are you a Soviet person? In that case you must *help* us.") And a shop like that is a wonderful place for gathering denunciations from citizens! And for a personal meeting with the Security chief there is the Sidorov apartment, second floor, three rings, from 6 to 8 P.M.

The poetry of recruitment of stool pigeons still awaits its artist.

There is a visible life and there is an invisible life. The spiderwebs are stretched everywhere, and as we move we do not notice how they wind about us.

Selecting tools available for recruitment is like selecting master keys: No. 1, No. 2, No. 3. No. 1: "Are you a Soviet person?" No. 2 is to promise that which the person being recruited has fruitlessly sought by lawful means for many years. No. 3 is to bring pressure to bear on some weak point, to threaten a person with what he fears most of all. No. 4 . . .

You see, it only takes a tiny bit of pressure. A certain A.G. is called in, and it is well known that he is a nincompoop. And so to start he is instructed: "Write down a list of the people you know who have anti-Soviet attitudes." He is distressed and hesitates: "I'm not sure." He didn't jump up and didn't thump the table: "How dare you!" (Who does in our country? Why deal in fantasies!) "Aha, so you are not sure? Then write a list of people you can guarantee are one hundred percent Soviet people! But *you are guaranteeing*, you understand? If you provide even one of them with false references, you yourself will *go to prison* immediately. So why aren't you writing?" "Well, I . . . can't guarantee." "Aha, you can't? That means you know they are anti-Soviet. So write down immediately the ones you know about!" And so the good and honest rabbit A.G. sweats and fidgets and worries. He has too soft a soul, formed before the Revolution. He has sincerely accepted this pressure which is bearing down on him: Write either that they are Soviet or that they are anti-Soviet. He sees no third way out.

A stone is not a human being, and even stones get crushed.

There are more master keys in freedom because life is more varied. In camp they are of the simplest sort. Life has been simplified, laid bare, and the threading of the screw and the diameter of its head are well known. No. 1, of course, remains: "Are you a Soviet person?" It is very applicable to the loyalists, and the screwdriver will never slip, and the screw head starts immediately and keeps going. No. 2 also works very well indeed: a promise to have the prisoner taken off general work and to have trusty work arranged for him in the camp compound and to see that he gets supplementary grits, and some pay, and has his term reduced. That's all life. And every such little step preserves life! (During the war years *stool-pigeoning* really got to be conspicuously small-time stuff; objects got more expensive and people got cheaper. Souls were *sold* for just a pack of tobacco.) And No. 3 works even better: We will take your trusty status away! We will send you out to general work! We will transfer you to a penalty camp! Every one of those steps was a step toward death. And the person who could not be coaxed upward by a piece of bread could still shudder and beg for mercy if he was pushed into the abyss.

This does not mean that finer, more skillful work did not exist or was never needed—great ingenuity was sometimes required. Major Shikin had to gather material against the prisoner Gertsenberg, a Jew. He had grounds for thinking that Anton, an inexperienced, seventeen-year-old German lad, could provide the material he wanted. Shikin called in young Anton and began to water the Nazi shoots implanted there: how repulsive the Jewish nation was and how it had destroyed Germany. Anton got steamed up and betrayed Gertsenberg. (And why wouldn't the Communist Chekist Shikin have become, under altered circumstances, a dependable interrogator for the Gestapo?)

Or take Aleksandr Fillipovich Stepovoi. Before his arrest he was a soldier in the MVD armies and he had been arrested under Article 58.[1]

He was not an orthodox Communist at all, just an ordinary lad from the working classes. And in camp he came to be

---

1. This is the only chance I will have to tell the story of his arrest. He was conscripted as a boy and sent off to serve in the MVD armies. First—into battle against the Ukrainian partisans, the "Banderists."* Having received information (from informers) as to when the "Banderists" were coming out of the forest to attend mass, the MVD surrounded the church and took them as they came out. (On the basis of photographs.) Later they also guarded (in civilian clothing) people's deputies in Lithuania when the latter went to election meetings. ("One of them was very bold and always declined to have a guard with him!") Later still they guarded a bridge in Gorky Province. They themselves mutinied over poor food and as punishment were sent to the Turkish border. But by this time Stepovoi had already been imprisoned. He used to draw pictures as a hobby, even on the covers of notebooks in political indoctrination courses. On one occasion he drew a pig, and then someone next to him asked: "Can you draw Stalin?" "I can." And he drew a picture of Stalin on the spot. And he turned in his notebook to be checked by the instructor. That was already quite enough to warrant his arrest, but beyond that, at target practice in the presence of a general he had scored seven out of seven bull's-eyes at a distance of four hundred yards and got leave to go home. When he returned to his unit, he reported there were no fruit trees left. All the orchards had been cut down because of the tax on them imposed by Zverev. At his court-martial in Gorky Province he shouted: "Oh, you scoundrels! ·If I am an enemy of the people, why don't you try me in front of everyone—what are you hiding from?" Then. . . . Burlepolom and Krasnaya Glinka (a cruel strict-regimen camp consisting only of 58's who worked on tunneling).

ashamed of his former service and carefully concealed it, realizing that it would be dangerous for him if it became known. So how was he to be recruited as an informer? Well, he was to be recruited with just that: "We will let it be known that you are a 'Chekist.'" They would even wipe their asses with their own banner—anything in order to recruit! (He insists that he nonetheless stood up against them.)

Someone else might, as the saying goes, be nothing at all, but merely want to be a stoolie—someone like that could be had without any difficulty. For another it might be necessary to cast the bait several times before he swallowed it. To anyone who wavered and squirmed on the grounds that it was difficult for him to gather exact information, they would explain: "Give us what you have and we will check it out." "But if I'm not at all sure?" "What does that mean—that you're a real enemy?" And in the end they would explain quite honestly: "What we need is five percent truth and the rest can be your imagination." (The Dzhida security chiefs.)

But sometimes it did happen that the "godfather"[2] would keep trying and trying without landing his prey either on his third try or on his fifth. This was rare, but it happened. Then the "godfather" had his spare noose left: a signature on nondisclosure. Nowhere—either in the Constitution or in the Code—did it ever say that such signatures exist or that we are obliged to give them, but . . . we have got used to everything. How can we refuse this either? We certainly will give all of them. (Yet, at the same time, if we didn't give them, if, on crossing the threshold, we were to announce to one and all our conversation with the "godfather," then indeed the demonic strength of the Third Section would be dispelled. It is on our cowardice that their secrecy and they themselves are founded!) And then a liberating and happy notation is put into the prisoner's camp file: "*Not to be recruited*." That is after try "ninety-six" or at least "eighty-four," but it is a long time before we learn about it, if we survive at all. We can make a guess, however, from the fact that all that scum subsides from us and never clings to us again.

However, most often of all the recruitment succeeds. Crudely

2. The word "kum" in Dal's dictionary is given as meaning "one in a state of *spiritual* kinship, the godfather of one's child by *christening*." And so the transfer of this term to the camp security officer was very precise and quite in the spirit of the language. But with that touch of irony customary with the zeks.

and simply, they put on more and more pressure, so much that you can neither beg nor growl your way out of it.

And soon afterward the new recruit brings in a denunciation.

And as often as not the denunciation tightens the noose of a second term around someone's neck.

And camp squealing turns out to be the strongest form of camp struggle: "You croak today, me tomorrow!"

Out *in freedom* stool-pigeoning was a totally safe occupation for an entire half-century or forty years; there was no answering threat from society, and neither exposure nor punishment could occur.

In the camps it was somewhat different. The reader will recall how the stool pigeons were exposed and exiled to Kondostrov by the Administrative Section of Solovki. But, for decades after, things were seemingly free and easy for the stool pigeons. But at occasional rare intervals and in occasional rare places a small group of resolute and energetic zeks would join forces and continue the Solovetsky tradition in hidden form. Sometimes they would beat up (and kill) a stool pigeon on the pretext of lynch law: a crowd stirred up against a thief caught stealing. (In camp terms lynch law was almost lawful.) Sometimes—as in Camp No. 1 of Vyatlag during the war—the work trusties would expel the most malevolent of the stool pigeons from their own construction project "for the sake of efficiency." It was hard for the security chief to help in that kind of case. Other stool pigeons caught on and clammed up.

High hopes were placed in the front-line soldiers when they arrived—they would go after the stoolies! Alas, the military reinforcements were a disappointment to the camp warriors; outside their army these warriors, artillerymen, and scouts went totally sour and were good for nothing.

But what was required was more tolling of the bell, more passage of time, before the extermination of stoolies would get under way in the Archipelago.

■

I do not have enough material for this chapter. For some reason old camp hands are not very eager to tell me about how they were recruited. I will therefore speak about myself.

Only with my later camp experience, as I became a veteran, did I look back and comprehend how pettily, how insignificantly, I had begun my term. Having become used, in my officer's pelt, to an undeservedly high position among those around me, in camp, too, I kept climbing into positions of some kind and immediately falling out of them. And I clung tightly to that pelt—to my field shirt, britches, greatcoat. How hard I tried not to exchange it for the dark camp camouflage! In new conditions I made the mistake of the new recruit. I drew attention to myself in a new locality.

And the sniper's eye of the very first "godfather," at Novy Iyerusalim, noticed me right off. And at Kaluga Gates also, just as soon as I got out of the painters' brigade and became an assistant to the norm setter, I dragged out that uniform once again—oh, how one wants to be masculine and handsome! Furthermore, I lived in that chamber of monstrosities where even the generals didn't doll up like that.

I had forgotten to wonder about how and why I had written my autobiography in Novy Iyerusalim. One evening I was reading a physics text, half-lying on my cot. Zinovyev was frying something and telling a story. Orachevsky and Prokhorov were lying there with their boots on the foot rail of the cots when in came the senior jailer, named Senin. (Evidently this was not his real name but a camp pseudonym.) He seemed not to notice the hot plate or the boots sticking out there—and he sat down on someone's cot and joined in the general conversation.

I didn't like either his face or his manner, that Senin. He used to flash his soft eyes too much, but he was oh, so cultured! So well-mannered! So different from all the rest of our jailers—boors, incompetents, illiterates. Senin was no more and no less than a *university student!* A fourth-year student, but I simply don't remember in which faculty. He was evidently quite ashamed of his MVD uniform, fearing his fellow students might run into him on the street when he was wearing his blue shoulder boards, and therefore when he came for his duty periods, he put on his uniform at the gatehouse, and when he left, he took it off. (Now here is a contemporary hero for our novelists! Could one imagine a progressive student in Tsarist times moonlighting as a jailer in a prison!) However, cultured or not, it cost him no trouble at all to send an old man scurrying on errands or to hand out three days in punishment block to a slogger.

But he very much liked to conduct an intellectual conversation in our room—so as to show that he understood our delicate souls, and so that we ourselves would value the delicacy of his soul. So it was this time—he was telling us something fresh about the life of the city, something about a new film, and suddenly, imperceptibly to the others, he clearly motioned to me—to go out into the corridor.

I went out, not understanding. After a certain number of polite sentences so it wouldn't be obvious, Senin also got up and came after me. And he instructed me to go immediately to the office of the security officer. The stairway leading there led nowhere else—so one would not run into anyone on it. There sat the old hoot owl.

I had not yet met him. I went with a sinking heart. What was I afraid of? I was afraid of what every camp inmate fears: that he might start to paste a second term on me. Not a year had passed since my interrogation. And everything within me still ached from the mere sight of an interrogator behind a desk. And what if my previous *case* were to be delved into again: a few pages more from my diary, maybe some letters?

Knock, knock, knock.

"Come in."

I opened the door. A small, cozily furnished room, as if it were not in Gulag at all. There was even enough room for a small divan (maybe he was bringing our women in here too) and for a "Philips" radio on a book stand. Its bright-colored little tuning "eye" gleamed and some soft, very pleasant melody was pouring gently out of it. I had become quite unused to such purity of sound and such music. I instantly softened: somewhere life was going on! My Lord, we had grown so used to believing that our own life was life itself, but it was going on somewhere out there, somewhere *out there*.

"Sit down."

On the desk was a lamp beneath a calming shade. The security chief sat in an armchair behind the desk—like Senin, he had that same intelligent, dark-haired, impenetrable appearance. My chair was also semiupholstered. How pleasant it was if only he wouldn't begin to accuse me of anything, if only he wouldn't begin dragging all that old nonsense out again.

But no, his voice was not hostile at all. He asked me in general about my life, how I was feeling, how I was adjusting to the camp, whether it was comfortable for me in the trusties' room. No, that was not how they began an interrogation. (And where had I heard that beautiful melody?)

And then came a quite natural question—it could even have been out of just plain curiosity:

"Well, and after everything that has happened to you, after everything you have suffered, are you still a Soviet person? Or not?"

Well? What could I answer? You, my descendants, will never be able to understand this: what should I answer now? I hear, yes, I can hear you normal, free people, shouting at me from 1990: "Go ahead and send him to ———! [Or perhaps my descendants will no longer express themselves in that kind of language? I think—in Russia—they will!] So they imprisoned you, they cut your throat, and they still want you to be a Soviet person!"

In actual fact, after all my prisons, after all my encounters with others, when I was engulfed with information from the whole world—how on earth could I still be a Soviet person? Where and when has anything Soviet ever been able to withstand completeness of information?

And if I had already been *re-educated* as much by prison as I had been *educated* by it, I ought to have cut him off then and there, of course: "No! Go to ———! I'm tired of beating my brains out over you! Let me rest after work!"

But then we had all grown up to be obedient fellows! After all, when it came to "Who's against? Who abstains?" there was absolutely no way you could raise your hand, no way. So how could even a convicted man twist his tongue around the words "I am not a Soviet person"?

"In the OSO decree it stated that I was anti-Soviet," I said evasively.

"The OSO!" And he waved it away without the slightest respect. "But you yourself, what do you feel? Are you still a Soviet person? Or have you changed, and become embittered?"

That melody continued to play softly and so purely, and our syrupy, sticky, and inconsequential conversation didn't stick to it. Lord, how pure and how beautiful human life can be, but because of the egotism of those who have power we are never able to attain it. Was it Moniuszko? No, it wasn't Moniuszko. Or

Dvořák? No, it wasn't Dvořák? Go away and let me be, dog, and let me listen.

"Why should I be embittered?" I acted astonished. (Why indeed? For ten letters or so—eight years, and that was not even a full year for each letter. "To be embittered" was quite out of the question—it would already smell of a new term.)

"And so that means you are Soviet?" the security chief pressed at me, sternly but encouragingly.

The important thing was not to answer sharply. Not to disclose what I had become by then. Say now you are anti-Soviet, and a new camp case would be set in motion, and they would solder a new term onto you, very easily.

"In your own heart, inside—how do you think of yourself?"

It was so fearsome—winter and blizzards, going to the Arctic. And here I had everything well arranged. I had a dry place to sleep, and it was warm, and there were even bedclothes. In Moscow my wife came to visit me and brought parcels. . . . Where would I be sent? And why should I go if I could stay behind? . . . What was there shameful in saying, "Soviet"? The system was socialist.

"I, uh, for myself . . . yes, well . . . Soviet . . ."

"Aha, so you are Soviet! Now that's something else again." The security chief was gladdened. "So now you and I can talk as two Soviet people. That means you and I share the same ideology —we have common goals. [Only our lodgings were different.] And you and I must act in unity. You *help* us and we will help you."

I felt I had already slipped downward. . . . And there was still that music. . . . And he kept tossing and tossing his neat little nooses: I had to help him keep in touch with what was going on. I might choose to overhear certain conversations. I was to report on them. . . .

Well, that was something I would never do. Coldbloodedly inside myself I knew that quite well! Whether I was Soviet or not was immaterial: Don't sit around waiting for me to report political conversations to you! However—caution, caution! Somehow I had to cover my tracks delicately.

"That's something I . . . wouldn't be able to do," I replied to him with something sounding like regret.

"Why not?" My ideological colleague grew more severe.

"Well, because . . . it's not in my character. . . . [How can I put this to you politely, you bastard?] Because . . . I don't listen. . . . I don't remember. . . ."

He noted there was something between me and the music—and clicked off the radio. Silence. The warm, bright-colored eye of the good world was extinguished. In the office—just the hoot owl and myself. It was in deadly earnest now.

If only they had known the rules of chess: If moves are repeated three times in a row, a draw is declared. But no! They were lazy in everything else but not in this; a hundred times he monotonously checked me from one and the same square of the chessboard, and a hundred times I hid behind the same pawn and then sallied out from behind it again. He had no taste at all . . . but he had all the time in the world. And I had put myself in eternal check by declaring myself a Soviet person. Of course, there was some slight variation each of the hundred times: a different word, a different intonation.

An hour passed and another. In our cell they were already asleep, but there was no need for him to hurry. This was his work. How could I get shut of him? What sticky people they are! He had already hinted at a prisoner transport and at general work, and he had already expressed his suspicion that I was an inveterate enemy, and had gone back again to the hope that I was an inveterate friend.

Yield I couldn't. Neither did I want to go on a prisoner transport in winter. And with heavy heart I wondered how it all would end.

All of a sudden he switched the conversation to the thieves. He had heard from the jailer Senin that I had spoken out sharply* against the thieves, that I had had a run-in with them. I came to life—this was a new move. Yes, I did hate them. (But I know that *you* love them.)

And in order to go right at my tenderest point, he drew the following picture. I have a wife in Moscow. Without a husband she has to walk the streets by herself, sometimes even at night. People on the street often have their clothes taken off them. By those very same thieves who escape from camp. (No, by those you amnesty!) So would I really refuse to report to the security chief if I should happen to learn of preparations for escape by the thieves?

Well, that was different, the thieves were enemies, pitiless enemies, and against them maybe any methods were good. . . . Anyway, good or not, the main thing was that it was a good out for me. At least it seemed so.

"I could. That I could do."

You said it! You said it! And the devil only needs one little word! And instantly a clean sheet of paper fluttered onto the table in front of me:

PLEDGE

I, the undersigned, pledge to report to the camp security officer any escapes planned by prisoners. . . .

"But we were talking only about the thieves!"

"And who escapes except the thieves? And how am I going to write the word 'thieves' in an official document? That's slang. It makes sense just as it is."

"But the entire meaning is changed!"

"No, now I see that you are *not one of us*, and that it is necessary to talk with you *in an entirely different way—and not here.*"

Oh, what fearsome words! "Not here." When there is a blizzard outside the window, when you are a trusty and live in a friendly chamber of monstrosities. Where is that "not here"? In Lefortovo? And what does it mean, "in an entirely different way"? Anyway, in the last analysis, there hadn't been a single escape during my time in this camp, it was about as likely as a meteorite falling. And if there were going to be escapes, what fool would talk about them ahead of time? And that meant I would never know. And that meant there would be nothing for me to report. In the last analysis, this wasn't a bad way out of it. . . . But . . .

"Couldn't we really get along without that paper?"

"That's the system."

I sighed. I reassured myself with unspoken qualifications and put my signature down, selling my soul. Selling my soul to save my body. All done? Can I go?

Oh, not at all. There was also one "on nondisclosure." But farther up the same piece of paper.

"You must choose a pseudonym for yourself."

A pseudonym? Aha, you mean a *conspiratorial nickname!* Yes, yes, yes, of course. All informers have to have a conspiratorial nickname! Good Lord, how swiftly I had fallen. He had outplayed me after all. The chessmen had moved, and it was checkmate.

And all my imagination fled and my mind went blank. I can always find names for dozens of heroes. Now I couldn't think up even one little nickname. Mercifully he suggested to me: "Well, what about Vetrov?"

And finally I wrote, at the end of the "pledge": "*Vetrov.*" Those six letters are branded in shameful grooves on my memory.

After all, I had wanted to die among human beings! I had been prepared to die among human beings! How did it turn out that I had remained to live among curs?

And the commissioner tucked my pledge away in the safe— this was his output for the night shift. And he courteously explained to me that I must not come to his office, that this would cause suspicion. The jailer Senin was a trustworthy person and all my reports (*denunciations!*) could be transmitted secretly through Senin.

That's how birds are snared. Beginning with the tiny little claw.

That particular year I probably wouldn't have been able to stop myself at that edge. After all, if you can't hold on to the mane, you'll not be able to hold on by the tail either. Once you start sliding down, you'll slide down further.

But something helped me to hold back. Whenever I met Senin he used to urge me on: "Well, well?" I used to spread my hands: I had heard nothing. I was regarded with hostility by the thieves and was unable to get close to them. And then, as if out of spite, although there had been no escapes at all, all of a sudden a lousy thief escaped from our camp. All right then, report on something else! On the brigade! On the room! Senin insisted. I kept insisting that I hadn't promised to report on anything else. (By now it was already getting on toward spring.) Nonetheless I had gained a little by giving too narrow a pledge.

And at this point I was jerked out of the camp and into a sharashka on special orders from the Ministry. And that's how I got by. Never again did I have to sign as "Vetrov." But even today I shudder when I encounter that name.

Oh, how difficult it is, how difficult it is, to become a human being! Even if you have survived the front and bombing and been blown up by land mines, that's still only the very beginning of heroism. That is still not the whole thing. . . .

Many years passed. I had been in sharashkas and Special Camps. I bore myself independently, ever more impudently, and never again did the Security Section spoil me with its good offices, and I grew used to living with the gay conviction that on my case file they had stamped: "Do not recruit!"

I was sent into exile. I lived there for nearly three years. The dispersal of the exiles had already begun too, and several of the exiled nationalities had already been liberated. By this time those of us who remained used to joke when we went to report in at the commandant's headquarters. The Twentieth Congress* had also passed. And everything seemed gone once and for all. I made jolly plans for my return to European Russia as soon as I was released. And suddenly when I was leaving the school courtyard one day, a well-dressed Kazakh (in civilian clothes) greeted me by name and patronymic, and hurried over to shake my hand.

"Let's go and talk." He nodded amiably in the direction of the commandant's headquarters.

"I have to have my lunch." I waved him away.

"And will you be free later this evening?"

"I won't be free this evening either." (In my free evenings I was writing a novel.)

"Well, when will you be free tomorrow?"

He had caught me. And I had to fix an appointment for the next day. I thought he would have something to say about my case being reconsidered. (Just before this I had made a mistake. I had written a petition to the higher-ups, just like the orthodox Communists, which meant I had got myself into the situation of a petitioner. That was something State Security couldn't let by!) But the province Security officer had triumphantly taken over the office of the district MVD chief, had locked the door, and was clearly preparing for a conversation that was to last many hours, and that was rendered all the more complicated by the fact that he didn't speak Russian very well. Despite this, by the end of the first hour I realized that he was interested not in reconsideration of my case but in recruiting me as an informer. (Evidently, with the release of a section of their exiles, the ranks of the informers had grown sparse.)

I found all this both ridiculous and vexing: vexing because I regarded each half-hour as very precious, and ridiculous because in March, 1956, this kind of conversation grated on me with its bad timing like the clumsy scraping of a knife across a plate. Very gently I tried to explain this untimeliness to him, but he would have none of it. Like a serious bulldog, he tried not to let up on his grip. Every sort of relaxation in the Soviet Union always reaches the provinces after a delay of three, five, or ten years. And it is only tightening up which is instantaneous. He hadn't the slightest idea of what 1956 was to be like! Then I reminded him that the MGB had been abolished, but he eagerly and happily demonstrated to me that the KGB was exactly the same thing, with the same personnel, and the same tasks.

But by that year I had already developed some sort of cavalier carelessness toward their glorious institution. I felt that it would be quite in the spirit of the epoch to send him exactly where he and his colleagues deserved. I feared no direct consequences for myself—they couldn't happen during that glorious year. And it would have been great fun simply to leave, slamming the door behind me.

But I stopped to think first. What about my manuscripts? For whole days at a time they lay there in my tiny hut, protected only by a weak little lock, yes, and concealed on the inside with an additional small ruse. At night I would get them out and write away. If I were to enrage the KGB, they would look for a chance of revenge, something compromising, and they might just find my manuscripts?

No, I simply had to bring this to an end peaceably.

Oh, my country! Oh, my accursed country, where in its very freest months the human being most inwardly free could not permit himself to antagonize the gendarmes! . . . He could not fling in their faces everything he thought.

"I am gravely ill, that's the problem. My illness doesn't allow me to look around and snoop. I have enough troubles! Let's leave it at that."

Of course, this was a pitiful way of getting out of it. Because I was recognizing their actual right to recruit. And what I should have done was to ridicule and deny that right. It was a refusal . . . on my knees.

And he still didn't accept it, the smart aleck! For half an hour more he kept trying to prove to me that even a gravely ill person also ought to collaborate! But when he saw that I was totally immovable, he took another tack:

"Do you have an extra certificate?"

"What kind?"

"Certifying that you are so ill."

"Yes, I have a certificate."

"Then bring it to me."

Yes, he had to have his "output," too, for his own workday! Justification that I had been correctly selected as a candidate, but that they had not known that this person was gravely ill. The certificate was required not merely for him to read, but to be stapled into the case file, and thereby to end the whole attempt.

I gave him the document, and with that we were quits.

Those were the freest months in our country in a whole half-century!

And what about the person who had no medical excuse?

■

The skill of the security officer consisted in immediately picking the right master key. In one of the Siberian camps, a native of one of the Baltic countries, U., who knew Russian well (which was why the choice fell on him), was summoned "to the chief." And there in the chief's office sat an unfamiliar captain with an aquiline nose and the hypnotic gaze of a cobra. "Shut the door tight!" he warned very gravely, as if enemies were about to burst in, without lowering his burning eyes, which stared at U. from beneath shaggy brows—and inside U. everything wilted, something burned and suffocated him. Before summoning U., of course, the captain had gathered all the information available about him, and without even having seen him had determined that keys 1, 2, 3, and 4 would all be of no avail, that here only the last and strongest key could be used, but he kept staring for several minutes into U.'s unclouded, defenseless eyes, checking him out with his own eyes and at the same time depriving him of his will power, and already invisibly raising above him that which would immediately descend upon him.

The security chief took time for only the briefest introduction, speaking not in the tone of an abstract political catechism, but tensely, as if something were about to explode today or tomorrow right there in their own camp. "Do you know the world is divided into two camps, and one will be defeated, and we know very well which it will be? Do you know which? So that's how it is: if you want to survive, you must break away from the doomed capitalist shore and swim across to the new shore. Are you familiar with Latsis' *To the New Shore?*"* And he added a few more such phrases, and did not for a moment lower his hot threatening gaze, and having finally confirmed in his own mind the number of the key, he then asked with alarmed seriousness: "And *what about your family?*" And one by one, without ceremony, he reeled off all their names! And he knew the ages of the children too! That meant he had already familiarized himself with the family—that was very serious! "You understand, of course," he pronounced hypnotically, "that you and your family are a single whole. If you make a mistake and perish, your family will immediately perish too. We do not permit *the families of traitors* [his voice grew more meaningful] to go on living in the healthy Soviet environment. So make your choice between the two worlds! Between life and death! I am offering you an opportunity to pledge to assist the Security Section! In case you refuse, your entire family will be immediately imprisoned in camp! In our hands we have full power [how right he was!] and we are not accustomed to backtrack on our decisions. [Once again he was right!] Since we have chosen you, you *will* work with us!"

All this was loosed suddenly on U.'s head. He was not prepared for it. He would never have thought of it. He had considered that only scoundrels became informers. But that they might approach him? A blow—direct, without waste motion, without the cushion of time—and the captain was waiting for his answer, and was about to explode right then, and then everything would explode! And U. took thought: What is there that is really impossible for them? When have they ever spared anyone's family? They didn't hesitate to liquidate the "kulak" families right down to tiny children, and they even wrote about it proudly in the newspapers. U. had also seen the work of the Organs in 1940 and 1941 in the Baltic States, and had gone to the prison yards to look at the pile of executed prisoners during the Soviet retreat. And in 1944 he had heard the Baltic broadcasts from Leningrad. Like the captain's gaze at this moment, they had been full of threats and had breathed revenge. They promised reprisals against *all*, against every last person who had aided the enemy.[3]

And so what was there to compel them to show mercy now? To ask for it was useless. It was necessary to choose. (But here is what U., himself a victim of the myth of the Organs, did not yet realize: That machine possessed no such magnificent coordination and interlinked responsiveness as would ensure that when he refused today to become an informer in a Siberian camp his family would be hauled off to Siberia in a week's time. And there was one more thing he didn't realize either. No matter how poor his opinion of the Organs, they were even worse than he thought: the hour would soon strike when all these families, all these hundreds of thousands of families, would troop off into common exile, where they would perish, without any reference to how the fathers were behaving in camp.)

Fear for himself would not have shaken him. But U. pictured his wife and daughter in camp conditions—in these same barracks where lechery wasn't even curtained off, where there was no defense whatever for any woman under sixty. And . . . he shuddered. The correct key had been picked. None other would have opened the door, but this one did.

But he still dragged things out a bit: "I have to think it over." "All right, think it over for three days, but don't talk it over with even a single person. *You will be shot for disclosure!*" (And U. goes to get advice from a fellow national—the very same, in fact, against whom he is being told to write his first denunciation, and, in fact, they edit it together. For this friend admits it is impossible to risk his family.)

On his second visit to the captain, U. signs the devil's receipt, and receives his assignment and his contact: he is not to go to

3. But every teacher, every factory worker, every streetcar conductor, everyone who had had to earn his bread with his work, had one and all aided the enemy. The only persons who didn't aid the enemy were the speculator at the market and the partisan in the forest! The extreme tone of these thoughtless Leningrad broadcasts pushed several hundred thousands of persons into flight into Scandinavia in 1944.

the office any more; he is to conduct all his business through the unconvoyed trusty Frol Ryabinin.

This is an important constituent of the work of the camp security chief: These "residents"* are scattered throughout the camp. Frol Ryabinin is the most vociferous of all "among the people," a prankster. Frol Ryabinin is a popular personality. Frol Ryabinin has some sort of under-the-counter work or other, and a separate cabin of his own, and always has money. With the security chief's help he has got into the depths and currents of camp life, and he hovers in them, comfortably at home. Such "residents" as he are the cables on which the whole network hangs.

Frol Ryabinin instructs U. that he must transmit his reports in a dark nook. ("In *our* work the main thing is conspiracy.") He summons him to his private quarters: "The captain is dissatisfied with your report. You have to write so that there's *material* against a person. I'm going to teach you how."

And this stinking snoot teaches the wan, depressed intellectual U. how to write filth against people! But U.'s downcast look leads Ryabinin to his own conclusion: it is necessary to liven this ninny up, to heat him up a little! And he says to him in a friendly way: "Listen, your life is a hard one. You sometimes want to buy something to add to your bread ration. The captain wants to help you. Here, take this!" And he takes a fifty-ruble bill from his billfold. (And this is the captain's! And that is how free of auditors *they* are, and maybe they are the only ones in the whole country!) And he shoves it at U.

And suddenly, at the sight of this pale-green toad which has been pushed into his hands, all the spells cast by the cobra captain, all the hypnosis, all the constraint, even all the fear for his family—all that has taken place, its entire meaning, is objectified in this loathsome bill with its greenish phlegm, these commonplace Judas silver pieces. And without even stopping to think what will happen to his family, with the natural gesture of warding off filth, U. pushes away the fifty-ruble bill, and the uncomprehending Ryabinin shoves it at him again, and U. throws it on the floor and gets up, already relieved, already *free* both of the moral teachings of Ryabinin and of his signature given to the captain, free of those paper conditions in the face of the great duty of a human being! He leaves without asking permission! He walks through the camp compound on legs light as air: "I'm free! I'm free!"

Well, not entirely so. A stupid security chief would have kept on hauling him in. But the cobra captain understood that the stupid Ryabinin had spoiled the threading, had used the wrong key. And the pincers no longer sought out U. in that camp, and Ryabinin would pass him without greeting. U. calmed down and was glad. And at this point they began to send the 58's off to the Special Camps, and he was sent to Steplag. And he thought that this prisoner transport would break the chain all the more.

But not at all! A notation evidently remained in his file. At his new place U. was summoned to a colonel: "They tell me you agreed to work with us but that you *do not deserve our trust.* Perhaps they didn't explain it to you clearly."

However, this colonel inspired no fear in U. And, in addition, U.'s family, like the families of many of the inhabitants of the Baltic States, had been resettled in Siberia by this time. There was no doubt about it: he had to get them off his back. But what pretext could he use?

The colonel turned him over to a lieutenant for the latter to work him over. And this lieutenant jumped up and down and threatened and promised while U. kept trying to find a way of forcefully and decisively turning them down.

Though he was an enlightened and irreligious person, U. discovered that the only defense against them was to hide behind Christ. This was not very honest, but it was a sure thing. He lied: "I must tell you frankly that I had a Christian upbringing, and therefore it is quite impossible for me to work with you!"

And that ended it! And all the lieutenant's chatter, which had by then lasted many hours, simply stopped! The lieutenant understood he had drawn a bad number. "We need you like a dog needs five legs," he exclaimed petulantly. "Give me a written refusal." (Once again "written"!) "And write just that, explaining about your damned god!"

Apparently they have to close the case of every informer with a separate piece of paper, just as they open it with one. The reference to Christ satisfied the lieutenant completely: none of the security officers would accuse him subsequently of failing to use every effort he could.

And does the impartial reader not find that they flee from Christ like devils from the sign of the cross, from the bells calling to matins?

And that is why our Soviet regime can never come to terms with Christianity! And the French Communists' promises to the contrary mean nothing.

Chapter 13

■

Hand Over Your Second Skin Too!

Can you behead a man whose head has already been cut off? You can. Can you skin the hide off a man when he has already been skinned? You can!

This was all invented in our camps. This was all devised in the Archipelago! So let it not be said that the *brigade* was our only Soviet contribution to world penal science. Is not *the second camp term* a contribution too? The waves which surge into the Archipelago from outside do not die down there and do not subside freely, but are pumped through the pipes of the second interrogation.

Oh, blessed are those pitiless tyrannies, those despotisms, those savage countries, where a person once arrested cannot be arrested a second time! Where once in prison he cannot be reimprisoned. Where a person who has been tried cannot be tried again! Where a sentenced person cannot be sentenced again!

But in our country everything is permissible. When a man is flat on his back, irrevocably doomed and in the depths of despair, how convenient it is to poleax him again! The ethics of our prison chiefs are: "Beat the man who's down." And the ethics of our Security officers are: "Use corpses as steppingstones!"

We may take it that camp interrogations and camp court were born on Solovki, although what they did there was simply to push them into the bell-tower basement and finish them off. During the period of the Five-Year Plans and of the metastases, they began to employ the second camp term instead of the bullet.

For how otherwise, without second (or third or fourth) terms, could they secrete in the bosom of the Archipelago, and destroy, all those marked down for destruction?

The generation of new prison terms, like the growing of a snake's rings, is a form of Archipelago life. As long as our camps thrived and our exile lasted, this black threat hovered over the heads of the convicted: to be given a new term before they had finished the first one. Second camp terms were handed out every year, but most intensively in 1937 and 1938 and during the war years. (In 1948–1949 the burden of second terms was transferred outside: they *overlooked*, they missed, prisoners who should have been resentenced in camp—and then had to haul them back into camp from outside. These were even called *repeaters*, whereas those resentenced inside didn't get a special name.)

And it was a mercy—an automated mercy—when, in 1938, second camp terms were given out without any second arrest, without a camp interrogation, without a camp court, when the prisoners were simply called up in brigades to the Records and Classification Section and told to sign for their second terms. (For refusing to sign—you were simply put in punishment block, as for smoking where it wasn't allowed.) And they also had it all explained to them in a very human way: "We aren't telling you that you are guilty of anything, but just sign that you have been informed." In the Kolyma that's how they gave out tenners, but in Vorkuta it was even less severe: eight years plus five years by the OSO. And it was useless to try to get out of it as if, in the dark infinity of the Archipelago, eight was in any way distinct from eighteen, or a tenner at the start from a tenner at the end of a sentence. The only important thing was that they did not claw and tear your body today.

Now we can understand: The epidemic of camp sentences in 1938 was the result of a directive from above. It was there at the top that they suddenly came to their senses and realized that they had been handing out too little, that they had to pile it on (and shoot some too)—and thus frighten the rest.

But the epidemic of camp cases during the war was stimulated by a happy spark from *below* too, by the features of popular initiative. In all likelihood there was an order from above that during the war the most colorful and notable individuals in each

35. Captain Lebedev, a "godfather"

camp, who might become centers of rebellion, had to be suppressed and isolated. The bloody local boys immediately sensed the riches in this vein—their own *deliverance from the front*. This was evidently guessed in more than one camp and rapidly taken up as useful, ingenious, and a salvation. The camp Chekists also helped fill up the machine-gun embrasures—but with other people's bodies.

Let the historian picture to himself the pulse of those years: The front was moving east, the Germans were around Leningrad, outside Moscow, in Voronezh, on the Volga, and in the foothills of the Caucasus. In the rear there were ever fewer men. Every healthy male figure aroused reproachful glances. Everything for the front! There was no price too big for the government to pay to stop Hitler. And only the camp officers (and their confreres in State Security) were well fed, white, soft-skinned, idle—all in their places in the rear. (In Illustration No. 35—this camp "godfather," for example. How badly he needed to stay alive.) And the farther into Siberia and the North they were, the quieter things were. But we must soberly understand: theirs was a shaky prosperity. Due to end at the first outcry: Bring out those rosy-cheeked, smart camp fellows! No battle experience? So they had ideology. And they would be lucky to end up in the police, or in the behind-the-lines "obstacle" detachments,* but it could happen otherwise; otherwise it was into officer battalions and be thrown into the Battle of Stalingrad! In the summer of 1942 they picked up whole officer-training schools and hurled them into the front, uncertified, their courses unfinished. All the young and healthy convoy guards had already been scraped up for the front. And the camps hadn't fallen apart. It was all right. And they wouldn't fall apart if the security officers were called up either! (There were already rumors.)

Draft deferment—that was life. Draft deferment—that was happiness. How could you keep your draft deferment? Easy—you simply had to prove your *importance!* You had to prove that if it were not for Chekist vigilance the camps would blow apart, that they were a caldron of seething tar! And then our whole glorious front would collapse! It was right here in the camps in the tundra and the taiga that the white-chested security chiefs were holding back the Fifth Column, holding back Hitler! This was their contribution to victory! Not sparing themselves, they conducted interrogation after interrogation, exposing plot after plot.

Until now only the unhappy, worn-out camp inmates, tearing the bread from each other's mouths, had been fighting for their lives! But now the omnipotent Chekist security officers shamelessly entered the fray. "You croak today, me tomorrow." Better you should perish and put off my death, you dirty animal.

And so they cooked up a "rebel group" in Ust-Vym: eighteen persons! They wanted, of course, to disarm the Militarized Guard, get its weapons away from it (half a dozen old rifles)! What then? It is hard to picture the scale of the plan: They wanted to raise the entire North! To march on Vorkuta! On Moscow! To join up with Mannerheim! And telegrams and reports flew to the top. A big plot had been neutralized. There was unrest in the camps! The security staff had to be strengthened.

And what was this? Plots were discovered in every camp! More plots! Still more! Ever larger in scale! And ever broader! Oh, those perfidious last-leggers! They were just feigning that they could be blown over by the wind—their paper-thin, pellagra-stricken hands were secretly reaching for the machine guns! Oh, thank you, Security Section! Oh, savior of the Motherland—the Third Section!

And a whole gang sat there in that Third Section in the Dzhida camps of Buryat-Mongolia: Chief of the Security Operations Section Sokolov, Interrogator Mironenko; Security Officers Kalashnikov, Sosikov, Osintsev: We've fallen behind! Everyone else has plots, and we have fallen behind! We do have a major plot, of course, but what kind? Well, of course, "the Militarized Guard is to be disarmed"; yes, of course, "they are going abroad"—after all, the border was close and Hitler was far away. With whom should they begin?

And just as a well-fed pack of hounds tears a sick, skinny, and mangy rabbit to bits, so did this sky-blue pack hurl itself on the unfortunate Babich, former Arctic explorer, former hero, now a last-legger covered with ulcers. It was he who at the outset of the war had nearly turned over the icebreaker *Sadko* to the Germans—so all the threads of the plot were obviously in his hands. It was his scurvy-racked dying body that was to save their well-nourished ones.

"Even if you are a bad Soviet citizen, we will still make you do as we wish, you will kiss our boots!" "You don't remember? We will remind you!" "You can't write? *We'll help you!*" "You want time to think? Into the punishment cell on ten and a half ounces!"

And here is what another security man told him: "I'm very sorry. Of course, you will come to understand later on that it would have been sensible to do as we demand. But it will be too

late, when we can break you *like a pencil* between our fingers."
(Where do they get this imagery? Do they think it up themselves
or is there a selection of such phrases in Chekist textbooks composed by some unknown poet?)

And here is the interrogation by Mironenko. Hardly had they
brought Babich in than he was hit by the smell of tasty food.
And Mironenko made him sit quite close to the steaming meat
borscht and cutlets. And as though unaware of that borscht and
those cutlets or even that Babich could see them, he gently cited
dozens of arguments to relieve his conscience and justify not only
the possibility but also the necessity of giving false testimony.
He reminded Babich amiably:

"When you were arrested the first time, in freedom, and tried
to prove your innocence, you did not after all succeed, did you?
No, you didn't succeed! Because your fate had already been
decided before your arrest. That's how it is now. That's how it
is now. Well, well, eat the lunch. Go ahead: eat it before it gets
cold. . . . If you are not stupid, we will get along very well. You
will always be well fed and provided for. . . . Otherwise . . ."

And Babich shuddered! Hunger for life had turned out to be
stronger than the thirst for truth. And he began to write down
everything dictated to him. And he slandered twenty-four people,
of whom he knew only four! And for the entire period of the
interrogation he was fed, but never given enough, so that at the
first sign of resistance they could lean on his hunger again.

Reading the record of his life written before his death sends
shivers down your spine: from what heights and into what depths
can a brave man fall! Can all of us. . . .

And so it was that twenty-four people who knew nothing about
anything were taken to be shot or to get new terms. And before
the trial Babich was sent off to a state farm as a sewage-disposal
worker, and then gave testimony at the trial, and then was given
a new *tenner*, with his previous term erased, but he died in camp
before completing his second term.

What about the gang from the Dzhida Third Section? Well,
will someone investigate that gang!? Anyone! Our contemporaries! Our descendants! . . .

And—you? You thought that in camp at least you could unburden your soul? That here you could at least complain aloud:
"My sentence is too long! They fed me badly! I have too much

work!" Or you thought that here you could at least *repeat* what you got your term for? But if you say any of this aloud—you are done for! You are doomed to get a new "tenner." (True, once a new camp tenner begins, at least the first is erased, so that as it works out you serve not twenty, but some thirteen or fifteen or the like. . . . Which will be more than you can survive.)

But you are sure you have been silent as a fish? And then you are grabbed anyway? Quite right! They couldn't help grabbing you no matter how you behaved. After all, they don't grab *for something* but *because*. It's the same principle according to which they clip the wool off *freedom* too. When the Third Section gang goes hunting, it picks a list of the most noticeable people in the camp. And that is the list they then dictate to Babich. . . .

In camp, after all, it is even more difficult to hide, everything is out in the open. And there is only one salvation for a person: to be a zero! A total zero. A zero from the very beginning.

To stick you with a charge presents no problem. When the "plots" came to an end after 1943 (the Germans began to retreat), a multitude of cases of "propaganda" appeared. (Those "godfathers" still didn't want to go to the front!) In the Burepolom Camp, for example, the following selection was available:

- Hostile activity against the policy of the Soviet Communist Party and the Soviet government (and what it was you can guess for yourself!)
- Expression of defeatist fabrications
- Expression of slanderous opinions about the material situation of the workers of the Soviet Union (Telling the truth was slander.)
- Expression of a desire (!) for the restoration of the capitalist system
- Expression of a grudge against the Soviet government (This was particularly impudent! Who are you, you bastard, to nurse grudges! So you got a "tenner" and you should have kept your mouth shut!)

A seventy-year-old former Tsarist diplomat was charged with making the following propaganda:

- That the working class in the U.S.S.R. lives badly
- That Gorky was a bad writer (!!)

To say that they had gone too far in bringing these charges against him is out of the question. They always handed out sentences for Gorky; that's how he had set himself up. Skvortsov, for example, in Lokchimlag (near Ust-Vym), harvested fifteen years, and among the charges against him was the following:

• He had unfavorably contrasted the proletarian poet Mayakovsky with *a certain* bourgeois poet.

That's what it said in the formal charges against him, and it was enough to get him convicted. And from the minutes of the interrogation we can establish who that *certain* bourgeois poet was. It was Pushkin! To get a sentence for Pushkin—that, in truth, was a rarity!

After that, therefore, Martinson, who really did say in the tin shop that "the U.S.S.R. was one big *camp*," ought to have sung praise to God that he got off with a "tenner."

As ought those refusing to work who got a "tenner" instead of execution.[1]

But it was not the number of years, not the empty and fantastic length of years, that made these second terms so awful—but *how* you got them. How you had to crawl through that iron pipe in the ice and snow to get them.

It would seem that arrest would be a nothing for a camp inmate. For a person who had once been arrested from his warm domestic bed—what did it matter to be arrested again from an uncomfortable barracks with bare bunks? But it certainly did! In the barracks the stove was warm and a full bread ration was

1. It was such a pleasure to hand out second terms, and it lent such meaning to the lives of the Security Operations Sections, that when the war was at an end, and it was no longer possible to believe either in plots or even in defeatist moods, they began to paste on terms under nonpolitical articles. In 1947, in the agricultural camp Dolinka, there were show trials in the compound every Sunday. They tried potato diggers for baking some potatoes in bonfires; they tried people for eating raw carrots and turnips in the fields. (What would some nobleman's serfs have said if tried for something like that?!) And for all this they handed out terms of five and eight years under the recently issued great "Decree of Four-sixths." One former "kulak" was already coming to the end of his "tenner." He was in charge of the camp bull calf, and he couldn't any longer stand to see it starve. He fed this camp bull calf—not himself!—with beets—and got eight years for it. Of course, a "socially friendly" zek would not have undertaken to feed the bull calf! And that is how in our country, over decades, natural selection operated, deciding who would live and who would die.

given. But here came the jailer and jerked you by the foot at night. "Gather up your things!" Oh, how you didn't want to go! People, people, I love you. . . .

The camp interrogation prison. What kind of a prison will it be and how can it possibly advance your confession if it isn't worse than your own camp? All these prisons are invariably cold. If they aren't cold enough, then they keep you in the cells in just your underwear. The famous Vorkuta *Number Thirty* (a term borrowed by the zeks from the Chekists, who called it that because of its telephone number, 30), a board barracks beyond the Arctic Circle, was heated with coal dust when it was 40 degrees below zero outside, one washtubful a day, and not because they lacked coal in Vorkuta, of course. And they tormented them with more than that—they didn't issue them matches. And for kindling there was one little chip the size of a pencil. (Incidentally, escapees who had been caught were kept in this Number Thirty *stark naked*. After two weeks anyone who had survived was given summer clothes but no padded jacket. And there were no mattresses and no blankets. Reader! Try it, just try to sleep like that for one night! In the barracks it was approximately 40 above.)

And that was how the prisoners were kept throughout the several months of interrogation! Even before that, of course, they had been worn down by many years of hunger and by slave labor. And now, it was much easier to finish them off. What did they feed them? As the Third Section instructed: in some places eleven and a quarter ounces a day, and in some places ten and a half ounces, and in Number Thirty seven ounces of bread, sticky as clay, a piece little bigger than a matchbox, and once a day a thin gruel.

But you still wouldn't get warmed up right away even if you signed everything, if you admitted everything, if you surrendered, and if you agreed to spend another ten years in this dearly beloved Archipelago. Until your trial they moved you from Number Thirty to the Vorkuta "interrogation tent"—no less famous. This was a plain ordinary tent, yes, and full of holes to boot. It had no floor. The floor was the Arctic earth. Inside it was seven by twelve yards, and in the center was an iron barrel instead of a stove. There were single-decker lattice bunks on one level and those next to the stove were always occupied by the thieves.

The political plebeians . . . had to sleep around the outside or on the ground. You would lie there and see the stars above you. And you would pray: "Oh, the sooner they try me the better! The sooner they sentence me the better!" You awaited that trial as a deliverance. (People will say: No person can live like that beyond the Arctic Circle, unless he is fed chocolate and dressed in furs. But in our country . . . he can! Our Soviet man, our Archipelago native . . . can! Arnold Rappoport spent many *months* like that— the Provincial Assizes kept delaying its journey from Naryan-Mar.)

Or here, for your delectation, is one more interrogation prison—the penalty camp of Orotukan in the Kolyma, 315 miles from Magadan. It was the winter of 1937–1938. A wood and canvas settlement, in other words, tents with holes in them but overlaid with rough boards. The newly arrived prisoner transport, a bunch of new interrogation fodder, saw even before being led in through the door: every tent in the settlement *was surrounded with piles of frozen corpses* on three out of four sides, except where the door was. (And this was not to terrify. There was simply no way out of it: people died, and snow was six feet deep, and beneath it there was only permafrost.) And then came the torment of waiting. You had to wait in the tents until you were transferred to the log prison for interrogation. But they had taken on too much and too many. They had herded in too many rabbits from the whole of the Kolyma, and the interrogators couldn't cope with them, and the majority of those brought here were simply destined to die without even getting to their first interrogation session. The tents were congested, there was no room to stretch out. You lay there on the bunks and on the floor, and you lay there for many weeks at a time. ("Do you really call that congestion?" responds the Serpantinka. "Here they wait to be shot—true, only for several days at a time—but *standing* the whole time in a shed, so that when they *give them a drink*—that is, throw pieces of ice over their heads from the doorway—it is so crowded that it is impossible to stretch out a hand to catch the pieces, and instead you have to try to catch them with your mouth.") There were no baths, nor any outdoor exercise periods in the fresh air. Bodies itched. Everyone scratched frantically, and everyone kept on *searching* for lice in padded cotton britches, padded jackets, shirts, underwear shorts, but they searched without undressing because of the cold. The big, white, bloated lice reminded you of plump suckling piglets. And when you crushed them, they splashed your face, and your nails were covered with ichor.

Before lunch the duty jailer would shout through the door: "Are there any stiffs?" "Yes." "Whoever wants to earn a bread ration—drag them out!" They were dragged out and placed on top of the pile of corpses. And *no one bothered to ask the names of the dead!* The bread rations were issued on the basis of the total count. And the ration was ten and a half ounces. And one bowl of gruel a day. And they would also issue humpbacked salmon rejected by the sanitation inspector. It was very salty. You were very thirsty after it, but there was never any hot water, never. Just barrels of icy water. You had to drink many cups to quench your thirst. G.S.M. used to try to persuade his friends: "Turn down the humpbacked salmon—that's your only salvation! You spend all the calories you get from your bread on warming that icy water inside you!" But people simply couldn't turn down a piece of free fish—so they kept on eating it and then drinking. And they trembled from inner cold. M. himself didn't eat it, so it's he who now tells us about Orotukan.

It was so congested in the barracks—yet it kept steadily thinning out. After a certain number of weeks the survivors of the barracks were driven outside for a roll call. In the unaccustomed daylight they saw one another: pale, their faces overgrown with stubble, beaded with nits, hard, dark blue lips, sunken eyes. They called the roll by file cards. The answers were barely audible. The cards to which there was no response were put aside. And that is how they established who was left there in the piles of corpses—avoiding interrogation.

All who survived Orotukan say they would have preferred the gas chamber.

The interrogation? It proceeded according to the plans of the interrogator. And those in whose cases it didn't are not about to tell us. As the security chief Komarov said: "All I need is your right hand—to sign the testimony." Well, yes, there were tortures, of course, homemade and primitive. They would crush a hand in the door, and it was all in that vein. (Try it, reader.)

The court? Some sort of *camp collegium*—this was a permanent camp court subordinate to the Próvincial Court, like the people's court in the district. Legality was triumphant! And there would be witnesses, bought by the Third Section for a bowl of gruel.

In Burepolom the brigadiers often testified against their brigade members. The interrogator—a Chuvash named Krutikov—forced them to. "Otherwise I will remove you from your position as brigadier and send you to Pechora!" And so a brigadier named Nikolai Ronzhin from Gorky stepped forward to testify: "Yes, Bernshtein said that Singer sewing machines were good and that Podolsk sewing machines were bad." Well, that was enough! Enough at least for the assizes of the Gorky Provincial Court (Chairman Bukhonin, and two local Komsomol girls, Zhukova and Korkina). Ten years!

In Burepolom there was also a smith, Anton Vasilyevich Balyberdin (local, from Tonshayevo), who used to be a witness at all camp trials. Should you run into him, please shake his honest hand!

Well, and then finally . . . there was one more prisoner transport to another camp, to make sure you didn't take it into your head to get even with the witnesses against you. This was a short transport—four hours or so on an open flatcar on the narrow-gauge railroad.

And then it was into the hospital. And if you could still put one foot in front of the other, tomorrow, first thing in the morning, you'd be pushing a wheelbarrow.

All hail the Chekist vigilance which saved us from military defeat, and saved the security officers from the front!

■

Few were shot during the war (if we exclude the republics from which we retreated in haste), and for the most part new terms were passed instead: what the Chekists needed was not the annihilation of these people, merely the disclosure of their crimes. The convicted could then labor or they could die—this was a matter of economics.

In 1938, there was an extreme impatience to shoot on the part of the higher-ups! They shot as many as they could in all the camps, but they shot the most in the Kolyma (the "Garanin" executions) and in Vorkuta (the "Kashketin" executions).

The Kashketin executions were tied up with the skin-grating name of the Old Brickyard. That was what the station of the narrow-gauge railroad twelve miles south of Vorkuta was called.

After the "victory" of the Trotskyite hunger strike in March, 1937, and the deception perpetrated on its participants, the "Grigorovich Commission" was sent from Moscow for investigation of the strikers. South of Ukhta, not far from the railroad bridge across the Ropcha River in the taiga, a long stockade was set up, and a new isolator—Ukhtarka—was created. This is where the interrogation of the Trotskyites of the southern section of the trunk railroad line was conducted. And commission member Kashketin was sent to Vorkuta itself. Here he dragged the Trotskyites through the "interrogation tent" (they were flogged with whips!). And without even insisting that they admit their guilt, he drew up his "Kashketin lists."

In the winter of 1937–1938 they began assembling at the Old Brickyard the Trotskyites and also the "detsisty"—the "democratic centralists"—from various concentration points—from tents at the mouth of the Syr-Yaga, from Kochmes, from Sivaya Maska, from Ukhtarka (some of them without any interrogation whatever). Several of the most prominent were taken to Moscow in connection with trials there. By April, 1938, the rest of them at the Old Brickyard numbered 1,053 persons. In the tundra, off to the side of the narrow-gauge railroad, stood a long old shed. They began to settle the strikers in it, and then, as additional groups arrived, they also set up next to it two tattered old tents, which had nothing to reinforce them, for 250 persons each. We can guess what the conditions were from what we know about Orotukan. In the middle of the six-by-twenty-yard tent like that stood one gasoline drum in place of a stove, for which one pail of coal per day was allotted, and in addition the zeks would throw their lice in to add a little to the heat. A thick layer of hoarfrost covered the inside of the canvas wall. There were not enough places on the bunks and the zeks took turns lying down and walking. They were given ten and a half ounces of bread a day and one bowl of gruel. Sometimes, though not every day, they were given a piece of codfish. There was no water and they were given pieces of ice as part of the ration. It goes without saying, of course, that they were never able to wash themselves and that there was no bath. Patches of scurvy appeared on their bodies. But what made this more oppressive than Orotukan was that they sicked on the Trotskyites the camp storm troopers—thieves, murderers included, who had been sentenced to death. They were instructed that these political bastards had to be squeezed, in return for which the thieves would get relaxation of their sentences. The thieves set to with a will to carry out instructions so pleasant and so completely to their taste. They were named monitors and assistant monitors—the nickname of one has been preserved: "Moroz" ("Frost")—and they went around with clubs, beating up these former Communists and mocking them in every way they knew: compelled them to carry them piggyback, grabbed their clothes, defecated in them, and burned them in the stove. In one tent the politicals hurled themselves on the thieves and tried to kill them, but the thieves raised an outcry, and the convoy opened fire from outside to protect the "socially friendly" elements.

It was, above all, this humiliation by the thieves that broke the unity and will of the recent strikers.

At the Old Brickyard, in cold and tattered shelters, in the wretched unwarming stove, the revolutionary gusts of two decades of cruelty and change burned themselves out.

And the Russian tradition of political struggle also, it seems, lived out its last days.

Nonetheless, thanks to the eternal human trait of clinging to hope, the prisoners in the Old Brickyard waited to be sent to some new project. For several months they had endured agonies there, and it was quite unbearable. And then truly, early on the morning of April 22 (we are not fully certain of the date, but that, after all, was Lenin's birthday), they began to assemble a prisoner transport—of two hundred persons. Those summoned were given their bags, which they placed on sledges. The convoy guards led the column east, into the tundra, where there was no dwelling nearby, though Salekhard lay in the distance. The thieves rode in back on the sledges with the things. Those who remained behind noticed only one unusual thing: occasionally bags would fall off the sledges, but no one bothered to pick them up.

The column marched along in good spirits. They were expecting some kind of new life, some kind of new activity, which, even if fatiguing, would be no worse than all that waiting. The sledges had fallen far behind. The convoy itself began to fall behind—no longer ahead or at their sides but only at their rear. So what! This laxity of the convoy was a good sign.

The sun shone.

Then all of a sudden, rapid machine-gun fire began to descend on the black moving column of zeks, from invisible emplacements, from out of the blinding snowy wastes. Some prisoners started to fall, while others still stood, no one understanding a thing.

Death came in sunny and snowy garments, innocent, merciful.

All this was a fantasy on the subject of the coming war. From snow-covered temporary emplacements the murderers rose up in their Arctic cloaks (they say the majority of them were Georgians) and ran to the column and finished off with revolvers all those still alive. Not far off were the previously prepared pits to which the newly arrived thieves began to drag the corpses. To the chagrin of the thieves, the dead men's things were burned.

On the twenty-third and the twenty-fourth of April, another 760 persons were shot in the same place in the same way.

And ninety-three were transported back to Vorkuta. These were the thieves, and, evidently, the stoolie provocateurs.[2]

Such were the main "Kashketin" executions.[3]

But some transports of condemned zeks arrived too late, and they continued to arrive with five to ten people at a time. A detachment of killers would receive them at the Old Brickyard station and *lead* them to the old bathhouse—to a booth lined with three or four layers of blankets inside. There the condemned prisoners were ordered to undress in the snow and enter the bath naked. Inside, they were shot with pistols. In the course of one and a half months about two hundred persons were destroyed in this way. The corpses were burned in the tundra.

The Old Brickyard shed and Ukhtarka were burned down. (And the "bath" was put onto a railroad flatcar and taken to the 191st milepost of the narrow-gauge railroad and dumped. There it was found and studied by my friend. It was saturated with blood on the inside, and its walls were riddled with holes.)

But the executions of the Trotskyites did not end there. Some

2. The names of some of them were Roitman, Istnyuk, Model (an editor in Goslitizdat), Aliyev. And one of the thieves was called Tadik Nikolayevsky. We cannot say for sure precisely why each of them was spared, but it is hard to imagine any other cause.

3. I collected this information from two zeks with whom I was imprisoned. One was *there* and had been spared. The other was a very inquisitive person, who at that time was passionately determined to write the whole story, and who had been able to see these places by tracking down the warm trails and questioning whoever he could about it.

thirty or so others who had still not been shot were gradually assembled and then executed not far from Number Thirty. But this time it was done by other people. And the first detachment of killers, those Chekists and convoy guards, and also those thieves, who had participated in the "Kashketin executions," were also shot soon afterward as witnesses.

In 1938 Kashketin himself was awarded the Order of Lenin "for special services to the Party and the government." And one year later he was shot in Lefortovo.

Nor could one say this was the first time this had happened in history.

A. B——v has told how executions were carried out at Adak —a camp on the Pechora River. They would take the opposition members "with their things" out of the camp compound on a prisoner transport at night. And outside the compound stood the small house of the Third Section. The condemned men were taken into a room one at a time, and there the camp guards sprang on them. Their mouths were stuffed with something soft and their arms were bound with cords behind their backs. Then they were led out into the courtyard, where harnessed carts were waiting. The bound prisoners were piled on the carts, from five to seven at a time, and driven off to the "Gorka"—the camp cemetery. On arrival they were tipped into big pits that had already been prepared and *buried alive*. Not out of brutality, no. It had been ascertained that when dragging and lifting them, it was much easier to cope with living people than with corpses.

This work went on for many nights at Adak.

And that is how the moral-political unity of our Party was achieved.

Chapter 14

■

Changing One's Fate!

To defend yourself in that savage world was impossible. To go on strike was suicide. To go on hunger strikes was useless.

And as for dying, there would always be time.

So what was left for the prisoner? To break out! To go *change one's fate!* (The zeks also called escape "the green prosecutor." It was the only popular prosecutor among them. Like all the other prosecutors, he, too, left many cases in their previous situation or in an even worse situation than before—but sometimes he freed them outright. He was the green forest. He was the bushes and the greensward.)

Chekhov used to say that if a prisoner was not a philosopher who could get along equally well in all possible circumstances (or let us put it this way: who could retire into himself) then he could *not* but wish to escape and he *ought to* wish to.

He could not but wish to! That was the imperative of a free soul. True, the natives of the Archipelago were far from being like that. They were much more submissive than that. But even among them there were always those who thought about escape or who were just about to. The continual escapes in one or another place, even those that did not succeed, were a true proof that the energy of the zeks had not yet been lost.

Here is a camp compound. (Illustration No. 36.) It is well guarded; the fence is strong and the inner cordon area is reliable and the watchtowers are set out correctly—every spot is open to view and open to fire. But all of a sudden you grow sick to death of the thought that you are condemned to die right here on this

36. Camp compound

bit of fenced-off land. So why not try your luck? Why not burst out and change your fate? This impulse is particularly strong at the beginning of your term of imprisonment, in the first year, and it is not even deliberate. In that first year when, generally speaking, the prisoner's entire future and whole prison personality are being decided. Later on this impulse weakens somehow; there is no longer the conviction that it is more important for you to be *out there*, and all the threads binding you to the outer world weaken, and the cauterizing of the soul is transformed into decay, and the human being settles into camp harness.

During all the years of the camps, there were evidently quite a few escapes. Here are some statistics accidentally come by: In the month of March, 1930, alone, 1,328 persons escaped from imprisonment in the R.S.F.S.R.[1] (And how inaudible and soundless this was in our society.)

With the enormous development of the Archipelago after 1937, particularly during the war years, when battle-fit infantrymen were rounded up and sent to the front, it became even more difficult to provide proper convoy, and not even the evil notion of self-guarding could solve all the problems of the chiefs. Simul-

1. TsGAOR, collection 393, shelf 84, file 4, sheet 68.

taneously with that there was the hankering to get from the camps as much economic profit and production and labor as possible—and this compelled, particularly in logging operations, the dispatch of work parties and subparties on distant assignments and their extension into more remote areas—and the guard supposedly surrounding them became ever more illusory, ever more unreal.

By 1939, on some of the auxiliary expeditions of the Ust-Vym Camp, instead of a perimeter fence surrounding the camp there were only pole or wattle palings and *no* nighttime illumination—in other words, at night no one kept the prisoners from departing! Even in the *penalty* camp in this camp complex, when the prisoners were taken into the forests for work, there was only one armed guard for a brigade of prisoners. It is obvious that he had no way to keep track of them. And seventy men escaped from there during the summer of 1939. (One even escaped twice in one day: before lunch and after lunch!) However, *sixty* returned. And there was no news of the rest.

But that was in the wilderness. In Moscow itself three very easy escapes took place while I was there: from the camp sector at Kaluga Gates during the day, when a young thief climbed the fence of the work compound (and, with his thief's talent for braggadocio, sent the camp a postcard the *next* day saying he was off to Sochi and sending his best wishes to the camp chief); from the Marfino minicamp near the Botanical Gardens, the girl I have already written about; and, from the same place, a young nonpolitical offender jumped on a bus and went off to the center of town. True, he had been left entirely without any guard at all; ganged up on us, the MGB took a cavalier attitude toward the loss of a nonpolitical offender.

In all likelihood they did some arithmetic in Gulag one bright day and became convinced that it was much cheaper to permit a certain percentage of zek losses than to establish a truly strict guard over all the many thousand points of imprisonment.

And at the same time they relied on certain invisible chains which kept the natives reliably in their place.

The strongest of these chains was the prisoners' universal submission and total surrender to their situation as slaves. Almost to a man, both the 58's and the nonpolitical offenders were hardworking family people capable of manifesting valor only in lawful ways, on the orders of and the approval of the higher-ups. Even when they had been imprisoned for five and ten years they could not imagine that singly—or, God forbid, collectively—they might rise up for their liberty since they saw arrayed against them the state (*their own* state), the NKVD, the police, the guards, and the police dogs. And even if you were fortunate enough to escape unscathed, how could you live afterward on a false passport, with a false name, when documents were checked at every intersection, when suspicious eyes followed passers-by from behind every gateway? And the universal mood in the corrective-labor camps was: Why are you standing there with your rifles, what are you watching us for? Even if you disperse, we'll make no move to go anywhere; we are not criminals, why should we escape? And we are going to be freed in a year anyway! (Amnesty . . .) K. Strakhovich relates that in 1942 his prisoner transport train was bombed while they were being taken to Uglich. The convoy scattered, and the zeks stayed right there, waiting for it to return. There are many such stories, like the story of the bookkeeper of the Ortaussky Division of Karlag: they sent him a distance of twenty-five miles with his financial report, accompanied by one convoy guard. And on the way back he not only had to haul the dead-drunk convoy guard in a cart, but also to take particular care of his rifle so the poor fool wouldn't be tried for losing it.

Another chain was *the death factory*—camp starvation. Although it was precisely this starvation that at times drove the despairing to wander through the taiga in the hope of finding more food than there was in camp, yet it was this starvation that also weakened them so that they had no strength for a long flight, and because of it it was impossible to save up a stock of food for the journey.

And there was another chain too—the threat of a new term. A political prisoner was given a new tenner for an escape attempt under that same Article 58 (and gradually it proved best to give Article 58-14—Counter-Revolutionary Sabotage). The thieves, it's true, were given Article 82 (pure escape) and two years in all, but up to 1947 they got no more than two years for theft and also robbery, so these were of comparable magnitude. Furthermore, camp was their "native home." In camp they did not starve, they did not work—their smartest move was not to escape but to serve out their term, all the more so because they might always benefit from special privileges or amnesties. Escape for a thief was merely the sport of a well-fed, healthy body and an explosion of impatient greed: to get out and go on a spree, to rob, drink, rape, show off. The only serious escapes among them were by bandits and murderers with long terms.

(The thieves love to lie about their nonexistent escapes or wildly embroider the ones they did carry out. They will tell you how *India* [the barracks of thieves] received the challenge banner for the best preparations for winter—for the substantial amount of earth piled around the barracks wall—and they will claim they were digging a tunnel at the same time and taking the earth out right under the chiefs' eyes. Don't believe them! All "India" wouldn't escape, and they wouldn't want to dig very long because they needed easier and quicker ways; and the chiefs weren't so stupid as not to see where they were getting the earth from. The thief Korzinkin, with ten convictions on his record, a commandant trusted by his chief, really did escape, well dressed, and really did pass himself off as an assistant prosecutor, but he had to add to that story how he spent the night in the same hut as the commissioner for catching escapees [they really did exist], stole his uniform, his gun, and even his dog one night—and from then on passed himself off as the commissioner. He is lying through his teeth about all this. In their fantasies and stories the thieves always had to be more heroic than they really were.)

Another thing restraining the zeks was not the compound but the privilege of going without convoy. The ones guarded the least, who enjoyed the small privilege of going to work and back without a bayonet at their backs, or once in a while dropping into the free settlement, highly prized their advantages. And after an escape these were taken away.

The geography of the Archipelago was also a solid obstacle to escape attempts—those endless expanses of snow or sandy desert, tundra, taiga. The Kolyma, even though it was not an island, was more bitter than any island; it was a piece torn off from the rest and where could you escape to from the Kolyma? People undertook escapes from there only out of desperation. It is true that there was a time when the Yakuts were hospitable to the prisoners and undertook to help them: "Nine suns—and I will take you to Khabarovsk." They took them there, too, on their reindeer. But then escaped thieves began to plunder the Yakuts and the Yakuts changed toward the fugitives and started to turn them in.

The hostility of the surrounding population, encouraged by the authorities, became the principal hindrance to escapes. The authorities were not stingy about rewarding the captors. (This was an additional form of political indoctrination.) And the nationalities inhabiting the areas around Gulag gradually came to assume that the capture of a fugitive meant a holiday, enrichment, that it was like a good hunt or like finding a small gold nugget. The Tungus, the Komis, and the Kazakhs were paid off in flour and tea, and in densely settled areas the trans-Volga people living near the Burepolom and Unzha camps were paid for each captured fugitive at the rate of two poods—seventy-two pounds —of flour, eight yards of cloth, and several pounds of herring. During the war years there was no other way to get herring, and local inhabitants simply nicknamed the fugitives *herrings*. In the village of Sherstka, for example, when any stranger appeared, the children would run along in a group shouting: "Mama! There's a herring coming!"

And what about the geologists? Those pioneers of the northern wastes, those brave, bearded, booted heroes, those Jack London bold-hearts! A fugitive had little hope of help from our Soviet geologists, and it was better not to come near their bonfires. The Leningrad engineer Abrosimov, arrested in the "Promparty" wave and sentenced to a "tenner," escaped from the Nivagres Camp in 1933. He wandered about in the taiga for twenty-one days, and he was delighted to meet up with some geologists. But they took him off to a settlement and handed him over to the chairman of the local trade union organization. (You can understand the geologists too: After all, they were not alone and they were afraid of being turned in by someone in their group. And what if the fugitive was really a criminal, a murderer—and would knife them in the night?)

A captured fugitive, if he was dead when taken, might be thrown near the camp mess hall to lie for several days with a rotting bullet wound—so the prisoners would value their thin gruel more highly. One taken alive might be set in front of the gatehouse, and whenever a column passed they would set the dogs on him. (And the dogs, depending on the command given, could suffocate a person, bite him, or merely tear his clothes off, leaving him naked.) And one could also make a placard in the Cultural and Educational Section, saying: "I escaped, but the dogs caught me." And this placard could be hung around the fugitive's neck and he could be ordered to walk around the camp wearing it.

And if he was beaten, then they had to burst his kidneys. If his hands were screwed into handcuffs, then it had to be done so that the feeling in his radial wrist joints would be lost for good (G. Sorokin, Ivdellag). Or if he was put into a punishment cell, he shouldn't come out without TB. (Nyroblag, Baranov, escape in 1944. After being beaten by the convoy he coughed up blood, and three years later they had to remove his left lung.)[2]

Properly speaking, to beat the fugitive to within an inch of his life and to kill him were the principal forms of combating escapes in the Archipelago.[3] And even if no escapes occurred for a long time—then they sometimes had to be manufactured. At the Debin goldfields in the Kolyma in 1951 a group of zeks was permitted to go out to gather berries. Three got lost—and disappeared. The camp chief, Senior Lieutenant Pyotr Lomaga, sent torturers. They loosed their dogs on the three sleeping men, then smashed their skulls with the butts of their rifles until their heads were a mass of pulp and their brains hung out—and in that state hauled them on a cart to the camp. Here the horse was replaced by four prisoners, who had to drag the cart past the whole line-up. "That's how it will be for everybody!" proclaimed Lomaga.

And who can find inside himself the desperation to keep from shuddering in the face of all that—and go on! and go on! and go on!——and arrive—but *arrive* where? There, at the end of the escape, when the fugitive attained his destined and designated goal —who was there who wouldn't be afraid to meet him, to hide him, to look after him? It was only the thieves who were awaited out in freedom at a prearranged *hangout*. For us 58's such an apartment would be called a *conspiratorial address*, and that was nearly an underground organization.

That is how many obstacles and pitfalls there were in the path of escape.

But the desperate heart sometimes did not weigh things. It

2. And today he is naïvely seeking to have his illness recognized as an *occupational* illness, for the sake of his pension. How could it be more occupational, one would think, for both prisoner and convoy! Yet they refuse to recognize it as such.

3. And it has become increasingly the principal form in the most recent, Khrushchevian, period as well. See Anatoly Marchenko's *Moi Pokazaniya (My Testimony).*

saw: the river was flowing and a log was floating down it—and one jump! We'll float on down. Vyacheslav Bezrodny from the Olchan Camp, barely released from the hospital, still utterly weak, escaped down the Indigirka River on two logs fastened together—to the Arctic Ocean! Where was he going? And what was he hoping for? In the end he was not so much caught as picked up on the open sea and returned over the winter road to Olchan to that very same hospital.

It is not possible to say of everyone who didn't return to camp on his own, who was not brought in half alive, or who was not brought in dead, that he had escaped. Perhaps he had only exchanged an involuntary and long-drawn-out death in camp for the free death of a beast in the taiga.

To the degree that the fugitives didn't so much escape as merely wander around and return on their own—the camp security chiefs even derived benefits from them: without any strain they would *wrap another term* around them. And if no escapes took place for a long time, they arranged provocations: some stoolie or other was given instructions to set up an "escape group," and all of them would be arrested.

But a man who seriously undertook to escape became very swiftly fearsome. Some of them set fire to the taiga behind them in order to get the dogs off their trail. And it would burn for weeks over dozens of miles. In 1949, on a meadow near the Veslyanka State Farm, a fugitive was detained with human flesh in his knapsack; he had killed an unconvoyed artist with a five-year term who had crossed his path, had cut his flesh off, and had not yet had the chance to cook it.

In the spring of 1947 in the Kolyma, near Elgen, two convoy guards were leading a column of zeks. And suddenly one zek, without any prior agreement with anyone, skillfully attacked the convoy guards on his own, disarmed them, and shot them both. (His name is unknown, but he turned out to have been a recent front-line officer. A rare and bright example of a front-line soldier who had not lost his courage in camp!) The bold fellow announced to the column that it was free! But the prisoners were overwhelmed with horror; no one followed his lead, and they all sat down right there and waited for a new convoy. The front-line officer shamed them, but in vain. And then he took up the rifles (thirty-two cartridges, "thirty-one for *them!*") and left alone. He killed and wounded several pursuers and with his thirty-second cartridge he shot himself. The entire Archipelago might well have collapsed if all former front-liners had behaved as he did.

In Kraslag a former soldier, a hero of Khalkhin-Gol, attacked a convoy guard with an ax, stunned him with the butt, took his rifle and thirty cartridges. The dogs were sent after him. He killed two of them and wounded the dog trainer. When they caught him, they didn't just shoot him but went crazy and avenged themselves and their dogs, riddling the corpse with their bayonets and leaving it to lie that way for a week by the gatehouse.

In 1951 in that same Kraslag, some ten long-termers were being convoyed by four infantrymen among the guards. Suddenly the zeks attacked the convoy, took away their automatic weapons, put on their uniforms (but they had mercy on the soldiers—the oppressed were often more magnanimous than the oppressors), and four of them, convoying *with braggadocio*, conducted their comrades to the narrow-gauge railroad. There was an empty car there, ready for timber. The false convoy went up to the locomotive and forced the crew to disembark. (One of them was a locomotive engineer.) They drove the train at full speed to the Reshoty Station on the trunk line of the Trans-Siberian. But they had about forty miles to cover. And meanwhile they had already been reported, starting with the guards they'd spared. Several times they had to shoot their way past groups of guards, and several miles before Reshoty the authorities succeeded in mining the track in front of them and put a battalion of camp guards into position. All the fugitives perished in the unequal battle.

The *quiet* escapes were usually more fortunate in their results. Some of them were surprisingly successful. But we rarely hear of these happy stories; *those who broke out* do not give interviews; they have changed their names, and they are in hiding. Kuzikov-Skachinsky, who escaped successfully in 1942, tells the story now only because he was caught in 1959—after seventeen years.[4]

And we have learned of the successful escape of Zinaida

4. Here is how he was discovered: The man who had fled with him got caught in another case. They managed to establish his true identity by his fingerprints. In this way they discovered that the fugitive had not perished, as they had formerly supposed. They started to track down Kuzikov too. For this they conducted careful inquiries in his home region and put his relatives under surveillance—and through a chain of relatives they got to him. And they spared neither effort nor time for all of this at seventeen years' remove!

Yakovlevna Povalyayeva because in the end it fell through. She got her term because she had stayed on as a teacher in her school during the German occupation. But she was not immediately arrested when the Soviet armies arrived, and before her arrest she was married to a pilot. Then she was arrested and sent to Mine No. 8 at Vorkuta. Through some Chinese working in the kitchen she established communication with freedom and with her husband. He was employed in civil aviation and arranged a trip to Vorkuta for himself. On an appointed day Zina went to the bath in the work zone, where she shed her camp clothing and released her hair, which had been curled the night before, from under her head scarf. Her husband was waiting for her in the work sector. There were security officers on duty at the river ferry, but they paid no attention to a girl with curly hair who was arm in arm with a flier. They flew out on a plane. Zina spent one year living on false papers. But she couldn't resist the desire to see her mother again—and her mother was under surveillance. At her new interrogation she managed to convince them she had escaped in a coal car. And they never did find out about her husband's participation.

In 1946 Janis L——s walked from his camp in Perm to Latvia, speaking fractured Russian the whole way and barely able to explain himself. His departure from camp was simple: he sprinted, broke through a rickety fence, and stepped over it. But later in a swampy forest—with bast sandals on his feet—he had to live for a long time on berries alone. One day he managed to take a village cow off into the woods and kill it. He ate his fill of beef and managed to make himself some primitive shoes from the cow's hide. In another place he stole a sheepskin coat from a peasant (a fugitive to whom the inhabitants are hostile unwillingly becomes the inhabitants' enemy). In populated places L——s claimed to be a Latvian conscript who had lost his documents. And although the universal inspection of passes had not yet been abolished that year, in Leningrad, which to him was a strange city, he managed without uttering a word to get to the Warsaw Station and to walk another two and a half miles along the tracks and board a train there. (But there was one thing L——s was firmly assured of: when he got to Latvia he would be fearlessly hidden—and that, of course, gave point to his escape.)

The kind of escape L——s undertook required a peasant's dexterity, grasp, and energy. But what about a city dweller, yes, an old man at that, sentenced to five years for repeating an anecdote, was he capable of escaping? It turns out that he was when a more certain death was the only outcome of staying in his own camp, a small camp, between Moscow and Gorky, for nonpolitical offenders on their last legs, which had been manufacturing shells since 1941. Well, five years was a "child's term," you might say, but the unfortunate anecdote teller would not have lasted out even five months if he was driven out to work without being fed. This escape was a gesture of despair, a brief impulse, for which there would have been neither the judgment nor the strength half a minute later. A routine train had been shunted into the camp and loaded with shells. And a convoy sergeant came marching along it, followed by a railroadman who had fallen several cars behind; the sergeant opened the door of each *red cattle car* and checked to be sure no one was in there, then shut the door, and the railroadman put a seal on it. And our ill-starred famished last-legger of an anecdote teller,[5] behind the back of the sergeant, who had gone on past and in front of the railroadman, scrambled into a car. It was not easy for him to clamber up, and it was not easy to push the door back noiselessly, and it was all very impractical, it was a sure failure, and he closed the door behind him, with his heart skipping a beat, he was already sorry he had started. The sergeant would return and would kick him with his boots and any moment now the railroadman would shout. Already someone was touching the door—it was the railroadman putting on the seal! (And I myself think: maybe the good railroadman saw him—and pretended not to?) The train moved off, out of the compound. The train moved off to the front. This fugitive was unprepared. He didn't even have a piece of bread. In the course of three days he would almost certainly die in this moving voluntary-punishment cell. He wouldn't get to the front, and it wasn't the front he needed. What was he to do? How could he save himself now? He saw that the shell boxes were packed with a steel band around them. With his naked defenseless hands he tore that steel ribbon, and with it sawed through the floor of the

5. All this happened in exactly this way, but his name has not been preserved.

railroad car in a place where there weren't any boxes. This was impossible for an old man? But was it possible to die? And if they opened it and caught him—was that possible? Furthermore, the boxes had wire loops attached to them, to carry them by. He cut off the loops, and out of them he made similar but much larger loops and tied them so that they hung down through the crawl hole he had cut. How exhausted he was! How hard it was to get his torn hands to do what he wanted them to! How dearly that repeated anecdote was costing him! He didn't wait for a station, but carefully let himself down through the hole while the train was in motion, and lay with both feet in one loop near r the rear of the train, and his shoulders in another. The tr n moved on, and the fugitive hung suspended there, rocking ba k and forth. The speed slackened, and at that moment he decided to let go; he dropped his feet, and his feet dragged along and dragg d the rest of him down. This was a sure death act, a circus act—but t, after all, they might send a telegram after the train and search the cars. After all, they would have missed him in the camp compound by now. He could not straighten out. He could not raise his head. He clung to the ties. He closed his eyes, ready for death. The accelerated clicking of the last cars—then lovely silence. The fugitive opened his eyes and rolled over: all he could see was the red light of the departing train! Freedom!

But that was not yet salvation. Freedom was freedom, but he had neither documents nor money, he was dressed in camp rags, and he was doomed. Swollen and torn, somehow he managed to get to a station, and there mingled with a recently arrived Leningrad train; evacuated semicorpses were being led by the hand and fed hot food at the station. But that would not have saved him either—except that in the train he found a dying friend and took his documents, and he knew all about his past too. They were all sent to a place near Saratov, and for several years, until the war was over, he lived there on a poultry farm. And then he was seized with a longing to see his daughter and went off to find her.

He looked for her in Nalchik, in Armavir, and he found her in Uzhgorod. During this time she had married a border guard. She had believed her father happily dead and buried, and now she listened to his story with horror and revulsion. Although she was quite devout in her civic conscientiousness, she nevertheless retained shameful vestiges of kinship and she did not denounce her father but merely drove him from her door. There were no other relatives of the old man left. He lived a meaningless existence, wandering like a nomad from city to city. He became a dope addict. In Baku he smoked hashish and was picked up by an ambulance and while under the influence of the drug gave his right name, though when he came to, he gave the name under which he had been living. It was one of our Soviet hospitals, which certainly couldn't treat him without first establishing his identity. A comrade was summoned from State Security—and in 1952, ten years after his escape, the old man got twenty-five years. (It was this that gave him the happy chance to tell his own story in prison cells and thus to enter history.)

Sometimes the subsequent life of a successful fugitive was more dramatic than the escape itself. That is how it must have been with Sergei Andreyevich Chebotaryov, who has already been mentioned more than once in this book. In 1914 he became an employee of the Chinese Eastern Railroad (the KVZhD). In February, 1917, he became a Bolshevik. In 1929, during the period of the KVZhD hostilities, he was imprisoned in a Chinese prison, and in 1931 he and his wife, Yelena Prokofyevna, and his sons, Gennady and Viktor, returned to their homeland. The Fatherland then operated in its usual way: Within a few days he himself was arrested; his wife went insane; his sons were turned over to *different* orphanages, and were given new patronymics and surnames, even though they well remembered their own and objected. At first Chebotaryov was given only three years by the Far Eastern troika of the OGPU (another *troika!*)—because of their inexperience; but soon he was seized again, tortured, and resentenced to ten years without the right of correspondence (what was there for him to write about now?), and even confinement under intensified guard during the revolutionary holidays. The severity of this sentence unexpectedly helped him. In 1934 he was moved to Karlag, where he worked on building a railroad to Mointy. While there, during the May holidays of 1936, he was confined in the penalty isolator, and they threw in with him the *free employee* Avtonom Vasilyevich Chupin under the same conditions as himself. Whether he was drunk or sober isn't clear, but at any rate Chebotaryov managed to filch his three-month identification certificate, which had expired six months earlier and which had been issued by his village soviet. This certificate virtually obliged him to escape! And on May 8 Chebotaryov left the Mointy Camp, dressed in civilian clothes, without a scrap of camp clothing on him or with him, and with two half-liter bottles in his pockets like a typical drunk, except that they held not vodka but water. Ahead of him stretched the salt-marsh steppes. Twice he fell into the hands of Kazakhs who were on their way to work on the railroad, but since he knew a little Kazakh, "I played on their religious feelings and they let me go."[6] At the western edge of Lake Balkhash he was detained by a Security Operations post of Karlag. Taking his document, they asked him to give all sorts of information about himself and his relatives, and the supposed Chupin answered correctly from memory. Here again he had a lucky accident (without such lucky accidents people probably get caught). The head of the operations group came into the dugout, and Chupin beat him to the draw: "Hey! Nikolai, how are you? Don't you recognize me?" (This split-second calculation was based on facial wrinkles and a contest in remembering faces: I recognize you all right, but if you recognize me, I'm a goner!) "No, I don't recognize you." "Well, how about that! We were traveling on a train together! Your name is Naidyonov, and you were telling me how you met Olya at the station in Sverdlovsk—you met in a train compartment and after that you got married." It was all true. Naidyonov was astonished; they had a smoke together and they let the fugitive go. (Oh, you bluecaps! Not for nothing do they teach you to keep silent! You must not give in to the human impulse to frankness. You told this story, not in a railroad car, but when you were on an assignment at the tree nursery of Karlag a year before, and you told it to the prisoners, just like that, out of foolishness, and you could never have remembered all the mugs of those who listened to the story. And in all likelihood he had told this story on a train too, more than once—it was the kind of story to tell on trains. And Chebotaryov's bold play was based on that!) Joyfully Chupin went farther along the highway to Chu Station,

6. Religion can have its uses even for an atheist! I affirmed earlier that orthodox Communists did not make escape attempts. Chebotaryov was not one. But he was not entirely devoid of materialism either. I imagine that among the Kazakhs the recollection of the Budenny repression of 1930 was still very much alive, because they were good to him. Things wouldn't be like that in 1950.

past the lake and on south. For the most part he traveled at night, and hid in the high reeds whenever automobile headlights approached. During the day he lay down in them (there were reed jungles there). There were fewer and fewer operations men about. At that time the Archipelago had not yet cast its metastases into those areas.[7] He had bread and sugar with him and he made them last, and for five days he went along without any water at all. After 125 miles of walking he reached the station and got on a train.

And then began his *free*—no, poisoned—years, because Chebotaryov couldn't risk settling down or staying too long in one place. That same year, several months later, he ran into his own *camp godfather* in the city park in Frunze! But that was in passing, it was a festive occasion with music and girls, and the godfather failed to recognize him. He had to leave the job he had found. (The senior bookkeeper questioned him and guessed the urgent reasons—but turned out to be a Solovki veteran himself.) He had to move on. At first he would not take the risk of seeking out his family, but afterward he worked out how to. He wrote to a woman cousin in Ufa: "Where are Lena and the children? Guess who is writing you. Don't tell *her* yet." And the return address was some kind of Zirabulak station, a man named Chupin. And the cousin replied: "The children are lost and your wife is in Novosibirsk." Then Chebotaryov asked her to go to Novosibirsk to tell his wife—but only face to face—that her husband had reappeared and wanted to send money. The cousin went—and now his own wife wrote to him: she was in a psychiatric hospital; her passport had been lost; she had to get through three months of forced labor; and she couldn't receive money sent general delivery. His heart leaped; he had to go to her! And her husband sent her an insane telegram: "Meet me on train such-and-such, car such-and-such." The heart is ever defenseless against emotion, but it is not, praise God, immune to premonitions. These premonitions so played on his mind while he was en route that he got off the train two stations before Novosibirsk and hitched a ride in a passing automobile. Having checked his luggage at the baggage room, he went recklessly to his wife's

7. But soon afterward the Korean exiles were sent there, and later the Germans, and then all the nations. Seventeen years later I ended up there myself.

address. He knocked! The door was open and there was no one in the house. (This first coincidence was an ill omen: the landlord had spent the whole day on guard in order to warn him about the ambush waiting for him—but at that very moment had gone out to get water!) He went on in. His wife was not there. On a cot lay a Chekist covered with his coat and snoring loudly. (This second coincidence was a benign omen!) Chebotaryov fled. At that moment he was hailed by the landlord—a fellow acquaintance from the KVZhD, not yet arrested. Apparently his son-in-law was a Security man and had brought the telegram home himself and shaken it in front of Chebotaryov's wife: This rat of yours, he's running right into our hands of his own accord! They had gone to the train—and hadn't found him; the second Security man had left for a moment and this other had lain down to rest. Nonetheless Chebotaryov managed to get hold of his wife, and they went several stations down the line in a car and got on a train to Uzbekistan. In Leninabad they registered their marriage again! That is, without divorcing Chebotaryov she now married Chupin! But they could not make up their minds to live together. They sent inquiries in every direction in her name in an attempt to find the children—but in vain. And that was the sort of separated and tormented life they led before the war. In 1941 Chupin was called up for military service and became a radio operator in the 61st Cavalry Division. On one occasion he was careless and called cigarettes and matches by their Chinese names, as a joke. In what normal country could something like that arouse suspicion—merely because a man knew some foreign words? In our country it did. And the stoolies were right there. And Political Commissar Sokolov, Security officer of the 219th Cavalry Regiment, was questioning him within the hour: "Where did you learn Chinese?" Chupin: "Only those two words." "Did you serve on the KVZhD?" (Service abroad is immediately viewed as a grave sin!) The Security officer also set the stoolies on him, but they found nothing. So, just to be certain, he arrested him under 58-10 anyway:

- Because he did not believe the Sovinformbureau communiqués
- Because he had said that the Germans had more equipment (as if everyone had not seen that with their own eyes)

Well, there's more than one way to skin a cat! Court-martial! Death sentence. And Chebotaryov was so fed up with life in the Fatherland *he didn't even petition* for mercy. But the state needed working hands, so he got ten years plus five muzzled. Once again he was back in his "native home." He served (with time off for work) *nine* years.

And there was yet another chance encounter. In camp another zek, N. F——v, called him over to a far corner of the upper bunks and there asked him quietly: "What's your name?" "Avtonom Vasilich." "And what province were you born in?" "Tyumen." "What district? What village soviet?" Chebotaryov-Chupin gave all the correct answers and heard: "You're lying. I worked on the same locomotive as Avtonom Chupin for five years, I know him as well as I know myself. Was it you who swiped his documents one day in May, 1936?" Now that's the kind of invisible underwater anchor a fugitive can rip open his belly on! What novelist would be believed if he were to think up an encounter like that? By that time Chebotaryov again wanted to survive and warmly shook that good man's hand when the latter said: "Don't be afraid, I won't go to the godfather. I'm not a bastard!"

And thus it was that Chebotaryov served out his second term, as Chupin. But to his misfortune his last camp was a top-secret one, one of that group of atomic projects—Moscow-10, Tura-38, Sverdlovsk-39, and Chelyabinsk-40. They were engaged in separating uranium-radium ores, and construction was proceeding according to Kurchatov's plans, and the construction chief was Lieutenant General Tkachenko, who was subordinate only to Stalin and Beria. Every quarter the zeks had to renew their pledges of "nondisclosure." But this was not the real trouble—the real trouble was that those released were not allowed to return home. The "released" prisoners were sent off in a large group in September, 1950—to the Kolyma! Only there were they relieved of convoy and declared to be *a particularly dangerous special contingent!* They were dangerous because they had helped make the atomic bomb! (How can one really keep up with all this and describe it? Chapters and chapters are necessary!) There were tens of thousands of similar ones scattered all over the Kolyma!! (Look through the Constitution! Look through the Codes! What do they say about *special contingents??*)

Well, at least he could send for his wife now! She came to him at the Maldyak goldfields. And from there they began to seek their sons again—but the replies were all negative: "No." "Not listed here."

Stalin kicked the bucket—and the old folks moved from the Kolyma to the Caucasus—to warm their bones. Things eased up, though slowly. And in 1959 their son Viktor, a Kiev lathe operator, decided to get rid of his hateful new name and declared himself to be the son of the enemy of the people Chebotaryov! And a year later his parents found him! And now the father's problem was to regain the name of Chebotaryov himself (*thrice* rehabilitated, by then he could no longer be charged for the escape). He came out into the open. His fingerprints were sent to Moscow for comparison. The old man got back his peace of mind only when all three of them were issued passports in the name of Chebotaryov; and his daughter-in-law also became Chebotaryov. (But a few years later he wrote to me that he already regretted having found Viktor; he abuses his father as a criminal and the source of all his misfortunes, and waves away the re-

37. The Chebotaryovs

habilitation certificates: "A fake!"[8] And his elder son, Gennady, never has been found.) (Illustration No. 37: the Chebotaryov family.)

From all the cases I have reported it is clear that even a successful escape still couldn't bring freedom, but merely a life constantly oppressed and threatened. This was very well understood by some of the fugitives—by those who in the camps had succeeded in breaking away from the Fatherland politically; by those, too, who lived by the ignorant illiterate principle of *just living!* And it was not altogether rare to find among the fugitives some (in case of failure, they had their answer ready: "We escaped in order to go to the Central Committee and ask to have our cases reopened") whose purpose was escape to the West and who considered only that kind of escape complete.

These escapes are the hardest of all to talk about. Those who did not make it are in the damp earth. Those who were caught again are silent. Those who left in some cases surfaced in the West but in some cases, because of someone left behind, are still silent. There were rumors that in Chukotka some zeks captured a plane and seven of them flew to Alaska. But what I think is: they merely tried to seize one and their plan failed.

All these cases will continue to languish in secrecy for a long time to come, and grow old, and lose their relevance, just like this manuscript, and like everything truthful written in our country.

Here is one such case, and once again human memory has failed to preserve the name of the heroic fugitive. He was from Odessa, and in his civilian profession he was a mechanical engineer, and in the army a captain. He finished the war in Austria and served in the occupation forces in Vienna. He was arrested in 1948 on the basis of a denunciation and was charged and sentenced under Article 58 to twenty-five years, as was the norm by then. He was sent off to Siberia, to a camp located 180 miles from Taishet, in other words far from the main line of the Trans-Siberian. He very soon began to weaken at logging. But he retained the will to fight for life and his memory of Vienna. And from there—yes, *from there*—he succeeded in escaping to Vienna! Incredible!

8. And now the old man has fallen silent. I fear . . . he may have died.

Their logging sector was bordered by a cut which was kept under surveillance from small watchtowers. On the chosen day he had a bread ration with him at work. He felled a thickly branched pine across the cut and beneath its branches crawled to its top. It wasn't tall enough to span the entire cut, but, continuing to crawl, he made it across successfully. He took an ax with him. It was summer. He made his way through the taiga in windfallen woods. The walking was very difficult, but on the other hand, he didn't run into anyone for a whole month. Tying up the sleeves and collar of his shirt, he caught fish in it and ate them raw. He collected cedar nuts, mushrooms, and berries. Half dead, he none-theless managed to get to the Trans-Siberian trunk line and hap-pily went to sleep in a haystack. He was roused by voices: they were picking up the hay with pitchforks and had already found him. He was fagged out and prepared neither to run away nor to put up a fight. And he said: "Well, all right, take me. Turn me in; I am a fugitive." There stood a railroad track walker and his wife. And the track walker said to him: "Oh, come on now, we are Russians. Just sit there and don't give yourself away." They went off. But the fugitive didn't believe them; they were, after all, Soviet people, they had to denounce him. And he crawled off into the woods. From the edge of the forest he watched and saw the track walker return, bringing clothing and food. That evening the fugitive walked along the track and at a forest whistle stop boarded a freight train, jumping off before morning and going into the forest for the day. Night after night he moved on in this way, and when he grew stronger, he even got off at every stop, hiding in the foliage or walking on ahead, getting in front of the train, and then jumping on it again while it was moving. That way he risked dozens of times losing an arm, a leg, his head. (That was how he paid for the few easy glides of the pen of the stoolie who had turned him in.) But on one occasion, just before reaching the Urals, he changed his rule and went to sleep on a flatcar carrying logs. He was wakened by a kick and a lantern shining in his eyes and a demand for "Documents!" "Just a minute!" He rose and with one blow knocked the guard off the car and jumped off the other side—and onto the head of *another* guard! He knocked that one off his feet and managed to make his getaway under the nearby trains. Outside the station he boarded a train while it was moving. He decided to bypass

Sverdlovsk by walking around it, and in the suburbs plundered a trade stall, got clothes for himself, put three suits on, and collected some food. At one station he sold one of the suits and bought a ticket from Chelyabinsk to Orsk and Central Asia. No, he knew where he was going—to Vienna! But he had to cover his tracks and let the pursuit die down. A Turkmen, chairman of a collective farm, met him at the bazaar, took him to work on the farm even though he had no documents. And his hands justified his calling as a mechanical engineer. He repaired all the farm machinery. After several months he took his pay and went to Krasnovodsk, near the border. After the train left Mary, a patrol came along, checking documents. At this point, our mechanical engineer went out on the car platform, opened the door, hung onto the toilet window, where they could not see him from inside because of the frosted glass, and only the toe of one shoe remained to support him and enable him to get back on the step. The patrol failed to notice the toe of a shoe in the corner of the door frame and went on into the next car. And so the awful moment passed. Having crossed the Caspian Sea without incident, the fugitive got on a train going from Baku to Shepetovka, and from there he made for the Carpathians. With great caution he started to make his way across the mountainous border at a remote, steep, forested place—but still the border guards caught him! How much had he had to sacrifice, to suffer, to invent, and to endure since his Siberian camp, since that first felled pine tree—and right at the very end everything was wrecked in one instant! . . . And his strength left him, just as it had back there in the haystack at Taishet, and he couldn't resist any longer, nor lie, and in a final fury he merely shouted: "All right, take me, you executioners! Take me, you are stronger!" "Who are you?" "A fugitive! From the camps! Take me!" But the border guards acted rather strangely: They blindfolded him, took him into a dugout, and there unbound his eyes —and questioned him again—and suddenly it emerged that they were friends: Banderists, Ukrainian nationalist partisans! (Fie, fie! educated readers will frown and wave their hands at me: "Well, you certainly picked some character—he regarded the Banderists as friends! A real rotten fruit, that one!" Well, all I can do is spread my hands myself: That's how he was. That's how he was when he escaped. That's what the camps had made of him. These camp people, as I can tell you, live on the basis of the swinish principle "Existence determines consciousness." Not by what the newspapers say. To camp inmates, friends are those with whom they were tormented in camp. And enemies are those who put the dogs on their trail. Lack of conscientiousness!) And so they embraced! The Banderists still had their own border crossings at that time, and they gently led him across.

And so there he was in Vienna again! But this time in the American zone. And submissive still to that enticing materialist principle, and not forgetting for one moment his bloody death camp, he no longer sought work as a mechanical engineer but, instead, went to the American authorities to unburden his soul. And he began to work for them in some capacity.

But! It is a human trait to relax one's vigilance as soon as the danger is past. He planned to send some money to his parents in Odessa, and to do that he had to exchange dollars for Soviet money. Some Jewish businessman invited him to his apartment in the Soviet zone of Vienna to make the deal. People used to shuttle back and forth all the time, paying no attention to the zones, but he should never have gone into the Soviet zone! He went, however—and was captured at the apartment of the money-changer.

Now this is a very Russian story of how superhuman feats are strung on and on and then thrown away for a glass of vodka.

Sentenced to death and in a cell of the Soviet prison in Berlin, he told the whole story to another officer and engineer—Anikin. This Anikin had himself been both in a German POW camp and on the verge of death in Buchenwald—and had been freed by the Americans, taken to the Soviet zone of Germany, and left there temporarily to assist in dismantling factories, and had run off to West Germany, and was engaged in building a hydroelectric power station near Munich, when he was kidnaped by the Soviet intelligence service (he was blinded with headlights and pushed into an automobile). And what was it all for? So that he could hear the story of the Odessa mechanical engineer and preserve it for us? So as to attempt fruitlessly to escape from Ekibastuz twice (about which there will be more in Part V)? And then be killed in the penalty lime factory?

Now that is predestination! Those are the twists of fate! And how can we then discern the meaning of one individual human life? . . .

We have not yet described the group escapes, and there were many of them too. They say that in 1956 a whole small camp escaped near Monchegorsk.

The history of all the escapes from the Archipelago would be a list too long to be read, too long to be leafed through. And any one person who wrote a book solely about escapes, to spare his reader and himself, would be forced to omit hundreds of cases.

Chapter 15

■

Punishments

Among the many joyous renunciations brought us by the new world were the renunciation of exploitation, the renunciation of colonies, the renunciation of obligatory military service, the renunciation of secret diplomacy, secret assignments and transfers, the renunciation of secret police, the renunciation of "divine law," and many, many other fairy-tale renunciations in addition. But not, to be sure, a renunciation of prisons. (They didn't break down the walls, but merely inserted a "new class content" inside them.) However, there was an unqualified renunciation of *punishment blocks*—that pitiless torture which could have been conceived only by the hate-filled minds of bourgeois prison keepers. The Corrective Labor Code of 1924 did allow, it is true, the isolation in a separate cell of especially troublesome prisoners, but it warned: This separate cell must in no wise resemble a punishment cell; it must be dry, well lit, and provided with the appurtenances for sleeping.

At that point it must have seemed ridiculous not only to the prison keepers but to the prisoners themselves that for some reason or other there was no punishment cell, that it should have been banned.

The Corrective Labor Code of 1933, which "was in effect" (i.e., not in effect) until the beginning of the sixties, turned out to be even more humane: it forbade even isolation in a separate cell!

But this was not because the times had become more complaisant but because other gradations of intracamp punishment had by this time been mastered and adopted by following the path of experiment. In them it was not loneliness but the collective that drove you mad, and on top of that those who were being punished had to *bend their backs:*

- Strict Regimen Companies ("RUR's"), which were subsequently replaced by
- Strict Regimen Barracks ("BUR's"), which were Penalty Work Brigades, and
- Strict Regimen Camp Compounds ("ZUR's"), penalty compounds.

And sometime later and somehow unnoticed they added—not punishment cells, oh, no! but—

- Penalty Isolators—*"ShIzo's"*

For if you didn't intimidate the prisoner, if there was no further punishment you could apply—how could he be compelled to submit to the regimen?

And where could you put the captured fugitives?

What was the ShIzo given for? For whatever they felt like: You didn't please your chief; you didn't say hello the way you should have; you didn't get up on time; you didn't go to bed on time; you were late for roll call; you took the wrong path; you were wrongly dressed; you smoked where it was forbidden; you kept extra things in your barracks—take a day, three, five. You failed to fulfill the work norm, you were caught with a broad —take five, seven, or ten. And for *work shirkers* there was even fifteen days. And even though, according to the law (what law?), fifteen days was the maximum in penalty cells (though according to the Corrective Labor Code of 1933 even that was impermissible!), this accordion could be stretched out to a whole year. In 1932 in Dmitlag (this is something Averbakh writes about —black on white!) they used to give *one year* of ShIzo for *self-mutilation!* And if one bears in mind that they used to refuse treatment in such cases, then this meant they used to put a sick, wounded person in a punishment cell to rot—for a whole year!

What was required of a ShIzo? It had to be: (a) cold; (b) damp; (c) dark; (d) for starvation. Therefore there was no heat.

(Lipai: not even when the temperature outside was 22 degrees below zero Fahrenheit.) They did not replace missing glass panes in the winter. They allowed the walls to get damp. (Or else they put the penalty-block cellar in moist ground.) The windows were microscopic or else there were none at all (more usual). They fed a *"Stalin" ration* of ten and a half ounces a day and issued a "hot" meal, consisting of thin gruel, only on the third, sixth, and ninth days of your imprisonment there. But at Vorkuta-Vom they gave only seven ounces of bread, and a piece of *raw* fish in place of a *hot* dish on the third day. This is the framework in which one has to imagine all the penalty cells.

It is very naïve to think that a penalty cell has of necessity to be like a cell—with a roof, door, and lock. Not at all! At Kuranakh-Sala, at a temperature of minus 58 degrees Fahrenheit, the punishment cell was a sodden frame of logs. (The free physician Andreyev said: "I, as a *physician,* declare it *possible* to put a prisoner in that kind of punishment cell.") Let us leap the entire Archipelago: at that same Vorkuta-Vom in 1937, the punishment cell for work shirkers was a log frame *without a roof.* And in addition there was *a plain hole in the ground.* Arnold Rappoport lived in a hole like that (to get shelter from the rain they used to pull some kind of rag over themselves), like Diogenes in a barrel. Here is how they were fed: The jailer came out of the gatehouse hut with the bread rations and called to the men inside the log frame: "Come out and get your rations!" But no sooner did they stick their heads out of the log frame than the guard on the watchtower aimed his rifle: "Stop. I'll shoot!" And the jailer acted astonished: "What, you don't want your bread? Well, then, I'll leave." And he simply hurled the bread and fish down into the pit in the rain-soaked clay.

In the Mariinsk Camp (as in many others, of course) there was snow on the walls of the punishment cell—and in such-and-such a punishment cell the prisoners were not allowed to keep their camp clothes on but were forced *to undress to their underwear.* Every half-hour the jailer would let down the food shelf in the door and advise I. V. Shved: "Hey, you won't last, you'll die! You would do better to go out logging!" And Shved decided he was right, that he would have the sheet pulled over his face more quickly if he stayed! He went out into the woods. Out of twelve and a half years in the camps Shved spent a total of 148 days in punishment cells. He had been punished for everything one could imagine! For refusing to be an orderly in *India* (the hoodlums' barracks) he got six months in a penalty camp. For refusing to allow himself to be transferred from a well-fed agricultural work party to logging—he was sentenced a second time for economic counterrevolution, 58-14, and got another ten years. Any thief not wanting to go to a penalty camp could strike the convoy chief, knock his revolver out of his hands, and he would be sent nowhere. The peaceful political prisoner, however, had no way out—he would have his head forced down between his legs. In the Kolyma in 1938 the punishment cells for the thieves were heated, unlike those for the 58's.

The "BUR's"—the Strict Regimen Barracks—were intended for longer imprisonments. Prisoners were kept there for a month or three months, for a half-year or a year, or without any limit to their term, simply because they were considered dangerous. Once you got yourself on the black list you would be pushed into the BUR at the first opportunity—every May Day and every November holiday, whenever there was an escape or any other unusual camp happening.

The BUR could be the most ordinary kind of barracks, set apart and fenced off by barbed wire, with the prisoners in it being taken out daily to the hardest and most unpleasant work in the camp. It could also be a masonry prison inside the camp with a full prison system—with beatings of prisoners summoned one by one to the jailers' quarters (a favorite method that didn't leave marks was to beat with a felt boot with a brick inside it); with bolts, bars, locks, and peepholes on every door; with concrete floors to the cells and an additional separate punishment cell for BUR inmates.

This was exactly what the Ekibastuz BUR was like (although they had the first type there as well). The prisoners confined in it were kept in cells without sleeping shelves. (They slept on the floor on padded jackets and pea jackets.) A "muzzle" made of sheet iron completely covered the tiny little window below the ceiling. There were nail holes in it, but in the winter the snow covered even these, and it became totally dark in the cell. The electric light was not turned on during the day, which meant that day was darker than night. There was never any ventilation of the cell. For *half a year*—in 1950—the prisoners were not taken on even one fresh-air walk. And so this BUR was very like a fierce prison, and it was hard to see what it had to do with a camp. The prisoners had to urinate inside their cell instead of being taken out to a toilet. The hauling out of the big latrine barrel was considered a privilege by the cell orderlies because it meant a chance to gulp down some fresh air. And a bath . . . was a holiday for everyone. The cell was tightly packed. There was room only to lie down but not to stretch your legs. And this —for half a year. The gruel was water, there were twenty-one ounces of bread and not a crumb of tobacco. If anyone got a parcel from home while he was in the BUR, anything in it which would spoil was "written off" (the administration grabbed it off or else sold it cheap to the trusties). And the rest was put into the storage room to be kept for many, many months. (Whenever such special-regimen prisoners were taken out to work again, they would get a move on to avoid being locked up again.)

Sometimes in this suffocation and immobility the prisoners just couldn't stand it any longer—particularly those being assimilated to the thieves' law who were nervous and self-assertive. (Thieves who got into Ekibastuz were also considered 58's and had no special privileges.) The most popular dodge of the BUR prisoners was to swallow the aluminum tablespoon provided for lunch. Everyone who did this was X-rayed. And only when it had been determined that he was not lying, that he really had a spoon inside him, did they put him in the hospital and cut open his stomach. Lyoshka Karnoukhy repeated this spoon-swallowing caper three times and there was nothing left of his stomach. Kolka Salopayev *played insane:* he hanged himself one night, but the other lads there "saw" him by agreement, tore down the noose, and he was taken to the hospital. Someone else contaminated a thread by pulling it between his teeth and then inserted it with a needle under the skin on his leg. Infection! Hospital! He didn't care whether it was gangrene or not—anything to get out of there.

But the convenience of also getting some work out of the punished prisoners compelled the bosses to set them apart in individual penalty compounds—the "ZUR's." In the "ZUR's," in the first place, the food was worse. For months at a time might be no second course, and the bread ration was reduced. In the bath even in winter there was a broken window, and the women barbers in their padded cotton trousers and padded jackets used to crop the naked prisoners. There might be no mess hall, but they didn't hand out the gruel in the barracks either— you had to go to the kitchen to get it and carry it to the barracks through the frost and eat it there cold. The prisoners died in droves, and the clinic was filled with the dying.

The mere enumeration of penalty compounds will someday constitute an historical investigation of its own, the more so because it will not be easy to carry out. Everything is being erased.

Here is the kind of work they assigned the penalty compounds: harvesting hay twenty miles away from the camp compound, where the prisoners would be quartered in shacks made of hay and had to scythe in swamps with their feet always in water. (When they had friendly guards, they could gather berries while they were at work; vigilant guards would shoot to kill, but they picked berries anyway. They so wanted to eat!) Or laying up silage in the same swampy places amid clouds of mosquitoes and without any protection from them. (Your face and neck were eaten up, covered with scabs, and your eyelids were swollen— a man almost went blind.) Or they might be sent to dig peat in the basin of the Vychegda River; in the winter, they had to open up the frozen strata of silt with a heavy sledge hammer and remove them, take the partly thawed peat from beneath them, and then haul it half a mile uphill on sledges, doing the pulling themselves. (The camp used to look after its horses.) Or they might be sent to work at ordinary earth-moving—in the "earth-moving camp" near Vorkuta, for instance. And then, too, there was the favorite penalty work—the lime quarry and the calcining of lime. And the stone quarries. There is no room to list everything. All the heaviest of the heavy jobs, all the most unbearable of the unbearable jobs—that was penalty labor. And every camp had its own.

The favored candidates for the penalty compounds were: religious believers, stubborn prisoners, and thieves. (Yes, thieves! Here the great system of indoctrination broke down because of the inconsistency of the local instructors.) They kept whole barracks of "nuns" there who had refused to work for the devil. (At the penalty camp for prisoners under convoy at the Pechora State Farm they held them in a penalty block up to their knees in water. In the autumn of 1941 they gave them all 58-14—economic counterrevolution—and shot them.) They sent the priest Father Viktor Shipovalnikov there on charges of conducting "religious propaganda" (he had celebrated vespers for five nurses on Easter Eve). They sent impudent engineers and other brazen intellectuals there. They sent fugitives who had been caught. And also, with sad hearts, they sent *socially friendly* elements who simply refused to assimilate the proletarian ideology. (Because of the complex mental task of classification, we will not reproach the administration for its sometimes unwitting confusion: From Karabas, for example, they sent two cartloads of religious women to the children's colony to look after the camp children there, and at the same time sent some women thieves and syphilitics to the Dolinka penalty sector, Konspai. But they got muddled over whose things to put on which cart, and the syphilitic women thieves were sent to look after the children and the "nuns" to the penalty sector. They later realized what had happened, but left them where they were.)

And often prisoners were sent to penalty compounds for refusal to become informers. The majority died there and naturally cannot speak about themselves. And the murderers from State Security are even less likely to speak of them. The soil scientist Grigoryev was sent to a penalty zone for that, but he survived. Also the editor of the Estonian agricultural magazine, Elmar Nugis.

There were stories of women in this context too. It is impossible to reach a sufficiently balanced judgment on these stories because some intimate element always remains hidden from us. However, here is the story of Irena Nagel as she told it herself. She worked as a typist for the Administrative Section of the Ukhta State Farm, in other words as a very comfortably established trusty. Heavy-set and imposing, she wore her hair in long braids wrapped around her head; and partly for convenience she went around in wide Oriental-type trousers and a jacket cut like a ski jacket. Whoever knows camp life will understand what an enticement this was. A security officer, Junior Lieutenant Sidorenko, expressed a desire to get more intimately acquainted. And Nagel replied: "I would rather be kissed by the lowliest thief in camp! You ought to be ashamed of yourself. I can hear your baby crying in the next room." Repulsed by her outburst, the security officer suddenly changed his expression and said: "Surely you don't really think I like you? I merely wanted *to put you to the test*. So here's the way it is: you must *collaborate* with us." She refused and was sent to a penalty camp.

Here are Nagel's impressions of the first night she spent there. In the women's barracks there were "nuns" and women thieves.[1] Five girls were walking about wrapped in sheets. Playing cards the day before, the women thieves had gambled and lost the girls' clothes and so had ordered them to take them off and turn them over. Suddenly a band of men thieves came in with a guitar —in underpants and felt hats. They sang their thieves' songs like some sort of serenade. All at once some other men thieves ran in in a rage, grabbed one of their own wenches, threw her on the floor, beat her with a bench, and trampled her. She screamed, but then couldn't scream any more and stopped. No one interfered and everyone just sat there and acted as if they didn't notice what was going on. Later the medical assistant came in. "Who beat you up?" "I fell off the bunk," answered the beaten-up girl. At cards that same evening they also "lost" Nagel, but she was saved by the *bitch* Vaska the Crooked: he squealed to the chief and the chief took Nagel to spend the night at the gatehouse.

The penalty work parties (like Parma Nyroblag, in the depths of the taiga) ·were also often regarded as penalty assignments both for enlisted men in the guards and for officers, and offenders were also sent there; even more often, however, they substituted trusty guards.

If there was no law and no justice in the ordinary camps, then all the more don't look for them in the penalty camps. The thieves played their dirty tricks just as they pleased and went around openly with knives. (The Vorkuta "Earth-Moving" Camp, in 1946.) And the jailers hid from the thieves outside the camp compound, and this was at a time when the 58's still constituted a majority.

At the penalty camp of Dzhantui near Pechora the thieves burned down two barracks out of mischief, stopped the cooking,

---

1. Who else in all world history ever equated them? What kind of person do you have to be to mix them together?

drove away the cooks, and cut the throats of two officers. The remaining officers there, even under threat of being demoted to the ranks, refused to enter the camp compound.

In cases like this, the chiefs saved themselves by resorting to the maxim "Divide and conquer"; they appointed as commandant of Dzhantui a *bitch* urgently brought in with his assistants from somewhere else. The very first night he and his gang knifed three thieves and things began to quiet down a little.

It takes a thief to catch a thief, as the proverb had long since foreseen. The fathers of the Archipelago, having, in accordance with the Progressive Doctrine, multiplied these socially friendly elements beyond all rhyme and reason, to the point where they themselves were being choked, could find no other way out of the situation than to split them up and sic them on each other in knife battles. (The war between the thieves and the bitches which shook the Archipelago in the postwar years.)

Of course, despite all their apparent bravado, the thieves themselves also had a hard time in penalty situations. This kind of debauchery was their way of trying to break out somehow. As with all parasites, it was more advantageous for them to live among those they could suck on. Sometimes the thieves cut off their fingers so as not to have to go on penalty work, as, for example, at the celebrated Vorkuta Lime Factory. (Certain recidivists in the postwar period actually had inscribed in their sentence: "To be confined at the Vorkuta Lime Factory." The screws were being turned from on high.)

There everyone went around with knives. The bitches and the thieves cut each other up every day. The cook—a bitch— served as he pleased: some got it thick, some got it thin, and some merely got a whack on the head with the ladle. The work assigner went about with an iron reinforcing rod and killed men on the spot with one single, whistling blow. The bitches kept young boys for pederasty. There were three barracks: the barracks of the bitches, the barracks of the thieves, and the barracks of the "suckers," a hundred in each. The suckers . . . worked: down below, near the camp, was a limestone quarry where lime was extracted; then it was carried in hand barrows up a cliff, where it was poured into cones, leaving flues on the inside; the lime was roasted; they then had to spread out the burning lime amid smoke, soot, and lime powder.

In the Dzhida camps, the penalty sector of Bayangol was famous.

To Revuchi, the penalty camp of Kraslag, even before it had any penalty prisoners, they had sent a "working nucleus" of 150 strong sloggers who had not committed any infractions. It's all very well to talk about penalty labor, but the chiefs have to fulfill their plan regardless! So they simply condemned ordinary sloggers to the penalty camp! They even sent thieves and also long-termers under Section 58—*heavyweights*. And the thieves were scared of these *heavyweights* too, because they had twenty-five-year sentences, and in the postwar situation they could kill a thief without having their prison term extended, and it was no longer considered (as at the canals) a sally of the class enemy.

The working day at Revuchi was supposed to be eleven hours, but in fact, what with marching for three or four miles to the forest and back, it turned out to be fifteen hours altogether. Reveille was at 4:30 A.M., and they got back to the camp compound toward 8 P.M. The zeks quickly began to become *last-leggers*, and, as a result, there were work shirkers. Following the general line-up in the morning they lined these malingerers up in the club, and the work assigner went down the line and picked out some for a *workover*. These malingerers in rope sandals ("shod for the season," 76 degrees below zero Fahrenheit) and thin pea jackets were pushed outside the compound—and five police dogs were set on them there with orders to "Get 'em!" The dogs tore them, clawed them, and knocked them down. The dogs were then called off and a Chinese came up on a young bull harnessed to a honey wagon, loaded the malingerers into it, carried them off, and dumped the cart from the roadbed into a hollow below. Down there waiting was the brigadier Lyosha Sloboda, who beat the malingerers with a club until they got up and began to work for him. He credited their output to his own brigade, while they got only ten and a half ounces each—a penalty-block ration. (Whoever thought up that whole graduated system was a real little Stalin!)

Galina Iosifovna Serebryakova! Why don't you write *about that?* Why is it that your heroes, sitting there in camp, do nothing, work nowhere, and only talk about Lenin and Stalin?

It was virtually impossible for an ordinary slogger from the 58's to survive in such a penalty camp.

At the penalty work subparty of SevZhelDorlag (chief—Colonel Klyuchkin) there was cannibalism in 1946–1947: people were cut up into meat, cooked, and eaten.

This was on the heels of our people's earth-shaking, historic victory.

Ah, Colonel Klyuchkin! Where did you build yourself your retirement villa?

Chapter 16

■

The Socially Friendly

Let my feeble pen, too, join in praise of this tribe! They have been hailed as pirates, as freebooters, as tramps, as escaped convicts. They have been lauded as noble brigands—from Robin Hood on down to operetta heroes. And we have been assured that they have sensitive hearts, that they plunder the rich and share with the poor. Oh, exalted confreres of Karl Moor! Oh, rebellious, romantic Chelkash! Oh, Benya Krik! Oh, barefoot Odessa lads and Odessa troubadours!

And, indeed, has not all world literature glorified the thieves? It is not for us to reproach François Villon; but neither Hugo nor Balzac could avoid that path; and Pushkin, too, praised the thief principle in his Gypsies. (And what about Byron?) But never have they been so widely glorified and with such unanimity and so consistently as in Soviet literature. (For this there were lofty Theoretical Foundations, it wasn't only a matter of Gorky and Makarenko.) Leonid Utyosov howled nasally from the variety stage—and his delighted fans howled back in response. And it was in speech heavily influenced by the thieves' jargon that the Baltic and Black Sea "little brothers" of Vishnevsky and Pogodin spoke. And it was precisely this thieves' jargon that gave most of the expressiveness to their humor. Who was there who was not breathless with sacred emotion in describing the thieves to us—their vivid, unreined nihilism at the beginning, and their dialectical "reforging" at the end—starting with Mayakovsky (and, in his footsteps, Shostakovich with his ballet *The Young Lady and the Hooligan*) and including Leonov, Selvinsky,

Inber—and you could go on and on? The cult of the thieves proved to be infectious in an epoch in which literature was drying up for lack of positive heroes. Even a writer so far from the official Party line as Viktor Nekrasov could find no better model to exemplify Russian heroism than the thief Master Sergeant Chumak (*In the Trenches of Stalingrad*). Even Tatyana Yesenina (*Zhenya, the Miracle of the 20th Century*) gave in to that same kind of hypnosis and drew for us the "innocent" figure of Venka, Jack of Diamonds. Perhaps it was only Tendryakov, with his capacity for looking at the world with an unprejudiced eye, who first expressed for us without licking his chops the essence of the thief, showing his spiritual loathsomeness—in *Three, Seven, Ace*. Aldan-Semyonov is supposed to have been in camp himself, but in his "Bas-Relief on the Cliff" he has invented absolute nonsense: He has a thief, Sasha Aleksandrov, influenced by the Communist Petrakov, whom all the bandits allegedly respect because he knew Lenin and helped destroy Kolchak (a totally fictitious motivation dating from Averbakh's time), who is supposed to have assembled a work brigade from the last-leggers without living off them! (But *they did live off them!* As Aldan-Semyonov knows very well!) And this thief even made sure they were properly fed! And for this he even won from the free employees at cards! As if he didn't really need those winnings for the money to buy enough tea for *a trip*. And what a stupid mothballed anecdote for the sixties!

Once in 1946 on a summer evening in the minicamp at the Kaluga Gates in Moscow, a thief lay stomach-down on the windowsill of the third floor and in a loud voice began to sing one thieves' song after another. His songs carried easily over the gatehouse and barbed wire and could be heard out on the sidewalks of Bolshaya Kaluga Street, at the trolleybus stop there, and also in the nearby section of Neskuchny Park. These songs glorified the "easy life"—of murder, burglary, assault. And not only did none of the jailers, instructors, or guards on watch interfere with him, but it didn't even occur to anyone to shout at him. This propaganda of the thieves' views, it seemed, in no way contradicted the structure of our lives or threatened it. I sat there in the compound and thought: What would happen if at this moment I were to climb up to the third floor and from the same window in as loud a voice sang something about the fate of the Russian POW, such as "Where Are You, Where Are You?," a song I had heard in counterintelligence headquarters at the front? Or what if I myself had composed something on the fate of the humiliated and trampled front-line soldier? What an uproar there would have been! How fast they would have come running! And right in all that hustle and bustle they would have run up the fire ladder to get me, not waiting until I was surrounded. They would have gagged me, tied my hands, and *pasted* a second *term* on me! Yet the thief went right on singing, and the free Muscovites listened—as if that were the most ordinary thing in the world.

Now, *historically*, as they never tire of saying in our country, this didn't happen all at once. In Old Russia there existed (just as there still exists in the West) an incorrect view of thieves as incorrigible, permanent criminals (a "nucleus of criminality"). Because of this the politicals were segregated from them on prisoner transports and in prisons. And also because of this the administration, as P. Yakubovich testifies, broke their licentiousness and their supremacy in the prisoners' world by forbidding them to occupy positions in the artels, income-producing positions, and by decisively taking the side of the other hard-labor prisoners. "Sakhalin swallowed them up by the thousands and never let them go." In Old Russia there was just one single formula to be applied to the criminal recidivists: "Make them bow their heads beneath the iron yoke of the law!" (Urusov.) And so it was that up to 1914 the thieves did not play the boss either in Russia as a whole or in Russian prisons.

But the shackles fell and freedom dawned. In the desertion of millions in 1917, and then in the Civil War, all human passions were largely unleashed, and those of the thieves most of all, and they no longer wished to bow their heads beneath the yoke; moreover, they were informed that they didn't have to. It was found both useful and amusing that they were enemies of private property and therefore a revolutionary force which had to be guided into the mainstream of the proletariat, yes, and this would constitute no special difficulty. An unprecedented multitude of newcomers also grew up to join them, consisting of the orphans of the Civil War and famine—homeless waifs or "besprizorniki,"* and hoodlums. They warmed themselves at asphalt caldrons during the New Economic Policy, and for their first lessons they learned to cut ladies' purses off their arms and lift suitcases through train windows with hooks. Reasoning on a social basis: wasn't the *environment* to blame for everything? So let us re-educate these healthy lumpenproletarians and introduce them into the system of conscious life! And the first communes came into existence for this purpose, and the first children's colonies, and the motion picture *The Road to Life*.* (But what they didn't notice was that the "besprizorniki" *were not full-blown thieves.* And the reforming of the "besprizorniki" did not say anything: they had not yet had time to be totally spoiled.)

And now, when more than forty years have gone by, one can look around and begin to have doubts: Who re-educated whom? Did the Chekists re-educate the thieves, or the thieves the Chekists? The urka—the habitual thief—who adopted the Chekist faith became a *bitch*, and his fellow thieves would cut his throat. The Chekist who acquired the psychology of the thief was an *energetic* interrogator of the thirties and forties, or else a *resolute* camp chief—such men were appreciated. They got the service promotions.

And the psychology of the urki was exceedingly simple and very easy to acquire:

1. I want to live and enjoy myself; and f—— the rest!
2. Whoever is the strongest is right!
3. If they aren't [beat]ing you, then don't lie down and ask for it.* (In other words: As long as they're beating up someone else, don't stick up for the ones being beaten. Wait your own turn.)

Beat up your submissive enemies one at a time! Somehow this is a very familiar law. It is what Hitler did. It is what Stalin did.

How much Sheinin has lisped into our ears about the "unique code" of the thieves, about the "honor" of their word. You read him and they all turn into Don Quixotes and patriots! But just wait till you meet those ugly mugs in a cell or a Black Maria. . . .

Come on now, stop lying, you mercenary pens! You who have observed the Russian thieves through a steamship rail or across an interrogator's desk! You who have never encountered the thieves when you were defenseless.

The thieves—the urki—are not Robin Hoods! When they want, they steal from last-leggers! When they want they are not squeamish about—taking the last footcloths off a man freezing to death. Their great slogan is: "You today, me tomorrow!"

But perhaps they really are patriots? Why don't they steal from the state? Why don't they plunder the *special* country villas? Why don't they stop the long black limousines? Is it because they expect to encounter the conqueror of Kolchak there? No, it is because those automobiles and dachas are well defended. And because stores and warehouses are shielded by the law. Because the realist Stalin understood long ago that all this was just a big buzz—this re-education of the urki. And he redirected their energy, sicked them on the citizens of his own country.

Here is what our laws were like for thirty years—to 1947: For robbery of the state, embezzlement of state funds, a packing case from a warehouse, for three potatoes from a collective farm —ten years! (After 1947 it was as much as twenty!) But robbery of a *free person?* Suppose they cleaned out an apartment, carting off on a truck everything the family had acquired in a lifetime. If it was not accompanied by murder, then the sentence was *up to one year*, sometimes six months.

The thieves flourished because they were encouraged.

Through its laws the Stalinist power said to the thieves clearly: Do not steal from me! Steal from private persons! You see, private property is a belch from the past. (But "personally assigned" VIP property is the hope of the future. . . .)

And the thieves . . . understood. In their intrepid stories and songs, did they go to steal where it was difficult, dangerous, where they could lose their heads? No. Greedy cowards, they pushed their way in where they were encouraged to push their way in—they stripped the clothes from solitary passers-by and stole from unguarded apartments.

The twenties, the thirties, the forties, the fifties! Who does not remember that eternal threat hovering over the citizen: Don't go where it's dark! Don't come home late! Don't wear your watch! Don't carry money with you! Don't leave the apartment empty! Locks! Shutters! Dogs! (And nowadays those writers of satirical columns who weren't cleaned out at the time ridicule these loyal watchdogs. . . .)[1]

1. In the consistent struggle against the individuality of a man, first they deprived him of one friend—the horse, promising a tractor in its place. As if a horse were only draft power for a plow, and not, instead, your living

How many citizens who were robbed knew that the police didn't even bother to look for the criminals, didn't even set a case in motion, so as not to spoil their record of completed cases—why should they sweat to catch a thief if he would be given only six months, and then be given three months off for good behavior? And anyway, it wasn't certain that the bandits would even be tried when caught. After all, prosecutors[2] "lowered the crime rate"—something demanded of them at every conference—by the curious method of simply quashing cases, especially if they foresaw that there would be many defendants.

Finally, sentences were bound to be reduced, and of course for habitual criminals especially. Watch out there now, witness in the courtroom! They will all be back soon, and it'll be a knife in the back of anyone who gave testimony!

Therefore, if you see someone crawling through a window, or slitting a pocket, or your neighbor's suitcase being ripped open—shut your eyes! Walk by! You didn't see anything!

That's how the thieves have trained us—the thieves and our laws!

In September, 1955, the *Literaturnaya Gazeta* (which delivers bold judgments on many matters—but not on literature) shed crocodile tears in a major article: At night on a Moscow street a man had been noisily battered to death beneath the windows of two families. It emerged later that both families (our! Soviet! families) were awake, looked out the window, but did not go to help: the wives did not allow their husbands to go. And one of the residents in the same house (maybe he, too, was wakened,

---

friend in sorrow and happiness, a member of your family, part of your own heart! And soon afterward they began a persistent campaign against his second friend—the dog. Dogs had to be registered; they were hauled off to the skinners; and often special teams from the local soviets simply shot dead every dog they came across. And there were no hygienic or miserly economic reasons for this—the basis was much more profound: After all, a dog doesn't listen to the radio, doesn't read the papers; he is a citizen who is, so to speak, beyond the control of the state, a physically strong one, moreover, but his strength goes not to the state but to defend his master as *an individual*, without regard to any kind of decree that might be issued against him in the local soviet and any kind of warrant they might come to him with at night. In Bulgaria in 1960 the citizens were told, and not as a joke either, to fatten up . . . pigs *instead of* their dogs! Pigs don't have principles. They grow their meat for everyone who has a knife. However, the persecution of dogs never extended to those dogs who were useful to the state—the Security and guard dogs.

2. Like the prosecutor Golushko, *Izvestiya*, February 27, 1964.

but the article says nothing about that), a member of the Party since 1916, a retired colonel (evidently languishing without anything to do), had taken on himself the duty of public accuser. He was going around to editorial offices and courts demanding that those two families be charged with *abetting* a murder. And the journalist thundered also: This didn't come within the terms of the Criminal Code, but it was a disgrace! A disgrace!

Yes, it was a disgrace, but *for whom?* As always in our prejudiced press, everything was said in this essay except the main thing. That:

1. "The Voroshilov Amnesty" of March 27, 1953, seeking to win popularity with the people, flooded the whole country with a wave of murderers, bandits, and thieves, who had with great difficulty been rounded up after the war. (To pardon a thief is to kill a good man.)

2. In the Criminal Code of 1926 there was a most stupid Article 139—"on the limits of necessary self-defense"—according to which you had the right to unsheath your knife only after the criminal's knife was hovering over you. And you could stab him only after he had stabbed you. And otherwise *you* would be the one put on trial. (And there was no article in our legislation saying that the greater criminal was the one who attacked someone weaker than himself.) This fear of exceeding the measure of necessary self-defense led to total spinelessness as a national characteristic. A hoodlum once began to beat up the Red Army man Aleksandr Zakharov outside a club. Zakharov took out a folding penknife and killed the hoodlum. And for this he got . . . ten years for plain murder! "And what was I supposed to do?" he asked, astonished. Prosecutor Artsishevsky replied: "You should have fled!"

So tell me, *who* creates hoodlums?!

3. The state, in its Criminal Code, forbids citizens to have firearms or other weapons, but *does not itself undertake* to defend them! The state turns its citizens over to the power of the bandits —and then through the press dares to summon them to "social resistance" against these bandits. Resistance with *what?* With umbrellas? With rolling pins? First they multiplied the bandits and then, in order to resist them, began to assemble people's vigilantes (druzhina),* which by acting *outside the legislation* sometimes turned into the very same thing. But then, how could

they "have simply forced them to bow their heads beneath the yoke of the law" from the very beginning! The One-and-Only True Teaching again blocked the path.

So what would have happened if those wives had let their husbands go out, and if the husbands had run out with clubs? Either the bandits would have killed them too—which is more likely—or else they would have killed the bandits—and gone to prison for exceeding the limits of necessary self-defense. The retired colonel taking his dog out for its morning walk could in both cases have relished the consequences.

Any genuine initiative like that shown in the French film *The Waterfront at Dawn*, in which the workers went about catching thieves and punishing them themselves without the knowledge of the authorities, would in our country have been suppressed as illicit! Could one even *imagine* that way of thinking and that sort of film in our country?

But that is not all! There is one more important feature of our public life which helps thieves and bandits prosper—*fear of publicity*. Our newspapers are filled with reports on production victories which are a big bore to everyone, but you will find no reports of trials or crime in them. (After all, according to the Progressive Doctrine, criminal activity arises only from the presence of classes; we have no classes in our country, therefore there is no crime and therefore you cannot write about it in the press! We simply cannot afford to give the American newspapers evidence that we have not fallen behind the United States in criminal activity!) If there is a murder in the West, photographs of the criminal are plastered on the walls of buildings, they peer out at one from the counters of bars, the windows of streetcars, and the criminal feels himself a persecuted rat. If a brazen murder is committed here, the press is silent, there are no photographs, the murderer goes sixty miles away to another province and lives there in peace and quiet. And the Minister of Internal Affairs will not have to answer questions in parliament as to why the criminal has not been found; after all, no one knows about the case except the inhabitants of that little town. If they find him—well and good; if not—that is all right too. The murderer . . . hasn't violated the state border, so he isn't dangerous enough (to the state) to justify proclaiming a countrywide search for him.

It was the same with criminal activity as it was with malaria. It was simply announced one day that it no longer existed in our country, and from then on it became impossible to treat it or even to diagnose it.

Of course, both the police and the courts were inclined to *close cases*. But that led to formalities which played even more into the hands of the real murderers and bandits: they would accuse *anyone at all* of an unsolved case, whoever happened to be nearest at hand, and they were particularly fond of *hanging* several crimes on someone already guilty of one. It is worthwhile recalling here the case of Pyotr Kizilov[3] who was twice, without any clues or evidence, sentenced to be shot (!) for a murder he had *not* committed. Or the case of Alekseyentsev,[4] which was similar. If lawyer Popov's letter about the Kizilov case had come not to *Izvestiya* but to the *Times*, it would have resulted in a change of the queen's judge or a government crisis. But in our country, four months later, the provincial Party committee (why the provincial Party committee—was the court subordinate to it?) met and, taking into consideration the "youth and lack of experience" of the investigator (why do they entrust people's fates to such people?) and his "participation in the War of the Fatherland" (for some reason they didn't take it into consideration with *us* in our time!), entered an official reprimand in one person's record and wagged a threatening finger at somebody else. And for using *torture* (this being already after the Twentieth Congress), the chief executioner Yakovenko was allegedly sentenced to three years a full half-year later, but since he was "one of our own" and was acting on instructions, carrying out orders from above—is it likely that he was actually compelled to serve his sentence? Such vindictiveness? But defense lawyer Popov, for example, had to be dealt with and driven out of Belgorod: He should learn the thieves', the countrywide, principle "If they're not [beat]ing you—then don't lie down and ask for it."

And so it is that anyone who speaks out on behalf of justice comes to repent thrice over, eight times over, that he ever did so. This is how the system of punishment is turned around so as to be an encouragement to thieves. And for decades they flourished like an unruly mold on our freedom, and in prisons and in camps.

3. *Izvestiya,* December 11, 1959, and April, 1960.
4. *Izvestiya,* January 30, 1960.

■

And there is always that sanctifying lofty theory for every-thing. It was by no means the least significant of our literary fig-ures who determined that the thieves were our allies in the build-ing of Communism. This was set forth in textbooks on Soviet corrective-labor policy (there were such textbooks, they were published!), in dissertations and scientific essays on camp man-agement, and in the most practical way of all—in the regulations on which the high-ranking camp officials were trained. All this flowed from the One-and-Only True Teaching, which explained all the iridescent life of humanity . . . in terms of the class struggle and it alone.

And here is how it was worked out. Professional criminals can in no sense be equated with capitalist elements (i.e., engineers, students, agronomists, and "nuns"), for the latter are steadfastly hostile to the dictatorship of the proletariat, while the former are only (!) politically unstable! (A professional murderer is *only* politically unstable!) The lumpenproletarian is not a property owner, and therefore cannot ally himself with the hostile-class elements, but will much more willingly ally himself with the proletariat (you just wait!). That is why in the official terminol-ogy of Gulag they are called *socially friendly* elements. (Tell me who your friends are . . .) That is why the regulations repeated over and over again: *Trust* the recidivist criminals! That is why through the Cultural and Educational Section a consistent effort was supposed to be made to explain to the thieves the unity of their class interests with those of all the workers, to indoctrinate them in a "suspicious and hostile attitude toward the 'kulaks' and counterrevolutionaries," and the authorities were to "*place their hopes* in these attitudes"! (Remember Averbakh: He taught you to steal! You never would have stolen on your own! And re-member: Fan the class struggle in the camps.)

The "packed-up"[5] thief G. Minayev wrote me a letter in the *Literaturnaya Gazeta*:[6] "I was even proud that although a thief I

5. "Zavyazat"—"to knot up" (one's bag) = "to pack up"—was thieves' jargon for leaving the thieves' law with the consent of the underworld to join the life of the suckers.
6. November 29, 1962.

was not a traitor and betrayer. On every convenient occasion they tried to teach us thieves that we were not lost to our Motherland, that even if we were profligate sons, we were nonetheless sons. But there was no place for the 'Fascists' on this earth."

And the theory also held that it was necessary to study and make use of the *best traits* of the thieves. They loved romanticism? So "the orders of the camp chiefs must be enveloped in an aura of romanticism." They strove toward heroism? Give them the heroism of work! (If they would accept it . . .) They had an adventurous spirit? Give them the adventure of competition! (Those who know both the camps and the thieves find it hard to believe that all this was not written by imbeciles.) Were they conceited? Did they like to be the center of attention? Play up to their conceit with praise, with honors! Promote them into positions of leadership! Particularly the *ringleaders*, so as to employ their already established *authority* among the thieves for the purposes of the camp. (That is exactly what it says in Averbakh's monograph: the authority of the ringleaders!)

But when this elegant theory came down to earth in camps, here is what emerged from it: The most inveterate and hardened thieves were given unbridled power on the islands of the Archipelago, in camp districts, and in camps—power over the population of their own country, over the peasants, the petty bourgeoisie, and the intelligentsia, power they had never before had in history, never in any state in all the world, power which they couldn't even dream of out in freedom. And now they were given all other people as slaves. What bandit would ever decline such power? The *central thieves*, the top-level thieves, totally controlled the camp districts. They lived in individual "cabins" or tents with their own temporary wives. (Or arbitrarily picking over the "smooth broads" from among their subjects, they had the intellectual women 58's and the girl students to vary their menu. In Norillag, Chavdarov heard a moll offer her thief husband: "Would you like me to treat you to a sixteen-year-old collective-farm girl?" This was a peasant girl who had been sent to the North for ten years because of one kilo of grain. The girl tried to resist, but the moll soon broke her will: "I'll cut you up! Do you think . . . I'm any worse than you? I lie under him!") And they had their own *lackeys* too—servants from among the sloggers who carried out their chamber pots. They had their food prepared separately, using the little bit of meat and good fat issued for the common pot. The thieves who were one rank lower carried out the managerial tasks of the work assigners, the deputies for auxiliary services, and the commandants, and in the morning they used to stand in pairs, with clubs, at the exits from the tents for two and command: "Leave without the last one!" The lesser hoodlums were used to beat up the work shirkers— that is, those who no longer had the strength left to drag themselves to work. (The chief of Taimyr Peninsula used to drive up to the line-up in his sedan and admire the way the thieves beat up the 58's.) Lastly, the thieves who were able to "chirp"—in other words, to talk glibly—washed the dirt off their necks and were appointed *instructors*. They gave speeches, lectured the 58's on how to live, themselves lived on what they stole, and got time off sentence. On the Belomor Canal an ugly mug like that—an instructor from among the socially friendly—who understood nothing about the business of construction, could abrogate the construction orders of a socially hostile construction supervisor.

And this was not only a question of theory translated into practice, but also of the harmony of everyday life. It was better for the thieves that way. And it was quieter and easier for the chiefs that way: not to tire their arms (with beatings) or their throats, not to get involved in details, and even not to appear in the camp compound. And it was much better for the business of oppression; the thieves carried it out much more brazenly, much more brutally, and without the least fear of responsibility before the law.

But even in places where the thieves were not given such power, they were all, on the basis of this same class theory, very much favored. If the thieves left the camp compound, that was the biggest sacrifice that could be asked of them. At work they could lie about as much as they pleased, smoke, tell their stories (of victories, escapes, heroism), and warm themselves in the sun in summer and at the bonfire in winter. Their bonfires were never touched by the guards, but the bonfires of the 58's were scattered and stamped out. But the *cubes*—the cubic yards—of timber, earth, or coal were then stolen from the 58's.[7] And in addition

---

7. The custom of living off someone else's *cubage*—work output—is maintained by the thief after he is released too, even though at first glance this would contradict his adherence to socialism. In 1951 at Oimyakon (Ust-Nera), the

they even took thieves to the rallies of shock workers, which on the whole were rallies of the recidivists (Dmitlag, and the Belomor Canal).

Now here is one female thief—Beregovaya. (Illustration No. 38.) She got herself into the glorious chronicles of the Moscow-Volga Canal. She was the scourge of every jail she was ever in and raised hell in every police station. If she ever had a whim to do some work, she immediately destroyed whatever she had done. With her necklace of sentences she had been sent to Dmitlag in July, 1933. The chapter of legends continues: She went into the *India* barracks and, to her astonishment (and the only thing believable is that astonishment), heard no mother oaths and saw no card games. They were supposed to have explained to her that the thieves there enjoyed their work. And she *immediately* went off to the excavations and even began to work "well." (Read this to mean that they credited her with the cubic yards of other people—just look at that face!) And then comes the chapter of truth: In October (when it got cold) she went to the physician, and even though she was not ill she asked him (with a knife up her sleeve?) for several days off. The physician willingly agreed (he always had many places available!). And the work assigner was an old girl friend of Beregovaya named Polyakova, and on her own account she added two weeks of loafing by setting up fake workdays for her. (More cubic yards were stolen from the sloggers.) And right then and there, seeing the enviable life of a work assigner, Beregovaya decided she would like to become a *bitch* too. And that very day, when Polyakova wakened her to go out to line-up, Beregovaya declared she would not go out to dig dirt before she had exposed Polyakova's machinations with workdays, output, and rations. (She was not particularly held

---

thief Krokhalyov was freed and took on a job as a coal miner at that same mine. He never even lifted a sledge, but the mine foreman recorded a record output for him—by stealing from the zeks. Krokhalyov received from eight to nine thousand rubles per month, and he brought the zeks a thousand rubles' worth of food *to bolt*, and they were glad enough of this and kept their mouths shut. In 1953 the brigadier, a prisoner, Milyuchikhin, tried to break up this system. The free thieves cut him up, and he was charged with robbery. He was tried and got a renewal of his twenty years.

Now this note should not be understood as an amendment of the Marxist thesis that the lumpenproletarian is not a property owner. Of course he isn't! Krokhalyov didn't use his eight thousand to build himself a private house; he lost them at cards, drank them, or spent them on the broads.

back by any feeling of gratitude!) She managed to get called in to see the security officer. (The thieves were not afraid of the security officers, because no second term threatened them, but just let some KR women try to avoid going out to work!) And right away she became a brigadier of the lagging men's brigade (evidently she had promised to kick in the teeth of these last-leggers), and then . . . a work assigner in Polyakova's place, and then . . . an instructor in the women's barracks. (This expert in oaths, this card shark, this thief!) And then . . . chief of a con-struction detachment. (She was already ordering engineers around.) And all the red bulletin boards of Dmitlag displayed this toothy *bitch* smiling there (see the picture) in a leather jacket and with a field pouch (filched from someone). Those hands of hers were skilled at beating men. The eyes are those of a witch. This woman was praised by Averbakh!

So easy were the paths of the thieves in camp: a bit of scandal, a bit of betrayal, and from there on beat and stomp.

People will object that it was only the *bitches* who accepted positions, while the "honest thieves" held to the thieves' law. But no matter how much I saw of one and the other, I never could see that one rabble was nobler than the other. The thieves knocked gold teeth out of Estonians' mouths with a poker. The thieves (in Kraslag, in 1941) drowned Lithuanians in the toilet for refusing to turn over a food parcel to them. The thieves used to plunder prisoners sentenced to death. Thieves would jokingly kill the first cellmate who came their way just to get a new inter-rogation and trial, and spend the winter in a warm place, or to get out of a hard camp into which they had fallen. So why men-tion such petty details as stripping the clothes or shoes from some-one out in subzero temperatures? And why mention stolen ra-tions?

No, you'll not get fruit from a stone, nor good from a thief.

The theoreticians of Gulag were indignant; the kulaks (in camp) didn't even regard the thieves as real people (thereby, so to speak, betraying their true bestial colors).

But how can you regard them as people if they tear your heart out of your body and suck on it? All their "romantic bravado" is the bravado of vampires.[8]

8. People in educated circles who have not themselves encountered thieves on their narrow path may object to such a merciless estimate of the thieves' world:

38. Beregovaya

■

But enough! Let us say a word in defense of the thieves also. They had their own "original code" and their own original concept of honor. But it was not a question of their being patriots, as our bureaucrats and writers would have liked to have it, but of their being absolutely consistent materialists and consistent pirates. And even though the dictatorship of the proletariat was so assiduous in courting them, they did not respect it even for one minute.

This tribe came into this world . . . to *live!* And since they were destined to spend as much time in prison as in freedom, then they wanted to gather life's flowers in prison too; and what did they care about—the purpose for which the prison was planned or the suffering of others beside them there? They were unruly, and they enjoyed the fruits of that unruliness there—so why should they worry about the man who bowed his head and died a slave? They had to eat—so they took whatever they could see that was edible and tasty. They had to drink—so they sold the convoy guards the things they had taken from their neighbors for vodka. They had to sleep on something soft—and, despite their manly looks, it was considered quite honorable for them to carry their own pillow with them, as well as a padded blanket or feather quilt. (The more so because one could hide a knife in it very well.) They loved the rays of the beneficent sun, and if they couldn't take a trip to a Black Sea resort, they tanned themselves on the roofs of their construction projects, in the stone quarries, at the mine entrances. (Let someone stupider go down into the mines.) They

---

Was it not a secret love of private property that motivated those whom the thieves so irked? I insist on my own expression: vampires sucking your heart. They defile absolutely everything that for us pertains to the natural sphere of humanity. But is it really so hopeless? After all, the thieves are not born with these traits. But where is the good side of their hearts? I don't know. Probably it has been killed and suppressed by the thieves' law in accordance with which the rest of us are not people. We have already written about the threshold of evildoing. Evidently, the thief who has absorbed the thieves' law has irreversibly crossed some moral threshold. People will also object: But you saw only the petty thieves. The important real thieves, the big shots of the thieves' world, were all shot in 1937. And, in truth, I did not see the thieves of the twenties. But I simply do not have imagination enough to picture them as moral beings.

had magnificent, well-fed muscles, bunched in rippling knots. They surrendered their bronze skin to tattooing and in this way gradually satisfied their artistic, their erotic, even their moral needs: on one another's chests, stomachs, and backs they could admire powerful eagles perched on cliffs or flying through the sky. Or *the big hammer*, the sun, with its rays shooting out in every direction; or women and men copulating; or the individual organs of their sexual enjoyment; and, all of a sudden, next to their hearts were Lenin or Stalin or perhaps both (and this meant exactly the same as the crucifix around a thief's neck). Sometimes they would laugh at a droll stoker hurling coal into their rear orifice, or a monkey engaged in masturbation. And they would read slogans on each other which, even if they were already familiar, they nonetheless dearly loved to repeat! "———— all the girls in the mouth!" And it sounded as triumphant as "I am King Assargodon!" Or else on a girl thief's stomach there might be: "I will die for a hot ————!" And even the modest and tiny moral on an arm, an arm which had already buried a dozen knives in somebody's ribs: "Remember your mother's words!" Or else: "I remember caresses. I remember my mother." (The thieves had a mother cult, a formality, however, which did not mean faithfulness to her teachings.)

In order to intensify their sensations in their swift-running lives they used to love taking drugs. The easiest drug to get was "anasha"—marijuana—from hemp. It was also known among them as *plantchik* and was rolled into a smoke. They even used to sing about it gratefully in their songs:

> Plantchik, plantchik, God's grass tall,
> Joy of pickpockets, one and all.*

Yes, they do not recognize the earthly institution of private property, and in this respect they really are hostile to the bourgeoisie and to those Communists who have dachas and automobiles. Everything they come across on life's path they take as their own (if it is not too dangerous). Even when they have a surfeit of everything, they reach out to grab what belongs to others because any unstolen article makes a thief sick at heart. They wear the clothes they have stolen while they have novelty, until they tire of them, and soon afterward lose them at cards. Card games that last for several nights on end give them their

most powerful sensations, and in this respect they have far outdone the Russian nobility of past eras. They can even gamble *an
eye* for stakes (and tear out the loser's eye on the spot). And
they can also play for *beneath themselves*—the stakes being the
right to use the loser for perverted enjoyment. And when they
lose, they declare a general *frisking* on a barge or in a barracks—
until they find something else belonging to one of the suckers.
And then the game goes on.

The thieves don't like to work, and why should they when
they get food, drink, and clothing without it? Of course, this
constitutes a barrier between them and the working class. (But
does the working class love work that much either? Isn't it for the
bitter money that the working class strains its sinews, having no
other way to earn it?) Not only can the thieves not "be carried
away by their enthusiasm for labor," but labor is repulsive to
them, and they know how to express this dramatically. For example, if they are sent off on an agricultural work party and
forced to leave the camp compound in order to rake up vetch
and oats for forage, they don't simply sit down and rest, but
they gather all the rakes and forks in a heap and set fire to them
and then warm themselves at the bonfire. (Socially hostile foreman! Make a decision. . . .)

When they tried to compel them to fight for their Motherland,
it was useless. Their Motherland is the whole earth. The conscripted thieves went off in transports singing their song as they
swayed back and forth:

> Our cause is right!
> Our cause is left!
> Why is everyone on the lam?
> Why, why indeed?

And then they would steal something, get themselves arrested,
and take a familiar prisoner transport back to prison in the rear.
Even the surviving Trotskyites applied from camp to be allowed
to serve at the front; the thieves did not make any such applications. But when the operational armies began to surge into
Europe, and the smell of booty grew strong, they put on uniforms
and went off to plunder at the heels of the army. (They jokingly
called themselves "The Fifth Ukrainian Front.")

But—and in this, too, they were much more principled than
the 58's—no Zhenka Zhogol or Vaska Kishkenyá, with rolled-

down boot tops, respectfully pronouncing that sacred word "thief," with a one-sided grimace, would ever be caught helping to *strengthen the prison*—digging in posts, stringing barbed wire, trenching the no-man's land at the camp perimeter, repairing the gatehouse, fixing the perimeter lighting. In this lay the thief's honor. Prison had been created as the enemy of his freedom— and he could not work for prison! (However, he did not run any risk of getting Article 58 for refusing to work, whereas the poor enemy of the people would immediately have had Counter-Revolutionary Sabotage hung on him. The thieves were bold and impudent because of their own impunity, for, as the saying goes: Whoever has been mauled by a bear is likely to be afraid of a stump.)

It was totally out of the question to see a thief with a newspaper. The thieves held firm to their belief that politics was twaddle, without relation to real life. Neither did they read books, or at least only very rarely. But they loved oral literature, and any storyteller who could endlessly *string out "novels"* for them after curfew would always be well fed out of their booty and held in esteem by them, as are all storytellers and singers among primitive peoples. These "novels" were a fanciful and rather monotonous amalgam of dime novels about life in high society (obligatorily high society!), peopled with titled viscounts, counts, and marquises, and with their own thieves' legends, their own self-magnification, their own thieves' jargon, and their thieves' concepts of the luxurious life which the hero always had to achieve in the end: the countess would lie down on his "cot," he would smoke only the very best "Kazbek," would own an "onion" —a watch—and his prokhorvá (his boots) would be shined to a high gloss.

Nikolai Pogodin was sent on an official visit to the Belomor Canal and probably used up no small amount of Soviet government money—yet he didn't see through the thieves, didn't understand them, and told lies about everything. Since in our literature nothing has been written about the camps for forty years except Pogodin's play—and the subsequent film—we have to comment on it.

The wretchedness of the KR engineers who stared into the mouths of their instructors and thereby learned how to live does not even require comment. But his *aristocrats*, his thieves, do. Pogodin even contrived not to notice in them their simple characteristic of *robbing by the right of the strong*, not secretly like a pickpocket. He portrayed them all to a man as petty pickpockets, and more than a dozen times he points this up in the play to the point of nausea, and he has the thieves steal from the thieves (utter nonsense! they steal only from the suckers and turn everything over to their ringleader). Neither did Pogodin understand (or he did not wish to understand) the real stimuli of camp work—hunger, beatings, and the collective responsibility of the brigade. He did not even distinguish between the camp inmate who was a "comrade" and the one who was a "citizen." He latched on to only one thing: the "socially friendly" character of the thieves. (Which he was prompted to by the canal administration in Medvezhyegorsk, and even before that by Gorky in Moscow.) And he rushed to show the *"reforging"* of the thieves. And what came out was such an outrageous libel of the thieves that even I want to defend them against it.

They are much smarter than Pogodin shows them—or Sheinin either. And you couldn't buy them with some kind of cheap *reforging*, simply because their world outlook was closer to real life that that of the prison chiefs—it was more integrated and contained no elements of idealism whatever! Yet all those incantations to starving people to work and die at work—pure idealism. And if in speaking to a citizen chief or a correspondent from Moscow or at an absurd meeting, there appeared a tear in their eye and a tremor in their voice—that was because they were playing a well-calculated role aimed at getting them privileges or time off sentence. And inside himself meanwhile the thief was laughing the whole time! The thieves understood the joke very well indeed. (But the visiting writers from the capital didn't.) It was impossible for the *bitch* Mitya to enter the cell of a Strict Regimen Company unarmed, without a jailer, and for the local thief ringleader Kostya to crawl beneath the bunks to hide from him! Kostya, of course, had a knife ready, and if he hadn't, he would have hurled himself on Mitya to choke him, and one of the two would have been dead. Now that was no joke—just the opposite—but Pogodin creates a banal joke. The horrifying hypocrisy of the "re-education" of Sonya (why? what forced her to take up a wheelbarrow?) and through her Kostya too?! And the two thieves becoming guards? (The nonpolitical offenders could have done that, but not thieves!) And all that competition between brigades was quite out of the question for the cynical, sober thieves—except maybe for the sake of laughs at the free workers. And the most irritatingly false note of all was the thieves' asking to be given the rules for creating a commune!

It would have been impossible to slander the thieves more or to make them more stupid! The thieves asking for *rules!* The thieves knew their *own* rules perfectly well—from the first robbery to the last knife blow in the neck. When you could beat a person who was down on the ground. And when five could attack one. And when they could attack a person who was sleeping. And for *their own* commune they had rules which predated the *Communist Manifesto.*

Their commune, more precisely their world, was a separate world within our world, and the strict laws which for centuries had existed in it for strengthening that world did not in any degree depend on our "suckers" legislation or even on the Party Congresses. They had their own laws of seniority, by which their ringleaders were not elected at all, yet when they entered a cell or a camp compound already wore their crown of power and were immediately recognized as chiefs. These ringleaders might have strong intellectual capacities, and always had a clear comprehension of the thieves' philosophy, as well as a sufficient number of murders and robberies behind them. The thieves had their own courts ("pravílki"), founded on the code of thieves' "honor" and tradition. The sentences of the court were merciless and were executed implacably, even if the condemned person was quite out of reach and in a completely different camp compound. (The types of punishment inflicted were unusual; they might all jump in turn from the upper bunks onto a convicted person lying on the floor and thus break his rib cage.)

And what did their word "frayersky"—"of the suckers"— mean? It meant what was universally human, what pertained to all normal people. And it was precisely this universally human world, *our* world, with its morals, customs, and mutual relationships, which was most hateful to the thieves, most subject to their ridicule, counterposed most sharply to their own antisocial, antipublic *kubla*—or clan.

No, it was not "re-education" which began to break the back of the thieves' world (the "re-education" merely helped them return faster to new robberies); it was when, in the fifties, brushing off class theory and social friendliness, Stalin gave orders that the thieves be incarcerated in isolators, in solitary long-term cells, and even that new prisons be built for them (the "*shut-ups*," as the thieves called them).

In these "shut-ups," or isolators, the thieves swiftly wilted, sickened, and began to die. Because a parasite cannot live in isolation, by itself. It has to live *on somebody*, twining itself around the victim.

Chapter 17

■

The Kids

The Archipelago had many ugly mugs and many bared fangs. No matter what side you approached it from, there wasn't one you could admire. But perhaps the most abominable of all was that maw that swallowed up *the kids*.

The kids were not at all those besprizorniki or waifs in drab tatters who scurried hither and thither thieving and warming themselves at asphalt caldrons on the streets, without whom one could not picture the urban life of the twenties. The waifs were taken from the streets—not from their families—into the colonies for juvenile delinquents (there was one attached to the People's Commissariat of Education as early as 1920; it would be interesting to know, too, how things went with juvenile offenders before the Revolution), into workhouses for juveniles (which existed from 1921 to 1930 and had bars, bolts, and jailers, so that in the outworn bourgeois terminology they could have been called prisons), and also into the "Labor Communes of the OGPU" from 1924 on. They had been orphaned by the Civil War, by its famine, by social disorganization, the execution of their parents, or the death of the latter at the front, and at that time justice really did try to return these children to the mainstream of life, removing them from their street apprenticeship as thieves. Factory apprenticeship began in the labor communes. And this was a privileged situation in the context of those years of unemployment, and many of the lads there learned with a will. From 1930 on, for sentenced juveniles, Factory Apprenticeship Schools of a special type were created, under the People's Commissariat of

Justice. The young offenders had to work from four to six hours a day, for which they received wages on the basis of the All-Union Code of Labor Laws, and for the rest of their day they studied and played. And perhaps things might have been set to rights on this path.

But where did the young offenders come from? They came from Article 12 of the Criminal Code of 1926, which permitted children *from the age of twelve* to be sentenced for theft, assault, mutilation, and murder (Article 58 offenses were also included under this heading), but they had to be given moderate sentences, not "the whole works" like adults. Here was the first crawl hole into the Archipelago for the future "kids"—but it was not yet a wide gate.

We are not going to omit one interesting statistic: In 1927 prisoners aged sixteen (they didn't count the younger ones) to twenty-four represented 48 percent of all prisoners.[1]

What this amounts to is that nearly *half* the entire Archipelago in 1927 consisted of youths whom the October Revolution had caught between the ages of *six and fourteen*. Ten years after the victorious Revolution these same girls and boys turned up in prison and constituted half the prison population! This jibes poorly with the struggle against the vestiges of bourgeois consciousness which we inherited from the old society, but figures are figures. They demonstrate that the Archipelago never was short of young people.

But the question of *how* young was decided in 1935. In that year the Great Evildoer once more left his thumbprint on History's submissive clay. Among such deeds as the destruction of Leningrad and the destruction of his own Party, he did not overlook the children—the children whom he loved so well, whose Best Friend he was, and with whom he therefore had his photograph taken. Seeing no other way to bridle those insidious mischiefmakers, those washerwomen's brats, who were overrunning the country in thicker and thicker swarms and growing more and more brazen in their violations of socialist legality, he invented a gift for them: These children, from twelve years of age (by this time his beloved daughter was approaching that borderline, and he could see that age tangibly before his eyes), should

---

1. Vyshinsky, *op. cit.*, p. 333.

be sentenced *to the whole works* in the Code. In other words, "with the application of all measures of punishment," as the Decree of the Central Executive Committee and the Council of People's Commissars of April 7, 1935, elucidated. (Including, that is, capital punishment as well.)

Illiterates that we were, we scrutinized decrees very little at the time. More and more we gazed at the portraits of Stalin with a black-haired little girl in his arms. . . . Even less did the twelve-year-olds read the decrees. And the decrees kept coming out, one after another. On December 10, 1940, the sentencing of juveniles from the age of twelve for "putting various objects on railroad tracks." (This was training young diversionists.) On May 31, 1941, it was decreed that for all other varieties of crime not included in Article 12 juveniles were to be given full sentences from the age of fourteen on!

But here a small obstacle arose: the War of the Fatherland began. But the law is the law! And on July 7, 1941—four days after Stalin's panicky speech in the days when German tanks were driving toward Leningrad, Smolensk, and Kiev—one more decree of the Presidium of the Supreme Soviet was issued, and it is difficult now to say in what respect it is more interesting for us today—in its unwavering academic character, showing what important questions were being decided by the government in those flaming days, or in its actual contents. The situation was that the Prosecutor of the U.S.S.R. (Vyshinsky?) had complained to the Supreme Soviet about the Supreme Court (which means His Graciousness had heard about the matter), because the courts were applying the Decree of 1935 incorrectly and these brats were being sentenced only when they had *intentionally* committed crimes. But this was impermissible softness! And so right in the heat of war, the Presidium of the Supreme Soviet elucidated: This interpretation does not correspond to the text of the law. It introduces limitations not provided for by the law! And in agreement with the prosecutor, the Presidium issued a clarification to the Supreme Court: Children must be sentenced and the full measure of punishment applied (in other words, "the whole works"), even in cases where crimes were committed not intentionally but as a result of *carelessness*.

Now that is something! Perhaps in all world history no one has yet approached such a radical solution of the problem of children! From twelve years on for carelessness . . . up to and including execution![2] And that is when all the escape holes were shut off to the greedy mice! That is when, finally, all the collective-farm ears of grain were saved! And now the granaries were going to be filled to overflowing and life would flourish, and children who had been bad from birth would be set on the long path of correction.

And none of the Party prosecutors with children the same age shuddered! They found no problem in stamping the arrest warrants. And none of the Party judges shuddered either! With bright eyes they sentenced little children to three, five, eight, and ten years in general camps!

And for "shearing sheaves" these tykes got not less than eight years!

And for a pocketful of potatoes—one pocketful of potatoes in a child's trousers!—they also got eight years!

Cucumbers did not have so high a value put on them. For a dozen cucumbers Sasha Blokhin got five years.

And the hungry fourteen-year-old girl Lida, in the Chingirlau District Center of Kustanai Province, walked down the street picking up, mixed with the dust, a narrow trail of grain spilled from a truck (doomed to go to waste in any case). For this she was sentenced to only *three* years because of the alleviating circumstances that she had not taken socialist property directly from the field or from the barn. And perhaps what also inclined the judges to be less harsh was that in that same year of 1948 there had been a clarification of the Supreme Court to the effect that children need not be tried for theft which had the character of childish mischief (such as the petty theft of apples in an orchard). By analogy the court drew the conclusion here that it was possible to be just a wee bit less harsh. (But the conclusion we draw is that from 1935 to 1948 children *were* sentenced for taking apples.)

And a great many were sentenced for running away from Factory Apprenticeship Training. True, they got only six months for that. (In camp they were jokingly called *death-row prisoners.*

---

2. In March, 1972, all England was shocked when in Turkey a fourteen-year-old adolescent was sentenced to six years for dealing in *large* amounts of *narcotics*—how could it be??! And where were the hearts and eyes of your leftist leaders when they read the Stalinist laws on kids? (Footnote of 1972.)

But joke or no joke, here is a scene with some such "death-row prisoners" in a Far Eastern camp: They were assigned to dump the shit from latrines. There was a cart with two enormous wheels and an enormous barrel on it, full of stinking sludge. The "death-row prisoners" were hitched up, with many of them in the shafts and others pushing from the sides and from behind [the barrel kept swaying and splashing them]. And the crimson-cheeked *bitches* in their twill suits roared with laughter as they urged the children on with clubs. And on the prisoner transport ship from Vladivostok to Sakhalin in 1949, the *bitches used* these children at knifepoint for carnal enjoyment. So even six months was sometimes enough too.)

And it was then that the twelve-year-olds crossed the thresholds of the adult prison cells, were equated with adults as citizens possessing full rights, equated by virtue of the most savage prison terms, equated, in their whole unconscious life, by bread rations, bowls of gruel, their places on the sleeping shelves—that is when that old term of Communist re-education, "minors," somehow lost its significance, when the outlines of its meaning faded, became unclear—and Gulag itself gave birth to the ringing and impudent word "kids." And with a proud and bitter intonation these bitter citizens began to use this term to describe themselves—not yet citizens of the country but already citizens of the Archipelago.

So early and so strangely did their adulthood begin—with this step across the prison threshold!

And upon the twelve- and fourteen-year-old heads burst a life style that was too much for brave men who were experienced and mature. But the young people, by the laws of their young life, were not about to be flattened by this life style but, instead, grew into it and adapted to it. Just as new languages and new customs are learned without difficulty in childhood, so the juveniles adopted *on the run* both the language of the Archipelago—which was that of the thieves—and the philosophy of the Archipelago—and whose philosophy was that?

From this life they took for themselves all its most inhuman essence, all its poisonous rotten juice—and as readily as if it had been this liquid, and not milk, that they had sucked from their mothers' breasts in infancy.

They grew into camp life so swiftly—not in weeks even, but in days!—as if they were not in the least surprised by it, as if that life were not completely new to them, but a natural continuation of their free life of yesterday.

Even out in freedom they hadn't grown up in linens and velvets; it had not been the children of secure and powerful parents who had gone out to clip stalks of grain, filled their pockets with potatoes, been late at the factory gate, or run away from Factory Apprenticeship Training. The kids were the children of workers. Out in freedom they had understood very well that life was built upon injustice. But out there things had not been laid out stark and bare to the last extremity; some of it was dressed up in decent clothing, some of it softened by a mother's kind word. In the Archipelago the kids saw the world as it is seen by quadrupeds: Only might makes right! Only the beast of prey has the right to live! That is how we, too, in our adult years saw the Archipelago, but we were capable of counterposing to it all our experience, our thoughts, our ideals, and everything that we had read to that very day. Children accepted the Archipelago with the divine impressionability of childhood. And in a few *days* children became beasts there! And the worst kind of beasts, with no ethical concepts whatever (looking into the calm and enormous eyes of a horse or caressing the flattened ears of a guilty dog, how can you deny that they have ethics?). The kid masters the truth: If other teeth are weaker than your own, then tear the piece away from them. It belongs to you!

There were two basic methods of maintaining kids in the Archipelago: in separate children's colonies (principally the younger kids, not yet fifteen) and in mixed-category camps, most often with invalids and women (the senior kids).

Both were equally successful in developing animal viciousness. And neither rescued the kids from being educated in the spirit of the thieves' ideals.

Take Yura Yermolov. He reports that when he was only twelve years old (in 1942) he saw a great deal of fraud, thievery, and speculation going on around him, and arrived at the following judgment about life: "*The only people* who do not steal and deceive *are those who are afraid to.* As for me—I don't want to be afraid of anything! Which means that I, too, will steal and deceive and live well." And yet for a time his life somehow developed differently. He became fascinated by the shining examples whose spirit he was taught in school. However, having got a taste of the Beloved Father (and laureates and ministers tell us that this was beyond their capacities), at the age of fourteen he wrote a leaflet: "Down with Stalin! Hail Lenin!" They caught him on that one, beat him up, gave him 58-10, and imprisoned him with the kids and thieves. And Yura Yermolov quickly mastered the thieves' law. The spirit of his existence spiraled upward steeply —and at the age of fourteen he had executed his "negation of a negation": he had returned to the concept of thievery as the highest and the best of all existence.

And what did he see in the children's colony? "There was even more injustice than in freedom. The chiefs and the jailers lived off the state, shielded by the correctional system. Part of the kid's ration went from the kitchen into the bellies of the instructors. The kids were beaten with boots, kept in fear so that they would be silent and obedient." (Here it is necessary to explain that the ration of the youngest juveniles was not the ordinary camp ration. Though it sentenced kids to long years of imprisonment, the government did not cease to be humane. It did not forget that these same children were the future masters of Communism. Therefore they added milk and butter and real meat to their rations. So how could the *instructors* resist the temptation of dipping their ladle into the kids' pot? And how could they compel the kids to keep silent, except by beating them with boots? Perhaps one of these kids who grew up in this way will someday relate to us a story more dismal than *Oliver Twist?*)

The simplest reply to the overpowering injustices was to create injustices oneself! This was the easiest conclusion, and it would now become the rule of life of the kids for a long time to come (or even forever).

But here is what's interesting! In giving the cruel world battle, the kids didn't battle against one another! They didn't look on each other as enemies! They entered this struggle as *a collective*, a united group! Was this a budding socialism? The indoctrination of the instructors? Oh, come on, cut the cackle, big-mouths! This is a descent into the law of the thieves! After all, the thieves are united; after all, the thieves have their own discipline and their own ringleaders. And the juveniles were the apprentices of the thieves, they were mastering the precepts of their elders.

Oh, of course, they were intensely indoctrinated! Their instructors came—with three stars, four stars, on their shoulder boards—and read them lectures on the Great War of the Fatherland, on the immortal feat of our people, on the Fascist atrocities, on the sunny Stalinist concern for children, on what a Soviet person should be. But the Great Teaching on Society, built on economics alone, knowing nothing of psychology, is ignorant even of that simple psychological law which says that the repetition of anything five and six times . . . already arouses disbelief, or even more than that—nausea. The kids were disgusted by whatever had been earlier rammed down their throats by their teachers and now by instructors who simultaneously stole from the kitchen. (And even the patriotic speech of an officer from a military unit —"Boys! You have been entrusted with the task of dismantling parachutes. This is valuable silk, the Motherland's property, try to take care of it!"—had no success. Rushing for overfulfillment of norms and to get extra dishes of cereal, the kids at Krivoshchekovo cut up all the silk into useless scraps.) And out of all the seeds sown among them, they took over only the seeds of hate —of hostility to the 58's and a feeling of superiority over the enemies of the people.

This was something that would come in handy later on, in the general camps. For the time being, however, there were no enemies of the people among them. Yura Yermolov was just the same kind of typical kid; he had long since exchanged the stupid political law for the wise thieves' law. No one could avoid being cooked up in that mash! No boy could remain a separate individual—he would be trampled, torn apart, ostracized, if he did not immediately declare himself a thieves' apprentice. And *all of them* took that inevitable oath. . . . (Reader! Put *your own* children in their place. . . .)

Who was the enemy of the kids in the children's colonies? The jailers and the instructors. The struggle was against them!

The kids knew their strength very well. The first element in their strength was unity, and the second impunity. It was only on the outside that they had been driven into here on the basis of the law for adults. But once in here, in the Archipelago, they were under the protection of a sacred taboo. "Milk, chief! Give us our milk!" they would howl, and beat on the door of the cell and break up their bunks and break all the glass in sight—all of which would have been termed armed rebellion or economic sabotage among adults. They had nothing to fear! Their milk would be brought them right away!

Or say they were marching a column of kids under armed guard through a city, and it seems even shameful to guard children so strictly. Far from it! They had worked out a plan. A whistle —and all who wanted to scattered in different directions! And what were the guards to do? Shoot? At whom? At children? . . . And so their prison terms came to an end. In one fell swoop 150 years ran away from the state. You don't enjoy looking silly? Then don't arrest children!

Our future novelist (the one who spent his childhood among the kids) will describe to us a multitude of kids' tricks—how they ran riot in the colonies, how they got back at and played nasty tricks on their instructors. Despite the seeming severity of the terms meted out to them and the camp regimen, the kids developed great insolence out of impunity.

Here is one of their boastful stories about themselves, which, knowing the typical pattern of the kids' actions, I fully believe. Some excited and frightened children ran to the nurse of a children's colony and summoned her to help one of their comrades who was seriously ill. Forgetting caution, she quickly accompanied them to their big cell for forty. And as soon as she was inside, the whole anthill went into action! Some of them barricaded the door and kept watch. Dozens of hands tore everything off her, all the clothes she had on, and toppled her over; and then some sat on her hands and on her legs; and then, everyone doing what he could and where, they raped her, kissed her, bit her. It was against orders to shoot, and no one could rescue her until they themselves let her go, profaned and weeping.

In general, of course, interest in the female body begins early among boys, and in the kids' cells it was intensely heated up by colorful stories and boasting. And they never let a chance go by to let off steam. Here is an episode. In broad daylight in full view of everyone, four kids were sitting in the compound of Krivoshchekovo Camp No. 1, talking with a girl called Lyuba from the bookbinding shop. She retorted sharply to something they had said. The boys leaped up, grabbed her legs, and lifted them in the air. She was in a defenseless position; while she supported herself on the ground with her hands, her skirt fell over her head. The boys held her that way and caressed her with their free hands. And then they let her down—and not roughly either. Did she slap them? Did she run away from them? Not at all. She sat down just as before and continued the argument.

These were sixteen-year-old kids, and it was an adult camp, with mixed categories. (It was the same one that had the women's barracks for five hundred where all the copulation took place without curtains and which the kids used to enter importantly like men.)

In the children's colonies the kids worked for four hours and then were supposed to be in school for four. (But all that schooling was a fake.) When transferred to an adult camp, they had a ten-hour working day, except that their work norms were reduced, while their ration norms were the same as adults'. They were transferred at the age of sixteen, but their undernourishment and improper development in camp and before camp endowed them at that age with the appearance of small frail children. Their height was stunted, as were their minds and their interests. They were sometimes maintained in separate brigades depending on the kind of work they were doing, and sometimes they were mixed into a general brigade with elderly invalids. Here, too, "reduced physical labor" was required of them, or simply native child labor.

After the children's colony their situation changed drastically. No longer did they get the children's ration which so tempted the jailers—and therefore the latter ceased to be their principal enemy. Some old men appeared in their lives on whom they could try their strength. Women appeared on whom they could try their maturity. Some real live thieves appeared, fat-faced camp storm troopers, who willingly undertook their guidance both in world outlook and in training in thievery. To learn from them was tempting—and not to learn from them was impossible.

For a *free* reader does the word "thief" perhaps sound like a reproach? In that case he has understood nothing. This word is pronounced in the underworld in the same way that the word "knight" was pronounced among the nobility—and with even greater esteem, and not loudly but softly, like a sacred word. To become a worthy thief someday . . . was the kid's dream. This was the elemental motivating force of their companionship. Yes, for even the most independent among them,

> For a young man, pondering life,

there was no destiny more reliable.

On one occasion, at the Ivanovo Transit Prison, I spent the

night in a cell for kids. In the next bunk to me was a thin boy just over fifteen—called Slava, I think. It appeared to me that he was going through the whole kid ritual somehow unwillingly, as if he were growing out of it or was weary of it. I thought to myself: This boy has not perished, and is more intelligent, and he will soon move away from the others. And we had a chat. The boy came from Kiev. One of his parents had died, and the other had abandoned him. Before the war, at the age of nine, Slava began to steal. He also stole "when our army came," and after the war, and, with a sad, thoughtful smile which was so old for fifteen, he explained to me that in the future, too, he intended to live only by thievery. "You know," he explained to me very reasonably, "that as a worker you can earn only bread and water. And my *childhood* was bad so I want to live well." "What did you do during the German occupation?" I asked, trying to fill in the two years he had bypassed without describing them—the two years of the occupation of Kiev. He shook his head. "Under the Germans I worked. What do you think—that I could have gone on stealing under the Germans? They shot you on the spot for that."

And in adult camps, too, the kids retained, as the principal characteristic of their conduct, their concerted action in attack and their concerted action in resistance. This made them strong and freed them from restrictions. In their consciousness there was no demarcation line between what was permissible and what was not permissible, and no concept whatever of good and evil. For them everything that they desired was good and everything that hindered them was bad. They acquired their brazen and insolent manner of behavior because it was the most advantageous form of conduct in the camp. And dissimulation and cunning served them very well in situations where strength could not carry the day. A kid could play the role of a boy saint. He could move you to tears. And all the while his comrades ransacked your bag behind your back. That rancorous company of theirs could wreak its vengeance on anyone at all—and just so as not to get mixed up with that horde, no one would come to the aid of their victim. When their purpose had been attained and their enemies divided, the kids would then hurl themselves in a pack on the single victim. And they were invincible! So many of them would attack at once that you couldn't even single them out, distinguish them, remember them. And you simply did not have enough hands and feet to beat them off.

Here, as recounted by A. Y. Susi, are several pictures from Krivoshchekovo (Penalty) Camp No. 2 of Novosiblag. Life was lived in enormous half-dark dugouts (for five hundred each) which had been dug into the earth to a depth of five feet. The chiefs did not interfere with the life inside the compound—no slogans and no lectures. The thieves and kids held sway. Almost no one was taken out to work. Rations were correspondingly meager. On the other hand, there was a surplus of time.

One day they were bringing a breadbox from the bread-cutting room under the guard of brigade members. The kids started a fake fight in front of the box itself, started shoving one another, and tipped the box over. The brigade members hurled themselves on the bread ration to pick it up from the ground. Out of twenty rations they managed to save only fourteen. The "fighting" kids were nowhere to be seen.

The mess hall at this camp was a plank lean-to not adequate for the Siberian winter. The gruel and the bread ration had to be carried about 150 yards in the cold from the kitchen to the dugout. For the elderly invalids this was a dangerous and difficult operation. They pushed their bread ration far down inside their shirt and gripped their mess tin with freezing hands. But suddenly, with diabolical speed, two or three kids would attack from the side. They knocked one old man to the ground, six hands frisked him all over, and they made off like a whirlwind. His bread ration had been pilfered, his gruel spilled, his empty mess tin lay there on the ground, and the old man struggled to get to his knees. (And other zeks saw this—and hastily bypassed the dangerous spot, hurrying to carry their own bread rations to the dugout.) And the weaker their victim, the more merciless were the kids. They openly tore the bread ration from the hands of a very weak old man. The old man wept and implored them to give it back to him: "I am dying of starvation." "So you're going to kick the bucket soon anyway—what's the difference?" And the kids once decided to attack the invalids in the cold, empty building in front of the kitchen where there was always a mob of people. The gang would hurl their victim to the ground, sit on his hands, his legs, and his head, search his pockets, take his makhorka and his money, and then disappear.

The big strong Latvian Martinson was careless enough to appear in the compound wearing the high brown leather boots of an English aviator which were laced over hooks up to knee height. He wouldn't even take them off at night and was confident of his strength. But they ambushed him when he lay down for a brief nap on the rostrum in the mess hall. The gang swooped swiftly to the assault, and fled just as swiftly, and he was without his boots! All the laces had been cut and the boots jerked off. Look for them? But where? The boots would have been sent outside the compound immediately, through one of the jailers(!), and there sold for a high price. (And what didn't the kids "float" out of the compound to be sold! Each time the camp chiefs, taking pity on their youth, issued them even slightly better footgear or duds, or some flattened-out pads for mattresses that had been taken away from the 58's—in several days it would all have been traded to the free employees for makhorka, and the kids would once more be going around in tatters and sleeping on bare boards.)

It was enough for a careless free worker to go into the camp compound with a dog and turn his head for one second. And he could buy his dog's pelt that very same evening outside the camp compound: the dog would have been coaxed away, knifed, skinned, and cooked, all in a trice.

There is nothing finer than thievery and brigandage! They provide nourishment. They are jolly. But young bodies also need simple exercise, innocent enjoyment, and relaxation. If they were given hammers to nail shell boxes together, they would brandish them about incessantly and, with huge enjoyment (even the girls), hammer nails into anything that came to hand—tables, walls, tree stumps. They used to be constantly fighting with each other—not just to knock over a breadbox, but, really fighting, they would pursue each other over bunks and in the aisles. And it didn't matter that they were stepping on legs, on belongings, spilling things, soiling things, waking people up, hurting others. They were playing!

All children play like that, but for all ordinary children there are nonetheless parents (in our epoch, unfortunately, no more than "nonetheless"), and there is some controlling force over them, and they can be stopped, they can be reached, punished, sent away. But in camp all that was impossible. To get through to the kids with words was simply impossible. Human speech was not for them. Their ears simply didn't admit anything that they themselves didn't need. If irritated old men started to grab them and pull them up short, the kids would hurl heavy objects at them. The kids found amusement in just about anything. They would grab the field shirt off an elderly invalid and play "Keep away"—forcing him to run back and forth just as if he were their own age. Does he become angry and leave? Then he will never see it again! They will have sold it outside the compound for a smoke! (And they will even come up to him afterward innocently: "Papasha! Give us a light! Oh, come on now, don't be angry. Why did you leave? Why didn't you stay and catch it?")

For adults, fathers and grandfathers, these boisterous games of the kids in the crowded conditions of camp could cause more anguish and be more hurtful than their robbing and their rapacious greed. It proved to be one of the most sensitive forms of humiliation for an elderly person to be made equal with a young whippersnapper—if only it were equal! But not to be turned over to the tyranny of the whippersnappers.

The kids' actions were unpremeditated, and they didn't mean to cause hurt or offense. They weren't pretending; *they simply did not consider anyone a human being* except themselves and the older thieves. That is how they came to perceive the world, and now they clung to that view. At the end of work they would break into a column of adult zeks who were utterly fagged out, hardly able to stand, sunk in a kind of trance or reverie. The kids would jostle the column, not because they had to be first— this meant nothing—but just for the fun of it. They used to talk noisily, constantly taking the name of Pushkin in vain. ("Pushkin took it!" "Pushkin ate it!") They used to direct obscene curses at God, Christ, and the Holy Virgin, and they would shout out all sorts of obscenity about sexual deviations and perversions, not even shamed by the presence of elderly women standing there—let alone the younger ones.

During their short camp stay they attained the peak, the summit, of freedom *from* society! During the periods of long roll calls in the camp compound the kids used to chase each other around, torpedoing the crowd, knocking people into one another. ("Well, peasant, why were you in the way?") Or they would run around a person, one after the other, as they might around a tree—and the person was even more useful than a tree, because you could shield yourself with him, jerk him, make him totter, tug him in different directions.

This would have been hurtful even when you were feeling cheerful, but when your whole life was broken, when a man had been cast into the distant pit of a camp to die, when death from hunger already hung over you, and your vision was darkening—it was impossible to rise above yourself and have sympathy for the youngsters and the fact that they could play such carefree games in so dismal a place. No, the tormented elderly people were possessed with rage, and they used to shout at them: "Plague on you, little skunks!" "Scum!" "Mad dogs!" "Drop dead!" "I could strangle them with my own hands!" "Worse rats than the Fascists!" "They've sent them to kill us!" (And there was so much hatred in those shouts of the elderly invalids that if words could kill . . . they would have.) Yes! And it really seemed that the kids had been set on them intentionally! Because after prolonged thought the camp chiefs could never have invented a more cruel whip. (And, just as in a successful chess game all the combinations suddenly begin to mesh of themselves and it seems as if they had been brilliantly thought out beforehand, so, too, a great deal succeeded in our System to the end of wearing people down more effectively.) And it seems that the little devil imps of Christian mythology must have been just the same as these and in nowise different!

All the more so since their chief amusement—their constant symbol, their sign of greeting, and their threat—was the *slingshot*: the index and middle fingers of the hand parted in a "V" sign—like agile, butting horns. But they were not for "butting." They were . . . for gouging. Because they were aimed always at the eyes. This had been borrowed from the adult thieves and indicated a seriously meant threat: "I'll gouge out your eyes, you shit!" And among the kids, too, this was a favorite game: All of a sudden, like a snake's head, a "slingshot" rises out of nowhere in front of an old man's eyes, and the fingers move steadily toward the eyes! They are going to put them out! The old man recoils. He is pushed in the chest just a bit, and another kid has already knelt on the ground right behind his legs—and the old man falls backward, his head banging the ground, accompanied by the gay laughter of the kids. And no one will ever help him up. And the kids don't even realize that they have done anything bad! It was merely fun! And you'd not catch those devils either, no way! And the old man, rising with difficulty, would whisper with rage: "If only I had a machine gun. I'd shoot them without pity!"

Old man T. nourished a burning hatred for them. He used to say: "Nothing good can come of them anyway. For human beings they are a plague. We have to annihilate them on the sly." And he worked out a means to this end: Whenever he succeeded in creeping up on a kid on the sly, he would hurl him to the ground and press down on the boy's chest with his knees until he could hear the ribs crack—but he didn't break them. He would let the kid up at that point. T. used to say that the kid wouldn't survive and that there wasn't a physician who could diagnose what was wrong with him. And by this means T. sent several kids to the next world before they themselves beat him to death.

Hate begets hate! The black water of hate flows easily and quickly along the horizontal. That was easier than for it to erupt upward through a crater—against those who condemned both the old and the young to a slave's fate.

That is how small stubborn Fascists were trained by the joint action of Stalinist legislation, a Gulag education, and the leaven of the thieves. It was impossible to invent a better method of brutalizing children! It was quite impossible to find a quicker, stronger way of implanting all the vices of camp in tiny, immature hearts.

Even when it would have cost nothing to soften the heart of a child, the camp bosses didn't permit it. This was not the goal of *their* training. At Krivoshchekovo Camp No. 1 a boy asked to be transferred so that he could be with his father in Camp No. 2. This was not permitted. (After all, the rules required families to be broken up.) And the boy had to hide in a barrel to get from one camp to the other and lived there with his father in secret. And in their confusion they assumed he had escaped and used a stick with spikes made of nails to poke about in the latrine pits, to see whether or not he had drowned there.

But it is only the beginning that is hard. For Volodya Snegiryov at fifteen it was somehow strange to be imprisoned. But later, in the course of six terms, he managed to collect nearly *a century* (including two terms of twenty-five years each). He spent hundreds of days in punishment blocks and prisons. (There his young lungs acquired TB.) For seven years he was on the All-Union wanted list. After this he was well set, of course, on the true thieves' path. (Today he is a Group Two invalid—without one lung and five ribs.) Vitya Koptyayev has been imprisoned *continually* since the age of twelve. He has been sentenced *fourteen* times, nine of them for escaping. "I have never yet lived in freedom legitimately." Yura Yermolov got work after his release but was fired—because it was more important to give the job to a demobilized soldier. And he was forced "to go on tour," with the end result a new prison term.

Stalin's immortal laws on kids existed for twenty years—until the Decree of April 24, 1954, which relaxed them slightly: releasing those kids who had served more than one-third . . . of their *first* term! And what if there were fourteen? Twenty years, twenty harvests. And twenty different age groups had been maimed with crime and depravity.

So *who* dares cast a shadow on the memory of our Great Coryphaeus?

■

There were nimble children who managed to *catch* Article 58 very early in life. For example, Geli Pavlov got it at twelve (from 1943 to 1949 he was imprisoned in the colony in Zakovsk). For Article 58, in fact, *no minimum age* existed! That is what they said even in public lectures on jurisprudence—as, for example, in Tallinn in 1945. Dr. Usma knew a six-year-old boy imprisoned in a colony under 58. But that, evidently, is the record!

Sometimes the arrest of the child was put off for the sake of appearances, but took place later anyway. For example, Vera Inchik, the daughter of a charwoman, and two other girls, all aged fourteen, discovered (Yeisk, in 1932) that in the course of the liquidation of the "kulaks," little children were being thrown out to die. The girls ("like the revolutionaries earlier") decided to protest. They wrote out their protests in their own handwriting on sheets of paper taken from their school notebooks and posted them in the marketplace themselves, expecting immediate and universal indignation. A doctor's daughter, it would appear, was arrested immediately. But the daughter of the charwoman was only noted on a list. When 1937 came, she, too, was arrested—"for spying on behalf of Poland."

And where, if not in this chapter, are we going to mention the children orphaned by the arrest of their parents?

The children of the women of the religious commune near Khosta were fortunate. When their mothers were sent off to Solovki in 1929, the children were softheartedly left in their own homes and on their own farms. The children looked after the orchards and vegetable gardens themselves, milked their goats, assiduously studied at school, and sent their school grades to their parents on Solovki, together with assurances that they were prepared to suffer for God as their mothers had. (And, of course, the Party soon gave them this opportunity.)

Considering the instructions to "disunite" exiled children and their parents, how many of these kids must there have been even back in the twenties? (Remember that 48 percent.) And who will ever tell us of their fate? . . .

Here is . . . Galya Benediktova. Her father was a Petrograd typesetter, an Anarchist, and her mother was a seamstress from Poland. Galya remembers very well her sixth birthday in 1933. They celebrated it joyfully. The next morning she woke up— her father and mother were gone, and some stranger in uniform was messing about among their books. True, a month later her mother returned to her; the women and children were to travel to Tobolsk on their own, as free people; only the men went on a prisoner transport. They lived there as a family, but they had not managed to complete the three-year term before her mother was arrested again and her father was shot. Her mother died in prison a month later. And Galya was taken to an orphanage in a monastery near Tobolsk. Conditions there were such that the young girls lived in constant fear of violence. Then she was transferred to an orphanage in the city. The director talked to her like this: "You are the children of enemies of the people, and nonetheless you are being clothed and fed!" (No! How humane this dictatorship of the proletariat is!) Galya became like a wolf cub. At the age of eleven she was already given her first *political* interrogation. Subsequently she got a *ten-ruble bill*, although she did not serve it out in full. At the age of forty she lives a lonely life in the Arctic and writes: "My life came to an end with my father's arrest. I love him so much to this very day that I am afraid even to think about it. That was a whole different world, and my heart is sick with love for him. . . ."

And Svetlana Sedova also remembers: "I can never forget the

day they took all our things out into the street and sat me there on top of them, and a heavy rain was falling. From the age of six I have been 'the daughter of a traitor to the Motherland.' And there can be nothing more awful in life that this."

They were taken into NKVD foster homes, into *Special* homes. The majority had their surnames changed, particularly those who had famous names. (Yura Bukharin learned his real name only in 1956. But the Chebotaryov name was not, it seems, particularly famous?) The children grew up totally purged of their parents' disgrace. Rosa Kovacs, a native of Philadelphia, brought here as a small child by her Communist father, after leaving an NKVD foster home, found herself during the war in the American Zone of Germany—what fates befall people!—and what happened? She returned to the Soviet Motherland and got her twenty-five years.

Even a superficial glance reveals one characteristic: The children, too, were destined for imprisonment; they, too, in their turn would be sent off to the promised land of the Archipelago, sometimes even at the same time as their parents. Take the eighth-grader Nina Peregud. In November, 1941, they came to arrest her father. There was a search. Suddenly Nina remembered that inside the stove lay a crumpled but not yet burned humorous rhyme. And it might have just stayed there, but out of nervousness Nina decided to tear it up at once. She reached into the firebox, and the dozing policeman grabbed her. And this horrible sacrilege, in a schoolgirl's handwriting, was revealed to the eyes of the Chekists:

> The stars in heaven are shining down
> And their light falls on the dew;
> Smolensk is already lost and gone
> And we're going to lose Moscow too.

And she expressed the desire:

> We only wish they'd bomb the school,
> We're awfully tired of studies.

Naturally these full-grown men engaged in saving their Motherland deep in the rear in Tambov, these knights with hot hearts and clean hands, had to scotch such a mortal danger.[3] Nina

3. Won't we ever someday, won't we ever, haul out at least one such mole who authorized the arrest of an eighth-grader because of a rhyme? To see what his forehead is like? And his ears?

was arrested. Confiscated for her interrogation were her diaries from the sixth grade and a counterrevolutionary photograph: a snapshot of the destroyed Vavarinskaya Church. "What did your father talk about?" pried the knights with the hot hearts. Nina only sobbed. They sentenced her to five years of imprisonment and three years' deprivation of civil rights (even though she couldn't lose them since she didn't yet have them).

In camp, of course, she was separated from her father. The branch of a white lilac tree tormented her: her girl friends were taking their examinations! Nina suffered the way a real criminal was supposed to suffer when being reformed: "What did my classmate Zoya Kosmodemyanskaya do? And how foul a thing am I!" The security officers pushed down hard on that pedal: "But you can still catch up with her! Just *help* us!"

Oh, you corrupters of young souls! How prosperously you are living out your lives! You are never going to have to stand up somewhere, blushing and tongue-tied, and confess what slops you poured over souls!

But Zoya Leshcheva managed to outdo her whole family. And here is how. Her father, her mother, her grandfather, her grandmother, and her elder adolescent brothers had all been scattered to distant camps because of their faith in God. But Zoya was a mere ten years old. They took her to an orphanage in Ivanovo Province. And there she declared she would never remove the cross from around her neck, the cross which her mother had hung there when she said farewell. And she tied the knot of the cord tighter so they would not be able to remove it when she was asleep. The struggle went on and on for a long time. Zoya became enraged: "You can strangle me and then take it off a corpse!" Then she was sent to an orphanage *for retarded children* —because she would not submit to their training. And in that orphanage were the dregs, a category of kids worse than anything described in this chapter. The struggle for the cross went on and on. Zoya stood her ground. Even here she refused to learn to steal or to curse. "A mother as sacred as mine must never have a daughter who is a criminal. I would rather be a political, like my whole family."

And she became a political! And the more her instructors and the radio praised Stalin, the more clearly she saw in him the culprit responsible for all their misfortunes. And, refusing to give in to the criminals, she now began to win them over to her views! In the courtyard stood one of those mass-produced plaster statues of Stalin. And mocking and indecent graffiti began to appear on it. (Kids love sport! The important thing is to point them in the right direction.) The administration kept repainting the statue, kept watch over it, and reported the situation to the MGB. And the graffiti kept on appearing, and the kids kept on laughing. Finally one morning they found that the statue's head had been knocked off and turned upside down, and inside it were feces.

This was a terrorist act! The MGB came. And began, in accordance with all their rules, their interrogations and threats: "Turn over the gang of terrorists to us, otherwise *we are going to shoot the lot of you* for terrorism!" (And there would have been nothing remarkable if they had: so what, 150 children shot! If He Himself had known about it, he would himself have given the order.)

It's not known whether the kids would have stood up to them or given in, but Zoya Leshcheva declared: "I did it all myself! What else is the head of that papa good for?"

And she was tried. And she was sentenced *to the supreme measure*, no joke. But because of the intolerable humanitarianism of the 1950 law on the restoration of capital punishment the execution of a fourteen-year-old was forbidden. And therefore they gave her a "tenner" (it's surprising it wasn't twenty-five). Up to the age of eighteen she was in ordinary camps, and from the age of eighteen on she was in Special Camps. For her directness and her language she got a second camp sentence and, it seems, a third one as well.

Zoya's parents had already been freed and her brothers too, but Zoya languished on in camp.

Long live our tolerance of religion!

Long live our children, the masters of Communism!

And let any country speak up that can say it has loved its children as we have ours!

Chapter 18

■

The Muses in Gulag

It was an accepted saying that *everything is possible* in Gulag. The blackest foulness, any twist and turn of betrayal, wildly unexpected encounters, love on the edge of the precipice—everything was possible. But if anybody should ever try to tell you with shining eyes that someone was re-educated by government means through the KVCh—the Cultural and Educational Section—you can reply with total conviction: Nonsense!

Everyone in Gulag was re-educated—re-educated under one another's influence and by circumstances, re-educated in various directions. But not even one juvenile, let alone any adult, was re-educated by means of the KVCh.

However, so that our camps might not be like "dens of depravity, communes of brigandage, nurseries of recidivists, and conductors of immorality" (this is how Tsarist prisons were described), they were equipped with such an appendage as the Cultural and Educational Section.

Because, as was said by the then head of Gulag, I. Apeter: "To the prison construction of capitalist countries, the proletariat of the U.S.S.R. counterposes its cultural [and not its camp!—A.S.] construction. Those institutions in which the proletarian state enforces deprivation of freedom . . . can be called prisons or by some other name—*it is not a matter of terminology.* . . . These are places where life is not killed off but, instead, gives forth new shoots. . . .[1]

I don't know how Apeter ended. There is a great likelihood, I

1. Vyshinsky, *op. cit.*, pp. 431, 429, 438.

think, that they soon wrung his neck, too, in those very places in which, as he said, life gives off new shoots. But it is not a matter of terminology. Has the reader now understood what the main thing was in our camps? *Cultural* construction.

And for every need an organ was created, and multiplied, and its tentacles reached out to every island. In the twenties they were called PVCh's—Political Educational Sections—and, from the thirties on, KVCh's. They were supposed in part to replace the former prison priests and prison religious services.

Here is how they were organized. The chief of the KVCh was a free employee with the authority of an assistant to the chief of camp. He picked out his own instructors (the norm was one instructor to 250 wards), who had to be from "strata close to the proletariat," which meant, of course, that intellectuals (the petty bourgeoisie) were unsuitable (it was more decent for them to be swinging a pick), so they recruited as instructors thieves with two or three convictions, urban swindlers, embezzlers, and seducers along with them. And so it was that a young fellow who had kept himself sort of clean and who had got five years for rape with mitigating circumstances might roll up his newspaper and go off to the barracks of the 58's to lead a little discussion on "The Role of Labor in the Process of Correction." The instructors had a particularly good outside view of that role because they themselves had been "released from the productive process." Similar such socially friendly elements made up the *activists' group of the KVCh*. But the activists were not released from work. (They could only hope that in time they would be able to do in one of the instructors and take over his job. This created a generally friendly atmosphere in the KVCh.) In the mornings the instructor had to see the zeks off to work; then he would inspect the kitchen (i.e., he would be well fed), and then he would go catch up on his sleep in his cabin. He would be ill-advised to tangle with or touch *the thief ringleaders* because, in the first place, it was dangerous, and, in the second place, the moment would come when "criminal cohesion would be transformed into a productive cohesion." And at that point the thief ringleaders would lead the shock brigades into storm assaults. And so, for the time being, let them, too, just sleep it off after their night-long card games. But the instructors are constantly guided in their activity by the general overall thesis that cultural and educational work in the camps is not cultural and educational work "with unfortunates," but cultural and productive work with a knife edge (we just can't get along without that knife edge), directed against . . . yes, you've guessed it: against the 58's. Alas, the KVCh "does not have the right to arrest" (now this was such a limitation on its cultural opportunities!) but "could make a request to the administration" (which would not refuse!). And, besides, the instructor "systematically presents reports on the *mood* of the zeks." (He who has an ear to hear, let him hear! At this point the Cultural and Educational Section delicately shades into the Security Section. But this is not spelled out in the instructions.)

However, we see that, carried away by our quotations, we have grammatically slipped into the present tense. We have to disappoint the reader with the fact that the matter concerns the thirties, the finest, most flourishing years of the KVCh, when a classless society was being built in the country, and when there had not yet occurred the awful outburst of class struggle that did occur the moment that society was achieved. In those glorious years the KVCh expanded into many important appendages: the cultural councils of those deprived of freedom; cultural and educational commissions; sanitary and living conditions commissions; shock-brigade staffs; inspection posts for fulfillment of the production and financial plan, etc. . . . Well, as Comrade Solts (the Curator of the Belomor Canal and Chairman of the Commission of VTsIK on particular amnesties) said: "Even the prisoner in prison must live by what the whole country is living by." (That foul enemy of the people, Solts, was justly punished by proletarian justice—I beg your pardon . . . that fighter for the great cause, Comrade Solts, was slandered, and perished in the years of the cult—oh, I beg your pardon . . . at the time of the insignificant phenomenon of the cult. . . .)

And how variegated and varied were the forms of work! Like life itself. Organization of competition. Organization of shock-worker movements. Struggle for fulfillment of the production and financial plan. Struggle for labor discipline. Storm assault on the liquidation of hold-ups. Cultural crusades. Voluntary collection of funds for airplanes. Subscription to loans. "Voluntary Saturdays" for strengthening the defense capabilities of the country. Exposure of fake shock workers. Conversations with malingerers. Liquidation of illiteracy (they went unwillingly).

Professional and technical courses for camp inmates from among the workers (the thieves pushed hard to learn to be drivers: freedom!). And fascinating lectures on the inviolability of socialist property! And simply reading the newspapers aloud! Evenings of questions and answers. And "Red Corners" in every barracks! Graphs of fulfillment of plan! Statistics on goals! And what posters! What slogans!

In this happy time the Muses soared over the gloomy expanses and chasms of the Archipelago—and the first and highest muse among them was Polyhymnia, the muse of hymns (and of slogans):

> The brigade that excels gets . . . praise and respect!
> Do your shock work—get time off your sentence!

Or:

> Work hard—your family waits for you at home!

You see how clever this is psychologically! After all, what do you have here? First: if you have forgotten about your family, this will start you worrying about them, and remind you of them. Second: if you are intensely alarmed, it will calm you down; your family exists and has not been arrested. And in the third place: your family does not need you *just for your own sake*, but needs you only through conscientious camp work. Lastly:

> Let's join in the shock assault in honor of the seventeenth anniversary of the October Revolution!

Who could resist that?

Then there were theatricals with politically relevant themes (a little bit from the muse Thalia). For example: the servicing of the Red Calendar! Or the living newspaper! Or propaganda mock trials! Or oratorios on the theme of the September Plenum of the Central Committee in 1930! Or a musical skit, "The March of the Articles of the Criminal Code" (Article 58 was a lame Baba-Yaga)! How this all brightened the life of the prisoners and helped them reach upward toward the light!

And the recreation directors of the KVCh! And then the atheistic work too! The choirs and glee clubs (under the shade of the muse Euterpe). And then those propaganda brigades:

> The shock workers swing their shoulders,
> Hurrying with their wheelbarrows!

39. Propaganda brigade

40. Propaganda brigade

You see what bold self-criticism this is! They were not even afraid to touch on the shock workers! In fact, it was quite enough for a propaganda brigade (Illustration No. 39) to come to a penalty sector and give a concert there:

> Listen, listen, River Volga!
> Night and day beside the zeks,
> On the site stand the Chekists!
> What that means is: never fear;
> The workers have a strong, strong arm,
> The OGPU men are Communists![2]

And all the penalty workers and in particular the recidivists would throw down their playing cards and rush off to work immediately!

And there were other measures as well: A group of the best shock workers would visit a Strict Regimen Company or a penalty isolator and take a propaganda brigade with them (for example, one like this—in Illustration No. 40). At the beginning the shock workers would reproach and shame the malingerers, *explain* to them the *advantages* of fulfillment of the work norms (they would get better rations). And then the propaganda brigade would sing:

> Everywhere the battles call,
> And the Moscow-Volga Canal
> Conquers snow and cold!

And then with total frankness:

> And so that we'll live better,
> *In order to eat, in order to drink—*
> We have to dig the ground better!

And they invited all volunteers not only to return to the compound but to transfer immediately into a *shock workers'* barracks (from the penalty barracks), where they would be fed right on the spot! What an artistic success! (The propaganda brigades, except for the central one, were not released from work themselves. They got an extra portion of grits on the days of their performances.)

And what about more delicate types of work? For example: "the struggle with the aid of the prisoners themselves against equalizing wages." You just have to ponder what a profound

2. This was in Yagoda's day.

thought is contained here! This means that at a brigade meeting a prisoner would stand up and say: Don't give him a full ration; he worked badly; you'd do better to give the seven ounces to me instead!

Or the comrades' courts? (In the first years after the Revolution these were called "moral comrades," and they embraced games of chance, fights, thefts—but were these really a business for a court? And the word "moral" smelled to high heaven of bourgeois morality, and it was abrogated. From the period of reconstruction [from 1928] these courts began to deal with absenteeism, with simulating illness, a poor attitude toward inventory, spoiled production, spoilage of materials. And so long as hostile-class elements among the prisoners did not worm their way into the comrades' courts [and only murderers, thieves converted to *bitches*, embezzlers, and bribe takers appeared there], the courts in their sentencing would petition the camp chief for such penalties as deprivation of visits, food parcels, time off sentence, release on parole, and the dispatch of incorrigibles on prisoner transports. What reasonable, fair measures these were, and how particularly useful it was that the initiative in applying them came from the prisoners themselves! [Though not, of course, without certain difficulties!] They commenced the trial of a former "kulak" in a comrades' court, and he said: "You have a comrades' court, and to you I'm a 'kulak,' not a comrade. So you have no right to judge me!" They were thrown into confusion. They consulted the Political Education Section of the Chief Administration of Corrective Labor Camps and received the reply: Try him! Try him! Don't fool around!)

What was the foundation of foundations of all the cultural and educational work in camp? "Don't leave the camp inmate to himself after work—so he will not revert to his former criminal tendencies." (Well, for example, so that the 58's wouldn't start thinking about politics.) It was important that "the prisoner should never get out from under the educational influences."

And in this regard advanced modern technical devices were very helpful, and in particular the loudspeakers on every pillar and in every barracks! They must never fall silent! They must explain to the prisoners constantly and systematically from reveille until taps how to advance the hour of freedom; they reported every hour on the course of the work, on the leading and lagging work brigades, on those who were hindering. And one could recommend another original format: a conversation on the radio with individual malingerers and slackers.

Well, and there was the press—of course, the press! The sharpest weapon of our Party. Now this was the real proof that in our country there was freedom of the press: the existence of a press in prisons! Yes! In what other country was it still possible for prisoners to have their own press?

First there were handwritten wall newspapers, and second, mimeographed or printed ones, and in both cases they had fearless *camp correspondents* who scourged faults (of the prisoners), and this self-criticism was encouraged by the Leadership. The extent to which the Leadership itself attributed significance to the free camp press is indicated even by Order 434 of Dmitlag: "The overwhelming majority of the criticisms arouse no response." The newspapers also published photos of the shock workers. The newspapers pointed the finger. The newspapers disclosed. The newspapers also exposed the sallies of the class enemy—so he could be hit harder. (The newspaper was the best collaborator of the Security Section!) And overall the newspapers reflected the flow of camp life and are invaluable testimony for descendants.

Here, for example, is the newspaper of the Archangel Prison in 1931, and it depicts for us the bounty and prosperity in which the prisoners were living: "Cuspidors, ashtrays, oilcloth on the tables, radio loudspeakers, portraits of the leaders, and slogans on the walls speaking vividly of the general Party line—these are the *well-earned fruits* which those deprived of freedom enjoy!"

Yes, dear fruits! And how did this affect the lives of those deprived of freedom? The same paper half a year later: "Everyone has set to work energetically. . . . The fulfillment of the production and financial plan has risen. . . . The food has decreased and worsened."

Well, that's all right! That, as it happens, is all right! The last element . . . could be corrected.[3]

And where, oh, where, has all that gone? . . . Oh, how transitory everything beautiful and perfect is on Earth. Such an intensive, hearty, optimistic system of education of the merry-go-round type, flowing from the very sources of the Progressive Teaching, promising that within a few years not one single crimi-

3. So far, the materials for this chapter have been drawn from the collection of articles edited by Vyshinsky, *op. cit.*, and from Averbakh, *op. cit.*

nal would be left in our country. (On November 30, 1934, it particularly seemed like that.)* And where then? All of a sudden the ice age set in (which, of course, was very necessary and absolutely indispensable!), and all the petals of those tender beginnings were scattered to the winds. And where did the shock-worker movement and socialist competition disappear to? And the camp newspapers? Storm assaults, collections of funds, subscriptions to loans, and unpaid Saturdays? Cultural councils and comrades' courts? Literacy drives and technical courses? What did it matter when they even issued orders that the portraits of the Party leaders and the loudspeakers should be removed from the camp compounds! (And they didn't go putting any more cuspidors around either.) And how the life of the prisoners suddenly paled! How it was suddenly thrown back whole decades, deprived of the most important revolutionary prison gains! (But we are not protesting, the measures of the Party were both timely and very much needed.)

No longer was the artistic-poetical form of slogans valued, and the slogans, too, were now only the simplest: Fulfill! Overfulfill! Of course, no one undertook to forbid directly aesthetic indoctrination or the fluttering of the muses, but the possibilities for this were greatly narrowed. Here, for example, is one of the camp compounds in Vorkuta. The nine-month winter came to an end, and the unreal, three-month-long, somehow pitiful summer set in. The chief of the KVCh was pained because the camp compound looked foul and dirty. In such conditions a criminal could not properly meditate on the perfection of the system from which he had excluded himself. So the KVCh proclaimed several working Sundays. In their free time the prisoners took great pleasure in making some "flowerbeds"—not out of anything growing, for nothing would grow there, but instead of planting flowers, they just decorated dead mounds skillfully with mosses, lichens, broken glass, crushed stone, slag, and broken-up brick. And then around these "flowerbeds" they set up little fences made of plasterer's lath. Though it turned out to be not quite so beautiful as the Gorky Park, nonetheless the Cultural and Educational Section was satisfied. Were you going to say that in two months' time the rains would fall and wash it all away? Well, so what, they would wash it away. Next year we will do it all over again.

Or what did the political chats turn into? A lecturer came to Unzhlag No. 5 from Sukhobezvodny (this in 1952). After work the zeks were herded to the lecture. The comrades, it is true, had no secondary education, but he delivered a necessary and topical lecture which was fully correct politically: "On the Struggle of the Greek Patriots." The zeks sat there sleepily, hiding behind each other's backs, without the slightest interest in it. The lecturer described the awful persecutions of the patriots and related how the Greek women, in tears, had written a letter to Comrade Stalin. The lecture came to an end, and Sheremeta, a woman from Lvov, who was simple-minded but cunning, rose and asked him: "Citizen Chief! Tell me, who should *we* write to?" And by this the positive influence of the lecture was reduced to zero.

The types of correctional and educational work which the KVCh retained were these: To a prisoner's petition to the camp chief they would add a notation on norm fulfillment and conduct; they would deliver to the various rooms letters released by the censor; they would bind newspapers in a file and hide them from the zeks so they couldn't use them for cigarette paper; three times a year they gave amateur theatrical programs; they procured paints and canvas for artists so the latter could provide decorations for the camp compound and paint paintings for the chiefs' apartments. And then they would help the security chief a bit, but that was unofficial.

After this it is not surprising that the workers of the KVCh themselves were not flaming, bold leaders but for the most part dimwits and sad sacks.

Yes! There was one more important type of work which they did! *Maintaining the boxes!* They had to be opened at intervals, cleaned out, and locked up again—small brownish-colored boxes hung in a prominent place in the compound. On the boxes were labels: "To the Supreme Soviet of the U.S.S.R.," "To the Council of Ministers of the U.S.S.R.," "To the Minister of Internal Affairs," "To the Prosecutor General."

Go ahead and write—you have freedom of speech here. And we will decide what goes to whom. There are special comrades here to read it.

■

What is put into these boxes? *Petitions asking pardon?*

Not only. Sometimes denunciations too (from beginners). The KVCh sorts out that they are not to go to Moscow but to the office next door. And what else? Well, the inexperienced reader is not going to guess! There were also inventions! The greatest inventions, intended to turn all modern technology upside down—or at any rate to liberate their inventors from camp.

There are many more inventors—as also poets—among plain ordinary people than we imagine. And in camp especially. One has to try to get released, right? Invention is a form of escape which doesn't involve the risk of a bullet or a beating.

At line-up before work and after, with hand barrows and picks, these servitors of the muse Urania (she is the closest you can come) wrinkle their brows and strive to invent something to astound the government and fire its greed.

Here is Lebedev, a radio operator from the Khovrino Camp. Now that he has been turned down there is nothing more to hide, and he admits to me that he discovered a deviation of the compass needle from the odor of garlic. From this he had envisioned a way to modulate high-frequency waves with an odor and thereby transmit an odor over a great distance. However, government circles did not see any military advantage in this project and were not interested. That meant it didn't come off. Either go on bending your back or think up something better!

One or another fellow—true, very rarely—would be suddenly taken off somewhere. He would not explain or say anything himself, so as not to spoil things, and no one in the camp could figure out why this particular person had been taken off somewhere. One might disappear forever, and another might be brought back after a time. He would still not say what it was about, so as not to become a laughingstock. Or he would put on an air of great mystery. This, too, was typical of the zeks: telling something to exaggerate their importance.

But having myself been on the Islands of Paradise, I had had the opportunity of seeing both ends of the pipeline: *where* this got to and how they read things there. And here I am going to allow myself to amuse the patient reader of this not-so-very-cheery book.

There was a certain Trushlyakov, formerly a Soviet lieutenant, shell-shocked in Sevastopol, taken prisoner there, dragged subsequently through Auschwitz, and as a result of all this a little touched. He managed to propose from camp something so intriguing that it led to his being brought to a scientific research institute for prisoners—i.e., a sharashka. There he proved to be a genuine fountain of inventions, and no sooner had the chiefs rejected one of them than he immediately proposed the next. And even though he did not get even one of these inventions to the calculating stage, he was so inspired, so impressive, spoke so little, and had such an expressive look, that not only did no one dare suspect him of swindling, but one of my friends, a very serious engineer, insisted that in the profundity of his ideas Trushlyakov was the twentieth-century Newton. I, it is true, did not follow up on all his ideas to the very end, but he was entrusted with working out and preparing a *radar absorber* which he himself had proposed. He demanded help in higher mathematics, and, as a mathematician, I was assigned to him. Here is how Trushlyakov set forth his idea:

In order not to reflect radar waves, a plane or a tank must be covered with a certain material made up of many separate layers. (What sort of material this was Trushlyakov never told me; either he had not yet selected it or else this was the inventor's main secret.) The electromagnetic wave had to lose all its energy through the multiple refractions and reflections back and forth at the edges of these layers. And now, without knowing the characteristics of the material, yet making use of the laws of geometrical optics and any other means available to me, I was supposed to prove that everything would work out as Trushlyakov had predicted—and in addition select the optimal number of layers!

Naturally, I could do nothing! Nor did Trushlyakov do anything either. Our creative alliance collapsed.

Soon afterward, Trushlyakov brought me in my capacity as librarian (I was also librarian there) a requisition for an interlibrary loan from the Lenin Library. Without indicating authors or publications, the requisition consisted of the following: "Something relating to the technology of interplanetary travel."

Since we were only in the year 1947 at the time, the Lenin Library had almost nothing to offer him other than Jules Verne. (People thought little of Tsiolkovsky at that time.) After an unsuccessful attempt to set up a flight to the Moon, Trushlyakov was expelled thence into the abyss—back to camp.

But the letters kept coming and coming. I was subsequently attached (this time as a translator) to a group of engineers investigating the piles of claims to inventions and patents coming in from the camps. A translator was required because many of the documents arriving in 1946 and 1947 were in German.

But these were not claims to patents! And they were not voluntary compositions either! It was shameful and painful to read them. They had been extorted, exacted, sweated out of German war prisoners. For it was clear that we could not succeed in holding these prisoners as war prisoners for all eternity. It might be three years or it might be five after the end of the war, but sooner or later they would have to be released "nach der Heimat." It was therefore necessary during the years they were here to squeeze out everything which could be useful to our country. We had to try to get even this pale reflection of those German patents that had been carted off to the Western zones.

I could easily picture how it had been done. The unsuspecting and dependable Germans were instructed to report their fields of specialization, where they had worked, and in what capacity. Then, naturally, the Security Operations Third Section summoned all the engineers and technicians into their office one at a time. They were first questioned with respectful attention (this flattered the Germans!) about the kind and nature of their prewar work in Germany. (They had already begun to think that perhaps they would be given more privileged work instead of camp work.) Then a signed agreement on nondisclosure was required of them. (And once something is "verboten" to a German he will not violate it.) And, finally, they were confronted with a harsh demand to set forth in writing all the interesting details of their field of production and describe any important technical innovations used there. Then the Germans came to realize belatedly what kind of trap they had been caught in by bragging about their former jobs! But they could not just write *nothing at all* now—for they were threatened in that event with never being allowed to return to their Motherland. (And in those years this seemed quite likely.)

With tormented consciences, depressed, barely pushing their pens, the Germans wrote. . . . The only thing that saved them and enabled them to avoid giving away serious secrets was the fact that the ignorant Security officers were incapable of fathoming the true nature of their testimony and valued it according to the number of pages. And we, going through it, were hardly ever able to find anything substantial; the information was either contradictory or buried in a scientific fog with omission of the main thing, or else they seriously described "technical innovations" of a type well known to our grandfathers.

But the claims to patents in Russian—what servility they sometimes reeked of! Once again one can easily picture how these were written: how there in camp, on a pitiful free Sunday, the authors of these claims carefully hid what they were writing from their neighbors, probably lying and saying they were writing *petitions for pardon.* Nor could their dim minds foresee that it was not the lazy, well-fed Leadership that would read their calligraphy addressed to the Sovereign, but plain ordinary zeks like themselves.

And we leafed through sixteen big pages (paper begged from the KVCh) of the most detailed proposals: (1) "On the use of infrared rays for guarding camp compounds." (2) "On the use of photoelectric elements for counting the number of prisoners departing through the gatehouse." And the son-of-a-bitch included drawings too, and technical elucidations. And the preamble was as follows:

Dear Iosif Vissarionovich!

Even though I have been sentenced for my crimes under Article 58 to a long term of imprisonment, even here I remain devoted to my beloved Soviet government and wish to assist in the secure guarding of the fierce enemies of the people who surround me. If I am summoned from the camp and receive the necessary means, I guarantee to make this system work.

Now this was a "political" for you! This treatise went from hand to hand among us, amid exclamations and obscenities (all of us there were zeks). One of us sat down to write a review of the project: The project was technically illiterate . . . the project did not take into consideration . . . the project did not provide for . . . unprofitable . . . unreliable . . . it could lead to a weakening rather than a strengthening of camp guard. . . .

What are you dreaming of today, Judas, at your distant camp? I'll shove a pole down your throat. Drop dead, rat!

And here came a packet from Vorkuta. The author complains that the Americans have an atomic bomb and our Motherland hasn't. He writes that at Vorkuta he often ponders this fact, and that up there, behind barbed wire, he wishes to help the Party and the government. And therefore he heads his project: "DAN—Disintegrating the Atomic Nucleus." But he has not perfected this project (a familiar picture) because of the lack of technical literature at the Vorkuta Camp. (As if there were any other literature there either!) And this savage merely asks us to send him in the meantime *instructions on radioactive disintegration*, after which he will undertake to complete his project for DAN.

Behind our desks we roll with laughter and almost simultaneously come to the same vulgar evaluation:

> This here DAN
> Is a ——ing sham.

And meanwhile really great scientists were done in and perished in camps. But the Leadership of our dear Ministry was in no hurry to seek them out there and to find worthier uses for them.

Aleksandr Leonidovich Chizhevsky served his whole term without ever being in a sharashka. Even before camp Chizhevsky was very much out of favor in our country because he had found a connection between revolutions on earth, biological processes on earth, and solar activity. His scientific scope was out of the ordinary: the problems he concerned himself with were unexpected and did not fit into the convenient, accepted classifications of the world of science; and it was not clear how they could be put to use for military and industrial purposes. Today, after his death, we read articles praising him: He established that the incidence of myocardiac thrombosis is sixteen times greater during electrical storms. He correctly predicted flu epidemics. He was in quest of a technique for the early discovery of cancer based on the graph of the subsidence reaction of red corpuscles. And he advanced the hypothesis of zeta radiation from the sun.

The father of Soviet space navigation, Korolev, was, to be sure, taken into a sharashka, but as an aviation scientist. The sharashka administration did not allow him to work on rockets, and he had to do that work at night.

(We don't know whether L. Landau would have been taken into a sharashka or shipped off to distant islands. He had already confessed, with a broken rib, to being a German spy, but was saved by the intervention of P. Kapitsa.)

Konstantin Ivanovich Strakhovich, the great Russian specialist in aerodynamics and an extraordinarily versatile scientific mind, after traveling on a prisoner transport from the Leningrad prison, became an auxiliary worker in the bath of the Uglich Camp. He now relates the whole story with his innocent childish laugh, which he amazingly retained throughout his whole tenner. After several months in a death cell, he then survived a serious attack of dystrophic diarrhea in camp. After that they assigned him to guard the entrance to the soaping room when the women's brigades were taking baths. (They had to assign stronger people to deal with the men—he couldn't have handled it.) His task was to be sure that the women entering the soaping room wore nothing and had empty hands, so that everything went to the fumigator, most of all the bras and panties, which the Medical Section considered the chief centers of lice infestation, and which the women tried particularly hard not to turn in and attempted to take through the bath with them. And Strakhovich looked like this: he had a Lord Kelvin beard and a forehead like a craggy cliff, with a brow double the ordinary height—you could hardly call it a forehead at all. The women pleaded with him and insulted him and grew angry at him and laughed at him and invited him to accompany them to a pile of twig brooms in the corner—nothing moved him and he was merciless. Then they unanimously and maliciously nicknamed him "The Impotent." And suddenly one fine day the authorities came and took this "Impotent" off to be in charge of no more and no less than the first turbojet engine project in the country.

But of those scientists who were allowed to die at general work we know nothing. . . .

And as for those arrested and destroyed in the heat of scientific discovery (like Nikolai Mikhailovich Orlov, who back in 1936 had worked out a method for the long-term preservation of foodstuffs), how are we to find out about them? After all, their discoveries *were shut down* following the arrest of the men who made them.

■

In the fetid, oxygenless atmosphere of the camps, the sooty flame of the KVCh would sputter and flare up, casting the merest glimmer. But people would be drawn from various barracks and from various brigades even to this little flame. Some came with a direct purpose: to tear paper from a book or newspaper to make a smoke, to get paper for a petition, or to write with the ink there. (Ink was not permitted in the barracks, and here, too, it was kept under lock and key; after all, ink can be used to forge rubber stamps!) And some came . . . just to put on airs: See how cultured I am! And some . . . to rub elbows and chatter with new people, someone other than their boring fellow brigade mates. And some came . . . to listen to the others and report to the "godfather." But there were others still who didn't themselves know why they were inexplicably drawn there for a short evening half-hour, tired as they were, instead of lying on their bunks, allowing their aching bodies to rest a little.

These visits to the KVCh brought the soul a mite of refreshment in imperceptible and unobvious ways. Even though those who stopped by were altogether the same sort of hungry zeks as the ones who stayed sitting on their brigade multiple bunks, here they didn't talk about rations, nor of portions of cereal, nor about norms. People here didn't talk about the things that made up camp life, and therein lay a protest of the heart and some relaxation for the mind. Here they talked about some kind of fabulous past which just could not have existed for these gray, famished, bedraggled people. Here, too, they talked about the indescribably blessed, free-moving life out in freedom of those fortunates who had somehow succeeded in not landing in prison. And people also talked about art here, sometimes so magically!

It was as if someone, when an evil spirit was raging, had drawn on the ground a weakly gleaming and foggily flickering circle—and it was just about to go out, but as long as it hadn't you could at least imagine that within that circle, for those half-hours, you were not in the power of the evil force.

Yes, and then, too, someone would sometimes be plucking at a guitar. Someone would be softly singing—a song that was not at all the kind permitted on the stage. And something would stir within you: Life . . . exists! It exists! And, looking happily around you, you, too, would want to express something to someone.

However, speak only guardedly! Listen, but keep pinching yourself. Take Lyova G——n. He was an inventor (and a student who had not completed the course in the auto engineering institute; he was planning to increase the efficiency of motors, but they took all his notes away when they searched his place).

He was also an actor and we were putting on Chekhov's *The Proposal* with him. He was a philosopher too, and was adept at such cute expressions as "I don't want to worry about future generations. Let them scratch around in the earth for themselves. I myself cling to life just like this!" He demonstrated by gripping the wood of the table with his fingernails. "Believe in lofty ideas? That's something to be said into a telephone with the wire pulled out. History is a disconnected chain of facts. Give me back my tail! An amoeba is more perfect than a human being: it has simpler functions." If you listened to him, he would explain in detail why he hated Lev Tolstoi, why he was intoxicated by Ilya Ehrenburg and Aleksandr Grin. He was also an obliging chap who didn't avoid hard work: he would hammer away at a wall with a cold chisel, true, in a brigade guaranteed 140 percent of norm. His father had been arrested and had died in 1937, but he himself was a nonpolitical offender imprisoned for forging bread-ration cards. However, he was ashamed of his own swindling article and tried to get closer to the 58's. He tried and tried to get closer. But then one day some camp trials began and this oh, so pleasant and interesting lad, "clinging to life," Lyova G———n, testified as a witness for the prosecution.[4] And it was a good thing if you hadn't said too much to him.

If there were eccentrics in camp (and there always were!), they could not avoid dropping in on the KVCh. They were bound to look in.

Take Aristid Ivanovich Dovatur—a real eccentric for you. A native of St. Petersburg, of French and Rumanian extraction, a classical philologist, for all the past and future a bachelor and a solitary. He was torn away from Herodotus and Caesar, like a cat from meat, and imprisoned in a camp. His heart was still full of unexpounded texts. And in camp he acted as if he were in a dream. He would have been finished off in the first week, but the doctors provided him with protection and set him up in the enviable position of medical statistician; and in addition, not without benefit to the freshly recruited camp medical assistants, Dovatur was instructed to give lectures twice a month! This was in camp—and they were in Latin! Aristid Ivanovich stood at a

4. And all those who "cling to life" too hard never particularly cling to the spirit.

small blackboard—and glowed, just as in his best university years! He wrote down strange columns of conjugations which had never ever loomed before the eyes of the natives, and at the sound of the crumbling chalk his heart beat voluptuously. His life was so quiet and so well set up! But disaster crashed on his head too: the camp chief considered him a rarity—an honest person! And he named him . . . manager of the bakery—the most lucrative of all camp positions! The man in charge of bread was in charge of men's lives! The road to this position was paved with the bodies and the souls of camp inmates—but few got there. And then and there this position fell from the heavens—to Dovatur, who was crushed by it. For one week he went about like a person condemned to death, even before taking over the bakery. He begged the camp chief *to have mercy on him* and to allow him to live, to keep his Latin conjugations and an unconfined spirit. And pardon came: a routine crook was named manager of the bakery.

And here is another eccentric who was always in the KVCh after work. Where else would he be? He had a big head and large features suitable for theatrical makeup, easily visible from far away. He had particularly expressive bushy eyebrows. And his look was always tragic. From a corner of the room he looked in dispiritedly on our skimpy rehearsals. This was Camille Leopoldovich Gontoir. In the first years after the Revolution he had come from Belgium to Petrograd to create a New Theater, a theater of the future. Who then could have foreseen how this future would go and that theater directors would be arrested? Gontoir fought both world wars against the Germans, the first in the West and the second in the East. And now he had been pasted with a tenner for treason to the Motherland. Which one? And when?

But of course the most noticeable people in the KVCh were the artists. They were the head men there. If there was a separate room, it was for them. If anyone was permanently released from *general work*, it was invariably they. Of all the servitors of the muses only they created real values—values you could feel with the fingers, hang up in apartments, sell for money. They did not, of course, paint their pictures out of their own inspiration. No one asked that of them, for how could a good painting come out of the head of a 58? They simply painted big copies from postcards. Some of them with a system of small squares and some without. And you couldn't find a finer piece of aesthetic merchandise in the entire taiga and tundra backwood: Just go ahead and paint, and we'll know where to hang it. Even if we don't like it right away. Vypirailo, the assistant commander of the platoon of guards, would come in and look at a copy of *Nero the Victor* by Deul:

"What d'ya call that? That a bridegroom there? Why is he so dark?"

But he would take it all the same. The artists also painted rugs with lovely ladies floating about in gondolas, with swans, sunsets, and castles—and all of it was very much in demand among the comrade officers. And not being fools, the artists also painted the same kind of rugs on their own, and the jailers sold them on the sly in the markets outside. They were in big demand. On the whole, the artists could make out in camp.

Sculptors had it worse. Sculpture for MVD personnel was something not pretty enough, not familiar enough, to be put in their homes—yes, and it took up room for furniture, and if you knocked it over, it would break. It was rare for sculptors to have work in camp, and when they did, it was usually combined with painting, as with Nedov. Even then Major Bakayev would walk in and see a statuette of a mother:

"Why did you make a weeping mother? In our country mothers don't weep!" And he reached out to break up the figure.

Volodya Klempner, a young composer, son of a well-to-do lawyer, and in terms of camp concepts still *an unbeaten newcomer*, took his own piano from home to the Beskudinovo Camp near Moscow. (This was unheard of in the Archipelago!) Allegedly he took it to strengthen mass cultural work, but in reality to continue his own composing. And he always had the key to the camp stage, and after taps he would play there by candlelight (the electricity had been shut off). Once he was playing there like that, writing down his new sonata, when he jumped at a voice behind him:

"It's sh-ack-les your music smells of!"

Klempner jumped up. From the wall where he had stood concealed, a major, the camp chief, an old Chekist, advanced on the candle—and behind him his immense black shadow grew. Now the major understood why this deceiver had sent for his piano.

He came up, took the music Klempner had written, and silently and gloomily began to burn it with the candle.

"What are you doing?" the young composer could not help but cry out.

"*Shove* your music!" the major declared still more positively through clenched teeth.

The ashes floated from the sheet and fell softly on the keyboard.

The old Chekist had made no mistake: that sonata really was written about the camps.[5]

If a poet announced himself in camp, he would be allowed to write captions beneath caricatures of prisoners and to compose jingles—also about violators of discipline.

No other theme was permitted either a poet or a composer. They were unable to make the camp chiefs anything tangible, useful, to be held in the hands.

And there were just no prose writers in camp because there were not supposed to be, ever.

When Russian prose departed for the camps, wrote B. Slutsky, it departed! And it never returned. It departed! And never emerged.

We shall never now be able to arrive at any judgment of the full scale of what took place, of the number who perished, or of the standard they might have attained. No one will ever tell us about the notebooks hurriedly burned before departures on prisoner transports, or of the completed fragments and big schemes carried in heads and cast together with those heads into frozen mass graves. Verses can be read, lips close to ear; they can be remembered, and they or the memory of them can be communicated. But prose cannot be passed on before its time. It is harder for it to survive. It is too bulky, too rigid, too bound up with paper, to pass through the vicissitudes of the Archipelago. Who in camp could make up his mind *to write?* A. Belinkov wrote, and his writings got to the "godfather"—and on the ricochet he got twenty-five years. There was M. I. Kalinina, no writer at all,

---

5. Soon they found an excuse to pin a new camp case on Volodya and sent him to the Butyrki for interrogation. He never returned to his camp, and his piano, of course, was never returned either. And did he survive himself? I do not know, but there is somehow no word of him.

who nonetheless wrote down in her notebook what was notable in camp life: "Perhaps it will be useful to someone someday." But it got to the security officer. And she was put in a punishment block. (But she got off easily.) Here is Vladimir Sergeyevich G——v, who, since he was not under convoy, while he was outside the camp compound, wrote over a period of four months somewhere there a chronicle of the camp, and in a dangerous moment he buried it in the ground, and he was sent away forever, and it remained in the ground. So inside the camp compound it was impossible, and outside the camp compound it was impossible, so where was it possible? Only in your head. But only verse can be written that way, prose can't.

It is impossible to estimate by extrapolating from the few who survived how many of us servitors of Clio and Calliope perished —because we, too, had no likelihood of surviving. (Going back over my own camp life, for example, I see that I was certain to die in the Archipelago—or else so to adapt myself in order to survive that even the need to write would have died. I was saved by a secondary factor, mathematics. And how could you take that into account in your calculations?)

From the thirties on, everything that is called our prose is merely the foam from a lake which has vanished underground. It is foam and not prose because it detached itself from everything that was fundamental in those decades. The best of the writers suppressed the best within themselves and turned their back on truth—and only that way did they and their books survive. And those who could not renounce profundity, individuality, and directness . . . inevitably had to lay down their heads during those decades, most often through camp, though some lost theirs through reckless courage at the front.

That's how our prose philosophers went beneath the ground. Our prose historians too. Our lyrical prose writers. Our prose impressionists. Our prose humorists.

And yet at the same time the Archipelago provided a unique, exceptional opportunity for our literature, and perhaps . . . even for world literature. This unbelievable serfdom in the full flower of the twentieth century, in this one and only and not at all redeeming sense, opened to writers a fertile though fatal path.[6]

6. I will be so bold as to elucidate this thought in its most general aspect. As long as the world has stood, there have always been until now two unmix-

Millions of Russian intellectuals were thrown there—not for a joy ride: to be mutilated, to die, without any hope of return. For the first time in history, such a multitude of sophisticated, mature, and cultivated people found themselves, not in imagination and once and for all, inside the pelt of slave, serf, logger, miner. And so for the first time in world history (on such a scale) the experience of the upper and the lower strata of society *merged*. That extremely important, seemingly transparent, yet

---

able strata of society: the upper and the lower, the ruling and the ruled. This is a crude division, like all divisions, but if one classifies among the upper stratum not only those superior in power, money, and social position but also those superior in education, obtained through either family efforts or their own, in a word all those who do not need to work with their hands, then the division will be almost across the board.

Therefore we can expect four spheres of world literature (and of art in general, and ideas in general). The first sphere: those in the upper stratum portraying (describing, pondering) the upper stratum, in other words themselves, their own people. The second sphere: the upper stratum depicting or pondering the lower stratum, "the younger brother." The third sphere: the lower stratum depicting the upper. And the fourth: the lower portraying . . . the lower, i.e., itself.

The upper stratum always had the free times, an excess or at least a sufficiency of means, the education, the training. Those among them who wanted to could always master the artistic techniques and the discipline of thought. But there is one important law of life: Contentment always kills spiritual striving in a human being. And as a result this first sphere contained within it many satiated artistic distortions and many morbid and self-important "schools"—sterile flowerings. And only when writers who were either profoundly unhappy in their personal lives or had an overwhelming natural drive toward spiritual seeking entered that sphere as the bearers of culture was great literature created.

The fourth sphere is all the world's folklore. Leisure time here was broken up into tiny pieces—and was available to individuals in different ways. And the anonymous contributions to this culture also came in different ways—unpremeditated, through lucky moments of glimpsing a perfected image or turn of speech. But the actual creators of it were innumerable, and they were almost always oppressed and dissatisfied people. Everything created then passed through selection, washing, and polishing a hundred thousand times over, passing from mouth to mouth and year to year. And that is how we have come to possess our golden store of folklore. It is never empty or soulless—because among its authors there were none who were unacquainted with suffering. The written literature belonging to the fourth sphere ("proletarian," "peasant") is altogether embryonic, inexperienced, unsuccessful, because individual know-how has always been lacking here.

The written literature of the third sphere ("looking upward from below") suffered from the same faults of inexperience, but even worse: it was poisoned by envy and hate—sterile feelings which do not create art. It made the same mistake that revolutionaries continually make: ascribing the vices of the upper class to the class itself and not to humanity as a whole, while failing to imagine how notably they themselves inherit these vices. Or else, on the other hand, it was spoiled by servile fawning.

Morally, the second sphere of literature promised to be the most fertile

previously impenetrable partition preventing the upper strata from understanding the lower—pity—now melted. Pity had moved the noble sympathizers of the past (all the enlighteners!) —and pity had also blinded them! They were tormented by pangs of conscience because they themselves did not share that evil fate, and for that reason they considered themselves obliged to shout three times as loud about injustices, at the same time missing out on any fundamental examination of the human nature of the people of the lower strata, of the upper strata, of all people.

Only from the intellectual zeks of the Archipelago did these pangs of conscience drop away once and for all, for they completely shared the evil fate of the people! Only now could an educated Russian write about an enserfed peasant *from the inside* —because he himself had become a serf.

But at this point he had no pencil, no paper, no time, no supple fingers. Now the jailers kept shaking out his things and looking into the entrance and exit of his alimentary canal, and the security officers kept looking into his eyes.

The experience of the upper and the lower strata had merged— but the bearers of the merged experience perished. . . .

And thus it was that an unprecedented philosophy and literature were buried under the iron crust of the Archipelago.

■

But the most populous of all the groups that visited the KVCh . . . were the participants in amateur theatricals. This particular function—directing amateur theatricals—still belonged to the

---

("looking down from above"). It was created by people whose goodness, striving for the truth, and sense of justice had proved stronger than their soporific prosperity, and whose artistry was at the same time mature and on a high level. But the fault of this sphere was *the incapacity genuinely to understand*. These authors sympathized, pitied, wept, were indignant—and precisely because of this could not *understand precisely*. They always looked at things from the sidelines and from above. They simply could not climb into the *pelts* of the members of the lower stratum. And any who managed to get one leg over the fence could never get the other over.

Evidently man's nature is so egocentric that this transformation can only take place, alas, with the help of external violence. That is how Cervantes got his education in slavery and Dostoyevsky his at hard labor. In the Gulag Archipelago this experiment was carried out on millions of heads and hearts all at once.

aged and decrepit KVCh, just as it had when it was young and vigorous.[7] On individual islands of the Archipelago amateur theatricals rose and disappeared in alternating ebb and flow, but unlike the tides of the sea, this did not take place with regularity but in fits and starts for reasons known to the chiefs but not to the zeks, and perhaps because the chief of the KVCh had to make a mark in his report once every six months, and perhaps because they were expecting someone from up top.

Here is how it was done at the remote camps: The chief of the KVCh (who was never ordinarily seen in the camp compound anyway, everything being managed for him by a prisoner instructor) would summon an accordionist and tell him: "Here's what! Round up a choir![8] And see to it that it performs in a month's time."

"But, Citizen Chief, I don't read notes."

"What the hell do you need with notes! You just play a song everyone knows, and let the rest sing along."

And so the recruiting of a choir was announced, sometimes along with a dramatics group. Where were they going to practice? The KVCh room was too small for this, they needed a more spacious one, and, of course, there was no clubroom at all. Ordinarily the usual domain for this was the camp mess halls—constantly stinking with the steam from gruel, the odor of rotten vegetables and boiled cod. On one side of the mess halls was the kitchen, and on the other side either a permanent stage or a temporary platform. After dinner the choir and the dramatic circle assembled here. (The surroundings were like those in the drawing by A. G——n. [Illustration No. 41.] Except that the artist has depicted not their own local amateur stage group but a touring "culture brigade." The last dishes are about to be gathered up

7. The universal concern for amateur theatricals in our country, something on which, incidentally, no small amounts of money are spent, does have some sort of intent, but what? One cannot say immediately. Is it the inertia left over from what was once proclaimed in the twenties? Or is it, like sport, an obligatory means of distracting the people's energy and interest? Or does someone believe that all these songs and skits actually help the required processing of feelings?

8. The political leadership *both* in the army and out in freedom has a superstitious faith in the primary indoctrinational significance of *choirs* in particular. All the rest of the amateur theatrical activity could wither, but there has to be a choir! A singing collective. Songs could easily be checked out, they were all *ours!* And whatever you sing . . . you believe.

41. Amateur theatricals

and the last-leggers are about to be kicked out—and then the audience will be let in. The reader can see how cheerful the serf actresses are.)

How was one to coax the zeks to join in the amateur theatricals? For out of perhaps five hundred prisoners in the compound there might be three or four genuine amateur singers—so how was one to put together a choir? Well, the main bait in mixed camp compounds lay in encounters at the choir! (Let's take a look again at Illustration No. 39. Well, isn't it clear why they are all in the KVCh?) A. Susi, who had been appointed choirmaster, was astonished at how rapidly his choir grew, so much so that he could never fully rehearse them in any single song. New participants kept coming and coming. They had no voices. They had never sung before. But they kept begging, and how cruel it would have been to refuse them, to ignore their newly awakened thirst for art! However, many fewer choir members turned up at the actual rehearsals. (The reason was that the participants in the amateur theatricals were permitted to move about the compound, to and from rehearsals, for two hours after the bed curfew. And so they used these two hours to wind up their own affairs.)

And it was not unheard of for things like this to happen: Just before the performance the only bass in the choir would be sent off on a prisoner transport (the transports were handled by a different department than the performance). Or the choirmaster—the same Susi—was summoned by the chief of the KVCh and told:

"We very much appreciate that you have worked so hard, but we can't let you perform at the concert, because a 58 doesn't have the right to lead a choir. So get a replacement ready; waving your arms around isn't like having a voice—you'll find someone."

And there were those for whom the choir and the dramatic circle were not merely a place to meet someone—but rather a counterfeit of life, or maybe not a counterfeit, but a reminder, instead, that life despite everything still exists, that it does go on existing. From the warehouse they would one day bring rough brown wrapping paper from cereal sacks—and it was handed round to write parts on. A time-honored theatrical procedure! And then, too, there was the distribution of roles! And the consideration of who would be kissing whom in the play! Who would be dressed in what! How to make up! How interesting it would look! On the night of the performance one could take a real mirror in one's hand and see oneself in a real dress from freedom and with rouged cheeks.

It was very interesting to dream about all that, but good Lord, the plays! What kind of plays they had there! Those special collections, inscribed "*For Use Only Inside Gulag!*" Why . . . "only"? Not "both for freedom and also for Gulag," but instead . . . "only inside Gulag." What this really meant was that it was such twaddle, such pigs' swill, that out in freedom they wouldn't swallow it, so pour it out for us! The stupidest and least talented writers deposited their most loathsome and rubbishy plays here! And if anyone wanted to put on a farce by Chekhov or something else, where was he supposed to find that play? It could not be found even among the free people in the whole settlement, and what the camp library had was Gorky, and even then pages had been torn out to roll smokes.

N. Davidenkov, a writer, assembled a dramatic circle in the Krivoshchekovo Camp. From somewhere he got an unusual playlet: it was patriotic and dealt with Napoleon's sojourn in Moscow! (And probably it was on a level with Rastopchin's posted proclamations!)* They distributed the roles, and the prisoners rushed to rehearsals with great enthusiasm. So what could interfere now? The main role was played by Zina, a former teacher, arrested after remaining behind in occupied territory. She acted well, and the director was satisfied with her. All of a sudden there was a quarrel at one of the rehearsals: the rest of the women rebelled against Zina's playing the main role. This was not exactly a new situation, and it was one with which a director can ordinarily cope. But here's what the women were shouting: "It's a patriotic role, and she ———— Germans on occupied territory! Get out, bitch! Get out, you German whore! Before you get stomped!" These women were socially friendly and also perhaps from among the 58's, but not on a charge of treason. Did they think this up themselves, or did the Third Section suggest it to them? The director, in view of his article, was in no position to defend his actress. So Zina departed sobbing.

Does the reader sympathize with the director? Does the reader think that the dramatic circle had got into an impossible situation —for who, at this point, could be given the role of heroine and when could she learn it? But there are no impossible situations for the Security Section! They had made a mess of everything—and they will straighten it out! Two days later Davidenkov himself was taken off in handcuffs—for trying to transmit something outside the compound in writing (another camp chronicle?), and there was to be a new interrogation and trial.[9]

9. This is a camp recollection about him. On the other hand, it was discovered by accident that L. K. Chukovskaya knew Kolya Davidenkov in the queues outside the Leningrad prisons in 1939 when, toward the end of the Yezhovshchina, he was exonerated by an ordinary court while his codefendant, L. Gumilyev,* remained imprisoned. They did not restore the young man to his place in the institute, but took him into the army. In 1941 he was taken prisoner by the Germans near Minsk. He then escaped from a German POW camp—to England . . . and while there published, under a pseudonym (in order to spare his family), a book about his imprisonment in the Leningrad dungeons in 1938. (One has to suppose that in those days love for the Soviet ally prevented English readers from giving due credit to that book. Afterward it was forgotten and lost. But *our people* did not forget him.) He fought on the Western Front in the International Anti-Fascist Brigade and, after the war, was kidnaped back to the U.S.S.R., where he was sentenced to be shot, but this was commuted to a sentence of twenty-five years. Evidently, however, he was actually executed on the basis of the second camp case against him. (Under capital punishment, which was returned to us by the Decree of January, 1950.) In May, 1950, Davidenkov managed to send off his last letter from camp prison. Here are several phrases from it: "It is impossible to describe my whole incredible life during these years. . . . I have a different purpose: over ten

And so it wasn't necessary to find anyone to play the principal role! Napoleon would not be put to shame once more, nor would Russian patriotism once more be glorified! There would be no play at all! And there would be no choir. And there would be no concert. So amateur theatrical activity was at an ebb. The evening gatherings in the mess hall and the lovers' rendezvous would cease. Till the next rising tide!

And so it lived by fits and starts.

And sometimes everything would have already been rehearsed, and all the participants would have been left intact, and no one would have been rearrested before the performance, but the chief of the KVCh, Major Potapov, a Komi* (SevZhelDorlag), would pick up the program and see there "*Doubts*, by Glinka."

"What's this! Doubts? No doubts! No, no, don't even ask me!"—and he crossed it out.

And I once planned to read my favorite monologue—Chatsky's speech: "But who are the judges?" I had been accustomed to reading it since childhood and I valued it purely for its rhetoric, failing to notice that it was about today. I had no such thoughts. But at any rate I had not gone so far as to write in the program: "But who are the judges?" for they would have crossed it out. The chief of the KVCh came to rehearsal and jumped up at the line which went:

> Their hostility to the free life was implacable.

---

years I have managed to accomplish something: my prose, of course, has all perished, but my verses remain. I have read them to almost no one—there was no one to read them to. I remember our nights at the Five Corners and . . . conceived the idea that my verses must be got . . . into your wise and skilled hands. . . . Read them and if possible preserve them. Of the future, as of the past—not a word. Everything is finished." And the verses are preserved entire in L.K.'s hands. How I recognize that tiny script (I, too, wrote like that)— three dozen poems on a double-sided notebook sheet—you have to work so much into such a small area! Just imagine this despair at the very end of his life: waiting for death in a camp prison! And he entrusted his last hopeless outcry to "illegal" mail:

> "I do not need clean bedclothes,
> Don't open up the door!
> And it must be true—
> I'm a cursed and savage beast!
> I know not what to do with you,
> Or how to address you:
> Shall I sing like a bird, or howl like a wolf,
> Shall I roar or shall I snarl?"

And when I declaimed:

> Where, point out to me, are the fathers of the fatherland?
> Are they not those, rich with plunder?

he stamped his feet and indicated that I get off the stage that instant.

In my youth I had almost become an actor, but a weakness of the throat prevented me. And now, in camp, I sometimes appeared in stage performances, and was drawn to refresh myself in that brief, unreal oblivion, to see at close range the faces of women excited by the performance. And when I heard that special theatrical troupes consisting of zeks freed from general work existed in Gulag—genuine serf theaters—I dreamed of getting into such a troupe and by this means saving myself and breathing a bit more easily.

Serf theaters existed in every provincial camp administration, and there were even several of them in Moscow. The most famous was MVD Colonel Mamulov's serf theater at Khovrino. Mamulov watched jealously to make sure that none of the notable performers of Moscow who had been arrested should slip by him through Krasnaya Presnya. And he had his agents searching in other transit prisons too. In this way he collected a large theatrical troupe in his camp and the start of an opera company too. His was the pride of an estate owner: "I have a better theater than my neighbor does." There was also a theater in the Beskudnikovo Camp, but it was inferior in most respects. The serf owners took their players to one another on visits in order to brag about them. At one such performance Mikhail Grinvald forgot in what key to accompany the singer. Then and there Mamulov pasted him with ten days of cold punishment cell—where Grinvald fell ill.

There were other such serf theaters in Vorkuta, Norilsk, Solikamsk, on all the big Gulag islands. And in those areas these theaters became almost municipal theaters, almost academic theaters, and gave performances for free people in a municipal theater. The local MVD big shots sat haughtily with their wives in the first rows and watched their slaves with curiosity and contempt. And the convoy guards sat behind the scenes and in the boxes with their automatic pistols. After the performances those players who had won applause were taken back to camp, and those who had fallen on their faces . . . to punishment block. Sometimes they were not even allowed to enjoy the applause. In the Magadan theater, Nikishov, the chief of Dalstroi, interrupted Vadim Kozin, a widely known singer at that time: "All right, Kozin, stop the bowing and get out!" (Kozin tried to hang himself but was taken down out of the noose.)

In postwar years many performers with famous names passed through the Archipelago: In addition to Kozin there were the actresses Tokarskaya, Okunevskaya, Zoya Fyodorova. There was a big to-do in the Archipelago over the arrest of the singer Ruslanova, and there were contradictory rumors about which transit prisons she had been at and to which camp she had been sent. They said that in the Kolyma she had refused to sing and had worked in the laundry. I do not know.

The idol of Leningrad, the tenor Pechkovsky, had been in an occupied area, at his dacha near Luga, at the beginning of the war and had subsequently performed for the Germans in the Baltic States. (His wife, a pianist, had been immediately arrested in Leningrad and had perished in the Rybinsk Camp.) After the war, Pechkovsky got a tenner for treason and was sent to Pech-ZhelDorlag. The chief maintained him there as a VIP in a separate little house of his own, with two orderlies attached to him. And butter, raw eggs, and hot port wine were included in his rations. He used to dine with the wife of the chief of the camp and the wife of the chief of camp regimen. And he used to sing there, but once, they say, he rebelled: "I sing for the people, not for Chekists!" And so he was sent to the Special Camp, Minlag. (After he had served out his term he was never allowed to rise to the heights of his former concerts in Leningrad.)

The well-known pianist Vsevolod Topilin was not spared in the roundup of the Moscow People's Volunteer Corps in 1941 and was thrown into battle in the Vyazma encirclement with an 1866 Berdan rifle.[10] But in German captivity a music-loving German major who was camp commandant took pity on him—

10. All that panic with the Moscow Volunteer Corps—what a diabolical piece of hysteria that was! To throw urban intellectuals with Berdan rifles of the last century against modern tanks! We had bragged for twenty years that we were "prepared" and that we were strong. But in animal terror in the face of the attacking Germans we shielded ourselves with the bodies of scientists and actors so that our nonentities in the leadership could survive a few extra days.

and helped get him reclassified as an East Zone worker, and he began to give concerts again. And for this, of course, Topilin then received from us the standard tenner. (And after camp he, too, never succeeded in rising again.)

The ensemble of the Moscow Administration of Corrective Labor Camps and Colonies, which went around giving performances in the camps and which had been housed at Matrosskaya Tishina, was suddenly transferred for a while to our camp at the Kaluga Gates. What luck! So now I could get to know them. And perhaps now I would force my way through to them.

What a strange sensation! To watch a performance of professional zek actors in a camp mess hall! Laughter, smiles, singing, white dresses, black frock coats . . . But what were their sentences? Under what Code articles had they been imprisoned? Was the heroine a thief? Or was she here under the "universally available 58"? Was the hero here for bribery or for "Seven-eighths"? An ordinary actor has one reincarnation only—in his role. But here was a double drama, a double reincarnation. First one had to pretend to be a free actor or actress, and only then play a role. And all that weight of prison, that consciousness that you were a serf, that tomorrow the citizen chief might send you to the punishment block for playing your role badly or for a liaison with a serf actress, or to logging, or six thousand miles to the Kolyma. What an added millstone that must be—over and above the whole burden the zek actor shared with the free actors—that destructive straining of the lungs and throat in order to force through oneself a mass of dramatized emptiness, the mechanical propaganda of dead ideas?!

The heroine of the ensemble, Nina V., turned out to be there for 58-10, on a five-year sentence. We quickly found a common acquaintance—our joint teacher in the art history department of the Moscow Institute of Philosophy, Literature, and History. She was a student who had not completed her course, and she was very young. Abusing the prerogatives of an actress, she spoiled herself with cosmetics and with those vile, cotton-padded shoulders with which all women out in freedom were destroying their beauty at that time. The women in the Archipelago had not suffered that fate, and their shoulders had developed only from hauling hand barrows.

In the ensemble Nina, like every prima, had her own beloved

(a dancer of the Bolshoi Theatre), but she also had there her own spiritual father in dramatic art—Osvald Glazunov (Glaznek), one of the senior disciples of Vakhtangov. He and his wife were—and perhaps they had wanted to be—captured by the Germans at a dacha near Istra outside Moscow. They had spent three years of the war in their tiny homeland in Riga, where they had performed in the Latvian theater. With the arrival of our Soviet forces they had received a tenner each for treason to the big Motherland. And now they were both in the ensemble.

Izolda Vikentyevna Glazunova was already old. It was already hard for her to dance. Once only did we see her in a dance which was unusual for our time, which I myself would have called impressionist, but I am afraid to offend connoisseurs. She danced in a dark silvery costume that covered her completely on a half-illuminated stage. This dance has remained in my memory. Most modern dances are a display of the female body, and that is almost all they are. But her dance was some kind of spiritual, mystical recollection, and reflected in certain of its elements her own belief in the transmigration of souls.

Suddenly, several days later, furtively, the way prisoner transports were always gotten together in the Archipelago, Izolda Vikentyevna was sent off on a transport, torn away from her husband, carried off to oblivion.

Among the serf-owning landed gentry this used to be their own special form of cruelty and barbarism: to separate serf families, to sell off the husband and wife separately. And for that they caught it from Nekrasov, Turgenev, Leskov, and from everyone. But with us this was not cruelty, it was simply a wise and reasonable move: the old woman did not earn her ration, yet she was occupying a staff unit.

On the day his wife was sent off on the prisoner transport Osvald came to our room (the chamber of monstrosities) with eyes vacantly wandering, leaning on the shoulder of his frail adopted daughter, as if she were the only thing that gave him support. He was nearly insane, and one feared he might do away with himself. Then he fell silent and his head drooped. Then he gradually began to speak, to recall his entire life: He had for some reason created two theaters: because of his art he had left his wife all alone for years. He wished now he could relive his entire life differently. . . .

I remember them now as if they were sculptured: how the old man drew the girl to him by the back of her head, and how she looked up at him from under his arm, without stirring, suffering with him and trying not to weep.

But what is there to say—the old woman had not been worth her bread ration. . . .

■

Despite all my efforts, I did not succeed in becoming a member of that troupe. Soon afterward they left the Kaluga Gates and I lost sight of them. A year later I heard a rumor at the Butyrki that they had been traveling on a truck to one of their regular performances and had been hit by a train. I do not know whether Glazunov was there or not. But so far as I myself was concerned, I once more realized that the ways of the Lord are imponderable. That we ourselves never know what we want. And how many times in life I passionately sought what I did not need and been despondent over failures which were successes.

I remained there in the modest little amateur theatrical group at the Kaluga Gates along with Anechka Breslavskaya, Shurochka Ostretsova, and Lyova G. We did manage to put on something before they broke us up and sent us away. I now recall my participation in that amateur theatrical activity as a lack of spiritual toughness, as a humiliation. The worthless Lieutenant Mironov, if he had found no other distractions and entertainments in Moscow on a Sunday evening, could come to camp in his cups and give orders: "I want a concert in ten minutes." And the performers were routed out of bed or torn away from the camp hot plate if they happened at that moment to be engaged in cooking with relish something in their mess tins. And in a trice we would be singing, dancing, and performing on the brilliantly lit stage before an empty hall, in which the only audience was the haughty dolt of a lieutenant and a troika of jailers.

Chapter 19

∎

The Zeks as a Nation

AN ETHNOGRAPHICAL ESSAY
BY FAN FANYCH

In this study, if nothing prevents us, we intend to make an important scientific discovery.

In the development of our hypothesis we would in no way wish to come into conflict with the Progressive Teaching.

The author of these lines, attracted by the enigma of the native tribe populating the Archipelago, undertook a lengthy scientific expedition there and collected abundant material.

And as a result it is very easy to prove that the *zeks* of the Archipelago constitute a *class* of society. For, after all, this multitudinous group (of many millions) has a single (common to them all) relationship to *production* (namely: subordinate, attached, and without any right to direct that production). It also has a single common relationship to the *distribution of the products* of labor (namely: no relationship at all, receiving only that insignificant share of the products required for the meager support of their own existence). And, in addition, all their labor is no small thing, but one of the principal constituents of the whole state economy.[1]

---

1. You could never say this of the outcasts in Western countries. There they are either languishing in individual isolation, where they do no work whatever, or else there are a few pockets of hard labor, whose output has no impact at all on the economy of their country.

But our ambition is greater than this.

It would be much more sensational to prove that these degenerate creatures (in the past undoubtedly human) are a totally *different biological type* in comparison with homo sapiens.[2] However, these conclusions are not yet ready. Here it will be possible only to offer certain hints to the reader. Imagine that a man is forced suddenly and against his will, yet out of implacable necessity and without hope of any return, to make a transition into the category of bear or badger. (We are not going to employ here that overused image of the wolf.) And should it turn out that he proved physically able to make it (and anyone who cashed in his chips would not be in demand there anyway), how could he possibly remain a human being while leading a new life among the badgers? We think he could not, and that he would become a badger: fur would grow; his snout would lengthen and sharpen, and he would no longer want or need anything cooked or fried: and he would be quite content to bolt things raw.

Picture to yourself that the island environment differs so sharply from the normal human one and so cruelly confronts a man with the choice of immediate adaptation or immediate death that it grinds and masticates his character much more thoroughly than could a foreign national or a foreign social environment. And the only thing it can be compared with is a transmutation into the animal world.

But we will postpone this until our next work. Here we will set ourselves only the limited task of proving that the zeks constitute a special separate *nation*.

Why is it that classes do not become nations within nations in ordinary life? Because they live commingled on the same territory with other classes. They encounter them on the streets, in stores, on trains and steamers, at theaters and places of entertainment, and they converse and exchange ideas by voice and through the printed word. The zeks, on the contrary, live totally isolated on their islands, and their life passes in communication solely with one another. (The free employers, their chiefs, they in the majority do not even see, and when they do, they hear nothing from them except orders and oaths.) Their ostracism is made all

2. Perhaps they are, in fact, the "missing link" of the theory of evolution.

the more profound by the fact that the majority of them have no clear possibility of ever abandoning this state before death, in other words, of making their way out and up into other, higher classes of society.

Who among us did not learn by heart back in secondary school the one-and-only scientific definition of a nation given by Comrade Stalin, namely: A nation is an historically formed community of people (but one neither racial nor tribal), possessing a common territory, a common language, and a commonly shared economic life, a community of psychological outlook which is manifested in a community of culture? Well, now, the natives of the Archipelago satisfy all these requirements completely, and even more too! (We are particularly free to reach these conclusions because of Comrade Stalin's brilliant remark that a racial or tribal community of blood is not obligatory at all!)

Our natives occupy a fully defined *common territory* (even though it is broken up into islands, but this does not surprise us in the Pacific Ocean, for example) on which other peoples do not live. *Their economic way of life* is standardized to an astonishing degree; it can, in fact, be described completely and exhaustively on two typewritten sheets of paper (the differential ration system and the directions to the bookkeeping office to credit the zeks' imaginary wages to maintaining the camp compound, the guard, the leadership of the islands, and to the state). If one includes in the economy also the tenor of their *daily way of life*, then it is uniform on all the islands to such a degree (like nowhere else!) that zeks who have been moved from one island to another are never surprised, do not ask silly questions, and at once set about their affairs flawlessly from the very first. ("To eat on a scientific basis, to steal whenever you can.") They eat *food* which no one else on earth eats any more. They wear *clothes* which no one else wears any more. And even their *daily schedule* is identical on all the islands and obligatory for every zek. (Now what ethnographer is able to point to any other nation, all of whose members have uniform daily schedules and uniform food and clothing?)

What is comprehended under the heading of community of *culture* in the scientific definition of nations? This has been inadequately spelled out for us. We cannot require of the zeks any unity of science or belles-lettres for the simple reason that *they have no written language*. (But then this is also the case with most other island natives, in the majority of cases for lack specifically of culture, but among the zeks . . . because of superfluity of censorship.) At the same time we hope to be able to demonstrate amply in our essay the zeks' community of *psychology*, the uniformity of their *day-to-day conduct*, even the uniformity of their *philosophical views*, of which other peoples could only dream and which is not provided for in the scientific definition of nations. It is in particular their clearly expressed *national character* that is immediately noted by the scholarly student of the zeks. They have their own folklore and their own hero images. Finally, they are tightly united by one more corner of culture indissolubly linked with *language*, and which we can describe only approximately by the pale term "matyorshchina"—mother cursing—(from the Latin *mater*). This is that special form of expressing the emotions which is even more important than all the rest of their language because it permits the zeks to communicate with one another in a more energetic and briefer form than that provided by the usual linguistic means.[3] The permanent psychological state of the zeks finds its best release and most accurate expression precisely in this highly organized mother cursing. And therefore all the rest of their language seems to recede into the background. But in this, too, we can observe from Kolyma to Moldavia the surprising similarity of expressions representing one and the same linguistic logic.

Without special study, the language of the natives of the Archipelago is quite as incomprehensible to the outsider as any foreign language. (Well, now, how for example would the reader understand such expressions as these:

"Skin the rag!"
"I'm still clicking!"
"Give a glimmer [about something]."
"To pick it off a lamppost!"
"Crook with crook and suckers out!")*

Everything said permits us to affirm boldly that the native condition in the Archipelago is a special national condition in which the former nationality of a human being is extinguished.

We can foresee an objection. They will ask us: Is this a

3. The economy of this means of communication compels one to ponder whether it does not contain the rudiments of the Language of the Future.

people if its ranks are not replenished by the usual method of child-bearing? (Incidentally, in the one-and-only scientific definition of nations which we have cited, no such criterion is stipulated!) Let us reply: Yes, its ranks are replenished by the technical method of *jugging* (and, out of some strange caprice, its own infants are turned over to neighboring peoples). However, chicks, after all, are hatched in an incubator, yet we do not, for this reason, cease to regard them as chickens when we use their meat.

But even if some sort of doubt does arise as to how the zeks *begin their existence*, at least there can be no doubt whatever as to the method by which they *cease* to exist. They die, like everyone else, only more densely and more prematurely. And their funeral rite is gloomy, meager, harsh.

Two words about the term *zek* itself. Up to 1934 the official term for them was "Lishonnye Svobody"—"Deprived of Freedom." This was abbreviated to L/S, and no evidence has been preserved as to whether the natives worked these initials "L" and "S" into "*elesy,*" but from 1934 on the term was changed to "prisoners"—"zaklyuchennye." (Let us recall that the Archipelago had begun to harden by then, and even the official language adapted itself to this and could not tolerate there being more *freedom* than prison in the definition of the natives.) And they began to abbreviate the term: in the singular Z/K ("zeh-káh"), and in the plural Z/K Z/K ("zeh-káh, zeh-káh"). And this was pronounced very often by the natives' guardians and was heard by all, and all became accustomed to it. But this bureaucratic word could not be declined either by case or by number. It was a worthy offspring of a dead and illiterate epoch. The living ear of the alert natives could not reconcile itself to this situation, and in a spirit of mockery, on various islands, in various localities, they began to adapt it for themselves: in some places they said "Zakhar Kuzmich," or, in Norilsk, "Zapolyarnye Komsomoltsy" (Arctic Komsomols); in others (for instance, Karelia) they tended toward "zak," which was the most correct etymologically, and in others (for instance, Inta) they preferred "zyk." What I heard was "zek."[4] And in all such instances the new

---

4. The old Solovetsky Islands prisoner D.S.L. assures me that as far back as 1931 he heard a convoy guard ask a native: "Who are you? A zek?"

word thus brought to life was declined both by number and by case. (But in the Kolyma, insists Shalamov, they adhered in conversation to the official term "zeh-káh." One can only regret that the Kolyma ear must have been numbed by the cold.)*

■

The *climate* of the Archipelago . . . is always Arctic, even if a particular islet has intruded itself into the southern seas. The climate of the Archipelago is *twelve months of winter, the rest summer.* And the air itself there scorches and pricks one, not only because of the frost, not only because of nature.

Even in summer the zeks are dressed in the soft gray armor of padded jackets. This in itself, along with the men's cropped scalps, gives them a uniformity of *external appearance* smacking of severity, impersonality. But after observing the zeks even only a little, you will be equally astonished by the common elements in their facial expressions—always guarded, sullen, without the slightest good will, easily slipping into hardness and even cruelty. Their facial expressions look as if they have been cast from a swarthy, copper-colored material (the zeks evidently belong to the Indian race), rough-textured, almost not of flesh, so as to be able to march facing into the wind, expecting at every step to be bitten from the right or the left. You notice also that in action, at work, in a fight, their shoulders are squared, and their chests braced for resistance, but as soon as a zek is left in a state of inaction, by himself, buried in his thoughts, his neck ceases to support the weight of his head, and his shoulders and his back immediately express an inveterate stoop, as if he were born with it. The most natural position his hands adopt when free is clasped behind the back if walking, or simply hanging limply when sitting down. His stoop and his depressed air will remain with him when he approaches you—a free person and therefore a possible boss. He will try not to look you in the eyes and will instead look at the ground, but if he is forced to look at you—you will be surprised by his blank, stupid stare, even though it will indicate willingness to carry out your orders. (Do not trust it, however; he will not carry them out.) If you order him to take off his cap (or if he himself understands he should), his shaven scalp will surprise you unpleasantly anthropologically with its bumps, hollows, and asymmetry of a clearly degenerate type.

In conversation with you he will be laconic, speaking without expression—either monotonously and dully or else with servility —if it is necessary to ask you for something. But if you somehow happen invisibly to overhear the natives when they are talking with one another, you will probably remember forever their special *manner of speech*—as if pushing the sounds out, maliciously mocking, brusque, and never heartfelt. This is so rooted in the natives that even when a man native is left alone with a woman native (which, incidentally, is strictly prohibited by the Archipelago laws) it is impossible to imagine his ridding himself of that manner of speech. In all probability he expresses himself to her too in a pushy, peremptory sort of way, for it is quite impossible to imagine a zek speaking tender words. But it is also impossible not to recognize the great energetic force of the zeks' language. In part this is because it is free of all kinds of superfluous expressions, of introductory phrases such as "pardon me," or "please," or "if you do not object," and also from superfluous pronouns and interjections. The speech of the zek moves straight to its goal, just as he himself pushes into the Arctic wind. He speaks as if he were punching his companion in the mug, beating him with words. Just as an experienced fighter invariably tries to knock his enemy off his feet with the very first blow, so the zek tries to confound his companion, to render him mute, and even to compel him to wheeze from the very first phrase. And he will flatly brush off any question directed at him.

Even today the reader may encounter this repellent manner in unforeseen circumstances. For example, when you are waiting at a trolleybus stop in a strong wind, your neighbor will spill a large hot ash on your new overcoat, threatening to scorch it. You demonstratively brush it off, but he continues to spill ashes on you. And you say to him: "Listen, comrade, how about being more careful with your smoking, eh?"

Not only does he not ask your pardon, and not only does he take no precautions with his cigarette, but he barks curtly: "Haven't you any insurance?"

And while you are trying to find an answer (you aren't going to find one), he already succeeds in clambering ahead of you onto the trolleybus. Now that is very much like the native manner.

Apart from their straight multisyllabic curses, the zeks evidently have a collection of ready-made expressions, which will paralyze any intelligent outside interference and directions. Such expression as: "Don't needle me, I'm of a different religion!"

"If they're not [beat]ing you, don't lie down and ask for it!"* (Here in brackets we have used a substitute for another—obscene—word, from which the second verb in the phrase also immediately acquires a quite indecent sense.)

Similar repellent expressions make a particularly indelible impression when coming from the mouths of the native women, since it is they in particular who make the most liberal use of erotically based metaphors. We regret that the bounds of morality do not permit us to embellish this inquiry with still other examples. We will venture to cite just one more illustration of the speed and deftness of the zeks in the use of language. A certain native named Glik was brought from an ordinary island to a special island—to a secret scientific research institute (certain natives are naturally developed to such a degree that they are even suitable for conducting scientific research)—but because of certain personal considerations the new and privileged place did not suit him and he wished to return to his former island. He was summoned before a very high-ranking commission, with big stars on their shoulder boards, and there they announced to him: "You are a radio engineer and we would like to make use of you—"

Without allowing them to finish their sentence with "in your profession," he straightened up sharply: *"Make use of me? So what do you want me to do—turn around and bend over?"*

And he reached for his belt buckle and made a motion as if to adopt the indicated position. Naturally the commission was struck dumb, and there was no deal. Glik was dismissed straightaway.

It is curious to note that even the natives of the Archipelago realize very well indeed that they arouse great interest on the part of anthropologists and ethnographers, and they even brag of this—it seems to increase their value in their own eyes. Among them there is a widespread, frequently told legendary anecdote about a certain professor of ethnography, evidently a predecessor of ours, who spent his whole life studying the breed of zeks and wrote a thick dissertation in two volumes in which he came to the final conclusion that *the prisoner is lazy, greedy, and sly.* (At this juncture of the story both the storyteller and his listeners laugh complacently, as though admiring themselves from the sidelines.) But soon after, apparently, they *jugged* the professor himself. (This is a very unhappy ending, but since no one is imprisoned in our country unless guilty, then there must have been something to it.) Then after jostling his way through the transit prisons and when he himself became *a last-legger on general work*, the professor came to understand his error and to realize that in actual fact *the convict is rowdy, crafty, and transparent*. (And this is an extremely apt description and once again one that is somehow flattering. And they all laugh once again.)

We have already said that the zeks have no written language. But through the personal example of the veteran islanders, in oral tradition, and in folklore, the entire code of *correct* zek conduct has been elaborated and is transmitted to newcomers—basic precepts relating to their work, to their employers, to those around them, and to themselves. All this code, taken as a whole, is imprinted on and exemplified in the moral structure of the native, and produces what we can call *the zek national type*. The imprint of this affiliation is driven deep inside the human being once and for all. Many years later, if he turns up outside the Archipelago, the first thing you will recognize in the human being is the zek—and only secondarily the Russian, Tatar, or Pole.

In the rest of our exposition we will try to examine here trait by trait in complex detail the constituents of the folk character, the life psychology, and the normative ethics of the nation of zeks.

■

Attitude toward government *work*. The zeks have an absolutely false concept of work as something designed to suck their whole lives from them, which means that their chief salvation is this: while working, not to become absorbed in the work. It is well known to a zek that you can't do all the work (never rush, thinking that the sooner you finish, the sooner you can sit down and take a rest; the moment you sit down, you will immediately be given other work to do). *Work loves fools*.

But how do you do it? Do you flatly refuse to work? That is the worst thing the zek can do! He will rot in punishment blocks, die of starvation. Going to work is unavoidable. But once there, during the workday, what he has to do is not *slog away*, but "fiddle about," not *bend the back*, but *loaf, goldbrick* (which is to say, not work anyway). The native will never openly or flatly refuse to perform any order—that would be the end of him. Instead, what he does is . . . *stretch the rubber*. "Stretching the rubber" is one of the principal concepts and expressions of the Archipelago; this is the zek's main salvation and achievement. (Subsequently widely adopted by the sloggers out in *freedom* as well.) The zek listens carefully to all the orders he is given and nods his head affirmatively. And . . . he goes off to carry out those orders. But . . . he does not carry them out! Most often of all . . . he does not even begin! This sometimes leads to despair on the part of the purposeful and inexhaustible commanders of production! And naturally the desire arises . . . to hit him with a fist in the nose or on the back of the neck, this stupid dumb animal in tatters—after all, he has been told in the Russian language! What doltish obtuseness is this? (But that's the point: the Russian language is ill understood by the natives, and a whole series of contemporary concepts such as "workers' honor" and "conscientious discipline" have no equivalents in their wretched language.) However, no sooner has the chief rushed in for the second time than the zek obediently bends his back beneath the cursing and immediately begins to carry out the orders. The heart of the employer softens a little, and he goes on with his multitudinous urgent tasks of management—and the zek, behind his back, immediately sits down and stops working. (If there is no brigadier's fist hanging over his head, if he is not threatened with being deprived of his bread ration today, and also if there is no bait in the shape of time off sentence.) It is difficult for us normal people to understand this psychology, but that is how it is.

Obtuseness? Quite the contrary, it is the highest degree of understanding and adaptation to conditions. What can he count on? After all, work does not get done by itself, and if the chief comes around once more, will that be any worse? But here is what he is counting on: Most likely of all, the chief won't come around for the third time today. And you have to survive until tomorrow.

Tonight the zek might be sent off on a prisoner transport, or transferred to another brigade, or put in hospital, or imprisoned in the punishment block—and whatever he has done today will then be credited to someone else. Or tomorrow that same zek and that same brigade might well be transferred to some other work. Or else the chief might decide that what they were doing isn't necessary, or ought to be done quite differently. And on the basis of many such cases the zeks had firmly mastered the truth: *Do not do today what you can do tomorrow.* Or in zek lingo: *Wherever you sit down is where you get off.* He is fearful of expending an extra calorie where it maybe doesn't need to be expended. (Incidentally, the concept of calories is well known and very popular among the natives.) And that is how the zeks talk frankly among themselves: *The one who pulls is the one they urge on.* (And the one who doesn't, supposedly, is let off with a shrug.) In general the zek works *just to get through the day to the night.*

(But at this point scholarly integrity obliges us to admit a certain weakness in our course of reasoning. First of all, because the camp rule of "The one who pulls is the one they urge on" turns out to be simultaneously an old Russian proverb. And we also find in Dal[5] another purely zekish expression: *"He lives just to get through the day to the night."* Now this coincidence arouses a whole whirlwind of thoughts in us: The theory of borrowing? The theory of migratory themes? A school of mythology? Continuing these dangerous comparisons, we find among the Russian proverbs and sayings which took shape under serfdom and were already well established by the nineteenth century the following:

"Don't do the work, don't run from work." [Astonishing! This is the very principle of camp *"rubber."*]

"May God grant we know how to do everything, but not do it all."

"You will never finish the master's work."

"A zealous horse doesn't live long."

"They'll give you a chunk of bread, and for that you'll have to thresh for a whole week." [This is very much like the zeks' reactionary theory that even a big bread ration doesn't make up for the expenditure of energy in labor.]

So what conclusion is to be drawn from all this? That across

5. V. Dal, *Poslovitsy Russkogo Naroda* (*Proverbs of the Russian People*), Moscow, 1957, p. 257.

all the bright boundary lines of our emancipatory reforms, our enlightenment, our revolutions, and our socialism, the serfs of the Empress Catherine's time and the zeks of Stalin's time, notwithstanding their complete dissimilarity in social position, reach out to shake each other's black and horny hands? That is impossible!

At this point our erudition breaks down and we will return to our exposition.)

From the zek's relationship to his work there follows also his *relationship to his chiefs.* Outwardly the zek is very obedient. For example, one of the zek "commandments" is *Don't stick your neck out!* In other words, never talk back to the chiefs. In appearance the zek is very much afraid of the chief, bends his back when a chief scolds him or even just stands near him. But in fact this is a simple calculation: to avoid unnecessary punishments. In actual fact the zek utterly despises the bosses—both the camp chiefs and the production chiefs—but covertly conceals it so as not to suffer for it. Departing in a throng after any sort of work announcements, reprimands, or official rebukes, the zeks laugh quietly among themselves: *It may have been said, but we'll manage to forget it!* The zeks inwardly consider themselves to be the superiors of their chiefs—both in literacy and in their mastery of work skills, and in their general level of comprehension of the circumstances of life. And one has to admit that that is how it often is, but here in their self-satisfaction: the zeks fail to see that, on the other hand, the administration of the islands possesses a *permanent* superiority over the natives by virtue of its *world outlook.* That is why the naïve concept of the zeks that the chiefs' principles are *I do as I please!* or *The law here is me!* is really quite unfounded.

However, this gives us a convenient opportunity to draw a distinction between the native status and the Old Russian serfdom. The serf-peasant did not like his nobleman-owner, and made fun of him, but had grown accustomed to feeling something superior in him, as a result of which there was a multitude of characters like Savelich and Firs who were dedicated slaves. But now this spiritual slavery has ended once and for all. And among the tens of millions of zeks it is quite impossible to imagine even one who sincerely worships his chief.

And in this respect there is an important national difference between the zeks and your and my compatriots, dear reader:

The zeks do not strive for praise, nor for honorary diplomas, nor to have their names posted on Red Bulletin Boards of Honor (unless these are directly tied in with supplementary rations). Everything that is called the glory of labor out in freedom is for the zeks, in their stupidity, only a dull and hollow sound. In this they are all the more independent of their guardians and of the necessity to please.

As a generalization, the entire *scale of values* is topsy-turvy among the zeks, but this need not surprise us if we recall that it is always that way among savages: for a tiny little mirror they are willing to part with a big fat pig; for cheap little beads, with a basket of cocoa beans. Those things that are precious to us, dear reader, such as ideological values, self-sacrifice, dedication, and the desire to labor selflessly for the future, these are not only quite absent among the zeks but are even considered worthless. It is enough to say that the zeks are *totally deprived of patriotic sentiment* and do not like their own native islands in the least. Let us recall the words of their own folk song:

> Be thou damned, O Kolyma!
> Snakes invented this planet!

Because of this they rarely undertake long and risky journeys in search of happiness, which are called, in their dialect, *escapes*.

Most highly esteemed of all among the zeks, occupying first place in terms of the value placed on it, is the *bread ration*—a piece of black bread with additives in it, badly baked, which you and I would be unwilling to eat. And among the zeks the bigger and heavier the ration is, the more precious it is. Anyone who has ever seen the greed with which the zeks hurl themselves on their morning bread ration, almost devouring their hands along with it, will have a difficult time ever erasing that unaesthetic recollection from his mind. Second place among them is occupied by makhorka, or home-grown tobacco, and the rates of exchange involving these things are wildly arbitrary, and don't pay the least heed to the amount of socially useful labor invested in the one or the other. This is all the more monstrous in that among them makhorka occupies the place, so to speak, of a universal currency. (There is no monetary system on the islands.) Third place is occupied by gruel (which is an island soup without fats, without meat, without grits or vegetables, in accordance with native customs). Probably even the marching of grenadiers on parade, in exact step with one another, in gleaming uniforms and flourishing weapons, does not leave such a fearsome impression on the viewer as does the evening entry of a brigade of zeks into the mess hall to get their gruel—those shaven heads, those slapdash caps, tatters tied together with strings, those mean crooked faces (how do they get those muscles and sinews from that gruel?). And in they go, with twenty-five pairs of shoes and rope and bast sandals—tup-tup, tup-tup, left, right, *give us our ration, bosses!* Anyone who's not of our faith, get out of the way! And on the twenty-five faces at the moment of seizing their prey the *national character* of the zeks is disclosed to you distinct and clear.

We note the fact that in reaching conclusions about the zeks we can hardly imagine them as individuals, their separate personalities and names. But that is not a fault of our method. It is a reflection of that *herd structure of life* in which this outlandish people lives, renouncing family life and the creation of heirs, which are so traditional among other peoples. (They are convinced that their population will be replenished by other means.) This collective way of life is extremely characteristic of the Archipelago—be it an inheritance from primitive society or the dawn of the future. Probably it is the future.

The next most highly valued thing among the zeks is sleep. A normal human being can only be astounded at how much a zek is capable of sleeping and in what varied circumstances. One hardly need say that insomnia is quite unknown among them. They take no sleeping pills. They sleep every night through without waking. And if they happen to get a day free of work, they sleep right through it. It has been reliably established that they are able to fall asleep when seated beside empty hand barrows while the latter are being loaded. They are able to fall asleep out at line-up with their legs spread wide apart, and they are also able to fall asleep even when marching under guard to work, but not all of them—some of them keel over and wake up. And the basis of all this is: during sleep the *sentence* passes more quickly. And, in addition: *the night is for sleep, and the day is for rest!*[6]

Let us return to the image of the brigade stamping in to get

6. It is paradoxical, but the Russian people have similar proverbs: "I eat while I'm marching, and sleep while I'm standing." "Where there's a nook or cranny there's a bed."

its "lawful" (as they call it) gruel. We see an expression here of one of the principal national traits of the zek people—*vital drive*. (Nor does this contradict their inclination to keep dropping off to sleep. That is, in fact, why they sleep, so as to have the strength for their drive in the interim!) This drive is both literal and physical, and continues right up to the finish line of their goals—food, a warm stove, a clothes drier, shelter from the rain. And in all that pushing and shoving the zek does not hesitate to stick his shoulder in his neighbor's side. And if two zeks are going to pick up a tree trunk, both of them head for the top end, so that the other will get the thick end. And this drive exists in a more general sense—a drive to get the most advantageous position in life. In the cruel island conditions (so close to the conditions of life in the animal kingdom that we can without fear of contradiction apply here the Darwinian "struggle for life"*) life itself often depends on success or failure in the struggle for a place—and in driving a path for oneself at the cost of others, the natives acknowledge no restraining ethical principles. They themselves say straight out: *"Conscience? It got left in my case file."* In taking vital decisions they are guided by the well-known rule of the Archipelago: *It is better to be a son-of-a-bitch than to suffer.*

But this drive can be successful only if it is accompanied by practical agility and resourcefulness in the most difficult situations.[7] The zek has to manifest this quality every day, for the simplest and the most insignificant purposes: to safeguard his pitiful dregs of property—some dented mess tin, stinking rags, a wooden spoon, his handy needle. However, in the struggle for an important position in the island hierarchy—even this resourcefulness must become calculated *trickery* of a superior, more subtle, more ingenious order. So as not to weigh down this inquiry—here is one example. A certain zek managed to secure the important position of chief of the camp workshops. Certain kinds of work were successfully carried out in his workshops, and others not, but the strength of his position depended not so much on the successful completion of his work as on his ability *to bluff*. Some MVD officers came to his office and saw some

7. The Russians say: "He bows with his front, watches out with his side, and feels his way with his rear."

ceramic cones on his desk. "What are they?" "Seger cones." "What are they for?" "To determine the temperature inside the ovens." "Aha!" drawled out the chief, thinking to himself: "Well, I certainly put a good engineer in the job." But those cones could not be used to determine temperatures through their melting point, because they weren't made of standardized clay and their composition was unknown. The cones started to become overfamiliar—and soon the chief of the workshops had a new toy on his desk—an optical instrument without a single lens (where in the Archipelago would you find a lens?). And again everyone was astounded.

And the zek's mind had continually to be occupied with such sideways feints as these.

According to the circumstances, and his psychological appraisal of the enemy, the zek had to demonstrate *flexibility of conduct*—ranging from a crude move with fist or voice up to the most delicate kind of pretense, from total shamelessness to sacred fidelity to a promise given face to face, which one would not think to be at all compulsory. (Thus for some reason all zeks were as faithful as saints to their promises of secret bribes and exceptionally patient and conscientious in carrying out private commissions. When we see some wonderful Archipelago handicraft work with carving and inlays, the likes of which can otherwise be seen only in the Ostankino Museum,* it is impossible to believe that this was done by those same hands which turned over to the foreman work that was held together only by a peg so that it would fall apart immediately.)

This flexibility of conduct was also reflected in the famous zek rule: *"If they give—take it; if they beat—beat it."*

The most important condition of success in the life struggle of the Gulag islanders is their *secretiveness*. Their character and their intentions are so profoundly hidden that to the inexperienced novice employer it seems at the outset as if the zeks bend like a blade of grass—beneath the wind and the boot.[8] (Only subsequently does he become bitterly convinced of the cunning and insincerity of the islanders.) Secretiveness is almost the most characteristic trait of the zek tribe. The zek has to hide his intentions and acts, both from the employers and from the jailers,

8. Compare the proverb of the Russians: "It is better to bend than to break."

and from the brigadiers and from the so-called "stoolies."[9] He has to conceal his successes so that they will not be outdone. He has to conceal his plans, his calculations, and his hopes, whether he be preparing for a big "escape" or has figured out where to collect shavings for a mattress. In the zek life it is always the case that to disclose means to lose. . . . One native, whom I treated to makhorka, explained it to me this way (I present it here in translation): "If you disclose a warm place to sleep where the foreman won't find you, everyone will rush there, and the foreman will smell it out. If you disclose that you have sent a letter out through a free person,[10] then everyone else will hand his letters to that free person, and they will catch him with the letters. And if the storeroom clerk has promised to exchange your torn shirt—shut up till you have exchanged it, and when you have, shut up some more: you won't give him away, and he will be useful to you later on."[11] With the years the zek becomes so accustomed to hiding everything that he no longer has to exert any effort at all to this end; the natural human desire to share what he has experienced dies in him. (Should we perhaps recognize in this secretiveness some sort of defense reaction against the *secret course of events* in general? After all, they also do all they can to conceal from him information concerning his own fate.)

The secretiveness of the zek flows also from his all-round *mistrustfulness*; he mistrusts everyone around him. An act that appears to be unselfish arouses his especially strong suspicion. *The law of the taiga*—that is how he formulates the highest imperative of human relationships. (On the islands of the Archipelago there really are great tracts of taiga.)

The native who in the highest degree combines and manifests these tribal qualities—the drive for life, pitilessness, resourcefulness, secretiveness, and mistrustfulness—calls himself, and is called by others, *a son of Gulag*. This, among them, is like the title "honorary citizen," and it is acquired, of course, through long years of life on the islands.

9. An insignificant phenomenon of the Archipelago upon which we consider it superfluous to dwell in this essay.

10. An official postal service does exist on the islands of the Archipelago, but the natives prefer not to make use of it.

11. Compare this proverb among the Russians: "If you have found something, shut up, and if you have lost something, shut up too." Frankly speaking, the parallelism of these rules of life leave us somewhat puzzled.

A son of Gulag believes himself impenetrable, and also that he, on the contrary, can see right through those around him and, as the phrase goes, six feet beneath them too. Maybe this is so, but at this point it becomes apparent that even the most penetrating of the zeks possesses a narrow range of outlook, a *short view* ahead. While judging very soberly actions close to them, and while very precise in calculating their behavior in the hours immediately ahead, the rank-and-file zeks and even the sons of Gulag, too, are incapable either of thinking abstractly or of grasping phenomena of a general nature, or even of speaking about the future. Even in their grammar the future tense is very rarely used; even with regard to the morrow it is applied with a conditional nuance—and still more carefully to the subsequent days of the same week, and you will never hear from a zek such a sentence as "Next spring I will . . ." Because they all know that they still have to make it through the winter, and that any day fate can hurl them from one island to another. In real truth: "My day is my epoch!"

The sons of Gulag are also the chief bearers of the traditions and the so-called *zek commandments*. On the various islands the number of these commandments varies, and they are not always formulated the same way either. And to work toward their systematization would be a very interesting subject for a separate inquiry. These commandments have nothing in common with Christianity. (The zeks are not only an atheistic people, but in general nothing is sacred to them, and they always hasten to ridicule and degrade anything lofty. And this, too, is reflected in their language.) But as the sons of Gulag affirm: If you live according to their commandments, you will not perish in the Archipelago.

There are certain precepts, such as: *Don't squeal!* (How is one to understand this? Evidently they are desirous of avoiding superfluous noise?) And: *Don't lick the bowls*; in other words, do not descend to slops, something they consider a swift and abrupt way to die. And: *Don't scavenge.* And others.

There is an interesting commandment: *Don't shove your nose in someone else's mess tin!* This seems to us to represent a great achievement of native thought; you see, this is the principle of negative freedom; it is the slogan "My home is my castle!" turned around, so to speak, and even improved upon, because it is a matter not of one's own mess tin but of someone else's (and yet "one's own" is, of course, understood). Knowing the native conditions, we have to understand here the term "mess tin" in the broadest sense—not merely as a dented and sooty dish, nor even as the specific unappetizing dishwater contained in it, but also as all the means of getting something to eat, all the means in the struggle for existence, and even more broadly: as the zek's *soul*. In a word, "Let me live as I wish, and you live as you wish"— that is what this precept means. A hard and cruel son of Gulag, under this precept, undertakes the obligation not to use his strength and drive out of empty curiosity. (But at the same time he frees himself of any kind of moral obligation: "Even if you are croaking right next to me, it's none of my affair." This is a cruel law, yet it is much more humane than the law of the thieves— —the island cannibals: "You today, me tomorrow." The cannibal-thief is not in the least indifferent to his neighbor; he will speed up the latter's death so as to put off his own or sometimes just for the hell of it or even for the amusement of watching it.)

Finally, there is one composite commandment: *Don't trust, don't fear, don't beg!* In this commandment the common, national character of the zek is cast, like a piece of sculpture, with sharp definition.

How can one (in freedom) rule over a people which is totally steeped in such a proud commandment? It is awesome even to think of it!

This commandment leads us to consider not so much the life style of the zeks as their psychological essence.

The first thing we note from the start in a son of Gulag, and then observe more and more frequently, is *spiritual equilibrium*, psychological stability. In this regard the zek's general, overall philosophical view of his place in the universe is highly interesting. As distinct from the Englishman or the Frenchman, who is proud all his life of having been born an Englishman or a Frenchman, the zek is not at all proud of his national affiliation; on the contrary, he perceives it as a cruel trial, but a trial he wishes to endure with dignity. The zeks have a particularly notable myth, which holds that somewhere there exist "the gates of the Archipelago" (compare with the pillars of Hercules in antiquity), and that on the outside of these gates there is a sign for those who enter: "DO NOT LOSE HEART!" And on the other side there is a sign for those who are leaving: "DO NOT BE OVERJOYED!" And the main thing, the zeks add, is that these signs are visible only to the wise, and fools do not see them. Often this myth is expressed as a simple rule of life: *"Newly arriving, do not be sad; newly departing, do not be glad."* It is in this key that the views of the zeks on the Archipelago and on the life taking place in the space abutting on it must be perceived. Such a philosophy is the source of the zek's psychological stability. No matter how darkly circumstances may be stacked against him, he knits the brows of his rough and weathered face and says: *"They cannot drop me any deeper than a mine."* Or they comfort each other: *"It could be worse."* And in reality, this conviction "It could be even worse!" clearly supports and encourages them in the most profound suffering of famine, cold, and spiritual depression.

The zek is always *expecting it to be worse.* That is how he lives, constantly awaiting the blows of fate and stings of the evil spirit. And, on the other hand, he perceives every temporary relaxation as an oversight, a mistake. In this constant expectation of misfortune the austere soul of the zek matures, stoically hardened to its own fate, and pitiless toward the fates of others.

The zek's deviations from his state of equilibrium are very minor—either on the dark side or the bright side, either on the side of despair or on the side of happiness.

This was felicitously expressed by Taras Shevchenko (who spent a little time on the islands in prehistoric times): "I now have almost neither grief nor gladness. On the other hand, there is a moral calm like the cold-bloodedness of a fish. Is it possible that constant suffering can rework a human being in this way?"[12]

Indeed! Yes. Indeed it can. A *stable, indifferent state of mind* is the zek's indispensable defense so he can survive long years of grim island life. If he does not attain this smoldering, lusterless state of mind in his first year in the Archipelago, ordinarily he dies. Once he has attained it, he continues to live. In a word: If you don't kick the bucket—you'll become an adept.

All the zek's feelings are dulled, and his nerves coarsened. Having become indifferent to his own grief, and to the punishments which the guardians of the tribe have laid upon him, and even, by then, almost to his whole life—he does not experience any spiritual sympathy for the grief of those around him either.

12. In a letter to Repnina.

Somebody's outcry of pain or even women's tears barely compel him to turn his head—so dulled have his reactions become. Often the zeks show no mercy to inexperienced newcomers and laugh at their errors and misfortunes—but do not judge them severely for this: they are not doing it out of malice—their sympathies have simply atrophied, and all that remains noticeable to them is the funny side of events.

The most prevalent world outlook among them is *fatalism*. This is their profound, universal trait. It is to be explained by their dependent situation, their total lack of knowledge of what will happen to them even in the most immediate future, and their actual inability to influence events. Fatalism is even necessary to the zek because it confirms him in his spiritual stability. The son of Gulag believes that the most tranquil course is to put his faith in fate. The future is a cat in a sack, a pig in a poke, and not understanding it clearly, and having no idea what's going to happen to you in the possible variations of life lying ahead, you don't need to strive too insistently for something or reject something too obstinately—be it a transfer to another barracks, or brigade, or camp. Maybe it will be for the better, maybe for the worse, but you are free of self-reproaches; let it be worse for you, but it wasn't done by your own hands. And this is how you preserve that precious feeling of dauntlessness, how you save yourself from fussing and ingratiating.

Given such a dark fate, the zeks have many strong *superstitions*. One of them is closely bound up with their fatalism: If you worry too much about your conditions or even your own comfort, you are bound to *get burned by a prisoner transport*.[13]

The fatalism widely prevalent among them extends not only to their personal fate but also to the overall course of things. The last thing in their mind is that *the overall course* of events could be changed. They imagine that the Archipelago has existed *for all eternity* and that earlier it was even worse.

But probably the most interesting psychological twist here is the fact that the zeks perceive their own stable state of equanimity in these primitive and wretched circumstances as a victory for

---

13. *Fires* in their literal sense don't frighten the zeks. They don't value the shelters they live in, and they don't even try to save burning buildings, since they are certain that they will always be replaced. *To get burned* is a phrase used only in the sense of their personal fate.

love of life. It is quite enough for the sequence of misfortunes to slow down a little, for the blows of fate to slacken just a little, for the zek to express his *satisfaction with life* and take pride in his own conduct in it. Perhaps the reader will find it easier to believe in this paradoxical trait if we cite Chekhov. In his story "In Exile," the boatman Semyon Tolkovy expresses this feeling as follows:

I . . . have brought myself to the point where I can sleep naked on the earth and eat grass. *And may God grant everyone a life like that.* [Our italics.] I need nothing, and I fear no one, and I understand myself so well that no man is richer and freer than I.

These astonishing words still ring in our ears; we have heard them many times from zeks of the Archipelago. (And the only surprise is, where could Chekhov have picked them up?) "And may God grant everyone a life like that!" How would you like that?

Up to the present, we have been speaking of the positive aspects of the national character. But we cannot shut our eyes to its negative aspects, to certain touching national weaknesses which seem to stand as exceptions and contradictions of the foregoing.

The more dauntless and stern the disbelief of this atheistic people (which, for example, completely ridicules the Gospel teaching which says, "Judge not, that ye be not judged," holding that judgments—in other words, sentences—don't depend on that), the more feverishly is it afflicted nonetheless by attacks of thoughtless gullibility. Here one can draw a distinction: Within that closely circumscribed field of vision where the zek can see well, he believes in nothing. But deprived of an abstract vision, deprived of historical perspective, he swallows with the innocence of a savage any farfetched rumor, any native miracles.

An ancient example of native *trustfulness* was the hope placed in Gorky's arrival on Solovki. But there isn't any need to go that far back. There is an almost permanent and almost universal religion in the Archipelago; this is faith in the so-called *Amnesty*. It is difficult to explain just what this is. It is not the name of a goddess, as the reader might have thought. It is something akin to the Second Coming among Christian peoples, it is a burst of such blinding radiance that the ice of the Archipelago will melt and even the islands themselves will dissolve, and all the natives will be swept on warm waves to sunny regions where they will immediately find their nearest and most beloved. Probably this is a somewhat transformed faith in the Kingdom of Heaven on earth. This faith, which has never yet been confirmed by one single real miracle, is nonetheless very much alive and persistent. And just as other peoples connect their important rituals with the winter and summer solstices, so, too, the zeks mystically await (always in vain) the first days of November and May. If a south wind blows on the Archipelago, they will immediately whisper from ear to ear: "There's bound to be an amnesty! It is already under way!" And when the winter winds set in in earnest, the zeks warm their numbed fingers by breathing on them, rub their ears, stamp up and down, and encourage one another. "That means there will be an amnesty. Otherwise we'll freeze to ————! [Here there is an untranslatable expression.] Evidently it's going to come now."

The harmfulness of every religion has long since been demonstrated and proved—and we see the same thing here too. These beliefs in Amnesty seriously weaken the natives, inducing in them an uncharacteristic state of dreaminess, and there are periods of epidemic when necessary and urgent government work quite literally falls from the zeks' hands—which, practically speaking, is the same effect as that produced by the opposite kind of rumor about "prisoner transports." For everyday construction work it is much more advantageous for the natives not to experience any ups and downs of feeling.

And the zeks also suffer from a certain national weakness, which in some incomprehensible fashion they retain despite the whole structure of their life. This is their *secret thirst for justice.*

Chekhov, too, observed this strange feeling on an island which, in fact, did not belong to our Archipelago at all: "The hard-labor prisoner, no matter how profoundly depraved and unjust he himself was, loved justice above all, and if it was not to be found among the people placed over him, then year after year he fell into a state of anger, into extreme mistrust."

Even though Chekhov's observations do not in any respect refer to our case, yet they astonish us with their accuracy.

Beginning with the zeks' arrival in the Archipelago, every day and every hour of their life here is one continual injustice, and in this situation they themselves commit only injustices—and one would think it had long since been time for them to grow used to it and to accept injustice as the universal norm of life. But no, not at all! Every injustice on the part of the elders in the tribe and the tribal guardians continues to wound them, and to wound them just as much as it did on their first day. (But injustice which rises from the bottom to the top provokes their hearty and approving laughter.) And in their folklore they do not create legends so much about justice as, in an exaggeration of this feeling, about unjustified magnanimity. (And thus it was that the myth about magnanimity to F. Kaplan was created and lasted for decades in the Archipelago—alleging that she had not been shot but confined for life in various prisons, and there were even many witnesses to be found who had been with her on prisoner transports or had received books from the Butyrki Prison library from her.[14] One asks why the natives needed this nonsensical myth. Only as an extreme case of inordinate magnanimity in which they wanted to believe. They then in their mind's eye could apply it to themselves.)

Instances are also known of a zek's coming to love his work in the Archipelago (A. S. Bratchikov: "I am proud of what I made with my own hands"), or at least not disliking it (the zeks of German origin), but these cases are so exceptional that we are not going to offer them even as an eccentricity, let alone a universal trait of the people.

And let not the already cited native trait of secretiveness seem in contradiction with another native trait: *a love of telling stories about the past.* Among all backward peoples this is a custom of the old men; and people of middle age actively dislike talking about the past and are even afraid to (particularly women, and particularly people filling out security questionnaires, yes, and in general everyone). In this regard the zeks behave like a nation

14. Not long ago the Commandant of the Kremlin, Comrade Malkov, officially repudiated these rumors and described how he had shot Kaplan at the time. And Demyan Bedny was present at the execution too. And her absence as a witness at the trial of the SR's in 1922 ought to have convinced the zeks! But they don't remember that trial at all. We suppose that the rumor about the life imprisonment of F. Kaplan arose from the life imprisonment of Berta Gandal. This woman, suspecting nothing, arrived in Moscow from Riga on the very day of the attempted assassination of Lenin, when the brothers Gandal (who had been waiting in an automobile for Kaplan) were shot. And that was why Berta got life imprisonment.

consisting only of old men. (In another respect—since they have *instructors*—they are, on the contrary, maintained like a nation of children.) You wouldn't be able to squeeze a word out of them about the petty secrets of today's daily life—such as where to warm up one's mess tin, or who's got makhorka to barter—but they will tell you everything about the past without concealment, disclosing everything: how they lived before the Archipelago and with whom and how they *got here*. (For hours at a time they listen to stories of how other zeks "got here," and they are never bored in the least by these monotonously similar stories.) And the more accidental, the more superficial, the briefer the encounter between two zeks (one night next to each other in a transit prison), the more extended and detailed are their hurried accounts of themselves to one another.

It is very interesting at this point to draw comparisons with Dostoyevsky's observations. He noted that each prisoner bore silently and suffered out within himself the story of how he got into the "House of the Dead"—and found it was not acceptable among them to talk about it. This is something we can understand: people got put in the "House of the Dead" for *crime*; and for those hard-labor prisoners it was hard to think back on it.

The zek gets to the Archipelago by an inexplicable move of fate or by an evil concatenation of vengeful circumstances—but in nine cases out of ten he doesn't feel he has committed any "crime"—and therefore there are no stories in the Archipelago more interesting, and none which arouse a livelier sympathy in the audience, than those of *"how I got here."*

The zeks' abundant stories about the past, which filled all the evenings in their barracks, had another purpose and meaning as well. The more uncertain the zek's present and future, the more unshakable is his past. No one can ever take his past away from the zek, and everyone was something bigger in the past than he is now in the Archipelago (since it is impossible to be lower than a zek, and even a drunken tramp outside the Archipelago is addressed as *Comrade*). And in his recollections, therefore, the zek's self-esteem reclaims those peaks from which life has toppled him.[15] His recollections are, in addition, invariably embellished,

---

15. And the self-esteem of an old deaf tinker or of a pipsqueak boy painter's apprentice in no way yields to that of a celebrated theater director of the metropolis.

and invented (but extremely plausible) episodes are inserted in them. And the zek storyteller (and his listeners) feel a life-giving *return of self-confidence*.

This self-confidence is strengthened in another way too—by multitudinous folk tales about the cleverness and luck of the zek people. These are rather crude stories, recalling the soldiers' legends of the times of Tsar Nicholas I (when soldiers were conscripted for twenty-five years). They will tell you how a certain zek went to the chief to split wood for the kitchen—and how the chief's daughter ran out to him in the woodshed. Or how a sly orderly made a crawl hole underneath the barracks and put a pot under the drain in the floor of the parcel room. (There was sometimes vodka in parcels from outside, but there was a prohibition law on the Archipelago, and, with due documentation, they were supposed to pour out all the vodka right on the ground—but they never ever did pour it out—and so this duty orderly supposedly collected it in his pot and was always drunk.)

In general, the zeks value and love *humor*—and this is best evidence of all of the healthy psychological state of those natives who manage not to die during their first year. They proceed on the theory that tears will not justify you nor laughter get you into debt. Humor is their constant ally, without which, very likely, life in the Archipelago would be totally impossible. They value curses, too, particularly for their humor; the funnier they are, the more convincing to them. Their every reply to a question, their every judgment about their surroundings, is spiced with at least a mite of humor. Ask a zek how much time he has spent already in the Archipelago and he will not tell you, "Five years," but, instead, "Well, I've sat through five Januarys."

(For some reason they refer to their stay in the Archipelago as *sitting*, even though they spend least of all their time sitting.)

"Is it hard?" you ask him.

"Only the first ten years," he replies mockingly.

And if you sympathize with him because he has to live in such a difficult climate, he will reply: "The climate's bad, but the company's good."

And they will say about someone who has left the Archipelago: "They gave him three, he sat out five, and they released him ahead of time."

And when prisoners began to arrive in the Archipelago with

excursion tickets for twenty-five years: "Now you'll be looked after for the next twenty-five years."

And in general the zeks talk this way about the Archipelago: "Whoever hasn't been there yet . . . will get there, and whoever has been there . . . won't forget it."

(This is a case of an unlawful generalization; you and I, reader, do not intend to go there at all, right?) And wherever and whenever the natives hear someone ask *to be given more* of something (even if only hot water in a mug), they all immediately shout in a chorus: "The prosecutor *will give you more!*"

(In general, the zeks have an incomprehensible hostility toward prosecutors, and it frequently bursts out. For example, in the Archipelago the unjust expression is widespread: "The prosecutor is a chopper."

Beyond its exact rhyme, in Russian,* we do not see any meaning in this phrase. With deep regret we have to note here a case of the split between associative and causative connections which reduces the zek's thought processes below the average level common to all mankind. We will have more to say about this anon.)

Here are some additional examples of their cute, good-natured jokes:

"He sleeps and sleeps, but has no time for rest."

"If you don't drink your water, where will you get your strength?"

At the end of the working day (when the zeks are already exhausted and waiting for knocking-off time) they invariably joke about the detested work: "Well, the work just got going, but the day is too short."

And in the morning, instead of setting about work, they go from place to place and say: "The night should come sooner, so tomorrow [!] we could go to work!"

And here is where we see the *gaps in their logic*. There is a well-known native expression: "We didn't plant that forest, so we won't cut it down."

But if one reasons that way, the logging camps didn't plant the forest either, yet they cut them down very successfully indeed! So what we have here is a childishness typical of the native way of thought, an idiosyncratic form of dadaism.

Or here again, from the time of the Belomor Canal: "Let the bears do the work."

Well, how, speaking seriously, can one imagine a bear digging the great canal? The question of bears' working was adequately treated in the works of I. A. Krylov. If there were the slightest possibility of harnessing bears for useful work—do not doubt that it would have been done in recent decades and we would have whole bear brigades and labor camps for bears.

True, the natives have a parallel expression about bears, which is highly unjust but caustic: "The chief is a bear."

We cannot even understand what association of ideas could give rise to such an expression. We would not like to think so ill of the natives as to combine the two expressions and draw a conclusion on that basis.

Going on to the question of the zeks' *language*, we find ourselves in somewhat of a quandary. Without even mentioning the fact that each study of a newly discovered language always calls for a separate book and a special scientific course, there are specific difficulties in our case.

One of them is the . . . agglomerative combination of language with cursing, to which we have already referred. No one could possibly separate them (because one cannot divide a living thing!).[16] But at the same time we are restrained from setting down everything as it is in these scholarly pages out of concern for the morals of our young people.

There is another difficulty—the necessity of precisely distinguishing the language of the zek people from the language of the tribe of cannibals (otherwise known as the "thieves," the crooks) scattered among them. The language of the tribe of cannibals is a completely separate branch of the philological tree, which has nothing like it or akin to it. This subject is worthy of a separate inquiry, and we would only be confused by the incomprehensible cannibal lexicon (with such words as: "ksiva" —a document; "marochka"—handkerchief; "ugol"—suitcase; "lukovitsa"—a watch; or "prokhorya"—boots). But the problem is that there are other lexicographical elements of the cannibal

---

16. Only recently a certain Stalevskaya from the village of Dolgoderevenskoye of Chelyabinsk Province found a way: "Why did you not struggle for the purity of the language? Why did you not appeal *to the instructor for help in an organized way?*" This remarkable idea simply never crossed our minds when we were in the Archipelago; otherwise we would certainly have suggested it to the zeks.

language which have been taken over by the zek language and which have enriched it with their images:

"Svistet," meaning in Russian "to whistle, to sing," and in the zek language "to tell a lie, to shoot the bull"; "temnit," meaning in Russian "to darken, to obscure," and similarly in zek "to deceive, to confuse"; "raskidyvat chernukhu," meaning in Russian "to cast something black over," and in zek, similarly, "to deceive, to throw dust in one's eyes"; "kantovatsya," meaning in Russian "to be tipped over, turned upside down," and in zek "to loiter, loaf on the job, but slyly"; "lukatsya," meaning in Russian "to feel out," and in zek "to check out the action—but swiftly"; "filonit," meaning in zek "to be clever, to loaf"; "mantulit," which used to mean in Russian "to lick the plates of the master's table," and which now means in zek "to get stuck in, to slave away"; "tsvet," meaning in Russian "color," including skin color, and in zek "appertaining, belonging, to the Russian thieves' law"; "polusvet," meaning in Russian "half-breed, mulatto," and in zek "half-thief"; "dukhovoi," meaning in Russian "pertaining to the spirit" or "wind," as is wind instrument, and in zek "courageous, fearless, reckless"; "kondei," meaning in Russian and in zek "the cooler, the punishment block"; "shmon," meaning in zek "a frisk, a body search"; "kostyl," meaning "a crutch" in Russian, and in zek "the bread ration"; "fitil," meaning "a wick" in Russian, and in zek "a prisoner worn down and dying"; "shestyorka," meaning in Russian something with "six elements" or scoring "six points," and in zek "someone working for the camp administration or for the thieves or trusties"; "sosalovka," meaning in Russian "something sucked on or which sucks," and in zek "a starvation situation"; "otritsalovka," meaning in Russian "something which is a denial, a disclaimer," and in zek "a rejection of everything demanded by the camp chiefs," usually on the part of the central hard core of thieves; "s pontom," meaning in Russian "with the style of a card player who plays against the bank," and in zek very much the same, "bluffing but with braggadocio, with theatrics"; "gumoznitsa," meaning in zek "a prostitute, a camp lay"; "shalashovka," derived from the Russian "shalash," meaning "a lean-to shelter, a shack," and meaning in zek "a shack-up, a girl friend"; "batsilly," meaning in Russian "bacilli," and in zek "fats and oils"; "khilyat pod blatnogo," meaning in zek "to imitate the ways of the Russian thieves"; "zablatnitsya," meaning in zek "to take up the ways of the Russian thieves."

Many of these words, one must admit, possess precision, vividness, even a general comprehensibility. Their crowning glory, however, is the shout "Na tsirlakh!" This can be translated into Russian only by a complex description. To run or to serve something "na tsirlakh" means: "on tiptoe, and headlong, and with heartfelt zeal and eagerness"—and all of it simultaneously.

Now it seems clear to us that the contemporary Russian language is in real need of this expression—particularly because action of that kind is often encountered in life.

But such concern . . . is already, in fact, superfluous. The author of these lines, having completed his lengthy scientific journey through the Archipelago, was extremely worried about being able to return to his teaching in the ethnographic institute —not merely as regards his security clearance, but also as to whether he had fallen behind contemporary Russian language and whether the students would understand him all right. And suddenly, then and there, with astonishment and delight, he heard from the first-year students the very same expressions his ears had grown used to in the Archipelago and in which the Russian language had been so deficient till now: "s khodu," meaning "right away" or "with a rush" or "crashing on"; "vsyu dorogu," meaning "all the way, all the time"; "po novoy," meaning "once again"; "raskurochit," meaning "to rob, to clean out"; "zanachit," meaning "to stash, to swipe"; "frayer," meaning "a sucker" or "anyone not belonging to the thieves' law"; "durak i ushi kholodnye," meaning literally "a fool with cold ears—a hundred percent fool"; "ona s parnyami shyotsya," meaning literally "she gets herself sewed up with the boys, she makes out with the boys"; and many, many others!

What this indicates is the great energy of the zek language, which helps it to filter inexplicably into our country and first of all into the language of our young people. This offers the hope that in the future the process will accelerate and that all the words enumerated previously will also flow into the Russian language and will perhaps even be an ornament to it.

But this makes the task of the researcher even more difficult: to separate the Russian language and the zek language.

And then, too, conscientiousness prevents our bypassing a fourth difficulty: some primary and sort of prehistoric influence of the Russian language itself on the zek language, and even on the language of the cannibals (although now such an influence cannot be observed). How otherwise can it be explained that we find in Dal's dictionary analogies to such specifically Archipelago expressions:

"*zhit zakonom*": literally "to live in the law," and meaning (in the Kostroma district) "to live with a wife" (in the Archipelago: "to live with her in the law").

"*vynachit*": "to fish out of a pocket," in the Russian peddlers' language. (And in the Archipelago they switched the prefix: "zanachit," "to steal.")

"*podkhodit*" meant "to become impoverished, to become fagged out." (Compare "*dokhodit*" in the Archipelago, "to get fagged out to the point of death, to be a dying man, a last-legger.")

Or one can consider the proverbs collected by Dal as well:

"Cabbage soup is good people"—and a whole series of island expressions: "*moroz chelovek*," meaning "a frost person," if he is not strong; "*kostyor chelovek*," literally "a bonfire person," etc.

And we also find in Dal: "He doesn't catch mice."[17]

And the word "suka" ("bitch") meant a "spy" or "stoolie" back in the times of P. F. Yakubovich.

And then there is that remarkable expression of the natives "*to dig your horns in*" (referring to every kind of work stubbornly executed and in general to all stubbornness, to standing up for yourself). And then too: "*to knock his horns down*" or "*to knock his horns off*," which restores to contemporary life precisely the ancient Russian and Slavonic meaning of the word "horns"—conceit, haughtiness, disdain—despite the phrase borrowed and translated from the French, "put horns on" someone —describing a wife's unfaithfulness—a phrase which never caught on among the ordinary people and which even the Russian intelligentsia would have forgotten had it not been bound up with Pushkin's duel.

And all these innumerable difficulties force us for the time being to put off the linguistic portion of our inquiry.

In conclusion, a few personal lines. The zeks at first shied away from the author of this essay when he questioned them;

17. Dal, *op. cit.*, p. 357.

they supposed that these inquiries were being conducted for the benefit of the "godfather" (a guardian spiritually close to them, to whom, however, as to all their guardians, they are ungrateful and unjust). When they became convinced that this was not the case, and after they had been plied with makhorka to smoke from time to time (they do not smoke expensive varieties), they adopted a kindly attitude toward the researcher, disclosing their unspoiled inner natures. In some places they even began in a friendly way to nickname the researcher "Dill Tomatovich" and in others "Fan Fanych." It has to be pointed out that patronymics are not employed at all in the Archipelago, and that therefore this form of respectful address bore a humorous character. Simultaneously it expressed how inaccessible to their intellect was the meaning of this study.

The author considers that the present inquiry has succeeded and that his hypothesis has been fully proved, namely, that in the middle of the twentieth century a completely new nation has been discovered, unknown to anyone before, with the ethnic scope of many millions of people.

Chapter 20

∎

The Dogs' Service

The title of this chapter was not intended as an intentionally scathing insult, but it is our duty to uphold the camp tradition. If you think about it, they themselves chose this lot: their service is the same as that of guard dogs, and their service is connected with dogs. And there even exists a special statute on service with dogs, and there are whole officers' committees which monitor the *work* of an individual dog, fostering *a good viciousness* in the dog. And if the maintenance of one pup for a year costs the people 11,000 pre-Khrushchev rubles (police dogs are fed better than prisoners),[1] then the maintenance of each officer must cost even more.

And then throughout this book we have also had the difficulty of knowing what to call them in general. "The administration," "the chiefs," are too generalized and relate to freedom as well, to the whole life of the whole country, and they are shopworn terms anyway. "The bosses"—likewise. "The camp managers"? But this is a circumlocution that only demonstrates our impotence. Should they be named straightforwardly in accordance with camp tradition? That would seem crude, profane. It would be fully in the spirit of the language to call them *lagershchiki*— "camp keepers"; this distinguishes them every bit as well from the "lagernik"—"camp inmate"—as does "tyuremshchik"—"prison keeper"—from "tyuremnik"—"prison inmate." And it expresses an exact and unique sense: those who manage and govern the

---

1. All this about the dogs comes from Metter's novella "Murat," *Novy Mir*, No. 6, 1960.

camps. And so, asking forgiveness of my stricter readers for this new word (and it is not entirely new if a vacant spot was left for it in the language), I shall from now on make use of it from time to time.

And that is what this chapter is about: the "camp keepers" (and the "prison keepers" with them). We could begin with the generals—and it would be a marvelous thing to do—but we don't have any material. It was quite impossible for us worms and slaves to learn about them and to see them close up. And when we did see them, we were dazzled by the glitter of gold braid and couldn't make anything out.

So we really know nothing at all about the chiefs of Gulag who followed one another in turn—those tsars of the Archipelago. But if we come across a photo of Berman or a word or two of Apeter, we seize on it immediately. We know about those "Garanin executions"—but of Garanin himself we know nothing. All we do know is that he was not satisfied with simply signing; when he went around the camps, he was not loath to empty his Mauser into whatever mug he took a dislike to. We have written about Kashketin—but we never saw that Kashketin face to face. (Thank God!) We managed to collect a little material on Frenkel, but not on Zavenyagin. He, the recently deceased, escaped being buried with the henchmen of Yezhov and Beria. And the newspaper hacks wrote of him: "the legendary builder of Norilsk"! Did he lay bricks with his own hands? Realizing, however, that from up above Beria loved him dearly and that from down below him the MVD man Zinovyev spoke highly of him, we suppose he was an out-and-out beast. Otherwise he would not have built Norilsk. As for Antonov, the chief of the Yenisei Camp, we can be grateful that the engineer Pobozhy described him for us.[2] And we would advise everyone to read this portrayal: the unloading of lighters on the Taz River. In the depths of the tundra where the railroad has not yet extended. (Will it ever?) Egyptian ants are dragging locomotives across the snow, and up above, Antonov stands on a hill, watching over everything and setting them a time limit for unloading. He flew in by air and he is about to fly out by air immediately. His whole retinue dances around him. Napoleon had nothing like this—and his personal cook sets fresh tomatoes and cucumbers on a folding table right before him, in the midst of the Arctic permafrost. And the son-of-a-bitch shares with no one, shoving the whole lot into his own belly.

In this chapter we are going to cover those from colonel down. We'll chat a little about the officers and then go on to the sergeants, briefly cover the infantry guard—and that will be it. Let anyone who has noted more than we did write down more. Our limitation is this: when you are confined in prison or in camp, the personality of the prison keepers interests you only to the extent that it helps you evade their threats and exploit their weaknesses. As far as anything else is concerned, you couldn't care less. They are unworthy of your attention. You are suffering yourself, and those around you who are unjustly imprisoned are suffering, and in comparison with that sheaf of sufferings, which is too much for your outspread hands to encompass, what are these stupid people in their watchdog jobs to you? What are their petty interests to you, their worthless likes and dislikes, their successes and failures in the service?

And then later, too late, you suddenly realize that you didn't observe them closely enough.

Without even discussing the question of talent, can a person become a jailer in prison or camp if he is capable of the very least kind of useful activity? Let us ask: On the whole, can a camp keeper be a good human being? What system of moral selection does life arrange for them? The first selection takes place on assignment to the MVD armies, MVD schools, or MVD courses. Every man with the slightest speck of spiritual training, with a minimally circumspect conscience, or capacity to distinguish good from evil, is instinctively going to back out and use every available means to avoid joining this dark legion. But let us concede that he did not succeed in backing out. A second selection comes during training and the first service assignment, when the bosses themselves take a close look and eliminate all those who manifest laxity (kindness) instead of strong will and firmness (cruelty and mercilessness). And then a third selection takes place over a period of many years: All those who had not visualized where and into what they were getting themselves now come to understand and are horrified. To be constantly a weapon of violence, a constant participant in evil! Not everyone can bring himself to this, and certainly not right off. You see, you are trampling on others' lives. And inside yourself something tightens and bursts. You can't go on this way any longer! And although it is belated, men can still begin to fight their way out, report themselves ill, get disability certificates, accept lower pay, take off their shoulder boards—anything just to get out, get out, get out!

Does that mean the rest of them have got used to it? Yes. The rest of them have got used to it, and their life already seems normal to them. And useful too, of course. And even honorable. And some didn't have to get used to it; they had been that way from the start.

Thanks to this process of selection one can conclude that the percentage of the merciless and cruel among the camp keepers is much higher than in a random sample of the population. And the longer, the more constantly, and the more notably a person serves in the *Organs*, the more likely it becomes that he is a scoundrel.

We do not lose sight of the lofty words of Dzerzhinsky: "Whoever among you has become hardened, whose heart cannot respond sensitively and attentively to those who suffer imprisonment—get out of this institution!" However, we cannot relate these words in any way to reality. Who was this meant for? And how seriously? Considering that he defended Kosyrev? (Part I, Chapter 8.) And who paid any attention to it? Neither "terror as a means of persuasion," nor arrests on the grounds of "unreliability," nor the executions of hostages, nor those early concentration camps fifteen years before Hitler . . . give us the slightest feeling of those sensitive hearts or those knights in shining armor. And if some did leave the Organs *themselves*, on their own in those years, then the ones Dzerzhinsky invited to stay could not help but grow hardened. And whoever became hardened or was hard to begin with stayed. (And maybe a different kind of advice was given on another occasion, but we simply don't have the quotations.)

How adhesive are those fashionable expressions which we are inclined to take over and use without thinking or checking them! *An old Chekist!* Who has not heard these words, drawled with emphasis, as a mark of special esteem? If the zeks wish to distinguish a camp keeper from those who are inexperienced, inclined to fuss, who shout pointlessly and do not have a bulldog grip, they say: "And the chief there is an o-o-old Chekist!" (Like that major who burned Klempner's sonata about shackles.) The Chekists themselves were the ones who put this term into circulation, and we repeat it without thinking. "An old Chekist"— what that means at the least is that he was well regarded under Yagoda, Yezhov, and Beria. He was useful to them all.

But let us not digress and begin to talk about "Chekists in general." There has already been one chapter in this book on Chekists in the specific sense, the Chekists of the Security Operations–interrogation–gendarme persuasion. And the camp keepers merely like to call themselves Chekists, merely aspire to that title, or else have come here from those jobs for a rest—for a rest because here their nerves are not subject to such wear and tear and their health is not being undermined. Their work here does not require of them either that degree of development or that active pressure of evil demanded back there. In the Cheka-GB one must be sharp and quick and invariably hit the eye, but in the MVD it is enough to be dull and not miss the whole skull.

To our chagrin, we cannot undertake to explain why the slogan "the 'proletarianization' and the 'Communization' of camp personnel,"[3] which was successfully carried out, did not create in the Archipelago that fluttering love of man according to Dzerzhinsky. From the very earliest revolutionary years, in courses in the Central Penal Department and the provincial penal departments, the junior administrative staff (in other words, the internal custodial staff) trained for prisons and camps "without interrupting work" (in other words, on the job, already in prisons and camps). By 1925 only 6 percent of the Tsarist prison custodial staff remained (what hardened old servitors!). And even earlier the middle-rank camp command staff had become fully Soviet in composition. They continued to study: first at the *law* faculties of the People's Commissariat of Education (yes, the People's Commissariat of Education! And not faculties of lawlessness either, but of law!). From 1931 on these became the corrective-labor divisions of the law institutes of the People's Commissariat

3. And by October, 1923, the number of them in the R.S.F.S.R. was already twelve thousand, and by January 1, 1925, fifteen thousand. TsGAOR, collection 393, shelf 39, file 48, sheets 4 and 13; shelf 53, file 141, sheet 4.

of Justice in Moscow, Leningrad, Kazan, Saratov, and Irkutsk. The graduates were 70 percent workers in origin and 70 percent Communists! In 1928, by decree of the Council of People's Commissars and the never-objecting VTsIK, the powers over the prison regimen of these "proletarianized" and "Communized" chiefs of places of confinement were expanded still more.[4] Just imagine! Love of man somehow didn't happen! Many *more* millions of people suffered from them than from the Fascists—and they weren't POW's either, nor conquered peoples, but . . . their own compatriots, on their own native soil!

And who is going to explain that to us? We can't. . . .

Do a similarity of paths in life and a similarity of situations give rise to a similarity in characters? As a general thing it doesn't. For people with strong minds and spirits of their own it does not. They have their own solutions, their own special traits, and they can be very surprising. But among the camp keepers, who have passed through a severe negative-selection process—both in morality and mentality—the similarity is astonishing, and we can, in all likelihood, describe without difficulty their basic *universal* characteristics.

Arrogance. The camp chief lives on a separate island, flimsily connected with the remote external power, and on this island he is without qualification the first: all the zeks are abjectly subordinate to him, and all the free employees too. He has the biggest star on his shoulder boards of any there. No limits are set to his power, and it admits to no mistakes; every person complaining is always proven wrong (repressed). He has the best house on the island. The best means of transportation. The camp keepers immediately below him in rank are also raised extremely high. And since their whole preceding life has not given birth to any spark of critical capacity inside them, it is impossible for them to see themselves as other than a special race—of born rulers. Out of the fact that no one is capable of resisting them, they draw the conclusion that they rule very wisely, that this is their talent ("organizational"). Every day each ordinary event permits them visibly to observe their superiority: people rise before them, stand at attention, bow; at their summons people do not just approach

---

4. Vyshinsky, *op. cit.*, p. 421.

but run up to them; on their orders people do not simply leave but run out. And if he (Dukelsky of BAMlag) walks to the gates to watch the dirty rabble of his workers marching in a column surrounded by police dogs, he is the very image of a plantation owner—in a snow-white summer suit. And if they (Unzhlag) have taken it into their heads that they would like to ride out on horseback to inspect the work in the potato field, where women dressed in black are struggling and sinking into the mud up to their bellies, trying to dig potatoes (which, incidentally, were not removed in time and had to be plowed under in the spring for fertilizer), then these camp keepers are dressed up in gleaming jackboots and in faultless woolen uniforms as they, elegant horsemen, ride past their drowning female slaves like the original Olympians.

Stupidity always follows on the heels of smugness. Deified alive, each knows everything inside out, doesn't need to read or learn, and no one can tell him anything worth pausing over. Among the Sakhalin officials Chekhov met clever, energetic men, with scholarly leanings, who had studied the locality and local life thoroughly, and who had in fact written geographical and ethnographical studies. But even for a laugh it is impossible to imagine one such camp keeper in the whole Archipelago! And if Kudlaty, the chief of one of the Ust-Vym work parties, decided that the 100 percent fulfillment of state work norms was not 100 percent at all, and that instead what had to be fulfilled was his own daily norm (taken out of his head) and that otherwise he would put everyone on a penalty ration—there was no way to get him to change his mind. So, having fulfilled 100 percent, they all got penalty rations. In Kudlaty's office there were whole piles of volumes of Lenin. He summoned V. G. Vlasov and unctuously informed him: "Lenin writes what attitude one must take toward parasites." (He understood parasites to mean prisoners who had fulfilled the work norm by only 100 percent, and he understood by the term "proletariat" . . . himself. These two things fitted into their heads simultaneously: Here is my estate, and I am a proletarian.)

But the old serf-owning gentry were incomparably better educated; many of them had studied in St. Petersburg, and some of them even in Göttingen. From them, after all, came the Aksakovs, the Radishchevs, the Turgenevs. But no one ever emerged from our MVD men, and no one ever will. And the main thing was that the serf owners either governed their estates themselves or at least understood a tiny little part of their estate operation. But the presumptuous MVD officers, with all kinds of state benefits showered on them, just could not take on themselves the additional burden of business management. They were too lazy for that and too stupid. And they wrapped their inane idleness in a fog of severity and secrecy. And, as it turned out, the state[5] was compelled to erect, alongside their whole gold-shoulder-boarded hierarchy, a second such hierarchy out of the trusts and combines.[6]

Autocracy. Autotyranny. In this respect the camp keepers were fully the equals of the very worst of the serf owners of the eighteenth and nineteenth centuries. Innumerable are the examples of senseless orders, the sole purpose of which was to demonstrate their power. And the farther into Siberia and the North they were, the truer this was. But even in Khimki, just outside Moscow (today it's in Moscow), Major Volkov noticed on May 1 that the zeks were not cheerful. And he issued orders: "Everyone must cheer up immediately! Anybody I see unhappy will go off to the punishment block!" And to jolly up the engineers he sent third-termer girl thieves to sing them obscene ditties. People will say this was not tyranny but a political measure, so all right. They brought a prisoner transport to that same camp. One of the newcomers, Ivanovsky, was presented as a dancer of the Bolshoi Theatre. "What? A performer?" Volkov raged. "Twenty days in the punishment block! Go by yourself and report to the chief of the penalty isolator!" After some time had passed he telephoned: "Is the performer there?" "He is." "Did he come on his own?" "He did." "Well, then, let him out! I am appointing him assistant to the Commandant." (And that same Volkov, as we have already mentioned, ordered a woman's head shaved because she had beautiful hair.)

The surgeon Fuster, a Spaniard, did not play up to the camp chief. "Send him to the stone quarry." They did. Soon afterward the camp chief himself fell ill and needed an operation. There

5. The state is by no means always directed from the summit, as history well understands; it is very often the middle layer that, by its inertia, has determined the *non*development of the state.

6. But this didn't surprise anyone; what is there in our country, after all, which is *not* duplicated, beginning with the very power of the Soviets itself?

were other surgeons, and he could have gone to a central Moscow hospital, but no, he had faith only in Fuster! Bring him back from the quarry! "You are going to operate on me!" (But he died under the knife.)

And one camp chief made a real find: It turned out that a zek geological engineer, Kazak, possessed an operatic tenor voice. Before the Revolution he had studied in Petersburg with the Italian teacher Repetto. And the camp chief also discovered that he himself had a voice. It was 1941–1942 and the war was going on somewhere, but the camp chief was well protected from military service by his exemption, and he took singing lessons from his serf. The latter was sickly and dying, and was making inquiries in an effort to locate his wife, while his wife, O. P. Kazak, in exile, was trying to find her husband through Gulag. The search documents came together in the chief's hands, and he could have helped them re-establish communication. However, he did not do this. Why not? He "reassured" Kazak that his wife had been exiled but was living well. (Formerly a teacher, she worked first as a charwoman in the Grain Procurements Office and subsequently on a collective farm.) And he continued to take his singing lessons. And when, in 1943, Kazak was at death's door, the camp chief spared him, helped to get him released because of illness, and let him go to his wife to die. (So he was not really a vicious chief!)

A sense of possessing a patrimonial estate was typical of all camp chiefs. They perceived their camp not as a part of some state system but as a patrimonial estate entrusted them indivisibly for as long as they occupied their positions. Hence came all the tyranny over lives, over personalities, and hence also came the bragging among themselves. The chief of one of the Kengir camps said: "I've got a professor working in the baths!" But the chief of another camp, Captain Stadnikov, put him down with "And in my camp I've got an academician barracks orderly who carries out latrine barrels."

Greed and *money-grubbing*. Among the camp keepers this was the most *widespread* trait of all. Not every one was stupid, and not every one was a petty tyrant—but every last one was engaged in attempting to enrich himself from the free labor of the zeks and from state property, whether he was the chief in that camp or one of his aides. Neither I nor any one of my friends could recollect any disinterested camp keeper, nor have any of the zeks who have been corresponding with me ever named one.

In their greed to grab as much as possible, none of their multitudinous legitimate monetary advantages and privileges could satisfy them. Neither high pay (with double and triple bonuses for work "in the Arctic," "in remote areas," "for dangerous work"). Nor prize money (provided management executives of camp by Article 79 of the Corrective Labor Code of 1933—that same code that did not hinder them from establishing a twelve-hour workday without any Sundays for the prisoners). Nor the exceptionally advantageous calculation of their seniority (in the North, where half the Archipelago was located, one year of work counted as two, and the total required for "military personnel" to earn a pension was twenty years; thus an MVD officer on completing MVD school at age twenty-two could retire on a full pension and go to live at Sochi at thirty-two!).

No! Yet every channel, meager or abundant, through which free services, food products, or objects could flow was always used by every camp keeper graspingly and gulpingly. Even back on Solovki the chiefs had begun to expropriate cooks, laundresses, stable boys, woodcutters from among the prisoners. And from then on there was never any end to (and from up above never any prohibition against) this profitable custom. So the camp keepers also took for themselves cattle herdsmen, gardeners, or teachers for their children. And in the years of the most strident outcry about equality and socialism, in 1933, for example, any free employee in BAMlag, for a minuscule payment to the camp cashier, could acquire a personal servant from among the prisoners. In Knyazh-Pogost "Aunt" Manya Utkina looked after the cow of the camp chief—and for this was rewarded with *a glass* of milk per day. And under the Gulag way of life this was real generosity. (And it would have been more likely in the Gulag way of life for that cow not to belong to the chief, but to be kept for "improving the diet of the sick"—but the milk would have kept on going to the chief.)

Not by the glass either, but by the pailful and the bagful, everyone who could possibly get fed off the rations of the prisoners did so on principle! Read over, dear reader, Lipai's letter in Chapter 9 above, the outcry, one would gather, of a former storeroom clerk. After all, it was not out of hunger, not out of need, not out of poverty that those Kuragins, those Posuishapkas, those Ignatchenkos hauled out bags and barrels from the storeroom, but very simply thus: Why shouldn't they enrich themselves at the expense of the mute, defenseless, starving slaves? (And all the more so during wartime, when everyone else around was grabbing. Anyway, if you didn't live that way, everyone would laugh at you! I am not even going to make a special issue here of their betrayal of trusties who used to catch it because of the shortages.) And the Kolyma prisoners remember: Whoever was in a position to steal from the common food pot of the prisoners —the camp chief, the chief of regimen, the chief of the Cultural and Educational Section, the free employees, the duty jailers— all invariably stole. And the gatehouse guards . . . swiped sweetened tea at the gatehouse! Even just a spoonful of sugar, just so as to eat off the prisoners. What you take from a dying man is sweeter. . . .

The chiefs of the Cultural and Educational Sections are best not recalled. They were a big laugh. They all swiped, but it was all small-scale stuff (they were not permitted anything bigger). The chief of the KVCh would summon the storeroom clerk and give him a bundle—a pair of tattered cotton padded britches, wrapped up in a copy of *Pravda*. "Take them and bring me some new ones." And the chief of the KVCh in 1945–1946 at the Kaluga Gates Camp used to carry out of the compound a bundle of bits of firewood, gathered for him by the zeks on the construction project. (And he went through Moscow on a bus . . . in a greatcoat and with a bundle of bits of firewood—his wasn't such a sweet life either. . . .)

It was not enough for the camp bosses that both they and their families were clothed and shod by the camp craftsmen. (And once a special costume for a masquerade ball, a "dove of peace," was made for the fat wife of one camp chief in the camp workshops.) It was not enough for them that they had their own furniture manufactured there, as well as all other kinds of household supplies. It was not enough that they even had their own shotgun pellets cast there (for poaching in the nearby game preserve). It was not enough for them that their pigs were fattened by the camp kitchen. It was too little! They were distinguished from the old serf owners because their power was not for a lifetime and not hereditary. And because of this difference the serf owners did not have to steal from themselves, but the camp keepers had their heads occupied with one thing—how to steal something from their own enterprise.

I am sparing with examples so as not to encumber the exposition. The sullen hunchback Nevezhin never left our camp at the Kaluga Gates with empty hands, but used to walk out, just like that, in his long officer's greatcoat, carrying either a pail of linseed oil, or windowpanes, or putty, and all of it in quantities a thousand times exceeding the needs of any single family. And a paunchy captain, the chief of Camp 15 on Kotelnichesky Embankment, used to come each week in his passenger car for linseed oil and putty. (In postwar Moscow these were gold!) And all this had previously been stolen for them from the construction zone and taken into the camp compound—by those same zeks who had received ten years for a sheaf of straw or a packet of nails! But we Russians had long since *been reformed*, and become accustomed to how things were in our Motherland; and to us this only seemed funny. But here is how it was with the German POW's in the Rostov Camp! At night the chief of camp sent them to steal construction materials for him; he and the other chiefs were building houses for themselves. What could these submissive Germans make out of all this—when they knew that this same camp chief had had them court-martialed for taking a pot of potatoes and sentenced to ten or twenty-five years? The Germans figured it out: They went to the woman interpreter S. and supplied her with a document justifying their act, a declaration that on a certain date they were going to be compelled to go and steal. (And what they were building was railroad facilities, and because of the constant stealing of cement these were being built almost entirely of sand.)

Pay a visit nowadays to the home of the chief of the mine administration in Ekibastuz, D. M. Matveyev. (He is now in the mine administration because of the curtailment of Gulag, but he was chief of the Ekibastuz Camp from 1952 on.) His home is filled with paintings, carvings, and other things made for him for free, by the hands of natives.

Lasciviousness. This was not true of each and every one of them, of course, and it was closely tied to individual physiology. But the situation of camp chief and the absoluteness of his rights allowed harem inclinations full sway. The chief of the Burepolom

Camp, Grinberg, had each comely young woman brought to him immediately on arrival. (And what other choice did she have except death?) In Kochmes the camp chief Podlesny enjoyed nighttime roundups in the women's barracks (of the same sort we have already seen in Khovrino). He himself personally pulled the blankets off the women, allegedly searching for hidden men. In the presence of his beautiful wife he simultaneously bedded three zek mistresses. (And one day, having shot one of them out of jealousy, he shot himself.) Filimonov, the chief of the Cultural and Educational Department of all Dmitlag, was removed "for moral corruption" and sent to be reformed (in the very same position) to BAMlag. There he continued his heavy drinking and fornication on a formidable scale, and he promoted his mistress from the nonpolitical offenders . . . to be the chief of the Cultural and Educational Section. (His son, incidentally, joined up with some bandits and very soon afterward was himself imprisoned for banditry.)

Malice, cruelty. There was no curb, either practical or moral, to restrain these traits. Unlimited power in the hands of limited people always leads to cruelty. (And we cite here all this similarity in vices to those of the serf owners not merely for eloquent argument. This similarity, alas, demonstrates that the nature of our compatriots has not changed in the slightest in two hundred years; give as much power as that and there will be all the same vices!)

Tatyana Merkulova, a woman-beast, at the women's logging camp No. 13 of Unzhlag, rode on her horse among her female slaves like a savage plantation owner. Major Gromov, according to the recollections of Pronman, was actually ill on any day he had not imprisoned several prisoners in the punishment block. Captain Medvedev (Camp No. 3 of UstVymlag) stood in the watchtower himself for several hours each day and jotted down the names of the men who had gone into the women's barracks in order to follow up by imprisoning them. He loved always to have a full isolator. If the cells of the isolator were not packed full, he felt something lacking in his life. In the evening he loved to line up the zeks and read them such statements as "You have lost the game! There is never going to be any return to freedom for any of you, and don't dare to hope there will be." In that very same UstVymlag the chief of camp Minakov (a former deputy chief of the Krasnodar Prison, who had served two years for exceeding his power in that prison, and who had already been readmitted to the Party) personally hauled from their bunks prisoners who refused to go out to work. Among them were thieves who began to put up a resistance, to brandish boards at him; and at that point he ordered all the window frames taken out of the barracks (at 13 degrees below zero Fahrenheit), and then he ordered pailfuls of water to be poured in through them.

All of them (including the natives) knew that the *telegraph lines stopped here!* The plantation owners also developed anger with a twist, in other words, what is called sadism. A prisoner transport was lined up in front of Shulman, the chief of the special section of Burepolom. He knew that this transport was going right out to general work. Nonetheless he could not deny himself the satisfaction of asking: "Are there any engineers? Raise your hands!" A dozen hands were raised above faces shining with hope. "Ah, so that's how it is! And maybe there are some academicians? *Pencils* will be brought you immediately!" And they brought in . . . crowbars. The chief of the Vilna colony, Lieutenant Karev, saw among the newcomers Junior Lieutenant Belsky (still in officer's boots and a tattered officer's uniform). Not long before, this person had been just such a Soviet officer as Karev, had worn just such shoulder boards. Did the sight of this tattered uniform arouse sympathy in Karev? Did he, at least, maintain an attitude of indifference? No, there was the desire to single him out for humiliation! And he ordered that Belsky (exactly as he was, without changing his uniform for camp clothing) be put to hauling manure to the vegetable garden. In that same colony high-ranking executives of the Lithuanian Administration of Corrective Labor Camps came to the bath and lay down on the benches and and gave orders they be washed, not just by prisoners but by 58's only.

Well, just look at their faces. After all, they are still going about among us today. They may well turn out to be next to us in a train (though not in anything less than a first-class compartment). Or in a plane. They have a wreath in their lapel buttonhole, though what the wreath crowns it is impossible to say, and, it is true enough, their shoulder boards are no longer sky-blue (they are shy), but the piping is blue, or even red, or maroon. An oaken cruelty is etched into their faces, and they always have a gloomy, dissatisfied expression. It would seem as if everything was going well in their lives, but there is that expression of dissatisfaction. Perhaps they have the feeling that they are missing out on something better? Or perhaps God has marked them out infallibly for all their evildoings? On the Vologda, Archangel, and Urals trains, in first-class compartments the percentage of this kind of *military* is higher. Outside the window shabby camp watchtowers loom. "Is that your *establishment?*" asks a neighbor. The military man nods his head affirmatively, and says in a satisfied, even proud, way: "Ours." "Is that where you are going?" "Yes." "And does your wife work there too?" "She gets 90. Yes, and I get 250 myself. [This means he's a major.] Two children. You'll not get far on that." Now this one here, for example, even has city manners, and is a very pleasant person to talk to on the train. Collective-farm fields have flashed past, and he explains: "In agriculture things are going along much better. Nowadays they *sow whatever they want to.*" (And when for the first time men clambered out of their caves to plant crops on a burned-over spot in the forest, did they not sow "whatever they wanted to"?)

In 1962 I traveled through Siberia on a train for the first time as a free man. And it just had to happen! In my compartment there was a young MVD man, just graduated from the Tavda school, traveling under orders from the Irkutsk Administration of Corrective Labor Camps. I pretended to be a sympathetic idiot, and he told me how they went through probationary work in contemporary camps, and how impudent, feelingless, and hopeless the prisoners were. On his face there had not yet set in that constant, permanent cruelty, but he triumphantly showed me a photo of the third graduating class at Tavda, in which there were not only boys—but also veteran camp keepers finishing up their education (in training dogs, in criminal investigation, in camp management and in Marxism-Leninism) more for the sake of their pensions than for the sake of service. And even though I had been around, nonetheless I exclaimed! Their blackness of heart stands out on their faces! How adroitly they pick them out from all humanity!

In a POW camp in Ahtme, in Estonia, there was an incident. A Russian nurse became intimate with a German POW, and they were found out. Not only did they evict her forthwith from their noble midst. Oh, no! For this woman who wore Russian officer's shoulder boards, they nailed together a plank booth with a tiny window near the gatehouse outside the camp compound (they spared no work and effort on this). They kept her in this booth for a week, and every free employee on his way "to work," and on his return, would throw stones at the booth, and shout: "You German whore!" And spit at her.

That is how they are chosen.

Let us help history preserve the names of the Kolyma camp-keeper butchers who (at the end of the thirties) knew no limits to their power and inventive cruelty: Pavlov, Vishnevetsky, Gakayev, Zhukov, Komarov, M. A. Kudryashev, Logovinenko, Merinov, Nikishov, Reznikov, Titov, Vasily "Durovoi." Let us also recall Svetlichny, the famous torturer of Norilsk, responsible for the loss of many zek lives.

Others, without our help, will tell about such monsters as Chechev (dismissed from the MVD in the Baltic States and sent to be chief of Steplag); Tarasenko (the chief of Usollag); Korotitsyn and Didorenko from Kargopollag; the fierce Barabanov (chief at the end of the war at Pechorlag); the chief of regimen at PechZhelDorlag Smirnov; Major Chepig (chief of regimen of Vorkutlag). Just a list of these famous names would take up dozens of pages. It is not for my lonely pen to pursue them all to the end. And they still have their former power. They have not yet set aside an office for me in which to gather all these materials, or offered me broadcast facilities for appeals over the All-Union radio networks.

One thing more about Mamulov, and that will suffice. This is that same Mamulov of the Khovrino Camp whose brother was the chief of Beria's secretariat. When our armies had liberated half of Germany, many of the MVD big-shots rushed there, Mamulov among them. From there he sent back whole trainloads of sealed cars—to his own Khovrino Station. The cars were shunted into the camp compound so that free railroad workers would not see what was in them—officially described as "valuable factory equipment"—and Mamulov's own zeks unloaded them. No one cared whether they saw. Shoved in there, in bulk, was everything that crazed looters grab: chandeliers ripped from ceilings, antique and ordinary furniture, table services wrapped up in wrinkled tablecloths, kitchen utensils, evening dresses and housedresses, women's and men's underwear and linens, dress coats, silk hats, and even canes! Here all this was sorted out, and whatever remained whole was carried off to apartments and distributed among friends. Mamulov also brought from Germany a whole parking-lotful of confiscated automobiles. He even gave his son an Opel Kadett, the son being twelve years old (the age of a camp kid!). For whole months long the tailor and shoemaker shops in camp were piled high with loot which had to be altered. Yes, and Mamulov had more than one apartment in Moscow and more than one woman, too, whom he had to provide for! But his favorite apartment was in the suburbs, at the camp. Sometimes Lavrenti Pavlovich Beria himself came here to visit. They brought out from Moscow a makeshift Gypsy chorus and even let two of the zeks in on these orgies—the guitarist Fetisov and the dancer Malinin (formerly from the Red Army Ensemble for Song and Dance). And they were warned: If you ever say a word anywhere, I'll see to it you rot! Here is the kind of person Mamulov was: They were returning from a fishing trip and dragged their boat through the vegetable garden of some old man, trampling all over it. The old man, it seems, began to protest. And how did they reward him? Mamulov beat him up with his own fists to the point where the old man lay there, groaning into the ground. "It belongs to me, and for that they beat me," as the saying goes.[7]

But I feel that my tale is becoming monotonous: Does it seem that I am repeating myself? Or is it that we have already read about this here, there, and elsewhere?

I hear objections! I hear objections! Yes, there were such individual facts. . . . But for the most part under Beria . . . But why don't you give some of the bright examples? Just describe some of the good ones for us! Show us our dearly beloved fathers. . . .

But no! Let those who saw them show them. I didn't see them. I have already deduced the generalized judgment that a camp keeper *could not be a decent person*—either he had to change direction or they got rid of him. Let us suppose for just one moment that a camp keeper decided to do good and to replace

7. When Beria fell in 1953, Mamulov was in bad trouble, but not for long, because after all he did belong to the ruling elite. He came out unscathed and became one of the chiefs of the Moscow Construction Trust. Then he got into trouble again for black-marketing apartments. And once again he rose to the top. And by now it is ample time for him to be on a pension.

the currish regimen in his camp with one that was humane: Would he be allowed to? Would they permit it? Would they let this happen? You might just as well leave a samovar out in the frost to heat up.

Now I am willing to accept certain things: There were "good" men who kept trying unsuccessfully to get out, who had not yet left, but who were going to leave. For example, the director of a Moscow shoe factory, M. Gerasimov, had his Party card taken from him, but they did not expel him from the Party. (This form of discipline did actually exist.) And in the meantime where could they send him? To Ust-Vym to be a camp keeper. And they say that he was very unhappy and depressed in this position and was easy on the zeks. In five months' time he got out of the job and left. And this I can believe: that for those five months he was good. And then, too, supposedly, in Ortau in 1944 there was a camp chief named Smeshko who was not known to have done anything bad—and he, too, was trying to get out of his job. In the Administration of the Northeastern Corrective Labor Camps the former pilot Morozov, section chief in 1946, had a decent attitude toward the zeks, and for that he was in the bad books of the administration. Or Captain Siverkin in Nyroblag was, they say, a decent man. And what came of that? They sent him to Parma, a penalty-work party. And he had two occupations there: he drank hooch and listened to the Western radio. In these localities the jamming was weak (1952). And then my neighbor in the railroad car, the Tavda graduate, he also possessed good impulses: There was a young fellow in the corridor who had no ticket and who had been standing a whole day. And so this fellow said: "Shall we make room for him, give him a place? Let him get some sleep?" But just give him a year's service as a chief, and he will do something else again— he will go to the conductor: "Get rid of that fellow without a ticket!" Isn't that right?

Well, I will speak honestly. I knew one very good MVD man —true, not a camp keeper but a jail keeper—Lieutenant Colonel Tsukanov.* For a brief while he was the chief of the Special Prison at Marfino. Not only I but all the zeks there admit that no one suffered evil and all experienced good from him. Whenever he could bend the order in the zeks' favor . . . he invariably did. And whatever he could ease up on . . . he invariably did.

And what happened? They reclassified our Special Prison into a stricter classification—and he was removed. He was not a young man and had served a long time in the MVD. And how he had done it I don't know. It is a riddle.

And Arnold Rappoport assures me that Colonel of Engineers Mikhail Mitrofanovich Maltsev, an army field engineer, who from 1943 to 1947 was chief of Vorkutlag—both the construction project and the camp—was, supposedly, a good man. In the presence of Chekists he shook the hands of zek engineers and addressed them politely. He could not stand career Chekists, and he held in contempt the chief of the Political Branch, Colonel Kukhtikov. And when he was commissioned with a State Security rank—General Commissar, Third Rank—he refused. (Can that be?) He said: "I am an engineer." And he got his way. He became an ordinary general. During the years of his administration, Rappoport assures me, not one single camp *case* was ever set in motion in Vorkuta. (And these, after all, were the war years, the very period for all those camp *cases*.) His wife was the prosecutor for the city of Vorkuta and succeeded in paralyzing the creative work of the camp security officers. This is a very important piece of evidence, if only A. Rappoport is not exaggerating involuntarily because of his own privileged position as an engineer at that time. Somehow I find it hard to really believe it; why, then, did they not get rid of this Maltsev? After all, he must have been *in everyone's way*. Let us hope that someone someday will establish the truth here. (Commanding a division of field engineers at Stalingrad, Maltsev could summon a regimental commander in front of the line-up and shoot him himself. He was sent to Vorkuta in disfavor, but not for that, for something else.)

In this and in other similar cases faulty memory and extraneous personal impressions sometimes distort recollections. And when they speak about *good men*, one wishes to ask: Good to whom? To all?

And former front-line officers were by no means an improvement as replacements for veteran MVD men. Chulpenyov bears witness that things got no better, but even worse, when an old camp dog was replaced, at the end of the war, by a front-line officer invalided out, like Regimental Commissar Yegorov. Understanding nothing at all of camp life, they issued careless, superficial orders and then went out of the camp compound on a drinking spree with some broads, turning the camp over to the scoundrels from among the trusties. /

However, those who *shout* particularly loudly about "good Chekists" in camps—these being the loyalist orthodox Communists—do not have in mind "good" in the sense in which we understand it; they don't mean those who tried to create a generally humane condition for all imprisoned there, at the cost of deviating from the savage instructions of Gulag. No, they consider those camp keepers "good" who honestly carried out all the currish instructions, who tore to pieces and tormented the whole crowd of prisoners, but did favors for the former Communists. (What breadth of view the loyalists have! They are always the heirs of universal human culture! . . .)

There actually were, of course, such "good" camp keepers as these, and no few of them. For example, Kudlaty with his volumes of Lenin—wasn't he such a one? Dyakov tells about one, and here was his nobility: During a business trip to Moscow the chief of camp visited the home of one of the orthodox Communist prisoners serving time in his camp, and returned—and immediately went right on carrying out all his currish duties. And General Gorbatov recalls a "good" Kolyma camp keeper: "People are accustomed to consider us some sort of monsters of cruelty, but this opinion is erroneous. We, too, enjoy communicating good news to a prisoner." (But the letter from Gorbatov's wife in which the passage where she warned him about the reconsideration of his case was blacked out by the censor—why did they deprive themselves of the enjoyment of communicating good news? But Gorbatov sees no contradiction in this: the chiefs say it, and the army general believes it.) And what that "good" Kolyma cur was worried about . . . was that Gorbatov might say something "up top" about the tyranny in his camp. That was why that pleasant conversation took place. And at the very end: "Be careful in your conversations." (And Gorbatov again understood nothing at all. . . .)

And here in *Izvestiya* (September 6, 1964) Levkovich writes a so-called *passionate*—but in our opinion assigned—article: She had known several good, intelligent, strict, sad, tired, etc., Chekists, and a certain Kapustin in Dzhambul had tried to arrange jobs for the exiled wives of Communists and because of this was forced to shoot himself. Now this is total delirium. Nonsense! The commandant *is obliged* to arrange work for exiles, even by compulsion. And if he really did shoot himself—what this means is that it was because he had either embezzled or got in a mess with some broads. But what was the central organ of the former VTsIK, *Izvestiya* (the very same that had approved of all the Gulag cruelties), trying to prove? It was saying that if there were some good serf owners, then there had never been any serfdom in general. . . .

Yes, and here is another "good" camp keeper: our Ekibastuz Lieutenant Colonel Matveyev. Under Stalin he showed and clacked his sharp teeth, but once Papa Stalin had died and Beria had had it—Matveyev became a leading liberal, the father of the natives! Well, until the next change of wind anyway. (But on the quiet, even during that year, he instructed the brigadier Aleksandrov: "If someone doesn't obey you—punch him in the snoot. Nothing will happen to you, I promise!")

No, "good" men like that are "good" only until the wind changes! All that kind of "good" men—are good and cheap! In our view they were good only when they themselves served time in camp.

And . . . some did serve time. But what they were tried for was not for *that*.

■

The camp custodial staff was considered the junior command staff of the MVD. These were the Gulag noncoms. And that was the kind of assignment they had—to worry the prey and not let go. They were on the same Gulag ladder, only lower. As a result they had fewer rights and they had to use their own hands more often. However, they were not sparing of their hands, and if they were required to bloody someone up in the penalty isolator or in the jailers' room, three of them would boldly beat up on one even until they had knocked him out. Year by year they coarsened in the service, and you couldn't observe in them the least cloudlet of pity toward the soaked, freezing, hungry, tired, and dying prisoners. In relation to them the prisoners were just as deprived of rights, and just as defenseless, as in relation to the big chiefs. And they could bring pressure to bear on the prisoners in the same way—and feel themselves to be high up.

And they could vent their malice and display cruelty—they encountered no barriers. And when you start beating with impunity—once you've started you don't want to stop. Tyranny incites you and you feel yourself to be so ferocious that you are afraid even of yourself. The jailers willingly copied their officers in their conduct, and in character traits too—but they didn't have that gold on their shoulder boards and their greatcoats were dirtyish, and they went everywhere on foot, and they were not allowed prisoner-servants, and they dug in their own gardens, and looked after their own farm animals. Well, of course, they did manage *to haul off* a zek to their places for half a day now and then—to chop wood, to wash floors—this they could do, but not on a lavish scale. And not using the working zeks either, but those resting. (Tabaterov—in Berezniki in 1930—had only just lain down after a twelve-hour night shift when the jailer awakened him and sent him to his house to work. And just try not to go! . . .) The jailers had no *patrimonial estates;* the camp for them, after all, was not a patrimonial estate, but their service, and therefore they did not have either that arrogance or that despotic scope. And there were obstacles in the way of thievery too. This was an injustice; even without thievery the chiefs had plenty of money—and they could steal much too, and the custodial staff had much less—and were allowed to steal less too. No one was going to give you a full bag from the storeroom —hardly even a small pouch. (Right now I can see before my eyes, as if it were today, the big-faced, flaxen-haired Sergeant Kisilyov; he came into the bookkeeping office in 1945 and ordered: "Don't issue one ounce of fats and oils to the zek kitchen! Only to the free employees!" There were not enough fats. And this was their whole advantage—fats according to the norm. . . .) In order to have something sewn for them in the camp tailor shop, they had to have the camp chief's permission and wait their turn. Well, at work you could make the zek do a small task for you—solder, cook, hammer, or sharpen something. Anything larger than a stool you'd not always manage to carry out. This limitation on thievery deeply affronted the jailers, especially their wives, and because of this there was much bitterness against the chiefs, because of this life seemed very unjust, and within the jailer's breast there stirred not so much sensitive heart strings as a sense of unfulfillment, an emptiness echoing a human groan. And sometimes the lower-ranking jailers were capable of talking sympathetically with the zeks. Not so often, but not all that rarely either. In any case, among both prison and camp jailers it was possible to find human beings. Every prisoner encountered more than one in his career. In an officer it was virtually impossible.

This, properly speaking, was the universal law of the inverse ratio between social position and humaneness.

The real jailers were those who had served in camp fifteen and twenty-five years. Whoever had once settled down in those accursed distant places . . . would never be able to clamber out again. Once they had memorized the statute and daily routine, there was nothing else in their whole lives that they had to read or know, and all they did was to listen to the radio, the Moscow program No. 1. And it was their corps that constituted for us the vacantly expressionless, unwavering face of Gulag, inaccessible to any thought.

Only during the war years was the composition of the jailers' staff distorted and muddied. The military authorities in their haste disregarded the sanctity of the custodial service, and took some of them away to the front, and in place of them began to send soldiers from army units released from hospitals—but even from these they selected the stupidest and cruelest. And old men turned up as well, mobilized straight here from home. And among these gray-mustached fellows were many good-hearted, unprejudiced people—they spoke gently, searched perfunctorily, confiscated nothing, and even joked. They never registered complaints nor reported people to be sent to the punishment cell. But after the war they were soon demobilized and there weren't any more of them.

There were unusual individuals among the jailers (in wartime too) like the student Senin, about whom I have already written, and one other Jewish jailer in our camp at Kaluga Gates—elderly, with a very civilian appearance, very calm, not fault-finding, and no one suffered misfortune from him. He was so mild in his bearing that on one occasion I was bold enough to ask: "Tell me, what is your civilian profession?" He took not the slightest offense, looked at me with calm eyes, and quietly replied: "Merchant." During the war before coming to our camp he had served in Podolsk, where, as he related, thirteen or fourteen people had died every day of the war from starvation. (And that alone makes twenty thousand deaths!) He evidently lasted out the war in the "armies" of the NKVD, and now he had to be nimble and not get stuck there for good.

But take Master Sergeant Tkach, the dreaded assistant to the chief of regimen of the Ekibastuz Camp, who fitted in with the jailers just as if he had been specially cast in a mold, as if from his diapers on he had served only there, as if he had been born along with Gulag. His was always an immobile, ominous face beneath a black forelock. It was frightening merely to be next to him or to run into him on a camp path; he would not walk past without doing a person harm—ordering him to turn back, compelling him to work, taking something away from him, scaring him, punishing him, placing him under arrest. Even after the evening roll call, when the barracks were all locked but, in summertime, the barred windows were left open, Tkach would creep silently up to the windows, listen there, then peer in—the whole room would be rustling—and from outside the windowsill, like a black bird of night, he would announce punishments through the grating: for not sleeping, for talking, for making or using something forbidden.

And all of a sudden . . . Tkach disappeared for good. And the rumor swept through camp (it was impossible to check it out, nonetheless such persistent rumors as this were usually correct) that he had been exposed as a Fascist executioner on occupied territory, that he had been arrested and had received a whole *quart*—twenty-five years. This was in 1952.

How had it happened, however, that a Fascist executioner (for no more than three years, certainly) had for seven years after the war been in the best graces of the MVD?

You tell me!

■

"The convoy opens fire without warning!" This invocation encompassed the whole special statute of the convoy[8]—and its power over us on the other side of the law.

8. When we say "convoy," we are using the everyday term of the Archipelago; they used to say too, and even more often in the Corrective Labor Camps, the VOKhR—the Militarized Guards—or simply OKhR. Their full title was Militarized Guard Service of the MVD, and "convoy" was only one of the possible services of the VOKhR, along with service "on watch duty," "perimeter duty," "patrol duty," and "in battalion."

Convoy service—even when there was no war—was like front-line service. The convoy had nothing to fear from any investigation, and did not have to give any explanations. Every convoy guard who fired was right. Every prisoner killed was guilty—of wanting to escape or of stepping across the line.

Take two murders at the Ortau Camp. (And you can multiply them by the total number of camps.) A guard was leading a group under convoy, and a person not under convoy went up to his girl friend in the group and walked along beside her. "Move away!" "Is it doing you any harm?" A shot. Killed. A comedy of a trial, and the guard was acquitted: he had been insulted while carrying out service duties.

At the gatehouse, a zek ran up to another guard with a release document (he was going to be released the next day) and asked: "Let me through, I am going to the laundry [outside the camp compound]. I'll only be a minute!" "You can't." "But tomorrow I'm going to be free, fool!" The guard shot him dead. Killed. And there wasn't even a trial.

And how easy it was for a prisoner not to notice in the heat of his work those blazes on the trees which constituted an imaginary dotted line, a forest cordon instead of barbed wire. For example, Solovyov (a former army lieutenant) cut down a fir tree and, moving backward, was cleaning the branches off it. He saw only his felled tree. And a convoy guard, "a Tonshayevo wolf," squinted and waited. He wouldn't call out to the zek, "Watch out!" He just waited, and Solovyov, not noticing, crossed the line of the work zone, continuing to back his way down the tree trunk. A shot! An explosive bullet and a lung was blown apart. Solovyov was killed—and the Tonshayevo wolf got a hundred-ruble prize. ("Tonshayevo wolves" . . . were the local inhabitants of Tonshayevo District near Burepolom, who had all enlisted in the VOKhR during the war, so as to be closer to home and not go to the front. This was the same Tonshayevo District where the children used to shout: "Mama! Here comes a *herring!*")

This absoluteness in the relations between the convoy and the prisoners, this continual right of the guards to use a bullet instead of a word, could not fail to influence the character of the VOKhR officers and the VOKhR enlisted men as well. The lives of the prisoners were given into their power, though not for the whole day, yet totally and profoundly. To them the natives were not people. They were some sort of lazy animated scare-crows, whom fate had given them to count, to drive to work and from work as swiftly as possible, and to keep at work as densely crowded together as possible.

But tyranny was even more intense among the officers of the VOKhR. These young whippersnappers of lieutenants had ac-quired a balefully despotic sensation of power over existence. Some were only loud-mouthed (Senior Lieutenant Chorny in Nyroblag), others reveled in cruelty and even let it carry over to their own soldiers (Lieutenant Samutin, in the same camp); still others did not recognize any limitations on their omni-potence. The Commander of VOKhR, Nevsky (Camp No. 3 at Ust-Vym), discovered the loss of his dog—not a service dog, but his beloved little lap dog. He went to look for it, of course, in the camp compound, and it was his luck to catch five natives dividing up the carcass. He pulled out his pistol and shot one dead on the spot. (There were no administrative consequences of the incident, except punishment of the remaining four zeks in the penalty isolator.)

In 1938 in the area west of the Urals a forest fire flew with the speed of a hurricane along the Vishera River—and from the forest into two camps. What was to be done with the zeks? The decision had to be made instantly—there was no time to consult with higher jurisdictions. The guard refused to release them—and they all burned to death. That was the easy way. If they had been released and escaped, the guards would have been court-martialed.

There was only one limitation in VOKhR service on the bubbling energy of its officers: The platoon was the basic unit, and all that omnipotence came to an end above the platoon, and in rank *above* lieutenant. Advancement in the battalion simply had the effect of separating the officer from the actual and real power of the platoon, and was a dead-end street.

And as a result, the most power-hungry and powerful of the VOKhR officers tried to leapfrog into the internal service of the MVD and to get their promotion there. Certain famous Gulag biographies consisted indeed of this. The already mentioned Antonov, the ruler of the "road of the dead" in the Arctic, had risen from a VOKhR commander, and his whole education was . . . through the fourth grade.

There is no doubt that inside the Ministry the selection of the infantry guard of the MVD was considered of great importance, and the military conscription centers had secret instructions on this. The military conscription centers conduct a great deal of secret work. Yet we take a benign attitude toward them. Why, for example, has there been such a determined rejection of the twenties concept of territorial armies (the project of Frunze)? And why is it, exactly to the contrary, that the newly called recruits are sent with exceptional persistence to serve in armies that are as far as possible from their own region—Azerbaijanians to Estonia, Latvians to the Caucasus, etc.? Because the armies must be alien to the local population, and preferably even of a different race (as was tested in Novocherkassk in 1962). And so in the selection of convoy troops there was, not without design, a higher percentage of Tatars and other minority nationalities; their inferior education and their lack of information were valuable to the state, they were its fortress.

But the real scientific organization and training of these armies only began at the same time as the Special Camps—the Osoblagi—at the end of the forties and the beginning of the fifties. They began to take only nineteen-year-old boys and immediately would subject them to intense ideological irradiation. (We are going to discuss this convoy separately.)

But until then it somehow seemed to be beyond their reach in Gulag. The truth was that not all our people, even though socialist, had yet risen to that steadfast cruel level necessary for a worthy camp guard! The VOKhR staff was uneven, and ceased to be the wall of horror it was intended to be. It softened up especially in the years of the Soviet-German war; the very best trained (in "good viciousness") of the young fellows had to be surrendered to the front, and sickly reservists were dragged into VOKhR, too unhealthy to be suitable for the active army, and too untrained in viciousness for Gulag (they were not brought up in the right years). In the most mercilessly hungry war years in camp this relaxation of the VOKhR (wherever it took place; it didn't take place everywhere) at least partially eased the life of the prisoners.

Nina Samshel recollects her father, who, in 1942, was called up into the army at an advanced age and sent to serve as a guard in a camp in Archangel Province. His family joined him there. "At home my father spoke bitterly about life in camp, and about the good people who were there. When my papa had to guard a brigade all by himself at a prison farm [this, too, was wartime—one guard for the whole brigade: wasn't that a relaxation?], I often went to see him there and he allowed me to talk with the prisoners. The prisoners had a lot of respect for my father; he was never rude to them, and he let them go to the store, for example, when they asked, and they never tried to escape from him. They said to me: 'Now if only all the convoy guards were like your father!' He knew that many innocents had been imprisoned,[9] and he was always indignant, but only at home—in the platoon he could say nothing. They imprisoned people for that." At the end of the war he was immediately demobilized.

But one cannot consider Samshel a typical wartime model. His subsequent fate shows it. In 1947 he himself was arrested under Article 58! And in 1950 he was released because he was dying and allowed to return home, where he died five months later.

After the war this loose sort of guarding still lasted a year or two, and it somehow began to happen that many of the VOKhR guards also began to talk of their service as their "sentence": "When I finish my sentence." They understood the shame of their service, the kind of service you could not talk about to the family at home. In that same Ortau, one convoy guard intentionally stole something from the KVCh, and was dismissed from the service and convicted and immediately amnestied—and the other guards envied him: He had found the way! Smart boy!

N. Stolyarova recalls a guard who caught her at the beginning of an escape attempt—and concealed her attempt. And she was not punished. One other shot himself out of love for a zechka sent off on a prisoner transport. Before the introduction of real severities in the women's camps, friendly, good, yes, and even loving relations between the women prisoners and the convoy guards had often begun. Not even our great state had managed to stamp out goodness and love everywhere!

The young reinforcements of the postwar years also did not become immediately what Gulag wanted them to be. When a member of the Nyroblag infantry guards, Vladilen Zadorny,

9. The guard Samshel knew, but our elite writers *did not know!*

mutinied (we will have more to say about him), his mates in the service who were of his age took a very sympathetic attitude toward his resistance.

Self-guarding constitutes a special area in the history of the camp guard. Back, indeed, in the first postrevolutionary years it was proclaimed that *self-watch* was a duty of Soviet prisoners. This was employed at Solovki, not without success, and very widely on the White Sea–Baltic Canal, and on the Moscow-Volga Canal; every socially friendly prisoner who did not wish to push a wheelbarrow could take up a rifle against his comrades.

We will not affirm that this was a special, diabolical plan for the moral disintegration of the people. As always in the half-century of our most recent modern history, a lofty, bright theory and creeping moral vileness somehow got naturally interwoven, and were easily transformed into one another. But from the stories of the old zeks it has become known that the prisoner trusty guards were cruel to their own brothers, strove to curry favor and to hold on to their dogs' duties, and sometimes settled old accounts with a bullet on the spot.

And this has also been noted in our literature on juris-prudence: "In many cases those who were deprived of freedom carried out their duties of guarding the colonies and maintaining order *better* than the staff jailers."[10]

And so tell me—what bad is there that one cannot teach a nation? Or people? Or all humanity?

That particular quotation came from the thirties, and Zadorny confirms it as being also true for the end of the forties: the trusty guards were vicious toward their comrades, used formal reasons for entrapment, and shot them. And in Parma, the penalty expedition of Nyroblag, the only prisoners were the 58's and the trusty guards were also 58's. Politicals . . .

Vladilen tells about the trusty guard Kuzma, a former chauffeur, a young fellow little more than twenty years old. In 1949 he had received a tenner for 58-10. How was he to survive? He could find no other way. In 1952 Vladilen found him working as a trusty guard. His situation tormented him, and he said he could not bear the burden of his rifle. When he went out on guard duties, he often didn't load it. At night he wept, calling himself

10. Vyshinsky, *op. cit.*, p. 141.

a mercenary coward, and he even wanted to shoot himself. He had a high forehead, a nervous face. He loved verses, and he went off with Vladilen into the taiga to recite them. And then again he used to take up his rifle. . . .

And he knew a trusty guard named Aleksandr Lunin, who was already well along in years and whose gray locks formed a wreath about his forehead, and who had a kind, good-natured smile. In the war he had been an infantry lieutenant—and then the chairman of a collective farm. He had received a tenner (under a nonpolitical article) because he had refused to give in to the demands of the District Party Committee and had arranged distributions to the collective farmers on his own. Which means he was that kind of man! His neighbors were dearer to him than he himself was. And there in Nyroblag he became a trusty guard, and even earned a reduction in his term from the chief of the Promezhutochnaya Camp.

The bounds of a human being! No matter how you are astounded by them, you can never comprehend. . . .

Chapter 21

■

Campside

Like a piece of rotten meat which not only stinks right on its own surface but also surrounds itself with a stinking molecular cloud of stink, so, too, each island of the Archipelago created and supported a zone of stink around itself. This zone, more extensive than the Archipelago itself, was the intermediate transmission zone between the small zone of each individual island and the Big Zone—the Big Camp Compound—comprising the entire country.

Everything of the most infectious nature in the Archipelago —in human relations, morals, views, and language—in compliance with the universal law of osmosis in plant and animal tissue, seeped first into this transmission zone and then dispersed through the entire country. It was right here, in the transmission zone, that those elements of camp ideology and culture worthy of entering into the nationwide culture underwent trial and selection. And when camp expressions ring in the corridors of the new building of the Moscow State University, or when an independent woman in the capital delivers a verdict wholly from out of camp on the essence of life—don't be surprised: it got there via the transmission zone, via campside.

While the government attempted (or perhaps did not attempt) to re-educate the prisoners through slogans, the Cultural and Educational Section, censorship of mail, and the security chiefs —the prisoners more swiftly re-educated the entire country through campside. The thieves' philosophy, which initially had conquered the Archipelago, easily swept further and captured the All-Union ideological market, a wasteland without any stronger ideology. The camp tenacity, its cruelty in human relations, its armor of insensitivity over the heart, its hostility to any kind of conscientious work—all this effortlessly tamed campside without difficulty, and then went on to make a deep impression on all *freedom*.

Thus it is that the Archipelago takes its vengeance on the Soviet Union for its creation.

Thus it is that no cruelty whatsoever passes by without impact.

Thus it is that we always pay dearly for chasing after what is cheap.

■

To give a list of these places, these hick towns, these settlements, would be almost the same as recapitulating the geography of the entire Archipelago. There wasn't a single camp compound which could ever exist on its own—next door to it there had to be a settlement of free people. Sometimes this settlement at some temporary logging camp or other would stand there several years—and disappear along with the camp. Sometimes it would put down roots, get a name, a town soviet, a branch line—and stay there forever. And sometimes famous cities would grow up out of these settlements—like Magadan, Dudinka, Igarka, Temir-Tau, Balkhash, Dzhezkazgan, Angren, Taishet, Bratsk, Sovetskaya Gavan. These settlements festered not only in the outposts of the wilderness, but also in the very torso of Russia— around the mines of the Donbas and Tula, next to peat diggings, next to agricultural camps. Sometimes entire districts were infected and belonged to the world of campside, like Tonshayevo. And when a camp was injected into the body of a big city, even Moscow itself, campside also existed—not in the form of a special settlement, but in the form of those separate individuals who flowed away from it every night on trolleybuses and motorbuses and who were drawn back into it again every morning. (In these cases the transmission of the infection proceeded outside at an accelerated rate.)

There were also such towns as Kizel (on the Perm mining and metallurgical branch line); they had begun their existence before there was any Archipelago, but subsequently turned out to be surrounded by a multitude of camps—and thus were transformed into provincial capitals of the Archipelago. Such a city would be permeated by the camp atmosphere. The camp officers and groups of the camp guards would go afoot or ride through it in droves, like occupying forces; the camp administration would be the city's main institution; the telephone network would not belong to the city but to the camps; the bus routes would all lead from the city's center to the camps; and all the town inhabitants would earn their living off the camps.

The largest of such provincial capitals of the Archipelago was Karaganda. It was created by and filled with exiles and former prisoners to such a degree that a veteran zek could not walk the street without running into old acquaintances. The city had several camp administrations. And individual camps were scattered all around it like the sands of the sea.

Who lived in campside? (1) The basic indigenous local inhabitants (there might be none). (2) The VOKhR—the Militarized Camp Guards. (3) The camp officers and their families. (4) The jailers and their families—and jailers, as distinct from camp guards, always lived with their families, even when they were listed as on military service. (5) Former zeks (released from the local camp or one nearby).[1] (6) Various restricted persons—"half-repressed" people, people with "unclean" passports. (Like the former zeks, they, too, were here not of their own free will, but of necessity; even if the particular place had not been assigned them as though they were exiles, it would be worse for them anywhere else in regard to both work and housing, and they might not even have been allowed to live anywhere else anyway.) (7) The works administration. These were highly placed people and constituted in all only a few people in a big settlement. (And sometimes there were none at all.) (8) Then, too, there were the *free employees*—the *volnyashki*—proper, all the tramps and riffraff—all kinds of strays and good-for-nothings and seekers after easy money. After all, in these remote death traps you could work three times as poorly as in the metropolis and get four times the wages—with bonuses for the Arctic, for remoteness, and for hardship, and you could also steal the work of the prisoners. And, in addition, many flocked there under recruitment programs and on contract, receiving moving and

---

1. The Stalinist epoch has gone, and various warm and cold breezes have blown over us—but many former zeks never did leave campside, never left their backwoods localities—and they were right not to. There they are at least half people, whereas here they would not be even that. They will stay there till they die, and their children will assimilate like the local inhabitants.

traveling expenses as well. For those able to pan the gold out of the work sheets campside was a real Klondike. People swarmed there with forged diplomas; adventurers, rascals, and money-grabbers poured in. It was particularly advantageous here for those who needed the free use of someone else's brains. (A semiliterate geologist would have zek geologists to carry out his field observations, work them up, draw all the conclusions, and then he himself could go defend his dissertation in the metropolis.) They sent here the total failures, and those who were simply hopeless drunks. Men came here after their families had broken up or to avoid alimony. Then, too, there were the young graduates of technical schools who had failed to get themselves into cushy spots when obligatory jobs were being assigned. But from the very first day of their arrival here they began to try to get back to the civilized world, and whoever couldn't manage it in one year's time would certainly be able to do it in two. But there was also quite a different category among the free employees: the elderly, who had already lived in campside for whole decades and had become so assimilated to its atmosphere that they no longer needed some other, sweeter world. If their camp shut down, or if the administration stopped paying them what they demanded—they left. But invariably they would move to some other such zone near a camp. They knew no other way to live. This was the situation of Vasily Aksentyevich Frolov, a great drunkard, a cheat, and a "famous master of casting," about whom I could tell many tales, except that I have already described him. Without any diploma, and despite the fact that he had drunk down his last skill as a master, he never received less than five thousand pre-Khrushchev rubles a month.

In the most general sense the word "*volnyashka*" means just any free person, in other words any citizen of the Soviet Union not yet arrested or already released, and therefore every citizen of campside. But most often this word was used in the Archipelago in the narrow sense: a "volnyashka" is that particular kind of free person who worked alongside prisoners in the same work compound. By this token those in groups 1, 5, and 6 above who came to the camp work compound to work were also "volnyashki."

"Volnyashki" were hired as construction superintendents, foremen, head foremen, warehouse managers, and norm setters. In addition, they were hired for those posts in which the employment of zeks would have made the work of the convoy much more difficult: drivers, draymen, dispatchers, tractor drivers, excavator operators, scraper operators, electrical linemen, night firemen.

These second-class "volnyashki," ordinary sloggers like the zeks, made friends with us right away without nonsense, and did everything forbidden by the camp regimen and by criminal law: they willingly deposited the zeks' letters in the *free* mailboxes of the settlement; they took and sold at the local free markets clothes the zeks had pinched in camp and kept the money, bringing the zeks some grub; together with the zeks they also plundered the project: they brought vodka into the work compound. (Despite very strict inspection at the gatehouse, they would drop flasks of vodka with tarred necks into the gasoline tanks of automobiles.)[2]

And wherever it was possible to credit the zeks' work to free people (the foremen and the head foremen were not at all squeamish about crediting themselves too), this was invariably done; after all, work credited to a prisoner did nothing for anyone. No one paid any money for it, but only gave them a bread ration. And that was why in unrationed times it made good sense to complete the zek's work sheet any old way, just so there was no serious trouble, and to credit the zek's work to a free man. The "volnyashka" got money for it, and he ate and drank himself, and gave his own zeks something to eat as well.[3]

---

2. And if it happened that the guard found them, there would still be no official report filed with the chief; the Komsomol guards preferred to drink any contraband vodka themselves.

3. The great advantage of working in campside could easily be observed even among the free employees of the Moscow camps. At our camp at the Kaluga Gates in 1946 there were two free bricklayers, one plasterer, one painter. They were listed as being employed at our construction project. As far as work went, they did almost none, because the project could not pay them large wages; there were no special bonus wages here, and all the areas were measured off exactly. For plastering one square yard they got thirty-two kopecks, and it was simply impossible to charge one and a half rubles per yard or to inflate the square yards to three times more than the room measured. But, in the first place, our free employees hauled off cement, paint, linseed oil, and glass, and, in the second place, they got a good *rest* during their eight-hour workday, and so at night and on Sundays they could really put their hearts into their main work—their work "on the left," private work—and there they made their money up. For the same square yard of wall space, that same plasterer got not thirty-two kopecks but ten rubles from a private person, and in the course of one evening he would earn two hundred rubles!

After all, as Prokhorov said: *"Money nowadays comes in two stories."* What Westerner could comprehend "two-story money"? A lathe operator dur-

And so in general you could not call the relations between the zeks and the "volnyashki" hostile. Instead, they were friendly. And these lost, half-drunken, ruined people were more sensitive to the grief of others, were capable of paying heed to the grief of a prisoner and the injustice of his arrest. The eyes of an unprejudiced human being were open to what the eyes of the officers, jailers, and guards were closed to because of their position.

The relations between the zeks and the foremen and the head foremen were more complex. As "commanders of production" they were put there to squeeze the prisoners and drive them. But they were answerable for the course of the work, and the work couldn't always be carried out in a condition of direct hostility between them and the zeks. Not everything can be got by hunger and the stick. Some things require willing agreement, both by inclination and by imagination. And the only foremen who were successful were those who reached an understanding with the brigadiers and with the best of the skilled craftsmen among the prisoners. And the foremen themselves were not just drunks and not simply enfeebled and poisoned by the constant employment of slave labor; they were also illiterate, and either knew nothing of their line of work or else knew it very badly, and because of this were even more dependent on the brigadiers.

And how interestingly Russian fates sometimes intertwined there! A carpenters' foreman, Fyodor Ivanovich Muravlyov, came to us in his cups before a holiday and bared his soul to the brigadier of painters, Sinebryukhov, an outstanding master of his trade, a serious, steadfast fellow who was serving out his tenth year:

"What? *You're serving time*, you kulak's son? Your father kept plowing away at the land and accumulated cows and figured

---

ing the war received, after deductions, eight hundred rubles a month, and bread cost 140 rubles on the open market. And that meant that in the course of one *month* he did not earn enough for even *six kilos* of bread, over and above his ration. In other words, he could not bring home even seven ounces a day for the whole family! But at the same time he did . . . live. With frank and open impudence they paid the workers an unreal wage, and let them go and seek "the second story." And the person who paid our plasterer insane money for his evening's work also got to the "second story" on his own in some particular way. Thus it was that the socialist system triumphed, but only on paper. The old ways—tenacious, flexible—never died out, as a result of either curses or persecution by the prosecutors.

he would take it all off to the kingdom of heaven. And where is he now? He died in exile? And they imprisoned you too? No, my father was smarter than that; from his earliest years he drank down everything and our hut was empty, and he didn't even give his chickens to the collective farm because he didn't have any or anything else—and right off they made him a brigadier. And I take after him—drinking vodka, and I know no grief."

And as it turned out he was right: Sinebryukhov, after serving out his sentence, would be sent off to exile, and Muravlyov . . . would become the chairman of the trade union committee on construction.

True, the construction superintendent, Buslov, could not wait to get rid of this chairman of the local trade union committee and foreman. (It was impossible to get rid of him; it was the personnel department that hired, not the construction superintendent, and the personnel department would often select loafers and dolts out of a feeling of kinship.) The construction superintendent answered for all the materials and wage fund out of his own pocket, but Muravlyov, out of illiteracy, or else because he was a simpleton (and he was not at all a malicious character, and because of this the brigadiers used to *carry* him), would squander that wage fund, sign unexamined work vouchers (which the brigadiers would fill in themselves), and accept badly done work, which would then have to be broken up and done over again. And Buslov would have been glad to replace that kind of foreman with a zek engineer who was working there with a pick, but because of vigilance the personnel department did not permit this.

"Well, now, tell me: what length beams do you have at the moment on the site?"

Muravlyov sighed deeply. "For the time being I hesitate to tell you exactly."

And the drunker Muravlyov got, the more impudently he used to speak to the construction superintendent. And at that point the construction superintendent decided to besiege him with paper work. Despite the time it cost, he began to put all his orders in writing (keeping carbons in a file). These orders were not executed, of course, and a fearsome case was being built up. But the chairman of the local union was not at a loss. He got himself a half-sheet of wrinkled notebook paper, and took half an hour to scrawl out with difficulty, clumsily:

i bring toyr information That all mechanisms which are for carpeny work in not working order whichis in a Bad state and exclusively do not work.

The construction superintendent was quite a different level of work management. For the prisoners he was a constant oppressor and a constant enemy. The construction superintendent would not enter either into friendly relations with the brigadiers or into deals with them. He used to *cut back* their work sheets, expose their "tukhta" (to the extent that he was smart enough), and he could always punish a brigadier and any prisoner through the camp administration:

To Camp Chief Lieutenant:
   I request you to punish in the severest manner—preferably in punishment cell—but with his being taken out to work—the brigadier of the cement workers, the prisoner Zozulya, and the foreman, the prisoner Orachevsky, for casting slabs thicker than the indicated measurement, in which was expressed an overexpenditure of cement.
   Simultaneously I wish to inform you that this day in dealing with me on the question of registering the volume of work in the work sheets the prisoner brigadier Alekseyev insulted the foreman Comrade Tumarkin, calling him a *jackass*. Such conduct on the part of the prisoner Alekseyev, which undermines the authority of the free administration, I consider extremely undesirable and even dangerous and beg you to take the firmest measures up to and including his being sent away on a prisoner transport.
                            Senior Construction Supervisor Buslov.

This very same Tumarkin had in a suitable moment been called a jackass by Buslov himself, but the zek brigadier, on the basis of his worth, deserved a prisoner transport.

Buslov sent the camp chiefs such notes nearly every day. He saw the camp punishments as the highest form of work stimulus. Buslov was one of those work bosses who had worked himself into the Gulag system and who had adapted himself to the ways of getting things done. That's what he said at meetings: "I have long experience of work with the zeks, and I do not fear their threats to flatten me with a brick." But, he regretted, the Gulag generations had changed for the worse. The people who came to camp after the war, and after Europe, turned out to be disrespectful types. "But working in 1937, you understand, that was pure pleasure. For example, when a free employee entered, the zeks invariably rose to their feet." Buslov knew both how to deceive the prisoners and how to put them in dangerous situations, and he never spared their strength, nor their stomachs, nor, still less, their vanity. Long-nosed, long-legged, wearing yellow American oxfords donated to needy Soviet citizens, which he had received through UNRRA, he perpetually rushed around the floors of the construction, knowing that otherwise the lazy, dirty beings called ze-ka ze-ka would be sitting in all his corners and crannies, lying, warming themselves, looking for lice, or even copulating, notwithstanding the urgency of the short ten-hour working day, and the brigadiers would be crowding the norms office and writing up "tukhta" (false figures) on work sheets.

And out of all the foremen there was only one on whom he partially relied—Fyodor Vasilyevich Gorshkov. He was a puny old guy with bristling gray mustaches. He had a keen understanding of the construction, and he knew both his own work and that contiguous to his, and his principal and unusual trait among the "volnyashki" was the fact that he had an honest interest in the outcome of the construction—not a pocket interest, like Buslov (would they fine him or give him a bonus? curse him out or praise him?), but an inner interest, just as if he were building the whole enormous building for himself and wanted it to be as good as possible. He was a careful drinker too, and never lost sight of the construction. But he had one major shortcoming: he had not adjusted to the Archipelago, and he was unaccustomed to keeping the prisoners in terror. He also liked to go around the construction and peer searchingly with his own eyes; however, he did not rush about like Buslov, and he was not trying to catch those who were cheating, and he liked to sit down and chat with the carpenters on the beams, with the bricklayers at their bricklaying, with the plasterers at their mixing box. Sometimes he shared candies with the zeks—a wondrous thing to us. There was one kind of work which even in his old age he simply could not get along without—glass cutting. He always had his own diamond glass cutter in his pocket, and if someone started cutting glass in his presence, he would begin to hoot right off that they were cutting it wrong, and he would push the glass workers away and cut it himself. Buslov went off for a month to Sochi— and Fyodor Vasilyevich replaced him, but he refused flatly to sit in Buslov's office, and remained right in the foremen's common room.

The whole winter Gorshkov went about in an old Russian short "poddyovka"—a waisted coat. Its collar had grown threadbare, but the outside material was remarkably well preserved. They used to say of that "poddyovka" that Gorshkov had been wearing it for going on thirty-one years without ever taking it off, and that before that his father had worn it for some years on holidays— and thus it developed that his father, Vasily Gorshkov, had been a *government foreman*. And then it was understandable why Fyodor Vasilich liked brick and wood and glass and paint so much—from childhood he had grown up on construction works. But even though the foremen were then called government foremen, and even though they are not called government foremen now, the time they actually became "government foremen" is now, whereas before they were . . . artists.

And Fyodor Vasilich would even now praise the old ways: "What's a construction superintendent nowadays? He isn't able to shift even one kopeck from one place to another. In the old days the contractor would come to the workers on Saturday. 'Well, boys, will it be *before* the bath or *after?*' And they would answer, 'Afterward, uncle, afterward!' 'Well, here's your bath money, and from there to the tavern.' The boys would pour out of the baths in a crowd, and the contractor would be waiting for them with vodka, snacks, and a samovar. . . . Just try after all that to work badly on Monday!"

For us today everything has a name, and we know everything about everything; this was the speedup system, merciless exploitation, playing on the lowest human instincts. And the drinks and the spread that went with them weren't worth what was squeezed out of the worker the following week.

And a bread ration, a wet bread ration, hurled by indifferent hands from the window of the bread-cutting room, now . . . was that really worth any more? . . .

■

So all eight of these classifications of free inhabitants elbowed one another on the crowded square inch of campside: between camp and forest, between forest and swamp, between camp and mine. Eight different categories, various ranks and classes—and all had to fit into that stench-ridden crowded settlement. They were all "comrades" to each other, and they sent their children to the same school.

The kind of comrades they were was such that, like saints in the clouds, up above everyone else two or three local magnates floated. (In Ekibastuz their names were *Khishchuk* and *Karashchuk*,* the director and the chief engineer of the trust— and I did not think up those names!) And then in descending order, with sharp lines of division carefully observed: the chief of camp, the commander of the convoy battalion, other ranking officials of the trust, and officers of the camp, officers of the battalion, and, in places, the director of the Workers' Supply Section, and, in places, the director of the school (but not the teachers). And the higher they went, the more jealously the walls separating them were guarded, and the greater the significance attached to which woman could go to visit whom, so that they could sit and chew sunflower seeds together. (They were not princesses, nor even countesses, and so they looked around all the more vigilantly to make sure their position had not been degraded!) Oh, what a doomed state it was to live in this narrow world far away from other well-provided-for families living in comfortable, spacious cities. Here everyone knew you, and you couldn't just get up and go to the movies without lowering yourself, and, of course, you could not go to a store. (The more so since they brought the best and the freshest things to your home.) It even seemed improper to keep your own piglet; it was demeaning for the wife of so-and-so to feed it with her own hands! (That is why it was necessary to have a servant from the camp.) And in the several wards of the settlement hospital how difficult it was to keep apart from the tatterdemalions and trash and to lie among decent neighbors. And you had to send your nice children to sit behind the same desks with whom?

But further down, these dividing walls quickly lost their precision and their significance, and there were no longer any troublemaking meddlers to keep watch over them. Further down, the categories inevitably commingled, encountered each other, bought and sold together, ran to get in lines, and argued about the New Year's tree gifts from the trade unions, sat all mixed up together any which way at the movies—both genuine Soviet people and those totally unworthy of this title.

One spiritual center of such settlements was the main "Tea Room" in some rotting barracks near which the trucks lined up and from which the drunkards, howling out songs, belching and stumbling, wandered around through the whole settlement. And among the very same mud puddles and mass of squshy mud was the second spiritual center—the Club, its floor covered with hulls of spat-out sunflower seeds, scuffed by boots, with a fly-blown wall newspaper from the previous year, with the constantly grumbling loudspeaker over the door, with the good old mother curses at the dances, and the knife fights after the film show. The style and tone of the local places was "Don't be out late," and if you took a girl to a dance, the safest thing to do was to put a horseshoe in your mitten. (Yes, and some of the girls there were such that even a gang of seven youths would flee from them.)

This club was a knife in the officers' hearts. Naturally, it was quite impossible for officers to go to dances in a shed like that among people of that kind. The enlisted men of the guard went there when they were on leave passes. But the trouble was that the young, childless officers' wives were drawn there too, even without their husbands. And they would end up dancing with the enlisted men! Rank-and-file soldiers embraced the officers' wives! So how could you expect faultless obedience from them on duty the next day! After all, this was equality, and no army can stand up under those conditions! Unable to prevent their wives from going to the dances, the officers managed to get the dances declared out of bounds to enlisted men. (Let some dirty "volnyashki" embrace their wives!) But what this did was to introduce a crack in the symmetry of the political indoctrination of the enlisted men: that we are all happy and equal citizens of the Soviet State, and that our enemies are, you see, behind barbed wire.

Many such complex tensions were hidden in campside, and many contradictions among its eight categories. Mingling in everyday life with the repressed and semirepressed, honest Soviet citizens would not neglect to reproach them and put them in their place, especially when it was a matter of a room in a new barracks. And the jailers, as wearers of the MVD uniform, claimed to be on a higher plane than the ordinary free people. And then there were invariably women in everyone's bad books, because all the single guys would have been lost without them. And there were also women who had plans for getting a permanent man. That kind would go to the camp gatehouse when they knew there would be a release—and they would grab complete strangers by the sleeve: "Come to my place! I have a place, and I will keep you warm. I will buy you a suit! Well, where are you going? After all, they'll just jug you again."

And there was also a security surveillance over the whole settlement. The settlement had its own "godfather." And its own stoolies, and they would flex their muscles: just who was taking letters from the zeks to be mailed outside, and who was selling camp clothing behind the corner of the barracks.

And then, too, of course, there was less sense of the presence of the Law among the inhabitants of campside than anywhere else in the Soviet Union, or that their barracks room was a castle. Some had "unclean" passports, and others had no passports at all, and others had been imprisoned in camp themselves, and others were members of families. And thus all these independent unconvoyed citizens were even more obedient than the prisoners to the command of a man with a rifle, even more meek in the face of the man with a revolver. When they saw one, they did not throw back their proud heads and declare: "You don't have the right!" They would shrink and bow their heads—and slink past.

And this sense of the unlimited power of the bayonet and the uniform hovered so confidently over the expanses of the Archipelago and campside, so communicated itself to everyone who entered the region, that the free woman (P——china) who flew to Krasnoyarsk with her little girl to visit her husband in camp allowed herself to be searched and patted all over at the first demand of the MVD officials in the plane, and allowed her child to be completely undressed. (Since then the little girl has wept every time she has seen the Skyblues.)

But if someone now says that there is nothing sadder than these camp environs and that campside is a sewer, we will reply: That depends on the individual.

A Yakut named Kolodeznikov got three years in 1932 for rustling reindeer, and, under our perspicacious relocation policy, was sent from his native Kolyma to serve his time near Leningrad. He served out his time and was in Leningrad itself, and he brought his family some bright-colored dress materials, yet for many years after complained to his fellow tribesmen and to the zeks who had been sent from Leningrad: "Oh, it's boring where you come from! It's awful!"

Chapter 22

■

We Are Building

After everything that has been said about the camps, the question simply bursts out: That's enough! But was the prisoners' labor profitable to the state? And if it was not profitable—then was it worthwhile undertaking the whole Archipelago?

In the camps themselves both points of view on this were to be found among the zeks, and we used to love to argue about it.

Of course, if one believed the leaders, there was nothing to argue about. On the subject of the use of the prisoners' labor, Comrade Molotov, once the second-ranking man in the state, declared at the Sixth Congress of the Soviets of the U.S.S.R.: "We did this earlier. We are doing it now. And we are going to go on doing it in the future. It is profitable to society. It is useful to the criminals."

Not profitable to the state, note that! But to society itself. And useful to the criminals. And we will go on doing it in the future! So what is there to argue about?

Yes, the entire system of the Stalin decades, when first the construction projects were planned, and only afterward the recruitment of criminals to man them took place, confirms that the government evidently had no doubt of the economic profitability of the camps. Economics went before justice.

But it is quite evident that the question posed needs to be made more precise and to be split into parts:

- Did the camps justify themselves in a political and social sense?
- Did they justify themselves economically?

• Did they pay for themselves (despite the apparent similarity of the second and third questions, there is a difference)?

It is not difficult to answer the first question: For Stalin's purposes the camps were a wonderful place into which he could herd millions as a form of intimidation. And so it appears that they justified themselves politically. The camps were also profitable in lucre to an enormous social stratum—the countless number of camp officers; they gave them "military service" safely in the rear, special rations, pay, uniforms, apartments, and a position in society. Likewise they sheltered throngs of jailers and hard-head guards who dozed atop camp towers (while thirteen-year-old boys were driven into trade schools). And all these parasites upheld the Archipelago with all their strength—as a nest of serf exploitation. They feared a universal amnesty like the plague.

But we have already understood that by no means only those with different ideas, by no means only those who had got off the trodden path marked out by Stalin, were in the camps. The recruitment into camps obviously and clearly exceeded political needs, exceeded the needs of terror. It was proportionate (although perhaps in Stalin's head alone) to economic plans. Yes, and had not the camps (and exile) arisen out of the crisis unemployment of the twenties? From 1930 on, it was not that the digging of canals was invented for dozing camps, but that camps were urgently scraped together for the envisioned canals. It was not the number of genuine "criminals" (or even "doubtful persons") which determined the intensity of the courts' activities —but the requisitions of the economic establishment. At the beginning of the Belomor Canal there was an immediate shortage of Solovetsky Islands zeks, and it became clear that three years was too short and too unprofitable a sentence for the 58's, that they had to serve out two Five-Year plans taken together.

The reason why the camps proved economically profitable had been foreseen as far back as Thomas More, the great-grandfather of socialism, in his *Utopia*. The labor of the zeks was needed for degrading and particularly heavy work, which no one, under socialism, would wish to perform. For work in remote and primitive localities where it would not be possible to construct housing, schools, hospitals, and stores for many years to come. For work with pick and spade—in the flowering of the twentieth century. For the erection of the great construction projects of socialism, when the economic means for them did not yet exist.

On the great Belomor Canal even an automobile was a rarity. Everything was created, as they say in camp, with "fart power."

On the even larger Moscow-Volga Canal (seven times bigger in scale of work than the Belomor Canal and comparable to the Panama Canal and the Suez Canal), 80 miles of canal were dug to a depth of over sixteen feet and a top width of 280 feet. And almost all of it with pick, shovel, and wheelbarrow.[1] The future bottom of the Rybinsk Sea was covered with forest expanses. All of them were cut down by hand, and nary an electric saw was seen there, and the branches and brushwood were burned by total invalids.

Who, except prisoners, would have worked at logging ten hours a day, in addition to marching four miles through the woods in predawn darkness and the same distance back at night, in a temperature of minus 20, and knowing in a year no other rest days than May 1 and November 7? (Volgolag, 1937.)

And who other than the Archipelago natives would have grubbed out stumps in winter? Or hauled on their backs the boxes of mined ore in the open goldfields of the Kolyma? Or have dragged cut timber a half-mile from the Koin River (a tributary of the Vym) through deep snow on Finnish timber-sledge runners, harnessed up in pairs in a horse collar (the collar bows upholstered with tatters of rotten clothing to make them softer and the horse collar worn over one shoulder)?

True, the authorized journalist Y. Zhukov[2] assures us the Komsomols built the city of Komsomolsk-on-the-Amur (in 1932) thus: They cut down trees without axes, having no smithies, got no bread, and died from scurvy. And he is delighted: Oh, how heroically we built! And would it not be more to the point to be indignant? Who was it, hating their own people, who sent them to build in such conditions? But what's the use of indignation? We, at least, know what kind of "Komsomols" built Komsomolsk. And today they write[3] that those "Komsomols" founded Magadan too!

---

1. So each time you ride along the canal in a motorboat—remember those who lie on its bottom.
2. *Literaturnaya Gazeta*, November, 1963.
3. *Izvestiya*, July 14, 1964.

And who could be sent down into the Dzhezkazgan mines for a twelve-hour workday of dry drilling? The silicate dust from the ore there floated about in clouds, and there were no masks, and in four months they were sent off to die of irreversible silicosis. Who could be sent down coal mine shafts on lifts without brake shoes, into mine tunnels without pit props, without protection against flooding? For whom alone in the twentieth century was it unnecessary to spend money on wasteful workmen's safety precautions?

And how was it then that the camps were economically unprofitable?

Read, read, in the "The Dead Road" by Pobozhi,[4] that description of how they disembarked from and unloaded the lighters on the Taz River, that Arctic Iliad of the Stalinist epoch: how in the savage tundra, where human foot had never trod, the antlike prisoners, guarded by an antlike convoy, dragged thousands of shipped-in logs on their backs, and built wharves, and laid down rails, and rolled into that tundra locomotives and freight cars which were fated never to leave there under their own power. They slept five hours a day on the bare ground, surrounded by signboards saying, "CAMP COMPOUND."

And he describes further how the prisoners laid a telephone line through the tundra: They lived in lean-tos made of branches and moss, the mosquitoes devoured their unprotected bodies, their clothing never dried out from the swamp mud, still less their footgear. The route had been surveyed hit or miss and poorly laid out (and was doomed to be redrawn); and there was no timber nearby for poles, and they had to go off to either side on two- and three-day expeditions (!) in order to drag in poles from out there.

There was unfortunately no other Pobozhi to tell how before the war another railroad was built—from Kotlas to Vorkuta, where beneath each tie two heads were left. And what kind of a *rail* road was it when before that railroad they laid alongside it a simple road of ties through an impenetrable forest—built by skinny arms, dull axes, and do-nothing bayonets!

Now who would have done that without prisoners? And how on earth could the camps not be profitable?

The camps were uniquely profitable in terms of the submissiveness of the slave labor and its cheapness—no, it was not just cheap, it cost nothing, because in antiquity money did have to be paid for a slave, whereas no one paid anything to buy a camp inmate.

Even at the postwar camp conferences, the industrial serf owners admitted that "the Z/K Z/K played a big role in the work in the rear, in the victory."

But no one will ever engrave their forgotten names on a marble tombstone placed over their bones.

How irreplaceable the camps were was discovered in Khrushchev's time, during the bothersome, vociferous Komsomol appeals for volunteers for the virgin lands and construction projects in Siberia.

The question of the camps' *paying for themselves* was, however, a different question. The state's saliva had been flowing over this for a long time. As long ago as the "Statutes on Places of Confinement" in 1921 there had been the plea that "places of confinement must, if possible, pay their way with the labor of the prisoners." From 1922 on, certain local executive committees, going against their worker and peasant character, manifested "tendencies of an apolitical pragmatism," and in particular: not only did they seek to have the places of confinement pay their own way, but they tried in addition to squeeze *profits* out of them for the local budget, to make them self-supporting plus. The Corrective Labor Code of 1924 also demanded that places of confinement be self-supporting. In 1928 at the First All-Union Conference of Penitentiary Executives there was stubborn insistence that there must be an obligatory "reimbursement to the state by the entire network of enterprises of places of confinement of expenditures by the state on these places of confinement."

They so wanted to have their little camps—and free too! From 1929 all the corrective-labor institutions of the country were included in the economic plan. And on January 1, 1931, it was decreed that all camps and colonies in the Russian Soviet Federated Socialist Republic and the Ukraine were to become completely self-supporting.

And what happened next? Instant success, of course! In 1932 the jurists proclaimed triumphantly: "The expenditures on corrective-labor institutions have been *reduced* [this can be believed] and the conditions in which those deprived of freedom are maintained *are improving with each year* [?]."[5]

We would be surprised, and we would try to find out why this happened and how? If we ourselves hadn't experienced on our own backs just exactly how that maintenance improved later on . . .

But if you come to think about it, it wasn't so very difficult at all! What was required? To make expenditures on camps equal the income from them? The expenditures, as we read, were being reduced. To increase income was even simpler: by squeezing the prisoners! If, in the Solovetsky Islands period of the Archipelago, an official 40 percent discount was applied to forced labor (the assumption being, for some reason, that labor performed under a club was not so productive), then as early as the Belomor Canal, when the "stomach scale" of compensation was introduced, the scholars of Gulag discovered that, on the contrary, forced and hungry labor was the most productive in the world! The Ukrainian Camp Administration, when ordered to become self-supporting in 1931, decided directly: to increase the productivity of labor in the coming year by neither more nor less than 242 percent (two hundred forty-two percent!) in comparison with the preceding years—in other words, by two and a half times, and without any mechanization![6] (And how scientifically this worked out! Two hundred forty and another two percent! The only thing the comrades did not know was: What this is called is *"The Great Leap Forward Beneath Three Red Banners."*)

And you see how Gulag knew in which direction the wind was blowing! Right then was when the immortally historic Six Conditions of Comrade Stalin poured forth—among them *self-support!* But we in Gulag already have it! We already have it! And once again: the use of specialists! But for us this was the easiest of all: to take the engineers off general work! Assign them to posts as work trusties! (The beginning of the thirties was the most privileged period for the technical intelligentsia in the Archipelago; almost none of them were forced to drag out an existence at general work, and even newcomers were immediately

5. Vyshinsky, *op. cit.,* p. 437.
6. Averbakh, *op. cit.,* p. 23.

established in their field of specialization. Up to that time, in the twenties, engineers and technicians perished for nothing on general work because they were not deployed or made use of. After this period, from 1937 right up to the fifties, self-support was forgotten, and all the historic Six Conditions along with it, and the main thing historically then became Vigilance—and the infiltration of the engineers, one by one, into trusty ranks alternated with waves of expelling them all to general work.) Anyway it was cheaper, too, to have a prisoner engineer rather than a free person; no wages had to be paid him! Once again profit, once again self-support! Once again Comrade Stalin was right!

So this line had been drawn out of the distant past, and they had carried it on correctly too: the Archipelago had to cost nothing!

But no matter how they huffed and puffed and broke all their nails on the crags, no matter how they corrected the plan fulfillment sheets twenty times over, and wore them down to holes in the paper, the Archipelago did not pay its own way, and it never will! The income from it would never equal the expenses, and our young workers' and peasants' state (subsequently the elderly state of all the people) is forced to haul this filthy bloody bag along on its back.

And here's why. The first and principal cause was the lack of conscientiousness of the prisoners, the negligence of those stupid slaves. Not only couldn't you expect any socialist self-sacrifice of them, but they didn't even manifest simple capitalist diligence. All they were on the lookout for was ways to spoil their footgear —and not go out to work; how to wreck a crane, to buckle a wheel, to break a spade, to sink a pail—anything for a pretext to sit down and smoke. All that the camp inmates made for their own dear state was openly and blatantly botched: you could break the bricks they made with your bare hands; the paint would peel off the panels; the plaster would fall off; posts would fall down; tables rock; legs fall out; handles come off. Carelessness and mistakes were everywhere. And it could happen that you had to tear off a roof already nailed on, redig the ditch they had filled in, demolish with crowbar and drill a wall they had already built. In the fifties they brought a new Swedish turbine to Steplag. It came in a frame made of logs like a hut. It was winter, and it was cold, and so the cursed zeks crawled into this frame between the beams and the turbine and started a bonfire to get warm. The silver soldering on the blades melted—and they threw the turbine out. It cost 3,700,000 rubles. Now that's being self-supporting for you!

And in the presence of the zeks—and this was a second reason—the free employees didn't care either, as though they were working not for themselves but for some stranger or other, and they stole a lot, they stole a great, great deal. (They were building an apartment building, and the free employees stole several bathtubs. But the tubs had been supplied to match the number of apartments. So how could they hand over the apartment building as completed? They could not confess to the construction superintendent, of course—he was triumphantly showing the official acceptance committee around the first stair landing, yes, and he did not omit to take them into every bathroom too and show them each tub. And then he took the committee to the second-floor landing, and the third, not hurrying there either, and kept going into all the bathrooms—and meanwhile the adroit and experienced zeks, under the leadership of an experienced foreman plumber, broke bathtubs out of the apartments on the first landing, hauled them upstairs on tiptoe to the fourth floor and hurriedly installed and puttied them in before the committee's arrival. And it was their lookout if they let the wool be pulled over their eyes. . . . This ought to be shown in a film comedy, but they wouldn't allow it: there is nothing funny in our life; everything funny takes place in the West!)

The third cause was the zeks' lack of independence, their inability to live without jailers, without a camp administration, without guards, without a camp perimeter complete with watchtowers, without a Planning and Production Section, a Records and Classification Section, a Security Operations Section, a Cultural and Educational Section, and without higher camp administrations right up to Gulag itself; without censorship, and without penalty isolators, without Strict Regimen Brigades, without trusties, without stockroom clerks and warehouses; their inability to move around without convoy and dogs. And so the state had to maintain at least one custodian for each working native (and every custodian had a family!). Well and good that it was so, but what were all these custodians to live on?

And there were some bright engineers who pointed out a

fourth reason as well: that, so they claimed, the necessity of setting up a perimeter fence at every step, of strengthening the convoy, of allotting a supplementary convoy, interfered with their, the engineers', technical maneuverability, as, for example, during the disembarkation on the River Taz; and because of this, so they claimed, everything was done late and cost more. But this was already an *objective* reason, this was a pretext! Summon them to the Party bureau, give them a good scolding, and the cause will disappear. Let them break their heads; they'll find a solution.

And then, beyond all these reasons, there were the natural and fully condonable miscalculations of the Leadership itself. As Comrade Lenin said: Only the person who does nothing makes no mistakes.

For example, no matter how earth-moving work was planned —rarely did it take place in the summer, but always for some reason in the autumn and winter, in mud and in freezing weather.

Or at the Zarosshy Spring in the Shturmovoi goldfields (the Kolyma) in March, 1938, they sent out five hundred people to drive prospecting shafts to a depth of twenty-five to thirty feet in the permafrost. They completed them. (Half the zeks kicked the bucket.) It was time to start blasting, but they changed their minds: the metal content was low. They abandoned it. In May the prospecting shafts thawed, all the work was lost. And two years later, again in March, in the Kolyma frosts, they had another brainstorm: to drive prospecting shafts! In the very same place! Urgently! Don't spare lives!

Well, that's what superfluous expenditures are. . . .

Or, on the Sukhona River near the settlement of Opoki—the prisoners hauled earth and built a dam. And the spring freshets carried it away immediately. And that was that—gone.

Or, for example, the Talaga logging operation of the Archangel administration was given a plan to produce furniture, but the authorities forgot to assign supplies of lumber with which to make the furniture. But a plan is a plan, and has to be fulfilled! Talaga had to send out special brigades to fish driftwood out of the river—logs which had fallen behind the timber rafting. There was not enough. Then, in hit-and-run raids, they began to break up whole rafts and carry them off. But, after all, those rafts belonged to someone else in the plan, and now they wouldn't have enough. And also it was quite impossible for Talaga to write up work sheets to pay those bold young fellows who had grabbed the timber; after all, it was thievery. So that's what self-support is. . . .

Or once in UstVymlag (in 1943) they wanted to overfulfill the plan for floating individual logs downstream, and brought pressure on the loggers, drove out all those able and unable, and accumulated too much timber in the timber-floating port—260,-000 cubic yards. They didn't manage to fish it out before the winter and it froze into the ice. And down below the harbor was a railroad bridge. If the timber did not break up into individual logs in the spring, and if it went off in a mass, it would wipe out the bridge, just like that, and the chief would be tried. And therefore they had to requisition whole carloads of dynamite, sink it to the bottom of the river, blow up the icebound log raft and then drag the logs ashore as quickly as possible—and burn them. (By spring they would not be usable as lumber.) The entire camp was occupied with this work, two hundred persons. For their work in the icy water they received a ration of fat bacon. But none of this could be covered by work vouchers, because it was all superfluous. And the burned-up timber—gone. Now that's what self-support is.

All PechZhelDorlag was engaged in constructing the railroad to Vorkuta—winding every which way. And only afterward did they begin to straighten out the already built road. Who paid for that? And the railroad from Lalsk on the River Luza to Pinyug (they even planned to extend it to Syktyvkar)? In 1938, what enormous camps were driven out there, and they built twenty-eight miles of that railroad—and abandoned it. . . . And so it all went to waste.

Well, of course, these small mistakes are inevitable in any work. No Leader is immune to them.

And all that railroad from Salekhard to Igarka started in 1949 —after all, it all turned out to be superfluous. There was nothing there to be hauled on it. And they abandoned it too. But then one quails to say *whose* mistake that was. It was, after all, His Own. . . .

And sometimes they carried this business of self-support to such a length that the camp chief didn't know where to hide from it, how to tie up the loose ends. There was a camp for invalid zeks at Kacha near Krasnoyarsk (fifteen hundred invalid zeks!), which after the war was told to go over to self-support: to manufacture furniture. And these invalids cut timber with bow saws. (It wasn't a logging camp—and no mechanical equipment was provided.) They hauled the timber to the camp on cows. (Transportation was not provided either, but there was a dairy farm.) The cost of manufacturing a divan turned out to be eight hundred rubles, and its sale price—six hundred! . . . And thus the camp management itself had a material interest in transferring as many invalids as possible into Group 1, or else in classifying them as ill and not sending them out of the compound, for then they would immediately shift from a debit balance on self-support to the reliable state budget.

Due to all these causes not only does the Archipelago not pay its own way, but the nation has to pay dearly for the additional satisfaction of having it.

The economic life of the Archipelago was also complicated by the fact that, even though this great statewide socialist self-support was needed by the entire state, and by Gulag too—yet the chief of camp couldn't care less—so they might scold a bit, pinch off his bonus money (but they would give it to him anyway). The main income, and the main scope, the main convenience and satisfaction for every chief of an individual camp . . . was to have his own independent economy in kind, to have his own cozy little estate, a patrimony. As in the Red Army, so, too, among the MVD officers, not at all as a joke, but very seriously, the circumstantial, respectful, proud, and pleasant word, the "*Master*," developed and established itself firmly. Just as one *Master* stood way up on top above the entire country, so the commander of every individual subdivision necessarily had to be a *Master* too.*

But, given that cruel comb of Groups A, B, C, and D which the merciless Frenkel had stuck forever into Gulag's mane, the Master had to twist and turn cunningly in order to drag through that comb a sufficient number of workers, without whom the economy of his patrimonial manor could in no wise be built. Wherever there was supposed to be one tailor on Gulag tables of organization, it was necessary to construct an entire tailor shop, wherever one shoemaker, a whole shoemaker's shop, and how many other very useful kinds of craftsmen one would wish to have right at hand! Why, for example, should one not have hothouses, and hothouse greens for the officers' table? Sometimes, even, a wise chief would set up a large auxiliary vegetable farm to feed vegetables over rations even to prisoners too. They would make up for it in work, it was simply quite advantageous for the Master himself, but where could he get the people?

But there was a way out—to overload all those same prisoner sloggers, and to deceive Gulag a little, and to cheat on the work a little too. For large-scale work inside camp, some construction project or other, all the prisoners could be compelled to work Sundays or evenings after their (ten-hour) workdays. For regular work, they inflated the statistics on brigades leaving the camp: workers remaining inside camp were listed as going out of it with their brigades to work. And the brigadiers had to bring back from there *their percentages*, in other words, part of the output stolen from the rest of the brigade members (who even so were not fulfilling the norms). The sloggers worked harder and ate less—but the manor economy grew and strengthened, and the comrade officers had a less monotonous and pleasanter life.

And in certain camps the chief had great breadth of economic vision, and he also found an engineer with imagination—and a powerful "Khozdvor," a complex of workshops, grew in the compound, even with official documentation after a while, even with unconcealed staffs, and accepting industrial assignments for fulfillment. But it could not push its way into the planned supply of materials and tools, and therefore, having nothing, it had to make everything it required itself.

Let us speak about one such Khozdvor—at the Kengir Camp. We won't mention the tailor, furrier, carpentry, and other auxiliary workshops—they are a mere bagatelle. The Kengir Khozdvor had its own foundry, its own metalworking shop, and even—in the middle of the twentieth century—manufactured hand-made drilling and grinding lathes! True, they were unable to manufacture their own turning lathe, but in this *camp lend-lease* was employed: a lathe was stolen in broad daylight from an industrial plant. Here's how it was arranged: They drove up a camp truck and waited till the chief of the plant section left—and then a whole brigade hurled itself on the lathe, dragged it onto the truck, which had no trouble driving right on past the gatehouse guard, because everything had been arranged with the guard—the guards' battalion was also MVD—and then they drove the lathe right into the camp, and once in there none of the "volnyashki" had access to it. And that was that! What could you get out of the stupid, irresponsible natives? The chief of the section raged and beat his breast—where had the lathe gone? But the zeks knew nothing: What lathe? We didn't see any. And the most important tools arrived in the camp in the same way—but more easily. In the pocket or under overcoat flaps.

The camp workshops once undertook to cast covers for sewer manholes for the ore enrichment factory of Kengir. They could do it, they found. But they ran out of pig iron—and where could the camp procure it in the last resort? So then the prisoners were given orders to steal some first-class English cast-iron brackets (relics of the prerevolutionary concession) *from that very same ore enrichment plant.* In camp these were melted down and carried off to the ore enrichment plant as manhole covers, for which the camp was paid.

And by this time the reader has come to understand how such an energetic "Khozdvor" as this strengthened self-support and also the entire economy of the nation.

And what was there that these camp workshops wouldn't undertake to manufacture—not even Krupp would have undertaken it all. They undertook to make large earthenware pipes for sewage disposal. A windmill. A chaff cutter. Locks. Water pumps. To repair meat grinders. To sew transmission belts. To mend sterilizers for the hospital. To sharpen drills for trepanning the skull. After all, necessity is the mother of invention! When you get good and hungry, you'll figure things out. After all, if you should say, "We aren't able to, we can't do it"—tomorrow they'll drive you out to general work; whereas in the camp workshops things are much more free and easy: no line-up, no marching under convoy, and you can work more slowly, and make something for yourself too. The hospital will pay for an order with two days' "sick leave," the kitchen with "something added," someone else with makhorka, and the management will throw in a little government bread.

And it's funny, and amusing. The engineers were constantly racking their brains: Out of what? How? A piece of suitable iron, found somewhere on the dump, often changed the entire planned design. They made a windmill, and they couldn't find a spring to keep it turned to the wind. They had to tie two strings to it and give orders to two zeks: When the wind changes, run and turn the mill with the two cords. And they made their own bricks too; with a metal wire, a woman cut a moving strip of clay the length of the future bricks, and they were carried farther on a conveyor which this woman had to keep moving. But with what? After all, her hands were occupied. Oh, immortal inventiveness of cunning zeks! They dreamed up a pair of shafts which hugged the woman's pelvis on either side, and while using her hands to cut the bricks, she simultaneously moved the conveyor belt with a strong and frequent motion of her pelvis back and forth! Alas, we are unable to show the reader a photograph of this.

And the Kengir estate owner finally became convinced for once and for all that there was nothing in the world that his "Khozdvor" could not make. And one day he called in the chief engineer and ordered him to begin the production of glass for windows and carafes immediately. How to make it? They looked in a volume of the encyclopedia lying there. General phrases, no formula. Nonetheless they ordered soda, found quartz sand somewhere, and brought it in. And for the main thing—they asked their friends to bring them broken glass from the "new city under construction." They broke a lot there. They put all this into the stove. They melted it, mixed it, drew it out, and they got sheets of window glass! But at one end it was one centimeter thick and at the other it got as thin as two millimeters. To recognize even a good friend through window glass like that was quite impossible. And the time limit was approaching . . . to show the output to the chief. How does a zek live? One day at a time: If only I can get through today, I will somehow manage tomorrow. And so they stole manufactured window panes from the site, with the glass already cut, brought them to the camp workshops, and showed them to the camp chief. He was satisfied: "Good boys! It's just like the real thing! So now start mass production!" "We can't make any more, Citizen Chief!" "But why not?" "You see, window glass must have molybdenum. We had only a tiny bit and it is all used up." "Can't you get it anywhere?" "Nowhere." "That's too bad. But can you make carafes without that molybdenum?" "We can probably make carafes." "Well, get going." But the carafes, too, all turned out lopsided, and for some reason they all broke apart. A jailer took one of these carafes to get milk, and he was left with just the neck in his hand,

and the milk spilled. "Oh, those bastards!" he cursed. "Wreckers! Fascists! You should all be shot!"

When they were clearing space for new buildings on Ogaryov Street in Moscow and they broke up the old ones, which had stood there for more than a century, not only did they not throw out the floor beams they found there, or even use them for firewood—but they used them for woodwork! They consisted of clean, *ringing* wood. That's what seasoning meant to our greatgrandfathers.

We hurry at everything. We never have time for anything. Does anyone think we should wait for beams to season? At Kaluga Gates we used to smear the beams with the latest antiseptics—and the beams rotted all the same, and fungi appeared on them, and so quickly, too, that even before the buildings were officially turned over it was necessary to tear up the floors and replace the rafters as we went.

Therefore, one hundred years from now everything that we zeks built, and in all probability the whole country as well, will not ring like those old beams from Ogaryov Street.

On that day when the U.S.S.R., with trumpets blaring, loosed into the heavens the first artificial earth satellite—opposite my window in Ryazan two pairs of *free* women, dressed in dirty zek pea jackets and padded britches, were carrying cement up to the *fourth floor in hand barrows.*

"True, true, that's so," they will object. "But what can you say? *Nonetheless it orbits!*"

And that you cannot take away from *it*, the devil take it! It orbits!

∎

It would be appropriate to finish this chapter with a long list of the projects completed by the prisoners for at least the period from the beginning of the First Stalinist Five-Year Plan up to the time of Khrushchev. But I, of course, am not in a position to compile that list, I can only begin it, so that those desiring to can make the necessary insertions and continue it.

The Belomor Canal (1932)
The Moscow-Volga Canal (1936)
The Volga-Don Canal (1952)

The Kotlas-Vorkuta Railroad, and the branch to Salekhard

The Rikasikha-Molotovsk Railroad[7]

The Salekhard-Igarka Railroad (abandoned)

The Lalsk-Pinyug Railroad (abandoned)

The Karaganda-Mointy-Balkhash Railroad (1936)

The Volga River Right-Bank Railroad

The lateral railroads paralleling the Finnish and Iranian borders

The Trans-Siberian second tracks (1933–1935, about 2,500 miles)

The Taishet-Lena Railroad (the beginning of BAM)

The Komsomolsk–Sovetskaya Gavan Railroad

The Sakhalin Railroad from Pobedino to join the Japanese network

The railroad to Ulan-Bator, and highways in Mongolia[8]

The Minsk-Moscow highway (1937–1938)

The Nogayevo-Atka-Nera highway

Construction of the Kuibyshev Hydroelectric Station

Construction of the Lower Tuloma Hydroelectric Station (near Murmansk)

Construction of the Ust-Kamenogorsk Hydroelectric Station

Construction of the Balkhash Copper Smelting Complex (1934–1935)

Construction of the Solikamsk Paper Combine

Construction of the Berezniki Chemical Complex

Construction of the Magnitogorsk Complex (in part)

Construction of the Kuznetsk Complex (in part)

Construction of factories and open hearths

Construction of the Lomonosov Moscow State University (1950–1953, in part)

Construction of the city of Komsomolsk-on-the-Amur

Construction of the city of Sovetskaya Gavan

Construction of the city of Magadan

Construction of the city of Norilsk

Construction of the city of Dudinka

7. Camps on the Kudma River, on Yagry Island, in the Rikasikha settlement.
8. During the construction of this railroad the unguarded prisoners were ordered to tell the Mongols that they were Komsomol members and volunteers. When the Mongols heard this, they replied: Take back your railroad, give us back our sheep.

Construction of the city of Vorkuta

Construction of the city of Molotovsk (Severodvinsk) (1935 on)

Construction of the city of Dubna

Construction of the port of Nakhodka

Construction of the pipeline from Sakhalin to the mainland

Construction of nearly all the centers of nuclear industry

Mining of radioactive elements (uranium and radium—near Chelyabinsk, Sverdlovsk, and Tura)

Work on isotope separation and enrichment plants (1945–1948)

Radium mining in Ukhta; petroleum refining in Ukhta; the manufacture of heavy water

Coal mining in the basins of the Pechora and the Kuznetsk, of the deposits at Karaganda and Suchan, etc.

Ore mining in Dzhezkazgan, Southern Siberia, Buryat-Mongolia, Shoriya, Khakassiya, and on the Kola Peninsula

Gold mining on the Kolyma, in Chukotka, in Yakutia, on Vaigach Island, in Maikain (Bayan–Aul district)

Apatite mining on the Kola Peninsula (1930 on)

Fluorspar mining in Amderma (1936 on)

Rare-metals mining (the "Stalinskoye" ore deposit in Akmolinsk Province) (up to the fifties)

Timber cutting for export and for internal needs. All the European Russian North and Siberia. We are not able to enumerate the countless logging camps. They constituted half the Archipelago. We will realize this with the very first listing of names: the camps on the River Koin; on the Uftyuga Dvinskaya River; on the River Nem, a tributary of the Vychegda (exiled Germans); on the Vychegda near Ryabova; on the Northern Dvina near Cherevkovo; on the Lesser Northern Dvina near Aristovo. . . .

But is it possible to draw up such a list? . . . On what maps or in whose memory have all these thousands of temporary logging camps been preserved, camps established for one year, for two, for three, until all the woods nearby had been cut, and then removed lock, stock, and barrel? And then why only the logging camps? What about a complete list of all the little islands of the Archipelago which ever surfaced—the famous camps lasting for decades, and the migratory camps following the line of a construction route, and powerful central prisons for long-termers, and transit camps made of tents and poles? And would anyone undertake to place on such a map all the preliminary detention cells and prisons in each city (several in each)? And then, too, the agricultural colonies with their haying and their herding outposts? And, in addition, the tiny industrial and construction colonies scattered like seeds through the cities? Moscow and Leningrad would each have to have enclaves marked throughout them on a large-scale map. (Do not forget the camp located a quarter-mile from the Kremlin—the beginning of the construction of the Palace of the Soviets.) Yes, and in the twenties the Archipelago was one thing, whereas in the fifties it was quite a different thing and in quite different places. How would one indicate its march through time? How many maps would be required? And Nyroblag, or UstVymlag, or the Solikamsk or the Potma camps would have to be a whole province of crosshatching —but who among us ever walked those boundaries?

But we hope to see such a map yet.

Loading of timber onto ships in Karelia (till 1930; after the appeal of the English press not to accept timber loaded by prisoners, the zeks were hastily taken off this work and removed to the inner depths of Karelia)

Supplying the front during wartime with mines, ammunition, packing for them, and with uniforms

The construction of state farms in Siberia and Kazakhstan

And even leaving out the whole of the twenties, and the output of prisons, reformatories, and corrective-labor prisons, what was it that *the hundreds of industrial colonies* spent their time on, what did they manufacture in the quarter-century from 1929 to 1953? There was no decent city in the whole country that did not have them.

And what did the hundreds and hundreds of agricultural colonies grow and harvest?

It is indeed much easier to enumerate the occupations the prisoners never did have: the manufacture of sausages and confectionary goods.

END OF PART III

PART IV

The Soul and Barbed Wire

■

"Behold, I shew you a mystery; we shall not
all sleep, but we shall all be changed."

I Corinthians, 15:51*

Chapter 1

■

The Ascent

And the years go by. . . .

Not in swift staccato, as they joke in camp—"winter-summer, winter-summer"—but a long-drawn-out autumn, an endless winter, an unwilling spring, and only a summer that is short. In the Archipelago . . . summer is short.

Even one mere year, whew, how long it lasts! Even in one year how much time is left for you to think! For 330 days you stomp out to line-up in a drizzling, slushy rain, and in a piercing blizzard, and in a biting and still subzero cold. For 330 days you work away at hateful, alien work with your mind unoccupied. For 330 evenings you squinch up, wet, chilled, in the end-of-work line-up, waiting for the convoy to assemble from the distant watchtowers. And then there is the march out. And the march back. And bending down over 730 bowls of gruel, over 730 portions of grits. Yes, and waking up and going to sleep on your multiple bunk. And neither radio nor books to distract you. There are none, and thank God.

And that is only one year. And there are ten. There are twenty-five. . . .

And then, too, when you are lying in the hospital with dystrophy—that, too, is a good time—*to think*.

Think! Draw some conclusions from misfortune.

And all that endless time, after all, the prisoners' brains and souls are not inactive?! In the mass and from a distance they seem like swarming lice, but they are the crown of creation, right? After all, once upon a time a weak little spark of God was breathed into them too—is it not true? So what has become of it now?

For centuries it was considered that a criminal was given a *sentence* for precisely this purpose, to think about his crime for the whole period of his sentence, be conscience-stricken, repent, and gradually reform.

But the Gulag Archipelago knows no pangs of conscience! Out of one hundred natives—five are thieves, and their transgressions are no reproach in their own eyes, but a mark of valor. They dream of carrying out such feats in the future even more brazenly and cleverly. They have nothing to repent. Another five . . . *stole* on a big scale, but not from people; in our times, the only place where one can steal on a big scale is from the state, which itself squanders the people's money without pity or sense—so what was there for such types to repent of? Maybe that they had not stolen more and divvied up—and thus remained free? And, so far as another 85 percent of the natives were concerned—they had never committed any crimes whatever. What were they supposed to repent of? That they had thought what they thought? (Nonetheless, they managed to pound and muddle some of them to such an extent that they did repent—of being so depraved. . . . Let us remember the desperation of Nina Peregud because she was unworthy of Zoya Kosmodemyanskaya.) Or that a man had surrendered and become a POW in a hopeless situation? Or that he had taken employment under the Germans instead of dying of starvation? (Nonetheless, they managed so to confuse what was permitted and what was forbidden that there were some such who were tormented greatly: I would have done better to die than to have earned that bread.) Or that while working for nothing in the collective-farm fields, he had taken a mite to feed his children? Or that he had taken something from a factory for the same reason?

No, not only do you not repent, but your clean conscience, like a clear mountain lake, shines in your eyes. (And your eyes, purified by suffering, infallibly perceive the least haze in other eyes; for example, they infallibly pick out stool pigeons. And the Cheka-GB is not aware of this capacity of ours to see with the eyes of truth—it is our "secret weapon" against that institution. And State Security slips up here with us.)

It was in this nearly unanimous consciousness of our innocence that the main distinction arose between us and the hard-labor prisoners of Dostoyevsky, the hard-labor prisoners of P. Yakubovich. There they were conscious of being doomed renegades, whereas we were confidently aware that they could haul in any free person at all in just the same way they had hauled us in; that barbed wire was only a nominal dividing line between us. In earlier times there had been among the majority . . . the unconditional consciousness of personal guilt, and among us . . . the consciousness of disaster on a mammoth scale.

Just not to perish from the disaster! It had to be survived.

Wasn't this the root cause of the astounding rarity of camp suicides? Yes, rarity, although every ex-prisoner could in all probability recall a case of suicide. But he could recall even more escapes. There were certainly more escapes than suicides! (Admirers of socialist realism can praise me: I am pursuing an optimistic line.) And there were far more self-inflicted injuries, too, than there were suicides! But this, too, is an act indicating love of life—a straightforward calculation of sacrificing a portion to save the whole. I even imagine that, statistically speaking, there were fewer suicides per thousand of the population in camp than in freedom. I have no way of verifying this, of course.

But Skripnikova recalls how a man thirty years old hanged himself in 1931 in the women's toilet in Medvezhyegorsk—and hanged himself on the very day he was to be released! So maybe it was out of a feeling of disgust for the *freedom* of that time? (Two years earlier his wife had abandoned him, but he had not hanged himself then.) Well, the designer Voronov hanged himself in the club of the main camp center of Burepolom. The Communist Party official Aramovich, a second-termer, hanged himself in 1947 in the garret of the machinery-repair factory in Knyazh-Pogost. In Kraslag during the war years Lithuanians who had been reduced to a state of total despair—mainly because nothing in their former lives had prepared them for our cruelties—marched on infantrymen so as to get themselves shot down. In 1949, in the interrogation cell in Vladimir-Volynsk, a young fellow stunned by his interrogation tried to hang himself, but Boronyuk pulled him down in time. At the Kaluga Gates a former Latvian officer who was hospitalized in the camp infirmary began to creep stealthily up some stairs—they led to the incomplete, empty upper stories. The "zechka" nurse saw him and went in pursuit. She caught up with him on the open balcony of the sixth floor. She caught him by the bathrobe, but the suicide slipped off the robe and stepped off into nothingness dressed in his underwear—and flashed past like a white streak of lightning in plain sight of busy Bolshaya Kaluzhskaya Street on a sunny summer day. When Emmi, a German Communist, learned about her husband's death, she left the barracks in sub-zero weather undressed so as to catch cold. The Englishman Kelly, in the Vladimir Special Purpose Prison, very skillfully cut his veins with the door wide open and the jailer right there on the threshold.[1]

I repeat: there are many others who can recount similar cases —but nonetheless, out of tens of millions who have served time, their total number will be small. Even among these examples, it is clear that a much greater proportion of suicides is accounted for by foreigners, Westerners; for them the transition to the Archipelago . . . was a more shattering blow than for us, so they put an end to it. And suicides were frequent among the loyalists too (but not among the hard-heads). And one can understand why—after all, their heads must have got thoroughly mixed up and filled with incessant buzzing. How could they stand it? (Zosia Zaleska, a Polish noblewoman who had devoted her entire life to the "cause of Communism" by serving in the Soviet intelligence service, tried to commit suicide three times during her interrogation: she tried to hang herself—they pulled her down; she cut her veins—but they stopped her; she jumped onto the window sill on the seventh floor—but the drowsy inter-rogator managed to grab hold of her by her dress. They saved her life three times—so they could shoot her.)

And, anyway, what is the correct interpretation of suicide? Ans Bernshtein, for example, insists that suicides are not at all cowards, that great will power is required for suicide. He him-self wove a rope out of bandages and throttled himself by lifting his feet off the floor. But green circles appeared before his eyes and there was a ringing in his ears—and each time he involun-

---

1. He did it with a piece of enamel from the washbasin. Kelly hid it in his shoe and his shoe stood by his bed. Kelly dropped his blanket over the shoe to cover it, got out the piece of enamel, and cut his wrist vein beneath the blanket.

tarily put his feet back on the ground. During his last try the homemade rope broke—and he felt glad that he was still alive.

I am not going to dispute that perhaps even in the most extreme despair you still need will power to commit suicide. For a long time I would not have taken it upon myself to pass judgment on this at all. All my life long I was absolutely convinced that I would never consider suicide in any circumstances whatever. But not so long ago I dragged my way through gloomy months when it seemed to me that my whole life's cause had perished, especially if I remained alive. And I remember very clearly indeed the revulsion against life that came over me and the sensation that to die . . . was easier than to live. In my opinion, in a state like that it requires more strength of will to stay alive than to die. But, in all probability, with other people, in a different extremity, this turns out differently. And that is why from time immemorial the two opinions have existed.

It is a very spectacular idea to imagine all the innocently outraged millions beginning to commit suicide en masse, causing double vexation to the government—both by demonstrating their innocence and by depriving the government of free manpower. And maybe the government would have had to soften up and begin to take pity on its subjects?—well, hardly! Stalin wouldn't have been stopped by that. He would have merely picked up another twenty million people from freedom.

But it did not happen! People died by the hundreds of thousands and millions, driven, it would seem, to the extremity of extremities—but for some reason there were no suicides! Condemned to a misshapen existence, to waste away from starvation, to exhaustion from labor—they did not put an end to themselves!

And thinking the whole thing over, I found that proof to be the stronger. A suicide is always a bankrupt, always a human being in a blind alley, a human being who has gambled his life and lost and is without the will to continue the struggle. If these millions of helpless and pitiful vermin still did not put an end to themselves—this meant some kind of invincible feeling was alive inside them. Some very powerful idea.

This was their feeling of universal innocence. It was the sense of an ordeal of the entire people—like the Tatar yoke.

■

But what if one has nothing to repent of—what then, what then does the prisoner think about all the time? "Poverty and prison . . . give wisdom." They do. But—where is it to be directed?

Here is how it was with many others, not just with me. Our initial, first prison sky consisted of black swirling storm clouds and black pillars of volcanic eruptions—this was the heaven of Pompeii, the heaven of the Day of Judgment, because it was not just anyone who had been arrested, but I—the center of this world.

Our last prison sky was infinitely high, infinitely clear, even paler than sky-blue.

We all (except religious believers) began from one point: we tried to tear our hair from our head, but our hair had been clipped close! . . . How could we? How could we not have seen those who informed against us?! How could we not have seen our enemies? (And how we hated them! How could we avenge ourselves on them?) And what recklessness! What blindness! How many errors! How can they be corrected? They must be corrected all the more swiftly! We must write. . . . We must speak out. . . . We must communicate. . . .

But—there is nothing that we can do. And nothing is going to save us! At the appropriate time we will sign Form 206. At the appropriate time the tribunal will read us our sentence in our presence, or we will learn it in absentia from the OSO.

Then there begins the period of transit prisons. Interspersed with our thoughts about our future camp, we now love to recall our past: How well we used to live! (Even if we lived badly.) But how many unused opportunities there were! How many flowers we left uncrumpled! . . . When will we now make up for it? If I only manage to survive—oh, how differently, how wisely, I am going to live! The day of our future *release?* It shines like a rising sun!

And the conclusion is: Survive to reach it! Survive! At any price!

This is simply a turn of phrase, a sort of habit of speech: "at any price."

But then the words swell up with their full meaning, and an awesome vow takes shape: to survive *at any price.*

And whoever takes that vow, whoever does not blink before its crimson burst—allows his own misfortune to overshadow both the entire common misfortune and the whole world.

This is the great fork of camp life. From this point the roads go to the right and to the left. One of them will rise and the other will descend. If you go to the right—you lose your life, and if you go to the left—you lose your conscience.

One's own order to oneself, *"Survive!,"* is the natural splash of a living person. Who does not wish to survive? Who does not have the right to survive? Straining all the strength of our body! An order to all our cells: Survive! A powerful charge is introduced into the chest cavity, and the heart is surrounded by an electrical cloud so as not to stop beating. They lead thirty emaciated but wiry zeks three miles across the Arctic ice to a bathhouse. The bath is not worth even a warm word. Six men at a time wash themselves in five shifts, and the door opens straight into the subzero temperature, and four shifts are obliged to stand there before or after bathing—because they cannot be left without convoy. And not only does none of them get pneumonia. They don't even catch cold. (And for ten years one old man had his bath just like that, serving out his term from age fifty to sixty. But then he was released, he was at home. Warm and cared for, he burned up in one month's time. That order— "Survive!"—was not there. . . .)

But simply "to survive" does not yet mean "at any price." "At any price" means: at the price of someone else.

Let us admit the truth: At that great fork in the camp road, at that great divider of souls, it was not the majority of the prisoners that turned to the right. Alas, not the majority. But fortunately neither was it just a few. There are many of them— human beings—who made this choice. But they did not shout about themselves. You had to look closely to see them. Dozens of times this same choice had arisen before them too, but they always knew, and knew their own stand.

Take Arnold Susi, who was sent to camp at the age of about fifty. He had never been a believer, but he had always been fundamentally decent, he had never led any other kind of life— and he was not about to begin any other. He was a "Westerner." And what that meant was that he was doubly unprepared, and kept putting his foot into it all the time, and getting into serious difficulties. He worked at general work. And he was imprisoned in a penalty camp—and he still managed to survive; he survived as exactly the same kind of person he had been when he came to camp. I knew him at the very beginning, and I knew him . . . afterward, and I can testify personally. True, there were three seriously mitigating circumstances which accompanied him throughout his camp life: He was classified as an invalid. For several years he received parcels. And thanks to his musical abilities, he got some additional nourishment out of amateur theatricals. But these three circumstances only explain why he survived. If they had not existed, he would have died. But he would not have changed. (And perhaps those who died did die because they did not change?)

And Tarashkevich, a perfectly ordinary, straightforward person, recalls: "There were many prisoners prepared to grovel for a bread ration or a puff of makhorka smoke. I was dying, but I kept my soul pure: I always called a spade a spade."

It has been known for many centuries that prison causes the profound rebirth of a human being. The examples are innumerable—such as that of Silvio Pellico: Through serving eight years he was transformed from a furious Carbonaro to a meek Roman Catholic.[2] In our country they always mention Dostoyevsky in this respect. And what about Pisarev? What remained of his revolutionary rebelliousness after imprisonment in the Peter and Paul Fortress? One can certainly debate whether this is good for revolution, but these transformations always proceed in the direction of deepening the soul. Ibsen wrote: "From lack of oxygen even the conscience will wither."[3]

By no means! It is not by any means so simple! In fact, it is the opposite! Take General Gorbatov: He had fought from his very youth, advanced through the ranks of the army, and had no time at all in which to think about things. But he was imprisoned, and how good it was—various events awakened within his recollection, such as his having suspected an innocent man of espionage; or his having ordered by mistake the execution of a quite innocent Pole.[4] (Well, when else would he have remembered this? After rehabilitation he did not remember such things very much?) Enough has been written about prisoners' changes

2. S. Pellico, *Moi Temnitsy* (*My Prisons*), St. Petersburg, 1836.
3. Henrik Ibsen, *An Enemy of the People*.
4. *Novy Mir*, 1964, No. 4.

of heart to raise it to the level of penological theory. For example, in the prerevolutionary *Prison Herald* Luchenetsky wrote: "Darkness renders a person more sensitive to light; involuntary inactivity in imprisonment arouses in him a thirst for life, movement, work; the quiet compels profound pondering over his own 'I,' over surrounding conditions, over his own past and present, and forces him to think about his future."

Our teachers, who had never served time themselves, felt for prisoners only the natural sympathy of the outsider; Dostoyevsky, however, who served time himself, was a proponent of punishment! And this is something worth thinking about.

The proverb says: "Freedom spoils, and lack of freedom teaches."

But Pellico and Luchenetsky wrote about *prison*. But Dostoyevsky demanded punishment—in prison. But *what kind of* lack of freedom is it that educates?

Camp?

That is something to think about.

Of course, in comparison with prison our camps are poisonous and harmful.

Of course, they were not concerned with our souls when they pumped up the Archipelago. But nonetheless: is it really hopeless to stand fast in camp?

And more than that: was it really impossible for one's soul to rise in camp?

Here is E.K., who was born around 1940, one of those boys who, under Khrushchev, gathered to read poems on Mayakovsky Square, but were hauled off instead in Black Marias. From camp, from a Potma camp, he writes to his girl: "Here all the trivia and fuss have decreased. . . . I have experienced a turning point. . . . Here you harken to that voice deep inside you, which amid the surfeit and vanity used to be stifled by the roar from outside."

At the Samarka Camp in 1946 a group of intellectuals had reached the very brink of death: They were worn down by hunger, cold, and work beyond their powers. And they were even deprived of sleep. They had nowhere to lie down. Dugout barracks had not yet been built. Did they go and steal? Or squeal? Or whimper about their ruined lives? No! Foreseeing the approach of death in days rather than weeks, here is how they spent their last sleepless leisure, sitting up against the wall:

Timofeyev-Ressovsky gathered them into a "seminar," and they hastened to share with one another what one of them knew and the others did not—they delivered their last lectures to each other. Father Savely—spoke of "unshameful death," a priest academician—about patristics, one of the Uniate fathers—about something in the area of dogmatics and canonical writings, an electrical engineer—on the principles of the energetics of the future, and a Leningrad economist—on how the effort to create principles of Soviet economics had failed for lack of new ideas. Timofeyev-Ressovsky himself talked about the principles of microphysics. From one session to the next, participants were missing—they were already in the morgue.

That is the sort of person who can be interested in all this while already growing numb with approaching death—now that is an intellectual!

Pardon me, you . . . love life? You, you! You who exclaim and sing over and over and dance it too: "I love you, life! Oh, I love you, life!" Do you? Well, go on, love it! Camp life—love that too! It, too, is life!

> There where there is no struggle with fate,
> There you will resurrect your soul. . . .

You haven't understood a thing. When you get there, you'll collapse.

Along our chosen road are twists and turns and twists and turns. Uphill? Or up into the heavens? Let's go, let's stumble and stagger.

The day of liberation! What can it give us after so many years? We will change unrecognizably and so will our near and dear ones—and places which once were dear to us will seem stranger than strange.

And the thought of freedom after a time even becomes a forced thought. Farfetched. Strange.

The day of "liberation"! As if there were any liberty in this country! Or as if it were possible to liberate anyone who has not first become liberated in his own soul.

The stones roll down from under our feet. Downward, into the past! They are the ashes of the past!

And we ascend!

■

It is a good thing *to think* in prison, but it is not bad in camp either. Because, and this is the main thing, there are no *meetings*. For ten years you are free from all kinds of meetings! Is that not mountain air? While they openly claim your labor and your body, to the point of exhaustion and even death, the camp keepers do not encroach at all on your thoughts. They do not try to screw down your brains and to fasten them in place.[5] And this results in a sensation of freedom of much greater magnitude than the freedom of one's feet to run along on the level.

No one tries to persuade you *to apply* for Party membership. No one comes around to squeeze membership dues out of you in *voluntary* societies. There is no trade union—the same kind of protector of your interests as an official lawyer before a tribunal. And there are no "production meetings." You cannot be elected to any position. You cannot be appointed some kind of delegate. And the really important thing is . . . that they cannot compel you to be a propagandist. Nor—to listen to propaganda. Nor—when someone jerks the string, to shout: "We demand! . . . We will not permit! . . ." Nor—will they ever drag you off to the electoral precinct to vote freely and secretly for a single candidate. No one requires any "socialist undertakings" of you. Nor—self-criticism of your mistakes. Nor —articles in the wall newspaper. Nor—an interview with a provincial correspondent.

A free head—now is that not an advantage of life in the Archipelago?

And there is one more freedom: No one can deprive you of your family and property—you have already been deprived of them. What does not exist—not even God can take away. And this is a basic freedom.

It is good to think in imprisonment. And the most insignificant cause gives you a push in the direction of extended and important thoughts. Once in a long, long while, once in three years maybe, they brought a movie to camp. The film turned out to be—the cheapest kind of "sports" comedy—*The*

5. Except for the unfortunate period of the White Sea–Baltic Canal and the Moscow-Volga Canal.

*First Glove.** It was a bore. But from the screen they kept drumming into the audience the moral of the film:

The result is what counts, and the result is not in your favor.

On the screen they kept laughing. In the hall the audience kept laughing too. But blinking as you came out into the sunlit camp yard, you kept thinking about this phrase. And during the evening you kept thinking about it on your bunk. And Monday morning out in line-up. And you could keep thinking about it as long as you wanted. And where else could you have concentrated on it like that? And slow clarity descended into your brain.

This was no joke. This was an infectious thought. It has long since been inculcated in our Fatherland—and they keep on inculcating it over and over. The concept that only the material result counts has become so much a part of us that when, for example, some Tukhachevsky, Yagoda, or Zinoviev was proclaimed . . . a traitor who had sidled up to the enemy, people only exclaimed in a chorus of astonishment: *"What more could he want?"*

Now that is a high moral plane for you! Now that is a real unit of measure for you! "What more could he want?" Since he had a belly full of chow, and twenty suits, and two country homes, and an automobile, and an airplane, and fame—what more could he want?!! Millions of our compatriots find it unthinkable to imagine that a human being (and I am not speaking here of this particular trio) might have been motivated by something other than material gain!

To such an extent has everyone been indoctrinated with and absorbed the slogan: "The result is what counts."

Whence did this come to us?

In the first place—from the glory of our banners and the so-called "honor of our Motherland." We choked, cut down, and cut up all our neighbors in our expansion—and in our Fatherland it became well established that: The result is what counts.

And then from our Demidovs, Kabans and Tsybukins. They clambered up, without looking behind them to see whose ears they were smashing with their jackboots. And ever more firmly it became established among a once pious and openhearted people: The result is what counts.

And then—from all kinds of socialists, and most of all from the most modern, infallible, and intolerant Teaching, which consists of this one thing only: The result is what counts! It is important to forge a fighting Party! And to seize power! And to hold on to power! And to remove all enemies! And to conquer in pig iron and steel! And to launch rockets!

And though for this industry and for these rockets it was necessary to sacrifice the way of life, and the integrity of the family, and the spiritual health of the people, and the very soul of our fields and forests and rivers—to hell with them! The result is what counts!!!

But that is a lie! Here we have been breaking our backs for years at All-Union hard labor. Here in slow annual spirals we have been climbing up to an understanding of life—and from this height it can all be seen so clearly: It is not the result that counts! It is not the result—but *the spirit!* Not *what*—but *how*. Not what has been attained—but at what price.

And so it is with us the prisoners—if it is the result which counts, then it is also true that one must survive at any price. And what that means is: One must become a stool pigeon, betray one's comrades. And thereby get oneself set up comfortably. And perhaps even get time off sentence. In the light of the Infallible Teaching there is, evidently, nothing reprehensible in this. After all, if one does that, then the result will be in our favor, and the result is what counts.

No one is going to argue. It is pleasant to win. But not at the price of losing one's human countenance.

If it is the result which counts—you must strain every nerve and sinew to avoid *general work*. You must bend down, be servile, act meanly—yet hang on to your position as a trusty. And by this means . . . survive.

If it is the essence that counts, then the time has come to reconcile yourself to *general work*. To tatters. To torn skin on the hands. To a piece of bread which is smaller and worse. And perhaps . . . to death. But while you're alive, you drag your way along proudly with an aching back. And that is when—when you have ceased to be afraid of threats and are not chasing after rewards—you become the most dangerous character in the owl-like view of the bosses. Because . . . what hold do they have on you?

You even begin to like carrying hand barrows with rubbish (yes, but not with stone!) and discussing with your work mate how the movies influence literature. You begin to like sitting down on the empty cement mixing trough and lighting up a smoke next to your bricklaying. And you are actually and simply proud if, when the foreman passes you, he squints at your courses, checks their alignment with the rest of the wall, and says: "Did you lay that? Good line."

You need that wall like you need a hole in the head, nor do you believe it is going to bring closer the happy future of the people, but, pitiful tattered slave that you are, you smile at this creation of your own hands.

The Anarchist's daughter, Galya Venediktova, worked as a nurse in the Medical Section, but when she saw that what went on there was *not healing* but only the business of getting fixed up in a good spot—out of stubbornness she left and went off to general work, taking up a spade and a sledge hammer. And she says that this saved her spiritually.

For a good person even a crust is healthy food, and to an evil person even meat brings no benefit.

(Now that is no doubt how it really is—but what if there is not even a crust? . . .)

■

And as soon as you have renounced that aim of "surviving at any price," and gone where the calm and simple people go— then imprisonment begins to transform your former character in an astonishing way. To transform it in a direction most unexpected to you.

And it would seem that in this situation feelings of malice, the disturbance of being oppressed, aimless hate, irritability, and nervousness ought to multiply.[6] But you yourself do not notice how, with the impalpable flow of time, slavery nurtures in you the shoots of contradictory feelings.

6. The revolutionaries of the past left many traces of this. Serafimovich, in one of his stories, describes the society of the exiles in this way. The Bolshevik Olminsky writes: "Bitterness and spite—these feelings are so familiar to the prisoner, so close to his soul." He used to pour out his anger on those who came to visit him. He writes that he lost all taste for work too. But then the Russian revolutionaries (in the overwhelming mass) did not get and did not serve out any *real* (long) sentences.

Once upon a time you were sharply intolerant. You were constantly in a rush. And you were constantly short of time. And now you have time with interest. You are surfeited with it, with its months and its years, behind you and ahead of you—and a beneficial calming fluid pours through your blood vessels—patience.

You are ascending. . . .

Formerly you never forgave anyone. You judged people without mercy. And you praised people with equal lack of moderation. And now an understanding mildness has become the basis of your uncategorical judgments. You have come to realize your own weakness—and you can therefore understand the weakness of others. And be astonished at another's strength. And wish to possess it yourself.

The stones rustle beneath our feet. We are ascending. . . .

With the years, armor-plated restraint covers your heart and all your skin. You do not hasten to question and you do not hasten to answer. Your tongue has lost its flexible capacity for easy oscillation. Your eyes do not flash with gladness over good tidings nor do they darken with grief.

For you still have to verify whether that's how it is going to be. And you also have to work out—what is gladness and what is grief.

And now the rule of your life is this: Do not rejoice when you have found, do not weep when you have lost.

Your soul, which formerly was dry, now ripens from suffering. And even if you haven't come to love your neighbors in the Christian sense, you are at least learning to love those close to you.

Those close to you in spirit who surround you in slavery. And how many of us come to realize: It is particularly in slavery that for the first time we have learned to recognize genuine friendship!

And also those close to you in blood, who surrounded you in your former life, who loved you—while you played the tyrant over them . . .

Here is a rewarding and inexhaustible direction for your thoughts: Reconsider all your previous life. Remember everything you did that was bad and shameful and take thought—can't you possibly correct it now?

Yes, you have been imprisoned for nothing. You have nothing to repent of before the state and its laws.

But . . . before your own conscience? But . . . in relation to other individuals?

. . . Following an operation, I am lying in the surgical ward of a camp hospital. I cannot move. I am hot and feverish, but nonetheless my thoughts do not dissolve into delirium—and I am grateful to Dr. Boris Nikolayevich Kornfeld, who is sitting beside my cot and talking to me all evening. The light has been turned out—so it will not hurt my eyes. He and I—and there is no one else in the ward.

Fervently he tells me the long story of his conversion from Judaism to Christianity. This conversion was accomplished by an educated, cultivated person, one of his cellmates, some good-natured old fellow like Platon Karatayev. I am astonished at the conviction of the new convert, at the ardor of his words.

We know each other very slightly, and he was not the one responsible for my treatment, but there was simply no one here with whom he could share his feelings. He was a gentle and well-mannered person. I could see nothing bad in him nor did I know anything bad about him. However, I was on guard because Kornfeld had now been living for two months in the hospital barracks without going outside, because he had shut himself up in here, at his place of work, and avoided moving around camp at all.

This meant . . . he was afraid of having his throat cut. In our camp it had recently become fashionable—to cut the throats of stool pigeons. This has an effect. But who could guarantee that only stoolies were getting their throats cut? One prisoner had had his throat cut in a clear case of settling a sordid grudge. And therefore . . . the self-imprisonment of Kornfeld in the hospital did not yet prove at all that he was a stool pigeon.

It is already late. All the hospital is asleep. Kornfeld is ending up his story thus:

"And on the whole, do you know, I have become convinced that there is no punishment that comes to us in this life on earth which is undeserved. Superficially it can have nothing to do with what we are guilty of in actual fact, but if you go over your life with a fine-tooth comb and ponder it deeply, you will always be able to hunt down that transgression of yours for which you have now received this blow."

I cannot see his face. Through the window come only the scattered reflections of the lights of the perimeter outside. And the door from the corridor gleams in a yellow electrical glow. But there is such mystical knowledge in his voice that I shudder.

These were the last words of Boris Kornfeld. Noiselessly he went out into the nighttime corridor and into one of the nearby wards and there lay down to sleep. Everyone slept. And there was no one with whom he could speak even one word. And I went off to sleep myself.

And I was wakened in the morning by running about and tramping in the corridor; the orderlies were carrying Kornfeld's body to the operating room. He had been dealt eight blows on the skull with a plasterer's mallet while he still slept. (In our camp it was the custom to kill immediately after rising time, when the barracks were all unlocked and open and when no one yet had got up, when no one was stirring.) And he died on the operating table, without regaining consciousness.

And so it happened that Kornfeld's prophetic words were his last words on earth. And, directed to me, they lay upon me as an inheritance. You cannot brush off that kind of inheritance by shrugging your shoulders.

But by that time I myself had matured to similar thoughts.

I would have been inclined to endow his words with the significance of a universal law of life. However, one can get all tangled up that way. One would have to admit that on that basis those who had been punished even more cruelly than with prison —those shot, burned at the stake—were some sort of super-evildoers. (And yet . . . the innocent are those who get punished most zealously of all.) And what would one then have to say about our so evident torturers: Why does not fate punish *them?* Why do they prosper?

(And the only solution to this would be that the meaning of earthly existence lies not, as we have grown used to thinking, in prospering, but . . . in the development of the soul. From *that* point of view our torturers have been punished most horribly of all: they are turning into swine, they are departing downward from humanity. From that point of view punishment is inflicted on those whose development . . . *holds out hope.*)

But there was something in Kornfeld's last words that touched a sensitive chord, and that I accept quite completely *for myself.* And many will accept the same for themselves.

In the seventh year of my imprisonment I had gone over and re-examined my life quite enough and had come to understand why everything had happened to me: both prison and, as an additional piece of ballast, my malignant tumor. And I would not have murmured even if all that punishment had been considered inadequate.

Punishment? But . . . whose?

Well, just think about that—*whose?*

I lay there a long time in that recovery room from which Kornfeld had gone forth to his death, and all alone during sleepless nights I pondered with astonishment my own life and the turns it had taken. In accordance with my established camp custom I set down my thoughts in rhymed verses—so as to remember them. And the most accurate thing is to cite them here—just as they came from the pillow of a hospital patient, when the hard-labor camp was still shuddering outside the windows in the wake of a revolt.

> When was it that I completely
> Scattered the good seeds, one and all?
> For after all I spent my boyhood
> In the bright singing of Thy temples.
>
> Bookish subtleties sparkled brightly,
> Piercing my arrogant brain,
> The secrets of the world were . . . in my grasp,
> Life's destiny . . . as pliable as wax.
>
> Blood seethed—and every swirl
> Gleamed iridescently before me,
> Without a rumble the building of my faith
> Quietly crumbled within my heart.
>
> But passing here between being and nothingness,
> Stumbling and clutching at the edge,
> I look behind me with a grateful tremor
> Upon the life that I have lived.
>
> Not with good judgment nor with desire
> Are its twists and turns illumined.
> But with the even glow of the Higher Meaning
> Which became apparent to me only later on.

And now with measuring cup returned to me,
Scooping up the living water,
God of the Universe! I believe again!
Though I renounced You, You were with me!

Looking back, I saw that for my whole conscious life I had not understood either myself or my strivings. What had seemed for so long to be beneficial now turned out in actuality to be fatal, and I had been striving to go in the opposite direction to that which was truly necessary to me. But just as the waves of the sea knock the inexperienced swimmer off his feet and keep tossing him back onto the shore, so also was I painfully tossed back on dry land by the blows of misfortune. And it was only because of this that I was able to travel the path which I had always really wanted to travel.

It was granted me to carry away from my prison years on my bent back, which nearly broke beneath its load, this essential experience: *how* a human being becomes evil and *how* good. In the intoxication of youthful successes I had felt myself to be infallible, and I was therefore cruel. In the surfeit of power I was a murderer, and an oppressor. In my most evil moments I was convinced that I was doing good, and I was well supplied with systematic arguments. And it was only when I lay there on rotting prison straw that I sensed within myself the first stirrings of good. Gradually it was disclosed to me that the line separating good and evil passes not through states, nor between classes, nor between political parties either—but right through every human heart—and through all human hearts. This line shifts. Inside us, it oscillates with the years. And even within hearts overwhelmed by evil, one small bridgehead of good is retained. And even in the best of all hearts, there remains . . . an unuprooted small corner of evil.

Since then I have come to understand the truth of all the religions of the world: They struggle with the *evil inside a human being* (inside every human being). It is impossible to expel evil from the world in its entirety, but it is possible to constrict it within each person.

And since that time I have come to understand the falsehood of all the revolutions in history: They destroy only *those carriers* of evil contemporary with them (and also fail, out of haste, to discriminate the carriers of good as well). And they then take to themselves as their heritage the actual evil itself, magnified still more.

The Nuremberg Trials have to be regarded as one of the special achievements of the twentieth century: they killed the very idea of evil, though they killed very few of the people who had been infected with it. (Of course, Stalin deserves no credit here. He would have preferred to explain less and shoot more.) And if by the twenty-first century humanity has not yet blown itself up and has not suffocated itself—perhaps it is this direction that will triumph?

Yes, and if it does not triumph—then all humanity's history will have turned out to be an empty exercise in marking time, without the tiniest mite of meaning! Whither and to what end will we otherwise be moving? To beat the enemy over the head with a club—even cavemen knew that.

"Know thyself!" There is nothing that so aids and assists the awakening of omniscience within us as insistent thoughts about one's own transgressions, errors, mistakes. After the difficult cycles of such ponderings over many years, whenever I mentioned the heartlessness of our highest-ranking bureaucrats, the cruelty of our executioners, I remember myself in my captain's shoulder boards and the forward march of my battery through East Prussia, enshrouded in fire, and I say: "So were *we* any better?"

When people express vexation, in my presence, over the West's tendency to crumble, its political shortsightedness, its divisiveness, its confusion—I recall too: "Were we, before passing through the Archipelago, more steadfast? Firmer in our thoughts?"

And that is why I turn back to the years of my imprisonment and say, sometimes to the astonishment of those about me: *"Bless you, prison!"*

Lev Tolstoi was right when he *dreamed* of being put in prison. At a certain moment that giant began to dry up. He actually needed prison as a drought needs a shower of rain!

All the writers who wrote about prison but who did not themselves serve time there considered it their duty to express sympathy for prisoners and to curse prison. I . . . have served enough time there. I nourished my soul there, and I say without hesitation:

"*Bless you, prison*, for having been in my life!"

(And from beyond the grave come replies: It is very well for you to say that—when you came out of it alive!)

Chapter 2

■

Or Corruption?

But I have been brought up short: You are *not talking about the subject* at all! You have got off the track again—onto prison! And what you are supposed to be talking about is *camp*.

But I was also, I thought, talking about camp. Well, all right, I'll shut up. I shall give some space to contrary opinions. Many camp inmates will object to what I have said and will say that they did not observe any "ascent" of the soul, that this is nonsense, and that corruption took place at every step.

More insistent and more significant than others (because he had already written about all this) was Shalamov's objection:

In the camp situation human beings never remain human beings— the camps were created to this end.

All human emotions—love, friendship, envy, love of one's fellows, mercy, thirst for fame, honesty—fell away from us along with the meat of our muscles. . . . We had no pride, no vanity, and even jealousy and passion seemed to be Martian concepts. . . . The only thing left was anger—the most enduring of human emotions.

We came to understand that truth and falsehood were kin sisters.

Friendship is born neither of need nor of misfortune. If friendship does arise between human beings—it means that conditions are not that difficult. If misfortune and need have joined hands—it means they were not *in extremis*. Grief is insufficiently sharp and deep if it can be shared with friends.

There is only one distinction here to which Shalamov agrees:

Ascent, growth in profundity, the development of human beings, is possible in *prison.* But

> . . . camp—is wholly and consistently a negative school of life. There is nothing either necessary or useful that anyone derives from it. The prisoner learns flattery, falsehood, and petty and large-scale meanness. . . . When he returns home, he sees not only that he has not grown during his time in camp, but that his interests have become meager and crude.[1]

Y. Ginzburg also agrees with this distinction: "Prison ennobled people, while camp corrupted them."

And how can one object to that?

In prison, both in solitary confinement and outside solitary too, a human being confronts his grief face to face. This grief is a mountain, but he has to find space inside himself for it, to familiarize himself with it, to digest it, and it him. This is the highest form of moral effort, which has always ennobled every human being.[2] A duel with years and with walls constitutes moral work and a path upward (if you can climb it). If you share those years with a comrade, it is never in a situation in which you are called on to die in order to save his life, nor is it necessary for him to die in order for you to survive. You have the possibility of entering not into conflict but into mutual support and enrichment.

But in camp, it would appear, you do not have that path. Bread is not issued in equal pieces, but thrown onto a pile—go grab! Knock down your neighbors, and tear it out of their hands! The quantity of bread issued is such that one or two people have to die for each who survives. The bread is hung high up on a pine tree—go fell it. The bread is deposited in a coal mine—go down and mine it. Can you think about your own

---

1. Shalamov also considers it an indication of the human being's oppression and corruption in camp that he "lives there for long years subject to someone else's will, to someone else's mind." But this is something I have chosen to set aside in a footnote—because, in the first place, one can say just the same thing about many free people (not counting the scope for activity in minor details which prisoners have as well), and because, in the second place, the fatalistic character obligatorily instilled into the native of the Archipelago by his ignorance of his fate and his inability to influence it tends rather to ennoble him, to free him from fruitless bustle.

2. How interesting people become in prison! I have known people who became tiresome bores after their release, yet in prison you simply couldn't tear yourself away from conversations with them.

grief, about the past and the future, about humanity and God? Your mind is absorbed in vain calculations which for the present moment cut you off from the heavens—and tomorrow are worth nothing. You *hate* labor—it is your principal enemy. You hate your companions—rivals in life and death.[3] You are reduced to a frazzle by intense *envy* and alarm lest somewhere behind your back others are right now dividing up that bread which could be yours, that somewhere on the other side of the wall a tiny potato is being ladled out of the pot which could have ended up in your own bowl.

Camp life was organized in such a way that envy pecked at your soul from all sides, even the best-defended soul. Envy also extended to *terms* and to *release* itself. In 1945 we, the 58's, had to see the nonpolitical offenders off at the gates (as a result of Stalin's amnesty). What were our feelings toward them? Gladness for them because they were going home? No, it was envy because it was unjust to free them and to hold us. And V. Vlasov, who got a twenty-year term, served out his first ten years calmly, for who was not serving out ten years? But in 1947–1948 they began to release many others—and he envied them, got nervous, and was eating his heart out: How was it that he had received a sentence of twenty? How galling it was to have to serve that second tenner! (And I did not ask him, but I suppose that when these others began to return to camp as *repeaters*, he then must have calmed down.) And in 1955–1956 the 58's were being released on a mass scale, and the nonpolitical offenders were left in the camps. What did they feel at that point? A sense of justice because the long-suffering article, after forty years of incessant persecutions, had at long last been pardoned? No, in fact, there was universal *envy* (I received many letters of this sort in 1963): they had freed "the enemies who were far worse than us habitual criminals." And why then are we still here? For what?

And in addition you are constantly gripped by *fear*: of slipping off even that pitifully low level to which you are clinging, of losing your work which is still not the hardest, of coming a cropper on a prisoner transport, of ending up in a Strict Regimen Camp. And on top of that, you got beaten if you were weaker

---

3. P. Yakubovich declared: "Nearly every hard-labor convict dislikes every other one." Yet where he was there was no competition for survival.

than all the rest, or else you yourself beat up those weaker than you. And wasn't this corruption? *Soul mange* is what A. Rubailo, an old camp veteran, called this swift decay under external pressure.

Amid these vicious feelings and tense petty calculations, when and on what foundation could you ascend?

Chekhov, even before our Corrective Labor Camps, observed and identified this soul corruption on Sakhalin. He wrote correctly that the vices of prisoners arose from their lack of freedom, enslavement, terror, and constant hunger. And their vices were dishonesty, slyness, cowardice, faintheartedness, stool-pigeoning, thievery. Experience had demonstrated to the hard-labor convict that in the struggle for existence deceit was the most reliable means.

And wasn't all this multiplied tenfold among us? So isn't it the right time not to object, and not to rise to the defense of some sort of alleged camp "ascent," but to describe hundreds, thousands of cases of genuine soul corruption? To cite examples of how no one could resist the camp philosophy of Yashka, the Dzhezkazgan work assigner: "The more you spit on people, the more they'll esteem you." To tell how newly arrived front-line soldiers (in Kraslag in 1942) had no sooner scented the thieves' atmosphere than they themselves undertook *to play the thief—to plunder* the Lithuanians and to fatten up off their foodstuffs and possessions: You greenhorns can go die! Or how certain Vlasov men began *to pass for thieves* out of the conviction that that was the only way to survive in camp. Or about that assistant professor of literature who became a thief Ringleader. Or to be astounded—via the example of Chulpenyov—at how infectious that camp ideology was. Chulpenyov stood it for seven years on general work at timbering and became a famous lumberjack, but landed in a hospital with a broken leg, and was subsequently offered a position as a work assigner. He had no need for this job. He could certainly have dragged out as a lumberjack the two and a half years he had still to serve since the management made a great fuss over him—but how could he turn down the temptation? After all, it is a rule of camp philosophy: "If they give, take it!" And Chulpenyov became a work assigner for just six months, which were the most restless, troubled, and dismal of his whole term. (And it is now a long time since his term was served out, and he will tell you with an openhearted smile about the tall pines—but there is a stone on his heart because of those who died as a result of his *slave-driving:* a Latvian six and a half feet tall, a captain who had sailed the seven seas—yes, and was he the only one?)

Conscious instigation of one prisoner against another can lead to just such awful "soul mange"! In Unzhlag in 1950, Moiseyevaite, who, even though she was touched in the head, was still being marched to and from work under convoy, paid no attention to the convoy and went off to look for "her mother." She was seized, tied to a post at the gatehouse, and it was announced that "because of her escape attempt" the whole camp would be deprived of the next Sunday (a standard trick)! And therefore as the brigades returned from work they spat at the trussed-up woman, and some even struck her: "Because of you, bitch, we don't have a rest day." Moiseyevaite only smiled benignly.

And how much corruption was introduced by that democratic and progressive system of "trusty watchmen"—which in our zek terminology became converted to *self-guarding*—introduced back in 1918? After all, this was one of the main streams of camp corruption: the enlistment of prisoners in the trusty guards! You —had fallen. You—were punished. You—had been uprooted from life—but you want to avoid the very bottom of the pile? You want to hover over someone else, rifle in hand? Over your brother? Here! Take it! And if he runs—shoot him! We will even call you *comrade.* And we will give you a Red Army man's ration.

And . . . he grows proud. And . . . he tightens his grip on his gun stock. And . . . he shoots. And . . . he is even more severe than the free guards. (How is one to understand this: Was it really a purblind faith in social initiative? Or was it just an icy, contemptuous calculation based on the lowest human feelings?)

After all, it was not just a matter of "self-guarding" either. There were also "self-supervision," and "self-oppression"—right up to the situation in the thirties when all of them, all the way up to the camp chief, were zeks. Including the transport chief. The production chief. (And how could it have been otherwise anyway—when there were only thirty-seven Chekists to 100,000 zeks on the White Sea–Baltic Canal?) Yes, and even *security chiefs* were zeks too. One could not have carried "self-supervision" any further than that: The zeks were conducting interrogations of themselves. They were recruiting stool pigeons to denounce themselves.

Yes, yes. But I am not going to examine those countless cases of corruption here. They are well known to everyone. They have already been described, and they will be described again. It is quite enough to admit they took place. This is the general trend, this is as it should be.

Why repeat about each and every house that in subzero weather it loses its warmth? It is much more surprising to note that there are houses which retain their warmth even in subzero weather.

Shalamov says: Everyone imprisoned in camp was spiritually impoverished. But whenever I recall or encounter a former zek, I find a real personality.

Elsewhere Shalamov himself writes that he wouldn't betray other zeks! He wouldn't become a brigadier and compel others to work.

Why is that, Varlam Tikhonovich? Why is it that out of a clear sky it appears that you would refuse to become either a stoolie or a brigadier—if it is the case that no one in camp can avoid or sidestep that slippery slope of corruption? Given the fact that truth and falsehood . . . are kin sisters? Does it mean that you did nonetheless grasp at some branch sticking out? Does it mean that you found a footing on some stone—and did not slide down any further? And maybe, despite everything, anger is not really the most long-lived feeling there is? Do you not refute your own concept with your character and verses?[4]

And how is it that genuine religious believers survived in camp (as we mentioned more than once)? In the course of this book we have already mentioned their self-confident procession through the Archipelago—a sort of silent religious procession with invisible candles. How some among them were mowed down by machine guns and those next in line continued their march. A steadfastness unheard of in the twentieth century! And it was

4. Alas, he decided not to refute it. . . . As if out of stubbornness, he continued this argument. . . . On February 23, 1972, in the *Literaturnaya Gazeta*, he published a renunciation (for some reason now that all the threats have passed): "The problematics of the *Kolyma Stories* have long since been crossed out by life." This renunciation was printed in a black mourning frame, and thus all of us understood that Shalamov had died. (Footnote of 1972.)

not in the least for show, and there weren't any declamations. Take some Aunt Dusya Chmil, a round-faced, calm, and quite illiterate old woman. The convoy guards called out to her: "Chmil! What is your article?"

And she gently, good-naturedly replied: "Why are you asking, my boy? It's all written down there. I can't remember them all." (She had a bouquet of sections under Article 58.)

"Your term!"

Auntie Dusya sighed. She wasn't giving such contradictory answers in order to annoy the convoy. In her own simplehearted way she pondered this question: Her term? Did they really think it was given to human beings to know their terms?

"What term! . . . Till God forgives my sins—till then I'll be serving time."

"You are a silly, you! A silly!" The convoy guards laughed. "Fifteen years you've got, and you'll serve them all, and maybe some more besides."

But after two and a half years of her term had passed, even though she had sent no petitions—all of a sudden a piece of paper came: release!

How could one not envy those people? Were circumstances more favorable for them? By no means! It is a well-known fact that the "nuns" were kept only with prostitutes and thieves at penalty camps. And yet who was there among the religious believers whose soul was corrupted? They died—most certainly, but . . . they were not corrupted.

And how can one explain that certain unstable people found faith right there in camp, that they were strengthened by it, and that they survived uncorrupted?

And many more, scattered about and unnoticed, came to their allotted turning point and made no mistake in their choice. Those who managed to see that things were not only bad for them, but even worse, even harder, for their neighbors.

And all those who, under the threat of a penalty zone and a new term of imprisonment, refused to become stoolies?

How, in general, can one explain Grigory Ivanovich Grigoryev, a soil scientist? A scientist who volunteered for the People's Volunteer Corps in 1941—and the rest of the story is a familiar one. Taken prisoner near Vyazma, he spent his whole captivity in a German camp. And the subsequent story is also familiar. When he returned, he was arrested by us and given a tenner. I came to know him in winter, engaged in general work in Ekibastuz. His forthrightness gleamed from his big quiet eyes, some sort of unwavering forthrightness. This man was never able to bow in spirit. And he didn't bow in camp either, even though he worked only two of his ten years in his own field of specialization, and didn't receive food parcels from home for nearly the whole term. He was subjected on all sides to the camp philosophy, to the camp corruption of soul, but he was incapable of adopting it. In the Kemerovo camps (Antibess) the security chief kept trying to recruit him as a stoolie. Grigoryev replied to him quite honestly and candidly: "I find it quite *repulsive* to talk to you. You will find many willing without me." "You bastard, you'll crawl on all fours." "I would be better off hanging myself on the first branch." And so he was sent off to a penalty situation. He stood it for half a year. And he made *mistakes* which were even more unforgivable: When he was sent on an agricultural work party, he refused (as a soil scientist) to accept the post of brigadier offered him. He hoed and scythed with enthusiasm. And even more stupidly: in Ekibastuz at the stone quarry he refused to be a work checker—only because he would have had to pad the work sheets for the sloggers, for which, later on, when they caught up with it, the eternally drunk free foreman would have to pay the penalty. (But would he?) And so he went to break rocks! His honesty was so monstrously unnatural that when he went out to process potatoes with the vegetable storeroom brigade, he did not steal any, though everyone else did. When he was in a good post, in the privileged repair-shop brigade at the pumping-station equipment, he left simply because he refused to wash the socks of the free bachelor construction supervisor, Treivish. (His fellow brigade members tried to persuade him: Come on now, isn't it all the same, the kind of work you do? But no, it turned out it was not at all the same to him!) How many times did he select the worst and hardest lot, just so as not to have to offend against conscience—and he didn't, not in the least, and I am a witness. And even more: because of the astounding influence on his body of his bright and spotless human spirit (though no one today believes in any such influence, no one understands it) the organism of Grigory Ivanovich, who was no longer young (close to fifty), grew stronger in camp; his earlier rheumatism of the joints disappeared completely, and he became particularly healthy after the typhus from which he recovered: in winter he went out in cotton sacks, making holes in them for his head and his arms—and he did not catch cold!

So wouldn't it be more correct to say that no camp can corrupt those who have a stable nucleus, who do not accept that pitiful ideology which holds that "human beings are created for happiness," an ideology which is done in by the first blow of the work assigner's cudgel?

Those people became corrupted in camp who before camp had not been enriched by any morality at all or by any spiritual upbringing. (This is not at all a theoretical matter—since during our glorious half-century millions of them grew up.)

Those people became corrupted in camp who had already been corrupted out in freedom or who were ready for it. Because people are corrupted in freedom too, sometimes even more effectively than in camp.

The convoy officer who ordered that Moiseyevaite be tied to a post in order to be mocked—had he not been corrupted more profoundly than the camp inmates who spat on her?

And for that matter did every one of the brigade members spit on her? Perhaps only two from each brigade did. In fact, that is probably what happened.

Tatyana Falike writes: "Observation of people convinced me that no man could become a scoundrel in camp if he had not been one before."

If a person went swiftly bad in camp, what it might mean was that he had not just gone bad, but that that inner foulness which had not previously been needed had disclosed itself.

M. A. Voichenko has his opinion: "In camp, existence did not determine consciousness, but just the opposite: consciousness and steadfast faith in the human essence decided whether you became an animal or remained a human being."

A drastic, sweeping declaration! . . . But he was not the only one who thought so. The artist Ivashev-Musatov passionately argued exactly the same thing.

Yes, camp corruption was a mass phenomenon. But not only because the camps were awful, but because in addition we Soviet people stepped upon the soil of the Archipelago spiritually disarmed—long since prepared to be corrupted, already tinged by it out in freedom, and we strained our ears to hear from the old camp veterans "how to live in camp."

But we ought to have known how to live (and how to die) without any camp.

And perhaps, Varlam Tikhonovich Shalamov, as a general rule friendship between people does arise in need and misfortune, even in extreme misfortune too—but not between such withered and nasty people as we were, given our decades of upbringing?

If corruption was so inevitable, then why did Olga Lvovna Sliozberg not abandon her freezing friend on the forest trail, but stay behind for nearly certain death together with her—and save her? Wasn't that an extreme of misfortune?

And if corruption was so inevitable, then where did Vasily Mefodyevich Yakovenko spring from? He served out two terms, had only just been released, was living as a free employee in Vorkuta, and was just beginning to crawl around without an escort and acquire his first tiny nest. It was 1949. In Vorkuta they began to rearrest former zeks and give them new sentences. An arrest psychosis! There was panic among the free employees! How could they hold on to their freedom? How could they be less noticeable? But Y. D. Grodzensky, a friend of Yakovenko from the same Vorkuta camp, was arrested. During the interrogation he was losing strength and was close to death. There was no one to bring him food parcels. And Yakovenko fearlessly brought him food parcels! If you want to, you dogs, rake me in too!

Why was *this man* not corrupted!

And do not *all* those who survived remember one or another person who reached out a hand to him in camp and saved him at a difficult moment?

Yes, the camps were calculated and intended to corrupt. But this didn't mean that they succeeded in crushing *everyone*.

Just as in nature the process of oxidation never occurs without an accompanying reduction (one substance oxidizes while at the same time another reduces), so in camp, too (and everywhere in life), there is no corruption without ascent. They exist alongside one another.

In the next part I hope still to show how in other camps, in the Special Camps, a different *environment* was created after a certain time: the process of corruption was greatly hampered and the process of ascent became attractive even to the camp careerists.

■

Well, and what about *correction?* How did things go with correction, after all? ("Correction" is a social and state concept and does not coincide with ascent.) All the systems of justice in the world, not just our own, dream that criminals will not merely serve out their term but will also become corrected in the process, in other words behave so as not to return to the defendant's bench in court, particularly for the same offense.[5]

Dostoyevsky exclaims: "Whom did hard labor ever correct?"

The ideal of correction existed in Russian legislation after the great reform. (The whole of Chekhov's *Sakhalin* grew out of that ideal.) But was it ever successfully implemented?

P. Yakubovich thought about this a great deal and wrote: The terrorist regimen of hard labor "corrects" only those who have not become depraved—but they would not commit a second crime even without it. Yet this regimen only depraves a corrupt person, compelling him to be sly and hypocritical, and to do his utmost not to leave any clues behind.

What can one say about our Corrective Labor Camps? Students of penology (Gefängniskunde) always believed that a prisoner must not be driven to total despair, that he must always be left hope and a way out. The reader has already seen that our Corrective Labor Camps drove prisoners only and precisely to total despair.

Chekhov spoke truly: "Soul-searching—that is what's truly needed for correction." But it was soul-searching that the managers of our camps feared most of all. The common barracks, brigades, work collectives, were all specially designed to disperse and dismember that dangerous soul-searching.

What sort of correction could there be in our camps! All they could do was damage: instill the thieves' morality, instill the

---

5. Nonetheless, they never strove to "correct" the 58's—in other words to avoid imprisoning them a second time. We have already cited the frank statements of the penologists on this subject. They wanted to exterminate the 58's through labor. And the fact that we survived was due to . . . our own initiative.

cruel camp ways as the general law of life. ("Criminogenic places" in the penologists' language—in other words, crime schools.)

I. G. Pisarev, when he was completing his lengthy prison sentence, wrote, in 1963: "It becomes particularly hard, because you leave here an incurable nervous wreck, with your health irreparably ruined by lack of proper food and by incessant incitement. Here people are corrupted once and for all. Maybe butter wouldn't have melted in a man's mouth before—but now you'd never manage to put salt on his tail. If you say 'pig' to a person for seven years, he will end up by grunting. . . . It is only the first year that punishes the prisoner; all the rest simply embitter him. He adapts to the conditions, and that is all. The law, with its long sentences and its cruelty, punishes the criminal's family more than it does him."

Here is another letter. "It is painful and frightening to leave life without having seen anything and without having done anything, and no one even cares about you except, in all likelihood, your mother, who never ceases to wait for you her whole life long."

And here is what Aleksandr Kuzmich K., who devoted much thought to the matter, wrote in 1963:

They commuted my sentence of execution to twenty years of hard labor, but, to be quite honest, I don't consider that to have been any favor to me. . . . I experienced those "mistakes," as it is now the style to call them, on my own skin and bones—and they were in no way any easier or better than those of Auschwitz or Majdanek. How is one supposed to distinguish dirt from truth? A murderer from an instructor? The law from lawlessness? An executioner from a patriot —when he moves upward, and from being a lieutenant becomes a lieutenant colonel, and the cockade he wears on his hat is very much like the one worn before 1917? . . . And how am I, emerging after eighteen years of imprisonment, supposed to decipher all the obfuscations? . . . I envy you educated people who have flexible minds and who do not have to spend a long time breaking your heads in order to figure out how you should proceed or how you should adapt, *which in fact I do not want to do.*

Well spoken indeed! "I do not want." With feelings like that on his release, can one say that he was corrupted? But was he then *corrected* in the state's sense? Of course not. For the state he has simply been ruined. See what he has come to understand: This was no different from Auschwitz, and the cockades are no different either.

The "correction" which the state would like (?) is by and large never attained in the camps. The "graduates" of the camp learn only to be two-faced, how to *pretend* to be corrected, and they learn cynicism—toward the appeals of the state, the laws of the state, and its promises.

And what if there is nothing for a person *to be corrected of?* If he is not a criminal at all in the first place? If he has been imprisoned because he prayed to God, or expressed an independent opinion, or became a prisoner of war, or because of his father, or simply to fulfill the prisoner-arrest quota—what then could the camps give him?

The Sakhalin prison inspector said to Chekhov: "If, in the final analysis, out of a hundred hard-labor prisoners fifteen to twenty emerge as decent men, the responsibility for this result lies not so much with the corrective measures we employ as with our Russian courts, which send so many good reliable elements to hard labor."

Well, that judgment can stand for the Archipelago too, provided we increase the proportion of the innocently sentenced to, say, 80 percent, without at the same time forgetting that in our camps the percentage of spoilage was also considerably higher.

If we are speaking not about the meat grinder for unwanted millions, not about the cesspool into which they were hurled without pity for the people—but about a serious correctional system—the most complex of questions arises: How is it possible to give monotonously uniform punishments on the basis of a single, unified criminal code? After all, externally *equal* punishments for *different* individuals, some more moral and others more corrupted, some more sensitive and some more crude, some educated and some uneducated, are completely *unequal* punishments. (See Dostoyevsky in many different places in his *The House of the Dead*.)

English thought has understood this, and they say there (I don't know how much they practice it) that the punishment must fit not only the crime but also the character of each criminal.

For example, the general loss of external freedom for a person with a rich inner world is less hard to bear than for a person who is immature, who lives more in terms of the flesh. This second person "requires more in terms of external impressions, and his instincts pull him more strongly in the direction of freedom." (Yakubovich.) The first finds it easier to be in solitary confinement, especially with books. (Ah, how some of us thirsted for that kind of imprisonment, instead of camp! When the body is confined, what broad horizons are opened to the mind and the soul! Nikolai Morozov did not seem in any way remarkable *either* before his arrest *or*, which is the more surprising, after it. But prison meditation provided him with the chance to conceive of the planetary structure of the atom—with its differentially charged nucleus and electrons—ten years before Rutherford! But *we* were never offered pencils, paper, and books, and even had every last one of them taken away from us.) The second kind of prisoner, on the other hand, might not be able to stand solitary confinement for even a year, and would simply wither away and die off. He would need someone, companions! And yet for the former kind of prisoner unpleasant company could be worse than no one. But camp (where they gave very little food) would be much easier for the latter to bear than for the former. As would a barracks where four hundred people were housed, all of them shouting, playing the fool, playing cards and dominoes, howling and snoring, and where, on top of all that, the radio, which was aimed at idiots, was constantly screeching away. (The camps in which I served time were *punished* by having no radio! What a salvation that was!)

Thus the system of Corrective Labor Camps in particular, with their obligatory and exhausting physical labor and their obligatory participation in the humiliating, buzzing ant heap, was a more effective means of destroying the intelligentsia than was prison. It was precisely the intelligentsia that this system killed off quickly and completely.

Chapter 3

■

Our Muzzled Freedom

But even when all the main things about the Gulag Archipelago are written, read, and understood, will there be anyone even then who grasps what our *freedom* was like? What sort of a country it was that for whole decades dragged that Archipelago about inside itself?

It was my fate to carry inside me a tumor the size of a large man's fist. This tumor swelled and distorted my stomach, hindered my eating and sleeping, and I was always conscious of it (though it did not constitute even one-half of one percent of my body, whereas within the country as a whole the Archipelago constituted 8 percent). But the horrifying thing was not that this tumor pressed upon and displaced adjacent organs. What was most terrifying about it was that it exuded poisons and infected the whole body.

And in this same way our whole country was infected by the poisons of the Archipelago. And whether it will ever be able to get rid of them someday, only God knows.

Can we, *dare* we, describe the full loathsomeness of the state in which we lived (not so remote from that of today)? And if we do not show that loathsomeness in its entirety, then we at once have a lie. For this reason I consider that *literature did not exist* in our country in the thirties, forties, and fifties. Because without the *full* truth it is not literature. And today they show this loathsomeness according to the fashion of the moment—by inference, an inserted phrase, an afterthought, or hint—and the result is again a lie.

This is not the task of our book, but let us try to enumerate briefly those traits of *free* life which were determined by the closeness of the Archipelago or which were in the same style.

1. *Constant Fear.* As the reader has already seen, the roster of the waves of recruitment into the Archipelago is not exhausted with 1935, or 1937, or 1949. The recruitment went on *all the time.* Just as there is no minute when people are not dying or being born, so there was no minute when people were not being arrested. Sometimes this came close to a person, sometimes it was further off; sometimes a person deceived himself into thinking that nothing threatened him, and sometimes he himself became an executioner, and thus the threat to him diminished. But any adult inhabitant of this country, from a collective farmer up to a member of the Politburo, always knew that it would take only one careless word or gesture and he would fly off irrevocably into the abyss.

Just as in the Archipelago beneath every trusty lay the chasm (and death) of general work, so beneath every inhabitant lay the chasm (and death) of the Archipelago. In appearance the country was much bigger than its Archipelago, but all of it and all its inhabitants hung phantomlike above the latter's gaping maw.

Fear was not always the fear of arrest. There were intermediate threats: purges, inspections, the completion of security questionnaires—routine or extraordinary ones—dismissal from work, deprivation of residence permit, expulsion or exile.[1] The security questionnaires were so detailed and so inquisitive that more than half the inhabitants of the country had a bad conscience and were constantly and permanently tormented by the approach of the period when they had to be filled out. Once people had invented a false life story for these questionnaires, they had to try not to get tangled up in it. But danger might strike suddenly: The son of the Kady Vlasov, Igor, regularly entered in his questionnaire the statement that his father was dead. And that way he got into a military school. Then one fine day he was summoned and he had three days to present a certificate of his father's death. And he had to do it!

---

1. In addition, there were such little-known forms as expulsion from the Party, dismissal from work, and dispatch to a camp as a free worker. That is how Stepan Grigoryevich Onchul was exiled in 1938. It was natural that such persons were listed as being very unreliable. During the war Onchul was conscripted into a work battalion, where he died.

The aggregate fear led to a correct consciousness of one's own insignificance and of the lack of any kind of *rights*. In November, 1938, Natasha Anichkova learned that the person she loved (her common-law husband) had been arrested in Orel. She went there. The enormous square in front of the prison was filled with carts. On them sat women in bast sandals, wearing their traditional peasant dress, with parcels which the authorities refused to accept. Anichkova pushed her way up to a window in a dreadful prison wall. "Who are you?" they asked her sternly. They heard her out. "Well, now, listen here, Comrade Muscovite, I am going to give you one piece of *advice:* get out of here today, because at night *they are going to come for you too.*" The foreigner finds all this quite incomprehensible: Why had the Chekist given her unsolicited advice instead of a businesslike answer to her question? What right did he have to demand of a free citizen that she leave immediately? And who was going *to come* and why? But what Soviet citizen will lie and say that this is incomprehensible to him or that it sounds like an improbable case? After advice like that you would be afraid to stay in a strange city!

Nadezhda Mandelstam* speaks truly when she remarks that our life is so permeated with prison that simple meaningful words like "they took," or "they put inside," or "he is inside," or "they let out," are understood by everyone in our country in only one sense, even without a context.

Peace of mind is something our citizens have never known.

2. *Servitude.* If it had been easy to change your place of residence, to leave a place that had become dangerous for you and thus shake off fear and refresh yourself, people would have behaved more boldly, and they might have taken some risks. But for long decades we were shackled by that same system under which no worker could quit work of his own accord. And the passport regulations also fastened everyone to particular places. And the housing, which could not be sold, nor exchanged, nor rented. And because of this it was an insane piece of daring *to protest* in the place where you lived or worked.

3. *Secrecy and Mistrust.* These feelings replaced our former openhearted cordiality and hospitality (which had still not been

destroyed in the twenties). These feelings were the natural defense of any family and every person, particularly because no
one could ever quit work or leave, and every little detail was
kept in sight and within earshot for years. The secretiveness of
the Soviet person is by no means superfluous, but is absolutely
necessary, even though to a foreigner it may at times seem superhuman. The former Tsarist officer K.U. survived and was never
arrested only because when he got married he did not tell his
wife about his past. His brother, N.U., was arrested—and the
wife of the arrested man, taking advantage of the fact that they
lived in different cities at the time of his arrest, hid his arrest
from her own *father and mother*—so they would not blurt it
out. She preferred telling them and everyone else that her husband had abandoned her, and then playing that role a long time!
Now these were the secrets of one family which I was told thirty
years later. And what urban family did not have such secrets?

In 1949 the father of a girl who was a fellow student of V.I.'s
was arrested. In these cases everyone would shun such a student,
and that was considered natural. But V.I. did not shun her, and
openly expressed sympathy with the girl, and tried to find ways
to help her out. Frightened by such unusual conduct, the girl
rejected V.I.'s help and participation, and lied to him, saying she
did not believe in the innocence of her arrested father, and that
he had evidently concealed his crime from his family all his life.
(And it was only during the times of Khrushchev that their
tongues were loosened: the girl told him she had decided he was
either a police informer or else a member of an anti-Soviet
organization out to rope in the dissatisfied.)

This universal mutual mistrust had the effect of deepening
the mass-grave pit of slavery. The moment someone began to
speak up frankly, everyone stepped back and shunned him: "A
provocation!" And therefore anyone who burst out with a sincere
protest was predestined to loneliness and alienation.

4. *Universal Ignorance.* Hiding things from each other, and
not trusting each other, we ourselves helped implement that
absolute secrecy, absolute misinformation, among us which was
the cause of causes of everything that took place—including both
the millions of arrests and the mass approval of them also. Informing one another of nothing, neither shouting nor groaning,

and learning nothing from one another, we were completely in the hands of the newspapers and the official orators. Every day they pushed in our faces some new piece of incitement, like a photograph of a railroad wreck (sabotage) somewhere three thousand miles away. And what we really needed to learn about, which was what had happened on our apartment landing that day, we had no way of finding out.

How could you become a citizen, knowing nothing about life around you? Only when you yourself were caught in the trap would you find out—too late.

5. *Squealing* was developed to a mind-boggling extent. Hundreds of thousands of Security officers in their official offices, in the innocent rooms of official buildings, and in prearranged apartments, sparing neither paper nor their unoccupied time, tirelessly recruited and summoned stool pigeons to give reports, and this in such enormous numbers as they could never have found necessary for collecting information. They even recruited obviously useless and unsuitable people who would most certainly not agree to report to them—for example, a religious believer, the wife of the Baptist minister Nikitin, who had died in camp. Nonetheless, she was kept standing for several hours while being questioned, then was arrested, and then transferred to worse work at her factory. One of the purposes of such extensive recruitment was, evidently, to make each subject feel the breath of the stool pigeons on his own skin. So that in every group of people, in every office, in every apartment, either there would be an informer or else the people there would be afraid there was.

I will give my own superficial speculative estimate: Out of every four to five city dwellers there would most certainly be one who at least once in his life had received a proposal to become an informer. And it might even have been more widespread than that. Quite recently I carried out my own spot check, both among groups of ex-prisoners and among groups of those who have always been free. I asked which out of the group they had tried to recruit and when and how. And it turned out that out of several people at a table *all* had received such proposals at one time or another!

Nadezhda Mandelstam correctly concludes: Beyond the purpose of weakening ties between people, there was another purpose as well. Any person who had let himself be recruited would, out of fear of public exposure, be very much interested in the continuing stability of the regime.

Secretiveness spread its cold tentacles throughout the whole people. It crept between colleagues at work, between old friends, students, soldiers, neighbors, children growing up—and even into the reception room of the NKVD, among the prisoners' wives bringing food parcels.

6. *Betrayal as a Form of Existence.* Given this constant fear over a period of many years—for oneself and one's family—a human being became a vassal of fear, subjected to it. And it turned out that the least dangerous form of existence was constant betrayal.

The mildest and at the same time most widespread form of betrayal was not to do anything bad directly, but just not to notice the doomed person next to one, not to help him, to turn away one's face, to shrink back. They had arrested a neighbor, your comrade at work, or even your close friend. You kept silence. You acted as if you had not noticed. (For you could not afford to lose your current job!) And then it was announced at work, at the general meeting, that the person who had disappeared the day before was . . . an inveterate enemy of the people. And you, who had bent your back beside him for twenty years at the same desk, now by your noble silence (or even by your condemning speech!), had to show how hostile you were to his crimes. (You had to make this sacrifice for the sake of your own dear family, for your own dear ones! What right had you not to think *about them?*) But the person arrested had left behind him a wife, a mother, children, and perhaps they at least ought to be helped? No, no, that would be dangerous: after all, these were the wife of an *enemy* and the mother of an enemy, and they were the children of an enemy (and your own children had a long education ahead of them)!

When they arrested engineer Palchinsky, his wife, Nina, wrote to Kropotkin's widow: "I have been left without any funds, and no one has given me any help, all shun me and fear me. . . . And I have found out what friends are now. There are very few exceptions."[2]

And one who concealed an enemy was also an enemy! And

2. A letter of August 16, 1929, manuscript section of the Lenin Library, collection 410, card file 5, storage unit 24.

one who abetted an enemy was also an enemy! And one who continued his friendship with an enemy was also an enemy. And the telephone of the accursed family fell silent. And they stopped getting letters. And on the street people passed them without recognizing them, without offering them a hand to shake, without nodding to them. And even less were they invited out. And no one offered to lend them money. And in the hustle of a big city people felt as if they were in a desert.

And that was precisely what Stalin needed! And he laughed in his mustaches, the shoeshine boy!

Academician Sergei Vavilov, after the repression of his great brother, became a lackey president of the Academy of Sciences. (That mustached prankster thought it all up too, to make a fool of him, and as a test for the human heart.) A. N. Tolstoi, a Soviet count, avoided not only visiting but even giving money to the family of his arrested brother. Leonid Leonov forbade his own wife, whose maiden name was Sabashnikova, to visit the family of her arrested brother, S. M. Sabashnikov.

And the legendary Georgi Dimitrov, that roaring lion of the Leipzig trial, retreated and declined to save and even betrayed his friends Popov and Tanev when they, who had been acquitted by a Fascist court, got sentenced to fifteen years each on Soviet soil "for the attempted assassination of Comrade Dimitrov." (And they served time in Kraslag.)

It is well known what the situation of an arrested man's family was like. V. Y. Kaveshan from Kaluga recalls it: "After the arrest of our father everyone avoided and shunned us, as if we were lepers, and I had to leave school because the *children tormented me*. [More betrayers were growing up! More executioners growing up!] And my mother was fired from her work. And we had to resort to begging."

One family of a Muscovite arrested in 1937—a mother and little children—was being taken to the railroad station by the police to be sent into exile. And all of a sudden, when they went through the station, the small boy, aged eight, disappeared. The policemen wore themselves out looking for him but couldn't find him. So they exiled the family without the boy. And what had happened was that he dived under the red cloth wound around the high pedestal beneath the bust of Stalin, and he sat there until the danger passed. And then he returned home—

where the apartment was sealed shut. He went to the neighbors, and to acquaintances, and to friends of his papa and mama—and not only did no one take that small boy into their family, but they refused even to let him spend the night! And so he went and turned himself in at an orphanage. . . . Contemporaries! Fellow citizens! Do you recognize here your own swinish faces?

But all that was only the minimal degree of betrayal—to turn one's back. But how many other alluring degrees there were—and what a multitude of people descended them! Those who fired Kaveshan's mother from work—did they not also turn their backs and make their own contribution? Those who harkened to the ring of the Security men and sent Nikitin's wife to manual labor, so that she would give in and become a stoolie all the sooner? Yes, and those editors who rushed to cross off the name of the writer who had been arrested the day before.

Marshal Blücher—he is a symbol of that epoch: he sat like an owl in the presidium of the court and judged Tukhachevsky. (And Tukhachevsky would have done the same to him.) They shot Tukhachevsky—and then they cut off Blücher's head too. Or what about the famous medical professors Vinogradov and Shereshevsky? Today we recall that they themselves were victims of the malevolent slander of 1952—but they themselves signed the no less malevolent slander against their colleagues Pletnev and Levin in 1936. (And the Great Laureate kept himself in training, both in theme and in individual souls. . . .)

People lived in the *field* of betrayal—and their best powers of reasoning were used in justification of it. In 1937 a husband and wife were awaiting arrest—because the wife had come from Poland. And here is what they agreed on: Before the actual arrest the husband denounced the wife to the police! She was arrested, and by the same token he was "purified" in the eyes of the NKVD and stayed free. And in that same glorious year, the prerevolutionary political prisoner Adolf Mezhov, going off to prison, proclaimed to his one and only beloved daughter, Izabella: "We have devoted our lives to Soviet power, and therefore let no one make use of your injury. Enter the Komsomol!" Under the terms of his sentence, Mezhov was not forbidden correspondence, but the Komsomol forbade his daughter to engage in any correspondence. And in the spirit of her father's testament the daughter renounced her father.

How many of those *renunciations* there were at that time! Some of them made in public, some of them in the press: "I, the undersigned, from such and such a date renounce my father and my mother as enemies of the Soviet people." And thus they purchased their lives.

Those who were not alive during that time, or who do not live today in China, will find it nearly impossible to comprehend and forgive this. In ordinary human societies the human being lives out his sixty years without ever getting caught in the pincers of that kind of choice, and he himself is quite convinced of his decency, as are those who pronounce speeches over his grave. A human being departs from life without ever having learned into what kind of deep well of evil one can fall.

And the mass mange of souls does not spread through society instantly. During all the twenties and the beginning of the thirties many in our country still preserved their souls and the concepts of the former society: to help in misfortune, to defend those in difficulties. And even as late as 1933 Nikolai Vavilov and Meister openly petitioned on behalf of all the arrested staff members of the All-Union Scientific Research Institute of Plant Breeding. There is a certain minimal necessary period of corruption prior to which the great Apparatus cannot cope with the people. This period is also determined by the age of those stubborn people who have not yet grown old. For Russia it took twenty years. When the Baltic States suffered mass arrests in 1949, their corruption had only had five or six years to establish itself, and that proved too little, and families that suffered from the government met with support on all sides. (Yes, and there was a supplementary cause there, strengthening the resistance of the Baltic peoples: social oppression there appeared simply as national oppression, and in this case people always fight back more firmly.)

In evaluating 1937 for the Archipelago, we refused it the title of the crowning glory. But here, in talking about *freedom*, we have to grant it this corroded crown of betrayal; one has to admit that this was the particular year that broke the soul of our *freedom* and opened it wide to corruption on a mass scale.

Yet even this was not yet the end of our society! (As we see today, the end never did come—the living thread of Russia survived, hung on until better times came in 1956, and it is now less than ever likely to die.) The resistance was not overt. It did not beautify the epoch of the universal fall, but with its invisible warm veins its heart kept on beating, beating, beating, beating.

And in that awful time, when in apprehensive loneliness precious photographs, precious letters and diaries, were burned, when every yellowed piece of paper in the family cupboard all of a sudden gleamed out like a fiery fern of death and could not jump into the stove fast enough, in that awful time, what great heroism was required *not* to burn things up night after night for thousands and thousands of nights and to preserve the archives of those who had been sentenced (like Florensky) or of those who were well known to be in disgrace (like the philosopher Fyodorov)! And what a blazing, underground, anti-Soviet act of rebellion the story of Lidiya Chukovskaya, *Sofya Petrovna,** must have seemed! It was preserved by Isidor Glikin. In blockaded Leningrad, feeling the approach of death, he made his way through the entire city to carry it to his sister and thus to save it.

Every act of resistance to the government required heroism quite out of proportion to the magnitude of the act. It was safer to keep dynamite during the rule of Alexander II than it was to shelter the orphan of an enemy of the people under Stalin. Nonetheless, how many such children were taken in and saved . . . Let the children themselves tell their stories. And secret assistance to families . . . did occur. And there was someone who took the place of an arrested person's wife who had been in a hopeless line for three days, so that she could go in to get warm and get some sleep. And there was also someone who went off with pounding heart to warn someone else that an ambush was waiting for him at his apartment and that he must not return there. And there was someone who gave a fugitive shelter, even though he himself did not sleep that night.

We have already mentioned those so bold as not to vote in favor of the Promparty executions. And there was also someone who went to the Archipelago for defending his unobtrusive, unknown colleagues at work. And sons followed in the footsteps of their fathers: the son of that Rozhansky,* Ivan, himself suffered in defense of his colleague Kopelev. At a Party meeting of the Leningrad Children's Publishing House, M. M. Maisner stood up and began to defend "wreckers in children's literature" —and right then and there he was expelled from the Party and arrested. And, after all, he knew what he was doing.[3] And in the wartime censorship office—in Ryazan in 1941—a girl censor tore up the criminal letter of a front-line soldier whom she did not know. But she was observed tearing it up and putting it into a wastebasket, and they pieced the letter back together—and *arrested* her. She sacrificed herself for a distant stranger! (And the only reason I heard about this was that it took place in Ryazan. And how many such cases were there unknown? . . .)

Nowadays it is quite convenient to declare that *arrest* was a lottery (Ehrenburg). Yes, it was a lottery all right, but some of the numbers were "fixed." They threw out a general dragnet and arrested in accordance with assigned quota figures, yes, but every person who *objected publicly* they grabbed that very minute! And it turned into a *selection on the basis of soul,* not a lottery! Those who were bold fell beneath the ax, were sent off to the Archipelago—and the picture of the monotonously obedient *freedom* remained unruffled. All those who were purer and better could not stay in that society; and without them it kept getting more and more trashy. You would not notice these quiet departures at all. But they were, in fact, the dying of the soul of the people.

7. *Corruption.* In a situation of fear and betrayal over many years people survive unharmed only in a superficial, bodily sense. And inside . . . they become corrupt.

So many millions of people agreed to become stool pigeons. And, after all, if some forty to fifty million people served long sentences in the Archipelago during the course of the thirty-five years up to 1953, including those who died—and this is a modest estimate, being only three or four times the population of Gulag at any one time, and, after all, during the war the death rate there was running *one percent per day*—then we can assume that at least every third or at least every fifth case was the consequence of somebody's denunciation and that somebody was willing to provide evidence as a witness! All of them, all those

---

3. There is evidence in our possession of a heroic case of mass steadfastness, but I require a second independent confirmation of it: in 1930 several hundred cadets of a certain Ukrainian military school arrived on Solovki in their own formation (refusing convoy)—because they had refused to suppress peasant disturbances.

murderers with ink, are still among us today. Some of them brought about the arrest of their neighbors out of fear—and this was only the first step. Others did it for material gain. And still others, the youngest at the time, who are now on the threshold of a pension, betrayed with inspiration, out of ideological considerations, and sometimes even openly; after all, it was considered a service to one's class to expose the enemy! And all these people are among us. And most often they are prospering. And we still rejoice that they are "our ordinary Soviet people."

Cancer of the soul develops secretly too and strikes at that particular part of it where one expects to find gratitude. Fyodor Peregud gave Misha Ivanov food and drink; Ivanov was out of work, and so Peregud got him a job at the Tambov railroad-car repair factory and taught him the trade. He had no place to live, so he let him move in with him, like a relative. And then Mikhail Dmitriyevich Ivanov sent a denunciation to the NKVD accusing Fyodor Peregud of praising German equipment at dinner at home. (You have to know Fyodor Peregud. He was a mechanic, a motor mechanic, a radio operator and repairman, an electrician, a watchmaker, an optician, a foundryman, a modelmaker, a cabinetmaker, master of up to twenty different skills. In camp he opened up a shop for precision mechanics. When he lost his leg, he made himself an artificial limb.) And so the police came to take Peregud and took his fourteen-year-old daughter to prison too. And M. D. Ivanov was responsible for all that! He came to the trial looking black. And what that meant was that a rotting soul sometimes emerges in the face. But soon after, he left the factory and began to work for State Security in the open. And subsequently, because of his lack of ability, he was made a fireman.

In a corrupt society ingratitude was an everyday, run-of-the-mill emotion, and there was almost nothing surprising in it. After the arrest of the plant breeder V. S. Markin, the agronomist A. A. Solovyov quite safely stole the variety of wheat which Markin had developed, "Taiga 49."[4] When the Institute of Buddhist Culture was destroyed (all its leading personnel were arrested) and its head, Academician Shcherbatsky, died, his

---

4. And when Markin was rehabilitated twenty years later, Solovyov was unwilling to yield him even *half* the payment he had received for it. *Izvestiya,* November 15, 1963.

student Kalyanov came to his widow and persuaded her to give him the books and papers of the deceased: "Otherwise things will go badly, because the Institute of Buddhist Culture turned out to be a spy center." Having taken possession of these works, he published part of them (as well as the work of Vostrikov) under his own name and thus acquired a reputation.

There are many scientific reputations in Moscow and in Leningrad that were also built on blood and bones. *The ingratitude of students*, cutting in a skewbald swath through our science and technology of the thirties and forties, had a quite understandable explanation: science passed out of the hands of the real scientists and engineers into the hands of the callow greedy *climbers*.

By now it is quite impossible to trace and enumerate all these appropriated works and stolen inventions. And what about the apartments taken over from those arrested? And what about their stolen possessions? And during the war did not this savage trait manifest itself as nearly universal: if there was someone bereaved, bombed out, their home burned down or being evacuated, the neighbors who had survived the disaster, plain Soviet people, tried in those very moments to profit from those who were stricken.

The aspects of corruption are varied, and it is not for us to cover them all in this chapter. The overall life of society came down to the fact that traitors were advanced and mediocrities triumphed, while everything that was best and most honest was trampled underfoot. Who can show me *one case* in the whole country from the thirties to the fifties of a noble person casting down, destroying, driving out a base troublemaker? I affirm that such a case would have been impossible, just as it is impossible for any waterfall to fall upward as an exception. After all, no noble person would turn to State Security, but for any villain it was always right there at hand. And State Security would not stop at anything, once it didn't stop at what it did to Nikolai Vavilov. So why should the waterfall fall upward?

This easy triumph of mean people over the noble boiled in a black stinking cloud in the crowded capital. But it stank, too, even way up north, beneath the honest Arctic storms, at the polar stations so beloved in the legends of the thirties, where the clear-eyed giants of Jack London should have been smoking pipes of peace. At the Arctic station on Domashni Island, off Severnaya Zemlya, there were just three people: the non-Party chief of the station, Aleksandr Pavlovich Babich, a much-honored old Arctic explorer; the manual laborer Yeryomin, who was the only Party member and who was also the Party organizer (!) of the station; and the Komsomol member (the Komsomol organizer!), the meteorologist Goryachenko, who was ambitiously trying to shove the chief aside and take his job. Goryachenko dug around among the chief's personal possessions, stole documents, and made threats. The Jack London solution would have been for the other two men simply to shove this scoundrel down through the ice. But no! Instead, a telegram was sent to Papanin in the Northern Sea Route headquarters about the necessity of replacing this employee. The Party organizer Yeryomin signed the telegram, but then he confessed to the Komsomol member, and together they sent Papanin a Party-Komsomol telegram just the opposite in content. Papanin's decision was: The collective has disintegrated; remove them to the mainland. They sent the icebreaker *Sadko* to get them. On board the *Sadko* the Komsomol man lost no time at all and provided the ship's political commissar with *materials*. Babich was arrested on the spot. (The principal accusation was that he intended to turn the icebreaker *Sadko* over to the Germans—that same icebreaker on which they were all now sailing! . . .) Once ashore, Babich was immediately put into a Preliminary Detention Cell. (Let us imagine for one moment that the ship's commissar was an honest and reasonable person and that he had summoned Babich and heard the other side of the question. But this would have meant disclosing a secret denunciation to a possible enemy! And in that case Goryachenko, through Papanin, would have also procured the arrest of the ship's commissar. The system worked faultlessly!)

Of course, among individuals who had not been brought up from childhood in the Pioneer detachments and the Komsomol cells, there were souls that retained their integrity. At a Siberian station a husky soldier, seeing a trainload of prisoners, suddenly rushed off to buy several packs of cigarettes and persuaded the convoy guards to pass them on to the prisoners. (And in other places in this book we describe similar cases.) But this soldier was probably not on duty, and was probably on leave, and he did not have the Komsomol organizer of his unit near him. If he had been on duty in his own unit, he would not have made up his mind to do it because he would have caught hell for it. Yes, and it was possible that even in the other situation the military police may have called him to account for it.

8. *The Lie as a Form of Existence.* Whether giving in to fear, or influenced by material self-interest or envy, people can't nonetheless become stupid so swiftly. Their souls may be thoroughly muddied, but they still have a sufficiently clear mind. They cannot believe that all the genius of the world has suddenly concentrated itself in one head with a flattened, low-hanging forehead. They simply cannot believe the stupid and silly images of themselves which they hear over the radio, see in films, and read in the newspapers. Nothing forces them to speak the truth in reply, but no one allows them to keep silent! They have to *talk!* And what else but a lie? They have to applaud madly, and no one requires honesty of them.

And if in *Pravda* on May 20, 1938, we read the appeal of workers in higher education to Comrade Stalin:

Heightening our revolutionary vigilance, we will help our glorious intelligence service, headed by the true Leninist, the Stalinist People's Commissar Nikolai Ivanovich Yezhov, to purge our higher educational institutions as well as all our country of the remnants of the Trotskyite-Bukharinite and other counterrevolutionary trash . . .

we certainly do not conclude that the entire meeting of a thousand persons consisted solely of idiots—but merely of degenerate liars acceding to their own arrest on the morrow.

The permanent lie becomes the only safe form of existence, in the same way as betrayal. Every wag of the tongue can be overheard by someone, every facial expression observed by someone. Therefore every word, if it does not have to be a direct lie, is nonetheless obliged not to contradict the general, common lie. There exists a collection of ready-made phrases, of labels, a selection of ready-made lies. And not one single speech nor one single essay or article nor one single book—be it scientific, journalistic, critical, or "literary," so-called—can exist without the use of these primary clichés. In the most scientific of texts it is required that someone's false authority or false priority be upheld somewhere, and that someone be cursed for telling the truth; without this lie even an academic work cannot see the light of day. And what can be said about those shrill meetings and trashy lunch-break gatherings where you are compelled to vote against your own opinion, to pretend to be glad over what distresses you (be it a new state loan, the lowering of piece rates, contributions to some tank column, Sunday work duties, or sending your children to help on the collective farms) and to express the deepest anger in areas about which you couldn't care less—some kind of intangible, invisible violence in the West Indies or Paraguay?

In prison Tenno recalled with shame how two weeks before his own arrest he had lectured the sailors on "The Stalinist Constitution—The Most Democratic in the World." And of course not one word of it was sincere.

There is no man who has typed even one page . . . without lying. There is no man who has spoken from a rostrum . . . without lying. There is no man who has spoken into a microphone . . . without lying.

But if only it had all ended there! After all, it went further than that: every conversation with the management, every conversation in the Personnel Section, every conversation of any kind with any other Soviet person called for lies—sometimes head on, sometimes looking over your shoulder, sometimes indulgently affirmative. And if your idiot interlocutor said to you face to face that we were retreating to the Volga in order to decoy Hitler farther, or that the Colorado beetles had been dropped on us by the Americans—it was necessary to agree! It was obligatory to agree! (And a shake of the head instead of a nod might well cost you resettlement in the Archipelago. Remember the arrest of Chulpenyov, in Part I, Chapter 7.)

But that was not all: Your children were growing up! If they weren't yet old enough, you and your wife had to avoid saying openly in front of them what you really thought; after all, they were being brought up to be Pavlik Morozovs, to betray their own parents, and they wouldn't hesitate to repeat his achievement. And if the children were still little, then you had to decide what was the best way to bring them up; whether to start them off on lies instead of the truth (so that it would be *easier* for them to live) and then to lie forevermore in front of them too; or to tell them the truth, with the risk that they might make a slip, that they might let it out, which meant that you had to instill into them from the start that the truth was murderous, that beyond the threshold of the house you had to lie, only lie, just like papa and mama.

The choice was really such that you would rather not have any children.

The lie as the continuing basis of life: A young, intelligent woman, A.K., who understood everything, came from the capital to teach literature in a higher-education institute in the provinces. Her security questionnaire had no black marks on it, and she had a brand-new candidate's degree. In her principal course she saw she had only one Party member and decided that this girl was the one who was bound to be the stool pigeon. (There had to be a *stool pigeon* in every course—of that A.K. was convinced.) And so she decided to become all buddy-buddy with this Party member and pretend friendship with her. (Incidentally, according to the tactics of the Archipelago this was a complete miscalculation. What she should have done, on the contrary, was to paste a couple of failing grades on her at the start and then any denunciations would have looked like sour grapes.) And so these two used to meet outside the institute and exchanged photographs. (The girl student carried A.K.'s photograph around in her Party card case.) During holiday time they corresponded tenderly. And in every lecture A.K. tried to play up to the possible evaluations of her Party student. Four years of this humiliating pretense went by, the student completed her course, and by this time her conduct was a matter of indifference to A.K., so when she made her first return visit to the school, A.K. received her with deliberate coldness. The offended student demanded her photograph and letters back and exclaimed (the most dolefully amusing thing about it was that she probably wasn't a stool pigeon): "If I finish my degree, I will never cling to this pitiful institute the way you do! And what lectures you gave—as dull as dishwater!"

Yes, by impoverishing everything, bleaching it out, and clipping it to suit the perceptions of a stool pigeon, A.K. ruined her lectures, when she was capable of delivering them brilliantly.

As a certain poet said: It wasn't a cult of personality we had, but a cult of hypocrisy.

Here, too, of course, one has to distinguish between degrees:

between the forced, defensive lie and the oblivious, passionate lie of the sort our writers distinguished themselves at most of all, the sort of lie in the midst of whose tender emotion Marietta Shaginyan could write in 1937 (!) that the epoch of socialism had transformed even criminal interrogation: the stories of interrogators showed that nowadays the persons being interrogated *willingly cooperated with them*, telling everything that was required about themselves and others.

And the lie has, in fact, led us so far away from a normal society that you cannot even orient yourself any longer; in its dense, gray fog not even one pillar can be seen. All of a sudden, thanks to footnotes, you figure out that Yakubovich's book *In the World of the Outcasts* was published, although under a pseudonym, *at the very same time* the author was completing his Tsarist hard-labor sentence and being sent off into exile.[5] Well, now, just add that up, just add that up and compare it with us! Compare that with the way my belated and shy novella managed to get out in the open by a miracle, and then they firmly lowered the barriers, bolted things up tightly, and locked the locks. And now it is forbidden to write not merely about something taking place in the present but even about things that took place thirty and fifty years ago. And will we ever read about them during our lifetime? We are destined to go to our graves still immersed in lies and falsehoods.

Moreover, even if they offered us the chance to learn the truth, would our *free people* even want to know it? Y. G. Oksman returned from the camps in 1948, and was not rearrested, but lived in Moscow. His friends and acquaintances did not abandon him, but helped him. But they did not want to hear his recollections of camp! Because if they knew about *that*—how could they go on living?

After the war a certain song became very popular: "The Noise of the City Cannot Be Heard." No singer, even the most mediocre, could perform it without receiving enthusiastic applause. The Chief Administration of Thoughts and Feelings did not at first grasp what was going on, and they allowed it to be performed on the radio and on the stage. After all, it was Russian and had a folk motif. And then suddenly they discovered what it was all

---

5. At the very time when that hard labor actually existed! It was about convict hard labor which was *contemporary with it*, and not allegedly in the irrevocable past.

about—and they immediately crossed it off the permitted list. The words of the song were about a doomed prisoner, about lovers torn apart. The need to repent existed still and it stirred, and people who were steeped in lies could at least applaud that old song with all their hearts.

9. *Cruelty*. And where among all the preceding qualities was there any place left for kindheartedness? How could one possibly preserve one's kindness while pushing away the hands of those who were drowning? Once you have been steeped in blood, you can only become more cruel. And, anyway, cruelty ("class cruelty") was praised and instilled, and you would soon lose track, probably, of just where between bad and good that trait lay. And when you add that kindness was ridiculed, that pity was ridiculed, that mercy was ridiculed—you'd never be able to chain all those who were drunk on blood!

My nameless woman correspondent, from Arbat No. 15, asks me "about the roots of the cruelty" characteristic of "certain Soviet people." Why is it that the cruelty they manifest is proportionate to the defenselessness of the person in their power? And she cites an example—which is not at all what one might regard as the main one, but which I am going to cite here anyway.

This took place in the winter of 1943–1944 at the Chelyabinsk railroad station, under a canopy near the baggage checkroom. It was minus 13 degrees. Beneath the shed roof was a cement floor, on which was trampled sticky snow from outside. Inside the window of the baggage checkroom stood a woman in a padded jacket, and on the nearer side was a well-fed policeman in a tanned sheepskin coat. They were absorbed in a kittenish, flirtatious conversation. Several men lay on the floor in earth-colored cotton duds and rags. Even to call them threadbare would be rank flattery. These were young fellows—emaciated, swollen, with sores on their lips. One of them, evidently in a fever, lay with bare chest on the snow, groaning. The woman telling the story approached him to ask who they were, and it turned out that one of them had served out his term in camp, another had been released for illness, but that their documents had been made out incorrectly when they were released, and as a result they could not get tickets to go home on the train. And they had no strength left to return to camp either—they were totally fagged out with diarrhea. So then the woman telling the story began to break off pieces of bread for them. And at this point the police-man broke off his jolly conversation and said to her threaten-ingly: "What's going on, auntie, have you recognized your relatives? You better get out of here. They will die without your help!" And so she thought to herself: After all, they'll up and haul me in just like that and put me in prison! (And that was quite right, what was to stop them?) And . . . she went away.

How typical all this is of our society—what she thought to herself, and how she went away, and that pitiless policeman, and that pitiless woman in the padded jacket, and that cashier at the ticket window who refused them tickets, and that nurse who refused to take them into the city hospital, and that idiotic free employee at the camp who had made out their documents.

It was a fierce and a vicious life, and by this time, you would not, as in Dostoyevsky and Chekhov, call a prisoner "an unfor-tunate," but, if you please, only "rot." In 1938 Magadan school pupils threw stones at a column of women prisoners (as Surov-tseva recalls).

Had our country ever known before, or does any other country know today, so many repulsive and divisive apartment and family quarrels? Every reader will be able to speak of many, and we will mention just one or two.

In a communal apartment on Dolomanovskaya Street in Ros-tov lived Vera Krasutskaya, whose husband was arrested and perished in 1938. Her neighbor, Anna Stolberg, knew about this, and for eighteen years—from 1938 to 1956—reveled in her power and tormented Krasutskaya with threats; catching her in the kitchen or in the corridor, she would hiss at Krasutskaya: "If I say so, you can go on living, but I only have to say the word and the *Black Maria* will come for you." And it was only in 1956 that Krasutskaya decided to write a complaint to the prosecutor. And Stolberg then shut up. But they continued to live together in the same apartment.

After the arrest of Nikolai Yakovlevich Semyonov in 1950 in the city of Lyubim, his wife, that very winter, kicked out his mother, Mariya Ilinichna Semyonova, who had been living with them: "Get out of here, you old witch! Your son is an enemy of the people!" (Six years later, when her husband returned from camp, she and her grown-up daughter, Nadya, drove him out into the street at night in his underpants. Nadya was so eager to do this because she needed the space for *her own* husband. And when she threw his trousers in her father's face, she shouted at him: "Get out of here, you old rat!")[6] When Semyonov's mother was kicked out of that apartment, she went to her childless daughter Anna in Yaroslavl. Soon the mother got on her daughter's and her son-in-law's nerves. And her son-in-law, Vasily Fyodorovich Metyolkin, a fireman, on his off-duty days, used to take his mother-in-law's face in the palms of his hands, hold it tight so she couldn't turn away from him, and amuse himself by spitting in her face till he had no spit left, trying to hit her in the eyes and mouth. And when he was really angry, he would take out his penis and shove it in the old woman's face: "Take it, suck it, and die!" His wife explained his conduct to her brother when he returned: "Well, what can I do when Vasya is drunk? . . . What can you expect from a drunk?" And then, in order to get a new apartment ("We need a bathroom because there is no place to wash our old mother and we certainly can't drive her out to a public bath"), they began to treat her tolerably well. And when—"because of her"—they had got a new apartment, they packed the rooms with chests of drawers and sideboards, and pushed her into a cranny between the wardrobe and the wall fourteen inches wide—and told her to lie there and not stick her head out. And N. Y. Semyonov himself, who was by then living with his son, took the risk, without asking his son, of bringing his mother home. The grandson came home. The grandmother sank down on her knees before him: "Vovochka, you're not going to kick me out?" And the grandson grimaced: "Oh, all right, live here until I get married." And it is quite apropos to add in regard to that same granddaughter Nadya—Nadezhda Nikolayevna Topnikova—that around this time she completed the course in the historical and philological faculty of the Yaroslavl Pedagogical Institute, entered the Party, and became an editor of the district newspaper in the city of Neya in Kostroma Province. She was a poetess as well, and in 1961, while she was still in Lyubim, she rationalized her conduct in verse:

> If you're going to fight, then really fight!
> Your father!? Give it to him in the neck!

---

6. V. I. Zhukov recounts an exactly similar story from Kovrov: his wife drove him out ("Get out, or I will have you jailed again!"), as did his stepdaughter ("Get out, jailbird!").

> Morals!! People dreamed them up!
> I don't want to hear of them!
> In my life I'll march ahead
> Solely with cold calculation!

But her Party organization began to demand that she "normalize" her relationship with her father, and she suddenly began to write to him. Overjoyed, the father replied with an all-forgiving letter, which she immediately ran to show her Party organization. And when they saw it, they put a check mark opposite her name, and that was that. And since then all he gets from her are greetings on the great May and November holidays.

Seven people were involved in this tragedy. And so there you have one little droplet of our *freedom*.

In better-brought-up families, they do not chase a relative who has suffered unjustly out onto the street in his underwear, but they are ashamed of him, and they feel burdened and imposed upon by his bitterly "distorted" world outlook.

And one could go on enumerating further. One could name in addition:

10. *Slave Psychology*. That same unfortunate Babich in his declaration to the prosecutor: "I understand that wartime placed more serious obligations and duties on the organs of government than to sort out the charges against individual persons."

And much else.

But let us admit: if under Stalin this whole scheme of things did not just come into being *on its own*—and if, instead, he himself worked it all out for us point by point—he really was a genius!

■

So there in that stinking damp world in which only executioners and the most blatant of betrayers flourished, where those who remained honest became drunkards, since they had no strength of will for anything else, in which the bodies of young people were bronzed by the sun while their souls putrefied inside, in which every night the gray-green hand reached out and collared someone in order to pop him into a box—in that world millions of women wandered about lost and blinded, whose husbands, sons, or fathers had been torn from them and dispatched to the Archipelago. They were the most scared of all. They feared shiny nameplates, office doors, telephone rings, knocks on the door, the postman, the milkwoman, and the plumber. And everyone in whose path they stood drove them from their apartments, from their work, and from the city.

Sometimes they trustingly based their hopes on the belief that a sentence "without the right of correspondence" was to be understood as meaning just that, and that when ten years had passed, *he* would write.[7] They stood in line outside prisons. They went distances of fifty miles and more to places where, they had heard, food parcels were accepted for mailing. Sometimes they themselves died before the death of their relative in prison. Sometimes they learned the date of death only from the notation on a food parcel that had been returned, which read: "Addressee died in hospital." Sometimes, as in the case of Olga Chavchavadze, who got to Siberia, carrying to her husband's grave a handful of the soil of his native land, they arrived on such a mission only to find that no one could tell them which mound he lay under together with three other corpses. Sometimes, as in the case of Zelma Zhugur, they kept on writing letters to be delivered by hand to some Voroshilov or other, forgetting that Voroshilov's conscience had died long before he died himself.[8]

And these women had children who grew up, and for each one there came a time of extreme need when they absolutely had to have their father back, before it was too late, but he never came.

A little folded triangle of school notebook paper with crooked handwriting. Red and blue pencils in turn, one after the other—in all probability a childish hand had put aside one pencil, rested, and then taken up a new one. Angular, inexperienced, tortuously written letters with breathing spaces between them and sometimes even within words:

Hello Papa I forgot how to write soon in School I will go through the first winter come quickly because it's bad we have no Papa mama

7. Sometimes there really were camps without the right of correspondence; not only the atomic factories of the period from 1945 to 1949, but also, for example, Camp 29 of Karlag allowed no correspondence at all for a year and a half.

8. He did not even have the courage to shield his closest adjutant, Langovoi, from arrest and torture.

says you are away on work or sick and what are you waiting for run away from that hospital here Olyeshka ran away from hospital just in his shirt mama will sew you new pants and I will give you my belt all the same the boys are all afraid of me, and Olyeshenka is the only one I never beat up he also tells the truth he is also poor and I once lay in fever and wanted to die along with mother and she did not want to and I did not want to, oh, my hand is numb from write thats enough I kiss you lots of times

Igoryok 6 and one half years

I already know how to write on envelopes and before mother comes from work I will drop the letter in the mailbox.

Manolis Glezos, "in a clear and passionate speech," told Moscow writers about his comrades languishing in the prisons of Greece.

"I understand that I have made your hearts tremble by my passionate speech. But I did it intentionally. I would like to have your hearts ache for those languishing in imprisonment. . . . Raise your voice for the liberation of the Greek Patriots."[9]

And those well-worn foxes—of course, they raised their voices! After all, a couple of dozen prisoners were languishing in Greece! And maybe Manolis himself did not understand the shamelessness of his appeal, and maybe, too, in Greece they do not have the proverb: "Why grieve for others when there is sobbing at home?"

In various parts of our country we find a certain piece of sculpture: a plaster guard with a police dog which is straining forward in order to sink its teeth into someone. In Tashkent there is one right in front of the NKVD school, and in Ryazan it is like a symbol of the city, the one and only monument to be seen if you approach from the direction of Mikhailov.

And we do not even shudder in revulsion. We have become accustomed to these figures setting dogs onto people as if they were the most natural things in the world.

Setting the dogs onto us.

---

9. *Literaturnaya Gazeta*, August 27, 1963.

Chapter 4

∎

Several Individual Stories

I have fragmented the fates of all the prisoners I have previously mentioned in this book, subordinating their stories to the plan of the book—to the contours of the Archipelago. I have steered away from biographical accounts; it would have been too monotonous, it's how they write and write, shifting all the burden of inquiry off the author's shoulders onto the reader's.

But precisely because of this I consider that at this point I have the right to cite several prisoners' stories in their entirety.

1. Anna Petrovna Skripnikova

The only daughter of an ordinary worker of Maikop, Anna Skripnikova was born in 1896. As we already know from the history of the Party, under the cursed Tsarist regime all paths to an education were closed to her, and she was condemned to the half-starving life of a female slave. And all this really did happen to her—but after the Revolution. At the time she was accepted in the Maikop gymnasium.

Anna grew up to become a big girl who also had a large head. A girl who was her gymnasium friend made a drawing of her which consisted solely of circles: her head was round (from all angles), she had a round forehead and round eyes which somehow expressed eternal perplexity. The lobes of her ears rounded off as they grew into her cheeks. And her shoulders were round. And her figure was a sphere.

Anna began to think about things too soon in life. As early as the third grade she asked her teacher's permission to take

Dobrolyubov and Dostoyevsky from the gymnasium library. The teacher was indignant: "It's too soon for you!" "All right, if you don't let me read them here, I'll get them in the city library." At the age of thirteen "she emancipated herself from God," and ceased to be a believer. At the age of fifteen she pored over the Church fathers—exclusively for the purpose of furiously refuting the priest in class—to the general satisfaction of her fellow students. However, she herself adopted the steadfastness of the Russian Church schismatics as her highest model. She learned: It is better to die than to permit one's spiritual core to be broken.

No one interfered with her receiving the gold medal she deservedly won.[1] In 1917 (what a time for study!) she went to Moscow and entered Chaplygin's Advanced School for Women in the department of philosophy and psychology. As a gold medalist she was paid, till the October coup, a State Duma scholarship. This department prepared teachers of logic and psychology for the gymnasiums. Throughout 1918, earning money by giving lessons, she studied psychoanalysis. She apparently remained an atheist, but she felt with her whole soul how

> . . . immovably on the fiery roses
> The living altar of creation smokes.

She managed to pay her dues to the poetical philosophy of Giordano Bruno and of Tyutchev and even at one time considered herself an Eastern Catholic. She changed faiths greedily, perhaps more often than her dresses. (There were no dresses, and she did not pay all that much attention to them anyway.) And, in addition, at the beginning she considered herself a socialist and that the blood of revolt and civil war was inevitable. But she could not reconcile herself to terror. Democracy, but not atrocities! "Let hands be steeped in blood, but not in mud!"

At the end of 1918 she had to leave the school. (And did the school exist any longer anyway?) With great difficulty she managed to make her way to her parents, where the food situation was better. She arrived in Maikop. An Institute of People's Education for adults and for young people had already been created there. Anna became no more and no less than an acting professor of logic, philosophy, and psychology. She was popular with the students.

1. But what if a schoolgirl challenged the basis of Marxism that way today?

During this period the Whites were living out their last days in Maikop. A forty-five-year-old general tried to persuade her to flee with him. "General, call off the show! Escape before you are arrested!" In those days, at a party for teachers, among themselves, a gymnasium history teacher proposed a toast: "To the great Red Army!" Anna rejected the toast: "Not for anything!" Knowing her leftist views, her friends' eyes popped out. "Because . . . notwithstanding the eternal stars . . . there will be more and more executions," she prophesied.

She had the feeling that all the best people were perishing in this war and only the opportunists were surviving. She already had a presentiment that her great moment was approaching, but she still did not know . . . what it would be.

Several days later the Reds entered Maikop. And a little later a meeting of the city intelligentsia was assembled. The chief of the Special Section of the Fifth Army, Losev, came out on the stage and, in a menacing tone, not far from cursing, began to abuse the "rotten intelligentsia": "What? Sitting on the fence, were you? Waiting for me to invite you? Why didn't you come on your own?" Getting wilder and wilder, he pulled his revolver out of its holster and, brandishing it, screamed: "Your whole culture is rotten! We are going to destroy it and build a new one. And if any of you interfere—we will eliminate you!"[2] And after that he proposed: "Who wants to speak?"

The hall was as silent as the grave. There was not one single bit of applause, and no hand was lifted. (The hall was silent because it was frightened, but the fright was not yet rehearsed, and people did not know that it was compulsory for them to applaud.)

In all probability Losev did not think that anyone would rise to speak, but Anna stood up. "I." "You?" said he rudely. "Well, climb up here, climb up." And she walked the length of the hall and mounted the stage. A big woman, with a big face, even with rosy cheeks, this twenty-five-year-old woman was of the generous Russian type (she got only an eighth of a pound of bread, but her father had a good garden). Thick auburn braids reached to her knees, but as an active professor she could not go around with them like that and had them twisted on top of her

2. Whoever has read Krylenko's speeches in Part I, Chapter 8, already knows all about this.

head, giving herself a second head. And she replied resoundingly:

"We have heard out your ignorant speech. You summoned us here, but it was not announced that it was to bury the great culture of Russia! We came here expecting to see a culture-bearer and found a gravedigger. You would have done better simply to curse us out than to say what you did today! And so are we supposed to understand that you speak in the name of Soviet power?"

"Yes," the already taken aback Losev nonetheless affirmed proudly.

"Well, if the Soviet government is going to have such bandits as you as its representatives, it will fall apart."

Anna had finished, and the whole hall applauded ringingly. (Being all together, they were not yet afraid.) And the evening came to an end on that note. Losev found nothing else to say. People came up to Anna, pressed her hand in the thick of the crowd, and whispered: "You are done for. They are going to arrest you right away, but thank you, thank you! We are proud of you, but you . . . are done for! What have you done?"

At home the Chekists were waiting for her. "Comrade teacher! How poorly you live—a desk, two chairs, and a cot—there's nothing to search. We have never arrested someone like you before. And your father is a worker. How is it that being so poor you could go over to the side of the bourgeoisie?" The Cheka had not yet got itself organized, and they brought Anna to a room in the chancellery of the Special Branch where the White Guard Colonel Baron Bilderling was already under arrest. (Anna witnessed his interrogation and his execution, and later on she went and told his widow: "He died honorably, be proud!")

They took her for questioning to the room where Losev was living and working. When she entered, he was sitting on his stripped bed in his field britches and an unbuttoned undershirt, scratching his chest. Anna immediately demanded of the guard: "Take me out of here!" Losev growled: "All right, I'll wash up and put on those kid gloves in which people make the Revolution."

For one week she awaited her death sentence in a state of ecstasy. Skripnikova now recalls this as the brightest week of her life. If these words are to be understood in their precise meaning, we can believe them completely. That is the kind of ecstasy which descends upon the soul as a reward when you have cast aside all hopes for impossible salvation and have steadfastly given yourself over to a great deed. (Love of life destroys this ecstasy.)

She did not yet know that the city intellectuals had delivered a petition asking that she be pardoned. (At the end of the twenties this would not have been of any help. And in the beginning of the thirties no one would have been willing to sign.) Losev began to take a conciliatory line in interrogating her:

"In all the cities I have captured, I have never met anyone as mad as you. The city is in a state of siege, and all power here is in my hands, and you called me—a gravedigger of Russian culture! Well, all right, we both lost our tempers. . . . Take back 'bandit' and 'hooligan.' "

"No. I still think the same about you."

"They keep coming to me from morning to night to ask for you. In the name of the honeymoon of Soviet power I am going to have to let you out. . . ."

They let her out. Not because they considered her speech harmless, but because she was a worker's daughter. They would not have forgiven a doctor's daughter that.[3]

That is how Skripnikova began her journey through prisons.

In 1922 she was held in the Krasnodar Cheka, confined there for eight months "for acquaintance with a suspicious individual." There was epidemic typhus and great congestion in that prison. They gave a bread ration amounting to somewhat less than two ounces per day, made from additives too. In her presence a child died in the arms of the woman sitting next to her. And Anna took an oath never to have a child under such socialism as this, never to let herself be tempted by motherhood.

She kept this oath. She lived out her life without a family, and her fate, her unwillingness to compromise, provided her more than once with the chance to return to prison.

Then began what was supposed to be a peaceful life. In 1923 Skripnikova went to enter the Institute of Psychology at Moscow State University. In filling out the security questionnaire, she wrote: "Not a Marxist." Out of kindness of heart her interviewers advised her: "Are you crazy? Who writes answers like that? State that you're a Marxist, and think whatever you please." "But I have no wish to deceive the Soviet government. I have simply never read Marx. . . ." "Well, all the more so in that case."

3. In 1920 Losev himself was shot for banditry and violence in the Crimea.

"No. When I get around to studying Marxism and *if* I accept it . . ." And for the time being she took a job teaching in a school for defectives.

In 1925 the husband of her close friend, an SR, fled to escape arrest. In order to force him to return, the GPU seized as hostages (in the midst of the NEP—hostages?) his wife and her friend, that is, Anna. She was just exactly the same round-faced, big-built woman with tresses that reached down to her knees when she entered her cell in the Lubyanka. (This is where the interrogator assured her: "All those flourishes of the Russian intelligentsia are out of date! *Just look after yourself.*") This time she was imprisoned about a month.

In 1927, for participating in a musical society of teachers and workers, doomed to be destroyed as a possible nest of freethinking, Anna was arrested for what was by then the *fourth* time. She got five years and served them out on Solovki and the Belomor Canal.

From 1932 on they did not touch her again for a long time, yes, and evidently she lived more carefully. Beginning with 1948, however, they began to fire her from her jobs. In 1952 the Institute of Psychology returned to her her already accepted dissertation ("The Psychological Conception of Dobrolyubov") on the grounds of her having received in 1927 a sentence based on Article 58! In this difficult time (she was already in her fourth year of unemployment) a hand reached out to help her from . . . State Security! Lisov, a representative of the central State Security apparatus (well, now, here is Losev again! Was he alive? How little had changed even in the letters! Just that he did not stick up his head openly, like an elk—"los"—but sniffed and darted like a fox—"lisa"), who had arrived in Vladikavkaz, proposed that she *collaborate*, in return for which work would be arranged for her and she would be allowed to defend her dissertation. Proudly she turned him down. Then they nimbly cooked up a charge that eleven years earlier (!), in 1941, she had said:

- that we had been poorly prepared for the war (and had we been well prepared?);
- that the German armies were deployed along our borders, and that we were sending them grain (and were we not?).

And on this occasion she got ten years and landed in the Special Camps, first Dubrovlag in Mordvinia, then Kamyshlag at Suslovo Station in Kemerovo Province.

Sensing that impenetrable wall in front of her, she thought up the idea of writing petitions not just anywhere, but . . . to the United Nations! During Stalin's lifetime she sent off three of them. This was not just some sort of trick—not at all! She actually, genuinely eased her eternally bubbling soul by speaking in her mind's eye with the UN. She actually, during these decades of cannibalism, had seen no other light in the world. In these petitions she lashed out at the savage tyranny in the Soviet Union and asked the UN to intervene with the Soviet government and request it either to reinvestigate her case or else to have her executed, since she could no longer go on living under this terror. She would address the envelopes "personally" to one or another of the Soviet leaders, and inside lay the request that it be sent on to the UN.

In Dubrovlag she was summoned by a clique of the infuriated bosses: "How dare you write to the UN?"

Skripnikova stood there, as always, erect, large, majestic: "Neither in the Criminal Code nor in the Code of Criminal Procedure nor in the Constitution itself is it forbidden. And you ought not to have opened envelopes addressed personally to members of the government!"

In 1956 an "unloading" commission of the Supreme Soviet was functioning in their camp. The only task of this commission was to free as many zeks as possible as quickly as possible. There was a certain modest procedure, which consisted in having the zek say several apologetic words and stand there a bit with drooping head. But no, Anna Skripnikova was not that kind! Her own personal release was nothing in comparison with common justice! How could she accept forgiveness if she was innocent? And she declared to the commission:

"Don't be so overjoyed! All accessories to Stalin's terror are going to have to answer to the people sooner or later. I do not know whom you were personally under Stalin, Citizen Colonel, but if you were an accessory to his terror, then you, too, are going to be sitting on the defendant's bench."

The members of the commission gulped in fury, shouted that

she was insulting the Supreme Soviet in their persons, that this would cost her plenty, and that she would just go on serving time from one toll of the gong to the next.

And in actual fact, because of her vain faith in justice, she had to serve three extra years.

From Kamyshlag she sometimes continued to write to the UN. (In seven years, up to 1959, she wrote a total of eighty petitions to various institutions.) In 1958, because of these letters, she was sent for one year to the Vladimir Political Prison. And there they had a rule: once in every ten days they would accept a petition directed to any authority. During a half-year she sent eighteen declarations from there to different institutions—including twelve to the UN.

And she got her way in the end. She got . . . not execution but a re-examination of her case—the cases of 1927 and of 1952. She said to the interrogator: "Well, what do you want? A petition to the UN is the only means of knocking a hole in the wall of Soviet bureaucracy and compelling the deaf Themis at least to hear something."

The interrogator jumped up and beat his breast: "All the accessories to the 'Stalinist terror'—as you for some reason [!] call the personality cult—will answer to the people? And what am *I* to answer for? What other policy could I execute at that time? Yes, I believed Stalin without any doubts and I did not know anything."

But Skripnikova kept hitting away at him: "No, no, you can't get away with that! One has to bear the responsibility for every crime! Who is supposed to answer for the deaths of millions of innocents? For the flower of the nation and the flower of the Party? The dead Stalin? The executed Beria? While you pursue your political career?"

(Her own blood pressure at this moment was rising to the danger point, she shut her eyes, and everything whirled and flamed.)

And they would still have detained her, but in 1959 a case of this sort was a real curiosity.

And in the years that followed—and she is alive right now —her life has been filled with solicitations on behalf of those still imprisoned or in exile, and those whose sentences still remain on the records—those whom she met in camps in recent years. She got several of them released. She got others rehabilitated. She has also undertaken the defense of those who live in her own city. The city authorities are afraid of her pen and the envelopes she sends off to Moscow, and in some degree they make concessions to her.

And if everyone were even one-quarter as implacable as Anna Skripnikova—the history of Russia would be different.

2. Stepan Vasilyevich Loshchilin

He was born in 1908 in the Volga region, the son of a worker at the paper factory. In 1921, during the famine, he was orphaned. He grew up to be a lad who was not very bold, and nevertheless at the age of seventeen he was already a member of the Komsomol, and at the age of eighteen he entered a school for peasant youth, and completed it at the age of twenty-one. At this time they were sent out to help in compulsory exactions of breadgrains, and in 1930 in his own native village he participated in the liquidation of the kulaks. He did not remain behind, however, to build the collective farm there, but "got a reference" from the village soviet and with it went off to Moscow. He had difficulty in finding a job . . . as a manual laborer at a construction project. (This was a period of unemployment, and people were swarming into Moscow especially at this time.) A year later he was called up into the army, and there he was accepted as a candidate member and later as a full member of the Party. At the end of 1932 he was demobilized and returned to Moscow. However, he did not wish to be a manual laborer and he wanted to acquire a skill, so he asked the district committee of the Party to assign him as an apprentice at a factory. But evidently he was a pretty incompetent sort of Communist because they turned down even this request, and instead offered him an assignment to the police.

And at this point—he refused. Had he taken a different turn, this biography wouldn't have been written. But this he refused.

As a young fellow he was ashamed to admit to the girls that he was only a manual laborer, that he had no profession. But there was nowhere he could get that profession! And he went to work at the "Kalibr" factory, once more as a manual laborer. At a Party meeting there he naïvely spoke out in defense of a worker whom the Party bureau had evidently marked down ahead of time for purging. They purged that particular worker just as they had planned, and they began to move in on Loshchilin. The Party dues he had collected from others were stolen from his barracks—and he was unable to make up the missing ninety-three rubles out of his own wages. At that point they expelled him from the Party and threatened to prosecute him. (Does the loss of Party dues really come under the terms of the Criminal Code?) Already in a state of depression, Loshchilin did not appear at work one day. He was fired for absenteeism. With a reference like that he could not get work anywhere for a long, long time. An interrogator kept after him for a while and then left him alone. He kept expecting a trial—but there was none. And suddenly a verdict in absentia was handed down against him: six months of forced labor with a fine of 25 percent of his pay, to be served through the municipal Bureau of Corrective Labor (the BITR).

In September, 1937, Loshchilin went to the buffet at the Kiev Station. (What do we know of our lives? What if he had just gone hungry for another fifteen minutes and gone to a buffet in a different place? . . .) Perhaps he had some sort of lost or seeking expression on his face? He himself does not know. A young woman in the uniform of the NKVD came toward him. (Is that the kind of thing you ought to be doing, woman?) She asked him: "What are you looking for? Where are you going?" "To the buffet." She pointed to a door: "Go on in there." Loshchilin, of course, obeyed her. (She should have spoken like that to an Englishman!) This was the office of the Special Branch. An official sat behind the desk. The woman said: "Detained during tour of the station." And she went out, and never in his life did Loshchilin see her again. (And we, too, will never learn anything about her! . . .) The official, without offering him a seat, began to question him. He took all his documents away from him and sent him to a room for detained persons. There were two men there already, and, as Loshchilin himself relates, "this time without permission [!] I sat down next to them on an unoccupied chair." All three kept silent for a long time. Policemen came and led them off to Cells for Preliminary Detention. A policeman ordered them to turn over their money to him, because, allegedly, in the cell "it would be taken from them anyway." (What a remarkable identity there is between the police and the thieves!) Loshchilin lied, saying that he had no money. They began to search him, and they took away his money once and for all. And gave him back his makhorka. With two packets of makhorka he entered his first cell, and put the makhorka on the table. No one else, of course, had anything to smoke.

They took him just once from the Cell for Preliminary Detention to the interrogator, who asked him whether he was a thief. (And what a rescue that would have been for him! He should have said then and there that, yes, he was a thief but never caught. And the worst that would have happened to him would have been to be sent out of Moscow.) But Loshchilin replied proudly: "I live by my own labor." And the interrogator directed no other charges at him, and the interrogation came to an end with that, and there was no trial!

He was imprisoned in the Cell for Preliminary Detention for ten days, and then at night they took them all to the Moscow Criminal Investigation Department on Petrovka Street. Here things were crowded and stifling, and it was impossible to get through. The thieves were the rulers here. They took things away from the prisoners and lost them at cards. Here for the first time Loshchilin was astonished by "their strange boldness, their insistence on some kind of incomprehensible superiority." One night the authorities began to haul them all off to the transit prison on Sretenka (that was where it was before Krasnaya Presnya). And there it was even more crowded. People sat on the floor and took turns on the bunks. To those who were only half-clothed—left in this state by the thieves—the police issued clothing—bast sandals and old police uniforms.

Among those sent there with Loshchilin were many others who also *had never been formally charged with anything*, never called to court or tried—but they were transported just like those who had been sentenced. They took them to Perebory, where they filled out an invoice for those who had arrived, and it was only when he got there that Loshchilin found his section: SVE—Socially Harmful Element, sentence four years. (To this very day he is in a state of dismay: After all, my father was a worker, and I myself am a worker, and why then was I an SVE? *It would have been a different matter* if I had been a trader. . . .)

Volgolag. Logging. A ten-hour workday and no days off except the November and May holidays. (And this was *three* whole years before the war!) And once Loshchilin broke his leg and had an operation and spent four months in the hospital and three on crutches. And then he was again sent to logging. And so it was that he served out his four-year term. The war began, but nonetheless he was not considered a 58, and in the autumn of 1941 he was released. Just before being released Loshchilin had his pea jacket stolen, but it was registered on his equipment card. And how he begged the trusties to write off that cursed pea jacket—but no! They refused to take pity on him! They took the cost of the pea jacket out of his "release fund"—double the cost, in fact! And the government inventory prices for those torn cotton-padded treasures were very dear. And so on a cold autumn day they let him out of the camp gates in a cotton camp shirt, with scarcely any money, or any bread or even a herring for the road. The gatehouse guards searched him at the exit and wished him good speed.

And so he was plundered on the day of his release, just as he had been on the day of his arrest.

When the documents were being written up in the office of the chief of the Classification and Records Section, Loshchilin managed to read upside down what was written in his *file*. What was written was: "Detained during tour of station . . ."

He arrived in the city of Sursk, his native area. Because he was ill the district military conscription commissariat exempted him from military service. And that, too, turned out to be bad. In the autumn of 1942, under Order No. 336 of the People's Commissariat of Defense, the district military commissariat conscripted all men of call-up age who could perform physical labor. Loshchilin landed in the *labor detachment* of the Apartment Maintenance Section of the Ulyanovsk garrison. What kind of detachment this was and what the attitude toward it was can be judged from the fact that it contained many young men from the West Ukraine, whom they had managed to conscript before the war, but who had not been sent to the front because they were unreliable. And so Loshchilin landed in another variety of the Archipelago again, a militarized unguarded camp geared to accomplish the same kind of annihilation as other camps—through exhausting the inmates' last strength.

A ten-hour workday. In the barracks two-story bunks without any bedding. (When they went out to work, the barracks was deserted.) They worked and went around in whatever of their own they had when they were taken from their homes and in their own underwear, without baths and without a change. They were paid a reduced wage, from which they were charged for bread (twenty-one ounces a day) and for their other food (which was bad and consisted of a first and second course served them twice a day). And they were even charged for the Chuvash bast sandals which they were issued.

Among the detachment members one was designated the commandant and another the chief of the detachment. But they had no rights. The whole show was bossed by M. Zheltov, the chief of the repair and construction office. He was like a prince who did exactly whatever he liked. When he gave orders, some of the detachment members were deprived of bread and lunch for one or two days at a time. ("Where was there a law like that?" Loshchilin asked. "Even in camp it wasn't like that.") And at the same time front-line soldiers recovering from wounds and still weak entered the detachment. There was a woman doctor attached to the detachment. She had the right to release prisoners from work because of illness, but Zheltov forbade her to. And being afraid of him, she wept, and she did not hide it from the detachment members. (That is *freedom!* That is our freedom, for you!) Everyone got infected with lice, and the bunks were swarming with bedbugs.

But then this was no camp! They could complain! And they did complain. They wrote to the provincial newspaper and to the provincial Party committee. And there was no answer from anywhere. The only response came from the municipal medical department, which carried out a thorough disinfection, gave everyone a good bath, and gave everyone a set of underwear and some bedding—all to be charged against their wages (!).

In the winter of 1944–1945, at the beginning of his third year in the detachment, Loshchilin's own footwear became simply unusable and he did not go to work. He was then and there tried for absenteeism—and given three months of corrective-labor work in that very same detachment with a fine of 25 percent deducted from his wages.

In the spring damp Loshchilin could no longer walk about in

bast sandals, and once again did not go to work. Once again he was sentenced—which, if one counts the other times he had been sentenced in absentia, made the fourth time in his life! This time he was sentenced in the so-called Red Corner of the barracks, and the verdict was three months of imprisonment.

But . . . they did not imprison him! Because it was unprofitable for the state to undertake the maintenance of Loshchilin! Because there was no form of imprisonment which could be worse than this labor detachment.

This was in March, 1945. And nothing worse would have happened, had it not been for the fact that earlier he had written a complaint to the Apartment Maintenance Section of the garrison to the effect that Zheltov had promised to issue secondhand footwear to all of them but did not do so. (And the reason that he alone wrote such a complaint was that any *collective* complaint was strictly forbidden. For any such collective complaint, since it was contrary to the spirit of socialism, they could have given sentences under 58.)

So they summoned Loshchilin to the Personnel Section: "Turn in your work clothes!" And the only thing that that mute slogger had ever gotten for his three years of labor—*his work apron*—Loshchilin took off and put quietly on the floor! And right there stood the precinct policeman who had been summoned by the Apartment Maintenance Section. He took Loshchilin off to the police station and, in the evening, to the prison, but the duty officer at the prison found something not in order in his documents and refused to accept him.

And the policeman then took Loshchilin back to the police station. And the road went past their detachment's barracks. And the policeman said: "Oh, go on, go there and rest; you aren't going to run off anywhere anyway. Wait for me one of these days."

April, 1945, came to an end. The legendary divisions had already rolled to the Elbe and surrounded Berlin. Every day the nation fired off salutes, flooding the heavens with red, green, and gold flares. On April 24 Loshchilin was imprisoned in the Ulyanovsk Provincial Prison. Its cells were just as overcrowded as they had been in 1937. Seventeen and a half ounces of bread, soup made from fodder turnips, or if from potatoes from small potatoes, unpeeled and poorly washed. May 9, Victory Day, he spent in his cell. (For several days they did not even know about the end of the war.) Just as Loshchilin had greeted the war behind bars, that is how he also bade it farewell.

After Victory Day they sent off to a work colony the *decree prisoners*—in other words, absentees, those tardy at work, and sometimes also those who had been caught at petty thievery at work. What they did there was earth-moving work, construction, and unloading barges. They fed them badly. The camp was a new one. There was no doctor in it and not even a nurse. Loshchilin got chilled and developed an inflammation of the sciatic nerve—and he was driven out to work anyway. He was on his last legs, and his legs had swelled up, and he was in a constant fever. They kept on driving him out to work all the same.

On July 7, 1945, the famous Stalinist amnesty struck. But Loshchilin did not have to last out until he was released under its terms—for on July 24 his own three-month term came to an end, and they let him out then and there.

"All the same," says Loshchilin, "in my soul I am a Bolshevik. When I die, consider me a Communist."

Maybe he's joking, but then again maybe he's not.

■

I do not have here the materials to complete this chapter the way I would like—to demonstrate the striking intersection of Russian lives and the laws of the Archipelago. And I have no hope that I will be granted another secure and unhurried period in which to carry out one more editing of this book, and at that time to include the missing life stories.

I think it would be very appropriate here to include a sketch on the life, prison and camp persecutions, and death of Father Pavel A. Florensky, perhaps one of the most remarkable men devoured by the Archipelago of all time. Well-informed people say of him that he was a scholar rare for the twentieth century, who had attained a professional mastery of a multitude of knowledge. He was educated as a mathematician, and in his youth he had experienced a deep religious conversion and become a priest. The book he had written in his youth, *The Pillar and the Affirmation of the Truth*, is only today coming into its own. He had to his credit many essays in mathematics (topological theorems, proved much later in the West), in art history (on Russian icons, on religious drama), and on philosophical and religious subjects. (His archive has been in the main preserved and has not yet been published. I have not had access to it.) After the Revolution he was a professor at the Electrical Engineering Institute (where he delivered his lectures in his priest's robes). In 1927 he expressed ideas anticipating those of Wiener. In 1932 he published in the magazine *Socialist Reconstruction and Science* an essay on machines for the solution of problems which were close in spirit to cybernetics. Soon after that he was arrested. His prison career is known to me only at several separate points, which I list with trepidation: exile in Siberia (in exile he wrote works and published them under a pseudonym in the works of the Siberian expedition of the Academy of Sciences), Solovki, and after Solovki was shut down the Far North, and according to some sources the Kolyma. In the Kolyma he studied flora and minerals (in addition to his work with a pick). Neither the place nor the date of his death in camp is known. But according to some rumors he was shot during wartime.

I certainly intended to cite here also the life of Valentin I. Komov from the Yefremov District, with whom I was imprisoned in the years 1950 to 1952 in Ekibastuz, but I simply do not recall enough about him, and I ought to have remembered more details. In 1929, when he was a seventeen-year-old boy, he killed the chairman of the local village soviet and fled. After that the only way he could exist and hide was as a thief. He was imprisoned several times, always as a thief. In 1941 he was released. The Germans carried him off to Germany. Did he collaborate with them? No, he ran away twice and as a result landed in Buchenwald. He was liberated from there by the Allies. Did he stay in the West? No, under his authentic family name ("The Motherland has forgiven, the Motherland calls you!") he returned to his own village, where he married and worked in the collective farm. In 1946 he was imprisoned under 58 for his 1929 crime. He was released in 1955. If this biography were set forth in detail, it would explain much to us about the Russian lives of those decades. In addition, Komov was a typical camp brigadier—a "son of Gulag." (And even in the hard-labor camp he was not afraid to shout at the chief at the general roll call, "Why do we have a Fascist system in our camp?")

Finally, it would have been appropriate to include in this

chapter the biography of some socialist who was exceptional—in personal qualities, in the steadfastness of his views—in order to show his peregrinations through the moves of the Big Solitaire over a period of many years.

And perhaps the biography of some inveterate MVD man—a Garanin, or a Zavenyagin, or else someone not so well known —would have been highly suitable here.

But evidently I am not fated to do all that. Breaking off this book at the beginning of 1967,[4] I do not count on having a chance to return to the theme of the Archipelago.

Anyway, it's enough. I have been with it . . . twenty years.

END OF PART IV

---

4. No, completing it a year later.

Translator's Notes

Page

ing peasants in rural areas. Hence the name Central Penal Department carried to Soviet ears an implication of terror.

18 **SLON:** This acronym for the Northern Special Purpose Camps is also the Russian word for elephant.

19 **"general work":** "General-assignment work." In Russian "obshchye raboty"—general work or common labor. The general work was whatever primary work the camp was established to perform—logging, construction, mining, heavy labor of any and all sorts.

23 **convoy:** The term in Russian is "konvoi"—escort guard.

25 **kremlin:** The Russian term "kreml" (kremlin) refers to any fortified urban center or citadel—not just the one in Moscow.

25 **capercaillies:** Also known as "cock of the wood"—a large European true grouse, the male of which is approximately the size of a wild turkey.

27 **"pyatina":** A "pyatina" was one of the five administrative territories into which the lands of Novgorod were divided at the end of the fifteenth century.

34 **passing marks:** The word here in Russian is "zachyoty." And there is a play on this term: on the one hand it means "passing marks" in an exam or a course in school, and on the other hand in Soviet prison life it means "time off sentence" given for good work.

35 **Metropole Restaurant:** Refers to the Metropole Hotel Restaurant in the center of Moscow near the Bolshoi Theatre.

43 **work assigner:** Work assignment supervisor. The term in Russian is "naryadchik."

44 **Berry-Yagoda:** In Russian the word "yagoda" means "berry."

59 **S. A. Malsagoff:** An Island Hell: A Soviet Prison in the Far North, translated by F. H. Lyon, London, Philpot, 1926, 233 pp.

81 **I. L. Averbakh:** In the Paris edition in Russian (p. 78) the initials of the second editor are given as A. L. Averbakh. In the actual book under reference the initials on the title page are given as I. L. Averbakh.

84 **Matvei Berman:** It was said by employees of the American Embassy in Moscow that the dacha or country house at Tarasovka, north of Moscow, rented by the Soviet government to the American Ambassador during World War II and the postwar period, had been built by Berman as his personal country residence.

145 **Below Shmidtikha:** This is no doubt a reference to Academician Otto Shmidt, famous Soviet polar explorer and scientist, and Chief of the Northern Sea Route from 1932 to 1939.

149 **"barshchina":** "Barshchina" was the Russian equivalent of corvée. It was the assessment paid the Russian serf owner by his serfs in the form of free labor on his lands, often amounting to three days out of a week. Not all Russians were under the "barshchina" system; about as many paid their assessment in the form of "obrok." See below.

153 **"obrok" system:** Russian serfs under the "obrok" system paid their assessment in the form of "obrok"—money and sometimes produce as well. Frequently the serfs had to work as hired laborers in factories or elsewhere, often at some distance from their native villages, in order to earn the money.

Page

154 **Arakcheyev:** Count Aleksei Arakcheyev, chief minister under Alexander I. His name became a synonym for cruel discipline, particularly because of his close association with the establishment of the military settlements, the first of which were created in 1810. Arakcheyev became Chief of Military Settlements in 1817 and remained in this post until his death in 1834. The military settlements lasted until 1857, when they were abolished. They were an effort to settle army units on the land under strict military discipline and regulation of all details of village and family life.

160 **"Rabsila":** This was intended to be an abbreviation for "labor force" (rabochaya sila), but it could also be envisioned as an abbreviation for "slave force" (rabskaya sila).

168 **Novy Iyerusalim:** Presumably at Istra, about thirty miles northwest of Moscow, where the Novo-Iyerusalim (New Jerusalem) Monastery is located.

186 **your leniency . . .:** These are verses by Pasternak from his poem "Lieutenant Shmidt." They were quoted previously in *The Gulag Archipelago*, Vol. I, Part II, Ch. 4. (Paris edition in Russian, p. 605; American edition in English, p. 614.)

214 **old works:** The reference is presumably to the seizure of manuscripts of *The First Circle* and some other of Solzhenitsyn's works, described in some detail in Zhores Medvedev, *Ten Years after Ivan Denisovich*, New York, Knopf, 1973, Chs. 6 and 7.

220 **a book:** The reference is to the novel by Ilf and Petrov, *The Golden Calf*, translated by John H. Richardson, New York, Random House, 1962.

221 **magara:** A millet-like plant; the seeds were made into a cereal for the zeks, who regarded it as one of the more repulsive of the many repulsive things they were given to eat.

224 **zechka:** "Zechka" is "zek" with a feminine suffix—and the term has a humorous twist.

232 **In my play:** The play referred to is that translated into English under the title *The Love Girl and the Innocent* by Nicholas Bethell and David Burg, New York, Farrar, Straus & Giroux, 1970.

251 **trusty:** The Russian term is "pridurok" (pl.: "pridurki"). For lack of a better word in English this has been translated throughout as "trusty." And this is the closest one can come. The Russian term includes all prisoners who got themselves what were by camp standards soft jobs, and thus did not have to go out and slog away at the general work. The Russian term also has a markedly contemptuous shade, and is closely related etymologically to a whole series of terms referring to half-wits and those who pretend to be half-wits. For instance, "pridurkovaty" means silly, daft, imbecile, etc.

256 **wage laborers:** The translation used here is Engels' revision of Samuel Moore's translation, bearing the date of 1888.

257 **(Memoirs of Survival):** In book form: Boris A. Dyakov, *Povest o Perezhitom*, Moscow, Sovietskaya Russiya Publishing House, 1966, 263 pp.

260 **the magic chain:** The full text: "the magic chain of Koshchei." Koshchei the Deathless is an evil sorcerer in Russian fairy tales. And the reference here is presumably to the famous fairy tale "Marya

Page

Moryevna," in which Koshchei broke the twelve chains binding him after he had been given three pails of water to drink successively by the story's hero, Prince Ivan.

260 **sharashka:** A "sharashka" was a special prison in which imprisoned scientists and technicians were put to work on important secret scientific assignments. Solzhenitsyn has described the Marfino "sharashka" in his novel *The First Circle*. (Also called a "sharaga.")

262 **Young Guard:** The reference is to the story told in A. Fadeyev, *The Young Guard, a Novel*, Moscow, Foreign Languages Publishing House, no date. The original version of this famous war story of young people who carried on underground resistance activities in the German rear in Krasnodon had to be rewritten by the author in the postwar period at the demand of the Party, to stress the role of the Komsomol and the Communist Party in directing underground resistance.

276 **Kleinmikhel:** The reference is to Pyotr Andreyevich Kleinmikhel, Minister for Ways of Communication, under Tsar Nicholas I, in charge of building the railway from St. Petersburg to Moscow, Russia's first major railway. Kleinmikhel had a reputation for ruthlessness and overexpenditure of government funds.

277 **this very same peasant who had fed the two generals:** The reference is to the short story by M. Y. Saltykov-Shchedrin, "A Story About How One Peasant Fed Two Generals."

277 **Dr. Pravdin:** "Pravda" in Russian means "truth."

287 **Sparrow Hills:** Rechristened the "Lenin Hills."

289 **by Stendhal:** The book referred to is not by Stendhal but about him, by the Russian literary scholar A. K. Vinogradov.

307 **If they're not raking you in . . .:** This is a paraphrase of the original: "If they're not fucking you . . ."

310 **Easter night:** Presumably this refers to much the same scene as that described in Solzhenitsyn's story "The Easter Procession."

317 **Trutnev(!):** The exclamation point underscores the fact that the name is derived from "truten," meaning "drone."

332 **(St. Luke, 11:50.):** The Russian edition has St. Luke, 11:51.

333 **(Matthew, 26:52):** The Russian edition has Matthew 25:52.

333 **Alalykin and Spiridonov—why did they now sign . . .:** This line is missing from the Russian edition.

334 **his grandfather:** Yevtushenko tells how his grandfather, who joined the Red Army, rose to the rank of Deputy Commander of Artillery of the Russian Republic, and was purged in 1938. (Yevgeny Yevtushenko, *A Precocious Autobiography*, New York, Dutton, 1963, pp. 15–16.)

338 **My friend Panin:** Panin is the real name of the individual who is described in *The First Circle* under the fictitious name Sologdin.

353 **seksoty:** "Secret collaborator" is "*sek*retny *sot*rudnik"—hence seksot.

357 **"Banderists":** Followers of the Ukrainian national leader Bandera.

364 **sharply:** In the Russian edition this is misprinted as "rarely" ("redko" instead of "rezko").

367 **The Twentieth Congress:** The Twentieth Congress of the Communist Party of the Soviet Union in February, 1956, at which Nikita Khrushchev launched his attack on Stalin's "personality cult."

Page

370 **To the New Shore:** Vilis T. Latsis, *K Novomu Beregu*, published in 1951. Latsis was Prime Minister of Soviet Latvia.

372 **"residents":** The term "resident" is used in Russian to indicate an important intelligence agent stationed in a nondiplomatic capacity on a long-term assignment in a foreign capital or country.

378 **"obstacle" detachments:** "Obstacle" detachments were used during the war to prevent retreats.

397 **My Testimony:** Anatoly Marchenko, *My Testimony*, translated by Michael Scammell, New York, Dutton, 1969.

427 **"besprizorniki":** In the wake of the war, Revolution, Civil War, and famine all Russia was inundated with a swarm of children who had no homes or parents. They descended on Soviet cities and lived as best they could, by begging and stealing and cadging. They were christened the "besprizorniki" (sing.: "besprizornik")—the homeless children.

428 **The Road to Life:** This Soviet motion picture attracted much attention in the West. It was based on the account of Anton S. Makarenko, *Pedagogicheskaya Poema*, and the film, one of the first Soviet sound films, was directed by N. Ekk and produced by Mezhrabpomfilm in 1931.

428 **ask for it:** See above note to page 307.

431 **(druzhina):** These groups of volunteer deputy policemen were created by decree in 1959, and their authority was strengthened by a subsequent decree of 1969. They operate "under the leadership and subject to the verification of Party organs."

441 **one and all:** A Russian slang word for pickpocket—"shirmach"— which comes from the thieves' language. In the Russian edition this is explained in a footnote, which has been omitted here as superfluous.

476 **On November 30, 1934:** On December 1, 1934, Kirov was assassinated in Leningrad, and Stalin set in motion the machinery of mass terror.

495 **Rastopchin's posted proclamations!:** Count Fyodor Rastopchin was left behind as the governor of Moscow when Tsar Alexander I abandoned the city to Napoleon in 1812.

495 **L. Gumilyev:** The son of the poetess Anna Akhmatova and the executed poet Nikolai Gumilyev.

496 **Komi:** The Komis are a small nationality in the northeast of European Russia.

505 **". . . suckers out!":** The author's point here is that these expressions are incomprehensible to the non-native of the Archipelago, and the translator has tried to preserve this element of outlandishness in the renderings while giving at least something of the real content. For example, the first of the expressions given here, translated as "Skin the rag!," means literally "Take off your jacket!" (i.e., "so that I, a thief, can steal it!").

507 **(cold):** At this point there is a sentence in the Russian text which has been left untranslated because it is meaningless to anyone unfamiliar with the Russian alphabet: "We write this word with the letter 'e' rather than the letter 'ye' in order to indicate the sound of a hard 'z.'"

Page
509 **"if they're not [beat]ing you . . ."**: See above note to page 307.

516 **"struggle for life"**: This phrase is in English in the Russian text.

517 **the Ostankino Museum:** The Ostankino Museum of Serf Arts, housed in what was once one of the estates of the noble Sheremetev family in Moscow.

528 **in Russian:** In Russian the phrase is "Prokuror—topor!"

551 **Lieutenant Colonel Tsukanov:** This is presumably the same individual who appears in *The First Circle* under the name Lieutenant Colonel Terentiev.

574 **Khishchuk and Karashchuk:** The name Khishchuk is derived from a Russian word meaning predatory, rapacious, greedy. The name Karashchuk has a very menacing sound to Russian ears, deriving from the juxtaposition of the root of "punish" and the root of "pike"—a vicious fish. Both names are presumably Ukrainian in origin.

587 **Master:** The Russian word here is "Khozyain," with a capital "K." During Stalin's times he was frequently referred to as the "Khozyain." The word means variously owner, proprietor, master, boss, etc. It carries with it a connotation not only of power, but also of ownership.

595 **I Corinthians, 15:51:** The translation given here is that of the King James version of the Bible. A literal translation of the Russian text given by the author indicates a difference between the Russian and English versions of this famous verse: "I tell you a truth: we shall not all die, but we shall all be changed."

608 **The First Glove:** *Pervaya Perchatka*, released by Mosfilm, 1946. Producer: A. Frolov; Director: B. Brozhkovsky.

634 **Nadezhda Mandelstam:** The author of *Hope Against Hope*, and widow of the purged poet Osip Mandelstam.

641 **Sofya Petrovna:** Published abroad in Russian: Lidiya Chukovskaya, *Opustely Dom*, Paris, Librairie des Cinq Continents, 1965; in English: Lydia Chukovskaya, *The Deserted House*. Translated by Aline B. Werth, New York, E. P. Dutton, 1967.

641 **Rozhansky:** See *The Gulag Archipelago*, Vol. I, pp. 48, 49.

Glossary

Agranov, Yakov Savlovich (?–1939). Deputy People's Commissar of Internal Affairs under Yagoda and Yezhov. Played role in preparing show trials. Shot in purges.

Aksakov, Ivan Sergeyevich (1823–1886). Essayist and poet; graduate of St. Petersburg Law School; leader of Slavophile school.

Aldan-Semyonov, Andrei Ignatyevich (1908–). Soviet writer; imprisoned in Far East camps, 1938–1953; author of memoirs.

Alksnis (Astrov), Yakov Ivanovich (1897–1938). Commander of Soviet air force after 1931; died in purges.

Alymov, Sergei Yakovlevich (1892–1948). Soviet poet; wrote popular songs on patriotic themes.

Arakcheyev, Aleksei Andreyevich (1769–1834). Adviser to Tsar Alexander I; known as a strict disciplinarian; fostered special military agricultural colonies for army men.

Aralov, Semyon Ivanovich (1880–1969). Bolshevik revolutionary; served as Soviet diplomat, 1921–1927; deputy director of State Literature Museum, 1938–1941.

Artuzov, (Frauci [?]) Artur Khristianovich (1891–1943). Secret police official, of Swiss Italian descent; head of counterintelligence.

Aseyev, Nikolai Nikolayevich (1889–1963). Futurist poet, wrote in the style of Mayakovsky in spirit of revolutionary romanticism.

Balitsky, Vsevolod Apollonovich (1892–1937). Ukrainian secret police chief, 1923–1930 and 1933–1937.

Bandera, Stepan (1909–1959). Ukrainian nationalist; led anti-Soviet forces in Ukraine after World War II; assassinated in Munich.

Bedny, Demyan (1883–1945). Soviet poet.

Belinkov, Arkady V. (1921–1970). Soviet writer; imprisoned in 1943 for his first novel; emigrated to United States.

Belinsky, Vissarion Grigoryevich (1811–1848). Literary critic and ardent liberal, champion of socially conscious literature.

Beloborodov, Aleksandr Georgiyevich (1891–1938). Bolshevik leader in the Urals; ordered execution of Tsar Nicholas and his family in 1918; expelled from Party as a Trotskyite; died in imprisonment.

Beria, Lavrenti Pavlovich (1899–1953). Georgian Bolshevik; headed secret police under Stalin after 1938; executed after his death.

Berman, Matvei (?–1938). One of the chiefs of Gulag; a Deputy Commissar of Internal Affairs, 1936–1938.

Berzin, E. P. (1888–1939). Commander of Latvian Rifles, a pro-Bolshevik military unit; secretary of Dzerzhinsky; chief of Dalstroi (Far East Camp Administration); arrested in 1937.

Biryukov, Pavel Ivanovich (1860–1931). Writer and biographer of Lev Tolstoi; preached Tolstoyan nonresistance to evil; lived mostly abroad after 1898.

Blücher, Vasily Konstantinovich (1890–1938). Commander of Far East Military District, 1929–1938; shot in purge.

Boky, Gleb Ivanovich (1879–1941). Secret police official; member of Supreme Court after 1927; arrested in 1937.

Bosh (Gotlibovna), Yevgeniya Bogdanovna (1879–1925). Bolshevik Revolutionary; held Ukrainian Party posts, 1917–1918; sided with Trotskyites in 1923; suicide.

Bruno, Giordano (1548–1600). Italian Renaissance philosopher.

Bubnov, Andrei Sergeyevich (1883–1940). Old Bolshevik, historian; Central Committee secretary, 1925–1929; chief political commissar of army, 1924–1929; Education Commissar of R.S.F.S.R., purged.

Budenny, Semyon Mikhailovich (1883–1973). Civil War hero; commander of Bolshevik cavalry; headed Southwest Front in World War II.

Bukovsky, Konstantin Ivanovich. Soviet journalist, essayist; father of the dissident Vladimir Bukovsky.

Campesino, El. Revolutionary name of Valentin y Gonzales, Spanish Civil War commander on Republican side; went to Soviet Union in 1939; spent time in camps; fled to France in 1949.

Chaadayev, Pyotr Yakovlevich (1794–1856). Russian philosopher; figured in dispute between pro-Westerners and Slavophiles; wrote critical analysis of Russian culture; declared insane.

Chaikovsky, Nikolai Vasilyevich (1850–1926). Populist revolutionary; organized anti-Bolshevik coup in Archangel during Allied intervention of 1918–1919; fled to Paris.

Chaplygin, Sergei Alekseyevich (1869–1942). Specialist in theoretical mechanics and hydrodynamics; director of Higher Women's

Courses, 1905–1918; member of Soviet Academy of Sciences after 1929.

Chernov, Viktor Mikhailovich (1876–1952). Socialist Revolutionary leader; served in Provisional Government; President of 1918 Constituent Assembly; went abroad in 1920.

Chernyshevsky, Nikolai Gavrilovich (1828–1889). Russian writer and economist; advocated utopian socialism; spent time in prison and exile.

Chudnovsky, Grigory Isaakovich (1894–1918). Bolshevik revolutionary; led storming of Winter Palace in Petrograd; killed on the Ukrainian front.

Chukovskaya, Lidiya Korneyevna (1907–   ). Soviet literary critic and writer (samizdat).

Dal, Vladimir Ivanovich (1801–1872). Russian lexicographer.

Demidovs. Dynasty of Urals industrialists under Peter the Great.

Denikin, Anton Ivanovich (1872–1947). Tsarist military leader; commanded anti-Bolshevik forces in South, 1918–1920; emigrated.

Dimitrov, Georgi Mikhailovich (1882–1949). Bulgarian Communist leader; chief defendant in 1933 Reichstag trial in Leipzig.

Dobrolyubov, Nikolai Aleksandrovich (1836–1861). Russian literary critic, influenced by German materialist philosophy; favored social criticism in literature.

Dombrovsky, Yuri (1910–   ). Soviet writer; spent time in camps; wrote about the Stalin period.

Dyakov, Boris Aleksandrovich (1902–   ). Soviet author of labor-camp memoirs.

Dybenko, Pavel Yefimovich (1889–1938). Soviet military commander; headed Central Asian, Volga, Leningrad military districts.

Dzerzhinsky, Feliks Edmundovich (1877–1926). First chief of the secret police; succeeded by Vyacheslav R. Menzhinsky.

Dzhaparidze, Lyusya. Daughter of Prokofi A. Dzhaparidze.

Dzhaparidze, Prokofi Aprasionovich (1880–1918). Azerbaijani revolutionary; member of Bolshevik government in Baku; among twenty-six Baku commissars executed in 1918 at time of British intervention in Caucasus.

Ehrenburg, Ilya Grigoryevich (1891–1967). Soviet writer and journalist; spent many years in Paris; author of memoirs.

Eideman, Robert Petrovich (1895–1937). Soviet military commander; headed Frunze Military Academy, 1925–1932; chief of Osoaviakhim, the civil deefnse agency, after 1932.

Eikhe, Robert Indrikovich (1890–1940). A founder of Latvian Communist Party; high Siberian official, 1925–1937; Soviet Agriculture Commissar, 1937–1938; arrested in purges.

Feldman, Boris Mironovich (1890–1937). Soviet defense official; chief of Main Administration of Red Army, 1931–1937.

Filipp. *See* Kolychev, Fyodor Stepanovich.

Finn, K. (Finn-Khalfin, Konstantin Yakovlevich) (1904–1973). Soviet writer, playwright.

Florensky, Pavel Aleksandrovich (1882–1943). Religious philosopher with broad scientific interests; anticipated development of cybernetics; died in camp.

Fonvizin, Denis Ivanovich (1744–1792). Russian satirist; wrote comedies about provincial nobility.

Frunze, Mikhail Vasilyevich (1885–1925). Bolshevik Civil War commander; helped organize the Red Army; Defense Commissar in 1925; died after an operation.

Fyodorov, Nikolai Fyodorovich (1828–1903). Russian religious philosopher; influenced Solovyev, Tolstoi, and Dostoyevsky.

Fyodorova, Zoya Alekseyevna (1912–). Soviet movie actress; imprisoned after she had child by U.S. naval officer, Jackson R. Tate.

Gannibal, Pavel Isakovich. Pushkin's uncle; sympathized with Decembrists; exiled in 1826 to Solvychegodsk, later to Solovetsky Islands; freed in 1832.

Gavrilovich, Yevgeny Iosifovich (1899–). Soviet screenwriter.

Gekker, Anatoly Ilyich (1888–1938). Soviet military commander; military attaché in China, 1922, and Turkey, 1929–1933; headed foreign relations department of General Staff, 1934–1937; executed in purges.

German (?–1478). Russian Orthodox saint; founded Solovetsky monastery with Savvaty.

Gershuni, Grigory Andreyevich (1870–1908). A founder and leader of Socialist Revolutionary Party.

Gershuni, Vladimir Lvovich (1930–). Nephew of Grigory Gershuni; Soviet dissident, sentenced in 1949 to ten years as member of anti-Stalin youth group; remanded to mental asylum in 1969.

Gikalo, Nikolai Fyodorovich (1897–1938). Soviet Party official; served as Party secretary in Belorussia, 1932–1937; purged.

Ginzburg, Yevgeniya. Soviet writer; spent eighteen years in prison camps; memoirs, *Journey into the Whirlwind*, appeared in West.

Glezos, Manolis (1922–). Greek Communist leader; led resistance under German occupation; repeatedly jailed after the war.

Glinka, Mikhail Ivanovich (1804–1857). Russian composer; wrote first Russian national opera.

Goloded, Nikolai Matveyevich (1894–1937). Soviet official; served as Premier of Belorussia after 1927; purged.

Golyakov, Ivan Terentyevich (1888–1961). Soviet jurist; assisted in Red Army purge, 1936–1938; chairman, Supreme Court, 1938–1949.

Gorbatov, Aleksandr Vasilyevich (1891–1973). Soviet military leader; sentenced to fifteen years in 1939, but freed two years later; commanded Third Army in 1943–1945, Soviet airborne forces in 1950–1954 and Baltic Military District in 1954–1958.

Gorky, Maxim (1868–1936). Writer; opposed Bolsheviks at first and lived abroad; returned to Russia in 1931; died under mysterious circumstances.

Grin, Aleksandr Stepanovich (1880–1932). Writer of romantic, fantastic adventure stories.

Gumilyev, Lev Nikolayevich (1912–   ). Soviet historian and ethnologist; at Leningrad University since 1961.

Herzen, Aleksandr Ivanovich (1812–1870). Liberal writer.

Inber, Vera Mikhailovna (1890–   ). Soviet writer; author of lyrical stories about Soviet themes and World War II.

Ivanov, Vsevolod Vyacheslavovich (1895–1963). Soviet writer, author of stories and plays about Civil War.

Ivanov-Razumnik (Ivanov, Razumnik Vasilyevich) (1876–1946). Left Socialist Revolutionary; served in Tsarist and Soviet prisons; went to Germany in 1941.

Ivanovsky (Ivanov), Nikolai Pavlovich (1893–1961). Soviet ballet dancer; director of Leningrad Choreographic School, 1940–1952.

Jasienski, Bruno (1901–1941). Polish Communist writer; emigrated to Paris in 1925 and deported by France in 1929; moved to Soviet Union in 1931; arrested in purges of 1937.

Johnson, Hewlett (1874–1966). British churchman; was chairman of a British-Soviet friendship society; backed Soviet causes.

Kabalevsky, Dmitri Borisovich (1904–   ). Prominent Soviet composer.

Kaganovich, Lazar Moiseyevich (1893–   ). Close associate of Stalin; headed Soviet railroad system. Ousted from leadership in 1957.

Kaktyn, Artur Martynovich (Kaktins, Arturs) (1893–1937). Latvian revolutionary; held Soviet economic posts; Deputy Premier of Tadzhik Republic after 1934; purged.

Kalinin, Mikhail Ivanovich (1875–1946). Nominal President of the Soviet Union, 1919–1946.

Kalyanov, V. I. Soviet Sanskrit scholar and Buddhologist.

Kapitsa, Pyotr Leonidovich (1894–   ). Soviet physicist; emigrated to Britain in 1921; returned to Soviet Union in 1935; became Director of Institute of Physics; worked on atomic bomb.

Kaplan, Fanya (Dora) (1888–1918). Left Socialist Revolutionary; executed after unsuccessful attempt on Lenin's life.

Katayev, Valentin Petrovich (1897–   ). Soviet novelist and playwright; won prominence in Soviet literature.

Kirov, Sergei Mironovich (1886–1934). Close Stalin associate; his murder, reputedly inspired by Stalin, set off the purges.

Kolchak, Aleksandr Vasilyevich (1873–1920). Tsarist admiral; led anti-Bolshevik forces in Siberia, 1918–1920; executed.

Kolnyshevsky, Pyotr (1690–1803). Last hetman of Zaporozhye Cossacks; exiled in 1775 to Solovetsky monastery for twenty-five years.

Kolychev (Filipp), Fyodor Stepanovich (1507–1569). Russian Orthodox Metropolitan of Moscow; a foe of Ivan the Terrible; exiled to Solovetsky monastery; executed by Malyuta Skuratov; canonized.

Kopelev, Lev Zinovyevich (1912–   ). Soviet specialist in German literature.

Kork, Avgust Ivanovich (1887–1937). Soviet military leader; commander of Moscow Military District, 1929–1935, and Frunze Academy, 1935–1937.

Kornilov, Lavr Georgiyevich (1870–1918). Commander in chief of Russian forces under Provisional Government; fought Bolsheviks in Don area; killed in battle.

Korolev, Sergei Pavlovich (1906–1966). Soviet scientist; leader of Soviet space exploration program.

Kosior, Stanislav Vikentyevich (1889–1939). Ukrainian Bolshevik leader; shot in purges.

Kosmodemyanskaya, Zoya Anatolyevna (1923–1941). Soviet woman guerrilla; tortured and executed by Germans in World War II.

Kovtyukh, Yepifan Iovich (1890–1938). Soviet military commander; legendary hero of Taman retreat in Civil War, 1918; purged.

Kozhevnikov, Innokenti Serafimovich (1879–1931). Bolshevik commander in Civil War; served as Deputy Foreign Minister of Far Eastern Republic before its annexation by Soviet Union in 1922.

Krizhanich, Yuri (1618–1683). Croatian priest; served as Vatican envoy in Eastern Europe; an advocate of Slavic unity.

Kropotkin, Pyotr Alekseyevich (1842–1921). Russian Anarchist leader; lived abroad most of his life.

Kruglov, Sergei Nikiforovich (1903–   ). Secret police official; served as Minister of Internal Affairs, 1946–1956.

Krupskaya, Nadezhda Konstantinovna (1869–1939). Wife of Lenin, whom she met in 1894 and married in exile in Shushenskoye in 1899; held education posts after 1921.

Krylenko, Nikolai Vasilyevich (1885–1938). Chief state prosecutor, 1918–1931; later People's Commissar of Justice; shot.

Krylov, Ivan Andreyevich (1769–1844). Russian classical fabulist.

Krzhizhanovsky, Gleb Maksimilianovich (1872–1959). Russian power engineer; drafted Russia's first electrification plan; headed State Planning Commission, 1921–1930.

Kun, Bela (1886–1939). Hungarian Communist leader; headed short-lived Hungarian Soviet Republic in 1919; then sought refuge in Soviet Union; died in purges.

Kurchatov, Igor Vasilyevich (1902–1968). Soviet physicist; headed development of atomic and hydrogen bombs.

Kurganov, I. A. Russian émigré statistician.

Kursky, Dmitri Ivanovich (1874–1932). Bolshevik revolutionary; served as People's Commissar of Justice, 1918–1928.

Kutyakov, Ivan Semyonovich (1897–1942). Soviet military leader; deputy commander, Volga Military District, 1936–1937.

Lakshin, Vladimir Yakovlevich (1933–). Soviet literary critic; wrote about Solzhenitsyn in the liberal monthly *Novy Mir*.

Landau, Lev Davidovich (1908–1968). Soviet physicist; won Nobel Prize in 1962; incapacitated in near-fatal auto accident in 1962.

Lapin, Boris Matveyevich (1905–1941). Soviet writer; wrote in collaboration with Zakhari Khatsrevin; killed while a war correspondent.

Latsis, Martyn Ivanovich (1888–1941). Early Cheka official, 1917–1921; director, Plekhanov Economics Institute, 1932–1937; arrested.

Latsis, Vilis (1904–1966). Latvian Communist novelist; served as Premier of Soviet Latvia, 1940–1959.

Leonov, Leonid Maksimovich (1899–). Soviet novelist; favored psychological and social novels in 1920's.

Leskov, Nikolai Semyonovich (1831–1895). Russian realist writer; known for social flavor of his stories; a master of style.

Levin, Lev Grigoryevich (1870–1938). Soviet physician; headed Therapy Department in Kremlin Hospital; accused in 1938 of causing death of Soviet officials; sentenced to death.

Likhachev, Dmitri Sergeyevich (1906–). Soviet cultural historian; specialist in ancient Russian literature.

Lomov-Oppokov, Georgi Ippolitovich (1888–1938). Soviet economic official; headed Russian oil industry and Donets coal basin in 1920's; later in State Planning Commission and Soviet Control Commission; died in prison.

MacDonald, James Ramsay (1866–1937). British statesman; served as Labourite Prime Minister in 1924 and 1929–1935; established relations with Soviet Union in 1929.

Makarenko, Anton Semyonovich (1888–1939). Educator; organized rehabilitation colonies for juvenile delinquents.

Malenkov, Georgi Maksimilianovich (1902–). Close associate of Stalin; after his death briefly Soviet Party leader, then Premier until 1955; expelled from leadership by Khrushchev in 1957.

Mannerheim, Carl Gustaf (1867–1951). Finnish general and statesman; commanded Finnish forces in World War II; President, 1944–1946.

Marchenko, Anatoly Tikhonovich (1938–). Soviet dissident; wrote about imprisonment, 1960–1966, in *My Testimony*, published in West; served a second term, 1968–1971.

Mayakovsky, Vladimir Vladimirovich (1893–1930). Futurist poet; committed suicide.

Metter, Izrail Moiseyevich (1909–). Soviet screenwriter; wrote on police themes.

Mihajlov, Mihajlo (1934–). Yugoslav writer; author of critical analyses of Soviet Union; in jail, 1966–1970; rearrested in 1974.

Molotov, Vyacheslav Mikhailovich (1890–). Close associate of Stalin; long Premier and Foreign Minister; ousted by Khrushchev in 1957.

Morozov, Nikolai Aleksandrovich (1854–1946). Self-taught Russian scientist; imprisoned in Schlüsselburg Fortress, 1881–1905; served as director of Natural History Institute in Leningrad, 1918.

Morozov, Pavlik (Pavel Trofimovich) (1918–1932). Russian farm boy, hailed by Soviet authorities as a hero of collectivization; he denounced his father for collaborating with kulaks, and was himself slain by peasants.

Nekrasov, Nikolai Alekseyevich (1821–1878). Russian poet.

Nekrasov, Viktor Platonovich (1911–). Soviet writer; active in psychological warfare; often criticized; left Soviet Union in 1974.

Nevsky (Krivobokov), Vladimir Ivanovich (1876–1937). Soviet historian; director of Lenin Library; arrested 1935.

Nikon (Minov, Nikita) (1605–1681). Patriarch of Russian Orthodox Church (1652–1666), whose reforms led to schism with Old Believers.

Nikulin, Lev Veniaminovich (1891–1967). Soviet author of revolutionary adventure stories and historical novels.

Oksman, Yulian Grigoryevich (1894–1970). Soviet literary critic; long imprisoned.

Okunevskaya, Tatyana Kirillovna (1919–). Soviet movie actress; popular in 1930's and 1940's.

Olminsky, Mikhail Stepanovich (1863–1933). Early professional revolutionary; journalist.

Ordzhonikidze, Grigory Konstantinovich (1886–1937). Close associate of Stalin; headed heavy industry; a suicide during purges.

Palchinsky, Pyotr Akimovich (1878–1929). Economist and mining engineer; chief defendant in Shakhty trial of 1928; shot.

Palitsyn, Avraami (Averki Ivanovich) (?–1626). Russian nobleman under Ivan the Terrible; in disfavor after 1588; exiled to Solovetsky monastery, where he became a monk.

Papanin, Ivan Dmitriyevich (1894–   ). Soviet Arctic explorer; headed first ice-floe station, 1937–1938.

Pechkovsky, Nikolai Konstantinovich (1896–   ). Soviet opera singer; popular in 1920's and 1930's.

Pellico, Silvio (1789–1854). Italian writer and patriot.

Peter the Great (1672–1725). Tsar of Russia, 1682–1725.

Peters, Yakov Khristoforovich (1886–1942). Secret police official; deputy chief of OGPU, 1925–1930.

Petlyura, Simon Vasilyevich (1879–1926). Ukrainian nationalist leader, 1918–1920; assassinated in Paris.

Petrovsky, Grigory Ivanovich (1878–1958). Bolshevik revolutionary; President of Ukraine, 1919–1939; purged in 1939 and became deputy director of Museum of the Revolution in Moscow.

Pigulevskaya, Nina Viktorovna (1894–   ). Soviet Orientalist.

Pisarev, Dmitri Ivanovich (1840–1868). Russian literary critic; influenced by German natural materialism.

Plekhanov, Georgi Valentinovich (1856–1918). Marxist philosopher and historian; became Menshevik leader and opposed Bolsheviks.

Pletnev, Dmitri Dmitriyevich (1872–1953). Soviet physician; sentenced to twenty-five years after 1938 show trial.

Pobozhi, Aleksandr. A Soviet railroad construction engineer.

Pogodin (Stukalov), Nikolai Fyodorovich (1900–1962). Soviet playwright; wrote plays about Lenin and White Sea Canal.

Popov, Blagoi (1902–?). Bulgarian Communist; a defendant in 1933 Reichstag trial; exiled to Soviet Union; disappeared in purges.

Postyshev, Pavel Petrovich (1887–1940). Ukrainian Bolshevik leader; arrested in 1938; died in prison.

Primakov, Vitaly Markovich (1897–1937). Soviet military commander; led pro-Bolshevik Cossacks in Civil War.

Priselkov, Mikhail Dmitriyevich (1881–1941). Soviet historian; studied ancient Russian chronicles.

Prishvin, Mikhail Mikhailovich (1873–1954). Russian writer; author of stories about environment and animal life.

Prokofiev, Sergei Sergeyevich (1891–1953). Soviet composer.

Prugavin, Aleksandr Stepanovich (1850–1920). Russian Populist author; wrote about Old Believers and other sects.

Pushkin, Aleksandr Sergeyevich (1799–1837). Russian classical poet.

Putna, Vitovt Kazimirovich (1893–1937). Soviet military commander; military attaché in Japan, Finland, Germany, Britain.

Pyatakov, Georgi Leonidovich (1890–1937). Bolshevik official; held high financial and industrial posts; executed.

Repetto (Elvira Trisolini). Italian coloratura soprano; sang with Italian opera in St. Petersburg, 1885–1887.

Rudzutak, Yan Ernestovich (1887–1938). Associate of Stalin; arrested in 1937 purge; died in prison.

Ruslanova, Lidiya Andreyevna (1900–). Russian folk singer.

Rykov, Aleksei Ivanovich (1881–1938). Close associate of Stalin; Soviet Premier, 1924–1930; shot after 1938 show trial.

Sablin, Yuri Vladimirovich (1897–1937). Soviet military commander.

Saltychikha (Saltykova, Darya Nikolayevna) (1730–1801). Woman landowner in Moscow Province; noted for cruel treatment of serfs.

Savvaty (?–1435). Russian Orthodox saint; founded, with German, the Solovetsky monastery in 1429.

Selvinsky, Ilya (Karl) Lvovich (1899–1968). Soviet writer; led constructivist school in 1920's.

Serafimovich (Popov), Aleksandr Serafimovich (1863–1949). Soviet writer; classical author of proletarian, revolutionary prose.

Serebryakova, Galina Iosifovna (1905–). Soviet writer; author of prison-camp memoirs.

Shaginyan, Marietta Sergeyevna (1888–). Soviet writer; author of detective stories and a novel on industrialization theme.

Shalamov, Varlam Tikhonovich (1907–). Soviet writer; spent seventeen years in Kolyma camps; author of *Kolyma Stories* (Paris, 1969).

Shcherbatsky, Fyodor Ippolitovich (1866–1942). Buddhologist.

Sheinin, Lev Romanovich (1906–1967). Soviet prosecuting and investigatory official; wrote spy stories after 1950.

Shekhter, Boris Semyonovich (1900–1961). Soviet composer.

Shereshevsky, Nikolai Adolfovich (1885–1961). Soviet physician; witness in 1938 purge trial; accused in "doctors' plot," 1952–1953.

Shevchenko, Taras Grigoryevich (1814–1861). Ukrainian classical poet; exiled for political activities, 1847–1857.

Shklovsky, Viktor Borisovich (1893–). Soviet writer and memoirist; founded formalistic school.

Shlikhter, Aleksandr Grigoryevich (1868–1940). Bolshevik revolutionary; agricultural economist; Ukrainian Commissar of Agriculture, 1927–1929; then director of Ukrainian Institute of Marxism-Leninism.

Shostakovich, Dmitri Dmitriyevich (1906–1975). Soviet composer.

Sikorski, Wladyslaw (1881–1943). Military leader of Polish exiles.

Skuratov, Malyuta (Belsky, Grigory Lukyanovich (?–1572). Aide of Ivan the Terrible; headed the Oprichnina, a policelike group.

Slutsky, Boris Abramovich (1919–   ). Soviet poet and translator.

Smirnov, Ivan Nikitovich (1881–1936). People's Commissar for Communications, 1923–1927; expelled from Party; shot after trial.

Sofronitsky, Vladimir Vladimirovich (1901–   ). Soviet pianist.

Solovyev, Vladimir Sergeyevich (1853–1900). Religious philosopher; sought synthesis of Orthodox faith and Western thought.

Solts, Aron Aleksandrovich (1872–1945). Soviet judicial and prosecuting official; member of Party's Central Control Commission; removed from all posts in 1938.

Spiridonova, Mariya Aleksandrovna (1884–1941). Russian revolutionary; condemned to hard labor in 1906 after assassination of a Tsarist official; leader of Left Socialist Revolutionaries after February, 1917; sentenced to year in jail in late 1918; amnestied; quit politics.

Starokadomsky, Mikhail Leonidovich (1901–1954). Soviet composer.

Steklov, Yuri Mikhailovich (1873–1941). Soviet historian; edited the newspaper *Izvestiya* in 1920's; purged.

Stuchka (Stucka), Pyotr Ivanovich (1865–1932). Latvian Bolshevik; headed short-lived Latvian Soviet Government, 1918–1919; served as chairman of Soviet Supreme Court, 1923–1932.

Tanev, Vasil (1898–?). Bulgarian Communist; a defendant in 1933 Reichstag trial; exiled to Soviet Union; disappeared in purges.

Tendryakov, Vladimir Fyodorovich (1923–   ). Soviet author; writes psychological stories on moral and social conflicts.

Tess (Sosyura), Tatyana Nikolayevna (1906–   ). Soviet journalist.

Tikhon, Patriarch (1865–1925). Head of Russian Orthodox Church after 1917; detained 1922–1923 on oppositionist charges.

Tikhonov, Aleksandr Nikolayevich (1880–1956). Soviet writer; was associated with Gorky; headed publishing houses after 1917 Revolution.

Timofeyev-Ressovsky, Nikolai Vladimirovich (1900–   ). Soviet geneticist; worked in Germany, 1924–1945; sent to prison camp on return to Soviet Union; rehabilitated under Khrushchev.

Todorsky, Aleksandr Ivanovich (1894–1965). Soviet military commander; headed Air Force Academy, 1934–1936; in prison camps, 1938–1953.

Tolstoi, Aleksei Nikolayevich (1882–1945). Soviet writer of psychological realistic school; emigrated after Revolution and returned in 1922; wrote major historical novels.

Trotsky, Lev Davidovich (1879–1940). Associate of Lenin; first

Soviet Defense Commissar; deported by Stalin; slain in Mexico City.

Tsiolkovsky, Konstantin Eduardovich (1857–1935). Russian inventor; laid groundwork for space travel.

Tukhachevsky, Mikhail Nikolayevich (1893–1937). Soviet military leader; shot in 1937 on trumped-up treason charges.

Tynyanov, Yuri Nikolayevich (1895–1943). Soviet writer and literary scholar.

Tyutchev, Fyodor Ivanovich (1803–1873). Russian writer of philosophical lyrical school.

Uborevich, Iyeronim Petrovich (1896–1937). Soviet military commander; headed North Caucasus, Moscow, and Belorussian military districts.

Ulyanov, Aleksandr Ilyich (1866–1887). Lenin's older brother; executed after unsuccessful attempt to assassinate Alexander III.

Unshlikht, Iosif Stanislavovich (1879–1938). Soviet official; worked in Cheka (1921–1923), State Planning Commission (1930–1933), and headed Soviet civil aviation, 1933–1935.

Urusov, Aleksandr Ivanovich (1843–1900). Russian lawyer; well known as a court orator.

Utyosov, Leonid Osipovich (1895–   ). Soviet orchestra leader and variety-stage star.

Vakhtangov, Yevgeny Bagrationovich (1883–1922). Innovative stage director; founded Moscow's Vakhtangov Theatre.

Vasilyev, Pavel Nikolayevich (1910–1937). Soviet poet; wrote about village themes; accused of idealizing kulaks.

Vavilov, Nikolai Ivanovich (1887–1943). Prominent plant geneticist; headed applied botany and genetics institutes; arrested 1940.

Vavilov, Sergei Ivanovich (1891–1951). Soviet physicist; brother of Nikolai Vavilov; director of Physics Institute, 1932–1945; president of Academy of Sciences, 1945–1951.

Vinogradov, Vladimir Nikitich (1882–1964). Soviet physician; witness in 1938 purge trial; figured in "doctors' plot," 1952–1953.

Vishnevsky, Vsevolod Vitalyevich (1900–1951). Soviet playwright and screenwriter; author of plays about Red Army.

Vlasov, Andrei Andreyevich (1900–1946). Red Army officer; captured by Germans in 1942; led forces against Soviet Union; executed.

Volkonskaya, Mariya Nikolayevna (1805–1863). Russian princess; wife of Sergei G. Volkonsky, a Decembrist, whom she followed into exile in Siberia in 1827, living there until 1855; wrote about hard-labor system.

Voloshin, Maksimilian Aleksandrovich (1878–1932). Symbolist poet and watercolorist; opposed Bolsheviks.

Voroshilov, Kliment Yefremovich (1881–1969). Close associate of Stalin; long Defense Commissar; Soviet President, 1953–1960.

Vyshinsky, Andrei Yanuaryevich (1883–1954). Lawyer and diplomat; chief prosecutor in show trials, 1936–1938; Foreign Minister, 1949–1953.

Yagoda, Genrikh Grigoryevich (1891–1938). Secret police official; People's Commissar of Internal Affairs, 1934–1936; executed.

Yakir, Iona Emmanuilovich (1896–1937). Soviet military commander; headed Kiev Military District, 1935–1937; purged.

Yakubovich, Pyotr Filippovich (1860–1911). Russian poet; translator of Baudelaire; wrote memoirs about his Tsarist exile.

Yegorov, Aleksandr Ilyich (1883–1939). Soviet military commander; military attaché in China, 1925–1926; headed Belorussian Military District, 1927–1931; chief of General Staff, 1931–1937.

Yenukidze, Avel Safronovich (1877–1937). Bolshevik official; secretary of Central Executive Committee, 1918–1935; shot in purges.

Yezhov, Nikolai Ivanovich (1895–1939). Secret police official; People's Commissar of Internal Affairs, 1936–1938.

Zaozersky, Aleksandr Ivanovich (1874–1941). Russian historian.

Zavenyagin, Avraami Pavlovich (1901–1956). Soviet metallurgical executive; headed Magnitogorsk steel plant, 1933–1937; Norilsk copper-nickel complex (after 1938), and nuclear weapons program, 1953–1956.

Zelinsky, Korneli Lyutsianovich (1896–1970). Soviet literary critic; a founder of constructivist school.

Zhuk, Sergei Yakovlevich (1892–1957). Soviet hydraulic engineer; supervised canal projects built with forced labor.

Zhukov, Georgi (Yuri) Aleksandrovich (1908–   ). Soviet journalist; headed State Committee for Cultural Relations with Foreign Countries, 1957–1962; then *Pravda* commentator.

Zinoviev (Apfelbaum), Grigory Yevseyevich (1883–1936). Associate of Lenin; expelled from Party in 1927; shot after 1936 show trial.

Zoshchenko, Mikhail Mikhailovich (1895–1958). Soviet satirist; known for his comic novellas; often in disfavor.

Zosima (?–1478). Russian Orthodox saint; first abbot of Solovetsky monastery.

Index

Page numbers in **boldface** refer to the Glossary